SELF AND SOCIETY

 IN MING

THOUGHT

by Wm. Theodore de Bary

and the Conference on Ming Thought

Columbia University Press   NEW YORK AND LONDON

*This book is dedicated to the senior member
of the Conference on Ming Thought*

WING-TSIT CHAN

*in anticipation of his seventieth birthday
and in recognition of his many contributions
to the study of Chinese thought.*

Copyright © 1970 Columbia University Press
ISBN 0-231-03271-4   *Clothbound*
ISBN 0-231-08313-0   *Paperback*
Library of Congress Catalog Card Number: 78–101229
Manufactured in the United States of America

This book is No. 4 in the *Studies in Oriental Culture*
series, edited at Columbia University.

PREFACE

The present volume has been produced through the cooperative efforts of several institutions concerned with the study of Chinese civilization. The American Council of Learned Societies, through its Committee on the Study of Chinese Civilization, planned and conducted a conference on Ming thought held in June, 1966, at Champaign, Illinois, with the co-operation and support of the University of Illinois. Most of the papers appearing herein were presented at that conference and subsequently revised for publication. Several of them were also discussed at an earlier seminar on Ming thought conducted at Columbia University in the spring of 1966 through the collaboration of the Department of East Asian Languages and Cultures and the Ming Biographical History Project, an activity of the Association for Asian Studies. The latter association also joined in sponsoring the conference.

As it happens, our manuscript goes to press just following the 600th anniversary of the founding of the Ming dynasty (1368–1644). While the appropriateness of celebrating such an anniversary might be questioned on several grounds, we take satisfaction in being able to signalize this great period of Chinese history, so long neglected within and without the country. Some of its pomps and works may seem to have been of the very devil and best left unexhumed. Nevertheless, the Ming has been poorly understood and badly underestimated in its contributions to Chinese culture and its significance for the development of modern China. In their own time the Ming vase, jar, and bowl were as much admired abroad as at home. How fitting then that the rediscovery of Ming thought should be an international affair—participated in by scholars from many parts of the world. We celebrate no narrow national achievement or evocation of China's past, but our own coming of age, our own accession to a common world inheritance.

The editor wishes to acknowledge the great assistance of Professor Robert Crawford in arranging the conference on Ming thought at the University of Illinois; of Professors Robert Ruhlmann and Chao-ying Fang in reading portions of the final manuscript and proofs; of Lien-che Tu Fang in drawing up the character lists; and of Miss Joanne Soderman in compiling the index. From the first planning of the Ming Thought seminar and conference to the preparation of the manuscript for the press, Mrs. Barbara Wichura has been of invaluable help to me, and I am glad for this opportunity to express my great indebtedness to her. I am grateful also to Miss Elisabeth L. Shoemaker of Columbia University Press for her work in editing a book of this length and complexity.

The papers of Professors Okada, Sakai, and Jen have been revised and in some cases expanded by the editor, partly on the basis of their published works in Japanese and Chinese. The undersigned bears responsibility for any misrepresentation of their views which may have resulted.

New York; January, 1968   *Wm. Theodore de Bary*

EXPLANATORY NOTE

The style of this book in sinological matters follows in general that of the Ming Biographical History, now in preparation, which in turn follows with slight modifications that of the basic reference work *Eminent Chinese of the Ch'ing Period*, edited by Arthur Hummel (Washington, 1943). One difference is that all Chinese characters are gathered in a list at the end of each paper, with alphabetical reference keys in the style of the *Journal of the American Oriental Society*. The special nature of a work on Chinese thought renders it more convenient for the reader to have the notes and character lists follow immediately after each paper, and in making each author's contribution thus self-contained it has been possible to respect certain individual preferences in matters of style and translation, rather than to insist on rigid standardization in all respects.

It might be considered a prime desideratum for any work on Chinese philosophy or thought to have a common glossary of terms with standard renderings in English. In a symposium, however, one encounters special problems arising from the nature of the Chinese language and the tendency in philosophical discussion for basic terms to be used in different senses by different writers or even by the same writer. For the Chinese the idea is not so much to analyze and define concepts precisely as to expand them, to make them suggestive of the widest possible range of meaning. Generally speaking, the more crucial or central the concept, the greater the ambiguity. This is bound to be reflected in translation; interpretation of a man's thought will often be bound up with one's rendering of such key concepts. Under these circumstances we must allow our writers some latitude, though we have discouraged needless diversity.

As an example, our policy has been to avoid excessive use of romanized terms, which put too great a burden on those unfamiliar with Chinese, and we have favored translations established in standard works, such as Professor Chan's "innate knowledge" for Wang Yang-ming's *liang-chih*. But the whole point of Professor Tang Chun-i's paper is to raise large questions as to the meaning and significance of this term, and one cannot deny him the use of the romanized form if that leaves him free to develop his argument unencumbered by the preconceptions or preferences of others.

Fortunately there are glossaries to which the interested reader can turn.

Wing-tsit Chan's *Source Book in Chinese Philosophy* (Princeton, 1963) contains a glossary including many terms important in Neo-Confucian philosophy. Another excellent glossary, in French, is found in Wang Tch'ang-che's *La Philosophie Morale de Wang Yang-ming* (Shanghai, 1936), which is more especially concerned with the philosophical vocabulary of this influential Ming thinker. A. C. Graham's *Two Chinese Philosophers* (London, 1958), though it deals with the earlier phase of Neo-Confucian philosophy, provides intensive and precise discussion of many terms used later by Ming thinkers (though not always in the same way). Needless to say, the results in each case differ somewhat. They suggest a range of possibilities, rather than establish a definitive norm. To some extent also the index to the present volume should serve the same purpose by providing cross references to different writers' handling of the same terms.

Against the current trend toward unlimited use of alphabetical abbreviations for sources cited, we have confined this practice either to standard works familiar to those working in Chinese studies, basic Ming sources, or works repeatedly cited within a given paper (and identified on first appearance in each). It seems an imposition on the reader to make him learn such an abbreviation for almost every work cited more than once, and often abbreviated titles will convey the necessary information without taking up much more space. The common abbreviations appearing herein are:

KHCPTS	Kuo-hsüeh chi-pen ts'ung-shu
MJCCTLSY	*Ming-jen chuan-chi tzu-liao so-yin*, National Central Library. Taipei, 1964
MJHA	*Ming-ju hsueh-an*
MS	*Ming shih*
SPPY	Ssu-pu pei-yao
SPTK	Ssu-pu ts'ung-k'an
TSCC	Ts'ung-shu chi-ch'eng
TT	Tao tsang

W. T. de B.

CONTRIBUTORS

WING-TSIT CHAN is Professor Emeritus of Chinese Philosophy and Culture at Dartmouth College and Anna R. D. Gillespie Professor of Philosophy at Chatham College. Representative of his numerous works on Chinese philosophy is his *Source Book in Chinese Philosophy* (1963), and of his interest in Ming thought is his translation *Instructions for Practical Living and Other Neo-Confucian Writings by Wang Yang-ming* (1963).

ROBERT CRAWFORD is Associate Professor of History, University of Illinois, and Director of its Center for Asian Studies. He is currently working on a book-length study of Chang Chu-cheng. His fields of special interest include the Han and Ming periods.

WM. THEODORE DE BARY is Carpentier Professor of Oriental Studies at Columbia University and President for 1969–70 of the Association for Asian Studies. He is the editor and co-author of *Sources of Chinese Tradition, Sources of Japanese Tradition,* and *Sources of Indian Tradition,* and of *The Buddhist Tradition in China, Japan and India.* Neo-Confucianism in China and Japan is his main field of study.

C. T. HSIA is Professor of Chinese Literature at Columbia University, and the author of two major studies in Chinese fiction, *The Classic Chinese Novel* (1968) and *A History of Modern Chinese Fiction* (1961). He obtained his Ph.D. in English Literature from Yale (1961).

RAY HUANG is Associate Professor of History at the State University College, New Paltz, New York. He earned the Ph.D. degree at the University of Michigan and has specialized in Chinese military and fiscal history.

LEON HURVITZ is Professor in the Department of Far Eastern Languages, University of Washington, Seattle. He is the author of a major work on the Chinese Buddhist thinker Chih-i, the subject of his doctoral research at Columbia, and of numerous other writings on Buddhism.

JEN YU-WEN is Honorary Fellow of the Centre for East Asian Cultural Studies, University of Hong Kong, and Fellow of the Institute of Modern History, Academia Sinica, Taiwan. He is a specialist in the history of the Taiping Rebellion, but has kept up a lifetime interest in the study of Ch'en Hsien-chang.

LIU TS'UN-YAN is Professor of Chinese at the Australian National University and has been a visiting professor at Columbia and Harvard. With a Ph.D. from the University of London, he is also a Fellow of the Royal Asiatic Society. Among his many writings are *Buddhist and Taoist Influences in Chinese Novels, Chinese Popular Fiction in Two London Libraries,* and *Wu-Ch'eng-en: His Life and Career.*

TAKEHIKO OKADA is Professor of Chinese at Kyūshū University, Fukuoka, Japan. A Doctor of Literature from the same university, he is the author of numerous books and articles in Japanese on Neo-Confucian thought in China and Japan. His current efforts are devoted to a massive, cooperative study of the Recorded Conversations of Chu Hsi (*Chu tzu yü-lei*).

TADAO SAKAI is Professor in the Faculty of Letters, Tōkyō Kyōiku University, and Chief Librarian of that university. An active leader in Japanese scholarly organizations, he has been a specialist in the study of Chinese popular religion and is the author of several major works in that field, including *Chūgoku zensho no kenkyū* (Researches in Chinese morality books).

ANNA SEIDEL was trained in Chinese history and religion at Munich and Hamburg, and received her doctorate from the Ecole Pratique des Hautes Etudes, Paris, with a thesis on La Divinisation de Lao Tseu dans le Taoisme des Han. She has been associated with the Sung project at the University of Munich and is currently a research associate of the Institut du Hōbōgirin, Kyōto.

TANG CHUN-I is Professor of Philosophy and Director of the Institute for Advanced Chinese Studies, New Asia College, Chinese University of Hong Kong. He was educated in China at the Sino-Russian University, Peking University, and the National Central University. He helped to found New Asia College, of which he served as dean from its inception until 1966. The most recent of his many books in Chinese philosophy is *Chung-kuo che-hsueh yüan-lun* (Studies in the origin and development of Chinese philosophical ideas), of which two volumes have already been published.

CONTENTS

明 In the three centuries since the fall of the Ming Dynasty (1368–1644) Ming thought has been in bad repute. Each of the great dynasties before it had made some enduring contribution—the Chou through the profusion and profundity of thought represented by the "Hundred Schools"; the Han through its synthesis of a Chinese world view; the Six Dynasties, Sui, and T'ang through the assimilation and development of Buddhist philosophy; and the Sung through the great Neo-Confucian revival in humane learning and, especially, in philosophy. The Ming period, by contrast, has been seen as one of general decline and aimless drifting, in the midst of which Wang Yang-ming stood out alone as an independent thinker. Indeed, to praise Wang was most often to deprecate Ming philosophy as a whole; to honor him was to reject the conventionality and mediocrity of most other thinkers of his age. Finally, indignities came at the hands of modern scholarship. The Sung and the early Ch'ing (under a foreign dynasty, no less) were seen by Hu Shih as periods of renaissance in Chinese thought, with the Ming as a long trough between.[1]

THE "EMPTINESS" OF MING THOUGHT

The firmness of this judgment seems to have become established very early. Few would dispute the opinion of a scholar like Ku Yen-wu [a] (1613–82), himself a survivor of the Ming and a towering figure in the world of classical scholarship, who compared the subleties of Ming thought unfavorably to the simple truths of Confucius' teaching:

It is a matter of great regret to me that, for the past hundred odd years, scholars have devoted so much discussion to the mind and human nature, all of it vague and quite incomprehensible. . . . They have set aside broad knowledge and concentrated upon the search for a single, all-inclusive method; they have said not a word about the distress and poverty of the world within the four seas, but have spent all their days lecturing on theories of the "weak and subtle," "the refined and the undivided." [2]

Ts'ui Shu [b] (1740–1816), another scholar who typified the finest in critical scholarship during the Ch'ing period, confirmed this judgment when he described the Neo-Confucian philosophy of the Sung and Ming:

As scholars who valued truth none can compare with the Sung Confucianists. Yet most of them concerned themselves with questions of the nature and principle of things and with moral philosophy. If one looks among them for men who devoted themselves to historical research, he will find no more than two or three out of ten. By Ming times scholarship had grown increasingly heterodox and it became so that if one hoped to write anything important he had to be conversant with Ch'an [Zen] doctrines and interlard his library shelves with Buddhist books.[3]

As a final example of this attitude we have in the early years of the present century Liang Ch'i-ch'ao (1873–1929). His *Intellectual Trends in the Ch'ing Period (Ch'ing-tai hsüeh-shu kai-lun)* [c] fixed in modern Chinese minds the authoritative interpretation of recent Chinese thought. He found much to admire in the early Ch'ing but prefaced it with a severe condemnation of the late Ming, in terms that by now were almost a convention:

When I went on to examine the substance of its thoughts, I found that the object of its study was simply too vague and intangible. A few outstanding and sincere scholars might have followed this path and achieved a state of repose for body and mind, but only rarely could ordinary mortals imitate them. It was too easy for superficial and pretentious men to pick up abstract phrases to brag about, and consequently there was a group in late Ming known as the *k'uang-ch'an* [d] ("wild Zen") [who thought] that "every street is full of sages" and that "wine, women, wealth, and passion do not block the road to enlightenment." Their ethics hit rock bottom. Moreover, the civil service examinations and the students' curriculum to prepare for them engaged the attention of all the nation; students needed only to learn this kind of dubious and imitative language in order to be ready to jockey for position, wealth, and reputation. The whole nation indulged in it prodigally and one man after another neglected his learning and the use of his mind.[4]

Here Liang repeats the charge that Ming thought was corrupted by Ch'an Buddhism, and adds to this an attack on the stereotyped civil service examination system as stultifying the intellectual life of the late Ming. This too is a familiar complaint, and much support for Liang's allegation can be found among qualified critics reaching back to the Ming itself.[5]

THE VITALITY AND DIVERSITY
OF MING THOUGHT

Nevertheless, the very existence of such criticism belies the common stereotype of Ming thought. If evils existed so did opposition to them. If education tended to become subservient to official recruitment, so was there a strong countertrend among individual thinkers and in the spread of private academies disavowing such purposes and nurturing independent thought. Indeed the irony of the situation is that many of those later described as given to empty speculation on the mind and nature were precisely those who resisted the prevailing pressures toward conformity.[6] They may appear to have been "escapists," but they sought a way out of real dangers. They were not simply avoiding troubles, but looking for a way to deal with them.

Thus, whatever one's ultimate judgment of the value of Ming thought, Liang Ch'i-ch'ao is certainly wrong in saying that the Confucians of the late Ming "neglected . . . the use of their minds." On the contrary the sixteenth and early seventeenth centuries may well have been one of the most creative and stimulating periods in the history of Chinese thought. In those distorted times there was no lack of challenge to thought. Evils, abuses, crises, conflicts—yes. But in the midst of such difficulties creative tensions existed such as had characterized earlier periods of social decadence and intellectual ferment. What we find, then, in the extremities of the Ming situation, is anything but a dull conformity of thought to established patterns and institutions; it is rather a picture of lively controversy and intellectual diversity.

From this point of view, whether or not one views Ming speculations on the mind and nature as "empty" depends on whether or not one understands the problems to which they sought an answer,

and whether or not one feels the importance and the urgency of
those problems as Ming thinkers did. To the successors of the Ming,
whose approach was frankly "empirical" and antimetaphysical, these
speculations seemed vapid and vague. Ch'ing thinkers for the most
part turned away from questions of this sort, to some extent out of
a sense of disillusionment with the general failure of the Ming. The
collapse of the old order and the fall of the dynasty, first to rebels
and then to the Manchus, were seen as consequences of the moral
decline and disorder of thought at the end of the period. Such a
causal connection, alluded to by Liang Ch'i-ch'ao above, may be
difficult to establish and no doubt reflects a typical Confucian
predilection for the moralistic interpretation of history. Nevertheless, whether as cause, symptom, or both, the apparent failure of
Ming thought and nerve loomed large in the minds of those who
sought to explain this catastrophe.

A notable exception to this line of thinking is found, however, in
the studies of Huang Tsung-hsi[e] (1610–95). He had suffered as
much as anyone from these tragic events and was deeply moved to
comprehend their meaning. Indeed, in his *Ming-i tai-fang lu*[f] Huang
was unsparing in his exposure of the failings of Ming rulers and
institutions. Loyalty to his own dynasty did not stand in the way of
a most searching analysis of its weaknesses and evils. Yet when he
came to compile his monumental survey of Ming Confucian thought,
the *Ming-ju hsüeh-an*,[g] Huang sought to preserve its contributions
from the neglect and indifference, if not the contempt, of the subsequent age. In his foreword he explains:

It is often said that the literary and practical accomplishments of the
Ming did not measure up to former dynasties. Yet in the philosophy of
Principle it attained what other dynasties did not. In everything Ming
scholars made the finest of distinctions and classifications, as if they were
sorting the hair of oxen or picking silk threads from a cocoon. They
thereby discovered what other scholars had failed to discover. Though the
Ch'engs and Chu Hsi [in the Sung] spent many words in refuting the
Buddha, they never got beneath the surface. Buddhism's specious reason-
ableness and confounding of truth they failed to point out. But Ming
scholars were so precise in their analysis that the Buddhists were completely exposed and trapped.[7]

What is important here is not Huang's evident hostility to Buddhism. It is true that his survey is motivated by a desire to uphold the orthodox Confucian tradition, but for the most part it is not marked by an unreasoning rejection of all things Buddhist and in later life his attitude grew increasingly tolerant of heterodox thought. What stands out is his claim that Ming thought came to grips with the challenge of Buddhism by a more precise clarification of issues, rather than by simply rejecting it out of hand. It acknowledges that Ming thinkers were concerned with the subtleties and refinements which his contemporary Ku Yen-wu had so little use for, but affirms that these enabled a more precise analysis of the fundamental problems at issue in the encounter of Confucianism and Buddhism. For ourselves, likewise, the mere fact that Ch'ing scholars took little interest in such questions is not a sufficient basis for regarding the Ming attempt as vain. We must try to understand, rather, why and how these questions assumed such importance in fifteenth- and sixteenth-century China.

THE SITUATION OF THE MING INTELLECTUAL

From the comments above we are aware of two problems facing the Ming Confucian scholar. One had to do with public service and the examination system. The other involved his confrontation with Buddhism and Taoism. Of the two the former was the more pressing, for intellectually Buddhism and Taoism were in a state of relative decline and institutionally in a weakened condition. They could not have compelled his attention except that, in wrestling with his own Confucian conscience, he could not ignore what they had to say to his inner self.

The question of first priority then, concerns the Ming Confucian in his dual role as scholar and official. With his traditional commitment to public service, it was natural that the scholar should be drawn to the business of government, and that this in turn should subject him to great political pressures, if it did not actually expose him to grave dangers.[8] But in the Ming, to an extraordinary degree, the Confucian found himself overshadowed by the power of the state and, whether in or out of office, felt his social conscience under great strain. Most historians, whatever their differences in other matters of interpretation, acknowledge the unprecedented concentration of power in the hands of the emperor and its despotic uses by those who acted in his name. It is not for us here to review the entire question of Ming "despotism," but simply to emphasize two related points: one is that autocratic and bureaucratic power existed in the situation, and the other is that men still attempted to defend themselves against it.[9]

Awareness of these conditions will help us to avoid a common error. We shall not mistake the seeming introversion of Ming thought and its apparent quietistic tendency as indicating that it had strayed from the "real" problems of life or lost interest in practical matters. Nothing was more real and practical for the thinker and scholar in that age than the preservation of his life, his integrity, and his fidelity to essential Confucian values in the face of such overwhelming odds. If to withdraw into reflective contemplation or solitary pursuits helped to achieve this, then, even if the withdrawal has the connotations of escapism, we must not think of it as useless or sterile. From this process of introspection and re-examination emerged not only the most deeply committed and personally effective of Confucian activists, Wang Yang-ming, but also at the end of the dynasty the most searching critique of political and social institutions China had ever known.

But let us consider, more concretely, the effects on Ming Confucians of the civil service system—an old problem in a new situation. Earlier, in the late T'ang and Sung, there had been protests against the type of Confucian scholarship encouraged and rewarded by the examinations. The integrity of Confucian teaching had constantly to be defended against the danger of debasement through its use as an official ideology or as a mere professional qualification. But if Liang Ch'i-ch'ao and others, like Chiang Fan,[h] the historian of seventeenth- and eighteenth-century thought, stress the particularly deleterious effects of the civil service examinations on Confucian thought in the Ming,[10] it is because during this period the system presented a more serious problem than ever before, and paradoxically so, since it was in many ways better organized and more widely effective.

The founder of the dynasty had sought to broaden the avenues of official recruitment, to extend the official school system so as to train more scholars, and to simplify the examinations so that men of practical ability need not demonstrate great erudition in order to qualify.[11] A concomitant of this effort at "democratization," however, was a further routinization and standardization of both training and recruitment. Simplification of the examinations resulted in a limiting of the scholar-official's intellectual horizons and placed almost no value on his commitment to Confucian ideals. Little more was demanded of him than rote memorization of the Classics (especially the Four Books), a mindless assimilation of the commentaries of Chu Hsi, and a technical mastery of the required essay and poetry forms.[12]

More thoughtful men naturally questioned whether this was true Confucian learning, or whether official service on this basis could be considered a fulfillment of the Confucian sense of duty to mankind. But the much larger numbers of candidates recruited under the new system, with all the implications of social leveling and a lowering of scholarly standards which that implied, greatly intensified the strain on the Ming Confucian. The tension increased between his egalitarian ideals and his elitist standards, between his commitment to public service and his revulsion at careerism on a mass scale among supposed Confucians devoid of genuine intellectual and moral worth.

And, quite apart from his own interior struggles in these matters, there was the constant political and social pressure to conform, to yield his scruples and high ideals in the service of a questionable master. To refuse was to find himself in an embattled minority. What was worse, it was a minority without status and with almost no cohesion as a group. In a sense it lacked even a *raison d'etre*. Within Confucianism the concept of a "minority" had no place.[13] The scholar stood alone, with comfort and support coming only from personal friends and distant admirers. He could only retire to his home ground, strive for economic self-sufficiency on the land (like Wu Yü-pi),[i] or devote himself to teaching.

Under such circumstances independence or resistance to the dominant power tended to be manifested in individualistic ways rather than through some interest group. In the early Ming, Fang Hsiao-ju is an excellent example of this. Rather than being a spokesman for the scholar-gentry as a class, he is representative of them in the sense of exemplifying the only kind of independence possible for them—individual heroism and individuality of thought—rather than in the conscious assertion of their interests as an opposition group.

It was among such individuals, thrown back upon themselves, that Ming thought in the true sense was born. Their inner conflicts, however, were of many sorts. It was one thing to defend one's own sense of the authentic Confucian tradition against a debased official "orthodoxy," as did even the Ch'eng-Chu school (e.g., Wu Yü-pi and Hu Chü-jen)[j] of the early Ming in holding itself aloof from the establishment. This was a conflict between the philosopher and the state as to what truly constituted orthodoxy. It was another thing that the philosopher felt within himself the stresses of time and change as they affected his understanding of the Confucian way. This was a conflict with the past and, again, even those who cherished orthodoxy experienced it. They suffered not only alienation from the established regime but also, in a more complex and indefinable way, estrangement from received tradition.

THE BURDEN OF CULTURE IN THE MING

This tradition Ming scholars received largely from the Sung (960–1279). Indeed, Ming China may be seen as the second phase of a far-reaching cultural development which had come to its first apex in the Sung. The Confucian revival in that period had been stimulated by forces which continued and were greatly intensified in the Ming—the strengthening and enlarging of the civil bureaucracy, expansion of commerce and industry, increasing urbanization and the growth of an urban culture of great diversity and refinement, the development of printing and the comparatively wide distribution of books, and the great extension of education, partly occasioned by increased social mobility and the participation of larger numbers of people in the competition for office if not in the civil service itself.[14]

The effect of this was not felt immediately in the democratization of learning on any large scale, or in a breaking down of the traditional distinction between the Confucian educated elite and the uneducated masses—though something of this was to come. The most direct effects were felt within the educated class itself—those who carried the burden of high culture and would be most sensitive to changes in the cultural situation. Until Chu Hsi it had been possible for the Confucian to conceive of himself as potentially a master of the arts, though even by his time signs of strain had appeared between interior moral cultivation and excessive involvement in external culture.[15] The enjoyment of arts and letters—aesthetic pursuits such as landscape painting, gardening, the collecting of bronzes, the furnishing of the scholar's studio with fine paper, brushes, and ink stones, and scholarly hobbies of an antiquarian sort—could sap completely the will of the Confucian to put the world in order. Still, somehow the Sung giants had found the energy to impose order on this fascinating diversity instead of denying it. Chu Hsi's all-embracing system had reunited the rational and moral orders; Ssu-ma Kuang had encompassed all history in a sweeping panorama of recorded fact and moral example; encyclopedists like Cheng Ch'iao, Wang Ying-lin, and Ma Tuan-lin had traced the development of social and cultural institutions from the primitive past to the complex present.

Yet they may have done their work too well for the Ming. Who could compete with such masters? Individuals found the problem too staggering; its magnitude now required large-scale cooperative effort such as was embodied in the massive Yung-lo Encyclopedia (1407). Printing and the dissemination of books, which made education more widely available, rendered mastery more difficult. To pursue the "investigation of things" and their principles in one thing or affair after another, in book after book, seemed an endless procedure. Indeed the Ming scholar was already confronted by the typical modern dilemma—how to keep up with the proliferation of literature, how to cope with more and more specialized branches of learning, and not lose the sense of human relevance. Was he not threatened with a loss of the intellectual and spiritual integration which had always been the aim of Confucian study?

Those who set the tone and direction of Ming thought, such as

Ch'en Hsien-chang [k] and Wang Yang-ming,[1] often voiced concern over the harmful effects of excessive involvement in book-learning and belles-lettres. This was indeed a crucial issue between Wang and his great predecessor Chu Hsi. The latter, Wang believed, had even learned to regret his own overindulgence in bookish pursuits:

[Chu] all along . . . directed his efforts only to intellectual investigations and writing. Naturally he would have had no time for these if he had given priority to self-cultivation with a sense of genuine and personal concern. . . . If he had really worried lest the doctrine not be made clear to the world, and, following the example of Confucius' retiring to edit the Six Classics, had eliminated superfluous works and confined himself to the simple and essential in order to enlighten later scholars, in general it would not have required him to do much investigation. When he was young he wrote many books and then repented doing so in his old age. That was doing things upside down.[16]

Reflected in this passage is the overpowering figure of Chu Hsi as a prodigious scholar, whose written work had left a monumental legacy to later generations. One might have thought that Chu's philosophy and his writings had been most impressive for their comprehensiveness. They had achieved the same remarkable balance of concern for philosophical inquiry, moral self-cultivation, cultural endeavor, and public service that had characterized Confucius himself. Yet it is that very comprehensiveness and complexity which disturbs Wang. He longs for the simplicity of the ancient sage, and puts forward his "innate knowledge" (*liang-chih*)[m] as a return to the irreducible essence of Confucius' teaching:

In learning to become a sage, the student need only get rid of selfish human desires and preserve the principle of nature (*t'ien-li*),[n] which is like refining gold and achieving perfection in quality. . . . Later generations [however] . . . seek sagehood only in knowledge and ability . . . and merely cripple their spirit and exhaust their energy scrutinizing books, investigating the names and varieties of things, and imitating the forms and traces of the ancients.[17]

Thus, through man's instinctive moral sense, based on Mencius' doctrine of the goodness of human nature, Wang seeks to redress the Confucian balance in the direction of moral cultivation in practice, as opposed to cultural activity and the accumulation of learning.

He is saying that the sage must be more a man of action than a scholar.

It would thus be possible to interpret this development within the context of Confucian humanism alone. Wang Yang-ming in his own experience of life is the Confucian as the man of action, the scholar who devoted more of his life to active official service than almost any other Sung or Ming thinker did, much of that activity being of the most strenuous and demanding sort. Indeed the official Ming History, which categorizes him as a statesman rather than a scholar, credits him with the greatest military achievements of any civil of- ficial in the Ming period.[18] Chu Hsi, by comparison, saw little active service. For the most part he either held sinecures involving cultural activities and very little active administration, or else he was out of favor at court and living in "retirement" as a scholar.[19] Wang Yang- ming complains in the quotation above that Chu wrote too much. And it is true that he devoted his life mainly to intellectual inquiry and writing, rather than to the active expression of his Confucian concerns in public service. In terms, then, of the traditional function of the Confucian as both scholar and official, or of Confucianism as upholding both culture and morality, there is some basis for saying that Wang Yang-ming manifests the instinct within Confucianism to restore this balance in the direction of moral action.

But what Wang expresses here is what other Ming thinkers before him had also sensed. The emphasis on interiority rather than intel- lectuality is already found in his predecessors, Wu Yü-pi, Hu Chü- jen, Ch'en Hsien-chang, and Lou Liang,° as Professor Chan's paper in this volume makes clear. Ch'en in particular had stressed the dispensability of book learning, and even the obstacle it might put in the way of achieving sagehood.[20] And yet their role in life was quite different from Wang's. They tended to be reclusive and not to engage in active official life as he did.[21] Hence we know that this fundamental difference between Chu Hsi and Wang Yang-ming arose not simply from the former's more scholarly way of life and the latter's more activist approach, but more broadly from a height- ened awareness of the burdens of culture which was common in the Ming, as well as from that deeper preoccupation with the true nature of the self to which both political and cultural pressures drove the

Ming thinker. In other words, the tensions which existed in Confucian thought between morality and culture, action and quiescence, political involvement or disengagement all focused on the underlying problem of man's nature: was it static or dynamic, metaphysical or physical, an abstract ideal or an active force, a moral norm or a trans-moral perfection? How was the individual to understand that nature in relation to his actual self and his society?

THE MING EXPERIENCE OF THE SELF

In a very concrete sense Ming thought proper originates in an experience of the self. Ch'en Hsien-chang and Wang Yang-ming, generally acknowledged to be leaders and exemplars of new thought in the Ming, each underwent a personal experience which had a decisive effect on his thinking. In both cases there is an atmosphere of intense spiritual crisis surrounding the event. Ch'en had returned from Peking, having failed twice in the metropolitan examinations, and entered upon a prolonged program of concentrated study and meditation, broken only by a brief period of study with Wu Yü-pi in Kiangsi. Extensive reading characterized the earlier phase of this program; later the emphasis shifted to quiet-sitting in meditation as Ch'en became convinced that self-realization could not come from books. Finally his solitary effort resulted in an experience of "enlightenment," described in terms of seeing his essential self and its identity with all things, and drawing from this realization a sense of unlimited power in dealing with the world. A feeling of overflowing joy and unshakable self-confidence ensued.[22]

Wang Yang-ming's experience came after his banishment to Kuei-chou, a period of extreme hardship less significant for its physical difficulties than for the intellectual and spiritual isolation he suffered. A man of tremendous energy and strong commitment to public service, he found his activities severely restricted. With a brilliant mind and a fondness for intellectual discourse, he had little company among the aboriginals, exiled criminals, and emigrés of little education who surrounded him. In such circumstances Wang was pushed to the limit of his spiritual resources. His *Life Chronology* (*Nien-p'u*) reports how he was driven in upon himself: "He had already given up and put behind him all thought of personal success or failure, honor or disgrace, and only the question of life and death remained to be overcome. Thus day and night he stayed in silent, solitary meditation. . . ." Then late one night as he was pondering what a sage would do in such circumstances, he suddenly had a "great enlightenment." In it was revealed to him the real meaning of "the investigation of things and the extension of knowledge" which earlier had eluded him as he tried to apprehend the principle of things through contemplation of the bamboo in his father's garden. Transported by his discovery, he called out exultantly and his feet danced for joy. His companions, awakened from sleep, were amazed at his behavior. Thus he first learned, it is said, "that the way to sagehood lies within one's own nature." [23]

Such experiences were common in the Ming, but recent historians have treated them with considerable reserve. Those of a rationalistic and critical bent tend to dismiss such accounts as conventional hagiography, and others, who find that they do not fit the picture of Wang Yang-ming as a "pragmatic" philosopher or man of action, have preferred not to emphasize the religious overtones. The similarity to Ch'an experience was also disturbing to find in a supposedly proper Confucian. But a phenomenon so widespread, or even a convention so well established, requires some explanation. No doubt the lingering influence of Ch'an helped to produce an atmosphere in which some extraordinary experience of "enlightenment" lent authority to one's views. In Wang Yang-ming's case, the references to his confrontation of "life and death" and his prolonged absorption over many years with the "investigation of things," almost as if this were a *kōan* for him that awaited some flash of illumination, lend some plausibility to this interpretation. But if Wang was not unfamiliar with the ways of Ch'an and Taoist meditation, he had long since repudiated his own experiments with it, and while feeling no compulsion constantly to attack Buddhism, he made clear his rejection of it as incompatible with Confucian principles.[24] There are, moreover, indications that his experience and that of other Confucians in the Ming falls into a broader category of mysticism which need not always be labeled "Ch'an." Indeed the possibility of a distinctive Confucian mysticism can by no means be ruled out.

On this particular occasion Wang Yang-ming was preoccupied not only with the problem of apprehending "the principle of things" but in an intensely personal way with the question of how to become a sage. In his pioneering work, *Chūgoku ni okeru kindai shii no zasetsu* (The frustration of modern thought in China), Shimada Kenji [p] has drawn attention to the special urgency with which Ming thinkers felt this need.[25] What for Chu Hsi and the Sung school had been seen as an ideal for all, though achievable in fact by only a few, had become for them—and this includes Ch'en Hsien-chang, his teacher Wu Yü-pi, and Wang's teacher Lou Liang, as well as Wang Yang-ming himself—an overriding necessity. It was, one might say, as if their salvation depended on it. Men had become persuaded that sagehood should no longer be thought of as a remote, lofty and awesome ideal, exemplified by a few great figures in the past. It must be something realizable here and now by anyone.

THE EXPERIENCE OF ONENESS WITH ALL CREATION

One key to the Ming experience of the self and of sagehood is the Neo-Confucian doctrine that "the humane man forms one body with Heaven-and-earth and all things." [q] A development from the earlier Confucian idea of the unity of Heaven and man, this doctrine had been put forward by Ch'eng Hao and was often associated with Chang Tsai's mystical vision of man's essential harmony with the universe expressed in his celebrated "Western Inscription." [26] According to this view, man in his essential nature (*hsing*)[r] is identical with all nature (*t'ien-ti*)[s] and of the same substance as all things. Theoretically this identity is based on the equation of humanity or man's nature with life itself. The fundamental characteristic of the universe or Way is seen as its creativity or productivity, and man too is seen as creative in his very essence.

It was especially in relation to Buddhism that Neo-Confucians stressed the importance of this doctrine. As they saw it, Buddhism identified life with suffering and illusion; it insisted that man could could discover his true identity only by negating and then transcending his ordinary humanity, that is, recognizing it as an unreal distinction in an illusory world. For the Neo-Confucian, on the other hand, self-transcendence should be attained not by denying one's humanity but by affirming it, by overcoming selfishness in one's daily life, identifying with others, and coming to an awareness of man's ethical and cultural activity as participating in the creative process of Heaven-and-earth.

In the Ming the importance of this conception is evident in the frequency with which it is employed to describe both man's role in the world of action and his experience in the life of contemplation.[27] Overtones of it are found in Professor Jen's discussion of Ch'en Hsien-chang, and particularly in the lines: "Standing between Heaven-and-earth, what dignity this body of mine possesses," and "This body of mine, small though it is, is nevertheless bound up with ethical principles. The pivot is in the mind." [28]

Man's bodily self and his moral mind are at the center of the creative process and therefore play an exalted role. "Man forms one body with Heaven-and-earth," Ch'en says. "Hence the four seasons proceed and all things are produced. If one gets stuck in one place how can one be the master of creation?" [29]

To be a sage, then, was to be the master of all creation. For Wang Yang-ming and many of his followers, the sagehood to which any man might aspire was no less cosmic in its significance. With a belief in the direct attainment of sagehood, and a vision of man standing at the center of creation, the ingredients of a spiritual revolution were at hand. In some ways this development is comparable to the proclamation of universal Buddhahood through the Mahāyana in China, Japan, and Korea centuries earlier, and especially to those forms (Chen-yen and Ch'an) which emphasized the attainment of Buddhahood in this life and this body. There is a great difference, however, in the Ming exaltation of life, creativity, and the potentialities of the human individual.

QUIETISM AND ACTIVISM

If the mystical quality of Ming thought is inspired by this sense of man's oneness with all creation, it has important implications for both self-cultivation and man's proper activity in the world. This is an ethical mysticism, of which the natural expression is an impulse toward action in behalf of all mankind. As we have seen in the case of Wang Yang-ming's experience of sagehood, there has been a tendency to interpret such mystical phenomena, especially where they involve the cultivation of "quiescence" (*ching*) or the practice of "quiet-sitting" (*ching-tso*),[t] as showing the influence of Buddhism and Taoism. Nor can there be much doubt that, in a general way, Buddhist ideals of nonattachment and peace of mind along with Taoist meditative practices exerted a strong attraction on Neo-Confucians of both Sung and Ming. Quiet-sitting was approved and encouraged by Chou Tun-i, the Ch'eng brothers, and Chu Hsi. Though a practice without precedent in earlier Confucian tradition, its sanction by these Sung masters was sufficient to justify and encourage its use among orthodox scholars from Wu Yü-pi in the early Ming to Kao P'an-lung in the late Ming. Thus it seems indisputable that the Buddhist-Taoist example exerted a magnetic pull on the growth of Neo-Confucianism, causing it to develop along lines which would have been improbable except in a climate permeated by such influence.

On the other hand, as we have just seen, Neo-Confucianism from the start had felt compelled to reject the basic assumptions of Buddhist nonattachment or Taoist vacuity. A detached attitude toward things might be admirable, but the Confucian conception of human life and the self did not allow the individual to be seen in isolation from his social environment or the moral imperatives of Heaven. It was unrealistic, wrong, and selfish to conceive of human existence apart from the concrete relationships and obligations inescapably involved in the production and sustaining of human life. One could not renounce these obligations and cares even if to do so brought peace of mind. Anxiety, as Fan Chung-yen had implied, might be a higher state of mind than the peace of Nirvana.[30]

Confucian detachment, therefore, was sought in another direction. Virtue, humaneness, love, in their fullness and perfection, could express detachment in the midst of human involvement. Unselfish performance of duty to others was a discipline of ordinary life leading to both self-transcendence and self-fulfillment. An example of this is found in Professor Jen's study of Ch'en Hsien-chang. The latter is said to have abandoned the wearing of silk after the death of his mother, to whom he had been deeply devoted. One might have taken this as a sign of utter desolation over his loss: Ch'en had become so identified with his mother and emotionally dependent upon her that the rest of his life was overshadowed by his sense of mourning. Yet Ch'en's own explanation was of another sort. His preference in dress, he says, had always been for the utmost simplicity. He had put on finer robes only to please his mother and, though he continued for years to humor her, with her passing he was free to please himself. We may have doubts today as to how well Ch'en understood what he was doing, or the extent to which hidden compulsions operated here. Yet such doubts are in one sense irrelevant. In his own mind he had no consciousness that subordination of self to filial duty involved the loss of his own identity. His own preferences, though submerged in hers for so long, remained intact and unimpaired, awaiting the proper time for their expression.

Thus, in most Neo-Confucian methods of cultivation, even those characterized by "quiescence," the object was to root out not desire itself but only selfish desires—desires which set one apart from others, from things, from the world, from Heaven. Chang Tsai's *Western Inscription* is the most eloquent statement of this ideal and its enduring popularity suggests how central to later Confucian thought was this mystical vision of man harmoniously united to all forms of life.

In the formulation of this view Neo-Confucians could draw upon the legacy of classical Confucian teaching for most of the essential ingredients, if not for the practice of quiet-sitting. Among these is the idea that involvement in life, the active cultivation of moral man, can lead to true repose. This is expressed in Confucius' memorable summation of his own experience of life:

At 15, I had my heart set on learning.
By 30, I had established myself (in its pursuit).
By 40, I had no perplexities.
By 50, I knew the will of Heaven.
By 60, I was ready to listen to it.
By 70, I could follow my heart's desire without transgressing.[31]

Here we find a confidence that human life can follow a meaningful pattern and by ordered stages of growth and maturity attain a freedom wherein one's spontaneous desires are naturally in accord with Heaven, the moral order and vital power in the universe. This is a freedom in which one's own desires have been brought into perfect relation to the means of their fulfillment, the desires and needs of others, and the creative purposes of Heaven as the source of all life. In the Ming it is an ideal and an aspiration intimately bound up with sagehood, and, as the latter came to be thought more readily attainable, so did this freedom. What it meant, however, to be able to "follow one's heart's desire without transgressing" depended greatly on one's understanding of the heart-and-mind of man. Hence the lively discussion of this problem—the mind and nature— throughout the Ming, and especially of this freedom among the existentialist followers of Wang Yang-ming, as shown in the papers of Professors Okada and de Bary.

At the same time, the ideal of freedom-in-action implied that active involvement in the world and personal commitment to doing Heaven's will need not require constant and compulsive action in the world. Obedience to Heaven's will called for quiet acceptance and resignation as often as for effort in behalf of right. The *Book of Changes* proffered a kind of moral science in which the conditions for "advancing" and "withdrawing," engaging and disengaging, were specified. Here too Ming scholars were more attracted by these "signs" as a guide to action than they were to the *Changes* as a cosmological system, as is shown, for example, in Professor Huang's study of the utilitarian thought of the late Ming statesman, Ni Yüan-lu.[11] The essential notion, however, is quite implicit in the *Analects* and *Mencius*. Mo Tzu saw it and condemned it as fatalism, but (as Professor T'ang Chün-i has brought out in his studies on the Will of Heaven in early Chinese thought) the Confucian conception was far more profound than Mo Tzu appreciated.[32] The decree of Heaven manifested itself in various forms and on different levels. One could not identify it wholly with a single course of action. One's moral nature, which was the endowment of Heaven, might prompt one to take action in a good cause, but Heaven's decree, as made known through the circumstances surrounding this action, might nevertheless thwart the accomplishment of one's objective or force a redirection of one's efforts before success could be achieved. Alertness was required to all the promptings of Heaven, whether internal or external, in a constant process of re-examination. There were times for action and times for quiescence.

Beyond this, moreover, there was a need for quiescence in action. This was an attitude of mind which not only took into account the circumstances favoring engagement or disengagement at any given time, but also accepted the necessity for continual striving in the face of continual disappointment. Confucius described himself as one who kept on trying even when he knew it was of no use. In other words he could be engaged in what he thought to be right and yet disengaged so far as his own expectations were concerned.

To sum up, then, Confucian cultivation was alert to the external signs that suggested whether to "advance" or "withdraw," and sensitive to the promptings of one's heart as to what was right in some circumstances, but not necessarily in all, or what one must hold to under any circumstances. Thus there could be stability of purpose and composure of mind in the midst of action, while there could also be active mental or spiritual contact with the world even when circumstances dictated a period of inactivity.

As applied to the Ming, therefore, or indeed any other period in Chinese history, we cannot expect from the Confucianist active involvement only of a kind which is highly visible or outwardly effective. Wang Yang-ming was outstanding as an active statesman and general, and some see this as exemplifying his doctrine of the unity of knowledge and action. Others cite it further as illustrating the more dynamic and active spirit of the Ming. But Wang was a most exceptional figure for his or any other age. For many Ming thinkers, confronted by difficult political choices, right action consisted in political disengagement. They chose deliberately to live in what would be known as official retirement, pursuing a life not dissimilar to that of Confucius as a teacher and scholar. Thus, if the spirit of Ming thought is to be thought of as "active" and "dynamic," the basis for it must be an involvement with life not exclusively political in character.

MIND, BODY, AND SELF

In the Ming, as its critics complained, there were as many ways of viewing the mind and nature as there were schools and thinkers. There were differences, for example, as to whether the substance of the mind (the nature) was static or dynamic, whether its cultivation should be active or passive, and, if active, whether the effort at cultivation (*kung-fu*)[v] should be applied to the substance of mind (*pen-t'i*)[w] or to its functioning (*yung*).[x] These differences are discussed in the paper of Professors T'ang and Okada. Most Ming thinkers agreed, however, that Confucian teaching in these matters differed from Buddhism in taking actual life as its starting point. For the Neo-Confucian life (*sheng*)[y] is the basic value. He is ever conscious of the intimate connection between it and man's nature. The nature is what fosters life, and action or conduct conforming to the true nature of man conduces to his total well-being—physical, emotional, spiritual—and ultimately to the welfare of all things. Thus a truly moral life builds one's morale and spirit, but also contributes to one's bodily health. Conversely, one's mental and moral capacities greatly depend on one's physical powers and drives for their development. Even the so-called School of the Mind does not see this mind as a disembodied spirit, but rather as a vital power manifested through the physical aspect of man, his material force or ether (*ch'i*).[z] Likewise, this school rejects the tendency in Ch'eng-Chu thought to distinguish an abstract essence of mind or moral nature, on the one hand, and an emotional, sensual self identified with the body on the other. The nature as principle is neither an immutable norm by which one judges the propriety of one's impulses and desires, nor a purely rational law standing over against man's physical drives and passions. The life-fulfilling nature and the vital power of material force are inseparable.

When we refer to the School of the Mind (*hsin-hsüeh*),[aa] then, we must remember that *hsin* represents both the heart and mind of man, his affective as well as his rational nature. To think of this school as a form of philosophical idealism or Neoplatonic mysticism is misleading. The mind here represents man's actual nature and, as Professor Okada's paper brings out, a major tendency in the school is undoubtedly existentialist. At the same time the very effort to overcome or to embrace the antithesis between ideal and actual, the spiritual and the material, the static and the dynamic creates its own ambiguities and precludes simple characterization. We do well to note the range of possibilities inherent in these concepts. Insofar as our word "spirit" designates the breath of life, its original and basic meaning in the West, it must be identified not with reason or principle but with the Chinese *ch'i*, material force or ether, which is constantly active in the universe, constantly emerging from an invisible state into a visible. So too in the mind the creative power of material force is constantly manifesting itself.

The moral nature, which is spoken of also as the "substance or essence of the mind" (*pen-t'i*), is the principle of unity and harmony between man and things. And the impulses, desires, and drives which arise in the mind are not necessarily evil, unless they impair or destroy that harmony. The problem of self-cultivation is to observe these impulses and ideas as they emerge from the formless state, and to insure that their expression (or functioning) conforms to this total harmony. Mind culture in the more orthodox thinkers consists in identifying these impulses at the point of inception (*chi*),[ab] and acting on them in such a way that the fundamental composure or harmony of the self is preserved and sustained. On the other hand, if one assumes, as Ming existentialists do, that the essential mind or nature is trans-moral in its perfection, then self-cultivation becomes a matter of true self-expression, rather than of moral judgment or self-restraint.

In either case the School of the Mind focuses on the active, living subject in contact with others and with things seen as one body with onself. Self-understanding, an apprehension of one's true self, or insight into the substance of the mind does not require withdrawal from the senses or from contact with the world. Knowledge and action involve a constant interaction between the self and others, the nature and the senses, the individual and the environment. Rightly or wrongly (and I cannot deal fully with the issues here), most Ming thinkers felt that this distinguished Confucian self-cultivation from the type of Buddhist contemplation which sought withdrawal into an inner self or a higher self, in which the flow of ideas, thought, and desires had been stopped.

This view of the mind or self was holistic in the sense that man and his universe were seen as an organic unity, whereas Buddhism asked man to disavow his distinctively human nature and establish his true nature in a state of nondependence on the world. According to Wang Yang-ming, this destroyed the essential unity of things by creating higher and lower spheres of existence, a transcendental and a mundane order. It did not help that Buddhism ultimately reconciled the two through insight into the identity of Nirvana and Samsara. Such a mystical insight afforded no way of dealing with the world in rational, human terms.

If, however, this life-affirming view was seen as opposed to Buddhism and Taoism, there were in Ming thought other tendencies toward reconciliation. The intuitionist and existentialist trend in the Wang Yang-ming school led close to Ch'an Buddhism, even if their original premises differed. There were points of convergence in the belief in sagehood and buddhahood being inherent in all men, and in the experience of enlightenment as the recognition of one's true selfhood being identical with the actual self. Further, the affirmation of the physical and affective side of man's nature opened the way to Taoist concepts and practices of self-cultivation through both physiological and psychological means, as is shown in Professor Liu's paper.

A NEW "LIBERALISM" AND "PRAGMATISM" IN THE LATE MING

In the widespread trend toward "Unity of the Three Teachings," so marked in the sixteenth century, there is no doubt a large element of traditional Chinese syncretism. But syncretism of this sort had usually operated on a low intellectual level as an aspect of popular religion. The striking feature of the new humanitarianism which developed out of the Wang Yang-ming school was that, drawing on the latter's liberal view of man, it brought together the upper and lower classes, deepening the level of social consciousness in the former and raising the level of moral consciousness in the latter, while also releasing new political and cultural energies throughout the society. In other words, this was not simply a popular religious phenomenon, but one which tended to unite and activate new forces on several levels, with leadership coming from an important segment of the educated elite. This is particularly apparent in popular literature and painting. Evidences of it are found in the new "morality books" discussed by Professor Sakai, on one hand, and in a very different way by Professor Hsia's discussion of the romantic trend in the dramatic literature of T'ang Hsien-tsu. Both of these developments arose partly out of contact with the so-called left wing of the Wang Yang-ming school. The morality books drew upon its view of the autonomy of the moral self, and romantic literature upon its recognition of the passionate and appetitive nature of the individual. The present writer's discussion of individualism in the late Ming brings out further the possibilities inherent in the optimistic and liberal view of the self found in this school.

There is still other evidence that what we find in the sixteenth century is a near-revolution in thought, rather than simply a passing mood of eclecticism. The new view of the self, stressing the actual nature of man and especially his physical life and concrete needs, tended to generate a new "pragmatism" which gave increasing attention to "practical" realities. Among our papers, those of Professor Crawford on Chang Chü-cheng and of Professor Huang on Ni Yüan-lu illustrate how this new "practicality" was applied to statecraft and fiscal administration.

Since this kind of thinking centered, philosophically speaking, around the concept of *ch'i* ("material force" or "ether"), it has been described as a kind of materialism. If we recall, however, the dual aspect of *ch'i* as both matter and "spirit," we are not surprised to find that its proponents in the late Ming are as readily drawn to Ch'an Buddhism as to anything resembling Western materialism. It is also significant that among Confucians upholding a monism of *ch'i* the emphasis on realism and practicality finds its concrete expression within the domain of the traditional Confucian concern for society, that is, primarily in government, rather than in the development of a thorough-going empiricism in either the physical or social sciences. At the same time, it is more an expression of Ming "activism" than it is of the kind of detached, theoretical speculation important to the development of science in the West.

It is for these reasons that I have spoken of a near-revolution in thought during the latter part of the Ming, recognizing both the new potentialities and opportunities it presented and also the failure of these to develop fully. By and large, the new trends were confined during the seventeenth century to the established areas of Confucian concern: self and society as understood essentially in humanistic and moralistic terms. Nevertheless, this could not mean simply a return of Chinese thought to the *status quo ante*. If a new empiricism and positivism failed to develop fully, still the Ming left its successors at a new stage. The antimetaphysical tone of Ch'ing thought is clearly the product of the increasing Ming emphasis on practical action, physical reality, and empirical study. In other words, Ch'ing thought is the direct heir of the Ming, even though it prefers not to acknowledge this indebtedness. Like the Ming itself in respect to the Sung, the Ch'ing attacks in its predecessor what the latter had taught it to be dissatisfied with. It washed its hands of the Ming in Ming water.

To discuss the failures and limitations of either Ming or Ch'ing thought is not the primary aim of this volume. Our task has been to rediscover what was there, and this we have only partially succeeded in doing. Large areas remain to be explored and the source materials are far from exhausted. But we hope enough has been done here to suggest the richness and complexity of Ming thought, to identify some of the main issues and conflicts, to suggest the relevance of China's intellectual development in the Ming to an understanding of modern China, and to show how "modern" (and not peculiarly Chinese) were some of the problems encountered by Ming thinkers.

NOTES

1. Cf. Hu Shih, *The Chinese Renaissance* (reprint of second edition, New York, 1963), pp. 66–70.
2. *T'ing-lin shih-wen-chi* [ac] 3/1a–2a (translated in *Sources of Chinese Tradition*, pp. 608–9).
3. Ts'ui Shu, *K'ao-hsin lu t'i-yao* [ad] (TSCC ed.), A/22 (translated in *Sources of Chinese Tradition*, p. 623).
4. Liang Ch'i-ch'ao, *Intellectual Trends in the Ch'ing Period*, translated by Immanuel Hsü (Cambridge, 1959), p. 28.
5. To cite only two prominent examples among many, there are Wang Yang-ming in his *Instructions for Practical Living*, tr. by Wing-tsit Chan (New York, 1964), pp. 119–20 and *passim*; Huang Tsung-hsi in his *Ming-i tai-fang lu* (as excerpted and translated in W. T. de Bary *et al.*, *Sources of Chinese Tradition* (New York, 1960), p. 593. Cf. also David Nivison, "Protest Against Conventions and Conventions of Protest," in Arthur F. Wright, ed., *The Confucian Persuasion* (Stanford, 1960), pp. 177–201.
6. As one apt example we might cite the discussion of the "refined and undivided" mind (so deprecated by Ku Yen-wu) by Ho Hsin-yin, one of the most original and "progressive" thinkers of the late Ming and one who suffered martyrdom for his opposition to the established regime. Cf. Jung Chao-tsu, *Ho Hsin-yin chi* [ae] (Peking, 1960), p. 33.
7. *Ming-ju hsüeh-an* (Wan-yu wen-k'u ed.), 1/Fan lei.
8. That this was the case from the outset of the Ming is admirably illustrated by Frederick Mote's study of Kao Ch'i's relations with the founder of the Ming dynasty and Kao's tragic end. Cf. *The Poet Kao Ch'i* (Princeton, 1962), espec. ch. 9.
9. The confrontation between Ming despotism and the Confucian conscience is well delineated in Charles Hucker, "Confucianism and the Censorial System" in David Nivison and Arthur Wright, eds., *Confucianism in Action* (Stanford, 1959), pp. 199–208. Cf. also R. B. Crawford *et al.*, "Fang Hsiao-ju in the Light of Early Ming Society," *Monumenta serica* XV, pp. 303–27.
10. Cf. Chiang Fan, *Han-hsüeh shih-ch'eng chi* [af] (Commercial Press ed., Shanghai, 1934), p. 13, Fan lei.
11. Cf. Ping-ti Ho, *The Ladder of Success in Imperial China* (New York, 1962), p. 216.
12. For a brief resumé of these changes and the nature of the Ming examinations, see Nivison, "Protest Against Conventions . . . ," pp. 193–94.
13. Obviously this is not a question of numerical minorities, but of an

organized group capable of acting in opposition to the dominant power or of representing some social segment or class. Any such alignment was condemned as factionalism, and while a Confucian could claim to speak in the general interest, he dared not identify himself as spokesman of a party or organized minority.

14. Cf. Ping-ti Ho, *The Ladder of Success in Imperial China*, pp. 212–14, 255–56, 258–59, 261.

15. Cf. Saeki Tomi, *Sō no shin bunka* [ag] (Tokyo, 1967), p. 384. There are already signs of it in Lu Hsiang-shan; cf., S. C. Huang, *Lu Hsiang-shan* (New Haven, 1944), pp. 32, 58, 62.

16. *Ch'uan-hsi lu* (in *Wang Yang-ming ch'üan-chi* [ah], Ta-t'ung ed.; Shanghai, 1935), 1/22; Wing-tsit Chan, *Instructions for Practical Living* (New York, 1963 [hereafter abbreviated as *Instructions*]), pp. 62–63.

17. *Ch'uan-hsi lu*, 1/22 [Ts'ai] Hsi-yüan wen; tr. adapted from Chan, *Instructions*, pp. 60–61.

18. *Ming shih* (Kuo-fang Yen--chiu Yüan ed.; Taipei, 1962), 195/2277 ts'an.

19. Cf. Conrad M. Shirokauer, "Chu Hsi's Political Career," in Arthur F. Wright and Denis Twitchett, eds., *Confucian Personalities* (Stanford, 1962), pp. 162–88.

20. *Pai-sha tzu ch'üan-chi* [ai] (Temple edition of 1771), V, 6/2b; see also Jen Yu-wen, "Ch'en Hsien-chang's Philosophy of the Natural," *infra*, pp. 56–57, 61, 79–80.

21. *Ming shih* 282/3171; 283/3181–82. To say that they were reclusive does not imply that their philosophies were necessarily quietistic: my point is simply that the retreat from book learning was a common response to a common problem among Confucians whose engagement with life took different forms.

22. *Pai-sha tzu ch'üan-chi*, 3/22b–23a; cf. *infra*, pp. 57, 70, 74.

23. *Nien-p'u* A/6 Cheng-te 3 in *Wang Yang-ming ch'üan chi*, Vol. 1.

24. Cf. Wing-tsit Chan, "How Buddhistic Is Wang Yang-ming?", in *Philosophy East and West*, XI, Nos, 3, 4; Kusumoto Fumio, *Ōyōmei no zenteki shisō kenkyū* [aj] (Nagoya, 1958).

25. Cf. Shimada Kenji, *Chūgoku ni okeru kindai shii no zasetsu* (Tokyo, 1949 [hereafter referred to as *Zasetsu*]), pp. 19–35.

26. Translated by Wing-tsit Chan in de Bary, ed., *Sources of Chinese Tradition*, pp. 524–25; and in his *Source Book in Chinese Philosophy* (Princeton, 1963), p. 497.

27. Among innumerable other references one might cite Wang Yang-ming's eloquent statement of the idea in the opening lines of his "Inquiry on the Great Learning" (*Ta-hsüeh wen*) [ak] (see Chan, *Instructions*, p. 272 n.).Cf. also Shimada's extensive discussion of this

theme in "Subjective Idealism in Sung and post-Sung China: The All Things are One Theory of *Jen*," *Tōhōgakuho*, No. 28 (March, 1958), pp. 1–80. Shimada sees this theory not only as a powerful force in Ming thought but as an influence on reformist thought at the end of the Ch'ing, especially in T'an Ssu-t'ung.

28. *Pai-sha tzu ch'üan-chi*, V, 6/2a.

29. *Ibid.*, III, 3/62b.

30. I.e., in his famous dictum that the noble man should be "first in worrying about the world's troubles and last in enjoying its pleasures." For the significance of this motto in relation to the Buddhist ideal of the Boddhisattva, see my article "Buddhism and the Chinese Tradition," *Diogenes*, No. 47 (1964), pp. 120–22.

31. *Analects* II/4.

32. Cf. his "The Heavenly Ordinance in Pre-Ch'in in China" in *Philosoophy East and West*, XI, No. 4; XII, No. 1; and his more recent *Chung-kuo che-hsüeh yüan lun* [a1] (Hong Kong, 1966), pp. 508–21.

GLOSSARY

a 顧炎武
b 崔述
c 梁啓超, 清代學術史概論
d 狂禪
e 黃宗羲
f 明夷待訪錄
g 明儒學案
h 江藩
i 吳與弼
j 胡居仁
k 陳獻章
l 王陽明
m 良知
n 天理
o 婁諒
p 島田虔次, 中國に於ける近代思
  惟の挫折
q 天地萬物一體之仁
r 性
s 天地
t 靜坐

u 倪元璐
v 工夫
w 本體
x 用
y 生
z 氣
aa 心學
ab 幾
ac 亭林詩文集
ad 崔述, 考信錄提要
ae 容肇祖, 何心隱集
af 江藩, 漢學師承記
ag 佐伯富, 宋の新文化
ah 傳習錄, 王陽明全集, 上海大東
  書局
ai 白沙子全集
aj 久須本文夫, 王陽明の禪的思想
  研究
ak 大學問
al 唐君毅, 中國哲學原論

WING-TSIT CHAN[a] *The Ch'eng-Chu[b] School of Early Ming*

明 This paper is an attempt to show that the Ch'eng-Chu school of early Ming (1368–1644) was not merely a faint echo of the Neo-Confucianism of Ch'eng Hao (Ming-tao,[c] 1032–85), Ch'eng I (I-ch'uan,[d] 1033–1107), and Chu Hsi[e] (1130–1200), but underwent significant changes, assumed a definite direction, and in these ways anticipated the rise of the School of Mind that culminated in Wang Yang-ming (Shou-jen,[f] 1472–1529).

The consensus on the growth and development of Ming thought has been that early Ming Neo-Confucianism differed very little from that of Sung (960–1279) and that the School of Mind rose independently. This tone was set by the official account in the *Ming shih*[g] (History of the Ming dynasty), which says:

Basically Confucianists of early Ming all represented minor branches and what were left of the followers of pupils of Chu Hsi. The transmission of doctrines from their teachers was clearly traceable and their patterns were in perfect order. Ts'ao Tuan (Yüeh-ch'uan,[h] 1376–1434) and Hu Chü-jen (Ching-chai,[i] 1434–84) earnestly practiced their own doctrines and carefully followed earlier prescriptions. They held on to the standard handed down to them by earlier Confucianists and dared not make any change. The division of systems of learning began with Ch'en Hsien-chang (Pai-sha or Po-sha,[j] 1428–1500) and Wang Shou-jen.[1]

Although only Ts'ao Tuan and Hu Chü-jen are mentioned here, the meaning is that the whole Neo-Confucian movement in early Ming was no more than a reflection of Sung Neo-Confucianism and had nothing to do with the rise of the School of Mind. This characterization was meant to apply to both Ts'ao Tuan and Hsüeh Hsüan (Ching-hsien,[k] 1392–1464) in the north, or the Ho-tung[l] School, so called because Hsüeh came from the Ho-tung (east of the Yellow River) region in Shansi, and Wu Yü-pi (K'ang-chai,[m] 1391–1469) and his pupil Hu Chü-jen in the south, or the Ts'ung-jen[n] School,

so called because Wu was a native of Ts'ung-jen.[2] These four philosophers are our main concern.

The author of the account in the *Ming shih* probably took a lead
from Huang Tsung-hsi [o] (1610–95). In the introduction to the chapter on Wang Yang-ming in his *Ming-ju hsüeh-an* [p] (Critical anthology of Ming Confucianists) he says,

The learning of the Ming dynasty started with Ch'en Hsien-chang but did
not achieve great glory until Wang Yang-ming. The reason was that
scholars before them learned well the established doctrines of earlier Neo-
Confucianists but never returned to themselves to realize their meaning
or extend their knowledge to discover their deep secrets. As we say, this
scholar merely transmitted Chu Hsi's ideas and that scholar also merely
transmitted Chu Hsi's ideas.[3]

In thus interpreting the development of Ming thought, Huang
himself most probably took a lead from Wang Yang-ming's pupil,
Wang Chi (Lung-hsi,[q] 1498–1583), who said: "The Neo-Confucianism of our dynasty started with Ch'en Hsien-chang and achieved
great brilliance in our Teacher." [4]

It is perfectly correct to say that Ming learning reached its greatest brilliance and achieved its highest glory in Wang Yang-ming,
for his philosophy opened a new chapter in Chinese thought, spread
over all parts of China, and dominated the philosophical scene for
about 150 years. In recognizing Ch'en Hsien-chang as the forerun-
ner, both Wang Chi and Huang Tsung-hsi showed a remarkably
unbiased spirit, for both were faithful followers of Wang Yang-ming
who himself did not acknowledge any debt to Ch'en and did not
mention him in his philosophical discussions. The absence of Ch'en's
name in Wang's *Ch'uan-hsi lu* [r] (*Instructions for Practical Living*)
is conspicuous.

Wang Chi's and Huang Tsung-hsi's intention was undoubtedly to
underscore the independent origin of the School of Mind. In this
respect, Huang was most likely influenced by his teacher, Liu Tsung-
chou (Chi-shan,[s] 1578–1645), who saw the spirit of independence in
a number of Neo-Confucianists. In commenting on Ts'ao Tuan, Liu
said that Ts'ao's learning was not derived from any teacher but was
rediscovered from ancient books. To him, Wu Yü-pi's learning was
attained through deep reflections at midnight and through sweat and

tears. Ch'en Hsien-chang single-handedly established a new school, he said, and Wang Yang-ming provided a link for the learning that had been cut off by the practices of literary composition and textual studies.[5]

This idea of independent origin was particularly stressed with great pride by Huang Tsung-hsi. He said that the learning of the Confucianists differed from that of the Buddhists who insisted that learning must pass from one generation to another. "The Grand Master [Confucius] did not learn [from any teacher]," [6] he said. "Lien-hsi [Chou Tun-i,[t] 1017–73] rose without depending on anybody, and we have never heard that Hsiang-shan [Lu Chiu-yüan,[u] 1139–93] received instruction from anyone." [7] In spite of the Confucian respect for authority, we have here a new spirit in Ming thought of great significance regardless of whether the feeling is justified by historical facts or not. Liu's observation of the independence of Ts'ao Tuan and Wu Yü-pi must be taken as a real insight, for it differed radically from the general view that they were but careful followers of Chu Hsi. While these philosophers were praised for their independent character, however, their possible influence on subsequent thought was altogether forgotten.

The result of this neglect has been that most historians of Ming thought have ignored altogether the four early Ming Neo-Confucianists or their bearing on the School of Mind. It is true that Huang Tsung-hsi began his *Ming-ju hsüeh-an* with the account of Wu Yü-pi, but he did so not because he thought Wu was the beginning of Ming philosophy, for he has said nothing to this effect. Nor because he was following a chronological order, for Fang Hsiao-ju,[v] (1357–1402), Ts'ao Tuan, and Hsüeh Hsüan were older than Wu. As Jung Chao-tsu [w] has suggested, Huang did so probably because he felt that Wang Yang-ming's philosophy came out of that of Ch'en Hsien-chang and that the latter grew out of that of Wu Yü-pi.[8] Huang was by and large quite fair in his evaluation of the Ming scholars but not entirely free from partisanship. In his preface to a later edition of the *Ming-ju hsüeh-an*, Mo Chin [x] (1761–1826) said that in Huang Tsung-hsi's subtle opinion the Wang Yang-ming school was the main movement but the Tsung-jen school was the initial light. There is nothing in what Huang had said of Hu Chü-jen to support this conclusion. Perhaps this was Mo's polite way of saying that Huang should have related the beginning of the School of Mind to early Ming Neo-Confucianism.

As to modern historians of Chinese thought, in his lengthy history of Chinese philosophy, Fung Yu-lan [y] omitted the four early Ming Neo-Confucianists entirely.[9] Hou Wai-lu [z] has done the same in his monumental work.[10] Jung Chao-tsu, who devoted lengthy sections to three of them, said that Hsüeh Hsüan provided only footnotes to Ch'eng I and Chu Hsi and that Wu Yü-pi was a strict follower of Chu Hsi. Although he has noted that Hu Chü-jen criticized both Chu Hsi and Ch'en Hsien-chang, he has said nothing about the possible influence of Hu Chü-jen on the latter.[11] Ch'ien Mu [aa] has allotted due space to the three early Neo-Confucianists but like other writers he has regarded them, especially Hsüeh Hsüan, as faithful followers of the Sung Neo-Confucianists.[12] In his recent work on Sung and Ming Neo-Confucianism, Kusumoto Masatsugu [ab] has devoted a whole chapter to Wu Yü-pi (but not to the other three), and has suggested that the concept of being natural (tzu-jan) [ac] in Ch'en Hsien-chang is none other than the "vacuity and enlightenment" (hsü-ming) [ad] of Wu Yü-pi.[13] The attempt to discover some relationship between the two thinkers is admirable but the resemblance just mentioned is accidental because the idea of "vacuity and enlightenment," expressed in one of Wu Yü-pi's poems, is by no means an important element in his system of thought. There are two paragraphs on Wu Yü-pi and Hu Chü-jen in Wu K'ang's [ae] work on Sung and Ming Neo-Confucianism but he is silent on any possible contribution by them to the emergence of the Philosophy of Mind.[14] Forke has included Hu Chü-jen in his voluminous work, but he does not understand the relationship of the Ming Neo-Confucianists for he has considered not only Hu Chü-jen but also Ku Hsien-ch'eng [af] (1550–1612) of the Tung-lin [ag] school as belonging to the Yang-ming school.[15]

It is clear that in the opinion of most scholars the Neo-Confucianism of early Ming was of little importance, whether in the history of the Ch'eng-Chu philosophy itself or in the development of the Philosophy of Mind. But if we examine the philosophies of the four philosophers, we shall find that they steered Ch'eng-Chu philosophy in a new direction and in doing so prepared an intellectual atmosphere conducive to the growth of the philosophies of Ch'en Hsien-chang and Wang Yang-ming.

There are several ways in which those followers of the Ch'eng-Chu school changed the direction of its philosophy. For one thing, some of the most important subjects have become insignificant or have disappeared in the discussions of the four philosophers, namely, those of the Great Ultimate, yin and yang,[ah] and the relation between principle (*li*)[ai] and material force (*ch'i*).[aj] These subjects are so important in Chu Hsi's system that they form the first chapter of his recorded conversations,[16] but they have hardly engaged the attention of his early Ming followers. To be sure, Ts'ao Tuan wrote a short treatise on Chou Tun-i's *T'ai-chi-t'u shuo*[ak] (Explanation of the diagram of the Great Ultimate), in which he took exception to Chu Hsi's theory of the relationship between principle and material force. In Chu Hsi's theory,

The Great Ultimate is principle whereas activity and tranquillity are matters of material force. As material force operates, so does principle. The two are always dependent on each other and have never been separated. The Great Ultimate is comparable to a man and activity and tranquillity to a horse. The horse is to carry the man and the man is to ride on the horse. As the horse goes in and out, so does the man with it.[17]

Ts'ao argues that if that was the case, "the man would be a dead man and could not be the most intelligent among creatures, and principle would be dead principle and could not be the source of all things."[18] Incidentally, this shows, to some extent at least, that Ts'ao was by no means a blind follower of Chu Hsi. But outside of this work he had almost nothing to say on the Great Ultimate, yin and yang, and principle and material force. In his *Tu-shu lu*[al] (Notes on reading) Hsüeh Hsüan commented on these subjects systematically, and followed Chu Hsi almost without deviation.[19] But these are his reading notes only. In his own works, however, no discussion of these subjects is to be found.

Closely related to the problem of principle is that of the investigation of things. In Chu Hsi's philosophy, to investigate things is to investigate the principles inherent in them. It should come as a surprise to many that Ts'ao Tuan remained almost completely silent on the subject. In his notes on the *Great Learning*, Hsüeh Hsüan went into a fairly lengthy discussion of it. The interesting thing is that here he departed from the Ch'eng-Chu formula. Ch'eng I had said that there were many ways to investigate things. "One way is to read books and elucidate moral principles. Another way is to discuss people and events of the past and present and to distinguish which are right and which are wrong. Still another way is to handle affairs and settle them in the proper way." [20] Chu Hsi, too, said, "There is no other way to investigate principle to the utmost than to pay attention to everything in our daily reading of books and handling of affairs. Although there may not seem to be substantial progress, nevertheless after a long period of accumulation, without knowing it, one will be saturated [with principle] and achieve an extensive harmony and penetration." [21] In his notes on the *Great Learning* Hsüeh Hsüan practically paraphrased Ch'eng and Chu on the subject. Like them he stressed reading and handling human affairs, saying,

From one's own body . . . to grass and plants, and insects and animals, one should investigate the principles embodied in them. One should extend further to the books of sages and worthies, the classics, and the political affairs of the various dynasties, all of which are things to be investigated. And one should investigate their moral principles.[22]

But he departed from Chu Hsi in two subtle but vastly important respects. One is that the intellectual element has become subordinate. According to Chu Hsi, the process of investigation "in regard to all things in the world, is to proceed from what knowledge one has of their principles, and investigate further until one reaches the limit." [23] He also said, "To investigate principle to the utmost means to seek to know the reason for which things and affairs are as they are and the reason according to which they should be." [24] While the moral emphasis is always present, the intellectual interest is paramount. In Hsüeh Hsüan, however, this is no longer so.

Furthermore, to Chu Hsi, one is to exercise one's intelligent mind to investigate the principles in things and in time one's understanding of principles will be complete. Hsüeh Hsüan, however, says:

Although principles are in things, when principles in one's own mind come into subtle union with them, all will be penetrated. At the initial penetration, one understands that each thing has its own principle. As penetration reaches the ultimate point, one realizes that the thousands and tens of thousands of things possess only one principle.[25]

It is no longer just the intelligent mind going out to discover principles but the principles embodied in the mind going out to form a union with the principles in things. Hsüeh Hsüan did not go as far as Lu Hsiang-shan who said that "the mind and principle can never be separated into two" and that "what permeates the mind, emanates from it, and extends to fill the universe is nothing but principle," [26] but in Hsüeh Hsüan principles are not only in things but also in the mind.

The Ho-tung school is generally regarded as the most faithful and orthodox Ch'eng-Chu school in early Ming, and yet we have found that both Ts'ao Tuan and Hsüeh Hsüan did not hesitate to differ from their masters. This tendency of deviation was even more pronounced in the Ts'ung-jen school, for both Wu Yü-pi and Hu Chü-jen showed almost no interest in the Great Ultimate, yin and yang, and principle and material force. Wu Yü-pi did not discuss the subject of the investigation of things. Hu Chü-jen did but with a new emphasis, as we shall see.

On the subject of principle, Wu Yü-pi declared that it is immanent in the mind. "Each of the Five Relations has its principle," he said, "and principle is sufficiently present in one's mind. It comes with birth. Man is a man because he possesses it. If one does not lose this principle which is in his mind but fulfills the principles of the Five Relations, one's life will not be amiss." [27] Of course, Chu Hsi also said that "the principle in the mind is the same as the Great Ultimate," that "the mind and principle are one," and that "the mind as a thing completely involves all principles." [28] In Chu Hsi, however, the mind and principles in things are of equal importance, while in Wu Yü-pi the mind occupies the central position.

The all-importance of the mind is even more obvious in Hu Chü-jen's doctrine of the investigation of things. In his essay on the subject, his basic point is that it must be done in the fulfillment of the Five Relations and in such things as governmental measures and education.[29] To him, "all principles are embodied in the mind" and "the investigation of things should be done only in one's own personal life." [30] He closely tied together the investigation of things and the preservation of the mind, that is, not losing the original mind in which all principles are embodied.[31] He said, "Preservation and nourishment [of the mind] both precede and follow the extension of knowledge." [32] "Since mind and principle are not separated," he said, "the preservation of the mind and the investigation of things must extend each other." [33] To him, "the fundamental of learning is none other than preserving the mind and investigating things." [34] Again, he said, "As one has successfully investigated principle in one's mind, one must preserve and nourish it and do so with seriousness (ching)." am [35]

From the foregoing, it is clear that while the early Ming Neo-Confucianists remained within the Ch'eng-Chu tradition, they struck out on their own and traveled in a new direction, thus opening up a new vista for Chinese philosophy. This fact becomes clearer when we look at the basic philosophy of each of the four thinkers.

Ts'ao Tuan was poor and devoted his life to teaching. He wrote a number of commentaries on ancient classics and Sung Neo-Confucian works, none of which is distinguished. His greatness lies instead in his earnest practice. But in his own philosophy of life, he formed a pattern that conditioned what was to come. Huang Tsung-hsi characterized him this way:

The Master held vigorous practice to be fundamental and he adhered to this principle strictly. . . . For he based his philosophy on seriousness and personally realized it through having no [selfish] desires. He said that "in everything one must devote one's effort to the exercise of the mind and that was the main road to the gate of Confucius." [36] It shows that his learning had a true foundation.[37]

The two words that underscore Ts'ao's thoughts are "seriousness" and "mind," and they are, of course, closely related. He said that "man can form a trinity with Heaven and Earth as the Three Powers solely because of his mind," that "if one can be respectful and serious, one's mind will be enlightened," and that "a student should be careful in his words so as to hold fast to and preserve the mind." [38] He also said, "One instance of sincerity will be sufficient to dispel ten thousand instances of insincerity and one instance of seriousness is sufficient to guard against a thousand depravities. There is nothing more to the point than this in what is called 'first building up the noble part of one's nature.' [39] " [40]

From these quotations, Ts'ao's central emphasis on the mind is unmistakable. Liu Tsung-chou was not exaggerating when he described Ts'ao Tuan's philosophy as "returning to search for principle in one's own mind," according to which "the mind is the ultimate, its activity and tranquillity are yin and yang, its dealings with daily affairs are the changes and union of the Five Agents." [41]

Like Ts'ao Tuan, Hsüeh Hsüan perpetuated the Ch'eng-Chu tradition but did so more vigorously. He copied the *Hsing-li ta-ch'üan* [an] (Great collection of Neo-Confucianism) in its entirety himself, and his *Tu-shu lu*, as already indicated, loyally reproduced the Sung Neo-Confucianists. Huang Tsung-hsi is perhaps justified in saying that "the learning of Hsüeh Hsüan is sincere but without excellence. He reverently adhered to the patterns of the Sung scholars." [42] But both Huang Tsung-hsi and the *Ming shih* agree that Hsüeh's teaching is to return to one's original nature.[43] He himself said, "In the pursuit of learning one must know one's original nature and must recover it." [44]

This doctrine was derived from Chang Tsai (Heng-ch'ü,[ao] 1020–77). According to Chang Tsai's doctrine of the transformation of physical nature, "With the existence of physical form, there exists physical nature. If one skillfully returns to the original nature endowed by Heaven and Earth, then it will be preserved." [45] The idea is that, because of physical nature, one's endowment is unbalanced, thus giving rise to moral defects. Through moral effort one can regain the harmony and balance and thus recover the original nature. Quoting Chang Tsai, Hsüeh Hsüan said that this passage means that when the nature endowed by Heaven and Earth becomes beclouded and turbid, it becomes physical nature, and that if one skillfully returns to his original nature by transforming his physical nature, his nature endowed by Heaven and Earth will become clear.[46] This interpretation is not at all original, but when it was made the foundation of his teaching it gained new significance.

The same is true of his stress on seriousness. The idea is not new.

It is an integral part of Sung Neo-Confucianism. Ch'eng Hao, Ch'eng I, and Chu Hsi all taught it.[47] But whereas for them it is one of the many items for moral cultivation, for Hsüeh Hsüan it became *the* item. It meant so much to him that he called himself Ching-hsien [ap] (Studio of seriousness). His individual sayings added nothing to what the Sung Neo-Confucianists had already said about it, but because of his central emphasis, it took on a new complexion and special meaning. He said, "If one does not hold seriousness to be fundamental, one's mind will drift and go in and out at every moment and one will not know how to stop it." "From ancient times on, nothing is more important in the pursuit of learning than seriousness. With seriousness, one's mind will have a master and all things can be done." "The mind is like a mirror and seriousness is like polishing. When the mirror is polished, the dust will be removed and brightness will grow. When the mind becomes serious, human selfish desires will disappear and the Principle of Nature will become brilliant." "When one always holds seriousness to be fundamental, one's mind will be preserved. As the mind is preserved, one can handle things without error." [48] One may quote many more sayings like these, but a few are sufficient to show the spirit. The significant point is that seriousness is now given special weight. Since seriousness is a quality of the mind, the more it is stressed, the more important the mind becomes.

When we turn to the Ts'ung-jen school, we find that seriousness and the mind occupy not only an important position but virtually an exclusive one. As Liu Tsung-chou said of Wu Yü-pi, "The Master's learning consisted of hard work and vigorous effort. Much of it was achieved through deep reflections at midnight and through sweat and tears. When he achieved something, he had something in which he found joy for himself and unwittingly danced with his hands and feet. For to him, his seven scores of years seemed like one day. Effort and joy produced each other. He may be said to have had the excellence of the mind of the sage. As to his way of learning, it lay essentially in cultivating one's nature and feelings and regarding self-mastery and contentment with poverty as the concrete steps. This is truly the way of Confucius and Yen Tzu [aq] to rise to a higher and higher level. He therefore did not engage in writing but his understanding of truth was genuine indeed." [49] Wu Yü-pi farmed for a living and refused to serve in the government. Thus his philosophy was that of personal demonstration instead of intellectual speculation. What he cherished most was tranquillity and ease of mind, and he cared least for formulating a philosophical system. And yet Hu Chü-jen, Ch'en Hsien-chang, and Lou Liang [ar] (1422–91) were all his pupils, and at least two of them directly contributed to the development of Wang Yang-ming's philosophy. (It was Lou Liang who directed Wang to study Sung Neo-Confucianism in 1489.) His sayings are reflections and advice on how to live a simple and peaceful life.[50]

Nevertheless, two central ideas clearly stand out, namely, seriousness and the cultivation of the mind. "Generally speaking," he said, "in the instructions of sages and worthies the important thing lies solely in seriousness. If one can be tidy in his attire and serious in his speech and movements, and control himself with rules of propriety, his mind will naturally be under control. Even if one does not study, he will improve much, though if he cultivates his mind through study and understanding principle, it will be even better." [51] "One's mind must have a place where it can rest in peace," [52] and "one must put his mind in order and make it pure and clear, and always be alert. Only this will do. This is the work of straightening one's inner life with seriousness. Alas! Without seriousness, the inner life will not be straightened and will be darkened and fall." [53]

Because of simple sayings like these, but more because of the influence of his personal life, his pupils were strongly affected by him. As the *Ssu-k'u ch'üan-shu tsung-mu t'i-yao* [as] (Essentials of the complete catalogue of the Four Libraries) has observed, his pupil Ch'en Hsien-chang learned from him quiet observation and self-cultivation and another pupil, Hu Chü-jen, learned from him earnest resolution and vigorous practice.[54]

Like Wu Yü-pi, Hu Chü-jen would not take the civil service examinations but was happy with a life of poverty and teaching. In the opinion of Huang Tsung-hsi, "His whole life was built on the strength of seriousness and consequently his practice of moral principles showed excellent results." [55] The *Ming shih* says of him, "In his learning the first thing is to 'hold loyalty and faithfulness to be fundamental,' [56] and the essential is 'to find the lost mind.' [57] In order to hold on to the mind and not to lose it, there is nothing more important than seriousness. He therefore named his study Ching-chai [at] (Study of seriousness)." [58] From these sayings we can see that seriousness became with him the chief factor in moral cultivation. He said, "When the Sage instructed people, he merely taught them to be 'loyal and faithful in words and sincere and serious in action,' [59] so that they can establish a foundation, and then their ability and scholarship can improve step by step." [60] The reason for this is because "Seriousness is the way to preserve and nourish [the mind]." [61] "The mind embodies all principles," he said. "Our trouble is that it may be confused, neglected, and lazy. Therefore we must hold seriousness to be fundamental. To 'concentrate on one thing and not to get away from it' [as Ch'eng I defined 'seriousness'] [62] is to restore order where there has been confusion and neglect, and to 'be orderly and solemn' [as Ch'eng I described seriousness] [63] is to overcome laziness. This is the essential method of preserving the mind." [64] Being serious, one's mind becomes absolutely intelligent, for "Intelligence and clarity of mind are results of seriousness. As soon as one concentrates on one thing, one becomes absolutely clear. When the mind is divided, it will be beclouded and confused." [65] "With seriousness," he said, "the mind becomes concentrated. When it is concentrated, it will be absolutely clear and therefore it will become intelligent. With seriousness, one's internal life becomes straightened. As one's internal ilfe becomes straightened, there will be no selfishness and one can therefore master oneself." [66] "Seriousness can remove becloudedness and laziness, correct evil and depravity, remove impurity and confusion, and establish one's great foundation." [67] If one can hold on to seriousness as fundamental and cultivate himself with it, it will be found that "the Principle of Nature is originally in his mind, intelligence will naturally grow, and moral principles will be increasingly clear to him." [68] When he was asked whether seriousness could become the master of the mind, he answered, "If the mind is not serious, it will be lost, but if it is serious, it will be preserved. Does this not mean that seriousness is the master of the mind?" [69] "When there is a master to preserve the mind, it can direct and control all things. When Mencius advocated seeking the lost mind, he was advocating a fundamental task." [70] On the other hand, "If the mind is without a master, it will not work when it is tranquil and it will not work when it is active. If it is without a master in the state of tranquillity, one's original nature will become either virtually nonexistent or beclouded. This is why one's great foundation cannot be established. If it is without a master in the state of activity, it will either become reckless and foolish in action or chase after material things and succumb to selfish desires. This is why the universal way cannot operate." [71]

In Hu Chü-jen's thinking, seriousness is so important that it must take precedence over the extension of knowledge. In the order of chapters of his *Chü-yeh lu* [au] (Records of occupying one's sphere of activity), the subject of seriousness follows immediately those on the substance of the Way and the pursuit of learning and comes ahead of the extension of knowledge.[72] This is a radical modification of Chu Hsi's order of learning and cultivation. In his *Chin-ssu lu* [av] (Reflections on things at hand), the first and standard anthology of Sung Neo-Confucian philosophy, chapters on the preservation of the mind and nourishment of one's nature come after that on the extension of knowledge.[73] Hu's primary interest in the mind and almost exclusive reliance on seriousness for its cultivation is surely a sharp departure from the orthodox Ch'eng-Chu position. The classical formula in that tradition is that of Ch'eng I's saying, "Self-cultivation requires seriousness; the pursuit of learning depends on the extension of knowledge." [74] There has always been an insistence on balancing the extension of knowledge with moral cultivation. In commenting on Ch'eng I's saying, Chu Hsi said, "If either is neglected, it will not do. In the extension of knowledge, we must cultivate ourselves, and in cultivating ourselves, we must extend our knowledge." [75] When asked if moral cultivation should not come before the extension of knowledge, Chu Hsi answered, "From the very beginning, moral cultivation comes first. People in ancient times cultivated themselves with seriousness from childhood. Their fathers and brothers gradually taught them to read and understand moral principles. If you say that we must wait until we have cultivated ourselves before we proceed to understand the extension of knowledge, when will the time be? We must make both efforts at the same time, cultivating ourselves on the one hand and extending knowledge on the other." [76]

Hu Chü-jen did not reject or ignore the extension of knowledge but he assigned it a definitely subordinate position. At least, he gave seriousness priority in time, in direct opposition to Chu Hsi. This is what he said of Ch'eng I's dictum: "Since it is said that self-cultivation requires seriousness and the pursuit of learning depends on the extension of knowledge, it means that before the mind knows anything it must be preserved and nourished so that it can engage in the extension of knowledge. It is also said, 'One should understand principle and preserve it with sincerity and seriousness.' [77] This shows that after the extension of knowledge one must preserve and nourish the mind so it will not get lost, for the effort at the extension of knowledge can be made from time to time but the effort at preservation and nourishment cannot stop." [78] In other words, cultivation is prior in time, embraces the extension of knowledge rather than vice versa, and occupies our whole life instead of periods of it.

From the above considerations of the four philosophers, brief though they are, we can readily see that early Ming Neo-Confucianism grew less and less interested in such intellectual aspects as metaphysical speculation and the doctrine of the investigation of things and more and more concerned with the mind, its cultivation and preservation, and seriousness as the means of achieving that goal. As we continue our survey, we also hear more frequently such phrases as "recovering one's nature," "seeking the lost mind," "returning to the original mind," "preserving and nourishing the mind," "first establishing the noble aspect of one's nature," and "the mind having a master." These should remind us of Lu Hsiang-shan, the greatest philosopher of mind in Sung times.[79] These ideas came from Mencius [80] but it was Lu who built a solid philosophy on them.

However, it would be wrong to suppose that the early Ming Neo-Confucianists were influenced by Lu. They did not get their inspiration from him. The chief issues of contention between Lu and Chu Hsi were those of the relationship between the mind and principle and the nature of the Great Ultimate. To Chu Hsi, mind is the function of human nature, and human nature is identical with principle. To Lu, however, mind *is* principle. Chu Hsi considered the

Great Ultimate as being above physical form and yin-yang as being with physical form but Lu refused to make the distinction.[81] The early Ming Neo-Confucianists did not continue the controversy and did not discuss the problems. Lu had very little to say about seriousnesses. In any case, after his pupil Yang Chien (Tz'u-hu,[aw] 1140–1228) Lu had no more successors. During the Yüan dynasty (1271–1368) Wu Ch'eng (Ts'ao-lu,[ax] 1249–1333) and Cheng Yü (Tzu-mei, Shih-shan,[ay] 1298–1358) attempted a compromise between the Chu and Lu schools, but by the end of that dynasty, whatever influence Lu had had came to an end.

The disappearance of Lu's philosophy of mind from the intellectual scene was chiefly due to the fact that his ideas are too close to those of Meditation Buddhism to suit the Confucianists. It may also have been due to the absence of any work by Lu which could form a basis for his followers to rally around. In the rational Neo-Confucianism of Ch'eng-Chu there were Chou Tun-i's *T'ai-chi-t'u shuo* and the *T'ung-shu* [az] (Penetrating the *Book of Changes*),[82] Chang Tsai's *Cheng-meng* [ba] (Correcting youthful ignorance),[83] the Ch'eng brothers' *I-shu* [bb] (Surviving works),[84] and Chu Hsi's *Chin-ssu lu* and commentaries on the Four Books, but there is no work by Lu Hsiang-shan which could serve as a focal point for his philosophy.

There was, of course, the factor of governmental promotion of the Ch'eng-Chu philosophy. In 1313 it was decreed that Chou Tun-i, the Ch'eng brothers, Chang Tsai, Chu Hsi, and other Sung Neo-Confucianists (but not Lu Hsiang-shan) be honored with religious sacrifices in the Confucian temple, and that Ch'eng I's and Chu Hsi's commentaries on the Confucian classics were to be the standard texts for the civil service examinations. The supremacy of Ch'eng-Chu Neo-Confucianism thus became complete. By the beginning of the Ming, all Neo-Confucianists were followers of the Ch'eng-Chu school.

There were additional reasons why the school particularly flourished at this time. With the overthrow of the Mongol dynasty, there was a resurgence of nationalism and a swing back to Chinese religion and philosophy, and the Ch'eng-Chu Neo-Confucianism represented them at their best. Astronomy, mathematics, medicine, architecture, and other practical arts had been developing in the Yüan dynasty and continued to grow, and the rational philosophy of Ch'eng I and Chu Hsi very well fitted this practical temper. A new dynasty needed reconstruction in many areas, and the Ch'eng-Chu system had much to offer, especially in the areas of society and government. The founder of the dynasty, T'ai-tsu [bc] (r. 1368–98), being a man of little education, depended greatly on the scholars of the time, and turned to the Neo-Confucianists. As the *Ming shih* says, "scholars served at court in large numbers." [85] Of these, Sung Lien [bd] (1310–81) was particularly prominent. He was the closest adviser to the emperor and the leading scholar as well as the leading official of his time. As the *Ming shih* has recorded, the emperor delegated to him virtually all important state matters, and he was the one who established the cultural institutions of the new dynasty.[86] And he was an ardent admirer of Chu Hsi. His pupil Fang Hsiao-ju, also a great scholar and a high official, further enhanced the influence of the Ch'eng-Chu tradition. All in all, the Ch'eng-Chu school monopolized Chinese thought at the beginning of the Ming. In other words, when changes took place in the school, they did not owe anything to Lu Hsiang-shan but were the results of forces at work within the school itself and in history. When the *Ssu-k'u ch'üan-shu tsung-mu t'i-yao* remarks that the learning of Wu Yü-pi lies between that of Chu Hsi and that of Lu Hsiang-shan,[87] it is correct only insofar as the outcome of his thinking happens to lie between them; it should not be understood to mean that Wu represented a direct transmission of ideas from Lu or had any historical connection with Lu's school.

What were the forces at work within the Ch'eng-Chu school and in history? First of all, Sung Neo-Confucianism developed a new metaphysics chiefly because of the challenge of Buddhism and Taoism. To counter the Buddhist concept of the Void and the Taoist concept of Nonbeing, the Neo-Confucianists had to construct their own cosmology and metaphysics, and this they did in terms of the Great Ultimate, principle, and material force. In the early Ming there was no longer such a challenge and consequently the Neo-Confucianists did not get excited over such problems as principle and material force.

Second, because of the new Neo-Confucian metaphysics, the Confucian horizon was extended beyond the mundane world and therefore the relationship between Heaven and man became the main consideration. That horizon had now become familiar and new horizons had to be discovered. Ming Neo-Confucianists found them in the relationships within man himself.

Third, the problem of the investigation of things had by this time been explored for several centuries. Had China had a tradition of pure science, the exploration might have been channeled to new intellectual fields. Lacking that tradition, the doctrine of the investigation of things found no new territory to expand into and became stale. It lost its attraction and gradually faded away.

Fourth, I have mentioned the growth of the practical spirit in the Yüan dynasty with the development of certain scientific subjects. Coupled with the new interest in the mind, it was natural, and perhaps inevitable, that the practical spirit was directed to the practical matter of living in terms of earnest practice and the actual demonstration of moral values.

In addition to these factors operating within the Neo-Confucian school itself, certain historical events added impetus to this tendency toward a philosophy of mind. In 1415 Hu Kuang [be] (1370–1418) and others compiled the *Hsing-li ta-ch'üan* by imperial decree. This monumental anthology contains the major works of the Ch'eng-Chu school and sayings by many Sung and Yüan Neo-Confucianists. It was designed not so much for the elucidation of the Neo-Confucian doctrine as to put an official jacket on it. The Ch'eng-Chu philosophy had become a state ideology and a rigid prescription for scholarship and truth. Its purpose was not a discovery of new insights but conformity with Neo-Confucian teachings in specific details. What was worse, the goal was not social progress and personal cultivation but worldly success in officialdom. Creative and self-respecting scholars refused to wear this jacket, shunned the civil service examinations, and sought independence and freedom in moral cultivation.

Last, there was the terrific impact of the martyrdom of Fang Hsiao-ju, a leading and much respected scholar. When a prince rebelled and captured the capital, the emperor, Hui-ti [bf] (r. 1399–1402), burned himself to death. The prince ordered Fang to draft an edict to legalize his assumption of rule. Rather than compromise his integrity and loyalty, Fang refused, knowing that he would die for it. His execution sent many scholars into soul searching, and his heroic spirit of righteousness inspired many more. It was a time not for dry and disinterested intellectual speculation but for moral choice and personal decision. In a climate like this, the philosophy of mind was an irresistible development. That was the case in mid-nineteenth-century Japan when the Meiji Restoration demanded determination and dedication. This is the case in present-day China, when the national crisis forces the best scholars to search within themselves for an explanation and a solution. In both cases the philosophy of mind came to the fore, just as in the early Ming.

In stressing the connection between the early Neo-Confucianists of the Ming and the rise of the philosophy of mind in Ch'en Hsien-chang and Wang Yang-ming, I am not suggesting that certain specific ideas of theirs have been derived from any of the four philosophers. In fact, one of the most important ingredients of early Ming thought, namely, seriousness, received very little attention from Ch'en and Wang. Furthermore, some of their most important ideas were not even hinted at by the four philosophers. Ch'en Hsien-chang taught meditation in order to see in the tranquil universe the spirit of life as expressed in the jumping of the fish and the flying of the hawk.[88] Wang Yang-ming strongly emphasized the extension of one's innate knowledge and the necessity of "always doing something." [89] None of these ideas was ever suggested by the early Ming Neo-Confucianists. Wang's doctrine of the unity of knowledge and action was, of course, all his own. If no specific idea has come from the early Ming, however, the general tendency toward the cultivation of the mind surely determined the direction and prepared the atmosphere in which Neo-Confucianism was to grow. Were not Ch'en's meditation and Wang's "always doing something" their own ways of exercising seriousness? At any rate, like the early Ming Neo-Confucianists, they were dedicated to the cultivation and realization of the moral nature of the mind.

NOTES

1. *Ming shih* (Ssu-pu pei-yao [bg] [Essentials of the Four Libraries] edition), 282/1b.
2. A county in Kiangsi Province.
3. *MJHA*, ch. 10.
4. *Lung-hsi Hsien-sheng ch'üan-chi* [bh] (The complete works of Master Wang Chi) (1615 edition), 10/35a.
5. *MJHA*, "Shih-shuo" [bi] (My teacher's words), pp. 1b, 2a, 3a, 4a.
6. *Analects*, 19/22.
7. *MJHA*, Explanatory Remarks, p. 1a.
8. *Ming-tai ssu-hsiang shih* [bj] (History of thought of the Ming dynasty) (Shanghai, K'ai-ming [bk] Bookstore, 1941), p. 19.
9. See his *A History of Chinese Philosophy*, trans. by Derk Bodde (Princeton University Press, 1953), Vol. II, chs. 14–15.
10. *Chung-kuo ssu-hsiang t'ung-shih* [bl] (A general history of Chinese thought) (Peking, Jen-min [bm] Publication Co., 1960), Vol. IV, pt. 2.
11. *Ming-tai ssu-hsiang shih*, pp. 14, 19, 23, 31.
12. *Sung-Ming li-hsüeh kai-shu* [bn] (A general account of the Neo-Confucianism of the Sung and Ming dynasties) (Taipei, Chung-hua Wen-hua Ch'u-pan Shih-yeh Wei-yüan Hui,[bo] 1953), chs. 38–40.
13. *Sōmin jidai jugaku shisō no kenkyū* [bp] (Studies on the Neo-Confucian thought of the Sung and Ming dynasties) (Kashiwa shi, Chiba ken, Japan, Hiroike Gakuen [bq] Press, 1962), p. 398.
14. *Sung-Ming li-hsüeh* [br] (The Neo-Confucianism of the Sung and Ming dynasties) (Taipei, Hua-kuo [bs] Publishing Co., 1955), pp. 289–90.
15. Alfred Forke, *Geschichte der neueren chinesischen Philosophie* (Hamburg, 1938), pp. 371–428.
16. See the *Chu Tzu yü-lei* [bt] (Classified conversations of Master Chu) (1880 edition), ch. 1.
17. *Ibid.*, 94/14b–15a.
18. *T'ai-chi-t'u shuo shu-chieh* [bu] (An account and an explanation of the *Explanation of the Diagram of the Great Ultimate*), p. 3b in the *Ts'ao Yüeh-ch'uan Hsien-sheng i-shu* (Surviving works of Master Ts'ao Tuan), pp. 17b–18a.
19. *Tu-shu lu* (Notes on reading) (*Cheng-i-t'ang ch'üan-shu* [bv] [The complete library of the Hall of Rectifying the Way] edition), 4/11b–16b.
20. *I-shu*, in the *Erh-Ch'eng ch'üan-shu* [bw] (The complete works of the two Ch'engs) (SPPY edition), 18/5b.
21. *Chu Tzu wen-chi* [bx] (Collection of literary works by Master Chu)

(SPPY edition, entitled *Chu Tzu ta-ch'üan* ^{by} [Complete literary works of Master Chu], 61/2a.

22. *Tu-shu lu*, 2/2b–3a.

23. Remarks on the fifth chapter of the *Great Learning*.

24. *Chu Tzu wen-chi*, 64/33a.

25. *Tu-shu lu*, 2/3a.

26. *Hsiang-shan ch'üan-chi* ^{bz} (The complete works of Lu Hsiang-shan) (SPPY edition), 1/3b, 34/21a.

27. *Wu K'ang-chai chi* ^{ca} (Collected works of Wu Yü-pi) (1526 edition), 8/27a. The Five Relations are those between ruler and minister, father and son, husband and wife, elder and younger brothers, and friends.

28. *Chu Tzu yü-lei*, 5/3b–4a.

29. *Hu Wen-ching Kung chi* ^{cb} (Collected works of Hu Chü-jen), 1504 edition, 2/21a.

30. *Chü-yeh lu* (Records of occupying one's sphere of activity), *Cheng-i-t'ang ch'üan-shu* edition, 2/9a–b.

31. *Ibid.*, 1/1b.

32. *Ibid.*, 8/21b.

33. *Ibid.*, 1/2b.

34. *Hu Wen-ching Kung chi*, 1/4b.

35. *Ibid.*, 2/10b.

36. *Lu-ts'ui* ^{cc} (Choice collection) in *Ts'ao Yüeh-ch'uan Hsien-sheng i-shu*, 1a.

37. *MJHA*, 44/1b.

38. *Lu-ts'ui*, 8b, 5a.

39. *Book of Mencius*, 6A/15.

40. *Lu-ts'ui*, 2a.

41. *MJHA*, "Shih-shuo," p. 1b. The Five Agents or Five Elements are Water, Fire, Wood, Metal, and Earth.

42. *MJHA*, 7/1a.

43. *Ibid.*, 7/3a, and *Ming shih*, 282/5a.

44. *Tu-shu lu*, 5/10b.

45. *Cheng-meng* (Correcting youthful ignorance), ch. 1, sec. 41.

46. *Tu-shu lu*, 5/3b.

47. For Ch'eng Hao's doctrine of seriousness, see the *I-shu*, 2A/2a, 5b–6a, 13b, 19a; 3/2a; 4/4b; 11/2a–3a, 7b, 11a. For Ch'eng I, see *ibid.*, 2A/23b; 3/5b; 15/1a, 8b, 11a; 18/3a, 5b, 6b. For Chu Hsi, see the *Chu Tzu yü-lei*, 9/3a–4a; 12/8a–17a; 17/1a–3a; 18/12a–14b; 30/2a–4b; 42/3b–6a; 44/27a–29a; 45/3a–4b.

48. Yen Tzu was the most virtuous pupil (521–490 B.C.) of Confucius; *Tu shu-lu*, 5/13b–15a.

49. *MJHA*, "Shih-shuo," p. 2a–b.

50. See his "Jih-lu" [cd] (Daily notes) in his *K'ang-chai Hsien-sheng wen-chi* [ce] (Collection of literary works by Wu Yü-pi), edition of *c.* 1600, ch. 11.

51. *Wu K'ang-chai chi*, 2/20a.

52. *Ibid.*, 1/19a.

53. *K'ang-chai Hsien-sheng wen-chi*, 11/13a. The idea of straightening the internal life with seriousness originated in the commentary on the second hexagram in the *Book of Changes* and was elaborated by the Ch'eng brothers. See the *I-shu*, 2A/5b–6a; 11/2a, 3a; 18/3a.

54. 1933 edition (Shanghai, Commercial Press), p. 3634.

55. *MJHA*, 2/1b.

56. *Analects*, 1/8.

57. *Book of Mencius*, 6A/11.

58. *Ming shih*, 282/6b.

59. *Analects*, 15/5.

60. *Chü-yeh lu*, 3/1a.

61. *Ibid.*, 2/2a.

62. *I-shu*, 1/5b; 11/3a; 15/5a–b, 20a.

63. *Ibid.*, 15/6b, 21a.

64. *Chü-yeh lu*, 1/4a.

65. *Ibid.*, 1/4b.

66. *Ibid.*, 2/12a.

67. *Ibid.*, 2/1a.

68. *Ibid.*, 2/2a.

69. *Ibid.*, 2/5a–b.

70. *Ibid.*, 1/4b.

71. *Ibid.*, 1/5a. For the great foundation and universal path, see the *Doctrine of the Mean*, ch. 1.

72. See the *Ssu-k'u ch'üan-shu tsung-mu t'i-yao*, p. 1927.

73. See Chu Hsi and Lü Tsu-ch'ien,[cf] comps., *Reflections on Things at Hand: The Neo-Confucian Anthology*, trans. by Wing-tsit Chan (New York, Columbia University Press, 1966).

74. *I-shu*, 18/5b.

75. *Chu Tzu yü-lei*, 18/14b.

76. *Ibid.*

77. Ch'eng Hao's words in the *I-shu*, 2A/3a.

78. *Chü-yeh lu*, 2/2a–b.

79. See the *Hsiang-shan ch'üan-chi*, 1/3a, 4a, 6b; 4/7b; 11/1a, 6a; 12/4b; 32/1b, 2a, 6a; 34/5a; 35/14a.

80. See the *Book of Mencius*, 6A/8, 10, 11, 15.

81. *Hsiang-shan ch'üan-chi*, 1/3b–4a, 11/5b–6a, 22/5a, 34/21a; *Chu Tzu wen-chi*, 36/4b–5a; 8a–9b, 16b; *Chu Tzu yü-lei*, 1/3b, 5/6a–10a.

82. For an English translation, see Wing-tsit Chan, comp. and trans., A

Source Book in Chinese Philosophy (Princeton University Press, 1963), ch. 28.

83. For selections, see *ibid.*, ch. 30.
84. For selections, see *ibid.*, chs. 31 and 32.
85. *Ming shih*, 282/1a.
86. *Ibid.*, 128/7b.
87. *Ssu-k'u ch'üan-shu tsung-mu t'i-yao*, p. 1729.
88. *Pai-sha Tzu ch'üan-chi* ^{cg} (Complete works of Ch'en Hsien-chang) (1769 edition), 1/14a, 22a, 29a; 3/12b, 23a.
89. *Instructions for Practical Living*, secs. 5/132–133, 137, 138, 147, 170.

GLOSSARY

a	陳榮捷	ad	虛明	bg	四部備要
b	程朱	ae	吳康	bh	龍溪先生全集
c	程顥, 明道	af	顧憲成	bi	師說
d	程頤, 伊川	ag	東林	bj	明代思想史
e	朱熹	ah	陰陽	bk	開明
f	王陽明, 守仁	ai	理	bl	中國思想通史
g	明史	aj	氣	bm	人民
h	曹端, 月川	ak	太極圖說	bn	宋明理學概述
i	胡居仁, 敬齋	al	讀書錄	bo	中華文化出版事業
j	陳獻章, 白沙	am	敬		委員會
k	薛瑄, 敬軒	an	性理大全	bp	宋明時代儒教思想
l	河東	ao	張載, 橫渠		の研究
m	吳與弼, 康齋	ap	敬軒	bq	千葉柏市廣池學園
n	崇仁	aq	顏子	br	宋明理學
o	黃宗羲	ar	婁諒	bs	華國
p	明儒學案	as	四庫全書總目提要	bt	朱子語類
q	王畿, 龍溪	at	敬齋	bu	太極圖說述解
r	傳習錄	au	居業錄	bv	正誼堂全書
s	劉宗周, 蕺山	av	近思錄	bw	遺書, 二程全書
t	濂溪, 周敦頤	aw	楊簡, 慈湖	bx	朱子文集
u	象山, 陸九淵	ax	吳澄, 草廬	by	朱子大全
v	方孝孺	ay	鄭玉, 子美, 師山	bz	象山全集
w	容肇祖	az	通書	ca	吳康齋集
x	莫晉	ba	正蒙	cb	胡文敬公集
y	馮友蘭	bb	遺書	cc	錄萃
z	侯外廬	bc	太祖	cd	日錄
aa	錢穆	bd	宋濂	ce	康齋先生文集
ab	楠本正繼	be	胡廣	cf	呂祖謙
ac	自然	bf	惠帝	cg	白沙子全集

JEN YU-WEN *Ch'en Hsien-chang's*

Philosophy of the Natural

明 In both the official Ming history and Huang Tsung-hsi's survey of Ming thought, the *Ming-ju hsüeh-an*, the importance of Ch'en Hsien-chang has been underscored by comparing him to Wang Yang-ming as one of the two fountainheads of Ming thought.[1] In later times, however, Ch'en has been largely neglected, and while innumerable works have been devoted to Wang Yang-ming or have focused attention on him as the leading Ming thinker, Ch'en's contribution to Ming thought—indeed, to the development of Chinese thought as a whole—is little known. Part of the reason for this is that Ch'en's own writings, especially those philosophical in character, are not extensive and much of his thought must be gleaned from his essays, poetry, and letters. This paper attempts for the first time to give a coherent account of his thought, based on the whole of his written work, in order to illuminate the original character of his ideas and his distinctive influence on Ming philosophy.[2]

THE BACKGROUND OF CH'EN'S
LIFE AND THOUGHT

Ch'en Hsien-chang[a] was born on November 27, 1428 (*Hsüan-te* 3:10:21) at the village of Tu-hui in Hsin-hui[b] County of Kwang-tung Province.[3] Later his family moved to the village of Pai-sha,[c] near the prosperous town of Chiang-men.[d] Hence he was known by the honorific title of Master of Pai-sha and the school of philosophy he founded was called the Chiang-men school.

Hsin-hui County, about 70 miles southwest of the provincial capital of Canton, was a comparatively newly developed area. In the Six Dynasties period it was referred to as an area inhabited by newly subjugated "barbarians," and in the Sui dynasty, when it became known by its present name, the district was a vast undeveloped region. In Ming and Ch'ing times the process of consolidation was still continuing, with the size of the district decreasing in extent as the population rose and subdivision became necessary. During Ch'en's time, in the fifteenth century, the region was still thinly populated in relation to the extent and fertility of the land. Settlers who had come down from the north enjoyed a prosperous life, in conditions that still resembled those of a frontier area.[4]

Ch'en Hsien-chang was a fifth-generation descendant of a settler who had moved to Hsin-hui from northern Kwangtung in 1273 in a migration with thirty-four other clans, including that of the present author. This completed a southward trek begun by the clan after it had fled North China to escape the Mongol invaders who set up the Yüan dynasty.[5]

The first two generations of the Ch'en family in Hsin-hui seem to have worked their newly occupied lands themselves, but gradually their holdings were extended to include scattered fields leased to others in neighboring districts. Ch'en Hsien-chang mentions that his family inheritance comprised about two *ching* (32.88 acres) of land yielding an average of 10–12,000 catties of rice annually. About one third of this product was in the form of rent. In Ch'en's poems he refers to male members of the family harvesting and collecting grain, and to female members spinning and weaving (VI, 8/16b, VII, 9/31a, VIII, 10/68b).[6] The family also had land in the village for the raising of vegetables, mulberries, hemp, poultry, and pigs.

Though by American standards such an estate would represent a modest one, by Chinese standards the income from it could support a good-sized family (about ten persons) and also provide an education for its sons. By the third generation, Ch'en's grandfather could afford to live the life of a scholar, free of worldly cares. "He was fond of reading the book of *Lao Tzu* and admired [the early Sung Taoist] Ch'en Hsi-i" (X, Mo/7 Hsing chuang). His father, a more orthodox Confucian scholar, studied Sung philosophy and was able to publish a volume of his own poetry.[7] Undoubtedly a library of some sort passed down to Hsien-chang and encouraged his scholarly inclinations.

Though little is known concerning Ch'en's early life, it is clear that he began his schooling when young, while at the same time helping out with the agricultural tasks of the family. Throughout his life he claimed to be half scholar and half farmer. A poem of his popular among the people of the region and, though unpublished, preserved by oral tradition, goes:

On market days at Chiang-men
I buy hoes and I buy books.
Ploughing the fields and reading the books
I am half farmer and half scholar.

The life of a scholar-farmer, who combines manual work in the fields with intellectual labors in his study, was also characteristic of his sons, whom he speaks of as contributing to the family's agricultural endeavors while at the same time they received schooling and passed the government examinations to attain the *hsiu-ts'ai* degree (X, Mo/11b).

The prosperity of the family may be inferred from the fact that Ch'en could afford to travel to Peking several times at his own expense, and to send his son to Hunan and a pupil to attend a sick friend in the north. He had the means to entertain frequent visitors, and to construct some buildings in his village and a fishing terrace in Chiang-men, four miles away. The annual tuition fees from his students provided at most a minor supplement to the regular family income, as tuition was generally low in those days.

Thus we may conclude from Ch'en's family background that he was a fairly typical representative of the independent local gentry, well enough off to afford the education required for an official career, but also self-sufficient enough to forgo such a career in favor of a scholar's life if he so chose. At the same time he had roots in the soil—rich, new soil in which Chinese culture was still not wholly established and the memory of the frontier still lived. A spirit of youth, adventure, and adaptation to new circumstances no doubt combined with the emigré's tenacity in preserving his cultural identity. From this standpoint it is understandable that Ch'en, as a thinker, should seek to reaffirm the values of Confucian tradition on the basis of a fundamental reevaluation of its meaning in new surroundings where Sung philosophy was hardly known.

BIOGRAPHICAL SKETCH

Ch'en's father, Ch'en Tsung[e] (H. Lo-yun, 1402–28), a scholar and poet, had died a month before his birth. His widowed mother (nee Lin, 1405–95) remained to bring up his elder brother Hsien-wen[f] (H. Ku-yu, 1422–86), then aged five,[8] and himself. In his childhood he was very weak and sickly. It is said that his mother did not wean him until he was nine. Throughout his life he felt toward her an extraordinary gratitude and devotion, discharging his filial duties with the utmost care.

As a student he was unusually bright and showed a strong memory. At the age of twenty, he passed the examination for the second official degree of *chü-jen*, shortly after having obtained the first (*hsiu-ts'ai*). In 1448 he went to Peking but, failing the examination for the advanced degree of *chin-shih*, he remained in the capital as a student in the Imperial Academy (*t'ai-hsüeh* or *kuo-tzu chien*). In 1451, when he was twenty-four, he failed again in the examination at Peking.

Returning home, Ch'en pursued his own studies in literature and philosophy and probably at this time began his career of teaching. At twenty-seven (1454) he made a long journey to Lin-ch'üan in Kiangsi Province for the purpose of studying under the philosopher Wu Yü-pi. An important seed for the development of his personal character and thought was planted there, but Ch'en admitted that, although he had learned much from Wu in the study of the classics and had been immensely inspired by Wu's personal example, he "still had not found the entrance gate to the pursuit of truth" (III, 3/22b).

On returning to his native place he earnestly applied himself to this search, following the customary approach of the Chu Hsi school through extensive book learning. He shut himself up in his home, studying every sort of literature available, ancient and modern. His reading included Buddhist and Taoist works, too, historical fiction and popular novels. He stayed up late at night reading and, when drowsy, would pour cold water over his feet to keep awake. In spite of this intensive effort, however, he seemed to get nowhere. One day, all at once, he came to a sudden realization: "Learning should be self-acquired. After the self-acquisition, it should be broadened with books. Then the words in the books will be my words. Otherwise, the books will remain books and I remain myself" (X, Mo/17a).

Thereupon he commenced a new method of study and self-cultivation, building a hall for himself in which he spent all his time practicing "quiet-sitting" (*ching-tso*).[8] This prolonged, self-imposed asceticism nearly caused a nervous breakdown, and he eventually moderated it somewhat.[9] Nevertheless, he continued this solitary life for fully ten years (1455–65, from the age of twenty-eight to that of thirty-eight). At long last his strenuous effort resulted in a kind of enlightenment, described by himself in the following terms:

After my return to Pai-sha, I stayed indoors without ever going out, devoting myself solely to a search for the proper method of [moral and spiritual] endeavor. Without the guidance of teacher or friend, I searched for it day after day in book after book, neglecting to sleep and eat. I went on this way for many years and still did not acquire anything. What I mean by "did not acquire anything" is that this mind of mine and this principle (*li*) did not converge and tally with one another [i.e., the opposition of subject and object was not overcome]. Then I forsook the complexities [of Chu Hsi's method] and sought, through quiet-sitting alone, for what was essential within myself. In time I was able to see the substance of my own mind reveal itself mysteriously, always as if it were a material object. Henceforth, in the daily round of social intercourse, everything followed my heart's desire, just like a horse guided by bit and bridle. Moreover, in the investigation and realization of the principles of things and in the examination of the sages' teachings, there was a clue and source for everything, just as water always has a source. Thereupon I gained great self-confidence and said, "Does not the effort to become a sage lie in just this?" (III, 3/22b–23a).

In this experience of enlightenment Ch'en felt that he had found the real nature of the human mind and established its freedom and independence. The mind, indeed, was the master of everything, even of the universe. It was a discovery crucial to the new philosophy which he went on to develop and elaborate for the rest of his life.

When Ch'en resumed teaching at Pai-sha, he came to enjoy a

high reputation as a scholar and many students already well advanced came to him for instruction in the classics, history, and literature and to learn the secret of his "self-acquisition." His method was not to indoctrinate the students with his own conceptions, but to inspire, evoke, and guide their own thinking toward their own self-acquired convictions.[10] His own accomplishment in literature, especially in poetry, was marked by elegance of style and beauty of language, but what distinguished him most from other poets, whose gifts were merely literary, was the depth of his thought and the richness of inner experience to which his poems gave expression.[11]

As Ch'en's fame spread throughout the province, more and more young scholars flocked to that obscure village to enlist in his academy. Even the commissioner of education in Kwangtung sent a number of choice scholars to study under him. Among these was Liang Ch'u [h] (1451–1527) of Shun-te County in Kwangtung, who later became a distinguished scholar and grand councilor in the imperial court.[12] A number of other students won high degrees and became officials, but an even larger number achieved distinction in scholarship and thought without pursuing an official career.

In 1466 an unexpected difficulty arose from Ch'en's teaching. He had introduced physical training into the curriculum in the form of archery practice. This was in accordance with the Classics, which mentioned archery as one of the six courses of study, but it gave rise to a rumor that he was gathering and training an armed band for a rebellion. People warned him of the danger to which he was exposing himself, but he took no heed of them. Finally, the magistrate of Shun-te, a well-known scholar who had great respect for Ch'en, counseled him in a friendly way to take leave and go north lest this ugly situation worry his aged mother. Thus Ch'en decided to make another trip to Peking, at the age of thirty-nine (X, Mo/8a).

Entering the Imperial Academy once more, he was given an examination requiring him to compose a poem which would rhyme with one by the Sung philosopher Yang Shih (1053–1135), the leading disciple of the Ch'eng brothers. In the poem Ch'en gave an account of his strenuous efforts in search of the Way. The following is a partial translation:

Enduring hunger makes one plan to raise millet;
Exposure to cold makes one think of planting mulberries [for silkworms].
In youth I conceived the rare ambition
Of reaching for the blue sky a hundred thousand feet above.
In dreams I saw the ancient sages—
Alas, time passes like a running stream.
My Way has a grand master,
The immortal Chu Tzu-yang [Chu Hsi].
He spoke of reverence [*ching*] [1] unceasingly,
Showing me the way to virtue.
Righteousness and profit diverge on separate paths,
But how slight the difference at the point of choice!
The learning of the sages need not be difficult.
It is all in using one's mind aright.
The "good beginnings" [of virtue] should be cultivated daily,
Lest they be choked off by material desires.
The Way and virtue are like rich fat,
While literature is merely chaff and husks.
Standing between Heaven and Earth,
What dignity this body of mine possesses! . . .
For the last sixteen years
I have absented myself from the arena of fame and profit.
Behind closed doors I have engaged in a search,
Putting away worldliness as if driving away sheep.
In my one room, ensconced on a stand,
I sat erect and composed, like [Chuang Tzu] "sitting in forgetfulness."
Strangely, in the midst of my travails,
My resolve proved not strong enough,
As if in crossing a great river
My progress were thwarted midway.
This body of mine, small though it is,
Is nevertheless bound up with ethical principles.
The pivot is in the mind;
To hold on or let go determines life and death.
Why then let dissipation wear it down?
Grievous indeed is such a loss.
Let each and all make utmost effort,
And in the end the raging tide will be turned back. (V, 6/2a–b)

It may be noted here that, as of this writing, Ch'en had not broken with the Ch'eng-Chu teaching, but still clung to the overriding idea of "reverence" so central to its method of self-cultivation.

As his disciple Chan Jo-shui [j] later commented, "This poem reflects things before he was forty, so the height of his achievement and the depth of his accomplishment are not yet expressed herein" (IX, 1/3a).

The chancellor of the academy admired his superb literary style and the depth of his thought. He exclaimed, "Even Yang Shih was not his equal." [13] Ch'en's reputation spread quickly in intellectual and political circles; celebrated scholars and influential officials befriended him and some even became his formal students. Unfortunately his popularity also caused him some distress. A vice-minister by the name of Yin Wen, [k] hearing of Ch'en's great reputation, sent his son to be his pupil, but Ch'en declined six or seven times to take him. Such a rigid refusal may seem unreasonable and inconsiderate of another's feelings, but Ch'en probably thought that taking Yin's son as a pupil might be misinterpreted as designed to win favors from a superior official. In any case Yin took it as an insult and cherished a deep hatred for him.

Shortly thereafter the Imperial Academy recommended Ch'en to the Ministry of Personnel and he was appointed a clerk in the ministry. There he performed his duties conscientiously until the following spring (1467), when he resigned his post and returned to Pai-sha to resume his teaching. Two years later, at the age of forty-two, he tried once more to pass the examination in Peking but failed. Returning home that autumn, he resolved to take no more examinations, but instead to devote the rest of his life to study and teaching.

Ch'en's pupils came from far and near to attend his academy. Some built houses for themselves in Pai-sha and studied under him for many years. High officials of Kwangtung and Kwangsi and even representatives of foreign countries passing through Canton made special trips to Pai-sha to pay their respects. Ch'en took a lively interest in all kinds of people, including Buddhists, Taoists, merchants, and servants, as well as the farmers and scholars with whom he normally associated. He received and conversed with them all with equal cordiality, answering their questions without reserve. In this way his influence reached beyond the circle of his own disciples.

A good illustration of his moral influence is found in a story recorded by the late Ming philosopher Liu Tsung-chou, [l] (1578–1645).

Once when Master Ch'en was traveling by boat he met with some robbers who took the money and belongings of his companions. From the rear of the boat Ch'en called out, "I still have some luggage here. Come and take it!" When they became aware of his identity, however, the robbers surprisingly enough apologized to him. "We mean fellows did not recognize you and insulted you—a real gentleman. Since the people on this boat are your friends, how can we rob them of their money?" They then returned everything they had taken and went away.[14]

By 1475, when he was forty-eight years old, Ch'en's philosophical views were well formulated. A long poem that year reveals the development of his thought after he had composed the poem cited just above.

The ancients cast away the dregs [of the classics];
These are not the genuine heritage of the past.
Trifling indeed is a ladleful of water,
But, accumulated, the water becomes a great stream.
Yet there is another kind, not produced by accumulation,
Whose source bubbles up of itself.
Utmost Infinity (*wu*) possesses utmost activity; [m]
What is nearest at hand is most divine.[n]
When it issues forth in activity, it is inexhaustible.
When hidden and stored, it is profound and deep.
Able to grasp the key to it [or the initial sign (*chi* [o])],
What need have I to pore over old books?
Learning is endangered by not using the mind,
But misusing it produces bondage to the letter.
Only when founded on emptiness can the structure be solid;
And the foundation must be established on the natural [*tzu-jan* [p]]
"Be watchful" and "apprehensive" [says *The Mean*].
This saying cannot be called wide of the mark.
Later scholars lacked discernment
And missed the Way at the crucial points.
Pass the word to men of understanding—
Nature's lute originally has no strings. (V, 6/2b)

Ch'en's break with the intellectual approach of the Chu Hsi school became further apparent in the summer of 1481, when he was honored by being invited to become the director of the Pai-lu Academy [q] in Kiangsi Province. This was the school in which Chu Hsi had taught and which the local authorities wished to restore. To accept such an honor was unthinkable for Ch'en, however, since he could not conscientiously expound the Chu Hsi teaching. Politely he asked, "How does it differ from trying to borrow hearing from the deaf or sight from the blind?" (II, 1/11b). Directly and frankly he replied to the Kiangsi officials: "I cannot accept the offer by any means" (III, 3/15b–16b).

Meanwhile high authorities in Kwangtung jointly recommended him to the emperor on the grounds that, as a scholarly treasure of the empire, he should be installed in office at court. Emperor Hsien-tsung approved the memorial and the local officials requested him to go to the capital, but he declined repeatedly on the grounds of illness and his mother's old age. In the autumn of 1482, when he was fifty-five, pressure from the governor finally obliged him to make the trip.

En route and on arrival at Peking in late spring of the next year, he was acclaimed as a living sage by many admirers in official and scholarly circles, as well as among the common people. However, on reporting to the Ministry of Personnel, he found the minister to be none other than Yin Wen, who still held a grudge against Ch'en for refusing to take his son as a pupil and who proceeded to subject him to all kinds of petty indignities and harassment.[15] Ch'en decided to return south and submitted a long memorial to the throne pleading illness and also reporting that his aged mother was seriously ill and longed for his return.[16] The emperor was touched. He granted Ch'en an honorary position at the Hanlin Academy (*Hanlin-yüan chien-t'ao* [r]), and released him on condition that he would return to service after he had recovered his health and was no longer needed by his mother. He arrived home in the winter and devoted the remaining years of his life to teaching. Despite many subsequent recommendations for his reinstatement, he had no intention of returning to official life.

During the last decade of his life, Ch'en enjoyed the enrollment of a distinguished pupil in his academy, Chan Jo-shui (H. Kan-ch'üan, 1466–1560) of Tseng-ch'eng [s] in Kwangtung. In 1494, two years after he obtained the *chü-jen* degree, Chan came to Pai-sha and stayed there until three years after the master's death. He became

Ch'en's favorite disciple, being recognized as the one who had the fullest understanding of his thought. Later Chan obtained the advanced degree in Peking and became an official of ministerial rank in Nanking. He was responsible for making Ch'en better known in the north through his establishment of Pai-sha academies, and he himself ranks as one of the most eminent philosophers of the Ming.[17]

If Ch'en's pupils were somewhat less numerous and influential than Wang Yang-ming's, it was partly due to the character of his teaching and personal example. Like Ch'en himself, many of them avoided the competition for honors in the examinations and official life. Huang Tsung-hsi says of them that they led lives of "simplicity, hardship, and independence." [18] The official Ming history also stated that "they were solitary in their conduct and independent in their views; hence their influence was not far-reaching." [19]

After the death of his mother in the spring of 1495 when he was sixty-eight, Ch'en never again wore silk or embroidered clothing. When asked the reason, he replied that he had worn them before only to please his mother. Practically it meant that he observed mourning for her the rest of his life. In subsequent years, though his own health was fading, he continued to teach, write poetry, correspond with friends and former pupils, and indulge his fondness for calligraphy, in which he had become quite expert. He used up so many brushes that it was difficult in that rural area to replace them. He then devised a method of making his own by gathering rushes in the wilderness and tying them together into a brush. From this he became known as the inventor of a new style of calligraphy called "rush-dragon" (*mao-lung* [t]). People treasured his work so much that it came to command a good price, as it still does. (It has been alleged that he was a good painter, as well, specializing in the drawing of flowering plums, but this has been proved untrue.)[20] For amusement, he played the Chinese lute and went fishing occasionally. Though unbending in matters of principle, he relaxed easily, enjoyed life, and was good company.

In 1499 some high officials once again recommended him for reinstatement at court, but before Emperor Hsiao-tsung's decree reached Kwangtung the following spring, he had passed away peacefully at home on March 9, 1500 (Hung-chih 13:2:10), at the age of seventy-three. He was survived by his second wife Chang, two daughters, a son by his first wife Lo who had died early, and three grandsons.

In 1585, during the reign of Shen-tsung (Wan-li 13), he was accorded the highest posthumous honor for a Confucian: his tablet was enshrined in the official temple of Confucius—he was the only Kwangtung man so honored in 2,000 years—and the honorific title of "Wen Kung" [u] was conferred upon him.

THE NATURAL (*TZU-JAN*)

"My learning is based on the natural" (III, 3/63a). This, indeed, is the keynote not only of Ch'en's philosophy, but also of his poetry, his approach to literature, his practical life, and even his calligraphy. In his poetry, for example:

> Who apprehends the real action and quiescence of the five agents?
> The ever-flowing of eternity originally is the natural (*Book of Changes*). (VIII, 10/39a)

> The illustrious books of sacred learning
> Teach me the rule of the natural. (V, 6/23a)

Chan Jo-shui, in a foreword to Ch'en's *Complete Works*, gives the best exposition of the latter's view of the natural in the following words:

His natural literature is produced from his natural mind and heart; his natural mind and heart are produced from natural learning; natural learning consists in [Mencius'] "neither forgetting nor assisting" (2A/2), just like the shining of the sun, the passing of clouds, the flowing of water, and, furthermore, like the blooming of Heaven's flowers—the red ones becoming red and the white ones becoming white—all by themselves, each forming its own form and each manifesting its own color. Who arranges it artificially? Who makes it that way? That is what is called the natural. (I/6b)

The original meaning of the word *tzu-jan* (the natural) in Chinese is "what is so of itself" (*tzu-jan erh jan*). As a philosophical term it is not found in any of the Confucian Classics, which generally use the term *T'ien* (Heaven) or *T'ien-ti* [v] (Heaven and Earth) to denote Nature in the sense of cosmos or universe. *Tzu-jan* is definitely of Taoist origin. Chuang Tzu used it twice in his "Inner Chapters," in the sense of the adjective "natural." In Lao Tzu's *Tao-te ching* "the natural" appears five times as a specific noun. Neo-Taoist thinkers in subsequent dynasties developed the conception of the natural in their cosmology and ontology, culminating in the formulation of a system of metaphysical naturalism. Kuo Hsiang (d. 312) may be considered the chief representative of this school.

The term "the natural" in Ch'en's philosophy was directly derived from Ch'eng Hao, who spoke about the "intuitive experience of the natural" (*ming-chiao tzu-jan* [w]); "Speaking of Heaven's naturalness (*t'ien chih tzu-jan*), it is called the Heavenly Way (*T'ien-tao*)" and "A yin and a yang are called the Way, which is the Way of the natural." [21] Most probably Ch'eng was influenced by the Neo-Taoists in his early years, as it is recorded that he dipped into various schools of thought, including Buddhism and Taoism, for ten years.[22] Chan Jo-shui was the first one to recognize the influence of Ch'eng Hao's concept of the natural on his master, but he failed to note other Taoist sources of Ch'en's thought. From Ch'en's own works it is evident that Chuang Tzu played an important role in the formation of his life outlook, but Lao Tzu and the Neo-Taoists were seldom if ever quoted: their influence on him was at most indirect.

Ch'en was the first Confucian to adopt the Taoist term "the natural" (*tzu-jan*) to denote the ontological character of Nature as the universe or cosmos (*t'ien-ti*). At the same time he continued to use the term Way (*Tao*), which was common to Confucianism and Taoism, as the abstract term for the universe and essentially identical in meaning with the natural (II, 2/1a, 2b). His general concept of the natural was similar to that of the Neo-Taoists in recognizing that it was at once self-caused, self-completing, self-existing, self-reproducing, and self-perpetuating. To him, the regular operations and processes of all phenomena were universal and eternal. In short, he held a realistic view of the natural and did away with the metaphysical theories of the Neo-Confucianists concerning such concepts as the five agents, eight trigrams, numbers and signs (*shu-hsiang*),[x] principle and ether (*li* and *ch'i* as an ontological dualism), yin and yang, the Great Ultimate (*t'ai-chi*) and Infinite (*wu-chi*),[y] the Great Void (*t'ai-hsü*)[z] or Great Harmony (*t'ai-ho*),[aa] and the metaphysical (*hsing-erh-shang*)[ab] and physical (*hsing-erh-hsia*).[ac] In early Confucianism, Hsün Tzu held this realistic and naturalistic view of Heaven,[23] but he did not use the term *tzu-jan*.

Though Ch'en adopted the term *tzu-jan* from Ch'eng Hao and the Taoists, his interpretation of the natural differed in important respects from theirs. In the first place, although the Taoists recognized the ever-changing and ever-moving character of the universe, they looked upon the natural as a great wheel revolving and return- ing to the same starting point. This is the meaning of Chuang Tzu's "heavenly wheel" (*t'ien-chün*),[ad] or "heavenly millstone" (*t'ien- ni*).[ae] [24] In other words, his picture of the universe is cyclical, a constant process of self-rotation and reversion, without advancing or progressing. Lao Tzu had practically the same view as Chuang Tzu, as he emphasized "returning" (*fan*)[af] and "reverting" (*fu*)[ag] to the original,[25] as in the expression: "Reversion is the action of Tao." [26] Ch'en rejected this view in favor of a developmental one, as we shall see below.

In the second place, Ch'en could not agree with Lao Tzu that "all things in the world come from being, and being from Noth- ing (*wu*).[ah] [27] In other words, Lao Tzu regarded "Nothing" as the ultimate reality and "being" as only a function of Nothing. The "Miscellaneous Chapters" of the *Chuang Tzu* developed this idea, arriving at the same conclusion; "being comes from Nothing." [28] This, too, Ch'en rejected.

In the third place, Taoism recognized no purpose, no will, and no principle whatsoever in the transformations and operations of the natural. In other words, the universe is amoral. Lao Tzu said: "Heaven and Earth are not humane; they regard all things as straw or dogs." [29] It meant that all things including man are produced by Nature, according to no purposive design. Man has no more value than a straw or a dog. Ch'en could not accept this, either.

The fourth point of Taoist teaching rejected by Ch'en is its in- sistence on acquiescence in the natural, as expressed in the doctrine of nonaction or effortless action (*wu-wei*).[ai] Such a concept is in- compatible with the meliorism and moralism of Confucianism to which Ch'en held fast.

The content of Ch'en's naturalism was essentially Confucian. He found in the *Analects* of Confucius, along with a predominantly humanistic outlook and a personalistic conception of Heaven (Nature), allusions to the naturalistic character of the universe. Once as Confucius observed the ever-flowing water he exclaimed: "What is going on is like this, never ceasing day or night" (*Analects* IX/16). This means that in the eternal movement and production of the universe he saw the explicit expression of the natural. Ch'en also drew heavily upon two other Confucian classics, *The Mean* (*Chung-yung*) and *The Book of Changes* (*I-ching*). In the former he found such teachings as "Therefore what is most real is unceasing" and "The way of Heaven and Earth may be completely described in one sentence: they are without any doubleness and so they produce things in an unfathomable way." [30] In *The Book of Changes* he drew inspiration from the following passages: "The movements of Heaven are vigorous; therefore the gentleman should likewise be energetic by himself unceasingly" (*ch'ien kua, hsiang-tz'u*). "Change means production and reproduction." [31] "The great virtue of Heaven is production." (*Hsi-tz'u*, II, 1). The next to last remark on the hexagrams (*tsa-kua*) is "Already completed" (*chi-chi*),[aj] but the last one is "Not yet completed" (*wei-chi*).[ak] These ideas together strongly affirm a developmental view of Nature and the natural, emphasizing the irreversible growth and productivity of Nature. Master Ch'en certainly had this in mind when he repeated the phrase "production, production and transformation, transformation" (*sheng-sheng hua-hua*) [al] as the essential characteristic of Nature.

In many of Ch'en's poems we find him likening the onward and unceasing process of the universe to the ever-flowing water of the river. One poem directly refers to Confucius' exclamation (as quoted above):

The Great Master [Confucius] then saw the running river.
He heaved a deep sigh, exclaiming that he knew not the [passing of the] years. (VIII, 10/26a)

In this way Ch'en conceived of Nature and the natural as monistic, unceasingly moving forward, and ever producing and transforming in an eternal process of creation (II, 2/3b,4a). True, he recognized patterns of recurrence in Nature, as with the four seasons, and quoted

The Book of Changes, Tsa-kua, where it is written that the *yang-ch'i* [am] (positive force) "recurs once in seven days." Nevertheless, recurrence for him does not mean a return to the past or to the point of origin as in Taoism; each time the recurrence of the seasons brings forth something new. To him, Nature is forever moving forward, producing and growing. This is the significance of his seemingly mystical epigram: "Utmost Infinity (*wu*) possesses utmost activity (*chih-wu yu chih-tung*)" [m] (V, 6/2b). It should be noted that Infinity (*wu*) here signifies the infinity of the universe, without beginning or end.

Master Ch'en's naturalistic view agrees with the last part of Lao Tzu's saying, namely, that Heaven and Earth "regard all things as straw or dogs," in the sense that all occurrences in the universe, including life and death in the human world, take place without regard to the individuals involved, according to "the natural" or the impersonal operations of Nature. It is an impartial process, giving life and death to all alike without any preconceived preference. He called this "natural fluctuation" (*tzu-jan hsiao-hsi*),[an] or "intimations of the natural," by which man is made aware of the fluctuations of the universe. Thus, he condoled with a friend on the death of his infant child with the following words: "You wrote that your child underwent transformation right after being born. The Great Earth is without mind. Things come and go of themselves. What is there sufficient to give your affection to?" (III, 3/54b). Again, in an essay mourning the death of a friend he wrote: "The Great Earth is without mind. Who should suffer an early death and who should enjoy longevity? The fluctuation is only natural. There is nothing to blame" (IV, 5/16a). In mourning the death of his cousin, he wrote: "Death and life are the same as day and night. all things are just 'straw or dogs'" (IV, 5/19b). Hence, Ch'en considered Nature as "without mind" (*wu-hsin*),[ao] meaning without a calculating and discriminating mind in the sense of having personal preferences. But he would not agree with Lao Tzu's interpretation that "Heaven-and-Earth is not humane [or kind]." In spite of his realistic and objective view of the natural process, he still adopted the idealistic view of Confucianism which sees the natural as intrinsically good and conducive to the sustaining of human life as a whole. Thus, he acknowledged "the kindness (*jen*)^{ap} of Nature (*t'ien-ti*) in being fond of life [or production]" (III, 3/21a).

PRINCIPLE AND MIND

Nature, as Ch'en saw it, was neither chaotic and disorderly nor muddy and unintelligible. To him, all the mechanical operations and natural processes in the human as well as the physical world were in perfect order, governed by definite principles (*li*) as though they were under strict regulation.

Ch'en derived his concepts of the Way and Principle mainly from the Sung Neo-Confucianists. Speaking of the Way (*tao*), he wrote:

The Way is [spoken of as] the greatest and Nature (Heaven-and-Earth) is also [spoken of as] the greatest. Nature and the Way appear to be equal to each other. However, if we compare the Way with Nature, the Way is the foundation of Nature, and if we compare Nature with the Way, then Nature (Heaven-and-Earth) is but a mere grain in the granary and a dipper in the ocean. How could it be equal to the Way? Since Nature, though great, cannot be equal to the Way, therefore the greatest of all is only the Way. (II, 2/1a)

Ch'en said little more concerning the Way than vaguely to recognize it as the over-all principle embodying all the principles of the separate parts of the whole. In regard to principle, however, he developed his own, original doctrine.

First, affirming the existence and significance of principle, Ch'en attacked Buddhism for its failure to recognize principle:

Men cannot but deal with the affairs of life;
Affairs cannot but be dealt with according to principles.
Both of these are called "obstructions" by the Buddhists.
How can we Confucianists accept this? (VII, 9/5b)

Since Ch'en has been thought to be strongly influenced by Buddhism, it is worth noting here that his adherence to objective principle clearly differentiates his philosophy from Buddhism.

Second, Master Ch'en's philosophy of principle also differs from that of the Ch'eng-Chu school and the school of Lu Hsiang-shan. He asserted that *li* was of primary and fundamental importance in the universe, not as a metaphysical substance, but because all natural processes, nonhuman and human, operated according to it.

All day and night, I endeavor vigorously and unceasingly to put this principle in order. This principle is involved in everything; with it there is no within and without, no end or beginning: there is no place where it does not reach, and not a single second when it does not function. If I understand this, then Nature is completely established by me, all its transformations emerge from me, and the universe is in me. Grasping this handle, what else do I need? Past and present, the four directions, above and below, all at once are strung together and all at once are put in order. There is no time or space which is not filled up with principle. . . . (IV, 4/12ab)

The significance of Ch'en's view of principle may be seen in contrast to Chu Hsi's view of it as metaphysical, abstract, and immutable. Although Ch'en shared with the Ch'eng-Chu school the concept of the eternal and universal principle in Nature, he did not agree with their rationalistic view of principle as a metaphysical entity or as the independent, absolute, and objective substance of the universe. To him, principle is the natural law in the physical as well as the moral and spiritual world, being both abstract and concrete. Again, he never spoke of the dualism of principle (*li*) and ether (*ch'i*). His Nature was monistic and his "principle" dynamic. Hence, he could not agree that "the nature (*hsing*) is principle" in the sense of its being immutable or above the mind. In fact, he regarded the mind as the active master of the whole universe, above all creation and even superior to principle in status. Thus, while Chu Hsi insisted on the need for principle "to put the mind in order," Ch'en taught that one should "put this principle in order" (*shou-shih tz'u-li*)[aq] with the mind. This is the most essential point of difference between his philosophy and that of Chu Hsi.

Ch'en often referred to principle as "material principle" (*wu-li*),[ar] signifying its nonmoral character as natural law, instead of using the term Heavenly Principle (*t'ien-li*)[as] as the Sung Neo-Confucianists did. Whenever he uses the term Heavenly Principle, he does so specifically to denote its moral and ethical character as applied to the human world. With this demarcation he freed himself from the confusion of the Ch'eng-Chu school which used "Heavenly Principle"

ambiguously to represent both the moral and the natural principle
at the same time.

On the other hand, Ch'en could not endorse Lu Hsiang-shan's view
that "Mind is principle," which denied the existence of principle in
Nature as an objective reality. In Ch'en's philosophy of mind, however, there were some points of agreement with Lu, because both of
them drew upon such teachings of Mencius as: "First, let a man set
up the nobler part of his constitution [meaning the mind]" (*Mencius*
VIA/15); "Seek after the lost mind" (VIA/11); and the doctrine
that every man has the four beginnings of virtue in his mind or
heart (IIA/6).

Ch'en's philosophy also differs from Wang Yang-ming's on the
same ground that it differs from Lu Hsiang-shan's philosophy of
mind, since both Lu and Wang denied the objective existence of
principle. Later, Chan Jo-shui had a long debate with Wang on this
issue, criticizing Wang's philosophy as having the "inner" (subjectivity) but not the "outer" (objectivity), while he himself insisted
on the union of the subjective and the objective, thus adhering to
the philosophy of his teacher, Ch'en.

Another contribution of Ch'en's is his solution of the important
problem of epistemology: how the mind acquires principle. Ch'eng
I's method of personal cultivation was a dual one, which he called
"two wings." In his own words: "For culture of the mind one must
employ reverence (*ching*), and for advancement in learning, one
must engage in the thorough acquisition of knowledge." [32] Following
the second method, it is necessary to "search for principle exhaustively and accumulate righteousness." Since principle is inherent in
all things one must "investigate all things" one by one, until he
achieves the final and thorough acquisition. Such an achievement
means the accumulation of righteousness in the mind to the fullest
extent. Then some day the mind will have a thoroughgoing understanding. In this way, Ch'eng I confused intellectual knowledge with
ethical and moral knowledge following his identification of the
natural principle with the ethical. Furthermore, he believed that,
although principle was inherent in all things and affairs, it was contained primarily in the classics. Therefore, to search for principle one
must study the classics. Chu Hsi's methodology in general followed

closely that of Ch'eng I's "two wings," but he extended the realm of "exhaustive search" for principle to cover the whole universe. According to his method of "investigating all things," emphasis is laid on "piling up," i.e., accumulating principle bit by bit and piece by piece, until some day one achieves complete understanding. He also believed that all moral principles were contained in the classics as handed down from the ancient sages. Accordingly, he laid even greater emphasis on studying books than Ch'eng I did. He taught that "to search exhaustively for principle, the study of books is essential." [33] Even what is acquired by one's own mind must be checked against the writings of the ancient sages to guard against error.

It was only from hard experience that Ch'en Hsien-chang discovered a new method of approach to the acquisition of principle. He had started by following in the footsteps of Chu Hsi, reading all kinds of books for many years, but failing in the end to achieve any union of the mind with principle; in fact, the more bookish learning he acquired, the more confused and distracted he became, as though he were constantly drawn in several directions at once, and the goal of personal integration was farther and farther away. He was lost, and finally he gave up the exhaustive search for principle and the slow accumulation of righteousness, in favor of quiet-sitting in meditation. At last, he rediscovered the actuality of his own mind, and thenceforth made mind the central focus of his study instead of principle. Thus he wrote: "Keep the mind constantly within, and when it sees principle clearly, great achievement will naturally follow" (II, 2/14a).

After all, how does the mind come to see or to acquire principle? Ch'en's new conviction was that *li* must be realized through personal experience in direct observation, meditation, and finally a personal experience of the principle of things (*t'i-jen wu-li*),[at 34] all within the mind. However, this method was not to be applied to the exclusion of others; it should be supplemented by "close examination of the sages' teachings" (*ch'i chu sheng-hsün*) [au] so that what was acquired could be checked and corroborated. However, in the acquisition of truth he let personal experience take priority over submission to the double authority of books and sages.

Principle, then, became the personally acquired truth, fully assimilated by the mind as one's own conviction. In this way, the mind and matter, the knower and the known, the subjective and the objective ultimately "converged" (*ts'ou-po*).[av] Truth inhered neither in the object (matter, *wu*) nor in the subject (mind, *hsin*). To Ch'en, principle became the unfailing truth only insofar as it could be realized and integrated in the mind. This is what he called "self-acquisition" (*tzu-te*)[aw]—with the main emphasis on the self.

This doctrine started with a "dualism of process," [35] i.e., the interaction of mind and matter in the monistic Nature. The coexistence of mind and matter, or the subjective and objective, was recognized, but through interaction the two aspects were united into one. Thus the aim of Confucian cultivation was fulfilled—the union of Heaven and man. With this attained Ch'en was at last able to exclaim triumphantly "The Way is in me!" and likewise, "I am in the Way!" In such a state, he said, there is "no internal or external," meaning the complete and harmonious merging of subject and object, the self and all things.

The basis for this doctrine is found in the following passage from *The Mean* (*Chung-yung*):

Before the feelings of pleasure, anger, sorrow, and joy are aroused it is called equilibrium (*chung*) [centrality, mean]. When these feelings are aroused and each and all attain due measure and degree, Heaven and Earth will attain their proper order and all things will flourish. (Ch. 1)[36]

This passage was interpreted by Ch'en in terms of the theory of *kan*[ax] and *ying*[ba] (impression and response, or stimulus and reaction). It means that, when the subjective mind is impressed or stimulated by objective phenomena, natural feelings are aroused and natural and proper responses are expressed; through this interaction, matter and mind, or the object and subject, the external and internal are merged together. In such a process the epistemological circuit is completed. This idea is expressed in Ch'en's stanza:

The Six Classics rest completely in empty Nothing (*hsü-wu*[bb])
All principles return to [the interaction of] *kan* and *ying*.
If one could see through this aspect,

Then one would know that my learning is just the teaching of *The Mean.* (VIII, 10/37a)

Subsequently, Ch'en established the clear supremacy of mind over matter. In one of his short poems he says:

The body resides amongst all matter,
But the mind transcends all matter. (VII, 9/5b)

The human mind, as the zenith of the creative development of the universe, is of the highest value in nature. It is what differentiates mankind from animals, as Ch'en wrote in a short essay: "Every man possesses a seven-foot body [according to ancient Chinese measurement], but without this mind together with this principle, there is nothing noble about him." (II, 2/9a)

Moreover, this mind, because of its functions in the cognition of principle, in the organization of all external impressions into ideas, and, most important of all, in the production and organization of things for the benefit of humanity and the world at large, is not only the master of the body (as Chu Hsi asserted) but also the real master of the universe, since the intellectual, moral, and spiritual efforts of man become the determining factor in shaping the course and destiny of human and nonhuman affairs. In fact, it may be said that the future of the entire universe is in man's hands. In a poem composed when he was still an adherent of Chu Hsi's philosophy, Ch'en had already suggested this exalted idea in the line: "The pivot is in the mind."

Furthermore, for Ch'en this new concept represented a declara-. tion of independence from the past.

Is there any idea not in one's own mind?
Why is it necessary to copy the ancients? (V, 6/26b)

The ancients were not necessarily better than the moderns, and the moderns are not necessarily inferior to the ancients. (III, 3/51a)

Chang Hsü, one of Ch'en's pupils, did not hesitate to claim that his master had superseded the giants of the Sung school: "How lofty and sublime is this genuine heritage of the Way of Confucius! And the teaching of the Ch'eng brothers is not worth mentioning [in comparison]." [37]

EMPTINESS AND QUIESCENCE

Ch'en Hsien-chang made a further contribution through his discussion of two fundamental principles for the cultivation of the mind, namely, emptiness (*hsü*,[bc] vacuity) and quiescence (*ching*,[bd] calmness). Huang Tsung-hsi observed correctly that "The teaching of the Master is to regard emptiness as the foundation and quiescence as the doorway." [38] These, of course, are not ends in themselves but merely means to the desired end.

Emptiness is the state in which the mind is unoccupied, self-forgetful, receptive, objective, being analogous to a piece of blank paper on which one can write words or draw pictures, or to an unfilled cup into which one can pour any liquid. Emptiness is the precondition for receptivity, and receptivity is essential for fulfillment. Ch'en wrote:

Only when founded on emptiness can the structure be solid.
And the foundation must be established on the natural. (III, 3/11b)
(V, 6/2b)

The utmost emptiness is the primal condition for receiving the Way. (V, 7/34a)

Emptying oneself is most difficult. If one can overcome the [selfishness of] ego-possession, one should progress ten thousand li a day. (III, 3/38b)

As Ch'en saw it, emptiness in the mind was the primary requisite for character development as well as learning. It is a quality emphasized in the classics: "Confucius was completely free from four things: he had no arbitrariness of opinion, no dogmatism, no obstinacy, and no egotism." [39] The *Book of Changes* (*ch'ien* hexagram) states that "Fullness causes disadvantages and modesty brings benefits," indicating that modesty, as opposed to fullness, was a kind of emptiness or receptivity. Ch'en's concept of emptiness denotes a condition in which the mind is ready to be filled up, as a prerequisite for objective apprehension of truth or principle. Furthermore, in Confucianism the word *hsü* is usually associated with the word *ming* (clear). Like an empty and clear mirror, the mind is ever ready to reflect any object presented to it. Emptiness is, therefore, merely a means to the end of acquiring principle. In Taoism the word is associated with Nothing (*wu*), and Empty Nothing (*hsü-wu*) represents the absolute state of undifferentiated being as an end in itself. In Buddhism the word is associated with void (*k'ung*)[be] and implies the illusory existence and disappearance of all beings. Therefore, to both Taoism and Buddhism *hsü* is an end in itself.

Propounding the doctrine of emptiness, Master Ch'en taught that the first requisite for one to empty his mind is to remove everything that blocks or covers it. In one of his poems he dwelt on the washing out of the "artificial obstructions" (VI, 8/32b). In another passage he wrote: "Covered, it [the mind] is dark; uncovered, it is bright" (II, 1/6b–7a). To him what obstructed and covered the mind from enlightenment and understanding of any new truth were established conventions, bookish learning, worldly habits, excessive desires, preconceptions, and prejudices.

The first step to take in removing obstructions and covers from the mind is to raise doubts as to preconceived notions and received opinion. In Ch'en's words:

According to the teaching of former scholars, for learning it is essential to doubt. Little doubts beget little progress and great doubts, great progress. To doubt is the key to [or initial sign of] enlightenment and comprehension. (III, 3/40b)

Doubt, then inquire. Inquire, then know. Know truthfully and then believe. Therefore doubt is the beginning of advancement towards the Way. Belief is what you have already possessed in your self.[40]

In this sense, doubting instead of blindly accepting the external authority of the past or present is not a negative attitude, but in reality positive, constructive, and creative, for its goal is to discover truth or principle and prove it by one's own experience. One may even see affinities to the spirit and method of modern science in the skepticism which constitutes the basis of Ch'en's doctrine of emptiness.

The other principle in Ch'en's method for the cultivation of the mind is quiescence (*ching*), as shown in the following quotations:

Get rid of worry and enter into quiescence. (IV, 4/35b)

A scholar must measure his own capacity. If he would not be seduced by Ch'an Buddhism, he should practice quiescence, and then he can gain entrance to the Way. If he is busy in his daily life, this is especially the medicine for the disease. (III, 3/82a)

The human mind should not retain a single thing in it [i.e., should avoid obsession with or fixation upon any one thing]. When it is attached to one thing only, there is an obstruction. For instance, the achievement of merit and great works is, of course, a good thing, but if every thought in the mind is centered on such achievement, then the mind cannot be broad and great, and it becomes a mind of entanglement. Therefore, the mind of a sage is empty of all things; when there is an impression, then there is a response; when there is not, there is no response. And not only is this so of the sages. The substance of the human mind is everywhere the same; you must just nourish it with quiescence and it will open wide.[41]

Quiescence is a normal and healthy state of mind, free from nervous tension, worry, vexation, perplexities, and entanglements in external affairs. Positively it means poise, calm, balance, relaxation, tranquillity, and clearheadedness. It is a condition prerequisite to the concentration of attention, penetrating meditation, the gaining of deep insight in any field of knowledge, a state of alertness in responding to any alarm or crisis, and the storing up of sufficient "surplus energy" to master any critical situation. Needless to say, it is a fundamental quality for success in any effort or project that one may engage in.

Ch'en, of course, did not originate this concept. It has a long history in Neo-Confucianism, and Ch'en acknowledged his special debt to Chou Tun-i in this connection:

When Master Chou was asked "Can anyone learn to be a sage?" he replied "Yes!" Being asked again "What is essential?" his answer was: "Oneness is the essential. By oneness is meant to have no desires (wu-yü).[bf] With no desires there is quiescence and emptiness, and action is straightforward. Then one can become a sage." (II, 2/13a) (III, 3/25a)

However, Ch'en, like Chou, did not regard quiescence as an end in itself, but only as a means to an end, which is action (tung).[bg] Ch'en recognized that the natural mind, like the universe itself, was made for action, but it should be directed lest it plunge into absurd and foolish actions (wang-tung).[bh] Therefore, quiescence must be cultivated as a prelude to correct and effective action. Unfortunately, his concept of quiescence was misinterpreted by some scholars, who took it as an end in itself and regarded it as his basic doctrine. Thus, he was denounced as a quietist and charged with being Taoistic or Buddhistic. In truth, however, he always retained and reaffirmed the Confucian commitment to action. "The country cannot be ruled without action; to rule it by action is the unanimous view of all sages and scholars." (III, 3/8b)

Quiescence, for Ch'en, was essentially a preparation for future tasks. This is the meaning of his doctrine of "quiescence before action" (hsien-ching hou-tung)[bi] and "quiescence pending action" (ching i tai tung).[bj] For this very reason Professor Wing-tsit Chan has stated recently that Ch'en made a unique contribution to Chinese philosophy by asserting that quiescence issuing in action results in the discovery and even the reconstruction of the entire universe.[42]

From the foregoing one can see how Ch'en taught that emptiness is necessary to the acquisition of truth or principle, while quiescence is essential to the mind as a preparation for action. To construct a solid structure on the foundation of emptiness and to enter into the world of action through the doorway of quiescence are the ends he advocated. This is what Huang Tsung-hsi meant when he said, "The teaching of the Master is to regard emptiness as the foundation and quiescence as the doorway." With this method of self-cultivation Ch'en rendered a distinct contribution to Chinese philosophy.

A final point of importance to his philosophy of mind is Ch'en's emphasis on constantly "sharpening the mind" (mo-hsin[bk]) like sharpening a sword (V, 6/14a) and "washing the mind" (hsi-hsin[bl]) (V, 6/3b) in order to help it preserve its emptiness and quiescence at all times. Thus the achievement of emptiness was not a matter of a single experience of enlightenment but a regular process of self-cultivation, and was a sustained effort in self-discipline rather than a passive quietism.

QUIET-SITTING

One of the practices which Master Ch'en performed regularly was "quiet-sitting" (ching-tso), generally but not necessarily in a cross-legged posture. Once he likened this practice to Chuang Tzu's "sitting in forgetfulness" (*tso-wang* ᵇᵐ).⁴³ But the practice of quiet-sitting was definitely of Buddhist origin and had been adopted by the Neo-Confucianists, including Ch'eng I, as an important method for self-cultivation. Ch'en once wrote to one of his pupils: "Every day, after eating my dinner I sit with closed eyes till the end of the day" (III, 3/34b).

He not only referred to this practice by the Buddhist term, *chia-fu* ᵇⁿ in two of his poems (VII, 9/21b, 9/32b), but he also urged his pupils to practice it.⁴⁴ Presumably in this posture one was to keep one's mind void of any content while still remaining conscious. Thus the mind could easily be concentrated and penetrate to a thorough understanding of principle. We have seen above how he spoke of achieving enlightenment through a long process of quiet-sitting after futile efforts in the study of books.

The desired effect of quiet-sitting was the recovery and revelation of the natural mind in order that the "beginnings" of virtue [spoken of by Mencius] could emerge from it. This method was emphasized by Ch'en in preference to the study of books, although he did not overlook the importance of book learning. Thus:

For learning, you must engage in quiet-sitting, from which will come forth a "beginning"; just then you will have a point for deliberation. . . . You should not rely on books alone. (III, 3/12b–13a)

Being wearied and confused by too much book learning, one has no means to comprehend the Way. Therefore, studying books to broaden your knowledge is not so good as quiet-sitting. (III, 3/79a)

A scholar pursuing learning should seek within his own mind; he must make this so-called empty and clear, quiet and single mind to be the master, and then slowly read the important works of the ancients so that there will be some union [of the truth in the mind and in books] and he will not let any shadow or echo [of external influence] attach to him lest he succumb to the weaknesses of falling in with others [external authority] and deceiving himself. This is the doorway to the philosophy of mind. (II, 2/16ab)

Now as one engages in learning, he desires to hear of the Way. When he desires to hear of the Way, if he seeks for it in books and the Way is there, then let him seek for it in the books. But if he seeks for it in books and fails to acquire it, and then returns to seek it in his mind and the Way is found there, then let him seek for it in his mind. How then can he become entangled by externals? This thing must be thoroughly understood; otherwise, even if one engages daily in study, it is only for [the sake of] others. . . . Now, as to cultivating the "good beginnings" through quiet-sitting and seeking for righteous principles in books, books may sometimes be dispensed with, but "good beginnings" must always be cultivated.[45]

Thus, in the study of books, the mind must ever exercise its own function in the process of selection, criticism, analysis, comparative evaluation, and final judgment. Only then is the knowledge obtained truly integrated into oneself. Ch'en further explained:

The learning of the Great Master [Confucius] was not what people after him have considered learning. Later scholars have only engaged in memorization and recitation [of earlier works]; it is nothing but words and phrases. What Heaven has endowed them with [their minds] they remain ignorant of. How can this be? The records and books of the past are too numerous, and diligent effort [in study] cannot be concentrated; the eyes and ears become confused, and intelligence is beclouded. No wonder the perceptive man is worried about it! . . . Moreover, I have heard that the Six Classics were the books of the Great Master, but if a scholar only reads the words and loses their real taste, the Six Classics become nothing but dregs. . . . If the scholar does not seek for principle only in books but also in his own mind, observing the initial sign (*chi*)[46] of being and Nothing, cultivating what is in himself, and not being confused by what he hears and sees, he will do away with the distracting effects of the ears and eyes and preserve the empty, all-embracing and unfathomable spirit. Then, when he opens a book, he acquires everything easily. It is not from the books that he acquires it, but from himself. For, if one studies the books with oneself, one will acquire benefits everywhere; but if one lets oneself be tied down with books, then, when the volume is laid aside, one will remain utterly ignorant. (II, 1/18a)

In the study of books, never be tied down to the text.
A thousand and ten thousand volumes are but dregs. (V, 6/35b)

The words of the sages are all contained in the books. You should take them and study them. Follow what is good and rectify what is not. (II, 1/19a)

Here we see clearly what distinguished Ch'en from the Ch'eng-Chu school philosophers. While the latter confused moral knowledge with intellectual knowledge and placed both in the category of Heavenly Principle (*t'ien-li*), the former made a distinction in the following passage:

Concerning learning, there is one kind which is achieved by accumulation and another kind which is not achieved by accumulation; one can be transmitted by words and the other cannot be transmitted by words. . . . Generally speaking, that which is achieved by accumulation can be transmitted by words and the other, which is not achieved by accumulation, cannot be transmitted by words. (III, 3/11a)

It is plain that knowledge in the intellectual sphere belongs to the first kind, which is achieved by accumulation and can be transmitted by words, while that of the moral and spiritual sphere cannot be so transmitted. This establishes the proper status of books as sources of information and means of edification. But even in the realm of intellectual or scientific knowledge the mind still plays the principal active role. Hence Master Ch'en's emphasis on the primacy of the mind.

SELF-ACQUISITION

The Chinese term *tzu-te* [aw] has two meanings. It may represent the feeling of spiritual joy, self-satisfaction, or being at ease with oneself, or it may represent the acquisition of the Way, principle, or truth by oneself, for oneself, and in oneself. "Self-acquisition" is a literal rendering of the Chinese term used by Ch'en Hsien-chang to denote the acquiring of principle by and for oneself. Master Ch'en's use of the term is probably derived from Mencius, who said that "A gentleman (*chün-tzu*) deeply cultivates himself with the Way, desiring to acquire it in himself (*tzu-te chih*)." Ch'en's doctrine of self-acquisition was similar to Chou Tun-i's: "When you see the great whole [quoting Mencius], your mind is calm (*chien-ta hsin-t'ai* [bo])" and to the popular Chinese saying: "When principle is acquired, the mind is at ease (*li te hsin-an* [bp])." The following quotations reveal the substance of his doctrine:

A scholar engaged in learning, when his work becomes profound and his endeavors reach the climax, is like the flower falling but the fruit remaining, achieving magnificent self-acquisition, so that he is oblivious even to the greatness of Heaven-and-Earth or the transformations of life and death. Still less does he care about his state in life—whether it be wealth and honor or poverty and low station, gain or loss, submitting or prevailing, gaining or losing. When one examines the content of his writing . . . one finds that he gives weight to the internal and esteems lightly the external. He advances [to office] reluctantly and withdraws easily, follows righteousness as though he might be too late [to catch up with it] but shrinks from selfish gain as though he were a coward. He stands erect, majestically alone, not gladdened by any material thing nor indulging himself in grief. For he approximates to what I call magnificent self-acquisition. (II, 1/5a)

Even though there were no ancient sages to serve as patterns, I still could not stop. Such then is the learning of self-acquisition. (III, 3/80b)

Scholars today, each boasting of the school he belongs to, do not seek self-acquisition. Even though there may be a great deal of reading and talking, nevertheless they are merely shadows and echoes. (III, 3/63b)

I forget myself and I become great. I do not seek to overcome material things and material things cannot disturb me. Mencius said: "I am good at nourishing the magnificent, inherent spirit" (IIA, 2). It is all the same whether I am in the mountain or the forest, whether at court or in the market. It is the same in the constant transformation of life and death. Again, it is the same whether my lot be wealth and honor or poverty and low station, or I be pressed by barbarians, adversaries, and calamities. None of these circumstances can disturb the mind. This is called self-acquisition. One who has accomplished self-acquisition is entangled neither by external things, nor by ears and eyes, nor by the pressures or dangers of the moment. Just as birds fly and fish jump, I hold the inner spring of action (*chi*). To know this is to be good in learning; not to know this is to derive no benefit from learning.[47]

However, self-acquisition is not only to be free from worry and entanglement by all external conditions and events. There is also a positive side: one's mind is full of "self-confidence" (*tzu-hsin* [bq]), "self-enjoyment" (*tzu-lo* [br]) and "self-ennoblement" (*tzu-kuei* [bs]), in Master Ch'en's words. These may be called the three manifestations of self-acquisition. For, when one has achieved a thorough understanding of principle and lives in accord with it, he is sure that the true Way of life towards a definite goal has been found. This self-confidence enables him to go forward in life's course bravely and calmly.

Ch'en profoundly believed that "The joy of the natural is the real joy" (III, 3/63b) and "The joy of self-acquisition is boundless" (II, 2/28a). For he found that his own mind was the genuine and unique spring of happiness (II, 1/51a) (V, 6/27b). This is why he pictured a really happy man as being like "the birds flying and the fish jumping." Because his self-acquisition had led him to the real happiness of self-enjoyment and appreciation of the natural, he has been likened to the Sung philosopher Shao Yung, who was known for his enjoyment of life.[48]

Another result of self-acquisition is the gaining of respect for the dignity of one's own person, without regard to one's station in life and without envy of others. Thus he sang:

Standing between Heaven and Earth,
What dignity this body of mine possesses! (V, 6/2a)

Who says an individual is trivial?
He can shake Heaven and Earth. (V, 6/10a)

The general condition for these spiritual attainments is "no waiting" (*wu-tai* [bt]), meaning nondependence. The idea derives from *Chuang Tzu* (ch. 1), but Master Ch'en elaborated its meaning in his own terms: "With sufficiency in the internal [mind], one need not wait upon anything external" (II, 1/51b). Thus when one has achieved self-sufficiency in the acquisition of principle, he has gained confidence, joy, and nobility within himself, without depending upon or needing anything from external sources. In this sense, no waiting means no wanting.

Once, after finishing a new padded garment, he composed a poem and sent it to one of his pupils, Li Hsüeh-ch'ing,[bu] who was an adherent of Buddhism. In it he expressed his joyful acceptance of life in sharp contrast to Buddhism's rejection of it:

Putting on this garment in the evening,
I sit and gaze at the moon over Mei-ts'un [a village near Pai-sha].
A beautiful girl offers me some wine.
I enjoy three small cups.
Half-intoxicated, I sing out merrily.
The tune and the moonlight are bright and penetrating.
This body is somehow empty and void (*hsü-k'ung*).
Oh, how joyous when life exterminates extermination! (V, 6/16ab)

Chan Jo-shui's commentary says:

"Somehow empty and void" is not really empty and void. For the Bud-
hists regard extinction, extermination, and insensibility as emptiness and
voidness, but we Confucianists regard adaptability or adjustment to everything which occurs, without being stuck in or impeded by matter, as being
"empty and void." They appear similar but in reality differ from each
other. The joy of the Buddhists lies in extermination, that is, to extermi-
nate life with extermination. But now, from gazing at the moon, enjoying
a little wine, and singing a song, joy emerges. Therefore, the Master's joy
lies in life; that is, in exterminating extermination with life. (IX, 2/10a)

Self-acquisition meant freedom and joy to him, but not at the expense of his responsibilities and duties to family and society. In one
of his poems he rejected Chuang Tzu's view of the true man as one
who leaves behind the cares of life through a transcendent flight of
the spirit:

There is something immanent in all the manifestations of nature,
Which yet does not fade away with these manifestations.
Just raise your eyes and look at it,
What need is there to chase after it on "the whirlwinds" [ninety thou-
    sand li up in the sky]? (*Chuang Tzu*, ch. 1) (V, 6/26b)

This is the meaning of Ch'en's epigram: "What is nearest at hand
is most divine." Remaining in the world, he lived and preached the
ethical life as the goal of all learning and self-cultivation. Chan
Jo-shui commented on this, "In the common life of husband and
wife, there is nothing but this mysterious principle, like birds flying
and fish jumping. Is it not true 'that what is nearest at hand [i.e.,
most intimate] is most divine'?" (IX, 1/11b)

On the other hand, Ch'en could not accept the moral dualism of
the orthodox Ch'eng-Chu school which identified ethical principles
with "Heavenly principles" (*t'ien-li*), while human desires were regarded as evil. As against this view of unceasing struggle to subju-
gate human desires to Heavenly principles, Ch'en asserted: "Under
Heaven, no one can secure an illustrious name in this age, nor can
his beautiful light shine in the future, if his life is not rooted in
Nature." (II, 2/19a)

In other words, one must live in accordance with the principles of
Nature. This is morality. According to such a view, there is no antithesis between Heavenly principle and human desires, for human

desires emerge from natural instincts, and are as much manifestations of Nature as are Heaven's principles. Only excessive, abnormal, or unnatural indulgence in satisfying one's desires is immoral.

UNION WITH THE UNIVERSE

"Union of Heaven and Man" has been the goal of spiritual and moral attainment cherished by most Neo-Confucians. Ch'eng Hao had been the first to expound this principle as "perfectly forming one body with all things" (*hun-jan yü wu t'ung-t'i* [bv]).[49] Ch'en adopted it as the aim of his own philosophy: "Man 'forms one body with Heaven-and-Earth.' Hence, the four seasons proceed and all things are produced. If one gets stuck in one place, how can one be the master of creation?" (III, 3/62b)

What he meant was that if a man becomes separated from the universe, as if he and it are opposing each other, he can no longer master it. Only by perfect union with it can he become the master of all things and pivot of creation.

How could a man be reunited with the universe? Ch'en advocated "following and responding to the natural" (*shun-ying tzu-jan* [bw]) (III, 3/50b). By this he meant to live a life in accordance with the principles of Nature. The prerequisite for this desired union, therefore, is accurate understanding of principle. But since the fundamental principle of the universe is dynamic action and creative production, a life in accordance with Nature cannot simply abide by principles conceived as static and external; it must involve active participation in the universe, so that, as *The Mean* (ch. 22) says: "One can assist the creative powers of Heaven-and-Earth and join in with Heaven-and-Earth."

For Ch'en harmonious union with the universe also meant joining oneself to all mankind and all creatures:

> Different bodies are all my bone-and-flesh kinsmen,
> All living creatures are my companions. (V, 6/26b)

This, of course, breathes the same spirit as Chang Tsai's famous "Western Inscription."[50] In this conception of universal brotherhood, everyone shares the fate, weal or woe, of all others; hence one must have a compassionate love for all men and exert one's energies for the betterment of society. In this respect Ch'en adopted the principle of humanity as interpreted by Ch'eng Hao, who, in turn, inherited it from Confucius himself.

Finally, as a corollary to the doctrine of union with the universe, Ch'en cherished the lofty and consoling idea that death did not mean the extinction of life. He wrote:

> Heaven-and-Earth have inexhaustible age.
> Inexhaustibly I shall also exist. (V, 6/26a)

> Imperishably, my Tao will live,
> For a hundred million years on end. (V, 7/40b)

With this thought he cherished a rational faith in an eternal life beyond death. In a religious sense, it was an eschatology much beyond the traditional Confucian conception of the three kinds of immortality—"to establish one's merits" (li-kung),[bx] "to establish one's words" (li-yen),[by] and "to establish one's virtue" (li-te).[bz] A life which is in complete union with the universe, participating in its creative evolution, will certainly enjoy eternal longevity with that same universe. Confucius himself had confessed, "I do not yet know life, how can I know death?" Ch'en Hsien-chang's creative philosophy, however, had brought him to the contemplation of life beyond death.

NOTES

1. *Ming shih* 282 (Wu-ying tien, I-wen ed.) p. 3096; Preface to *Ju-lin chuan*; *MJHA* (Wan-yu Wen-k'u ed.), 5/47; Preface to *Pai-sha hsüeh-an*.

2. Ch'en wrote no book or treatise expounding his philosophical thoughts systematically. He left only a number of short essays in prose, letters to friends, officials, and pupils, and some 2,000 poems in both old and new styles. Shortly after his death, about one fifth of his poems were printed in Shantung Province and about one twentieth in Wuchow, Kwangsi (dates unknown). Later on, efforts were made to collect all his works in prose and verse to be engraved on blocks and printed. Up to the present no less than eight editions of his collected works have been published. They are as follows:

1505 (Hung-chih 18). 20 *chüan*, published in Kwangtung by Lo Chiao ᶜᵃ of Chi-shui in Kiansgi Province (then Magistrate of Hsin-hui), entitled *Pai-sha hsien-sheng ch'üan-chi*.ᶜᵇ

1508 (Cheng-te 3). 20 *chüan*, published by Lin Ch'i ᶜᶜ of P'u-t'ien in Fukien Province. A revision of the first edition.

1533 (Chia-ching 12). 8 *chüan* printed at Yang-chou (Wei-yang) in Kiangsu Province by Kao Chien ᶜᵈ (H. Shan-feng) of Nei-chiang in Szechuan Province, a pupil of Chan Jo-shui. Kao made some additions and deletions of material in the two earlier editions, and changed the title to *Pai-sha tzu*.

1551 (Chia-ching 30). 9 *chüan*, printed by Hsiao Shih-yen ᶜᵉ (H. Yu-shan) also of Nei-chiang in Szechuan, entitled *Pai-sha hsien-sheng ch'üan-chi*.

1601 (Wan-li 29). Printed by Lin Yu-yang ᶜᶠ in Fukien Province, entitled *Pai-sha hsien-sheng chi*.ᶜᵍ

1612 (Wan-li 40). 9 *chüan*, printed by Ho Hsiung-hsiang ᶜʰ (H. Ch'ien-tsai) of Hsin-hui in Kwangtung, based on a good edition in Chan Jo-shui's possession, with title of *Pai-sha tzu ch'üan-chi*.ᶜⁱ

1710 (K'ang-hsi 49). 6 *chüan*, printed by Ho Chiu-ch'ou,ᶜʲ grandson of Ho Hsiung-hsiang. With the addition of 221 newly collected prose pieces and poems not contained in the previous editions, and entitled *Pai-sha tzu ch'üan-chi*.

1771 (Ch'ien-lung 36). 10 *chüan*, edited by Ch'en Yü-neng,ᶜᵏ a descendant of Ch'en Hsien-chang, and printed by the temple of the Ch'en clan (hence often called the Ch'ien-lung or Temple edition). Entitled *Pai-sha-tzu ch'üan-chi*; based on the 1710 edition with the addition of one volume of Chan Jo-shui's *Pai-*

sha-tzu ku-shih chiao-chieh [cl] (Commentaries on the old-style poems of Pai-sha-tzu) and one volume of appendices. (Cf. *Pai-sha hsüeh-k'an*,[cm] No. 2 [Hong Kong, March, 1965], p. 2.)

For a long time the 1505, 1508, and 1601 editions have not been extant. The 1710 edition, which is the best printing, is very rarely seen. Some years ago the Commercial Press of Shanghai reprinted by photocopy the 1533 edition. The 1771 edition, which has been re-printed several times, remains the most comprehensive and most widely circulated one. The original engraving blocks are still preserved in the Ch'en temple in Pai-sha. Recently, more of Ch'en's poems which had not been collected in earlier editions have been recovered from some of his handwritten scrolls in private collections. At present, a new edition is being prepared and is to be published by the Pai-sha Cultural and Educational Association of Hong Kong. This association also publishes the periodical *Pai-sha hsüeh-k'an*.

3. This biographical sketch is mainly drawn from the following sources:
   a. His official biography in *Ju-lin chuan* (*Ming shih*, 283).
   b. Chang Hsü, *Pai-sha hsien-sheng hsing-chuang*,[cn] in *Pai-sha-tzu ch'üan-chi* (1771 ed.), Vol. X, *chuan mo* (hereafter abbreviated as *Hsing-chuang* and *Ch'üan-chi*).
   c. Juan Jung-ling, *Ch'en Pai-sha hsien-sheng nien-p'u* (hereafter abbreviated as *Nien-p'u*), reprinted in *Pai-sha hsien-sheng chi-nien-chi* [co] (Hong Kong, 1952), compiled by Ch'en Ying-yao (hereafter abbreviated as *Chi-nien chi*).
   d. Juan Jung-ling, *Pai-sha men-jen-k'ao*,[cp] reprinted in *Pai-sha hsüeh-k'an*, No. 2 (Hong Kong, 1965) (hereafter abbreviated as *Men-jen-k'ao*).
   e. Juan Jung-ling, *Pai-sha ts'ung-k'ao* [cq] (Hsin-hui, Kwangtung, 1851) (hereafter abbreviated as *Ts'ung-k'ao*).
   Source references will be given to salient points only.
4. Huang Pei-fang, *Hsin-hui hsien-chih* [cr] (1840), 2/1–4, and Tan Piao, *Hsin-hui hsiang-t'u-chih* [cs] (late Ch'ing ed.; undated), 1/1–7, 6/lab, 7/1–4.
5. Chang Hsü, *Hsing-chuang*, X Mo/7.
6. All citations unless otherwise indicated are to *Pai-sha tzu ch'üan-chi* (1771 ed.) with the *ts'e* indicated in roman numerals, followed by *chuan* and page.
7. Huang, *Hsin-hui hsien-chih*, 8/15, 11/14b.
8. All ages given in this paper are according to Chinese reckoning.
9. Huang Tsung-hsi, quoted in *Nien-p'u*, p. 4.
10. Essay for Li Ch'eng-chi, *Ch'uan-chi* II, 1/22b.
11. Wang Hsiao-sheng, *Ch'en Pai-sha hsien-sheng chih li-hsüeh yü shih-hsüeh*,[ct] in *Chi-nien chi*, p. 52.

12. *Men-jen-k'ao*, p. 14.
13. Hsing-chuang, X, Mo/8a.
14. Liu Tsung-chou, *Jen-p'u*,ᶜᵘ VI (Commercial Press ed., 1939). Supplement V, p. 93.
15. *Nien-p'u*, pp. 21–22.
16. Full text in *Ch'üan-chi*, II, 1/1a–3b.
17. There is a separate *Kan-ch'üan hsüeh-an* ᶜᵛ in MJHA 37–42.
18. MJHA 5, preface to *Pai-sha hsüeh-an*.
19. *Ming shih* 282, preface to *Ju-lin chuan*.
20. *Ts'ung-k'ao*, 26ab.
21. *Ming-tao wen-chi*, 3/1.
22. Wing-tsit Chan, A *Source Book in Chinese Philosophy* (Princeton University Press, 1963), p. 519.
23. *Ibid.*, pp. 116 f.
24. *Chuang Tzu chuan-chien* (Ch'ien Mu ed.; Hong Kong, 1955), p. 14 Ch'i-wu lun.
25. *Tao-te-ching*, 16, 25.
26. Chan, *Source Book*, p. 160 (*Tao-te-ching* 40).
27. *Ibid.*
28. *Chuang Tzu*, Tsa-p'ien, Keng-sang-ch'u.ᶜˣ
29. Cf. Chan, *Source Book*, p. 141 (No. 5). I add the word "or" in the second sentence, according to the commentaries of Ho-shang-kung and Wang Pi who both regarded "straw" and "dogs" as two separate things. On the other hand, in *Chuang Tzu*, T'ien-yün, "straw dog" refers to only one thing.
30. Cf. Chan, *Source Book*, p. 109.
31. *Ibid.*, p. 226.
32. *I-shu*, V, 18, 7, in *Erh-Ch'eng ch'üan-shu*.ᶜʸ
33. Hsing-kung pien-tien tsou-tsa, in *Chu Wen Kung ch'üan-chi* ᶜᶻ (SPTK), II, 14/204.
34. Chan, *Source Book* (p. 790) gives a very accurate interpretation of the term *t'i-jen* in a general sense, although he does not refer specifically to Ch'en's doctrine.
35. I have borrowed this term from James B. Pratt, *Matter and Spirit* (New York, 1922), Lecture V, pp. 183 ff. What he calls "a dualism of process," not of substance, emphasizes the interaction of spirit and matter.
36. Chan, *Source Book*, p. 98.
37. Hsing-chuang, *Ch'üan-chi*, X, 18b.
38. Huang Tsung-hsi, MJHA 5/49.
39. Chan, *Source Book*, p. 35.
40. Huang, MJHA, 5/57, *Yü-lu*.
41. *Ibid.*, 5/54, Lun-hsüeh shu.

42. *Pai-sha hsüeh-k'an*, No. 2, pp. 28–29.

43. *Chuang Tzu*, ch. 6, Ta-tsung-chih. Here Chuang Tzu was supposedly referring to Yen Hui, favorite disciple of Confucius, who, according to the *Chuang Tzu*, practiced "sitting in forgetfulness." Ssu-ma Piao's commentary on *tso-wang* is "to sit and forget one's own body," quoted by Ch'ien Mu, *Chuang Tzu chuan-chien*, p. 60.

44. The regular term for this Buddhist practice is *chieh-chia-fu-tso* [da] (braided cross-legged sitting). One who practices it is to sit up straight with crossed legs, putting the back of the left foot on the right thigh and that of the right foot on the left thigh. This is called "full *chia-fu*"; when only one foot, left or right, is put up, it is called "half *chia-fu*." The Taoists, at least in modern times, also practice quiet-sitting called *ta-tso* [db] more as a method for the improvement, restoration, or preservation of health than as a method for moral cultivation. All those practicing quiet-sitting, whether Buddhists or Taoists, insist that the mind must be absolutely blank.

45. Jung Chao-tsu, *Ming-tai ssu-hsiang shih* [dc] (Taiwan reprint; 1962), p. 37, quoting Lin Kuang, *Nan-ch'üan ping-nieh ch'üan-chi,* [dd] Mo/12–13.

46. According to Chan (*Source Book*, p. 467), "The word *chi* means an originating power, an inward spring of activity, an emergence not yet visible, a critical point at which one's direction toward good or evil is set." (See also *ibid.*, p. 784, for other definitions.) The commentary on the word *chi* in *The Great Learning* is "the source of action." Perhaps no one word can adequately render this term in all its contexts. In some cases "spring" or "key" may be appropriate. I venture to translate it here as "initial sign" since it is the very beginning of a movement or development that can be observed as a "sign." By observing the initial sign one can direct one's own action to meet the developing situation for the benefit of oneself or a cause; e.g., the *Book of Changes* (Hsi-tz'u) says: *chien-chi erh tso* [de] (to see the initial sign and to take action accordingly).

47. Huang, *MJHA* 5/58, *T'i-pa*.

48. Shao Yung named his own abode "The Nest of Comfort and Happiness" (*An-lo wo* [df]) and called himself "Master of Comfort and Happiness."

49. *Erh-Ch'eng ch'üan-shu* (SPPY ed.), *I-shu*, 2A/3.

50. Chan, *Source Book*, p. 497.

GLOSSARY

a	陳獻章	ai	無為
b	新會都會	aj	既濟
c	白沙	ak	未濟
d	江門	al	生生化化
e	陳琮	am	陽氣
f	獻文	an	自然消息
g	靜坐	ao	無心
h	梁儲	ap	仁
i	敬	aq	收拾此理
j	湛若水, 甘泉	ar	物理
k	尹旻	as	天理
l	劉宗周	at	體認物理
m	至無有至動	au	稽諸聖訓
n	至近至神焉	av	湊泊
o	機	aw	自得
p	自然	ax	感
q	白鹿書院	ba	應
r	翰林院檢討	bb	虛無
s	增城	bc	虛
t	茅龍	bd	靜
u	文恭	be	空
v	天地	bf	無欲
w	明覺自然	bg	動
x	數象	bh	妄動
y	無極	bi	先靜後動
z	太虛	bj	靜以待動
aa	太和	bk	磨心
ab	形而上	bl	洗心
ac	形而下	bm	坐忘
ad	天鈞	bn	跏趺
ae	天倪	bo	見大心泰
af	反	bp	理得心安
ag	復	bq	自信
ah	無	br	自樂

bs　自貴

bt　無待

bu　黎雪青

bv　渾然與物同體

bw　順應自然

bx　立功

by　立言

bz　立德

ca　羅僑, 吉水

cb　白沙先生全集

cc　林齊

cd　高簡, 內江

ce　蕭世延

cf　林裕陽

cg　白沙先生集

ch　何熊祥

ci　白沙子全集

cj　何九疇

ck　陳俞能

cl　白沙子古詩教解

cm　白沙學刊

cn　張詡, 行狀

co　紀念集

cp　門人考

cq　叢考

cr　黃培芳, 新會縣志

cs　譚鑣, 新會鄉土志

ct　王韶生, 陳白沙先生之
　　　理學與詩學

cu　人譜

cv　甘泉學案

cw　錢穆, 莊子纂箋

cx　庚桑楚

cy　二程全書

cz　朱文公全集, 行宮
　　　偏殿奏剳

da　結跏趺坐

db　打坐

dc　容肇祖, 明代思想史

dd　林光, 南川冰蘗全集

de　見機而作

df　安樂窩

The Development of the

Concept of Moral Mind from Wang

Yang-ming to Wang Chi

CHU HSI'S SYSTEM OF MORAL MIND AS ONE SOURCE OF WANG YANG-MING'S TEACHING

明 In this essay, I shall discuss some important features of Wang Yang-ming's idea of moral mind, and how Wang-chi's ideas of moral mind were developed from the problems concerning moral cultivation which Wang Yang-ming left unresolved. However, I have to begin by tracing the problem of moral mind in Neo-Confucianism back to Chu Hsi and Lu Hsiang-shan and I shall try to explain, in a more definite way, what Yang-ming's idea of moral mind is, and how it synthesized and went beyond the thought of Chu and Lu.

Generally speaking, all the ideas of Neo-Confucianists about mind are closely related to the moral aspects of mind or moral cultivation; so we may consider all their ideas of mind as ideas of moral mind.

In the Sung dynasty, the ideas of moral mind of all the previous Neo-Confucianists converged and culminated in Chu Hsi's thought. In his thought, the mind is analyzed and explicated from three points of view. From the first point of view, which may be called a psychological point of view, the mind is taken as the spirituality of *ch'i*,[a] or the transparency and sensitiveness of *ch'i*. As *ch'i* animates our bodily life, the mind governs our whole life as its master. The mind which receives the impressions from its perceptions of external things and bodily life is affected thereby and responds to them with its different faculties, such as feelings, emotions, will, volitional ideas, and deliberations. All of them show the abilities of mind to form the actions and knowledge of man. From this point of view, the different faculties of the mind are known through its functional relation to the principles of Heaven, our body, and other things (including other people and natural things) as external objects in the so-called objective world.

From the second point of view, which may be called an ontological or metaphysical point of view, the mind contains the principles of Heaven (or *t'ien li* [b]), which are universal principles, as its inner nature. Thus the nature of mind has a cosmic significance, because the universal principles of Heaven prevailing in all things are permanent, immutable, and divine. In this sense, the nature of mind has its absolute dignity which transcends all things in the natural world. However, the principles of Heaven as mind's nature are not necessarily self-consciously known or realized and then expressed. That aspect of mind which contains the principles of Heaven, yet unexpressed, is described as *wei fa,* [c] which means that part of mind which is "still not" or "not yet" expressed. The unexpressed part of mind was considered by Chu Hsi to be static or quiet. In contrast, the other part of mind, described as the "expressed" part, denotes that in which its nature is expressed when it is affected by and responds to things of the ordinary empirical world, through its feelings, wills, desires, deliberations, volitional ideas, and so on, as mentioned above. This part of mind, as it is actually responsive to the things of the world through its faculties or functions, is described as active and affective. The technical term for it in Chinese is the *i-fa* [d] part or aspect of mind. As the unexpressed part of mind is found in inner intentions, feelings, etc., it is known only by oneself in solitude. When it is expressed in outer action, it may be known by other beings also. The inner part of mind is its transcendental or metaphysical part, because it is closely related to the principles of Heaven, or *li,* [e] and the outer part of mind is its empirical or physical aspect, because it is closely related to the *ch'i.* I shall not further discuss their relations to *li* and *ch'i* here.

From the third point of view, which may be called the axiological or purely moral point of view, the mind may be classified into two or three kinds, according to its level in the realization of moral values. The first kind of mind is called the mind of Tao. [f] Tao means the principles of Heaven or the nature of mind as actually expressed and realized in the mind's faculties or functions as feelings, will, and so on. This is a mind which is purely good. If a man has his mind of Tao fully realized to its utmost, he is a sage (*sheng*),[g] and if a man has his mind of Tao gradually transforming his other kinds of mind, he is a man of worth (*hsien*).[h] The second kind of mind is called the human mind (*jen-hsin*).[i] It means a kind of mind which just keeps its natural spirituality, natural transparency, and natural sensitiveness with its natural desires and instincts. Such a mind is cognitive, and responsive to ordinary things in a natural way. It is by itself neutral in moral value. However, when the natural desires or instincts of man conform to or are governed by and become the self-conscious embodiment of the principles of Heaven as our nature, then this mind is morally good. On the other hand, if these natural desires go uncurbed and depart from the principles of Heaven as our nature, then such desires become selfish or sensual desires. The human mind which is stained by such desires is a selfish mind too. Then it is evil. In Chu Hsi's thought, the human mind by itself stands in the middle. It may ascend to the level of expressing the principles of Heaven as its nature and transform itself into the mind of Tao which is morally good. It may also descend to the level of selfiish desires, and degenerate into the mind of an animal or a mind even worse than that of an animal.

From each of the above three points of view, Chu Hsi discussed mind in an analytical way, and the mind as a whole was differentiated into many different faculties or functions, inner and outer parts, and kinds and levels of existence that differed according to their moral value.

As Chu Hsi made many distinctions in regard to one's mind, he also made many distinctions in regard to the ways of moral cultivation or the moral task of man. In Chu Hsi's thought about the ways of moral cultivation, if one intends to transform his mind which is full of selfish desires, and then to elevate his human mind into the mind of Tao, he must have different ways of moral cultivation corresponding to the inner mind—the unexpressed part—and the outer mind—the expressed part.

Corresponding to the unexpressed part, one should have a way of moral cultivation which is designated by the technical term *han-*

yang [j] or *ts'un-yang*.[k] It roughly means the self-nourishment and self-preservation of mind in its static and quiet state. In this state of mind, though static and quiet, there is an inner activity which is self-circled, or self-conscious in its self-nourishment or self-preservation. So Chu Hsi called this way of moral cultivation the mind in its static function. In this way of moral cultivation, the mind in its static function is a pure consciousness which can reveal the principles of Heaven as its nature, as if it shed light on its nature and let its nature be revealed or made conscious of itself. This way of moral cultivation is the fundamental way of moral cultivation Chu Hsi expounded.

However, the mind should also have other ways of moral cultivation, corresponding to the expressed part of mind. On its expressed side, the mind, as perceiving and knowing the world and things, should have a way of moral cultivation which is called the investigation of things for the attainment of right knowledge about things. In the investigation of things, we have to know or to search for the principles of what things are to be and what actions should be done.

Corresponding to our selfish desires, and all our volitional ideas, deliberations, feelings, emotions, and wills, which are selfish and evil, we should have a way of moral cultivation which Chu Hsi calls *ko-chih*,[1] that is self-conquest or self-governing.

Corresponding to the feelings, ideas, wills, and so on, which appear to be neutral in their moral value, we should have a way of moral cultivation which Chu Hsi calls *sheng-ch'a*,[m] meaning self-observation, self-reflection, or self-examination. Through this way of moral cultivation we learn that what appears to be neutral in moral value, when self-observed or self-reflected, is actually either good or evil. When it is found to be evil, we have to conquer it; and when it is found to be good, we have to preserve and strengthen it in order to make all our feelings, will, and ideas perfectly good. In short, this is a way of moral cultivation which makes our will pure, sincere, or authentic.

Corresponding to the initial expression of our mind in our feelings, will, ideas, and so on, we should have a way of moral cultivation which Chu Hsi calls the way of *shen-tu*,[n] which means self-prudence or self-care of mind in its solitude and in the inception of activity from its unexpressed state to its expression. The self-prudence or self-care, when it is serious, is like self-fear, or self-dread, or the self trembling on a cliff. Here our mind may either ascend to the principles of Heaven, being conscious of them as our nature and thus expressing them in all good actions, or descend into the pit of selfish desires and commit the worst deeds.

On the basis of the foregoing, Chu Hsi's thought about moral mind and moral cultivation can be taken as the most comprehensive system, encompassing the whole field of morality, in the Neo-Confucianism of the Sung dynasty. Chu Hsi also interpreted the teachings on moral cultivation of *The Great Learning* in this way. He interpreted the investigation of things and the attainment of knowledge in *The Great Learning* as searching for the principles of things for the purpose of attaining knowledge. He interpreted the making of the moral will authentic as the result of *ko chih* and *sheng-ch'a*. He interpreted the rectification of mind (*cheng-hsin* º) as corresponding to his way of moral cultivation in the *han-yang*. Chu Hsi also interpreted the *shen-tu*, (the "self-carefulness in solitude") of *The Great Learning* through the thought of *The Mean*, placing it in a position between *han-yang* and *sheng-ch'a*, or between the *cheng-shin* and *ch'eng-yi* ᵖ of *The Great Learning*.

LU HSIANG-SHAN'S CONCEPT OF ORIGINAL MIND AS A BASIS FOR WANG YANG-MING'S "REALIZATION OF *LIANG-CHIH*"

In comparison with Chu Hsi's complicated system of morality, Lu Hsiang-shan's thought, although very simple and straightforward, is more penetrating and essential.

As to the first point of view from which Chu Hsi analyzed the mind's functions, Lu Hsiang-shan took no interest in it. In one dialogue of Lu Hsiang-shan, when Li Pa-ming, one of his disciples, asked about the distinction between mind, nature, feeling, and ability, Lu Hsiang-shan reproached him severely. He said that his disciple merely asked trivial questions and had never plunged into the sources and roots of learning. He also said that Li only wanted to define and to explain the terms etymologically, which is unnecessary for becoming a sage.[1]

As to the second point of view of Chu Hsi, which divided the mind into two parts, an inner-unexpressed˙and outer-expressed, Lu Hsiang-shan mentioned no distinction between the inner part and the outer part of mind. He said that the universe is our mind and our mind is the universe, and that all the things of the universe are rightly things in the domain of one's own sense of responsibility, and things in the domain of one's own sense of responsibility are rightly things of the universe also. The mind which is undifferentiated from the universe is a metaphysical mind or a cosmic mind, but it exists as a whole in one's individual and empirical self as well. Thus any distinction between the "unexpressed" and the "expressed" part of mind is of no importance. Lu Hsiang-shan's original mind contains not merely the principles of Heaven as its content, or substance, but also is existentially identical with the principles of Heaven. This is the reason why it is also a cosmic mind or metaphysical mind. As the mind is existentially identical with the principles of Heaven, which are also its nature, where there is any expression of the original mind there is the mind expressed simultaneously with the principles of Heaven as its nature. The original mind never just preserves its nature internally nor is it self-contained; it is always open and manifests its principles or nature without any reservation in its expressions.

In contrast to Chu Hsi's third point of view, which distinguished mind as of two or three kinds on different levels, Lu Hsiang-shan strenuously criticized the theory of mind which classified it as the mind of Tao and that of human selfish desires. He said that his theory originated in Taoistic thought and had been adopted into the chapter of the "Records on Music" in the *Record of Rites*. Chu Hsi in his dialogues and letters sometimes acknowledged Lu Hsiang-shan's criticism of this traditional theory. Nevertheless, Chu Hsi continued to follow this theory in the "Records on Music" and went further by making a distinction of the human mind into two kinds: one is the human mind by itself which is morally neutral; the other is the human mind stained by selfish desires which is evil, as has been explained above.

From Chu Hsi's conceptual analysis, there are not only two, but actually three kinds of mind. Hence his theory of mind is even more complicated than the theory of the "Records on Music." However, Lu Hsiang-shan insisted that there is only one original mind, which, as undifferentiated from the universe, is unlimited or infinite in its essence. But as an ordinary man may not know that he has such an original mind, so great, sublime, and lofty, the ordinary man's mind may be self-limited or narrowed down, and sunk in his private ideas or opinions, or in his egoistic sensual desires which only run after sense objects.

However, though the original mind may be sunk in these base things, it can still emancipate and liberate itself from this self-limitation. Thus it has a self-consciousness, self-illumination, or self-awakening. Therefore, from Lu Hsiang-shan's point of view, the original mind can either be unconscious of itself and descending, or self-conscious and self-awakened and ascending. Whether the mind is descending or ascending, it is the same one mind. The descending or ascending of the mind is determined by the mind itself. The mind has its self-determination and its self-mastering, and then has its self-establishment based on its moral self-cultivation; the foundation of moral cultivation is nothing other than the self-awakening of the original mind. In this sense, the original mind is absolutely free even in its descending actions because it can arise or reawaken again and nothing outside can be an obstacle or hindrance to the original mind, if it resolves to reawaken itself.

Lu Hsiang-shan, unlike Chu Hsi, who made distinctions in the mind from different points of view, has a simple and essential idea of the original mind which is existentially identical with the principles of Heaven. This original mind of Lu Hsian-shan is not merely a contemplative or knowing mind in the theoretical sense, it is also a practical and active mind. Therefore there is actually no distinction between his theory of moral mind and his theory of moral cultivation. The original mind of Lu Hsiang-shan has the power of self-awakening. It needs no other way of moral cultivation to assist its self-awakening. And we may say that any other way of moral cultivation, such as self-nourishment, self-preservation, self-care in solitude, self-examination, self-conquest, self-governing, and so on, which we find in Chu Hsi, are all only different modes or moments of man's self-awakening. Even the investigation of things and the search for the principles of things, which Chu Hsi emphasized, may be re-interpreted by Lu Hsiang-shan from his point of view. As all things are within the universe and the original mind is undifferentiated from the universe, the task of investigating things never goes outside the domain of the original mind's self-knowledge or self-conscious-ness and is just a task for its self-awakening.

The different ways of moral cultivation as taught by Chu Hsi were all united into one teaching of self-awakening of mind as taught by Lu Hsiang-shan. The original mind is what is greatest in the uni-verse and man. "To establish first this greatest" is a teaching of Mencius and is often quoted by Lu Hsiang-shan. Some people criti-cized Lu Hsiang-shan's teaching as being too simple and said, "Be-sides the phrase 'to establish this greatest,' Lu Hsiang-shan has no other teaching." When Lu Hsiang-shan heard this criticism, he said, "It is quite true, quite true." We have to say "quite true" also.

WANG YANG-MING'S "REALIZATION OF LIANG-CHIH" AS A SYNTHESIS OF CHU HSI'S AND LU HSIANG-SHAN'S MORAL MIND AND MORAL CULTIVATION

As to Wang Yang-ming's thought, it is ordinarily understood that Wang is a follower of Lu Hsiang-shan, and we always talk about the "Lu-Wang school" in contrast to the "Ch'eng-Chu school." Actu-ally, however, Wang Yang-ming also took over Chu Hsi's problems of moral cultivation. After his industrious study of such problems as the meaning of ko-wu,[q] which Chu Hsi interpreted as the investiga-tion of things, and also the relation of han-yang or ts'un-yang (self-preservation or self-nourishment) and sheng-cha (self-reflection or self-examination) as taught by Chu Hsi, he had a self-enlightenment about the way of being a sage which is similar to Lu Hsiang-shan's teaching about the awakening of the original mind. Therefore, from a historical point of view, Wang Yang-ming's thought may be taken as a synthesis of Chu Hsi's and Lu Hsiang-shan's thoughts. This is why I have had to explain the ideas of moral mind of Chu Hsi and Lu Hsiang-shan in the first two sections of this essay.

The central idea of Wang Yang-ming's thought is *liang-chih*,[r] which is a word difficult to translate. *Liang* means, etymologically, "innate" or "original." *Chih* means knowledge or consciousness, or awareness, as a noun; and means to know, to be conscious, or to be aware, as a verb. As a noun, *chih* is a concept of substance or essence. As a verb, *chih* combined with *liang* to form one word, *liang-chih*, may mean the innate knowledge or original knowing, original consciousness, or original awareness. I prefer to translate the word *liang-chih* as the original knowing or original consciousness. Yet, as the word *liang* has also its derivative meaning of "good," and what is good is also moral; we may also translate the word *liang-chih* as original-good-consciousness or original-good-knowing. Furthermore, *liang-chih* as a good consciousness is always knowing and sensitive to the value of goodness, and its contrary, evil; thus it is even better to translate *liang-chih* as original-good-conscientious or original-good conscientious-knowing. But as the romanized term *liang-chih* is simpler to use, I shall adopt this in the following discussion.

In Wang Yang-ming's thought, *liang-chih* was taken as a substance or essence of mind, and his thought about the ontological and moral status of *liang-chih* in the universe was very similar to Lu Hsiang-shan's thought about the status of original mind in the universe; therefore the meanings of these two terms are also very close to each other. However, the word *mind* is usually used as a noun to denote a substance, and the word *chih* is usually used to denote also a function or activity of mind. When Wang Yang-ming said that *liang-chih* is the substance of mind[s 3] and that "the self-illumination and self-consciousness of the principles of Heaven is *liang-chih*," [t 4] his intention seems to have been to replace Lu Hsiang-shan's idea of original mind by *liang-chih* as existentially identical with the principles of Heaven. As the word *mind* is just a name for substance, and the word *chih* is a name for function, when we say that *liang-chih* is a substance of mind, it implies that the function of the mind is identical with the substance of mind. Hence the most essential point of Wang Yang-ming's thought is to see the mind's substance functionally and then also to see the mind's function substantially; thus the substance and function of mind, or of *liang-chih*, can be taken as existentially identical in its being. This theory, like Chu Hsi's, uses the words of substance and function differently, and each has its logical meaning. Yet it differs from Chu Hsi's, as substance and function are thought to be existentially identical. This theory emphasizes the self-consciousness of *liang-chih* as the original substance of mind, as Lu Hsiang-shan emphasizes the self-awakening of the original mind as the substance of the so-called ordinary mind. But Lu Hsiang-shan never called his original mind *liang-chih* or original knowing, and never stated clearly that he saw the substance of mind through its function. Wang Yang-ming inherited Chu Hsi's distinction of substance and function in their logical meanings, but rejected Chu Hsi's distinction of substance and function in their existential meanings. He also inherited Lu Hsiang-shan's idea of original mind, but supplemented Lu's thought with the idea of seeing the substance of original mind through its function as knowing, and called it *liang-chih*. It is certainly a theory which synthesized Chu's and Lu's ideas of mind, as well as distinguishing itself from both of them. Chu Hsi, speaking metaphorically, said that the principles of Heaven, as the content and nature of our mind, are self-radiating, illustrious, and bright. This compares the principles with the sun shining. Lu Hsiang-shan, who took the original mind as existentially identical with the principles of Heaven, usually compared mind as a whole with the sun which shines through the whole universe. This seems to mean that, as light radiated from the sun also shines back on itself, so the awakening of the mind as it originates from the original mind makes the original mind itself self-awakened. In Wang Yang-ming's dialogues, he too compared *liang-chih* to the sun.[5] The sun functions in its enlightening as *liang-chih* functions in its knowing. Yet, in Wang-ming's thought, it seems not merely that the light radiated from the sun is shining back to the sun, but that the sun, when radiating the light, is itself immanent in its own light. If this is so, then in using the metaphor of sun and light, he means that while there is light, there is a sun; so where there is *liang-chih*'s knowing as its function, there is also *liang-chih*'s substance in its knowing. As the sun, immanent in its light, pervades the whole universe, the substance of *liang-chih*'s substance, as immanent in its function of knowing the whole universe, pervades the universe also.

As the distinctions among the three theories of Wang Yang-ming's *liang-chih,* Lu Hsiang-shan's original mind, and Chu Hsi's mind as containing the principles of Heaven may not be easily understood by everyone, it may be better to think of their ideas through the metaphor of sun and light.

Because Wang Yang-ming's thought that the substance and function of *liang-chih* are mutually seen through each other and existentially identical, in *liang-chih,* when it is unexpressed, there is an expression of the transcendental, because it is always knowing; and when it is expressed, there is the unexpressed immanent, because it is still *liang-chih* itself as the original substance of mind. The original substance of mind, as Wang Yang-ming said, is the principle of Heaven. Principles are always within the mind or *liang-chih,* and thus are always unexpressed principles within. Surely *liang-chih,* in its expression, is active, yet it is always at rest with its unexpressed principles within. Therefore, it never gets in motion, and is always static. As *liang-chih* is static, it is quiet (*chi*),ᵘ but as *liang-chih* is active, it is affective (*kan*).ᵛ Therefore, the unexpressed and the expressed, the static and the active, and the quiet and the affective, which are related concepts in Chu Hsi's system and show different parts of mind, are now just relative adjectives to qualify one absolute *liang-chih,* and all are existentially identical in their meaning.

Liang-chih is the substance of mind seen as a knowing function. *Liang-chih* as the substance of mind is always existing; therefore, as a knowing function, it is always knowing even with nothing to know. It is just like the sun always shining even with nothing to shine on. When *liang-chih* has nothing to know and is still knowing, this is called its expression in the unexpressed. In this state, the moral cultivation of *liang-chih* is nothing other than the self-continuity of its knowing, or its self-awakening, and thus its self-consciousness of its own existence. This corresponds to what Chu Hsi called the way of moral cultivation through self-preservation or self-nourishment. Wang Yang-ming used these terms also to indicate the state of *liang-chih* when it is always knowing, yet has nothing to know.

However, *liang-chih* usually has something to know, as the sun usually has something to shine on. In this state, *liang-chih* has its objects to be known. Yet the direct objects of *liang-chih* are not the things ordinary people call external objects. The direct objects of *liang-chih* are our volitional ideas, or *i-nien*,ᵂ which are intended for handling affairs or doing things concerning the so-called external objects. Thus the so-called external objects are merely indirectly related to *liang-chih*, or are merely the constituent elements of our affairs, or things which are intended by our ideas. So the word *chih* (knowing) in Wang Yang-ming is to be taken as quite different from ordinary knowing. It is not a purely intellectual activity, the purpose of which is to get theoretical knowledge about external objects through our psychological functions such as sensing, perceiving, imagining, abstracting, conceiving, and understanding. It is also a different knowing from Chu Hsi's knowing which knows both the principles of the external objects theoretically and the principles of our actions practically. Wang Yang-ming's *liang-chih* knows immediately the good or evil of ideas in one's solitude with an inner certainty and without any reflection. *Liang-chih* never errs in its knowing. If it errs, it is not the voice of *liang-chih*; but what knows that one errs is *liang-chih*. Nevertheless, *liang-chih* may know only partially about the principles of Heaven as its nature; its nature is gradually self-revealed in a continuous process, as I have said before.

The most important point of Wang Yang-ming's thought about *liang-chih* is that when *liang-chih* knows, it is through an immediate feeling of the good and evil of our volitional ideas as these ideas are confronted and felt by *liang-chih*. Here *liang-chih* favors what is good and resists what is evil, and then likes the former and dislikes the latter. *Liang-chih* knows simultaneously with its feeling and its feeling continues itself and extends into its action. This action is an action which avoids what is evil and does what is good. This is why Wang Yang-ming insisted that knowledge and action are one.

Liang-chih, when it knows the good and evil of its volitional ideas, which are the motives of our ordinary feelings, will, desires, deliberations, and so on, actually practices the same thing Chu Hsi called self-examination. As *liang-chih* is avoiding what is evil, it does the same thing as the mastery of oneself that Chu Hsi called self-conquest and self-governing. When it both knows and feels what is good or evil and does what is good and avoids what is evil, *liang-chih*, as a function, is *fully* realized and its substance is embodied, incarnated in its function and realized therein also; then all our volitional ideas become good and are the expressions of our moral will. Thus the realization of *liang-chih* is at the same time the making of our moral will, pure, sincere, genuine, and authentic.

Furthermore, as *liang-chih* is always knowing and is essentially liking what is good and disliking what is evil, even when it is unexpressed and there is nothing to be known, its self-continuation or self-preservation is still in a state of self-restraint (*chieh*),[x] self-care (*shen*),[y] self-fear (*k'ung*),[z] and self-dread (*chü*)[aa] for avoiding evil; and also in a state of self-orientation and self-establishment of one's moral will (*i-chih*)[ab] for doing good. This is the state of *liang-chih's* self-expression in the unexpressed, which rightly corresponds to the way of moral cultivation: self-care in solitude, as Chu Hsi taught.

The only way of moral cultivation which Wang Yang-ming seems not to give intensive attention to is the way of investigating things, or *ko-wu*, which Chu Hsi taught. Yet Wang Yang-ming also had his interpretation of *ko-wu*, which can include Chu Hsi's theory of *ko-wu* on a higher level of thought. In Wang Yang-ming's thought, when *liang-chih* is realized and what is evil is avoided, then all our volitional ideas are good and at the same time perfectly right, and any affairs or things originating from the right ideas are rectified and put in their right place by a right way. This is Wang Yang-ming's interpretation of the word *ko-wu*, which seems to be too subjective and has no such objective meaning as is contained in Chu Hsi's idea of *ko-wu*. However, Wang Yang-ming never denies that men should have knowledge of objective things, or so-called external objects. Yet this kind of knowledge originates from our senses and is called sense knowledge (*wen-chien chih chih*).[ac] It is not the knowing of *liang-chih* or the knowledge of our virtuous nature which originates from ourselves. Surely it is not enough for one to have merely the knowing of *liang-chih*, or the knowledge of virtuous nature in a narrow sense. Nevertheless, as our volitional ideas are related to our affairs or things concerned with objective things or so-called external objects, we can never have *liang-chih* without including some knowledge about objective things within the whole domain of its knowing.

When man is motivated by his *liang-chih* and is oriented toward something good, he must and should know the ways to accomplish those good things and then carry out these ways through objective things. In this case, the world of objective things should be observed, researched, and known from the moral obligations of *liang-chih* too. Thus the theory of *ko-wu*, according to Wang Yang-ming's thought, may actually include the way of *ko-wu* according to Chu Hsi's thought, as an aspect of or a moment in the process of realization of *liang-chih*. As the knowing of objective things is a moment of our doing something with them and our doing something is preconceived in our volitional idea as its content, the volitional ideas exist on a higher level than the knowing and doing. *Liang-chih* which knows the good and evil of the ideas exists on a still higher level, or on the highest level, and can include ideas known by itself as within itself also. Therefore, the realization of *liang-chih*, which stretches through ideas, affairs, and down to objective things, can definitely include also the investigation of objective things, such as Chu Hsi taught, on a higher level of thought. Although Wang Yang-ming may not put so much emphasis on knowing objective things as Chu Hsi did, and we may not be able to deduce all the implications clearly from his teaching, we still may insist that his teaching of the realization of *liang-chih* can include what Chu Hsi taught in principle.

In Wang Yang-ming's thought, objective things are not so objective or external to our mind as Chu Hsi and common sense suppose. Here the crucial point we have to understand is that our ideas are always to be carried out through the objective things, and our *liang-chih*'s substance is immanent in its function as knowing. From Chu Hsi's point of view, there are externally existing objective things, such as other persons and things in the natural world, which are outside our mind. These outside things are assumed to have their independent principles or *li* for their being, although metaphysically speaking these principles are also principles of our being. For Chu Hsi all principles, whether without or within, have to be searched out by our "investigation of things." This is a teaching for our empirical and ordinary consciousness. However, it is quite inadequate to a higher state of man's moral, metaphysical, or ontological self-consciousness, as Wang Yang-ming expressed it in his very profound and simple sayings. In such a self-consciousness, when we know or act morally toward objective things, we have to see these things as immanent in our moral consciousness at the same time that they are confronted as objects. Here not only is the principle of moral knowledge and action ours, but even what the actions and knowledge are directed toward as objects are inseparable from our action and knowledge, and are ours also. In Wang Yang-ming's thought, as *liang-chih's* substance is expressed and immanent in its function as knowing, therefore, where *liang-chih's* knowing is, its substance is also. Whatever is knowing, or enlightened by *liang-chih's* knowing or light, is penetrated by *liang-chih's* light and being enlightened. Thus Wang Yang-ming said that there is no substance of eyesight, and the substance of eyesight is in the color; there is no substance of mind and the substance of mind is in its affections and responses and judgments of the right or wrong of the myriad things in Heaven and Earth. These statements mean nothing other than that *liang-chih's* substance is in its knowing, which is the essence of its affections, responses, and judgments; its substance is in all the things in the universe, and all the things in the universe are within the domain of *liang-chih*. This is why Wang Yang-ming said that *liang-chih* is the spirit of the creative and transforming universe, and that nothing is outside the domain of *liang-chih*. This is an idealism which is very like Lu Hsiang-shan's idealism. Yet Lu Hsiang-shan's thought is based on the "self-awakening of the original mind," while the idea of Wang Yang-ming is based on his seeing the substance of *liang-chih* through its function as knowing and residing in what is known.

According to Wang Yang-ming's thought, all ways of moral cultivation, such as self-preservation, self-examination, self-conquest, rectification of the mind, making the will authentic, and the investigation of things which Chu Hsi taught, are aspects or moments of one process of the realization of *liang-chih*; thus all are expressions of *liang-chih's* substance in its function. Therefore, Wang Yang-ming also views the psychological functions or faculties which Chu Hsi analyzed into different kinds as simply different expressions of *liang-chih's* nature, or *liang-chih's* substance in its functions.

Wang Yang-ming frequently states that the nature, mind, will, ability, and knowing are the same thing, seen from different aspects, existentially identical and ontologically one. Now as Wang Yang-ming acknowledged also the differences of meaning in these psychological terms, he distinguished his attitude from that of Lu Hsiang-shan, who refused to discuss the meanings of these terms in answer to his disciple's question. However, as Wang Yang-ming thought these different functions were existentially one, he still belongs to the camp of Lu Hsiang-shan, who saw the original mind as one.

As to the distinction between the mind of Tao and the human mind, Wang Yang-ming had a view which seems to be a synthesis of Lu Hsiang-shan and Chu Hsi. Wang Yang-ming said that there is only one mind or one *liang-chih* in man, and that the mind which realizes the principles of Heaven as our nature is good, rational, and the mind of Tao, while the mind which does not do so is irrational and evil, a human mind with selfish desires.[6] This latter point is slightly different from Lu Hsiang-shan's thought, which insists that there is no distinction between the mind of Tao and the human mind. Wang Yang-ming still distinguished between the mind of Tao and the human mind of private opinion or selfish desires as originating from two contradictory directions of the same mind, and his thought is somewhat closer to Chu Hsi's idea of the human mind as standing midway between the mind of Tao and the human mind with selfish desires, and serving as a neutral medium for the mutual transformation of these two opposite kinds of mind.

WANG CHI'S INTERPRETATIONS OF *LIANG-CHIH* AS BEYOND IDEAS OF GOOD AND EVIL AND HIS TEACHING ABOUT "LEARNING PRIOR TO HEAVEN"

After Wang Yang-ming's death, his disciples were divided into different schools. The two most important of them were the Chiang-yu school and the Che-chung school.[ad] Yet all the thinkers of these two schools faced one important problem in the teaching of Wang Yang-ming. That is: how can sagehood really be attained by the realization of *liang-chih?*

According to Wang Yang-ming's teaching, there are volitional ideas, either good or evil, coming and going in our mind. The moral task of realization of *liang-chih* is to know them and evaluate them, and to do what is good and avoid what is evil. However, as the volitional ideas come and go indefinitely, we can never have the guarantee that all the evil volitional ideas will never come back; thus we have no self-confidence that we can attain sagehood. Again, the very coming and going of good and evil ideas is proof of our lack of moral stability or moral integration in the general sense. Furthermore, good and evil ideas, as known and evaluated by *liang-chih*, usually go ahead of *liang-chih*'s knowing. It seems that we have good and evil ideas first and then *liang-chih* follows their traces and knows them. It seems also that *liang-chih* is destined to remain a step behind these ideas, and thus always to be running after them. If this is so, how can it really master them, and how can its like and dislike of them necessarily be powerful enough to preserve or eradicate them absolutely? This is surely a very serious problem.

In dealing with this problem the thinkers of the Chiang-yu school, Ni Shuang-chiang [ae] and Lo Nien-an,[af] took "back to tranquillity" (*kuei-chi*)[ag] as their slogan. By the phrase "back to tranquillity" is meant a moral task which is temporarily separated from all affections, and thus stops all volitional ideas, and then abides in an inner state of tranquillity to meditate on the substance of *liang-chih*, which is quiet and transcendental. Here both Ni and Lo had very profound insights and experienced a deep spiritual enlightenment, which I shall not discuss here. I mention them only as a stepping stone to the discussion of Wang Chi's [ah] idea of moral mind.

Wang Chi disagreed with the Chiang-yu school's idea of substance and function as two distinct parts of *liang-chih*. He was more congenial than Ni and Lo to Wang Yang-ming's thought about the identity of substance and function. Nevertheless, Wang Chi saw also that the coming and going of good and evil ideas in our mind are disturbances of our moral mind, and therefore "passing beyond good and evil ideas" also became a central thought of Wang Chi.

From the historical point of view, Wang Yang-ming had already thought that the principle of Heaven is the substance of mind or *liang-chih* at rest with itself; therefore, in a sense, it may be taken as static and beyond the distinction of good and evil. This thought does not mean that one need not act according to the principles of Heaven, as the nature of *liang-chih*, or that the realization of *liang-chih* is not good; it only means that the principle as static and as the origin of our ordinary good is above ordinary good and it means also that when good is done for the realization of principle one should not still keep the idea of good as something reserved in one's mind. Wang Yang-ming compared the very idea of good kept in mind as bits of gold in our eyes which, though precious, obstruct the seeing power of our eyes. In our common sense, we all agree that a man who is really good does not think of himself as good. A man who always thinks of himself as good is a man of pride, which is not good. This proves that the utmost or supreme good of man may consist in the self-forgetting and self-transcending of the idea of his goodness. This proves also that the ideas of supreme good and of "beyond good and evil" are not incompatible ideas on a more profound level.

From this point of view, in talking about the nature or substance of *liang-chih* as the origin of our ordinary moral good, Wang Yang-ming took it both as supreme good and as beyond the distinction of good and evil. At the same time, in talking about the function of *liang-chih*, Wang Yang-ming never ceased to say that the function of *liang-chih* is to know the good and evil of our volitional ideas, to like and do what is good, and to dislike and avoid what is evil, and that the distinction of good and evil must be clearly known by *liang-chih* without any obscurity and confusion. In Wang Chi's thought, "passing beyond the distinction of good and evil" rightly became a thoroughgoing teaching for moral cultivation.

Concerning the problem of "Beyond the distinction of good and evil," there is a famous discussion of Wang Yang-ming, Wang Chi, and Ch'ien Te-hung,[ai] another disciple of Wang Yang-ming. The record of this discussion is called "The Record of Confirmation of Tao in T'ien-ch'üan." [aj] T'ien-ch'üan is a place name which literally means "the source originated from Heaven," and thus symbolically shows the importance of this discussion. However, the record by Wang Chi and that by Ch'ien Te-hung of this discussion were slightly different. The version in the *Ch'uan hsi-lu* [ak] was based on Wang Chi's record. A hundred years later Huang Tsung-hsi, who edited the *Ming-ju hsüeh-an*, also used the record of Wang Chi in the section on the latter's thought (*Lung-hsi hsüeh-an* [al]). Yet, in one of his other essays, he doubted that what was recorded by Wang

Chi was genuinely Wang Yang-ming's teaching. All these documents are of the utmost importance for our understanding of the development of thought in Wang Yang-ming's school. At one point in this famous discussion, both Wang Chi and Ch'ien Te-hung asked questions about the essence of their master's teaching of the realization of *liang-chih*, which were summarized in four sentences. My translation differs slightly from the translations of others, and my reasons for translating the four sentences this way will become apparent in the discussion that follows.

> Beyond the distinction of good and evil is the original substance of mind.
> There is either good or evil in the arising of volitional ideas.
> To know the good and evil of the volitional ideas is the "function" of *liang-chih*.
> Doing what is good and avoiding what is evil is to make things righteous.

According to our interpretation of Wang Yang-ming's thought in the last section, it is beyond question that these four sentences summarized most important features of Yang-ming's teaching. The first sentence represents Wang Yang-ming's ontological or metaphysical idea of *liang-chih* as a transcendental being. It means nothing other than that the substance of mind as the origin of our ordinary good is beyond distinctions of good and evil and is the supreme good, as I have said above.

The second sentence is a descriptive statement about our ordinary experience and consciousness of the moral value and lack of value, or good and evil, arising in our volitional ideas. Here the word *i* am does not mean moral will, which does only what is good and avoids what is evil. The moral will is purely good and not evil; therefore here the word *i* means simply "thoughts" (*i-nien*), which come and go in our ordinary consciousness and are only our volitional ideas, which may be either good or evil.

The third sentence says that the *liang-chih* which confronts the good or evil ideas knows them and evaluates them. Here *liang-chih* definitely has a higher level of existence and is master of the ideas. It is the substance of mind of the first sentence, where the emphasis is put on the substance of *liang-chih*, so the word "substance [of mind]" is used. In the third sentence the emphasis is put on the function of *liang-chih*. As the word *chih* means "knowing," which is the function of mind, the word *liang-chih* itself is used. The first sentence is an ontological statement which is intended to show that *liang-chih*, as the substance of mind, is beyond good and evil and transcends them. The third sentence says that *liang-chih* has its function in knowing ordinary good or evil ideas, and is immanent in its function. Thus it is also close to us in our moral practice.

The fourth sentence refers to things directly related to moral practice. Strictly speaking, doing what is good and avoiding what is evil and thus making things righteous is just the continuation of knowing good and evil in the process of realizing *liang-chih*, as I have explained before. Thus to make things righteous is nothing other than the last step in realizing *liang-chih*. Here one may ask, "What happens after the last step in realizing *liang-chih?*" or "What happens once the thing is already made righteous?" Wang Yang-ming did not answer this explicitly in his four sentences. However, according to the explanation of Wang Yang-ming's teaching in the preceding section, Wang Yang-ming would say that when *liang-chih* is realized and things are made righteous, no idea of good should be reserved in the mind and we should again go beyond the distinction of good and evil. This means that we have to return to the thought of the first sentence. Thus the meaning of the "four sentences" as a whole is just a description of the circular process of moral practice which begins from the realm beyond the distinction of good and evil, then proceeds to know the distinction of good and evil, and to do good and avoid evil, and ends in a state of mind again beyond the distinction of good and evil. This is rightly a very concise summary of Wang Yang-ming's teaching.

However, both Wang Chi and Ch'ien Te-hung had questions about the teaching of the four sentences. Both their questions were raised from points of view which are more logical than the teaching of the four sentences as such. Ch'ien Te-hung asked: If there are good and evil in our volitional ideas, and we have the knowledge and actions to do good and also avoid evil, then how can the substance of mind be beyond the distinction of good and evil? Thus it seems that there are good and evil in the substance of mind also. On the other hand, Wang Chi supposed that if the substance of mind is beyond the distinction of good and evil, then *liang-chih*'s knowing of volitional ideas and all things should also be beyond the distinction of good and evil. It is recorded by Wang Chi that, after these two questions were raised by the two disciples, Wang Yang-ming said he had two ways of teaching: one for men born with high or sharp intelligence (*li-ken*),[an] and the other for men born with ordinary intelligence (*tun-ken*),[ao] and that what Wang Chi said was implied by the first sentence was for the sharp minds, and what Ch'ien Te-hung spoke of as implied in the other three sentences was for ordinary men. Yet, according to Ch'ien Te-hung's record in his biography of Wang Yang-ming, Wang Yang-ming did not say that he had two kinds of teaching; he said only that there are few people who are of sharp intelligence and that the two disciples' understanding of his teaching should supplement each other, and he said also that his disciples should never forget the four sentences as a whole. As the records of Wang Chi and Ch'ien Te-hung are slightly different, we need to know which one is closer to the actual situation at T'ien-ch'üan. I assume that Ch'ien Te-hung was a more faithful disciple of Wang Yang-ming, while Wang Chi, who was a more brilliant student, may have interpreted his master's saying according to his own predispositions. I think that Huang Tsung-hsi is quite right in saying that Wang Yang-ming never said anywhere that he had two kinds of teaching, because the teaching of the four sentences, if understood as I have explained it above, is both sufficient and necessary for the summarization of Wang Yang-ming's teaching. I think also that the criticism implied by the questions of his disciples about the moral practice of moral mind is actually irrelevant, because the four sentences understood as a whole are descriptive statements and not a deductive system. I suppose that in this discussion, Wang Yang-ming merely said that each of his two disciples had understood only one side of his teaching, and that later Wang Chi interpreted the two sides of his master's teaching as two kinds of teaching. Therefore, when Wang Yang-ming died, the idea of "beyond the distinction of good and evil" was further developed by Wang Chi and became his central teaching.

In the discussion at T'ien-ch'üan, as stated above, Wang Chi just supposed that, if *liang-chih* is beyond the distinction of good and evil, our volitional ideas and knowing of *liang-chih* should be likewise. However, in his dialogues and letters we also find his theory of the abolition of volitional ideas. This is plainly a further thought naturally arising in his mind. His reason for the abolition of ideas seems to be that, as volitional ideas are actually either good or evil, if we want to go beyond the distinction of good and evil, we have to go beyond the volitional ideas themselves, and then abolish volitional ideas altogether. The belief in the abolition of volitional ideas was originally held by Yang Chien [ap] (1140–1226), the disciple of Lu Hsiang-shan in the Sung dynasty, and was adopted by Wang Chi as a disciple of Wang Yang-ming. However, Wang Chi not only took the abolition of volitional ideas (*i*) as a way for the realization of *liang-chih*, but also distinguished *liang-chih* from both volitional ideas (*i*) and ordinary consciousness (*shih*),[aq] and even thought, to transcend ordinary consciousness as well. This idea is not difficult to understand, if we know that our volitional ideas reside in our ordinary consciousness. The difference between the knowing of *liang-chih* and ordinary consciousness consists in there being a duality of subject and object in our ordinary consciousness, while there is no such duality in the knowing of *liang-chih*. The difference between *liang-chih* and volitional ideas consists in that volitional ideas come and go, appear and perish, and are transitory, while *liang-chih* is permanent. As volitional ideas appear and perish, they are rightly the origin of the birth and death of our life and mind. As consciousness has its subjective and objective sides, this is the basis of its inner world in contrast to the outer world, and the origin of the breaking of the identity of self and the world. So all consciousness and volitional ideas have to be abolished or transcended. Thus, in our moral consciousness, if there are still subjective good and evil ideas coming and going in opposition to the outer objective world, this is the stage of "consciousness and volitional ideas." In this stage even good ideas are limited to what we are conscious of and thus are not identical with the universe as a whole nor with the transcendental being of our moral mind itself. Therefore, Wang Chi said that we should have a moral task which transforms the conscious ideas into the moral mind or *liang-chih* itself, if we really take the moral life of the sage as our ideal. In the moral life of the sage there are surely many expressions of his which are expressions of the principles of Heaven. However, any sage's self-expression is natural and spontaneous, as it should be in accord with his present situation. So there is nothing added to the principles of Heaven as the unexpressed substance of his mind, nor is there anything remaining after the expression has passed; thus, though all his expressions are good, he also has no conscious idea about the goodness of his activity in the life of the sage, as there are no conscious ideas left after the expression of *liang-chih*. Here *liang-chih* is superconsciousness as Nothing (*wu*),[ar] and also as transcendental being, always unexpressed as well as always expressed, and supremely good as well as beyond good and evil. Therefore, when talking about *liang-chih* in this highest sense, Wang Chi in his terminology even cut off the word *liang*, which implies goodness. *Liang-chih* to Wang Chi is identical with *chih* or "pure knowing." This pure knowing passes beyond good and evil. This pure knowing itself is both being (*yu*)[as] and Nothing (*wu*). This pure knowing is like a vacant valley which echoes a sound, but in which nothing remains after the echo. It is like the void space through which a bird passes and leaves no trace. Thus, from our *liang-chih* as pure knowing, there may arise all kinds of good expressions in response to things which we confront, yet, when any good expression has passed, nothing remains, as in the vacant alley or void space. This is rightly the moral life of the sage, which passes through the ideas of ordinary good to realize the utmost or supreme good which is beyond good and evil.

On the basis of the foregoing, Wang Chi distinguished between two kinds of moral task in becoming a sage. One he called learning how to make the will authentic. He called this learning "the learning posterior to Heaven" because it is posterior to the arising of volitional ideas. Where we have an idea, there we have a world before us, and we have Heaven. Thus the learning posterior to an idea is posterior to Heaven. In my opinion, this kind of learning is actually similar to the teaching of Wang Yang-ming. The other kind of moral task for becoming a sage, which Wang Chi preferred, he called "the learning anterior to Heaven." This is actually the learning prior to the arising of ideas. As here ideas do not arise, no world or Heaven is before our mind. Yet the mind as pure knowing is still there, the mind which is Nothing as well as being, unexpressed as well as always expressing, beyond the distinction of good and evil, and the supreme good. Here the mind or *liang-chih* as pure knowing, though confronting nothing to be known, exists in its own right and is wholly righteous in itself. So this kind of learning is called by Wang Chi "learning how to put the mind in its right position," and it is in this that Wang Chi's thought went beyond Wang Yang-ming's thoughts about *liang-chih* as pure knowing, which is both Nothing and being, both unexpressed and expressed.

The word *cheng-hsin* [at] is usually translated as "rectification of mind." But in Wang Chi's so-called learning of *cheng-hsin*, there is nothing to be rectified, and it is perhaps better to translate his *cheng-hsin* as "putting the mind in its right position." Even this, however, is not adequate, because in Wang Chi's thought there is no action of "putting" beside the mind's knowing of itself. The only thing we can do is to let our mind stand as it is in its right position, which is actually no position, since the mind is universal being, as well as universal Nothing.

Wang Chi further attempted to synthesize the teachings of Buddhism and Taoism with Confucianism. In Wang Yang-ming's thought, there is already the germ of such a synthesis. Wang Chi, however, stated plainly that the meaning of *liang-chih* covers Buddhism and Taoism as generally understood, but that Confucianism is positivistic, while Buddhism and Taoism are negativistic. Now, in Wang Chi's thought, *liang-chih* as Nothing is negativistic, and as being is positivistic; it is not difficult to understand why Wang Chi took *liang-chih* to cover the essentials of the three teachings.

After Wang Chi there was still further development of the idea of *liang-chih* in the schools of Yang-ming's disciples, ending with the thinkers of the Tung-lin school and Liu Tsung-chou,[au] who criticized severely Wang Chi's idea of "Beyond good and evil" and his thought about the synthesis of the three teachings. They also have a profound idea of moral mind, but this is beyond the scope of this essay.

CONCLUDING REMARKS

Above I have said that Wang Yang-ming accepted the problem which Chu Hsi left, replaced Lu Hsiang-shan's idea of original mind with his *liang-chih*, and actually had a theory of mind which is a synthesis of the thought of Lu Hsiang-shan and that of Chu Hsi. Wang Chi took up the problem where Wang Yang-ming had left it and went beyond his master, even, in a sense, beyond Confucianism. While Wang Chi is usually considered close to Yang Chien, the disciple of Lu Hsiang-shan, he is also close to Lu Hsiang-shan himself. In the thought of Lu Hsiang-shan, one should have a self-awakening of the original mind. This requires a sudden jump in the moral task. Lu Hsiang-shan's concept of mind is simpler than Wang Yang-ming's. The teachings of both Lu Hsiang-shan and Wang Chi are illuminating and brilliant in talking about the higher level of the mind. But the teachings of Chu Hsi and Wang Yang-ming are closer to ordinary life and more easily practiced. This may be taken as a rough comparison of these four thinkers as I have discussed them in this essay. Although my exposition has emphasized Wang Yang-ming and Wang Chi rather than Chu Hsi and Lu Hsiang-shan, I feel that we can never understand Wang Chi adequately except through Wang Yang-ming, nor can we ever understand Wang Yang-ming without comparing him with both Lu Hsiang-shan and Chu Hsi.

NOTES

1. *Hsiang-shan hsien-sheng ch'üan-chi* (Shanghai, 1935), 35/447.
2. *Chu Tzu yü-lei* (Taipei, 1962), 8/4817.
3. *Ch'uan-hsi lu* (Shanghai, 1917), 2/19.
4. *Ibid.*, p. 28.
5. *Ch'uan-hsi lu*, 3/19.
6. *Ch'uan-hsi lu*, 3/12.

GLOSSARY

a	氣	y	愼
b	天理	z	恐
c	未發	aa	懼
d	已發	ab	意志
e	理	ac	聞見之知
f	道心	ad	江右, 浙中
g	聖	ae	聶雙江
h	賢	af	羅念菴
i	人心	ag	歸寂
j	涵養	ah	王畿
k	存養	ai	錢德洪
l	克治	aj	天泉
m	省察	ak	傳習錄
n	愼獨	al	龍溪學案
o	正心	am	意
p	誠意	an	利根
q	格物	ao	鈍根
r	良知	ap	楊簡
s	良知卽心之本體	aq	識
t	天理之昭明靈覺卽良知	ar	無
u	寂	as	有
v	感	at	正心
w	意念	au	劉宗周
x	戒		

TAKEHIKO OKADA *Wang Chi and the*

Rise of Existentialism

明 In the sixteenth century the Wang Yang-ming school developed into three main branches. The first was the Left Wing,[a] or existentialist school (*hsien-ch'eng p'ai*)[b]; the second was the Right Wing,[c] or quietist school (*kuei-chi p'ai*)[d]; and the third was the Orthodox school,[e] or cultivation school (*hsiu-cheng p'ai*).[f] In general, the Orthodox school understood Wang Yang-ming's thought correctly, but it was not completely free from the contemplative and quietistic tendency manifested in Sung thought. The Right Wing developed this tendency even further. These two schools failed to adapt themselves to the romantic, emotional, and sensual mood of the late Ming dynasty, which was represented by such works as the novel *Golden Lotus* (*Chin-p'ing-mei*), the poetry of Yüan Hung-tao, the painting of Hsü Wei, and the calligraphy of Tung Ch'i-ch'ang. On the other hand, the Left Wing prospered during this period through its successful adaptation to the trend of the times, though it did not escape harmful side effects.

Wang Yang-ming, in his later days, told his disciples, "The Way is innate knowledge (*liang-chih*), and from the beginning innate knowledge is complete and perfect. I regard what is right as right, and what is wrong as wrong. If we only rely on innate knowledge with regard to what is right and what is wrong, everything will be correct. This innate knowledge is after all your wise master." [1] The innate knowledge which each man possesses is as perfect as that of the sage. Consequently there is a sage in everyone. It is only man's lack of self-confidence that prevents his innate knowledge from reaching this. The potentiality originally belongs to man.[2] Wang asserted that, if man apprehends directly this innate knowledge, he can settle everything, just as "one gram of a holy medicine turns iron into gold." [3] This is the essential basis for the doctrine of existential innate knowledge. Thus among Wang Yang-ming and his disciples this saying became common: "The men in the street are all sages." [4] This is a phrase which the existentialist scholars popularized in their attempts to have people apprehend directly the innate knowledge.

The germ of this idea can be found in Lu Hsiang-shan. One day his disciple Ch'an Fu-min (Tzu-nan)[g] was sitting beside him, when suddenly Lu stood up. So did Ch'an. Thereupon the teacher asked, "Did you make a *special effort* in doing what you have just done?" At that time Ch'an Fu-min was making too much of an effort to arrive at the Principle. His master told him, "If only you believe in the actuality of your mind, you will be able to act freely and without any obstruction, just as a great bird flies with the wind or a large fish swims freely in the great sea." [5]

Chu Hsi had said that the Nature (of man) is Principle. This doctrine reflected his high idealism. He wanted to uphold the purity and objectivity of Principle. He also wished to examine the actual world in the light of a rigid moral standard. Lu Hsiang-shan criticized Chu Hsi's teaching as leading to a divided mind and overlooking the truth that Principle is to be found in the actual, living mind. Lu Hsiang-shan valued the natural state of mind, saying, "It is not only evil that harms the mind, but also the good" (insofar as one conceives of the good as outside oneself, as something to be achieved).[6] He explained that every man in himself possesses the self-confident mind that is his own master, and he therefore stressed the importance of self-reliance and self-confidence.

Chu Hsi criticized Lu's doctrine on the ground that it evinced a blind belief that one mind can know everything. Chu further asserted that Lu's doctrine could never rise above the state of moral relativism; there was a danger of accepting the world as it is and adjusting to it without subjecting it to moral judgment.[7] Wang Yang-ming, who succeeded Lu, attempted to clarify the source and substance of Lu's living, active mind and came to assert his own existentialist doctrine on the basis of his predecessor's theory: "Mind is Principle."

The Lu-Wang school of the mind takes the dynamic life of the mind as its pivot. According to this doctrine, substance (*pen-t'i*)[h] (or the nature) and effort (*kung-fu*,[i] or the moral task) are inseparable. As the question of the relationship between substance and effort came to be central to this philosophy of Wang Yang-ming, the doctrine of the mind was further articulated.

If we compare the Ch'eng-Chu doctrine which asserts that "Nature is Principle" with the Lu-Wang doctrine which asserts that "Mind is Principle," we may say that the former holds a position in which man devotes himself to effort in order to achieve principle (the substance or nature) while the latter holds a position in which man devotes himself directly to the substance of the mind itself.

When Chu's disciples criticized Lu, saying "Lu neglected effort" (in favor of direct enlightenment), Chu Hsi admonished them for being excessive in their criticism. Chu Hsi himself was, however, philosophically opposed to Lu's sense of the direct relation between self and substance. Chu complained that Lu disregarded the importance of effort while accepting what freely flows out of one's heart as the principle of Heaven. Thus Chu pointed out that it was Lu's emphasis on the mind as Nature (substance) that led him to disregard the significance of effort. Chu earnestly argued for the indispensability of effort.[8] It is recorded that even on his deathbed Chu Hsi said, "Man should always exert himself in seeking the substance"[9] (i.e., in apprehending the nature and striving for virtue).

If we compare Lu's doctrine with Wang Yang-ming's in terms of substance and effort, in Lu's doctrine of "Mind is Principle" one has difficulty finding a basis for the effort of self-cultivation, and as a result one tends either to give oneself over to elemental human nature or to fall into subjective illusion. But in Wang Yang-ming's doctrine, which stresses the effort to extend one's innate knowledge, the innate knowledge itself is the moral rule, the keen moral consciousness, and the source of mind. This means, therefore, that, according to Wang Yang-ming's doctrine, there is a foundation for effort. To "extend innate knowledge" is the self-improving function by which innate knowledge, as the substance of mind, constantly restores itself to the original state, but in a higher dimension. Therefore, we may also say that effort is the function of the mind's substance, and that effort transcends itself through drawing upon that substance. Thus Wang Yang-ming's doctrine is free from the defects found in Lu's teaching.

Consequently, according to Wang Yang-ming's view, substance

and effort are not separate or different; they are fundamentally one. In other words, substance is effort and effort is substance. As long as one understands the truth of the oneness of substance and effort, one may describe substance as effort and vice versa.

The Mean (*Chung-yung*) states: "The superior man does not wait till he sees things to be cautious, nor till he hears things to be apprehensive" (I, 4). It also states that substance is neither seen nor heard, and that caution and apprehension are the moral task or effort. Wang Yang-ming said, "Here you must believe that while original substance is neither seen nor heard [when not acting on something] it is still operative as caution and apprehension. Caution and apprehension are not anything to be added to what is not seen or heard. If original substance is truly understood, it will be all right to say that [the functions of] caution and apprehension refer to original substance and that what is not seen or what is not heard refer to effort." [10] He also said, "It is innate knowledge that can be cautious and apprehensive." [11] The Japanese Confucianist Satō Issai [j] said, concerning the above quotation, "From the word 'can' we understand that substance and effort are one." [12] His meaning is that innate knowledge itself has this function or capability; to be cautious and apprehensive is the effort as well as the substance of innate knowledge. Lo Ju-fang,[k] a later follower of Wang Yang-ming, said that if there is effort apart from substance, the function of the mind is obstructed; if there is substance apart from effort, the substance will be isolated (from actual life).[13] His explanation is clear and appropriate.

In Wang Yang-ming's terms, as long as one realizes the oneness of substance and effort, one may call effort substance and vice versa. Wang Yang-ming further explained this, using Buddhist terminology: "Wherever the mind is, there is the true state. Wherever the mind is not, there is the illusory state. At the same time, wherever the mind is not, there is the true state, and wherever the mind is, there is the illusory state." [14]

As mentioned above, Wang Yang-ming sometimes explained substance by effort or effort by substance. In this manner, he endeavored to show that substance and effort are not static, but are one completely unified living thing. One can realize personally such a doctrine only when one has in his own experience fully penetrated and realized this unity of the original substance of mind and effort.

It is said that even Ch'ien Te-hung,[1] the most learned of Wang Yang-ming's disciples, took several years before he finally came to understand this doctrine. Only the most talented scholar, Wing Chi, immediately understood his master's doctrine. Wang Chi interpreted the doctrine as follows:

When you say, "Wherever the mind is, there is the true state; wherever the mind is not, there is an illusory state," you are talking about effort from the point of view of the original substance of the mind. When you say, "Wherever the mind is not, there is the true state; and wherever the mind is, there is an illusory state," you are talking about the original substance from the point of view of effort.[15]

Although Wang Yang-ming approved Wang Chi's interpretation, he thought that direct realization of the nature or substance was not necessarily the basic purport of his doctrine. For he had observed that many highly talented scholars, regarding the acquisition of innate knowledge as a simple matter, sought direct realization in a kind of vacuum, and failed in concrete application. Consequently they fell into illusion without achieving the result originally desired.

Wang Yang-ming therefore added to "innate knowledge" the word "extension," i.e., putting innate knowledge into effort, extending it in action.[16] Other existentialist scholars such as Wang Ken [m] and Wang Tung [n] stated that Wang Yang-ming's basic intention was not to emphasize the extension of innate knowledge, but to explain innate knowledge itself. These scholars maintained that Wang Yang-ming was compelled to refer to the word "extension" because at that time there were those who, understanding innate knowledge to be "empty" (i.e., nonattached) and "vacuous" (i.e., unobstructed) sought only transcendence and regarded innate knowledge as easy and simple. Those people, according to Wang Ken and Wang Tung, asserted that wherever consciousness is, whether or not it is moral, there is the nature (*hsing*), which is manifested in man's natural desires. Consequently, they fell victim to the error of the moral indifference of human nature found in the doctrines of Kao Tzu and the Buddhists. According to Wang Ken and Wang Tung, this is the only reason why Wang Yang-ming was driven to refer to the "extension" of innate knowledge.[17]

Be this as it may, Wang Yang-ming's intention is clearly expounded in the Four Dicta ° which he taught his disciples. "In the original substance of the mind there is neither good nor evil. When the will becomes active, there is good and evil. The function of innate knowledge is to recognize good and evil. The investigation of things is to do good and reject evil." [18]

Tsou Shou-i,[p] however, recorded the First Dictum as "The substance of the mind is the supreme good and is free from evil." [19] This caused fervent controversies among scholars of later generations. However, if one clearly understands that Wang Yang-ming's innate knowledge is, actually, the consciousness which constitutes the moral rule, the one living thing which unifies the internal and external and makes original substance and effort into one, and the absolute Nothing which is simultaneously being and nothing or vice versa, it will become evident that one may call Wang Yang-ming's substance of the mind either the supreme good or something which is above good and evil, i.e., a faculty of moral judgment which is wholly good in itself, transcending any objective, practical choice between good and evil, whatever the extent of its actual operation or effectiveness.

As for the doctrine of the Four Dicta, Wang Chi said that the reason why Wang Yang-ming had said, "There is neither good nor evil in the original mind," rather than "the supreme good is the original substance of the mind," is because at that time some scholars identified human weakness with the nature and consequently misunderstood Mencius' doctrine that "human nature is originally good." Wang Yang-ming expounded his doctrine to correct these scholars' mistakes of subjectivity. Wang Chi thus concluded that Wang Yang-ming's real intention was to eradicate their subjective ideas and to lead them to the direct apprehension of the "Nothingness" (i.e., the nonduality or transmoral character) of innate knowledge.[20] Wang Chi regarded this doctrine of Wang Yang-ming's as a teaching fitted to a particular circumstance and stated, "Perhaps this is not the final conclusion." Wang Chi also said, "If we say that in the original substance, there is neither good nor evil, then neither can such a distinction be found in the will, in knowledge, or in things." [21]

This is what is called the doctrine of the Four Negatives (or Non-dualities, meaning the absence of good and evil, *ssu wu* q), or of "having no good" (*wu shan* r).

However, Ch'ien Te-hung asserted, "The substance of the mind is the Nature endowed in us by Heaven and there is originally neither good nor evil in it. But because we have a mind conditioned by evil customs and habits, we see in our thoughts distinctions between good and evil. The work of the investigation of things, the extension of knowledge, the making of the will sincere, the rectification of the mind, and the cultivation of one's person is aimed precisely at recovering that original nature and substance of the mind. If there were no good and evil involved in these tasks, what would be the necessity of such an effort?" In this way Ch'ien Te-hung faithfully followed Wang Yang-ming's doctrine of the Four Dicta.[22] This is what is called the doctrine of the Four Positives (*ssu yu* s), or of "having good" (*yu-shan* t).

Why did Wang Yang-ming say that in the original substance of the mind there is neither good nor evil? According to Ch'ien Te-hung, in the supreme good of the original substance of the mind, there is naturally neither evil nor good, for it is vacuous (devoid of selfish preferences or desires) and omnipotent, and brings everything in the world to perfection. Ch'ien Te-hung further stated that those who seek the supreme good externally seek it as a definite principle or standard in things, and they take it for granted that good exists in the originally vacuous and omnipotent mind. But this approach, according to Ch'ien Te-hung, obstructs the original vacuous and omnipotent substance of mind from working with complete freedom. He concluded, therefore, that it was to correct this error that Wang Yang-ming stated: "In the original substance of the mind, there is neither good nor evil." Ch'ien Te-hung also asserted that this doctrine of Wang Yang-ming's is a teaching to suit a particular circumstance.[23] I think Ch'ien Te-hung is right on this point.

According to the *Ch'uan-hsi lu* and the *Ch'ing-yüan-tseng-ch'u*,[u] Wang Yang-ming in general approved both Wang Chi's and Ch'ien Te-hung's interpretations. Wang Yang-ming is recorded as saying, "Wang Chi's view is the means I use in dealing with men of keen intelligence. Ch'ien Te-hung's view is for the men who are less well endowed. You should think of them as complementary, and not hold to one side." At the same time, Wang Yang-ming reasserted his doctrine expounded in the Four Dicta, and stressed the importance of Ch'ien Te-hung's view, which urges one to devote oneself to effort.

Wang Yang-ming told Wang Chi, "You should not show your interpretation to people. You cannot readily expect from them full realization of the unity of the original substance of the mind and effort. For it is not easy to find people of keen intelligence in this world. Otherwise they will imagine an original substance in a vacuum. Whatever they do will not be genuine. They will do no more than cultivate a mind of vacuity and quietness, and will make the mistake of skipping over [not following the proper steps]." [24]

On the other hand, according to Wang Chi, Wang Yang-ming said, "If one can realize the original substance in which there is neither good nor evil, one will know what absolute Nothing (wu) is. And then all will, knowledge, and things will emerge from Nothing. Once this is done, it settles everything. Effort is substance. This truth is simple and direct. It is neither too much nor too little. This is the secret to be passed from one mind to another. Now that you have grasped my secret, it can be divulged to others. I have no intention of keeping it to myself." [25]

If we examine this in the light of the development of the dynamic concept of life and living thought from Lu Hsiang-shan to Wang Yang-ming, and consider the direction of Wang Yang-ming's thought itself, the doctrine of the Four Negatives is the revelation and development of Wang Yang-ming's inner tendency. However, when we realize that Wang Yang-ming attained his doctrine of the innate knowledge only after experiencing indescribable agonies, we may say that the doctrine of the Four Positives is also in accord with the true aim of Wang Yang-ming. Here again we will find the reason why Wang Chi advocated the doctrine of the Four Negatives and rejected Ch'ien Te-hung's doctrine of the Four Positives, and this will give us a clue as to why Wang Chi came to assert the concept of direct enlightenment and the doctrine of existentialism.

Criticizing Ch'ien Te-hung, Wang Chi said that if one cultivates Nothing through being and seeks the original substance through accumulated efforts with a belief that there is good and evil in the will, knowledge, and things, one will inevitably become attached to being and one's mind will be unable to attain Nothing (nonattachment), and consequently one will not be able to arrive at the absolute, original substance of the mind. That is to say, one must realize that in the original substance of the mind there is no distinction between good and evil, and one must further realize what absolute Nothing is. Only in this way can all will, knowledge, and things emerge from Nothing.

If this is done, the mind will become no-mind, hiding itself deeply in secret, the will will become no-will, functioning with complete freedom, the knowledge will become no-knowledge, whose substance will be tranquil, and things will become no-things, whose functions will do wonders. Here lies the secret key of being being Nothing and Nothing being being.[26]

What Wang Chi here calls the "secret key" (hsüan-chi [v]) has the so-called a priori and spontaneous function,[w][27] and manifests the spiritual resonance or wonder-working power of Nature (tzu-jan chih shen-ying [x]).[28] It is intuitive action free of any selfish attachment or preconception and appropriate to every circumstance. Wang Yang-ming had done distinguished service to his state when he succeeded with his swift and decisive actions in suppressing the Ch'en Hao revolt. But he had never been boastful of his achievements or made any claims for himself. How could he attain this state of mind? Wang Chi thought that it was solely due to the work of Wang Yang-ming's existential innate knowledge which possessed the above-mentioned true secret key or spring. In other words, what made Wang Yang-ming what he was, was the existential innate knowledge that was Nothing then and there.[29] In short, Wang Chi rejected totally the accumulation of conscious effort and declared that it was the true object of Wang Yang-ming to realize at once the substance of the mind through effort which is a direct extension of the original mind.

A poem of Lu Hsiang-shan goes:

When small streams accumulate,
    A great ocean they become,
When small stones accumulate,
    A great mountain they become.[30]

This poem criticized sharply Chu Hsi's principle of investigation. Lu considered that Chu's doctrine became preoccupied with fragmentary and isolated details in his attempt to accumulate aimlessly wide knowledge. Lu, on the other hand, attempted to teach that the Way of governing and teaching the people of the world is after all the extension and amplification of such morality as is seen in a child's love for his parents and his propriety toward his elder brothers. According to Wang Chi, Wang Yang-ming regarded the above criticism as no more than Lu's personal opinion. Wang Chi claimed that Wang Yang-ming said: "One should know that a small stream is a great ocean and a small stone is a great mountain. This is the greatest of all the secret functions, by which one can fly without wings, walk without legs, and accomplish without accumulated effort." [31]

This statement means that the original substance of the mind is right then and there, it is self-sufficient then and there, and it is existential then and there. Therefore it stresses direct enlightenment as the sole means in learning, in complete rejection of gradual cultivation.

This might be Wang Yang-ming's final conclusion, but we know that he did not regard this as the basic purpose of his doctrine. Wang Chi, however, adopted this as the basic principle of his own doctrine and advocated it very earnestly. He described this direct enlightenment as something which cannot be consciously grasped or controlled. It is like "letting go of the overhanging cliff" [32] or trying to "catch a cloud or control a thunderbolt." [33] He referred to it as "consciousness without consciousness" (wu-chiao chih chiao[y])[34] and "uncaused enlightenment" (wu-yüan-ch'i chih wu[z]),[35] and as something which one must find out directly all by oneself. He also explained direct enlightenment as the mysterious function of the secret key or spring by which one attains the state of a sage, and as the great Way for which there is no fixed statute.[36] Wang Chi said that this is establishing one's foundation in the midst of "chaos," [37] and compared it to drawing a square and a circle using neither ruler nor compass. He concluded that in comparison to this, Wang Yang-ming's doctrine is no more than drawing a square and a circle with the help of ruler and compass.[38] Thus we may say that Wang Chi stressed even more strongly than his master the importance of direct enlightenment.

The above-mentioned stress on direct enlightenment is meant to emphasize a thoroughgoing realization of Nothing as the original substance of the mind, and the simultaneous realization of substance and effort. Lao Tzu, Chuang Tzu, and Lu Hsiang-shan's disciple Yang Chien [aa] all stressed Nothing as much as Wang Chi. We must, however, note that, while Yang Chien's, as well as Lao Tzu's and Chuang Tzu's, Nothing has an outward similarity to Wang Chi's, they are different in nature. Yang Chien considered that the original substance is Nothing, and strove to dissolve all being into Nothing. Wang Chi, on the other hand, though he also considered that the original substance is Nothing, at the same time affirmed all being, asserting that being in itself is Nothing. It was thus the intent of Wang Chi's doctrine to transcend being through a divine transformation. We must therefore say that, while both Yang Chien and Wang Chi regard direct enlightenment as their principle, their doctrines differ from each other.

Lo Ju-fang explained this difference clearly:

Throughout man's history, the Way has been attained through direct enlightenment. However, there are two approaches to the Way. One is to go from being to Nothing, and the other is to go from Nothing to being. The former gradually goes towards the mysterious and empty state, and the more profound its mysterious quality, the more inexhaustible are the results. The latter gradually enters into a fusion; and the longer effort is sustained, the greater the working of the nature. In this way man is able to administer the great world, establish the great foundation of virtue in the world, and know the transforming and sustaining forces of the world.[39]

Direct enlightenment by going from being to Nothing is equivalent to Yang Chien's enlightenment which stresses quietness and purity. Direct enlightenment which goes from Nothing to being is equivalent to Wang Chi's enlightenment which stresses unobstructedness and fusion. Why did Wang Chi maintain the direct enlightenment which goes from Nothing to being, rather than the direct enlightenment which goes from being to Nothing? It is because he thought that if the original substance of the mind is only defined negatively and not asserted existentially it cannot be absolute.

Since Wang Chi's enlightenment is the one attained by going from Nothing to being, it does not fall into emptiness and quiescence, but is a dynamic power which actively displays with utmost freedom the wonderful workings of Nature in dealing with the world. According to him, since the original substance is vacuous, it holds all things, and if this truth is realized, it will penetrate all things without being obstructed by material desires.[40] Therefore, Wang Chi declared that Wang Yang-ming's extension of innate knowledge means the extension of vacuity. He believed it wrong to regard the extension of innate knowledge as dealing with all changes in accordance with a definite rule.[41] At any rate, it is not without reason that Wang Chi thought that vacuity has the power to transform what is moribund or decadent into something miraculously alive.[42] Similarly there is a reason why he asserted, "Nothing creates being, this phrase is indeed exhaustive!" [43] We find the working of the dynamic life in this vacuity.[44] It therefore differs from Yang Chien's vacuity in calmness which dissolves all things. Consequently, Wang Chi criticized Yang Chien's doctrine of vacuity for being so vague that it is difficult to see any principle in it.[45]

Among Lu Hsiang-shan's disciples, there was Fu Meng-ch'uan,[ab] who is said to have most clearly grasped his master's secret of the dynamic life. People said that Fu Meng-ch'uan was capable of capturing the dragon and the phoenix, and possessed the ability to attain enlightenment in the twinkling of an eye.[46] Then, why is it that Fu Meng-ch'uan's doctrine was not transmitted down to later generations, while the doctrine of Yang Chien, who departed from his master's doctrine in advocating quiescence and vacuity, was transmitted? The answer will be found in the background of the times. The Sung spiritual climate was quietistic and contemplative. We may say that what Wang Chi was to the Wang Yang-ming school, Yang Chien was to the Lu school. The difference was that, while Yang Chien departed from his master's doctrine, Wang Chi developed his master's doctrine. We should not, therefore, treat them as identical.

Wang Chi's doctrine of vacuity was to let being display its own original colors, in other words, to let being truly be what it is, just as the vacuity of the sunlight lets the colors of things show through as they are.[47] Therefore, if vacuity is truly realized, being will not be obscured and Nothing will not fall into voidness or nonexistence, and through their mutual interaction they will display wonderful functions without end. Thus the governing of the world and the virtuous acts of man will be achieved without being obstructed by attachment, selfish desires, preconceptions, or artificiality. It was in these terms that Wang Chi refuted criticism of his doctrine of vacuity by some scholars who tended to identify his vacuity with the doctrine of the Ch'an Meditation school.

It is only natural that Wang Chi, who thought that effort creates being out of Nothing, advocated rectification of the mind, i.e., emphasis on a priori learning, while he rejected the attempt to make the will sincere, i.e., effort at a posteriori learning. For the former is conceived as the way to follow Nature, that is to say, to enter from Nothing to being, and the latter is conceived as the way to return to Nature, that is to say, to go from being toward Nothing. Wang Chi further explained that when man establishes a foundation upon the a priori original substance of the mind, even if the will moves, it will not become evil. The extension of knowledge naturally becomes easy and simple, and it is not necessary to make a great effort. But if man establishes a foundation on a posteriori ideas or will, he will fall into worldly and material desires; if man gets stuck there, the extension of knowledge will also become difficult, and as a result the task of returning to the a priori original substance of the mind will require great effort.[48]

Wang Chi's Nothingness of the original substance of the mind possesses an "incipient, activating force" or sign (*sheng-chi* [ac]) which creates and transforms all things. This is the subtle spring of action which exists between being and Nothing, and between tranquillity and feeling, and whose existence covers, penetrates, and transcends all. Wang Chi considered it as the moment at which the original substance of the mind manifests itself. It is only natural that Wang Chi, who attached special importance to the unity of the active and living original substance of the mind, should place special emphasis on this living, incipient, and activating force. Other existentialist thinkers too greatly stressed the importance of this living force, and such scholars as Nieh Pao [ad] and Wang Shih-huai [ae] of the quietist school also discussed it. Ch'en Hsien-chang, who held the doctrine of quiescence and vacuity, also touched on this point. It is a distinctive feature of Ming thought that it gave much attention to this living, incipient, and activating force in the mind. Wang Chi's view was, however, that the quietists actually made too much of a conscious effort to arrive at the incipient, activating force and consequently failed to grasp the truth. Thus he considered sitting in meditation wrong.[49]

In this connection Wang Chi rejected the doctrines of both the quietist and cultivation schools of his time. He believed that one should realize the substance of the mind directly through a priori learning and vacuity. It is true that the quietist school also preached the doctrine of a priori learning and vacuity, but the contents of their respective views are quite different. The quietist school divided the unity of the mind into the original substance and function, the prior and posterior, and the internal and external. It considered that one should make effort solely on the basis of the original substance of the mind, and not upon function at all. The quietists regarded function merely as the result of effort. One of them, Lo Hung-hsien, said, "As soon as the original substance of the mind is established, function naturally attains its perfection." This quietist criticized Wang Chi's doctrine of a priori learning and vacuity as falling into artificiality and a posteriori learning, for it had "neither head nor tail." [50] Wang Chi, however, retorted:

This doctrine of the quietist school is attached to mere circumstances and chases illusory phenomena. It not only commits the mistake of distorting the truth of the original substance of the mind by an artificial realization of it, but also seeks quiescence and avoids activity, being indifferent to the responsibility of governing. After all, it will not be able to save itself from falling into Taoism and Buddhism.[51]

Wang Chi, therefore, rejected both intellectual understanding through reasoning and cultivation of realization through sitting in meditation. He asserted that one should train and polish oneself in the actual affairs of life and he emphasized the importance of this activity as essential to complete enlightenment. He explained that as long as one follows intellectual understanding, i.e., the acquisition of objective knowledge, even if one has gained something by it, whatever he has gained will not become his in the sense of becoming thoroughly internalized, and as long as one follows cultivation for enlightenment, even if he has gotten something by it, whatever he has gotten is not completely free from elements of attachment. But if one achieves complete enlightenment, Wang Chi claimed, one will meet the source of being everywhere with both constant action and constant immovability and neither purity nor impurity can attach to this origin.[52] What Wang Chi refers to as training and polishing in the actual affairs of life is an effort in relation to the original substance. Otherwise, even if one exerts the best effort to eliminate one's desires, he will not be able to attain his objective. To Wang Chi, this thorough realization aimed at transforming decadence or atrophy into miraculous vitality; in other words, it was the easy and simple effort on the basis of the original source to transform being directly into Nothing. This is exactly the means whereby being arises from Nothing.

According to Wang Chi, the Nothingness of the original substance is then and there existential; effort is substance, being is Nothing. They are in complete unity and there is no space for a hair between them.

Wang Chi said,

If we seek it apart from being, we will sink into emptiness. On the other hand, if we attempt to cultivate it through being, we will fall into relativism. It is somewhere between being and Nothing and therefore difficult to pinpoint. It is like the trace of a bird flying in the air or the moon in the water. It appears to exist and at the same time it appears not to exist. It appears sinking and at the same time, it appears floating. If we decide after deliberation, we will be wrong, and if we chase after it, we will go against it. It manifests itself miraculously through its spiritual functioning. The original substance is empty. There are no definite steps or tracks to follow. If there were, we would wait for, and go back and forth with, traces of being arising in the mind, and we would fall into intellectual understanding. Consequently a variety of thoughts would arise pell-mell, and we would not be able to arrive at the absolute Way.

Here lies the reason why Wang Chi strongly rejected the subjectivity of the consciousness perceived through the intellect and the senses, and criticized the cultivation doctrine. He said: "All the selfish desires arise from thoughts (i). All causes grow out of the consciousness perceived through the faculties. When the thoughts grow strong, the mind becomes weak. When consciousness comes to light, knowledge becomes hidden."

If one does not believe in existential innate knowledge, and insists that innate knowledge should be cultivated in relation to events, things, and functions, it is impossible for one to avoid compounding thoughts with innate knowledge. When thoughts are compounded into innate knowledge, this cultivation doctrine, just like the quietist doctrine, will chase illusions and commit the mistake of distorting the truth of original substance.[53]

In accordance with Wang Chi's doctrine of original substance, i.e., direct enlightenment, original substance must be identical with effort, realization with cultivation, and nature with effort. In other words, original substance is entirely in accordance with effort, effort with substance, realization with cultivation, cultivation with realization, nature with effort, and effort with nature. Wang Chi concluded that, should there be even a bit of discrepancy between these, the way of unity and oneness would be lost. This is the standpoint from which he was critical of the quietist and cultivation schools, insofar as they tended to create a dichotomy between these concepts.

How then can one attain such direct enlightenment? Once Wang Chi wrote in a letter to Wang Ching-so: [af]

You must not depart from the present, but in one stroke should cast off all the distinctions of illusion and phases of things and stimulate all the substance, thus getting rid of all thoughts and selfish desires. Then you can arrive at the place where you will not go astray, and whatever you grasp will be the Way. Thus, you will be able to gain genuine results.[54]

"Stimulating all the substance" (ch'üan-t'i t'i-ch'i)[ag] means wakening the original substance of the mind by directly penetrating to it. Wang Chi also wrote: "Exert yourself for the present thought, that is, the intelligence which you alone as an individual possess, and with the help of the direct penetration of this intelligence, let everything go."[55]

"Letting everything go" (i-ch'ieh fang-hsia)[ah] means getting rid of all selfish desires and intellectual understanding. It is identical with "stimulating all the substance."[56] These expressions, "letting everything go," "direct penetration" (chih-ta liu-hsing),[ai] and "the present thought" (hsien-tsai chih i-nien),[aj] characterize the doctrine of existentialism, which totally rejects understanding through reasoning, decision based on deliberation, and longing for or straining after things.

On this basis Wang Chi also criticized forms of existentialism advocated by other scholars of the time. He said that those scholars failed to understand the truth of his direct enlightenment. He censured them for regarding their natural inclinations as the original substance and for ignoring the importance of effort to get rid of selfish desires.[57] No doubt the effort which Wang Chi emphasized was effort on the basis of the original substance of Nothing. According to Wang Chi, Nothing is both the original substance and effort. Nature (*tzu-jan*) too is both original substance and effort. Therefore, he took a different view from the quietist school of the phrase in the *Book of Changes*, "What is there to think about; what is there to deliberate about?" Wang Chi regarded this phrase as referring to effort itself as an activity or process and the object or result of such effort.[58] We must say, therefore, that when Wang Chi attempted to attain both the original substance and effort at one stroke by realizing the truth of the original substance, he was going through the experience of, so to speak, effort without effort or effort beyond effort. We know this because Wang Chi in his teaching of enlightenment advocated thoroughgoing enlightenment (*ch'e-wu* [ak]), which rejected intellectual understanding and consciousness perceived through the sense faculties. And yet, his way of apprehending straight from the original substance was not entirely free from the tendency to deny effort. And this was a tendency which grew among Wang Chi's followers, whose talent was much inferior to their master's. We can now see that Wang Yang-ming showed much foresight when he warned Wang Chi of this danger.

Wang Ken, whose existentialist philosophy had as important an influence upon later generations as Wang Chi's, was called by Ku Hsien-ch'eng [al] of the Tung-lin school a Tzu-hu [am] (Yang Chien) of Wang Yang-ming.[59] It is said that while Wang Chi's existentialism was attained mostly through direct intuition, Wang Ken's was gained mostly through action.[60] For this reason Wang Ken's existentialism was easier, simpler, and more direct than Wang Chi's. Wang Ken said: "The Way is one; the Way is the Mean, and the Way is the One. If one understands this, one will know that it is existential and omnipotent." [61] He stressed the importance of direct realization of the nature by rejecting all deliberation as the basis for action. How easy, simple, direct, and Buddhistic in flavor his doctrine was is clearly shown in the following discussion:

One evening Wang Ken and his disciple, Hsü Yüeh,[an] came to a stream. Wang Ken jumped over, and then turned back to Hsü Yüeh and said, "Why do you hesitate so?" Then Hsü Yüeh also crossed the stream, in a state of total absent-mindedness, as if he had lost his consciousness." [62] At that time, Hsü Yüeh was suffering from trying too hard.

Indeed, Wang Ken's method was as spirited as a falcon flying in the winter sky.[63] So much so that it had the tendency to pursue fantasies and ignore the importance of effort. Wang Ken considered that if one realized the nature (hsing), nothing obstructed one's way and the universe was at one's command. Wang Ken thus showed great self-confidence. He considered it unnecessary in seeking the Way to read books, to exert oneself to seek principle, or to improve oneself through association with learned friends. He asserted that one had better obey one's own pleasure, because the mind is originally full of joy and restricted only by partiality and selfish desires. Wang Ken said that joy is characteristic of the original substance of the mind and that to learn is to enjoy.[64] As a result, he sought a transcendent, emancipated, and eternal state of mind, just as did Tseng Tien in ancient times and Shao Yung in the Sung dynasty. However, Wang Ken's existentialism placed a high value on practice. He made much of filial piety and brotherly love. According to him, these are the most genuine elements of the nature. They represent not only the nature of man but also the Decree of Heaven and the foundation for governing the state.[65]

In the existentialist school, there were other scholars who made sincere and concrete effort without falling into attachment, seeking shallow knowledge, or chasing illusions. Some of them originated the Neo-Chu Hsi branch of the Tung-lin school, upholding moral principle. There was also Liu Tsung-chou [ao] of the Neo-Wang Yang-ming school, who advocated the theory of "making the will sincere" during the latter period of the Ming dynasty, regarding the will as the substance prior to the arousing of the feelings. Still others started a new school by regarding everyday activity as the ultimate arena of innate knowledge. These groups were critical of the prevailing trend in the existentialist school of the late Ming, which followed two main lines:

1. The school accepting Ch'an Buddhism and stressing the uncontrolled broad mind. While Lu and Wang were influenced to some extent by Ch'an, they consciously rejected it. The scholars of this school, however, openly accepted Ch'an. They were primarily advocates of Confucianism, but most of them asserted that Confucianism, Taoism, and Buddhism are one, as did Li Chih.[66] At this time, the Surangama Sutra (*Leng-yen ching* [ap]) was widely read, and the Patriarchal school of Ch'an Buddhism (*Tsu-hsih Ch'an* [aq]) prospered. Existentialist thinkers of this first type widely accepted these developments, for they sought the Way on the basis of accepting man's natural character and feelings. Among them there were scholars who delighted in the transcendent, emancipated, and eternal mind. This tendency was similar to the Ch'ing-t'an movement of the fourth and fifth centuries A.D.

2. The school stressing strong character and chivalry. The thinkers of this school, including Yen Chun and Ho Hsin-yin, emphasized the importance of strong character and gave themselves to deeds of chivalry. They believed in man's natural feelings and advocated respect for individuality. Arguing for the freedom and equality of man, they strove for his emancipation from traditional mores which were, in their view, restrictive of human freedom. They regarded traditional morality, status ethics, and moral principles as restrictions of the individual. They also regarded moral effort as an obstacle to self-realization and in their attempt to get away from it they deliberately shocked people with extravagant talk and eccentric conduct. As a result, they created disorder in society, and their speech and conduct had something about it which reminds us of modern revolutionaries. But their excesses also worked to prepare their own destruction. Only those who can heed the famous dictum of Tu Fu, "When water flows, the mind does not follow" [ar] (i.e., the mind remains detached and is not carried along by the feelings),[67] can correctly lead and regulate the natural feelings. Some Late Ming thinkers who came to realize the truth of this dictum tried to rescue the followers of the existentialist school from their own excesses, but, alas, their efforts were unavailing against the decadent trend of the times.

NOTES

1. *Ch'uan-hsi lu* [as] (Meiji Rangai ed. of Satō Issai), 3/15; tr. by W. T. Chan, *Instructions for Practical Living* (New York, 1963), p. 218.
2. *Ibid.*, 3/3, 15.
3. *Ibid.*, 3/4.
4. *Ibid.*, 3/26.
5. *Lu Hsiang-shan ch'üan-chi* [at] (Han-fen-lou ed. of Wang Tsung-mu), 35/50 Yü-lu.
6. *Ibid.*, 35/32 Yü-lu.
7. *Chu tzu Yü-lei* [au] (Cheng-chung shu-chü ed. of Li Ching-te), 124/4836.
8. *Ibid.*, 124/4836–37.
9. Wang Mou-hung, *Chu tzu nien-p'u* [av] (Ch'ing ed.), 4/52.
10. *Ch'uan-hsi lu*, 3/15.
11. *Ibid.*, 2/25 Ta Lu Yüan-ching.
12. *Ibid.*, 2/25 Commentary of Satō Issai.
13. *Chin-hsi tzu chi* [aw] (Ming ed. of Keng Ting-hsiang, *et al.*), T'ing hsun A/51.
14. *Ch'uan-hsi lu* 3/35; Chan, tr., *Instructions*, p. 258.
15. *Idem;* Wang Chi, *Wang Lung-hsi ch'üan-chi* [ax] (Edo ed. of Ting Pin), Lung-hsi hsien-sheng chuan, 3; *Ibid.*, 20/4 Ch'ien-chun Hsü-shan hsien-sheng hsing chuang.
16. *Wang Wen-ch'eng kung ch'üan-shu* [ay] (SPPY ed. of Hsieh T'ing-chieh), 5/16 Yü Lu Yüan-ching, 2; *Ibid.*, 6/32 Yü Ch'en Wei-chün; 8/15 Shu Chu Shou-ch'ien chuan; 27/8 Yü Ku Wei-hsien.
17. MJHA [az] (KHCPTS ed.), VI, 32/86 Wang I-an yü-lu.
18. *Ch'uan-hsi lu* 3/26.
19. *Tsou Tung-kuo hsien-sheng wen-chi* [ba] (Ming ed. of Tung Sui), 2/17 Ching yüan tseng-chu.
20. *Wang Lung-hsi ch'üan-chi* 3/20–21 Ta Chung-huai Wu tzu wen.
21. *Ch'uan-hsi lu* 3/26–27. There is a slight difference between Wang Chi's version in the *T'ien-ch'üan cheng-tao chi* (*Wang Lung-hsi ch'üan-chi* 1/1) and the obituary of Ch'ien Te-hung (*Ibid.*, 20/3). Such scholars as Hsü Fu-yüan, Hsüeh K'an, Fang Hsüeh-chin, Ku Hsien-ch'eng, Ch'ien I-pen, Liu Tsung-chou, *et al.*, questioned the accuracy of Wang Chi's account.
22. *Ch'uan-hsi lu* 3/27.
23. MJHA, II, 11/96–97 Ch'ien Hsü-shan lün-hsüeh shu, Fu Yang Hu-shan.
24. *Ch'uan-hsi lu* 3/27; *Tsou Tung-kuo wen-chi* 2/17 Ch'ing-yüan tseng-ch'u. Wang Chi doubted the accuracy of this account.

25. *Wang Lung-hsi ch'üan-chi*, Lung-hsi hsien-sheng chuan, 3.
26. *Ibid.*, 1/2 T'ien-ch'üan cheng-tao chi.
27. *Ibid.*, Lung-hsi hsien-sheng chuan, 6.
28. *Ibid.*, 1/33 Fu-chou I-hsien-t'ai hui-yü, Tzu-jan chih shen-chi.
29. *Ibid.*, 13/6–7 Tu hsien-shih tsai-pao Hai Jih-weng chi-an ch'i-ping hsü.
30. *Lu Hsiang-shan ch'üan-chi*, 25/2.
31. *Wang Lung-hsi ch'üan-chi*, 25/2 Fu-chou i-hsien-t'ai hui-yü.
32. *Ibid.*, 4/3 Kuo Li-ch'eng ta-wen.
33. *Ibid.*, 4/13 Tung-lin hui-yü.
34. *Ibid.*, 4/16 Liu-tu hui-chi.
35. *Ibid.*, 11/10 Yü Wang Ching-so.
36. *Ibid.*, 10/17 Ta Wu Wu-chai.
37. *Ibid.*, 4/13 Tung-yu hui-chi.
38. *Ibid.*, 10/17 Ta Wu Wu-chai.
39. *Chin-hsi tzu chi*, she, 27–28.
40. *Wang Lung-hsi ch'üan-chi*, 2/22–23 Wan-ling hui-yü.
41. *Ibid.*, 2/23.
42. *Ibid.*, 4/20 Liu-tu hui-chi.
43. *Ibid.*, 5/21 T'ien-chu shan fang hui-yü.
44. *Ibid.*, 5/20.
45. *Ibid.*, 9/17 Ta Chi P'eng-shan lung-ching shu.
46. *Chang Nan-hsien wen-chi* [bb] (Edo reprint of ed. of Shen Yün), 24/11 Yü Chu Yüan-hui yu; *Lu Hsiang-shan ch'üan-chi*, 34/15 Yü-lu.
47. *Wang Lung-hsi ch'üan-chi*, 10/17 Ta Wu Wu-chai.
48. *Ibid.*, 16/1 Lu Wu-t'ai tseng-yen; 10/12 Ta Feng Wei-ch'uan; 1/13 San shan li tse lu.
49. *Ibid.*, 4/12 Tung-yu hui-chi.
50. *Lo Nien-an ch'üan-chi* [bc] (Ching ed. of Lo Fu-chin), 3/54 Ta Wang Lung-hsi; *Wang Lung-hsi ch'üan-chi*, 2/17 Sung-yüan wu-yü; 10/18 Ta Wu Wu-chai; 16/28 Liu pieh Ni-ch'uan man yü.
51. *Ibid.*, 2/20–21 Sung-yüan wu-yü; 14/25–26 Shou Nien-an Lo ch'ang Sung-yüan wu-yü.
52. *Ibid.*, 4/15 Liu-tu hui-chi; 17/19 Wu shuo.
53. *Ibid.*, 8/23–24 I-shih chieh.
54. *Ibid.*, 11/10 Yü Wang Ching-so.
55. *Ibid.*, 9/35 Yü Chao Shang-chin.
56. *Ibid.*, 3/4 Chiu-lung chi hai.
57. Wang Chi classified and criticized eight different theories of innate knowledge at that time. Cf. *Ibid.*, 1/35–36; 2/6, 9–11 Chu yang hui-chi.
58. *Ibid.*, 7/6 Nan-yu hui-chi.
59. *Hsiao-hsin chai ta-chi* [bd] (Ch'ing ed. of Chang Ch'un-hsiu), 3/4–5.

60. *Chin-hsi tzu chi,* su/51.

61. *Wang Wen-chen kung ch'üan-chi* [be] (Edo ed. of Kasuga Senan), 3/10.

62. *MJHA,* VI, 32/80 Hsü Po-shih chuan.

63. Kasuga Senan, *Wang Wen-chen kung ch'üan-chi,* hsü/1.

64. *Ibid.,* 4/9 Ta-ch'eng k'o ch'i Lo Nien-an; 4/5 Lo-hsüeh k'o.

65. *Ibid.,* 5/5–7 Yü Nan-tu chu yu; 2/1 Hsiao chen.

66. *Li-shih fen-shu* [bf] (Yen-t'ai wen-k'u ed.), 1/5–6 Ta Teng Shih-yang; *Li shih shuo-shu* [bg] (Ming ed. of Li Chih), 8/39; *Lin tzu ch'üan-shu* [bh] (Ming ed. of Li Chih) Hsing-ming ta-yü, 7.

67. *Ch'üan T'ang shih* [bi] (Chung-hua shu-chü ed.), 226/2440.

GLOSSARY

a 左翼

b 現成派

c 右翼

d 歸寂派

e 正統派

f 修證派

g 詹阜民(子南)

h 本體

i 工夫

j 佐藤一齋

k 羅汝芳

l 錢德洪

m 王艮

n 王棟

o 四句教言

p 鄒守益

q 四無說

r 無善說

s 四有說

t 有善說

u 青原贈處

v 玄機

w 先天無爲之用

x 自然之神應

y 無覺之覺

z 無緣起之悟

aa 楊簡

ab 傅夢泉

ac 生機

ad 聶豹

ae 王時槐

af 王敬所

ag 全體提起

ah 一切放下

ai 直達流行

aj 現在之一念

ak 徹悟

al 顧憲成

am 慈湖

an 徐樾

ao 劉宗周

ap 楞嚴經

aq 祖師禪

ar 水流心不競

as 傳習錄欄外書, 佐藤一齋,
　　明治35年, 東京松山堂
　　參考和版
　　標註傳習錄, 三輪希賢,
　　　正德2年,
　　傳習錄講義,
　　　東敬治, 明治39年, 東京松山堂
　　譯註傳習錄,
　　　山田準等, 昭和11年,
　　　東京岩波書店
　　新譯漢文大系傳習錄,
　　　近藤康信, 昭和36年,
　　　東京明治書院

at 陸象山全集, 王宗沐編,
　　嘉靖32年, 上海涵芬樓影印

au 朱子語類, 黎靖德編,
　　成化9年, 影印,
　　正中書局
　　參考和版
　　朱子語類大全, 黎靖德編,
　　　朱吾弼校訂, 萬曆31年
　　鵜飼石齋校刊, 寬文8年,
　　　寬政3年重修, 京都風月堂,
　　　大坂崇高堂

av 朱子年譜, 戀竑纂王訂, 乾隆16
年, 浙江書局
參考和版
朱子年譜, 葉公回重刊, 宣德6年,
和版(江戶)

aw 近溪子集, 耿定向評本, 萬曆刊
參考和版
羅近溪先生明道錄, 詹事講重編,
萬曆13年, 和版(江戶)

ax 王龍溪全集, 丁賓編, 萬曆43年,
和版(江戶)

ay 王文成公全書, 謝廷傑編, 隆慶
6年, 上海涵芬樓影印四部叢
刊

az 明儒學案, 黃宗羲, 國學基本叢
書, 中華民國22年, 上海商務
印書館

ba 鄒東廓先生文集, 董燧編, 隆慶6
年, 佑啓堂藏版

bb 張南軒文集, 沈暉重刊, 弘治11
年, 寬文9年覆刻, 芳野屋

bc 羅念菴全集, 羅復晉重刊, 雍正
10年, 石蓮藏版

bd 小心齋箚記, 張純修編, 康熙37
年, 顧端文公遺書

be 王文貞公全集, 春日潛菴刊, 永
嘉元年, 京都聖華房

bf 李氏焚書, 李贄, 燕臺文庫, 貝葉
山房

bg 李氏說書, 李贄, 明版

bh 林子全書

bi 全唐詩, 彭定求等編, 康熙42年,
1960年重刊, 中華書局

WM. THEODORE DE BARY *Individualism and Humanitarianism in Late Ming Thought*

明 Individualism—the lack of it or the excess of it—has often been considered a major problem in the modernization of China. In the early decades of this century reformers championed individualism in opposition to traditional authority in both thought and social life, and especially in opposition to the "Confucian" family system.[1] Others contended that what thwarted China's modernization was not the absence of individualism but rather a surplus of it. Sun Yat-sen's experience trying to organize the Chinese people, first in a revolutionary movement and then in a modern state, convinced him that the excessive individualism of the Chinese made them just a "heap of loose sand" unable to achieve the cohesion necessary for true nationalism.[2] Still others, ardent exponents of greater individual freedom in the early reform movements, later found such freedom almost meaningless in a chaotic society, and acquiesced in more intense authoritarianism than China had known before.[3]

THE PROBLEM OF "INDIVIDUALISM"

The common term for "individualism" in modern East Asia (in Chinese *ko-jen chu-i*)[a] represents a Western idea, and implies that no such "ism" existed in traditional thought. Thus it symbolizes the challenge of a new idea to traditional values and suggests the conscious advocacy of change. Nevertheless, in the earlier Chinese tradition the problem of the "individual"—his relation to the group, his role in society, his "rights" in the sense of what is due him as a human being, or in such and such a status—has been the subject of as much thought and discussion as in the West. In this sense the problem of "individualism" has existed in China's past as well as its present.

It was particularly in the Ming period, however, that the question of individualism became a lively, and indeed crucial, issue, which came closer than at any other time, past or present, to the kinds of questions asked more recently about the nature and role of the individual in the modern West. Indeed, some Chinese and Japanese scholars are convinced that the Ming experience in this regard was crucial in determining the direction China would take in the modern world.[4]

My procedure here, instead of starting from a definition of individualism based on Western concepts or experience, will be to explore the developing awareness of the individual in Ming China in order to see how, in what context, and under what aspect the individual emerged as a central concern of Ming thinkers. Rather than a preconceived definition, what we require here are only a few distinctions as to our use of the term "individualism." For one thing we should distinguish between individualism and "individuality." The existence of the latter does not always imply the presence of the former. Many flourishing cultures have recognized individuality in arts and letters, for instance, without affirming an equal right to individuality of expression in other fields of endeavor or among all classes of society. Aristocratic societies have often encouraged more individuality among the elite than democracies have tolerated among the masses. Nor is it difficult to recognize the extraordinary degree of individual creativity or mastery exhibited by artists, craftsmen, and performers in traditional cultures. Japan, with its strong aristocratic tradition and hierarchical society, fostered this kind of individuality in the arts without conceiving of individualism as a value to be more widely extended. In China the great cultural flowering of the Sung is a similar case in point.[5]

Further, in regard to the assertion of individualism itself, we may distinguish two main types in traditional China. There is, first of all, the individualism of the hermit or recluse, who has largely withdrawn from society. This we might call a personal or "private" individualism. Though it has a positive aspect in affirming the individual's freedom from society and his own transcendent value, from the standpoint of society this is a "negative" individualism since it has no effect on the status of other individuals.[6] It makes no positive claim within society. It establishes the right not so much to dissent from the group or reform society as to secede from them. Both Taoism and Ch'an (Zen) Buddhism tend in this direction and historically their type of individualism has had little positive effect in terms of basic political or social institutions.

By contrast, there is a more "positive" and public individualism which seeks to establish the place of the individual or self in relation to others, to secure his rights or status in some institutional framework or on the basis of widely declared and accepted principles.[7] Here we face the paradox that, in order to establish and secure its own claims, such an individualism must be "social." Confucianism attempts this in relation to the family and state. In the process, some modern critics have complained, Confucianism made a bad bargain for the individual. He was made to sacrifice more to the group than he got in return, and there is a real question whether this kind of "individualism" could ever be equated with the types of individualism known in the West. Indeed some might prefer to call this "personalism," which does not set the individual over against society. However this may be, it remains true that the Confucian almost alone concerned himself with defining and establishing some positive role for the individual in Chinese society, and it was by virtue of this active social and political endeavor that Confucianism became a vehicle for the growth of a new humanitarianism and individualism in the Ming.

At the same time, the question of the relation between this new trend and "negative" tendencies deriving from Buddhism and Taoism, remains a real one throughout this period. This is because none of these systems falls wholly within one or the other of our categories. The Confucian conception of the self is not without a metaphysical aspect, nor the Buddhist and Taoist wholly without some social orientation. All three have a common ground in so far as they deal with one or another aspect of the human condition.

Another distinction which may be useful is between the advocacy and the effectuality of individualism. Confucius is reported in the *Analects* to have said: "In education there should be no class distinctions" (XV, 38). In principle this would seem to carry the implication that the individual's right to an education overrides social and economic differences. Yet Confucius and his followers, while asserting this as a seemingly universal principle, appear to have accepted the fact that social and economic circumstances would prevent many from receiving any formal education, and that politically effective learning would remain the business of an elite. In the Ming this assumption was openly challenged. And yet the question remains: how effectively was it challenged, how much actual change was brought about through the advocacy of the new individualism?

The type of individuality recognized by Confucianism, especially in terms of moral character and intellectual attainments, had been manifested to a remarkable degree by certain individuals in traditional Chinese society. In the Sung (960–1297), as we have said, we observe a striking increase in the number of independent and creative minds and an unprecedented expression of individual interests and tastes in art and culture. Nevertheless, this development too appears to have been confined largely to the social elite: the scholar-officials, the bureaucratic gentry, and such members of the merchant class as might approach the latter status. It becomes an appropriate question then what signs there are of this type of individuality finding wider expression in the Ming through the advocacy of a humanitarianism extending to all classes of society. Our concern with this humanitarianism, however, will be limited to its role in the development of individualism itself.

THE CONFUCIAN CONTEXT

Confucianism from the outset had been deeply involved with the problem of the individual, and Confucius himself had set guidelines for the discussion. An incident in the *Analects* reveals his basic stand. Once the Master was traveling with his followers (in the context of the book, if not of actual chronology, he had just left the court of an unworthy ruler), and one of his disciples went off to ask directions from a farmer. The latter, however, gave him advice of a different sort. "The whole world is swept as if by a torrential flood, and who can change it? As for you, instead of following one who flees from this man [i.e., the ruler] and that, you would do better to follow one who flees from this whole generation of men." When the disciple reported this to Confucius, the latter replied sadly, "One cannot flock with birds or herd with the beasts. If I am not to be a man among men, then what am I to be? If the Way prevailed in the world, what need would there be to change things?" (XVIII, 6).

"To be a man among men" is Confucius' fundamental aim. There can be no fulfillment for him in isolation from his fellow man. To think of himself as an island apart, or as an individual abstracted from mankind as a whole, is impossible. Nor is it just a matter of man's being a social animal; what distinguishes him from the birds and the beasts is his moral sense, his inborn, Heaven-endowed sense of a mission to make the Way prevail in the world, which compels Confucius to find his own fulfillment in the fulfillment of others.

Another passage elaborates this theme when Confucius is asked what it takes to be truly humane: "The humane man, if he seeks to establish himself, will help to establish others, and if he seeks to succeed himself, will help others to succeed. To be able to judge others by what one knows of oneself is the method of achieving humanity" (VI, 28).

Reciprocity, then, becomes the basis of self-cultivation. Man defines his "self" in relation to others and to the Way which unites them. Thus is constructed the web of reciprocal obligations or moral relations in which man finds himself, defines himself. Apart from these he can have no real identity. And yet these relations alone, it is equally important to recognize, do not define a man totally. His interior self exists at the center of this web and there enjoys its own freedom. Confucius was not constantly burdened by his responsibilities to others or his mission to the world. He not only "delighted in truth" with a joyful spontaneity (*Analects* VI, 18); he was enraptured by the music of Shao so that he lost his taste for anything else (VII, 13), and forgot all his worries in the enjoyment of learning (VII, 18). He said "Personal cultivation begins with poetry, is made firm by the observance of ritual, and is perfected in music" (VIII, 8). And his disciple Yen Hui said of Confucius that "he has broadened me with learning and restrained me with ritual" (IX, 10). Here learning stands for culture generally, and ritual for moral discipline. They are equally essential to self-cultivation, complementary aspects in the process of spiritual enlargement and self-control.

These few examples may suffice to illustrate how for Confucius the individual exists in a delicate balance with his environment, reconciling his own self-respect with respect for others, his inner freedom with his outer responsibilities, morality with culture, and the transcendent Way with an imperfect world. It is this delicate balance which becomes most central and most crucial, both in the self-development of the Confucian individual and in the development of Confucianism as a whole.

WANG YANG-MING: SAGEHOOD AND THE INDIVIDUAL

In the most general sense the problem of the individual is implicit in the whole Ming preoccupation with the self,[8] and its full dimensions can therefore be seen only in relation to the entire range of Ming thought. Here, however, we must limit ourselves to that trend of thought arising in the Wang Yang-ming school which brings most sharply into focus the debate over the nature and role of the individual in the sixteenth century. Among these ideas is Wang's conception of sagehood, which opened the way to a kind of "popular" movement involving a greater potential participation of ordinary men in the fulfillment of Confucian ideals.

It was possible so to popularize the notion of sagehood only because Wang had internalized or subjectivized it.[9] "How can the signs of sagehood be recognized? . . . . If one clearly perceives one's own innate knowledge, then one recognizes that the signs of sagehood do not exist in the sage but in oneself." [10] One could not recognize the qualities of the sage in anyone else unless they corresponded to a standard of perfection within one's own heart and mind. And the way to self-perfection was not to set up some idealized image so far beyond one as to be unattainable, as many scholars had done, "seeking to know what they cannot know and do what they cannot do." [11] It was to stop relying on external standards, to become completely identified with the principle of Nature (or Heaven) within oneself and thus become self-sustaining.[12]

This subjective approach opened up almost unlimited possibilities for individual development and self-expression, and it was the mission of the later Wang Yang-ming school to explore these possibilities to the limit. No doubt in some sense Wang himself was conscious of these possibilities, but for the most part his understanding of innate knowledge was based on the assumption of a common moral nature in all mankind. Indeed, its common character was almost Wang's fundamental article of faith; individual differences were for him of secondary importance, and the value of the individual in his uniqueness is not something Wang dwells on.

An immediate consequence of this fact, so far as Wang's own outlook is concerned, is that the achievement of his own ideal involved no radical social reforms. He sought to free the individual from within, not to set him against anything without. There was no question of breaking away from social obligations or restrictions, nor any consciousness of the kinds of conflict between the individual and society often found in modern individualism. Moreover, the principles and affairs which he discussed in relation to innate knowledge were the traditional moral virtues and concerns expressed in Mencius' formulation of the Four Beginnings: the sense of sympathy or commiseration, of shame, of deference to others, of right and wrong (IIA, 6). Each of these presupposed some interrelationship or interplay between the self and others. Wang Yang-ming accepted without question the contextual character of Confucian ethics whereby these virtues were linked concretely to existential human relationships.[13] We find him illustrating the principle of innate knowledge again and again with reference to the virtue of filial piety, and we know that a crucial experience in his own development had been his discovery, when he tried to practice a kind of Taoist-Buddhist meditation, that to detach himself from his parents would be inhuman and would amount to destroying his own nature.[14]

As a result Wang Yang-ming seems to have assumed that the

traditional Confucian relationships would remain intact. Innate knowledge would only confirm them, revivify them with the spontaneity of freely given assent, and assure them of sefless commitment on the part of the individual. Perhaps nowhere is this traditional character of Wang's social ideal so apparent as in the vision of the Golden Age described in his famous essay "Pulling Up the Roots and Stopping Up the Source":

The mind of a sage regards Heaven, Earth, and all things as one body. He looks upon all people of the world, whether inside or outside his family, or whether far or near, but all with blood and breath, as his brothers and children. He wants to make them secure, preserve, educate and nourish all of them, so as to fulfill his desire of forming one body with all things. Now the mind of everybody is at first not different from that of the sage. Only because it is obstructed by selfishness and blocked by human desires, what was originally great becomes small and what was originally penetrating becomes obstructed. . . .[15]

Concerned over this, says Wang, the sage sought to teach people how to overcome their selfishness. On its practical side this teaching was expressed in the terms of Mencius:

Between father and son there should be affection, between ruler and minister there should be righteousness, between husband and wife there should be attention to their separate functions, between old and young there should be a proper order, and between friends there should be faithfulness—that is all. (IIIA, 4)

At the time of Yao, Shun, and the Three Dynasties, teachers taught and students studied only this. At that time *people did not have different opinions, nor did families have different practices.* . . .[16]

This was possible, Wang says, because "there was no pursuit after the knowledge of seeing and hearing [i.e., sense-knowledge or secondary knowledge] to confuse them, no memorization and recitation to hinder them, no writing of flowery compositions to indulge in, and no chasing after success and profit. . . ." [17] Thus everyone was content with his own station in life, whether as farmer, artisan, or merchant. "Those who served also desired only to be united with their superiors in one mind and one character to bring peace to the people. [They were] all diligent in their various occupations, so as mutually to sustain and support the life of one another without any desire for exalted position or strife for external things." [18]

From this we see clearly that Wang's social ideal is based on moral self-reformation, not on any radical change in the traditional social relationships. It strongly emphasizes a community of interests as opposed to individual differences. Like so many other Confucian reformers, however, he invokes the past in order to censure the present.[19] In the lines just quoted the source of all evil in the world is identified in terms of the characteristic problems of his own age, and Wang goes on at much greater length in this essay to vent his moral indignation over these evils: people's involvement in and dependence on external knowledge and received opinion (i.e., in a more complex culture, where so much of one's knowledge is vicarious or derivative rather than based on one's own innate knowledge and experience), the memorization and recitation of the classics and the writing of "flowery compositions" (i.e., mastery of the literary skills necessary for the official examination and the writing of the stereotyped examination essays which only demonstrate one's technical competence in the mastery of literary forms, without expressing any genuine conviction); finally, the quest for fame and profit (i.e., the competition for official positions and emoluments, which lead the individual to think and do what will gain the approval of others rather than what his own conscience approves.

If we looked no further than this, Wang might seem a hopeless traditionalist and idealist, completely out of joint with civilization and his own times and naïvely addicted to moralistic solutions of complex cultural problems. His social views would also seem greatly to vitiate the promise of individual self-development implicit in the doctrine of innate knowledge. But if Wang shows himself unaware of the deeper historical and social implications of his doctrine, he is not one to despair of mankind and withdraw into his own world. His basic commitment, like that of the Sage, is to regard all things as himself and all men as his own family. More particularly, however, Wang's active commitment is to teaching and scholarly discussion (i.e., the traditional relationships of master-pupil and friend-friend). This, in the end, is what enables him both to achieve fulfillment as a

Confucian and to give practical expression to his belief that all hope for social improvement lies within the individual.

EDUCATION IN THE WANG YANG-MING SCHOOL

If Wang has little to say about the reform of social organization, he has much to say about educational reform. His own greatest talent may well have been that of a teacher, rather than a philosopher, scholar, or official. Perhaps no other figure in Chinese history (unless it be Confucius, about whom we know much less) has had such direct, personal influence as a teacher in terms of the number of his students, the schools established by him and by them, and the wide effect of this teaching on the thinking of the time. It is in this sphere, then, that Wang's brand of individualism manifested itself most clearly and authentically.

"Study," Wang said, "must be for one's own sake." [20] That is, there must be no self-deception, no learning simply to please others. As a teacher himself he was careful always to respect this basic principle, demonstrating a primary concern for the self-development of the individual. His *Instructions for Practical Living (Ch'uan-hsi lu)* which are in large part dialogues with students, reveal an active interest in what others have learned for themselves and what results they have achieved by their own efforts.[21] Unless we understand this, for instance, the following encounter might strike us as having a surprising, if not comic, twist to it.

Ou-yang Ch'ung-i said, "Sir, your principle of the extension of knowledge expresses all that is excellent and deep. As we see it, one cannot go any further."

The Teacher said, "Why speak of it so lightly? Make a further effort for another half year and see how it is. Then make an effort for another year and see how it is. The longer one makes an effort, the more different it will become. This is something difficult to explain in words." [22]

What would seem to have been the most whole-hearted praise cannot by Wang be accepted as a genuine compliment. It implies that the student has received from his master the full and final answer, which only shows that he has understood nothing. "Why speak of it so lightly" means "Don't think it's that easy." For Wang everything depends on continuing thought, effort, and reflection. The truth, since it is not an object or a statement, cannot be summed up in a formula but must be experienced in an intensely personal way.

There are here, one might suspect, strong overtones of Ch'an training, which it would be idle to deny since so much conscious reference is made to Ch'an in the *Instructions*. But if there are indeed similarities to Ch'an in the irreducibly personal method, the insistence on a life-and-death earnestness in the seeker, and the ineffability of ultimate truth, there is also a significant difference. Learning for Wang is never directed toward a special experience of "enlightenment." Such things may occur but are incidental. Learning for him is a simple day-to-day and life-long process. "Here is our innate knowledge today. We should extend it to the utmost according to what we know today. As our innate knowledge is further developed tomorrow, we should extend it to the utmost according to what we know then." [23]

Moreover, Wang refuses to set himself up as an authority or as one who sets his seal on another. Truth emerges in action, discussion, and constant self-criticism. Indeed, the insistence on authority in both patriarchal Ch'an and traditional Confucianism is called into question in a most fundamental way. The title of the *Ch'uan-hsi lu* suggests the passing on of a method of practice, not a received revelation or an inherited body of doctrine. If we render it as "Instruction," we must remember that it carries none of the traditional connotations of indoctrination. Otherwise we could not appreciate the extent to which general discussion as a means of arriving at truth became the most important feature of education in the Wang Yang-ming school.

The most radical challenge to authority was, of course, posed by the doctrine of innate knowledge itself. If Ch'en Hsien-chang had already declared his independence of intellectual authority, it was Wang who made it fully explicit:

If words are examined in the mind and found to be wrong, although they have come from the mouth of Confucius, I dare not accept them as correct. How much less those from people inferior to Confucius! If words are examined in the mind and found to be correct, although they have come from the mouth of ordinary people, I dare not regard them as wrong. How much less those of Confucius! [24]

At this point, however, we must remind ourselves that Wang's confidence in trusting one's own mind as the ultimate authority rests squarely on his faith that all men's minds reflect and express a common standard of truth. Thus he says:

The Way is public and belongs to the whole world, and the doctrine is also public and belongs to the whole world. They are not the private properties of Master Chu [Hsi] or even Confucius. They are open to all and the only proper way to discuss them is to do so openly.[25]

There is perhaps no more striking example than this of Wang's basically Confucian—and we might even say Chinese—outlook: for all his emphasis on personal intuition of truth, he retains a faith in the fundamental rationality of man, and for all his insistence on discovering right and wrong for oneself, it does not even occur to him that there could be any essential conflict between subjective and objective morality, or that genuine introspection could lead to anything other than the affirmation of clear and common moral standards.

Ch'an, though a distinctively Chinese form of Buddhism, nevertheless was true to its Indian and Taoist origins in seeking truth beyond the moral sphere and in withdrawing from the arena of rational debate in order to achieve it. Wang, on the other hand, not only challenges authority in public (as indeed the *koan* or "public case" did) but goes on to reestablish it in public.

Here is the underlying reason why Wang Yang-ming's Confucianism could have had such a quickening effect on the thought of those times and such an explosive impact on all levels of Ming society and culture—its tremendous moral dynamism, its enormous confidence in man, and its faith that life could be dealt with by opening people up to one another from within. This is also why Ch'an Buddhism, though it maintained a silent presence throughout the age, depended upon the vitality of Wang's teaching for a momentary reinvigoration of its own intellectual life during a long period of decline.[26]

Without Wang's passionate faith in humanity, and in the Heavenly reason implanted within man, his teaching might have been as lifeless and moribund, culturally speaking, as Ch'an at that time. With this faith in the underlying unity of man, however, Wang

Yang-ming was also able to accept the diversity manifested in the development of his individual students. Wang's strength as a teacher, and his weakness as a philosopher (from the analytic point of view), lies in his seemingly deliberate cultivation of ambiguities which could be explored by his own students and clarified by their own experience.[27] Had he not allowed these ambiguities to stand, there might have been far less discussion and debate within his school, less room for individual and regional differentiation, and perhaps no such ranges of opinion as justified making distinctions between right, center, and left.[28] Nor could we have found so many remarkable personalities, so many striking individualists, among his followers.

WANG KEN: THE COMMON MAN AS SAGE

Probably none of the influential followers of Wang Yang-ming exemplifies as well as does Wang Ken (1483?–1540),[29] both in his person and in his thought, the potential for individualism within this school—that is, for an individualism most nearly resembling that of the modern West. Claims might be made for others as being more faithful to other basic teachings of Wang Yang-ming or to the main line of Confucian tradition, but it is Wang Ken who carries forward most vigorously the idea of the common man as sage.

What distinguishes Wang Ken from the start is that he began life as the son of a salt maker and never sought or attained the status of a Confucian scholar-official. A man of tremendous energy and vitality, he seemed to draw strength and self-confidence as if through a taproot striking deep into the soil of China. Wang Yang-ming apparently appreciated this rugged quality of Wang Ken, when later he suggested that the latter change his name from Yin [b] (silver), to Ken for "stubborn strength" (symbolized by a mountain, but phonetically related to *ken* for "root").[30]

A native of T'ai-chou, in modern Kiangsu Province, Wang Ken had only five years of instruction at the village school before economic necessity forced him, at the age of eleven, to leave it and assist his father in the family business. Later, on repeated business trips to Shantung Province, he carried copies of the *Analects* of

Confucius, the *Classic of Filial Piety*, and the *Great Learning* in his sleeve, and discussed them with anyone he could find who might aid his understanding. His determination to become a sage was aroused, it is said, when he visited the shrine of Confucius at Ch'ü-fu and realized that the immortal Sage himself had been, after all, just a man.[31]

By the age of twenty-one he had become established as an independent salt dealer, and prospered enough so that he could devote more time to self-study. He developed the practice of shutting himself up in a room for quiet-sitting, meditating in silence day and night for long periods of time in a manner reminiscent of Ch'en Hsien-chang, by then not an uncommon method of seeking "enlightenment." In an age marked by a heightening of the mystical spirit and a widespread belief in dreams and visions, it is not extraordinary that Wang Ken's spiritual awakening should have followed a dream in which he saw the heavens falling and people fleeing in panic. Answering their cries for help, he stood forth, pushed up the heavens, and restored order among the heavenly bodies. People were overjoyed and thanked him profusely. When Ken awoke, bathed in perspiration, he suddenly had his enlightenment, described in terms of an experience of being united with all things through his humanity (*jen*) and of finding the universe within himself.[32] Here again the resemblance to both Ch'en Hsien-chang and Wang Yang-ming is obvious. Though he has not yet come directly under the influence of any teacher, he seems to breathe the same spiritual atmosphere as they, and spontaneously to manifest similar ideas and experiences.

What is of special interest in Wang Ken is the sense of mission which arose from this experience. He felt a vocation to become a teacher to mankind. But since he had had little formal education, his approach to learning was highly individual, and emphasized personal spirituality and activity as opposed to scholarly study. The classics he used simply to document his own experience. As he put it, "one should use the classics to prove one's own enlightenment, and use one's own enlightenment to interpret the classics." [33] In his daily life he combined teaching with solitary study and meditation, the active with the contemplative life. And, as if to confirm the contemporary theory that activity arises from quiescence, from the depths of Wang Ken's subjectivity arose dynamic ideas, dramatically expressed in his own actions.

As an example, at the age of thirty-seven, not long before he met Wang Yang-ming, Wang Ken's reading of *Mencius* and his reflections on the true meaning of sagehood in one's daily life produced a startling thought. "Mencius says, 'Can one speak the words of [the sage-king] Yao, and perform the actions of Yao and yet not wear the clothing of Yao?'" Whereupon, following some prescriptions found in the *Book of Rites*, he made himself a long cotton gown, a special hat and girdle to wear, and a ceremonial tablet to carry around with him.[34] Above his door he inscribed the declaration: "My teaching comes down through [the sages] Fu-hsi, Shen-nung, the Yellow Emperor, Yao, Shun, the Great Yü, Kings T'ang, Wen, and Wu, the Duke of Chou, and Confucius. To anyone who earnestly seeks it, whether he be young or old, high or low, wise or ignorant, I shall pass it on." [35] Many people laughed at this, but some were moved by Wang Ken's sense of active concern to make the ancient Way live in the present, and, ignoring the ridicule of others, took up the cause.

Involved here is something more than just a quaint and quixotic gesture on the part of an eccentric old scholar. Wang Ken is not in his dotage, not even much of a scholar, and not really an antiquarian. Like Wang Yang-ming he is struggling to discover, to work out for himself, the meaning of sagehood for his own time, to bring the conception of the sage down from the lofty heights and out of the remote past directly into the foreground of his own life. Wang Ken lacks the self-consciousness of Wang Yang-ming, and is not so tortured by doubt, but he undergoes something of the same tension that made Yang-ming cry out:

Whenever I think of people's degeneration and difficulties I pity them and have a pain in my heart. I overlook my own unworthiness and wish to save them by this teaching. And I do not know the limits of my ability. When people see me trying to do this, they join one another in ridiculing, insulting, and cursing me, regarding me as insane. . . . Of course there are cases when people see their fathers, sons, or brothers falling into a deep abyss and getting drowned. They cry, crawl, go naked and barefooted, stumble and fall. They hang onto dangerous cliffs and go down to save them. Some gentlemen who see them behave like this . . . consider them insane because they cry, stumble, and fall as they do. Now to stand aside and make no attempt to save the drowning, while mocking those who do, is possible only for strangers who have no natural feelings of kinship, but even then they will be considered to have no sense of pity and to be no longer human beings. In the case of a father, son, or brother, because of love he will surely feel an ache in his head and a pain in his heart, run desperately until he has lost his breath, and crawl to save them. He will even risk drowning himself. How much less will he worry about whether people believe him or not! Alas! The minds of all people are the same as mine. There *are* people who are insane. How can I not be so? There *are* people who have lost their minds. How can I not lose mine?" [36]

Wang Ken, though not the kind to experience such agonies, undoubtedly expects to be similarly misunderstood, if not thought quite mad. Yet there is a difference. Yang-ming found it trouble enough to be natural and humane; Wang Ken's eccentricities are of another sort. They reflect not only a difference in temperament from Wang Yang-ming—a deliberate self-dramatization—but a conflict which the latter never had to face. Wang Ken, after all, is a commoner, the uneducated son of a salt merchant; Yang-ming, a distinguished scholar-official and the son of a distinguished scholar-official. For Yang-ming to discover sagehood in his contemporaries meant ignoring the accidents of birth and status, stripping away the cultural and social adornments of the Confucian, and finding the essential moral man. For Wang Ken, however, the question is not whether "he will take off his clothing" to save mankind, but what clothing to put on: not whether he should "take the Way of Confucius upon himself," [37] (already answered in his fateful dream) but the next question to follow: how shall the commoner fulfill that mission in a world where Confucian virtue is everywhere identified with membership in the ruling class? He refuses to accept the superiority of the scholar-official, to ape the manners and dress of the so-called gentry, or even to acknowledge a debt to centuries of learned Confucians. Instead, he boldly clothes himself in the garments of the primordial sage, and though it may appear to the conventionally-minded a sign of eccentricity, for Wang Ken it is enough that at least it not be taken as a sign of affectation. Symbolically the simple cotton gown of Yao signifies the common man's direct access to sagehood, Ken's unwillingness to yield this responsibility to any official elite, and his life-long adherence to the status of commoner.

WHEN SAGES MEET

Wang Ken was already thirty-eight, and well-established in his own thinking, before he met Wang Yang-ming. He had been living intensely in his own small world while scholars and officials from all over that region flocked to hear the brilliant governor of Kiangsi lecture on innate knowledge. Then a friend, more in touch with scholarly thought than he, remarked to Wang Ken how similar his ideas were to the famous Wang Yang-ming's. "Is that so?" he said, and then went on with characteristic forthrightness: "But you say Mr. Wang teaches 'innate knowledge' while I teach 'the investigation of things.' If they are indeed similar, then Mr. Wang is Heaven's gift to the world and later generations. But if they differ, then Heaven is giving me to Mr. Wang!" [38]

If their ideas correspond, in other words, they share the same high mission; but to the extent that they differ each may have something to learn from the other.[39] With this remarkable combination of conviction, self-confidence and, at the same time, humility in pursuit of the Way, Wang Ken, dressed in his outlandish gown, set off to meet the governor. But having entered the latter's courtyard, he stopped at the middle gate and stood erect, holding aloft his tablet and refusing to come in as a mere client, until Wang himself came out and escorted him in. When that was done he strode in and took the seat of honor. Only after some debate did Wang Ken acknowledge Wang Yang-ming's superiority and move down to a lower seat, signifying his readiness to become the latter's pupil. "He is so simple and direct. I cannot equal him." [40] But even then, reflecting upon the day's debate that night, Wang Ken found himself not wholly convinced. He went back the next morning and said "I gave in too easily," resuming the seat of honor. Far from being offended, Yang-ming was delighted to find a man who would not yield assent too readily. But after further debate, Ken surrendered completely and made his submission as a disciple. Later Yang-ming told his disciples, "When I captured [the rebel Chu] Ch'en-hao, I was not a bit moved, but today I was moved by this man." [41]

Wang Ken was never wholly tamed, however, nor would Yang-ming have had it so—except perhaps once. Ken's active disposition made him restless to carry the true way to all men. He returned home, built himself a cart like the one Confucius allegedly used when he traveled to the courts of feudal princes, and went off to Peking. There his dress, his cart, and his somewhat pig-like appearance attracted much attention and great crowds came to hear him. Many people became convinced of his deep sincerity and were drawn to his ideas. In ruling circles, however, he was looked on either as a joke or else as a potential troublemaker. Some of Wang Yang-ming's disciples at court found it embarrassing. They urged him to leave, which he eventually did, but only after the Master himself ordered Ken out.[42]

On his return Yang-ming showed his displeasure by refusing to see him for three days. Contrite, Ken waited by his gate and, when Wang Yang-ming came to see a guest off, tried to make apologies. The Teacher would not listen, but as he turned to go back inside, Ken followed and cried out bitterly, "Confucius would not have carried things to such an extreme!" (quoting *Mencius* VB, 10), a telling reproach from someone charged with extremism. Yang-ming relented, helped him to his feet and took him in.[43]

Accounts differ as to how much of a change this worked in Ken,[44] but it is less of a problem when one recognizes that stubbornness and humility were complementary aspects of his personality. He seems to have settled down to a less spectacular role while Yang-ming remained alive, but thereafter resumed an active life as a teacher in his own school and had wide influence.

WANG KEN'S CELEBRATION OF SELF

Before visiting Wang Yang-ming, Wang Ken had described his own teaching as "the investigation of things," but recognized that his interpretation of it was similar to Yang-ming's "innate knowledge." The similarity lies in the fact that "investigation of things" means for both essentially the "rectification of affairs." In other words, the starting point of all self-cultivation as formulated in the *Great Learning* should be the application to all things, matters, actions, and events of one's own moral sense, so that they are made to conform to one's own sense of right and wrong, shame and deference, etc., and are thus "rectified." [45]

If there is a significant difference between the two, it is that Wang's "innate knowledge" stresses man's moral awareness whereas Ken's places more stress on the self as the active center of things. Simply stated, Ken's view was that the self and society were one continuum, with the self as the root or base and society as the branch or superstructure.

If in one's conduct of life there is any shortcoming, one should look for the fault wtihin himself. To reflect on oneself is the fundamental method for the rectification of things. Therefore, the desire to regulate the family, order the state and pacify the world [as in the *Great Learning*], rests upon making the self secure (*an-shen*).[d] The *Book of Changes* says: "If the self is secure, then the empire and state can be preserved." [46] But if the self is not secure, the root is not established.[47]

To make the self secure, one must love and respect the self, and one who does this cannot but love and respect others. If I can love and respect others, others will love and respect me. If a family can practice love and self-respect, then the family will be regulated. If a state can practice love and self-respect, then the state will be regulated, and if all under Heaven can practice love and self-respect, then all under Heaven will be at peace. Therefore, if others do not love me, I should realize that it is not particularly because of others' inhumanity but because of my own, and if others do not respect me, it is not particularly that others are disrespectful but that I am.[48]

This, according to Huang Tsung-hsi, is what was called the "Huai-nan [method of] the investigation of things," [e] so-called because Huai-nan is the classical name for Wang Ken's home region.[49] It is a recurrent theme in Ken's recorded conversations and writings [50] and rests on two cardinal Confucian principles: that reciprocity is the basis of all social relations, and that higher forms of social organization depend on the self-cultivation of individuals in the lower forms and ultimately on the individual himself.

On the other hand, there is implicit here a subtle shift of emphasis and of context. When the *Book of Changes* speaks of the preservation of the state being dependent on the security of the individual, it is speaking to the "gentleman" who is a member of the ruling class, if not the ruler himself. Wang Ken, however, is actualizing the theoretical potential in this principle, and broadening its significance to include the common individual as well as the traditional Confucian "gentleman." His intent is clearly to alter the balance in the reciprocal equations of Confucian politics and social relations, that is, to make the welfare and security of the individual the *sine qua non* in every case. Thus, starting from the premise of the individual's moral responsibility, and proceeding by a disarmingly simple reductionism of a type which appealed to Confucians, he established the welfare of the individual as the primary basis of the social order.

We must be careful not to exaggerate this shift. It keeps the individual well within the bounds of Confucian reciprocity and social responsibility. But within that context it does allow new possibilities for a fuller development of the conception of the individual. One of these is revealed in Wang Ken's brief essay entitled "Clear Wisdom and Self-preservation" (*Ming-che pao-shen lun*),[f][51] from which the following passage is drawn: (The reader is asked to bear with Wang Ken's simple style and repetitious argumentation, which reflects both his own homespun character and his desire to communicate to the simplest people.)

Clear wisdom is innate knowledge. To clarify wisdom and preserve the self is innate knowledge and innate ability. It is what is called "To know without deliberating and to know how without learning how." [52] All men possess these faculties. The sage and I are the same. Those who know how to preserve the self will love the self like a treasure. If I can love the self, I cannot but love other men; if I can love other men, they will surely love me; and if they love me, my self will be preserved. . . . If I respect my self, I dare not but respect other men; if I respect other men, they will surely respect me; and if they respect me, my self is preserved. If I respect my self, I dare not be rude to other men; if I am not rude to others, they will not be rude to me; and if they are not rude to me, then my self is preserved. . . . This is humanity! This is the Way whereby all things become one body!

If by this means I regulate the family, then I can love the whole family; and if I love that family, they will love me; and if they love me, my self is preserved. If by this means I rule a state, I can love the whole state; if I love that state, the state will love me; and if the state loves me, my self is preserved. Only when my self is preserved can I preserve the state. If by this means I pacify all under Heaven, I can love all under Heaven; and if I can love all under Heaven, then all who have blood and breath cannot but respect their kin, and if they all respect their kin, then my self is preserved. Only if my self is preserved can I preserve all under Heaven. This is Humanity! This is [the Mean's] unceasing Sincerity! This is [Confucius'] Way which threads through all things!

The reason men cannot fulfill it is because of the partiality which arises from their physical endowment and material desires, and this is also what makes them differ from the sage. Only when they differ from the sage do they need education. What kind of education? Education in clear wisdom and self-preservation—that is all.

If I only know how to preserve my self and do not know to love other men, then I will surely seek only to satisfy my self, pursue my own selfish gain, and harm others, whereupon they will retaliate and my self can no longer be preserved. . . . If I only know how to love others and do not know how to love my self, then it will come to my body being cooked alive or the flesh being sliced off my own thighs, or to throwing away my life and killing my self, and then my self cannot be preserved. And if my self cannot be preserved, with what shall I preserve my prince and father? [53]

When Wang Ken speaks of "my body being cooked alive or the flesh being sliced off my own thighs, throwing my life away," etc., he alludes to extravagant gestures of self-sacrifice, and protests against a highly idealized view of the self which called for heroic self-denial and an almost religious dedication to one's ruler or parents, so contrary to man's natural instinct for self-preservation.[54] His quarrel is not at all with loyalty or filial piety; he himself was known for his exemplary filiality and devotion to his father.[55] Rather he reminds his Confucian brethren of the true meaning of filial piety: that one's duty to Heaven and one's parents, from whom one receives life, is to nourish, preserve, and reproduce that life in its most fundamental biological form.[56]

Here then we observe a difference between Wang Ken and Wang Yang-ming which has important implications for those who follow them. Wang Ken's conception of the self is strongly physical—the bodily self or person (*shen*).[g] Wang Yang-ming's emphasis in innate knowledge is on the mind (*hsin*),[h] especially the identity of mind with principle or nature. Nature for Wang Ken is the physical self—not excluding, of course, the mind which was understood as of one substance with the body and which most often has the sense of "heart." Hence the terms "School of the Mind" or "Subjective Idealism" frequently used to designate the Wang Yang-ming school can be applied to Wang Ken and his followers only with substantial qualification.[57] Liu Tsung-chou, a later "revisionist" within the Yang-ming school, noted the crucial difference between Wang Ken and Yang-ming on this point, and asked whether it did not portend the abandonment of mind control and of the restraining influence of the mind over the bodily desires.[58]

SELF-MASTERY AND SELF-ENJOYMENT

In the passage above, Wang Ken does refer to material desires as giving rise to selfishness, a typically Neo-Confucian view, but he sees this tendency as essentially unnatural and remediable through nothing more than education in "clear wisdom and self-preservation," that is, by the exercise of innate knowledge through and for the self. The easy optimism with which he regards such selfishness in man springs from his identification of human nature (*hsing*)[i] with natural spontaneity (*tzu-jan*).[j][59] Action in accordance with nature is in direct response to innate knowledge, which, as we have seen, is "knowing without deliberation." It draws upon the unlimited creative power of nature. The only need is to see that one's actions are uninhibited by artificial restraints or devices (*wei*).[k]

Here, of course, Wang Ken uses the language of Taoism, but in a context that still suggests important Confucian overtones. Take, for instance, his equation of the Way (Tao) and self. These are fundamentally one. "To respect the self and not respect the Way is not [truly] to respect the self. To respect the Way and not respect the self is not [truly] to respect the Way. To respect both the Way and the self is the Highest Good." [60] But if one suspects a lapse here into a kind of quietism or passive acceptance of Nature, in Wang Ken the goal is seen as dynamic self-mastery, and approximates Ch'en Hsien-chang's aim of making the whole universe dependent on oneself, rather than oneself dependent on the universe.[61] The aim of all study should be precisely that "Heaven and earth and all things should be dependent on the self, rather than the self dependent on

Heaven and earth and all things. Any other way than this is the 'way of the concubine' " [spoken of by Mencius.] [62]

The "way of the concubine" is the way of dependence on others and loss of integrity. Instead of such a passive, feminine role in the world, the sage takes an active, masterful role. Being true to the Way means for him fulfilling the mission of the Confucian sage, who remakes his world to conform to the Way of moral and political order. "The sages put the world in order by means of this Way." And what is most worthy of respect in the self is man's capacity to "enlarge the Way" by putting it into effect in his life and in the world.[63] For this reason the Confucian sage does not hide himself, but comes out into the world and makes his principles plain. Does this mean, then, that the Way can be fulfilled only by ruling, by taking office in the government? Not at all. Confucius did it by cultivating his self and by teaching. The sage serves as "teacher to the ruler," as "teacher to all generations." [64] For him or for anyone else to compromise his self and his Way by taking office in questionable circumstances is again the "way of the concubine." [65]

If there is Taoist influence here, it is expressed in terms of the natural spontaneity and creative power of the Way manifesting itself through the individual, while the Confucian element is expressed in terms of that Way serving the needs of man. Wang Ken's activism draws heavily on both. He is alive with the spontaneous joy of the Tao and finds that joy in learning. Thus his paean of the "Enjoyment of Learning":

The human heart naturally enjoys itself
But one binds oneself by selfish desires.
When a selfish desire makes its appearance,
Innate knowledge is still self-conscious,
And once there is consciousness of it, the selfish desire forthwith disappears,
So that the heart returns to its former joy.
Joy is the enjoyment of this learning:
Learning is to learn this joy.
Without this joy it is not true learning;
Without this learning it is not true joy.
Enjoy and then learn,
Learn and then enjoy.

To enjoy is to learn, to learn is to enjoy.
Ah! among the joys of this world what compares to learning!
What learning in the world compares to this joy! [66]

Wang Ken is not the first Chinese thinker to find joy in life. This is a common theme among his predecessors, from Confucius and Chuang Tzu down through the Sung masters to Ch'en Hsien-chang and Wang Yang-ming.[67] But he is the first to express such rapturous joy in learning—that is, learning of a kind that is available to all and not just the secret delight of the scholar. Wang Ken's joy arises from the fact that learning is so simple and easy. It does not require any erudition or intellectual exertion; it is the operation of ordinary intelligence in everyday life, which should be effortless. Joy is spontaneous when one does not rely on one's own strength, but lets nature, innate knowledge, the Way be manifested freely through the self.[68]

THE COMMON MAN AND THE GRAND UNITY

During his mature years as a teacher Wang Ken laid special emphasis on making the Way answer to the everyday needs of the people (*pai-hsing jih-yung*).[1] [69] The substance of man's heavenly nature is manifested in people's ordinary desires and wants; there is nothing mysterious or transcendental about it. Just follow the way of "ignorant men and women" (*yü-fu yü-fu*),[m] [70] who, without education, go about their daily tasks.[71] The sage, like the ordinary man, must be concerned with what nourishes people's bodies and hearts. "What is nearest at hand," he says, echoing Ch'en Hsien-chang, "is divine." [72]

In recent years Wang Ken has attracted special attention from left-wing writers who have not unnaturally stressed the "popular" aspects of Wang Ken's character and teaching, his great concern for the needs of the poor, and his general antipathy toward those in power who failed to provide for these needs.[73] There can be no doubt that these points have a real basis in Wang Ken's thought, and that his school has historical significance as a kind of "protest movement" against the "establishment" (whether that be defined as "feudal" or bureaucratic). It is a school that engenders widespread popular interest and support, not just another current of scholarly thought.

Nevertheless, there is noticeably lacking in Wang Ken's writing or in what has been recorded of him any indication of a significant social or economic program, or any sign that he ever discussed the people's problems in other than the most immediate personal terms.[74] He shares Wang Yang-ming's vision of the primitive ideal of Grand Unity, which is thoroughly traditional, and bases it on the principle of "all things forming one body," which is so fundamental to Ming thought, but he is extremely vague as to how this is to be achieved except through the accumulation of individual actions performed in that spirit. One may argue that the paucity of sources renders any speculation as to his social and economic views inconclusive.[75] Still, such evidence as there is indicates that the main thrust of his teaching is typically Confucian: it is to deal with social problems primarily as problems of the individual person, and insofar as Wang Ken adds a new dimension to such discussion, it is to liberate the potentialities of the individual and satisfy his immediate needs, rather than to deal with the complex problems of a mature society.

THE NEW HEROISM

Wang Ken's egalitarian tendencies and his concern for the practical needs of the common man, like those of the early reformer Mo Tzu, are expressed in an idealistic vision of a society based on love, which evokes a kind of religious enthusiasm. His activist temperament and his conviction that man can master his own destiny also recall Mo Tzu's "antifatalism" and the dynamic quality which infused the latter's popular reformist movement. On the other hand, among the many differences which could be pointed to is the absence in Wang Ken of Mo Tzu's self-denying asceticism and puritanism. The *Chuang Tzu* had commented that this quality in Mo Tzu's teaching had called for a life of strenuous exertion and heroic self-sacrifice.[76] Wang Ken too calls for heroism, but without self-sacrifice.

In Wang Ken's "Ode to the Loach and Eel," [77] which is a kind of parable—indeed, almost a Confucian *jataka* tale—the loach saves the life of a floundering eel, but seeks no credit or thanks for it.[78] His is a spontaneous act of generosity, prompted by the suffering of a fellow-being but not tainted by self-importance or vainglory and not vitiated by the kind of pity which demeans its object. The observer of this scene asks himself where such humaneness and detachment can be found among men, and recalls the type of "great man" or "hero" spoken of by Mencius:

He who dwells in the wide house of the world, stands in the correct station of the world, and walks in the great path of the world; he who, when successful, practices virtue along with the people, and when disappointed, practices it alone; he who is above the power of riches and honors to corrupt, of poverty and mean condition to make swerve from principle, and of power and force to make bend—he may be called a great man! [79]

Applying this concept to his own time, Wang Ken sees the "great man" (ta-chang-fu)[n] as one who ranges widely over the land, helping people in distress, but doing so in a spirit of spontaneous self-fulfillment. Wang Yang-ming, after picturing the ideal society and contrasting with it the corrupt state of his own, almost despaired of setting things right. But—

Fortunately the principle of nature lies within the human mind and can never be obliterated; the light of innate knowledge shines through all ages. When they hear what I have to say about pulling up the roots and stopping up the source [of evil], some men will surely be touched and pained, and will rise up in indignation, like a river that cannot be held in check. To whom shall I look if not to heroic leaders (hao-chieh chih shih)[o] who will rise up without further delay? [80]

To his followers Wang Yang-ming himself was a heroic leader, but the quality in him that most impressed them was his combination of active commitment and personal detachment.[81] For Wang Ken the "great man" will manifest these qualities in the spontaneous joy with which he fulfills his human responsibilities, in his outgoing love for mankind and his ceaseless action in the world. He will be a Neo-Confucian Vimalakīrti, a layman who has achieved transcendent wisdom within the secular world, but also a kind of sage-savior whose activity within that world expresses the fullness of his humanity.[82] As Shimada has so aptly put it, Wang Ken's "great man" is one who "acts according to the nature of his inner self, whose absolute subjectivity is at once the basis of his perfect freedom and unlimited joy, and of his outgoing desire to rescue others from their sufferings." [83]

THE T'AI-CHOU SCHOOL AS A "MASS" MOVEMENT

From Wang Ken's teachings and personal example his school (named T'ai-chou [p] from his home town) drew remarkable vitality, and was able to exert a wide influence on sixteenth-century China. That it has been called the "left" or radical wing of the Wang Yang-ming school reflects both its popular character and the revolutionary nature of its ideas. Thus his school is the only one which can claim such a large number of commoners, including a woodcutter, a potter, a stonemason, an agricultural laborer, clerks, merchants, and so on.[84] A foremost student of social mobility in this period credits Wang Ken and his son with "carrying the intellectual torch to the masses. . . . Never before and never afterward, in traditional China, were so many people willing to accept their fellow men for their intrinsic worth or did they approach more closely the true Confucian ideal that 'in education there should be no class distinctions.' " [85]

Such a development could not have come about, of course, simply through the force of Wang Ken's ideas alone, or even those of the Wang Yang-ming school as a whole. Other factors contributed. Economic affluence had prepared the ground by raising the general level of subsistence and enabling more people to participate in the cultural life of the nation. The lower Yangtze valley area, in which T'ai-chou was situated, had for several centuries been a major area for economic production and commercial activity.[86] In the Sung and Yüan (as reported by Marco Polo) it was already the center of a flourishing culture, which allowed for the pursuit of individual interests, the satisfaction of individual tastes, and the expression of individuality in art and literature.[87] Though confined originally to a relative minority in the bureaucratic gentry, the base for this cultural activity had widened to include segments of the middle classes. In the Sung and Ming, for instance, the spread of high culture is shown in the existence of literary societies which sponsored the writing and printing of poetry in the classical *shih* form by merchants and artisans.[88] The reverse process is seen in the adoption by the literati (not wholly legitimized) of forms which developed in the market places and amusement centers—especially the popular drama and fiction which grew out of popular story-telling.[89]

This combination of economic strength and cultural activity was particularly marked in the lower Yangtze valley during the sixteenth and seventeenth centuries. Yang-chou, the prefecture in which T'ai-chou was situated, was a leading center of the salt industry, and the great Yang-chou salt merchants were munificent patrons of both classical and popular culture.[90] Nanking, across the Yangtze, was described by the Jesuit Matteo Ricci as far outdoing Peking or any other capital city in size, wealth, and splendor.[91] Nearby Soochow could also lay a claim to being the true economic and cultural capital of China. At the end of the sixteenth century it had a population of well over two million, paid one tenth of the total taxes collected in the empire—an amount equivalent to that paid by the whole province of Szechuan.[92] Indeed, Ricci spoke of it as a city "known for its wealth and splendor, for its numerous population and for about everything that makes a city grand. . . . When the Tartars were expelled and the kingdom taken over by the ancestor of the present reigning monarch, this city of Succu [Soochow] was stubbornly defended by its chiefs and up to today a tremendous tax is still levied on it as a rebellion city. . . . The whole province followed the capital city in opposition to the King, and even now it is heavily guarded, as the fear of rebellion from this quarter is greater than from anywhere else in the kingdom." [93]

This affluence and independence, however, were not associated with a single economic or social class. Increasing social fluidity was accompanied by strong political and cultural crosscurrents. The sixteenth and early seventeenth centuries saw the apogee of upward mobility from the merchant families into the bureaucracy. Among these families, as Wang Tao-kun said, "trade and studies alternated with each other." [94] Some old gentry families could survive only by going into business, while others, more fortunate in maintaining their position in the official class, participated in the culture of the non-official classes as sponsors of theatrical performances and collectors on a large scale of works of popular fiction and drama.[95]

In such circumstances the T'ai-chou school reflected a growing confusion of class roles and concepts. For all its "radical" or "progressive" character, it cannot be identified with the rise of one class such as the merchant or the "commoner." No doubt the growth of commerce and the economic strength of the middle classes contributed to the self-confidence and optimism that is characteristic of T'ai-chou thought, but on the whole this school defies description as a "bourgeois" or "middle class" phenomenon, much less a movement of the lower classes (and we remember, of course, that from the traditional or formal standpoint merchants were regarded not as in the middle but as at the lowest end of the social scale). Significant though the T'ai-chou school is as a movement led by a commoner to awaken the masses, in its membership as a whole the official class or bureaucratic gentry played a major role. Of 25 thinkers and teachers discussed by Huang Tsung-hsi in relation to the T'ai-chou school, 17 had a clear connection with officialdom, and no less than 11 won the advanced civil service (*chin-shih*) degree.[96] In several cases it was the protection afforded by persons in high places which enabled the more radical activists to escape or hold off official persecution.[97] Though some of these officials may well have originated from families of nonofficials, taken as a whole the official majority in the movement probably represents a typical cross section of the educated elite at that time.

As Kuei Yu-kuang (1506–71) observed, "the status distinctions among scholars, peasants, and merchants have become blurred." [98] In such a situation the infusion of new blood and the raw energy of men like Wang Ken is probably less significant as an expression of rising class consciousness than as a bold attempt to grapple with a common human problem: the search for identity at a time when traditional roles have been obscured by rapid change and new energies can no longer be channeled along established lines.

In the T'ai-chou school itself personal relationships crossed traditional class lines, intellectual associations crossed political lines, and educational work crossed religious lines. While the penetration of the movement to the lower levels of society is significant, as contrasted to the type of individuality cultivated almost entirely within the upper class of the Sung period,[99] its broad extension to all levels of society and to many areas of life is of more fundamental importance than its class character. That is, of importance not only to society but to the role of Confucianism in it. For with its primary engagement in education, and what might be called proselytizing and propaganda, in the T'ai-chou school Confucianism for the first time became heavily involved in the sphere traditionally occupied by the popular religions.

Huang Tsung-hsi, no admirer of the T'ai-chou school as a whole, says that, owing to the activities of Wang Ken and Wang Chi, the teachings of Wang Yang-ming "spread like the wind over all the land." [100] True to his self-declared mission as a teacher to the world, Ken traveled widely and stirred up discussion wherever he went. On his homemade touring car he had written that he would "travel to the mountains and forests in order to meet recluses and into the towns and villages in order to mix with ignorant commoners." [q][101] One of these uneducated commoners, the potter Han Chen, after his "conversion" and a period of study with Wang Ken's brother, took up the mission of spreading the new gospel among ordinary folk, and developed a large following among peasants, artisans, and merchants. After the fall harvest he would gather people together for lectures and discussion. When he had finished in one town he moved on to another. A regular feature of these gatherings was group singing: "With some chanting and others responding, their voices resounded like waves over the countryside." [102] The atmosphere of a religious revival prevailed, and Han Chen personally exemplified a kind of religious dedication to the cause. When at these meetings the talk turned toward partisan politics and personalities, he would ask, "With life so short, how can you spend time gossiping?" And when the discussion became too pedantically involved with the niceties of classical scholarship, he would ask if those so engaged thought they were on a scholarly lecture platform.[103]

Hou Wai-lu's researches, drawing on the writings, records, and letters of Wang Ken's disciples, indicate that as the movement spread in all directions it developed a kind of organization on the local and regional levels, with a corps of able and dedicated leaders helping in the planning, scheduling, and conducting of public meetings. The whole community participated: scholars, officials, Buddhists and Taoists, monks and laymen. The leaders were often men of outstanding reputation or influence, but a more important qualification was the receipt of a personal transmission of the true teaching from Wang Ken or his authorized successors. Wang attached great importance to a man's demonstrating a total dedication to the fulfillment of the Sage's teaching. Along with his public lecturing he had a more private communication through which he confided his deeper understanding of the Way only to those who were ready for it.[104]

Thus an esoteric quality and religious aura surrounds the legitimate transmission in this school and for the same essential reason as in Ch'an Buddhism: instead of the truth being defined in a set of doctrines it was seen as a living Way and a highly personal experience, culminating in a personal encounter between master and disciple which recognized the personality, capabilities, and insights of the individual. Hence in the very laicizing of Confucianism by the Wang Yang-ming school we find a new mystique of the secular order, discovering the divine (as Wang Ken had put it) in what is most commonplace and what is most intimately human.[105]

Huang Tsung-hsi had said of Wang Ken that, while he did not match Wang Chi in dialectical subtlety, there was no one more successful than he in awakening people to the living truth within them and to the Way as something which answers to the everyday needs of man.[106] Among the persons upon whom his earnest teaching made a deep impression was Yüan Huang (1533–1606), whose father had been an intimate acquaintance of both Wang Chi and Wang Ken and had traveled a great distance to attend the latter's funeral.[107] Yüan Huang's forebears had been professional Taoists for generations, and at one point he was overcome by a deep pessimism and fatalism when the prophecies of a Taoist wizard convinced him that he could never achieve the *chin-shih* degree and would die without a male heir. Subsequently Yüan was roused from this hopelessness and became persuaded that man, through moral action and the accumulation of meritorious deeds, could become the master of his own destiny. When eventually he succeeded in the examinations and also became the father of a boy, Yüan was confirmed in a mission to preach the value of moral effort as a means to personal success in life. He did this through his popular "morality books" (*shan-shu*) [8] and "ledgers of merit and demerit" (*kung-kuo ko*),[t] which were widely printed and sold, not only in China but even in Japan.[108]

Yüan's immediate conversion from fatalism was achieved by a Buddhist monk, Yün-ku,[u] but, having been a student of Wang Chi, Yüan expressed his philosophy of mastering one's own destiny through moral action in the language of the Wang Yang-ming school.[109] Also, while the morality books were of a type used earlier in popular Taoism, Professor Tadao Sakai has emphasized a significant difference in their employment by Yüan. In the earlier case reward and retribution were seen as meted out by the gods, and many superstitious practices were encouraged as means of winning divine favor. In Yüan Huang's case the system of moral reward and retribution was self-enforcing, a kind of ethical science. The good deeds prescribed pertained to the ordinary conduct of life, and the promised recompense answered to the ordinary needs of human life.[110] Though a somewhat mechanical system, with too quantitative an approach to the value of ethical acts, it nevertheless strengthened the confidence of the ordinary man that he could cope with the challenges and crises of life.

Another important proponent of the system of merits and demerits was the great Ch'an monk Chu-hung [v] (1535–1615), who helped to revive the declining fortunes of Buddhism at this time by his synthesis of Pure Land and Ch'an Buddhism.[111] In this way he allied the most popular form of devotional Buddhism with the more ascetic Meditation school. Through Chu-hung's efforts the Ledgers of Merit and Demerit for the first time became widely used as a means of moral reform among Buddhists.[112] In this case the direct influence of the T'ai-chou school might be difficult to prove, but Chu-hung had many associations with this school and indirectly its emphasis on the moral potentialities of the individual must have encouraged the belief, which Chu-hung's ledgers presupposed, that man could affect not only his karmic destiny in the afterlife but also his status and welfare in this life.[113] This tended to give lay Buddhism a more practical and humanized character, no doubt reflecting the new faith in man which Wang Yang-ming and his followers encouraged.

Though from a deeper ethical standpoint it would be hard to reconcile this system with the disinterested morality of either Wang Yang-ming and Wang Ken or the loftier forms of Buddhism, from the historical standpoint it represents something more than just another case of religious syncretism.[114] It is another concrete expression of the trend toward secularization of traditional teachings and the definition of an ethical common denominator in the midst of social and cultural change. To this extent it might have helped to widen the base for the growth of individualism.

The vitality of the T'ai-chou school is shown in the wide range of thinkers and personalities it produced.[115] Though it has been referred to as the "left wing" and as the "Wild Ch'an" movement within the Wang Yang-ming school, this is only because its more radical and extreme tendencies have readily attracted attention. The less spectacular side of the school shows a greater diversity and complexity of thought. Of those who were activists not all were radicals, and of those who turned toward Ch'an some were quite conservative in politics and morals.[116] A full study of individualistic philosophies in the late Ming would require far more extensive treatment of the available alternatives, not only within the Wang Yang-ming school as a whole, but even within the T'ai-chou school itself.

Nevertheless, among these diverse individualisms some tended in what we have called a "negative" direction, and offered little hope of establishing a more positive and widely extended individualism in Chinese society as a whole. They may have asserted their own independence or autonomy but not necessarily that of others. The radical wing at least was identified with a kind of social reformism which might conceivably have led to fundamental changes in the situation of the Chinese individual generally. Some recent writers in China and Japan have also considered it a real hope in sixteenth-century China for an indigenously generated force toward modernization.[117] I cannot enter into all aspects of this larger problem, but the question of individualism, since it arises naturally in Ming thought, is one way of approaching the larger issue from within the Chinese tradition.

HO HSIN-YIN: THE HERO AND
THE NATURAL MAN

The sixteenth-century historian Wang Shih-chen ʷ (1525–90) said that the popular lecturers of the Wang Yang-ming school

flourished and spread throughout the land in the Chia-ching [1522–1567] and Lung-ch'ing [1567–1572] periods. What led finally to their great excesses was that they used their lecturing to serve the cult of heroism, and used the cult of heroism to indulge their unrestrained selfishness. Their arts had basically nothing to them that might rouse men to action, and lacking any real conviction or concern they joined in beating the drums, blowing their horns, and flapping their wings, drawing crowds together and flashing here and there, until they came near to causing a disaster like the Yellow Turban and Five Pecks of Grain [movements at the end of the second century A.D.]. Now the change from Wang Yang-ming to T'ai-chou [Wang Ken] had not yet done too great damage, but with the change from Ta'i-chou to Yen Chün ˣ ¹¹⁸ everything rotted apart and it could not be put together again.¹¹⁹

Wang Shih-chen had great contempt for Yen Chün as an illiterate with little real knowledge of the classics, who was so fond of his own ideas that he did not hesitate to misconstrue the classical texts in support of them. "He believed," Wang says, "that man's appetite for wealth and sex all sprang from his true nature" and should not be repressed.¹²⁰ Wang then goes on to make many charges of licentiousness and sedition against Yen and other members of his following, especially Ho Hsin-yin (1517–1579).¹²¹ Huang Tsung-hsi, writing a couple of generations later in his preface to the T'ai-chou school in the *Ming-ju hsüeh-an*, says that most of the wild stories about Yen and Ho derive from Wang Shih-chen's partisan and one-sided accounts which are not to be trusted. Nevertheless, Huang himself shared the general feeling against the leaders of this movement as having brought the Wang Yang-ming school to disgrace and undermined public morality. His discussion of them is confined to his preface; he gives neither formal biographies of them nor excerpts from their writings. "After T'ai-chou his followers wanted to seize the dragon's tail with their bare hands [i.e., seize hold of life and truth without any help from past teachings]. As transmitted to Yen Chün and Ho Hsin-yin, it reached the point where they could no longer be restrained by traditional morality." [122]

According to Huang, Yen Chün had received the teaching of Wang Ken from Hsü Yüeh,[y] [123] who followed Ken's "Way of Self-respect."

Yen believed that man's mind was an unfathomable store of mysterious creativity and that his nature was like a transparent pearl, originally without flaw or stain. What need was there for "caution" and "apprehension" whenever one saw or heard something? In ordinary times one should simply follow wherever one's nature leads, trusting its spontaneity—this is what one calls the Way. Only if one should on occasion go to excess is it necessary to exercise "caution" or "self-watchfulness" or "apprehension" in order to correct such excess. All of the knowledge, principles, and norms of earlier Confucians suffice only to obstruct the Way.[124]

Huang also says that Yen followed the way of the *yu-hsia*,[z] imperfectly translated as "knight-errant," [125] a free spirit and daredevil who would risk anything to help a friend in distress or a sufferer from injustice. He and Ho Hsin-yin were both known for their extraordinary heroism in devotion to their friends. When Chao Chen-chi,[aa] a fellow student under Hsü Yüeh who became a grand secretary, was sent in official disgrace to a remote post for his outspokenness at court, Yen insisted on accompanying him, an act of loyalty which Chao is said to have appreciated deeply during his hour of trial. Also, when his teacher Hsü Yüeh died in battle in Yünnan (ironically as a result of his own imprudence) [126] Yen went to search for his remains and bring them back for burial.[127] Keng Ting-hsiang,[ab] a disciple of Ho Hsin-yin, said of Yen Chün that his "teaching was Confucian but his actions were those of a 'hero' or 'knight-errant' (*hsia*)." [128]

The description might well apply to Ho Hsin-yin [129] himself, whose abilities, Huang says, far exceeded those of Yen. In 1546 he won first place in the Kiangsi provincial examinations and was considered a person of great promise, but after learning the teachings of Wang

Ken from Yen Chün, he gave up all thought of an official career [130] and set out on an independent course, paying little respect to the views and counsels of the established scholars in his home town. Taking as his basis the teaching of the *Great Learning* that the ordering of the state depended on the regulation of the family, he conceived a new type of organization for his own clan which would have made it a self-sufficient, autonomous community. Through this organization, centering around a so-called Collective Harmony Hall (*Chü-ho t'ang*),[ac] he attempted to regulate clan life in the strictest detail. There were to be two leadership groups, one supervising the educational and cultural affairs of the clan, and the other its economic and social welfare. All clan affairs, including the rituals of capping, marriage, funerals, care of the aged, the collection of taxes, and the performance of labor service, were to be handled on a cooperative and egalitarian basis. Schooling was to be provided for the sons of all in the clan, irrespective of wealth or status. They would live together at school, carrying on a cooperative life and submitting to the same discipline. This meant, in effect, pioneering a kind of public education on the local level.[131]

Ho ran into difficulty trying to maintain the autonomy of his utopian community, however. When special taxes were imposed by local officials, he remonstrated against them and so antagonized the authorities that he was arrested and imprisoned. Only through the intervention of powerful friends did he escape banishment.[132] Thereafter he taught and lectured widely throughout the country and attracted a great following. He had many friends in officialdom, and enjoyed their hospitality for long periods. During a stay in Peking he became involved in a conspiracy to unseat the powerful and corrupt grand secretary Yen Sung, which succeeded in its object but resulted in Ho's becoming a hated and hunted man after his part in the plot became known. Yen Sung's party sought vengeance.[133] As a consequence he led a kind of nomadic existence for the rest of his life, taking refuge with his official friends and patrons wherever they happened to be, and having no fixed abode. His difficulties were increased by his having once antagonized Chang Chü-cheng, who subsequently became all-powerful at court. During a brief personal encounter he had bluntly challenged Chang's understanding of the real import of the *Great Learning*.[134] Moreover, as a leading exponent of public lecturing and a champion of the freedom of teaching and discussion, Ho was closely identified with the independent academies where such discussion was carried on, and on this account too he was at odds with Chang, who later ordered the suppression of the academies. Ho's fugitive life came to an end at the age of sixty-two when he was arrested and subsequently died at the hands of jailers in Wu-ch'ang who probably thought his elimination would ingratiate them with Chang Chü-cheng.[135]

FROM DESIRELESSNESS TO DESIREFULNESS

Ho's life was an exemplification of his philosophy. Following Yen Chün, he believed that self-expression was more important than self-restraint. Above all he valued a man's spirit (*i-ch'i*).[ad] Every man is endowed with this spirit—ideas and feelings and a natural passion to manifest these in his life. This is his share of the living Way, and it is precisely through his active self-assertion that the creative power of the Way asserts itself. All things in Heaven and earth, all beings from the sage to the least of men thus have the Way working in and through them.[136] Ho went so far as to reinterpret a famous passage in the *Analects*, wherein, according to the traditional reading, Confucius had seemed to be a model of self-effacing moderation: "There were four things from which the Master was entirely free. He had no foregone conclusions, no arbitrary predeterminations, no obstinacy and no egoism." (*Analects* IX, 4)

According to Ho's interpretation the passage really meant that Confucius would have nothing to do with nonegoism, noninsistence, nonobstinacy and having-no-ideas-of-one's-own. These attitudes represented the passivity of Lao Tzu, and Confucius rejected such Taoistic quietism as incompatible with his own activism in behalf of mankind. "He did away with these [attitudes] lest they harm the Way."[137]

From this we can see how Wang Yang-ming's conception of man's nature as an active principle within the mind and Wang Ken's emphasis on the physical as well as moral self have developed to the

point where Ho is ready to liberate man from traditional forms of
self-repression. In Wang Yang-ming innate knowledge had been
opposed not only to external knowledge and influence but also to
selfish desires. Ho Hsin-yin still recognizes selfishness as a problem,
but he refuses to identify it with man's desires. Indeed, he strongly
affirms the validity of the so-called material desires. Sense appetites
have their basis in the inborn nature of man, and are to be nurtured
and satisfied rather than denied and suppressed.[138] Further, he is
prepared to dispute the authority of Chou Tun-i, the great patriarch
of Neo-Confucian philosophy, on the validity of Chou's "desireless-
ness" (wu-yü),[ae] which he implies is a Taoistic intrusion into Confucian thought.[139] It is not possible for the mind-and-heart of man to
be without desires, for even the wish to be without desires is a desire.
On the other hand, if one recognizes that in any case it becomes a
question of choosing among desires rather than attempting to eradicate them, it will suffice for the preservation of man's mind-and-
heart if only the desires are reduced. He cites Mencius:

I like fish and I also like bear's paws. If I cannot have the two together,
I will let the fish go and take the bear's paws. Life too I like and also
righteousness, but if I cannot have the two together, I will let life go and
choose righteousness. . . . There are cases when men by a certain course
might preserve life and yet do not take that course, or when by certain
things they might avoid danger and yet will not do them. Therefore men
have that which they like more than life and that which they dislike more
than death. (VIA, 10)

"To love fish and love bear-paws," says Ho, "are desires. To do
without the fish and take the bear-paws is to reduce one's desires.
To love life and love righteousness are desires. To give up life and
choose righteousness is to restrict one's desires. But can one reduce
and reduce to the point of nothingness and still preserve one's mind-
and-heart?" [140] Thus, man's emotional desires and sense appetites,
like his moral or spiritual aspirations, are rooted in his inborn nature.
Without them he would dwindle to nothing. As undeniable expressions of the natural self, they cannot be left unnurtured, and even
when subordinated to man's higher instincts, the sacrifice must serve
the whole self, not some diminished self. Self-denial through a reduc-
tion of desires can be justified only as a means to self-fulfillment
through identification with others.

Neo-Confucianism in the Sung had rejected the Buddhist view of the essential self as transcending the world of desire and moral involvement, and had asserted the moral nature of man as precisely the means whereby he united himself with Heaven and earth and all things. This was the first step in reaffirming the Confucian view of the natural man—essentially as moral man. Chu Hsi, however, had distinguished between the two natures in man, the essential moral nature and the actual individual nature which might be obscured by differences in one's physical, psychic, and emotional makeup. This dichotomy Wang Yang-ming had then overcome by finding the moral nature as a living principle within the actual self. And the T'ai-chou school, especially as represented by Ho Hsin-yin, completed the process by broadening the conception of the natural man to include the most dynamic element in his actual nature—the drives and appetites that expressed the Chinese will to live in this world.

THE INDIVIDUAL AND THE COMMUNITY

To live in this world meant for Ho Hsin-yin what it had for Confucius: to be a man among men. And if to be a man, in his times, called for heroism, it was because only a hero could rectify the injustices and master the disorder which prevented other men from achieving self-fulfillment. One of Ho's arguments for the validity of human desires came from Mencius' urging the rulers of his time to take the people's desires as their own—that is, to provide for the satisfaction of their material wants.[141] From this we can see that he viewed the problem of self-satisfaction and self-fulfillment in a clear relation to that of others. Whatever extremity of means he might resort to as "hero" and master of his own destiny, he was not asserting his radical independence of society. Indeed, as in the case of Wang Yang-ming and Wang Ken, self for him meant primarily the common self of mankind, and only secondarily the individual as distinct from others.[142] Perhaps what most distinguishes his thought from that of other thinkers of the T'ai-chou school is his passionate concern for the common welfare, as well as his attempt to redefine man's relation to other men.

The virtues of humanity and righteousness had most often been defined within Confucianism in terms of some such definite relationship to others—in the family, the community, or the state. Ho argued for the broadest possible conception of these virtues. "Humanity regards all as one's own kind. . . The kinship between father and son is not the only kinship; kinship extends to all worthy of one's kindness—to all creatures that have blood and breath." Similarly, righteousness regards all as worthy of respect. It is not respect just for the ruler, but for all who have blood and breath. Thus, he argued, one should enlarge one's dwelling to include the whole world.

At first sight this might appear to be only a reiteration and rephrasing of the common Neo-Confucian theme: that "the humane man forms one body with Heaven and earth and all things." But for Ho this familiar phrase is no mere pious platitude or vague humanitarian sentiment. Nor can it be the basis of a purely interior illumination in which he attains a sense of oneness with the universe as did many other Ming thinkers. His experience of life makes him more conscious than most men of the individual's inescapable dependence on others. At the same time his vision of a larger world is strongly conditioned by his awareness of the individual's need to find security in some community. It is impossible to maintain himself otherwise. Most people achieve some measure of security through their family or clan, their class or profession. But what about the man who is neither peasant, merchant, artisan, nor official—especially the scholar who is unwilling to find his security in serving the state? [143] A wanderer himself much of his life, he knew what it meant to "dwell in a wider world," but also what it could mean to stand exposed to the world, facing alone the power of the state.

Ho first attempted to find that security in his autonomous clan community—a rather typical Chinese utopia of a kind which appeals to both Confucian decentralist thinking and the yearning for a totally ordered life.[144] It failed, and though we know nothing of its internal weaknesses, in any case the community could not withstand pressure from the local and central government. The cooperative, collective, and egalitarian features of this scheme have appealed to some modern writers,[145] but it is likely that Ho himself came to recognize its limitations in his situation. He seems to have made no further efforts to establish such communities elsewhere, and his main efforts at social and political reform were increasingly directed toward the scholarly community and the schools.

It is significant, however, that Ho thought of the wider community or collectivity not so much in terms of the highest level of generality or abstraction as in terms of an enlarged family system. He recognized the need for transcending the pettiness of traditional family loyalties, but wished to preserve and extend the basic values of the kinship system rather than dissolve them. His favorite expression for the group or collectivity was the "family" or "household" (*chia*), while the individual members or components of any higher-level organization were referred to as "selves" (*shen*).[146] In this he not only attempted creatively to adapt the kind of Confucian thinking found in the *Great Learning* to the needs of sixteenth-century Chinese society. He also foreshadowed one of the most typical Chinese responses to the challenge of modernization: the drive to adapt the kinship system itself to serve new functions, instead of yielding to the trend toward ever more rational and impersonal systems of organization.[147]

Ho believed that the narrow limits of the self and family could best be overcome through the relationship among friends, understood, as one might expect in the Ming context, as friendship among scholars with a common social commitment. Within this sphere the ultimate relation was between teacher and student, friends in the pursuit of truth and in the educating and leading of men. To stress such a deep bond was only natural for the Confucian; it corresponded to the actual facts of his life as an intellectual whose closest personal relations were with other scholars. But Ho goes further than this. In a society where the scholar is so dependent on the state, he sees a need for the scholars to organize in some kind of association that gives them collective strength, and not just personal intimacy.[148] They must be able to complement and, if necessary, check the ruling power; they must support one another as scholars, thinkers, and teachers so that the work of Confucius can go on:

The fulfillment of the Way starts with the relationship of ruler and minister on the highest level and ends with the relationship of friend and friend on the lowest. If there is intercourse between highest and lowest, then the way of parent and child, older and younger brother, husband and wife can be unified between them and achieve fulfillment. Though these latter relations are essential to fulfillment of the Way, they cannot unify all under Heaven. Only through the [cooperation of] ruler and minister can the heroes of the land be gathered together, humanity be made the basis of government, and thus extend to all under Heaven. . . . [On the other hand] only through the relation of friend and friend can the brave and talented in the land be gathered together in order to establish humanity as the basis of instruction and have all under Heaven naturally return to it.[149]

For this reason Ho makes a distinction between two types of sages, corresponding to a differentiation in function within society. Earlier the Confucian model had been the sage-king, combining intellectual and political functions, and the model Confucian had accordingly been both scholar and official. Ho distinguishes between Kings Yao and Shun as model rulers and Confucius as model teacher. They serve distinct but complementary functions. On occasion Ho even suggests that the latter may be more fundamental, since without the work of Confucius the true way of ruler and minister would have been lost.[150] Moreover, in his own day Ho felt it urgent that men of ability commit themselves to teaching and spreading the great Way, forgoing government service, as Confucius had, because education contributed more importantly to government than did official service in the bureaucracy.[151] Beyond this, he argued also for the necessity of scholarly associations and independent schools so that the Way could be discussed and spread even when the ruling power opposed it. By far his longest surviving work is an essay in defense of free lecturing and discussion in the schools.[152]

Li Chih, a great admirer of Ho, said that of the five Confucian relations Ho discarded four and kept only the relation between friend and friend.[153] The life Ho led, apart from his family and in opposition to the ruling power, no doubt strengthened this impression among his contemporaries. Others, less sympathetic than Li, accused Ho of heterodoxy, of resorting to magic (the plot against Yen Sung involved a Taoist adept who tricked the emperor), of utilitarianism (using questionable means to benefit his friends) and even of lapsing into Ch'anism.[154] This is not the place to evaluate such charges, which may well have some basis in his actual conduct and his belief in uninhibited self-assertion.[155] But Ho protested his own orthodoxy and compared the charges of heterodoxy against himself to the persecution of Chu Hsi in the Sung.[156] Like other T'ai-chou members he had frequent associations with Buddhists and Taoists, and was ready to enlist anyone in the "cause," but with him this reflected no tendency to equate the "Three Teachings as One." [157] For him Confucius' teaching, which affirmed self and human relations, was clearly superior to those of Lao Tzu and the Buddha, who repressed and denied them. Likewise he rejected all forms of quietism. He had no use for those who forsook the world and he criticized so-called scholars-in-retirement who took no active part in the common struggle.[158]

So far as Ho's thought is concerned, there is ample evidence that it kept within the essential Confucian tradition. In any case, as an example of individualistic thought in the Ming, it represents a significant attempt to redefine the place of the individual in Confucian terms. Having recognized the new potentialities of the individual, as well as the new demands of society upon him, Ho was forced to question whether either the family system or bureaucratic officialdom was an adequate instrument for the reform of society, the defense of the individual, or the perpetuation of Confucian values. The family was too weak and limited, as the inability of his own clan organization to contend with centralized power had demonstrated. Officialdom had lost its soul in the scramble for power. Unless some independent platform could be established, where the "brave and talented men of the land" might carry on free discussion, Confucian protests could not be heard and there would be no limit to the despotism of a totalitarian power structure—totalitarian in the sense, not that everything was controlled in detail from the top, but that in the absence of any alternative center of power or protection the insecurity of ordinary men would make them susceptible to even the imagined wishes of those in power, as Ho's jailers thought they might win favor with Chang Chü-cheng.

Ho Hsin-yin failed, perhaps as much from his own audacity as from the inherent weakness of his personal position, but his proposed solution was not totally lacking in realism. He sensed that in Ming society there was only one hope for establishing a vital Confucianism in the existing order: in the indispensable function of education, which even the bureaucracy and China's dynastic rulers had need of. And he pursued this hope with all the courage and conviction of Wang Yang-ming's "hero" or Wang Kên's "great man." In this respect then he represents the climax of the Confucian activism and humanitarianism generated within the Wang Yang-ming school, and is at the opposite pole from those other individualists of the time who retreated into quietism or withdrew into Ch'an.

LI CHIH, THE ARCH-INDIVIDUALIST

The tide of individualistic thought in the late Ming reached its height with Li Chih [af] (1527–1602),[159] who has been both condemned and acclaimed as the greatest heretic and iconoclast in China's history. He is in any case one of the most brilliant and complex figures in Chinese thought and literature.

Li was born and raised in the Chin-chiang district of the port city of Ch'üan-chou, Fukien Province. In earlier times Ch'üan-chou had been a center of foreign trade, with a somewhat cosmopolitan character. Li's forebears had been active in this trade, one of them traveling to Iran.[160] They were members of a Chinese Muslim community, and Li's wife too may have been a Muslim.[161] Some writers have seen special significance in Li's associations with a minority religious community and a non-Chinese value system, as well as in the commercial background of his family.[162] But in his voluminous writings Li makes no mention of Islam,[163] and he had very poor rapport with his wife, intellectually and spiritually. Moreover, his family, by virtue of their talents as interpreters and knowledge of foreign trade, had been drawn into official life—a not unnatural course for merchants in China, who considered themselves truly successful only when they had gained acceptance into the ranks of the bureaucratic gentry. This must have meant a closer identification with Confucian values, and no doubt a weakening in their adherence to Islam.[164]

The commercial atmosphere of Ch'üan-chou is vividly recalled in Li's writing by his frequent use of the language of the market place and by his aggressive, hard-driving mentality. But Ch'üan-chou's foreign trade had been largely cut off by the Ming seclusion policy; what survived was mostly illicit or severely regulated—trade of a kind that had the nefarious connotations of smuggling, the black market, official collusion, and squeeze. Its spirit could hardly have been that of the self-confident bourgeois, the expansive builder of a new world, but must rather have reflected a deep sense of frustration, ambivalence, and, probably, guilt.[165] This, it seems to us, is the characteristic spirit of Li Chih, whether it mirrors his Ch'üan-chou background, his mixed ancestral heritage, or the larger contradictions of life and thought in Ming China which he was to experience.

Li was given a classical Confucian training but, as he said later, he was a skeptic from his youth, repelled by anything or anyone—Confucian, Buddhist or Taoist—identified with an organized creed.[166] He felt a great revlusion, too, against the kind of mechanical learning required for the examinations to enter an official career, and though he managed to overcome his scruples and pass the provincial examinations in 1552, he did not go on to the higher examinations at the capital.[167] Financial difficulties may have combined with personal aversion in this decision, but whatever the reason his failure to achieve the *chin-shih* degree tended to limit his opportunities for official advancement. Such an attitude on Li's part hardly demonstrates a completely uncompromising independence, but it does suggest a recognizable pattern of alienation among members of the educated class in Ming and Ch'ing China, typified by the sensitive, highly intelligent child of a well-to-do family on the decline, who feels a fundamental conflict between his own individuality or intellectual integrity and what he must do in order to succeed in the world and discharge his family responsibilities.[168] Something of the same conflict, however, was widely felt in the sixteenth century by scholars of varying background and temperament, and Li's own subsequent development suggests important differences, as we shall see, from Wang Yang-ming, Wang Ken, and Ho Hsin-yin.

After his qualifying examination Li spent almost thirty years in the status of an official, going from one routine assignment to another, interrupted by periods of mourning for his father and grandfather and by periods in which he waited for reassignment. Though a somewhat frustrating life, marked by frequent conflict with his superiors, it was not without considerable leisure in which he could pursue his own studies. Assignments in Peking and Nanking gave him opportunities to meet with other scholars, in and out of office. He did an enormous amount of reading and his intellectual proclivities were greatly strengthened, but a profound spiritual unrest was at work within him. As he put it, he yearned to "hear the Way," [169] borrowing the phrase from Confucius: "Hearing the Way in the morning, one could die content in the evening" (Analects IV, 8). In other words, he too was searching for something worth living and dying for.

Thus through five years at the Board of Rites in Peking, Li's mind was little occupied with official duties but rather "sunk deep in the Way." [170] In the course of these years, he formed close associations with others who shared his serious interests, including members of the Wang Yang-ming school who introduced him to the teachings of Wang Yang-ming, Wang Chi, and the T'ai-chou school.

They told me the teachings of Master Lung-hsi (Wang Chi) and showed me the writings of Master Yang-ming. Thus I learned that the True Man who has attained the Way is deathless, and that he is one with the True Buddha and the True [Taoist] Immortal. Though an obstinate person, I could not but believe.[171]

One of these friends, Hsü Yung-chien,[ag] [172] participated in the public lecture meetings of Chao Chen-chi,[173] a leader of the T'ai-chou school, but Li had a strong antipathy to such meetings and would not go. Hsü therefore gave him a copy of the Diamond Sutra, one of the key texts of the Prajñā pāramitā philosophy of Buddhism. He said, "This is the learning that leads to deathlessness. Will you refuse to consider that too?" This, it is said, proved a turning point in Li's thinking.[174]

What kind of turning point? Li was nearly forty by this time. His personality and many of his attitudes must already have been well formed, and these experiences perhaps only confirmed the direction in which he was already headed. It is noteworthy, for instance, that they are intellectual experiences—spiritually significant but not described in deeply emotional or mystical terms, as was the case with Wang Yang-ming and Wang Ken. The feeling of oneness attained by Li is of the oneness of Truth, the identity of the Three Teachings.

It shows the influence of Wang Chi in particular, and an attitude in which the moral demands of the left wing yield to a more transcendental faith. Does this then leave Li Chih without the sense of mission that emerged from Yang-ming's and Wang Ken's experiences? We shall soon see.

Li's next long assignment was in Nanking, where he had close associations with other T'ai-chou members, notably the Keng brothers, Ting-hsiang [175] and Ting-li,[ah] [176] and Chiao Hung.[ai] [177] The latter became perhaps Li's closest friend, soul mate, and sworn brother. He was a distinguished scholar and historian, with a fine library and, like Li, a sharp, critical mind combined with a broad tolerance for the Three Teachings. In such company Li's thinking and studies were greatly stimulated, and when in 1578 he was reassigned to serve as a prefect in remote Yunnan, it was a great hardship for him to leave Nanking.

But if this brought on a personal crisis for him, such as Wang Yang-ming had experienced in the border region of Kweichou, for Li its resolution was of a different sort. Reduced to his essential self, Wang had discovered his moral identity with the uneducated or uncivilized men around him. His sympathies were enlarged, his effectiveness in dealing with men enhanced, and his mission of social and political action confirmed. For Li Chih, on the other hand, it brought a further withdrawal from the world, not into inactivity, but into an independent life of study and contemplation. At the end of his three-year term he resigned from official service.[178]

Without returning home, Li went to stay with the Keng brothers at Huang-an,[aj] in northeast Hu-kuang Province (modern Hupei). He preferred life as a house guest and family tutor to the social responsibilities and involvements that awaited him in Ch'üan-chou.[179] But a strain eventually developed in his intellectual and personal relations with Keng Ting-hsiang, partly owing to Li's belief that Keng, an influential official, had done all he could to save Ho Hsin-yin. Li moved out and took up residence in the Buddhist temple of Chih-fo yüan,[ak] at a lakeside retreat in the same county. He sent his wife and children home to Fukien, and, when a few years later he took the Buddhist tonsure, it signified as much as anything else his determination to make a complete break with family cares and social obligations.[180] Though not without some sympathy for his wife, he regretted that she was not more intellectually compatible, and in any case he wished to pursue his own interests unencumbered. Indeed, the expense he went to earlier in providing a suitable burial ground for his parents and grandparents is in striking contrast with his rather indifferent treatment of his immediate family.[181]

Li gave many different reasons for his decision to shave off his hair and become a monk, some of them perhaps only half serious and some apparently dubious rationalizations.[182] The most plausible is simply that he wished to escape the control of others and achieve a degree of personal freedom not possible for the layman. There can be no doubt of his serious interest in Buddhism, but he was as individualistic in this respect as in all others. In fact his desire "to be an individual" (*ch'eng i-ko-jen* [ad]) is given by Li as intimately involved in his decision to become a "monk." [183] Officially he was not a licensed monk, nor did he keep the monastic discipline. Instead he pursued even more intensively his scholarly interests. His friend and admirer Yüan Chung-tao [am] has described in detail his life in the temple, his devotion to his books, to his writing, and to a select group of friends with whom he kept up active intellectual relations. Yüan conceded that no one could hope to take Li as a master to follow, both because of his extreme idiosyncrasies and fastidiousness, and because of a capacity for scholarship no one else could match.[184]

Two years after becoming a "monk," in 1590, he published his *Fen-shu* [an] (A book to burn), the title of which acknowledged the dangerousness of its contents. It was a collection of letters, essays, prefaces, poems, etc., expressing his repudiation of traditional Confucian morality and Neo-Confucian philosophy, his belief in the essential identity of the Three Teachings, and his revolutionary views on history, literature, and a wide range of other subjects. He expected the book to be condemned as heresy and it was. But despite attacks upon it and mounting pressure against him, Li persisted in his course. He became even freer in his conduct, and though the charges of social and sexual misconduct made against him are undoubtedly exaggerated, he did not hesitate to relieve his intense scholarly efforts with pleasant diversions in and out of the temple.[185] Aware of the risks, and prepared for the most extreme persecution, he went ahead with the preparation of his voluminous study of Chinese history, the *Ts'ang-shu* ᵃᵒ (A book to be hidden away),[186] which was one long indictment of the Confucian record in public affairs. After its publication in 1600 a mob incited by local authorities burned down his residence at the temple, and he spent the remaining few years of his life taking refuge in the home of friend after friend in different places. Finally, in 1602, a memorial at the court in Peking charged him with a long list of offenses, and an edict was issued ordering his arrest and the burning of his books. In prison in Peking he made his last protest, committing suicide by slashing his throat.

INNOCENCE AND INTELLIGENCE

Li Chih was a passionate man, and he knew it. He had violent hatreds and unbounded enthusiasms. He said of himself that

his nature was narrow, his manner arrogant, his speech coarse, his mind mad, his conduct rash and imprudent. He did not mix much with others, but in peronal contacts could be warm and friendly. Towards others he was critical of their faults and little impressed with their good points: those he did not like he would have nothing to do with except wish them ill to his dying day.[187]

But if, in this self-characterization, he belligerently asserts his absolute independence of others, he was nonetheless a hero-worshiper. To him Wang Yang-ming and Wang Chi were sages, and Wang Ken was a hero followed by other heroes of the T'ai-chou school: Hsü Yüeh, Yen Chün, Chao Chen-chi, Lo Ju-fang ᵃᵖ and—greatest of them all—Ho Hsin-yin, the martyr to the Way, who was a "scholar for the whole world, a scholar for all ages." [188]

Li thus paid full tribute to those who inspired him, and there is no question of his debt to them: he clearly draws upon and carries forward some of the main ideas and tendencies generated within the Wang Yang-ming school.[189] On the other hand, since many of his attitudes must have been well formed by the time he came under their influence, the individuality of his thought is no less significant than his identification with any school. He does things with others' ideas which they had not done.

The first piece in Li's first published work, A Book To Burn, gives us a clue to this in a passage with a typically ironic touch:

Under Heaven there is no man in whom consciousness does not arise, no thing in which consciousness does not arise, no moment in which consciousness does not arise. Though some may be unconscious of it themselves, they can always be made conscious of it. It is only such things as earth, wood, tiles, and stones, which cannot be made conscious of it because they are unfeeling and cannot be communicated with, and there are also the wise and the foolish, who though not incapable of being made conscious of it, are difficult to communicate with precisely because they do have feelings. Excluding these two types, then even the different animals, in the depths of their suffering, can be reached and made conscious. . . .[190]

Some scholars see this as essentially a reformulation of Wang Yang-ming's innate knowledge, or have pointed to the classical source in the Mean (XX) of the term used by Li, sheng-chih,[aq] where it means "the knowledge one is born with." [191] In the Mean it signifies an awareness of human obligations, as innate knowledge does for Wang Yang-ming. But the chih here is the most generalized sort of consciousness, shared with other animate and even inanimate beings. It has no specific human or moral character. It is consciousness in the Buddhist sense, applicable to all sentient beings. This is clear from the continuation of the same passage, where Li says that the beings "can be made conscious, can be apprised of the way to Buddahood." "Those in whom consciousness has arisen are Buddhas; those in whom it has not are not yet Buddhas." [192]

This, then, is innate knowledge as mediated to Li through Wang Chi, and we recall that Li's introduction to the latter was simultaneous with his introduction to the Diamond Sutra. Innate knowledge as the transcendental perfection of Wang Chi was also, for Li, the Great Perfect Wisdom of the Prajñā Pāramitā:

All men possess the mirror of Great Perfect Wisdom (ta-yüan-ching chih [ar]), which is the "illustrious virtue" [of the Great Learning] shining within. It is one with Heaven above and Earth beneath, and with thousands of sages and worthies in between. They do not have more of it nor I less.[193]

In this apparent convergence of Confucian and Buddhist concepts, innate knowledge appears not in its moral aspect but in its universal and egalitarian aspect, which then combines with the undifferentiated consciousness of Mahāyāna Buddhism. One might interpret this process as showing the influence of Buddhist egalitarianism on Confucianism, but the interaction is mutual. In discussing the relative merits of Ch'an meditation and the invocation of Amitābha as a means of salvation, Li disputes the view of some Ch'anists that the former is higher and the latter lower, and he uses a typically Neo-Confucian argument: "As heaven, earth, and I have the same root, who is superior to me? As all things form one body with me, who is not as good as I?" [194] From the process of equation and interaction, then, we must be careful to observe what actual meaning "equality" can have in this new and somewhat confusing context. Is Li able to derive from it a more profound and universal humanism?

One very active ingredient in Li's thinking is the notion of Yen Chün and Ho Hsin-yin (in whom it has no Buddhistic connotations) that man's nature is originally pure and one should follow wherever it spontaneously leads. Li develops its implications in his celebrated essay on the "Childlike Mind" (*T'ung-hsin*).[as 195] The childlike mind, he says, is originally pure, but it can be lost if received opinions come in through the senses and are allowed to dominate it. The greatest harm results when moral doctrines are imposed upon it, and the mind loses its capacity to judge for itself. This comes mainly from reading books and learning "moral principles." [196]

Once people's minds have been given over to received opinions and moral principles, what they have to say is all about these things, and not what would naturally come from their childlike minds. No matter how clever the words, what have they to do with oneself? What else can there be but phony men speaking phony words, doing phony things, writing phony writings? Once the men become phonies, everything becomes phony. Thereafter if one speaks phony talk to the phonies, the phonies are pleased; if one does phony things as the phonies do, the phonies are pleased; and if one discourses with the phonies through phony writings, the phonies are pleased. Everything is phony, and everyone is pleased.[197]

Moreover, says Li, the phonies have seen to it that the best in literature was destroyed.

This was because the best in literature always came from the childlike mind, and if the childlike mind continued to exist in this way, moral principles would not be practiced, received impressions would not stand up, and the writing of any age, any man, any form, any style, and any language would all be accepted as literature.[198]

From this Li proceeds to argue against adherence to classical literary canons, and in favor of accepting the literature of every age as having its own value. Further to establish his point, he even calls into question the authenticity of the Confucian Classics as authoritative sources of the Sage's teachings. Indeed one may say without exaggeration that Li Chih anticipates in the sixteenth century the criticisms of the classical Confucian tradition which erupted in the twentieth century during the so-called New Culture movement, and like the modern reformers Li contributed significantly to the promotion of a contemporary vernacular literature in his own day, especially through his editing of The Water Margin (Shui-hu chuan).[199]

While arguing for a more spontaneous and less moralistic or rationalistic literature, however, Li is not necessarily anti-intellectual in his attitude. It was frequently charged against the T'ai-chou school and the so-called Wild Ch'an movement that they neglected book learning and scholarship. To some extent this may have been true. Ch'an itself is anti-intellectual to the extent that its spiritual training demands a thorough process of intellectual demolition and cultural de-conditioning. And though Li described himself as a skeptic from his youth, it is not unlikely that Ch'an irreverence toward scripture contributed to his debunking of the Confucian Classics. Still, even in the monastery Li devoted himself to scholarship, not Ch'an training. Moreover, what makes his attitude unorthodox or "wild" even as Ch'an Buddhism is his positive endorsement of the literature of the emotions, of a heroic and passionate approach to life. Thus for him The Water Margin and similar works of vernacular fiction were justified, not merely as harmless diversions but as exemplifications of heroic virtue in the common man and indeed as serious works of importance even to government.[200]

Li makes no pretense that the ancient sages did without books. Others might be corrupted by book learning, but the sages, "even when they did read many books, did so in such a way as not to lose their childlike minds." [201] Nor does Li's attack on artificiality involve a wholesale repudiation of culture. He does not pine nostalgically for a primitive, uncomplicated past, nor does he see all art, artifice, and technology as alien to man. Art and inspiration in the genuine sense are complementary.[202] And even ritual or decorum (*li*) has its natural place. The criterion is whether or not it is a spontaneous expression of inner feelings.

What comes forth from within may be called decorum; what comes from without is not decorum. What comes without studying, deliberation, premeditation, effort, intellection, or knowledge is called decorum; what comes through the eyes and ears, deliberation and calculation; what involves talk first and action later, or is based on some comparison with others, is not decorum.[203]

A NEW LOOK AT HUMAN RELATIONS

It is from this standpoint that Li undertakes a reevaluation of human relations and human morality. We have seen his comment on Ho Hsin-yin that "of the five human relations [as defined in Confucian tradition] he abandoned all but one—the relation of friend and friend." But Li proceeds to a more fundamental reexamination of all five relations than had been attempted by anyone before, and against the background of social change in the sixteenth century we can appreciate how he anticipated the modern dilemma of Confucianism: how can a moral philosophy based essentially on human relations survive in a world of rapid social change and mobility?

Many of Li's writings reflect his critical attitude on this question, but one devoted solely to an extensive treatment of it is the *Ch'u-t'an chi*.[at] Significantly, its general introduction discusses the primacy of the husband-wife relationship in an unusually abstract manner for Li, and has a philosophical importance transcending the concrete relationship. In effect, Li argues that the genesis of all human life—indeed of all life—depends upon the male-female relationship; all other relations derive from this because procreation is their precondition. On the moral level Li thus disputes the usual primacy given to the parent-child or ruler-subject relation which tend to exemplify a patriarchal or a paternalistic system, and stresses a relationship of equality or complementarity. Further, on the basis of the irreducibility of the male and female principles represented by yin and yang, Li denies the existence of any first principle at all. Most particularly he rejects any monism based on the Neo-Confucian concepts of the Supreme Ultimate (*t'ai-chi*) or principle (*li*).[204]

Two things stand out here. One is Li's attack on the rationalistic-moralistic mentality of the Neo-Confucians as represented by the concept of "principle." He seems to sense that male dominance in society is linked to the whole system of moral principles embodying that mentality. On the other hand, he is not wholly antirationalist. For him the intuitive mentality, represented by the female, is complementary to the rational mentality, as represented by the male, but—in a separate letter discussing male-female equality—he insists that the difference between the sexes is only one of degree, and that each possesses both types of intelligence, which each should be allowed to develop.[205]

The second point is the manner in which Li makes a philosophical issue of the question in his general introduction. Taking the contents of the *Ch'u-t'an chi* as a whole, little space is actually devoted to the husband-wife relationship (four chapters or *chuan*) and only ten altogether to the three relationships within the family, whereas the remaining two relations—between teachers and friends, and rulers and ministers—occupy twenty chapters. If then he has less practical interest in the familial relations than in the broader social ones, it seems clear that his interest in the male-female relation is of another sort. In fact, his final argument goes beyond both Neo-Confucian morality and metaphysics and any possible alternative to them. "I speak only of the duality of male and female, not of the 'One' or of 'Principle.' And if I speak not of the One, how much less would I speak of Nothingness; and if not of Nothingness, how much less of No-Nothingness." [206] In other words, beyond the cosmogonic dualism of male and female nothing whatever can be predicated, and Li therefore feels no urge to construct a new metaphysics of his own. Though it has definite overtones of Chuang Tzu and the Madhyamika dialectic of negation, this attitude also may be linked to the rising antimetaphysical temper of the fifteenth and sixteenth centuries. Li Chih, from his Ch'an monastery, sounds the death knell of metaphysics in the Ming.[207]

Generally speaking, in his discussion of human relationships Li attached the greatest importance to the relation of friendship, which for him tended to supersede all others. In other words, when speaking about Ho Hsin-yin in this regard, he was also speaking for himself. At the same time, however, there is a noticeable disillusionment even with the possibilities of true friendship. The fate of Ho himself, abandoned by his friends, is much in Li's mind. Moreover, a true, like-minded friend, though dearer than a kinsman, is extremely rare. Confucius searched all over and found only one, Yen Hui.[208] And if in the end the relation of friendship cannot be depended upon, the individual is thrown back entirely on his own resources. Li is therefore compelled to probe more deeply into the whole basis of human nature and the nature of the individual. How could one still hold to Confucius' ideal: to be a man among men?

THE IMPORTANCE OF BEING SELFISH

Li Chih's discussion of human nature is premised on the uniqueness of the individual and the necessity above all for being onself. "Each man Heaven gives birth to has his own individual function and he does not need to learn this from Confucius. If he did need to learn it from Confucius, then in all the ages before Confucius could no one have achieved real manhood?" [209] Indeed, even Confucius had not taught men to study Confucius, but had taught them to look within themselves. And since people differ in their capacities, they should not all be made to conform to the same pattern. "What people consider right and wrong can never serve as a standard for me. Never from the start have I taken as right and wrong for myself what the world thinks right and wrong." [210]

To others Li's stubborn independence seemed the most willful egotism and he was urged to have a greater respect for the feelings and opinions of others, to follow the example of the sage-king Shun, who was said to have "given up his own view and followed that of others," thus ruling according to the wishes of his people.[211] But to Li this makes little sense. How can one yield one's own opinion to that of others? In the final analysis, even if one yields, it must represent what one chooses to do and depends on knowing what one really wants. Yielding by itself solves nothing. If, whenever there was a conflict of wills or opinions, the rule were always to yield, everyone would have to accept the opposing opinion and the conflict would remain unresolved. Thus a solution can be found only by transcending the dichotomy of self and other, through a deeper understanding of what is common to the self and others. "Not to know onself and yet to speak of yielding one's opinion to others, not to know men and yet speak of following them—is it any wonder that each holds to his own opinion and will not yield, is stubborn and will not follow?" [212]

Another common idea among Neo-Confucians was "having no mind [of one's own]." [213] This notion came from Ch'eng Hao, and meant achieving a state of mind in which one has no self-conscious intent or ulterior motive in doing good. For Li this is the worst self-deception. "Selfishness is the mind-and-heart of man. Men must be selfish so that what is in their minds can be made known. If there is no selfishness, there is no mind." [214] Even to desire rectitude is a matter of self-interest. Thus the Way is made manifest through the desires of individuals to achieve something for themselves. "If I do not seek to achieve anything for myself, how and when will the Way be made manifest?" [215]

Li goes on further to develop Wang Ken's idea that the people's daily needs are the very substance of the Way. When Shun inquired into the desires of the people as a basis for his rule, he learned about

their desire for goods, for sexual satisfaction, for study, for personal advancement, for the accumulation of wealth; their desire to buy lands and homes for the sake of their posterity; their seeking out of the proper geomantic factors (*feng-shui*)[au] that will bring blessings to their children —all [of] the things which are productive and sustain life in the world, everything which is loved and practiced in common by the people, and what they know and say in common. . . .[216]

In this Li finds a new basis for human relations: "To wear clothing and eat food—these are the principles of human relations. Without them there are no human relations. . . . The scholar should learn only what is real and unreal in respect to these relations, and not impose other principles of human relations on top of them." [217]

The essential thing in social relations is to let people satisfy their own desires, to let them find their own natural place in the world.

Men have always found their own natural place [when left alone]. If they do not it is only because they are harassed by those who are greedy and aggressive and harmed by humanitarians (*jen-che*).[av] The humanitarians worry about everyone finding his place in the world, and so they have virtue and decorum to correct people's minds, and the state with its punishments to fetter their limbs. Then people begin to lose their place in a big way! [218]

THE INDIVIDUAL IN HISTORY

Li devoted the last years of his life to the massive study called *Ts'ang-shu* (A book to be hidden away), in which he attempted a re-evaluation of historical personages whom he thought Confucian historians had misjudged because of their moralistic biases. Or, to put it more accurately, whom he thought that earlier historians had failed really to judge.

For over eleven hundred years there have been no real judgments of right and wrong. Could there, then, have been no right and wrong among men? [No], it was because they all accepted what they thought to be Confucius' judgments as to right and wrong, and never had any right or wrong of their own. . . . Now the conflict of right and wrong is like the passing of the years and the seasons, or the alternation of night and day, which cannot be reduced to one. Yesterday's right is today's wrong. Today's wrong is right again tomorrow. Even if Confucius reappeared today, there is no way of knowing how he would judge right and wrong. So how can we arbitrarily judge everything as if there were a fixed standard? [219]

Just as in the case of literature each age has its own characteristics, so in history each age has its own conditions and needs. The achievement of the individual must be judged in each context. Although Li has his own view of the pattern of history, moving in cycles of roughness and refinement somewhat similar to those of the Arab historian Ibn Khaldun, it serves mainly to differentiate the kind of "morality" appropriate to each age. Nothing is so vain as trying to preach frugality in an age of luxury, or expecting cultural refinements and gentlemanly conduct in a desperate and disordered age.[220]

What standards, then, can be applied to such different situations? Basically it is a question of how one applies ordinary intelligence to provide for the security and material welfare of the people. In a letter to a friend Li says, "My book is [intended] for the achieving of peace and order throughout the ages." [221] To accomplish this, different talents and capabilities must be employed for different purposes; there is no single model for all of the wise and virtuous minister. Weak rulers and strong have different needs; the former require strong ministers, the latter able and talented ones. Some ages call for strong, activist policies, others for the laissez-faire approach. But always there must be a realistic attention to the uses of power. This Confucian ministers have been largely incapable of, mainly because they have neglected military affairs and considered it a virtue to confine themselves to civil administration and the polite arts. Though committed to the business of government, they are largely unfit to govern. "Again and again, though they have the capability of doing something, they are unwilling to exert their full efforts to achieve it, so worried are they lest others suspect them of seeking wealth, power, fame, or gain for themselves." [222]

In A Book To Be Hidden Away, despite the perverse delight Li Chih gets from exposing the failures of Confucian moralism, he is still very much the moralist himself, judging men in history. Some people have questioned whether Li can be considered a philosopher in the usual sense, and histories of Chinese philosophy barely mention him, if at all. But if he foreswears metaphysics and moral philosophy, he nevertheless writes as a moralist and critic.

Carsun Chang describes Li as "primarily a literary man," [223] and yet we find that he left no literary work of great distinction. This makes it all the more significant that so much of Li's writing should be in an historical vein. Whether he would qualify strictly as an historian is another question, but Li obviously still shares the Confucian belief that history provides the ultimate ground for verifying essential truths. Thus for him the written record and the right kind of book learning are of real importance. There is, as we have already indicated, much more of the scholar and intellectual in him than earlier thinkers of his school, who had virtually set aside scholarly study and cultural pursuits in order to assert the primacy of moral man and the demands of humanitarian activism.

Li is still heir to Wang Yang-ming and the ground has been prepared for him by the subjectivistic and pragmatic tendencies in the School of the Mind. Moreover, he is to some degree still moved by its spirit of activism in the pursuit of human welfare. But new and different uses have been found by him for the realistic criticism which his predecessors had directed at the cultural man. By this time the undermining of tradition has gone so far that even traditional morality can be called into question. All the moral values which Wang Yang-ming had so easily assumed were written on the heart of the essential man can now be re-examined in the light of reason and history. If culture must submit to moral judgment, so must morality submit to historical judgment.

Thus the scholarship which not long before had been deprecated within the Wang Yang-ming school has reappeared to haunt those who believed that morality could dispense with culture. This, in fact, is what makes Li Chih so dangerous a revolutionary. Though he was attacked for turning to Ch'an Buddhism, had he really disappeared into the silence of Ch'an meditation, Confucians would have had little to worry about from him. It was precisely his scholarship and his extensive use of history that made Li a more formidable antagonist, and at the same time a seemingly more traitorous and treacherous one, than any ordinary bonze could have been.

THE FAILURE OF HUMANITARIANISM

If Li Chih is a "realist," however, one still could not mistake him for a dispassionate scholar or objective historian. He is too embittered and vindictive for that. Indeed it is here that he seems almost a classic case of alienation from his whole society and culture. That he is disillusioned with official life is not surprising, nor is his rejection of all formal tradition. What really strikes us is his disillusionment even with the kind of moralism and humanitarianism that has emerged from the Wang Yang-ming school.

Li did not believe that morality could be taught. "Confucius, in his teaching of men, taught them only to seek humanity [within themselves]. If they sought it and failed to achieve it, that was that— nothing more could be said." [224] As regards the various virtues, these too could only develop naturally and spontaneously. It was all a matter of self-confidence and self-fulfillment. But now those who promote "lecturing" or "learning by discussion" (chiang-hsüeh [aw]) "think they can teach filiality, brotherliness, loyalty, and good faith by talking about them. This can only do great harm to people's natures." [225]

Li still had great admiration for some of the individual members of the T'ai-chou school, like Lo Ju-fang, who went out among the people but did not "preach" to them.[226] But, as we have seen, he had a strong aversion from the start to the kind of group philosophical discussion developed within the Wang Yang-ming school, and refused to attend such meetings. He showed great inner resistance to any moral pressure or any effort to "organize" him. It was apparent too that for him scholarship and book learning in private took priority over public discussion. But on top of this Li developed a disgust with anything that took the form of a "school," of a teacher with a following, of a group that wants to organize for political action. Undoubtedly, his own experience with Keng Ting-hsiang had much to do with this, as well as his bitterness over the fate of Ho Hsin-yin. In his eulogy and lament for the latter he castigated the "lecturers" (chiang-hsüeh che) for their failure to lift a finger to save Ho, and one of their great leaders, Keng, he charges with the worst hypocrisy.[227]

In Li's scathing attacks on these "hypocrites" one can see what has become of the grand humanitarian slogans of Wang Yang-ming and Wang Ken.

If there is something to be gained by it and they want to take charge of public affairs, then the "lecturers" will cite the saying that "all things are one body" [and it is their duty to serve mankind]; if they stand to lose by it, however, and they wish to avoid blame and censure, then they invoke the saying "The clearest wisdom is self-preservation" [in order to withdraw from threatening danger].[228]

Or again:

In ordinary times when there is peace, they only know how to bow and salute one another, or else they sit the day long in an upright posture [practicing quiet-sitting] like a clay image, thinking that if they can suppress all stray thoughts they will become sages and worthies. The more cunning among them participate in the meetings to discuss innate knowledge, secretly hoping to gain some recognition and win high office. But when a crisis comes, they look at each other pale and speechless, try to shift the blame to one another, and save themselves on the pretext that "the clearest wisdom is self-preservation." Consequently, if the state employs only this type of scholar, when an emergency arises it has no one of any use in the situation.[229]

Of their activities as teachers, he says the "lecturers" gather crowds of followers and take in students

to enhance their own name and fame and make themselves rich and honored, not realizing that Confucius never sought wealth or honors or to surround himself with disciples. . . . But the teachers of today—one day out of office and their disciples abandon them; one day without funds and their followers scatter.[230]

Again and again Li mocks the moralistic pretensions of those who preach the Way but have "their hearts set on high office and the acquisition of wealth." [231] He compares them with a type of literary man whom he considers equally "phony"—the so-called mountain-men (*shan-jen*)[ax] who affect the independence and eccentricity of artists and poets who live alone in the midst of nature.

Those who consider themselves sages today are no different from the mountain-men—it is all a matter of luck. If it is a man's luck that he can compose poetry he calls himself a "mountain-man"; if it is not and he cannot compose poetry and become a mountain-man, he calls himself a "sage." If it is a man's luck that he can lecture on "innate knowledge," he calls himself a "sage," but if it is not and he is unable to lecture on innate knowledge, he gives up being a sage and calls himself a "mountain-man." They turn around and reverse themselves in order to deceive the world and secure their own gain. They call themselves "mountain-men" but their hearts are those of the merchants. Their lips are full of the Way and virtue, but their ambition is to become "thieves of virtue." (*Analects* XVII, 13)

Those who call themselves "mountain-men," if considered as merchants would not be worth one copper cash and without the protection of high officials would be despised among men. And how do I know that I am any better? Who knows but that I too have the heart of a merchant and have put on Buddhist robes just to deceive people and make use of the name? [232]

Whatever people may think, says Li, at least he will have had the satisfaction that, by becoming a "monk," he will have spared himself worry over the acquisition of wealth and the danger of losing it, the buying of lands and houses, getting the right geomantic factors, etc., which other people trouble themselves with.

That the scholar-officials are worse than merchants and no better than cheats is a constant refrain in Li's writing. Outwardly they are sages, inwardly merchants. But the merchants in their business dealings could never compete with the scholar-officials, who are masters in the business of selling out dynasties, sacrificing rulers on the altar of the sage and then carrying their heads into the market place.[233]

One might indeed believe that Li Chih has the "heart of a merchant" if some contemporary writers are right in saying that Li's satirizing of the scholar-officials shows a sympathy for the merchants and reflects a "rising bourgeois capitalist spirit." [234] That he has such a sympathy is quite evident, especially in a passage which has been cited from a letter of Li to Chiao Hung wherein he expresses his compassion for the merchant who "is burdened with heavy loads, runs great risks and braves many dangers, endures many humiliations from the tax officers and insults in the market place. . . ." [235] What Li describes here, however, has been the typical lot of the Chinese merchant throughout history, and Li goes on in the same passage [236] to make clear that the condition he describes is of a depressed, not a "rising," bourgeoisie. For all their pains, he says, the merchants' gain is slight. They have to curry favor and enter into collusion with high officials to make even a little profit. They are despised as "profit-seekers," simply for seeking honest gain, while the scholars and poets, who are just as mercenary and less productive, sit with the high and mighty and thereby avoid all danger and harm.[237] Surely if this is the capitalism for which Li is cast as a spokesman, it is what Shimada has called, following Weber, "pariah capitalism." [238]

THE IDEALIST AND THE TOTALITARIAN

What we actually face here is an unresolved conflict between Li's philosophy of self-interest and his remaining Confucian idealism. Though he accepts self-interest and the laws of the market place as governing the dealings of most men, true sagehood of the kind that Confucius represented is a different matter; it is a priceless commodity which can be obtained only by total self-dedication.[239] There is no room for self-seeking here, only for self-sacrifice. Thus commercialism or the profit motive are things to be decried, not accepted or endorsed, when found in the Confucian scholar-official or moralist. They are a betrayal of the high idealism of Confucius.

Truly the strain is beginning to show, in the humanitarianism of the T'ai-chou school, between its belief that every man is a ready-made sage and its ideal of the "great man" who serves the welfare of the common man while preserving a lofty detachment himself. At heart Li is still deeply moved by that ideal, yet he is also shocked by the discrepancy between the ideal and the actuality as revealed in the self-professed "sages" around him. The latter stand in obvious contradiction to both these articles of the T'ai-chou faith. Sagehood is not all that easy to find or attain.

Whether Li is really conscious of this dilemma is difficult to say. Rather than face it, he prefers to denounce the "phony" sages as the source of all evil. How they have fallen into this state of utter depravity we are not told. In Li's sight they have become almost "non-men" or "non-people," but in the fundamentally Confucian sense that, not being humane, they have ceased to be human. As such, they are virtually deprived of any right to sympathy or the benefit of the doubt as to their intentions. Thus, to sustain his ever-narrowing but all the more intense idealism, to preserve his faith in the goodness of human nature so widely proclaimed by the T'ai-chou school in the face of the movement's moral degeneration, Li must attack and destroy the "hypocrites" who have betrayed the cause. But in destroying the "pharisees" with such demonic fury and savage wit, does not Li himself verge on a new phariseeism? Is not his self-righteousness more than a match for theirs?

To answer this question, or even to understand it better, we must first consider what happens to the common man at Li's hands. He becomes, really, two things. As one, he remains the naturally good man of Wang Ken and the rest, with emphasis on his biological self, his innate intelligence, and (with Li) his Buddha-consciousness. As the other, he is man subject to illusion, constantly falling victim to the hypocrites and moralists. It is only in some such terms that one may explain how every man can be a sage or possess the Buddha-nature, how "the streets are full of sages," and yet the sage turns out to be such a rare and lonely figure. Li says, "Confucius spoke of the noble man (*chün tzu*) being 'unaffected even though men take no note of him' (*Analects* I, 1). By men he means the common man. It is because the common man does not know me that I can be called a 'noble man.' If the common man knew me, I too would be a common man and no more." [240] The common man in this sense is obviously not the sage, but his direct antithesis. And elsewhere Li indicates that the noble man, like the Bodhisattva, has superior knowledge. Though all men have the capability for enlightenment, few attain it. [241]

The susceptibility of the ordinary man to prevailing opinion and conventional conduct also explains why one cannot actually look for sages among them, but must look for heroes—men who are wild and impetuous and ready to break the bonds of convention. Confucius, he says, set a high value on true humanity; unable to find heroes, he was "unwilling to sell himself cheap." [242] As for the majority of men, Li comes to doubt that they are any better than beasts. [243] He cannot even call them dogs—that would be unfair to the dog, who like man possesses the Buddha-nature but unlike man is capable of some loyalty.

Against this background we may better understand the significance of Li's political views. With his admiration for political realists goes also his pessimism about the judgment of ordinary men in political matters. He retains his faith in the ordinary man's ability to take care of his own affairs, and from that standpoint the problem of government is simply to provide conditions in which the individual can take care of himself. But this responsibility Li is ready to leave to strong rulers, who will use power ruthlessly when necessary and in any case with utter realism and efficiency. Hence his great esteem for the Legalist statesmen and authoritarian rulers of the past; hence his description of the first emperor of the Ch'in—the bane of all Confucians for his totalitarian policies—as the "greatest emperor of all time" and of Emperor Wu of Han—who emphasized military power and strong state control over the economy—as "the greatest sage of all time." [244]

Thus, for all his radical individualism, Li extends the rights or functions of the individual into politics only insofar as a few exceptional individuals may display their rare talents in ruling over the masses. The latter, he agreed with Lao Tzu, are better off completely ignorant of state policy and innocently unaware of what the ruler is doing, except that he makes their lives secure and their bellies full. To Li the one thing most needful for this is military power, and after that, for the people to know only what will bring certain rewards and inescapable punishment.[245]

Given Li's historical relativism, one must allow for the fact that he will not commit himself to one type of rule in all circumstances. Further, if we grant that in the transcendent freedom of his Buddhist enlightenment he remains forever uncommitted to any particular political philosophy, one may hesitate to call him a totalitarian. Yet it is evident that, while denying the moral constants of traditional Confucianism, he is not unwilling to generalize rather broadly about the constant power factors in human society, and to see biological man as best served by a powerful state.

Some have wondered how the gentle mysticism of Lao Tzu could have been appropriated so readily by the early Legalists and made to serve as a mystique of state power. Li Chih shows how tempting it is for the frustrated idealist, the believer in the natural goodness of man, to strike a bargain with the totalitarian, thinking that somehow the latter's realism will dispose of the messy human complications that prevent the fulfillment of his dream. Anarchism only needs a capable sponsor. And if Li's view of history does not enable him to envisage the "withering away of the state," his hatred and contempt of the moralists is enough to persuade him that in most ages the individual is better off with the despot than with the preacher or teacher.

THE MONK, THE MAN, AND THE MARTYR

For Li Chih as an individual, however, this still does not solve the problem entirely. He himself will be no statesman or general. A sage, perhaps, but no sage-king. His destiny is to be a hero. And if he has forsworn moral philosophy, the hero nevertheless carries with him a heavy moral burden—the psychological cost of having broken with his Confucian past and turned his back on his own class, the ruling elite. Though emancipated from tradition, he is still the servitor of a Confucian conscience which demands justification and vindication before his enemies. As the hero who has cut himself off from all the sources of power and influence, and as the sage who will not compromise with a corrupt world, he has sought the sanctuary of a monastery and shaved his head. But whatever freedom he has found there has not released him from his own inner compulsions.

Most modern writers, hero-worshipers no less than Li, have been loath to speak about him as a Buddhist and a Confucian. To them, he is a completely emancipated individual who has risen above all sectarianism and achieved heroic stature in a wider world. He has taken what was best in the Three Teachings, their common human denominator, and forged it into a philosophy for the modern man. As regards his "Buddhism" or "Confucianism" one need not probe too deeply into what, after all, he himself has discarded or transcended.

There is truth in this, as we have said: he was as individualistic in his "Buddhism" as in his "Confucianism." But if we assume that his becoming a "monk" is purely a matter of personal convenience and not at all a matter of conviction, we fail to reckon with the serious interest in Buddhism undeniably manifest in his writings. On the other hand, we must, if we take him as a genuine monk, confront the fact that he devoted his last years to scholarly work as if his salvation depended on it, and said that he was ready to be judged in history on the basis of his final work, A Book To Be Hidden Away, which is exclusively concerned with history and politics.[246] This in turn may seem to suggest that, after all, he was really more of a Confucian than anything else, a view which gains apparent support from the title of one of his essays: "The Three Teachings Converge in Confucianism."

Our concern here being with Li as an individualist who plainly had no use for orthodoxy, we do not pursue the matter as a question of his being one thing more than another. The essay just mentioned, however, throws some light on the enigma of Li Chih himself. The

Three Teachings are one, he says, because they all originate in the expectation of "hearing the Way." Confucius said that "if he could hear the Way in the morning, he could die content in the evening" (*Analects* IV, 8). Being bent on this alone, and unready to die until he had heard it, "he looked on wealth and rank as fleeting clouds and renounced the empire as if he were throwing away an old shoe." The Taoist, for his part, looks on wealth and rank as so much manure, and the Buddhist, as a snare and a trap through which man suffers a painful life and a painful death. The Three Teachings are thus one in their transcendence of the world and differ only in the degree of their contempt for it.[247]

The essential unity of the Three Teachings is then "their seeking for the Way in order to be delivered from this world, for only by escaping the world can they avoid the sufferings of wealth and rank." [248] Even in Confucius' time it was evident that most men, and even most of his disciples, could not match Confucius' dedication to the Way, and though Li goes on to detail the stages in the degeneration of the true teaching, it had been inevitable that the educated class would be corrupted by wealth and rank. There is nothing really strange in things' having deteriorated to the point reached in his own time, when scholars "outwardly pursue the Way but inwardly seek wealth and rank, dress themselves in Confucian robes but act like dogs and swine." [249]

Now, however, it has reached the point where no one can escape contamination. To succeed in the professedly Confucian world one must study moral philosophy, and even those who have no desire for wealth and rank, if they want to achieve anything in the world, cannot help getting involved in it. Consequently, concludes Li, for those who sincerely wish to study the Way in order to learn the essence of Confucianism, Buddhism, and Taoism and thus be delivered from the world, there is no alternative but to shave their heads and become monks.[250]

From this it is evident that the real essence of the Three Teachings is the heroic vocation pursued in a world of hopeless corruption and suffering—a strange combination of Confucian commitment to life and Buddhist pessimism concerning the world. And Li's withdrawal to the monastery is more than a convenient escape from the contamination of the world. It is his last desperate effort to reconcile the contradiction between his "realism" and his "idealism," between his philosophy of self-interest and his search for something holy, between his sanctioning of selfishness and his condemnation of the self-seeking moralists.

There are indications that in the monastery Li is somehow aware of and reconciled to the absurdity of his position. As was commonly the case in Chinese temples, the image of Confucius was worshiped in Li's along with other deities and Buddhas, and he comments:

People all think Confucius a sage and so do I. They all think Lao Tzu and Buddha are heretics and so do I. But people don't really know what sagehood and heterodoxy are. They have just heard so much about them from their parents and teachers. Nor do their parents and teachers really know what sagehood and heterodoxy are; they just believe what they hear from the scholars and elders. And the scholars and elders don't know either, except that Confucius said something about these things. But his saying "Sagehood—of that I am not capable" [as quoted in *Mencius* II A, 2] they take as just an expression of modesty, and when he spoke of "studying strange teachings [as] harmful" (*Analects* II, 16) they interpret this as referring to Taoism and Buddhism.

The scholars and elders have memorized these things and embroidered on them; parents and teachers have preserved and recited them, and children have blindly accepted them. . . . So today, though men have eyes, they do not use them. And what then about me? Do I dare use my eyes? I too follow the crowd and regard him as a sage, . . . I too follow the crowd in doing him honor at Chih-fo yüan.[251]

We have here the same sense of irony and absurdity found in the *Journey to the West* (or *Monkey*) by Wu Ch'eng-en, a contemporary of Li's who shares with him a fondness for the philosophy expressed in the Heart Sūtra.[252] But Wu's ironies and satire are most often gentle and compassionate. There is little of the bitterness and disillusionment that puts such a biting edge on Li's satire. Thus, if Li has achieved some self-transcendence in the monastery, at best he is still only a bodhisattva and not yet a Buddha. His Confucian karma has yet to spend itself before his final release from this world; his scholarly genius has yet to vindicate the renegade's rejection of his own class and abandonment of his family. Moreover, as a bodhisattva who shows compassion for the world essentially through the redemptive power of his enlightenment, he can now become a teacher to the world through his writings.

There is more than enough evidence in these writings to document his final view of life as a "sea of suffering," [253] and at the same time his conviction that the hero can triumph over this through his own martyrdom. Li's sympathies are strongly elicited by those who sacrifice themselves for a cause. He would wish them to be more realistic sometimes and not sacrifice themselves uselessly; also, as in the case of Fang Hsiao-ju in the early Ming, he would insist on distinguishing between simple martyrdom and actual political accomplishment.[254] But he pays loving tribute to Fang among three Ming martyrs whose writings he collected in a special anthology, entitled *San i-jen chi* (Works of three nonconformists). And in one of his essays he discusses five good ways to die, the best of which is to die a heroic death for a noble cause. It is a wasted death just to die at home in the bosom of one's family.[255] In death as in life there is nothing more worthwhile than to register one's protest and pour forth one's indignation against the evil in the world.[256] In one of his letters Li writes: "You can see that I have no fear of death, no fear of men, and that I have put no reliance in power and in influence. All men have just one death; you can't die twice!" [257]

CAUSE AND COUNTER-CAUSE

To what cause then did Li Chih die a martyr? Some might say to the cause of intellectual freedom. If so, they are putting it in modern Western terms and not those of Li himself. He has lived and died for the Way, which for him meant the cause of Truth. But "what is Truth?" Clearly his cause implies the affirmation of his own integrity as an individual and his faith in the ultimate victory of right over wrong. Yet it remains doubtful that he means to assert the equal right of all individuals to express themselves freely. In an abstract way he does believe that men should have the freedom to develop and express themselves with the least possible interference—Lao Tzu's freedom to be left alone. But in practice, as we have seen, he attaches no value to the general exercise of political freedom or pub-

lic discussion, and he applauds strong rulers who suppress such discussion. Moreover, he recognizes that the exercise of freedom by
some individuals will inevitably limit the freedom of others. As a
believer in the economic survival of the fittest, he expects that in-
equalities will necessarily result from difference in people's capabilities and the weak will be compelled to submit to the strong.[258] In
this light, then, we can say only that Li Chih died for his own
convictions, and not necessarily in the cause of intellectual freedom
for all.

The significance of Li's "martyrdom" must also be seen against
the background of the times. Among recent writers the view has
generally prevailed that Li's unconventionality and independence of
mind inevitably made him the object of remorseless attack by the
traditionalists, the ruling class ("feudalistic reactionaries" or entrenched bureaucrats, as you will), bigoted and hypocritical Confucianists—and so on down the list of those who could be identified
with the "establishment" and whose vested interests were threatened
by Li's revolutionary ideas. Moreover, his conduct "aroused a custom-
loving and conformist society to rise up and vilify him." [259]

Alongside such views one would have to put the comment of Li's
good friend and admirer Yüan Chung-tao, who, in a postface to a
1613 edition of Li's works, says: "When Cho-wu [Li Chih] was
arrested, there was some suppression of his books, but within a few
years they reappeared and circulated everywhere. In this one can see
how far the liberality of our dynasty towards its scholars exceeds that
of the Sung dynasty [which suppressed the works of Su Shih]." [260]

To the historian of the late Ming neither of these views adequately
represents the reality. In Yüan's statement there is no doubt some
calculated flattery. If the Ming had been as wholly liberal as he says,
he would not need to have said anything at all about the matter,
and Li Chih, instead of meeting so dramatic an end, would have had
to suffer the disappointment of dying a natural death in his own bed.
But of the two views Yüan's is certainly much closer to the truth.
The suppression of books in the late Ming was rarely so systematic
and prolonged as to be fully effective, and in any case Li's works
were quickly reprinted after his death. Yüan writes hardly more than
a decade after Li's demise and already Li's books are widely avail-

able. Many writers testify to their enormous popularity with all segments of the literate population.[261] A number found their way to
Japan and enjoyed a comparable popularity there. Indeed, so great
was his reputation and popularity that his name was attached to
many spurious works as a means of increasing sales.[262]

What really undid Li's reputation in the long run and deferred
for centuries the recognition he so confidently expected history to
bring, was in fact not the immediate smothering of his ideas and
destruction of his books by pharisaical censors, but their powerful
appeal to the taste for sensational and shocking literature among
the sophisticated reading public of the late Ming. This taste obviously extended to the ruling classes, for they comprised the majority
of literate persons. And if they delighted in Li's mordant wit and
unsparing ridicule of the Confucianists, his irreverence, disillusionment, and cynicism plainly reflected a deep deterioration of morale
and inner crisis within the ruling class itself.[263]

It was therefore not the conventionalism or the repressiveness of
late Ming society which undid Li Chih, but its decadence in the
eyes of the conquering Manchu dynasty, who did not wait long to
ban Li's books and enforce the ban with far more ruthless efficiency
than the Ming.[264] There is irony in this too, of course. For the
Ch'ing not only were masters in the art of governing through attrac-
tive rewards and unhesitating punishments, but they followed up
their military conquest with an administration which could hardly
be matched for its success in promoting the people's material welfare while sapping or suppressing all resistance among the educated
class. Li Chih would have found it hard to withhold his admiration.

But it would be misleading to imply that it was the Manchus who
really disposed of Li and his ideas. The real counterattack was
mounted by the scholars themselves, and among them men whose
reputation for intellectual integrity and moral courage is not easily
questioned. It is often said that Huang Tsung-hsi, Ku-Yen-wu,[ay] and
Wang Fu-chih [az] are the three leading thinkers and scholars of the
early Ch'ing period. Huang's attitude toward Li we have already
seen. Though probably the most objective of the early historians of
Ming thought, and certainly the most sympathetic in his approach

to it, his attitude toward Li is one of such profound hostility and resentment that he will not even dignify him with criticism.[265] Ku Yen-wu, on the other hand, devotes a section of his famous *Jih-chih lu* [ba] to Li and the corrupting influence of Ch'an and the left wing of the Wang Yang-ming school on public morality and the civil service in the late Ming. To him there had never been anyone in Chinese history so shameless and so audacious as Li in his rebellion against Confucian teaching.[266] Wang Fu-chih, though sharing many of Li's "progressive" views in philosophy, history, and politics, and notably his kind of quasi materialism, nevertheless reacted in horror to Li's total abandonment of moral standards. He describes him as a man who has lost all conscience, and says that Li's Book To Be Hidden Away has done incalculable harm.[267]

None of these judgments can be dismissed as simply conventional or unthinking. Huang, Ku, and Wang had maintained their complete intellectual independence of the Ch'ing establishment, refusing to serve the new dynasty, and it is much more likely that their own views on Li influenced the official one rather than the other way around.[268] Moreover, Wang cut himself off from the world far more than did Li.[269] To him it is Li who took the conventional path, who "followed the crowd," "catered to human passions," and made no distinction between legitimate and illegitimate, noble and base desires.[270]

These judgments reflect, in fact, a reaction already fully apparent in the late Ming dynasty. If Li's writings were widely read in the early seventeenth century, there were important segments of the scholarly community who saw Li's influence as a great danger to the whole social and moral fabric of Chinese life. These were men who took an active role in the political life of the time, and are important not because of their identification with the "establishment," but because as reformers they spoke out vigorously and courageously against the political corruption at court as well as the moral decadence within the educated classes. I refer, of course, to the Tung-lin [bb] school and party, and to colleagues of theirs like Liu Tsung-chou,[bc] the teacher of Huang Tsung-hsi. Although they tended to be wary of the cult of "heroism," because they associated it with opportunism, they too were great enemies of cant, conventionalism, and hypocrisy.[271] Many of them paid with their lives in Ming prisons for the courage of their convictions, as did Huang's own father.[272]

Since these were men of great courage and fierce dedication, it is perhaps understandable that their judgment of Li Chih was no less moralistic than his was of others. It became a "cause" with them to subdue the heresy of Li's moral spontaneity. Shih Meng-lin [bd] wrote:

Today the leaders of "philosophical discussion" (*chiang-hsüeh*) and education generally direct scholars to "live in the present." This is most solid advice. But if you ask how, they say it is like eating when hungry or sleeping when tired; one does these things naturally and spontaneously, completely without exertion. . . . [However] to give rein to one's feelings and lusts—so interpreted, "living in the present" becomes a deep pit to ensnare people. . . .

When Li Cho-wu [Li Chih] discoursed in Nanking on the philosophy of the mind, all his directions to his pupils consisted of "living in the present" and "spontaneity." He said that every man is a ready-made sage. When anyone spoke about loyal, chaste, filial, or righteous people, he said that all this was artificial. . . . The students were pleased by this easy formula and flocked to him like mad. . . . Therefore, not to recognize that "living in the present" truly means for the student to take up the immediate moral task is to cast men into a deep pit.[273]

A similar view is expressed by Tsou Shan,[274] of the moderate wing of the Wang Yang-ming school. When asked about the great popularity of Li Chih, he explained that according to Li "the desires for wine, sex, money, and power do not block the road to Buddhahood. Who would not want to follow someone who sanctioned such things?" [275]

The official indictment against Li had accused him of, among other things, disporting himself with worthless fellows and lewd women in the temple, bathing with them in broad daylight, and corrupting nuns and the wives and daughters of the gentry, who slept there with him.[276] Some of the charges have been discredited, and others are no doubt exaggerated.[277] At his age Li could never have written so many books had he engaged in that much dissipation. Yet Li himself made no pretense of following monastic discipline, and might not have considered it a favor to be exonerated of the charge if it meant that he was prepared to abide by such strict standards. Yüan Chung-tao, in his sympathetic portrait of Li, says,

"He had nothing much to do with music or women and little use for love and lust, and yet when his mood was so disposed and his affections aroused, he would enjoy to the fullest the company of some boy or girl amidst the flowers and the moonlight, as if to embellish his solitary existence." [278]

Li's attitude, then, was probably not too different from that of the Japanese monk Kenkō, who had a reputation as a "sexy monk" (*iro bōshi*),[bf] and whose *Tsurezuregusa* [bg] expresses a similarly epicurean attitude toward sexual indulgence, though Li's was probably more earthy and less refined.[279] In any case Li's commentary on the Heart Sūtra shows that, in principle, he did believe as Tsou Shan said that the passions are no obstacle to Buddahood, because they are in themselves empty. The enlightened one knows that the passions are no different from emptiness, and that there is no emptiness apart from the passions. Since he has no attachments, indulgence leaves on him no stain of sin. "There is no impurity in the passions; no purity in emptiness." [280] As a deep student of the Prajñā pāramitā literature, Li no doubt derives this view from Nāgārjuna's *Ta chih-t'u lun* [bh] (Treatise on the great perfect wisdom) which provides the scriptural basis for the doctrine that "Lustful desires are identical with the Way" (*yin-yü chi-shih tao*),[bi] [281] from which developed the saying that "the passions are enlightenment [or Buddahood] (*fan-nao chi p'u-t'i*)" [bj] [282]

That Li Chih took the full freedom which such a doctrine might allow is indicated by the criticism of him which came even from within Buddhist circles. The monk Chu-hung, whose approach to the unity of the Three Teachings reflects more the moral dynamism of the Wang Yang-ming school than the affirmation of man's physical and appetitive nature,[283] has these things to say about Li:

I respect Li Chih's superior talents and heroic spirit, but if I respect them I also have my regrets. For a man to have such great talents and spirit and yet not take the sages' teaching as a guide or traditional norms as a foundation, for him not to govern these powers with virtue and magnanimity or to restrain them with caution meant inevitably that his talk about "shocking the world in order to reform evil customs" would be only a matter of self-indulgence.[284]

Given the severity of Li's judgments on worthy men of the past, says Chu-hung, it was inevitable that "the fire he set should eventually burn him too." [285] He did not keep to the hills and forests, but enjoyed himself in the towns and cities." [286] Li's unrestrained actions and wild talk violated the norms of Buddhism. "A monk should think of his obligation to the state and not flout its laws. . . . To kill such a criminal is not contrary to the precepts of Buddhism." [287]

Chu-hung's stern repudiation of Li Chih is almost matched by the Ts'ao-tung sect monk Yüan-hsien,[bk] who accused Li Chih of "pursuing the Way through the passions. He never failed to indulge his passions. No matter how wide his learning became, nor how broad his knowledge grew, his egotism only thrived the more." [288]

In the light of these statements Li Chih's "cause" and the reaction it evoked cannot be interpreted in relation to traditional Confucianism alone, or to established convention, or to the Ming-Ch'ing "establishment." The individualism of which he is the final and most extreme expression arose as one tendency within the optimistic humanitarianism of the T'ai-chou school. It generated enthusiasm and energy from the fact that it appealed to common elements in the Three Teachings, and yet it also tended to generate a common reaction within at least two of them, Confucianism and Buddhism. The point of original convergence had been the goodness of human nature, a persistent belief of the Chinese [289] but intensified at this moment by the almost ecstatic view of this-worldly salvation which was such a powerful element in Ming thought. The exaltation of self and of the individual, based on the belief in every man's potentiality for sagehood, drew some of its plausibility from the Mahāyāna Buddhist idea of universal salvation, and more particularly from the Ch'an belief that the Buddha-nature is inherent in all beings. But in Li Chih we can see how the original moral basis of Confucian sagehood has disappeared, while the Buddhist awareness of egoism and selfish craving, which is the starting point of all its philosophy and discipline, has been largely ignored. As the original T'ai-chou optimism concerning human nature evaporated under the stresses of actual life, Li Chih himself reflects disillusionment, but it is the weaknesses and failings of others which he recognizes and not his own. Within both the Confucian and the Buddhist communities, on the other hand, there is a strong reassertion of the need for discipline, the one calling for moral effort and civic action, the other, for a renewed insistence on the rooting out of egotism and the dispelling of a delusory sense of freedom.[290]

Thus within both Confucianism and Buddhism there is a noticeable effort to recover their former balance. But it is a static balance, not a dynamic one, and we are left to ponder whether the new humanitarianism and individualism of the Ming remained only a momentary enthusiasm, without any real substance, or might still in some way have contributed to the enlargement of the Chinese spirit.

THE LIMITATIONS OF LI CHIH'S INDIVIDUALISM

When Li Chih died he left no disciples or school to carry on his work or further his "cause." This was as he intended it. He did not wish to become a teacher, gather students, start a school, or organize a movement. And it was not just a matter of personal preference, but one of principle.[291] On the other hand, this is another way of saying that his "cause" was a purely personal one, and did not aim at establishing within society any wider basis for the exercise of individual freedom.

It may be argued that in any case the historical situation did not allow for such a thing. Individualism of the Western type is a product of a different historical development. In China the extreme weakness of the middle class, the nondevelopment of a vigorous capitalism, the absence of a church which fought for its rights against the state, or of competing religions which sought to defend the freedom of conscience against arbitrary authority; the lack of university centers of academic freedom, deriving from their original function as monastic sanctuaries; the want of a free press supported by an educated middle class—the list, of course, is almost endless of the elements lacking in China which contributed in some way to the rise of Western types of individualism.

Carson Chang, in attempting an even-handed judgment of Li

Chih, balances his criticism of seventeenth-century China as a "custom-loving and conformist society" with the comment on Li Chih that "he had only himself to blame. His unconventionality could only have been tolerated in a country where fundamental rights were well-protected." [292] This, however, begs the question. What would one do who wished in China to establish such fundamental rights? Would not one run the same risks as Li Chih did in speaking out? Would he not be given the same advice that Li got from Keng Tinghsiang: that it is imprudent to insist on one's views if they are unpopular? But on the other hand, so far as the rights are concerned, may we not ask of Li Chih whether he had any intentions whatever in regard to "fundamental human rights"?

In view of all that has gone before, this is a question unlikely to be answered in the affirmative, and yet some aspects of it deserve to be considered. If we speak of "fundamental rights," some basis in law, custom, or institutions is implied. Li, however, has turned his back on custom and, for all his emphasis on the realities of political life and his admiration for the Legalists, he says almost nothing about the fundamental role of institutions, legal or otherwise. In one sense Li recognizes law as an aspect of state power, but whether his historical and moral relativism will allow him to establish a fundamental human basis for law, apart from the institutions that satisfy man's biological needs, is a real question.

To the extent that Li does liberate himself from Confucian moralizing he turns in the direction of a Buddhist "law" that may not offer much more hope for the assertion or defense of fundamental human rights. It is difficult to see how the moral relativism and the principle of indeterminacy implicit in Mādhyamika Buddhism could serve as the positive basis for law in the legal or constitutional sense.[293] The traditional position of the Buddhist clergy, moreover, is exemplified by the monk Hui-yüan, who argued for the religious freedom of the monk and his independence of state authority precisely on the ground that the monastic life represents a *different* life from that of the ordinary citizen or householder. He claimed a special status for the monk, an immunity from the demands which the ruler might legitimately make upon the ordinary man. In other words, he defends the monk's right to leave the world, while acknowledging and confirming the ruler's complete authority over those who remain in it.[294]

That Hui-yüan's view remained the predominant, if not the "orthodox" view among Ming Buddhists, is indicated by the quotation from Yüan-hsien above (p. 219), when he insists that the monk, in return for the special favor he enjoys in the pursuit of the religious life, is obliged to uphold the established laws and customs. By and large, therefore, the attitude of Ming Buddhists was negative toward social problems, possibilities for legal reform, or the establishment of any new order within the world of men.[295] Although there were a few exceptions, like the monk Ta-kuan [b1] who admired Li Chih and followed him in martyrdom, "the great mass of Buddhists shrank back into or persisted in an attitude of passivity and conformity." [296]

CONCLUSION

Li's individualism did then enable him to achieve a large measure of intellectual independence, to rise considerably above the traditional limits of his culture (above most of the cultural determinants of Buddhism as well as Confucianism) and to envisage a new world —one might almost say a modern world—transcending most of the parochial limits of traditional culture. Nevertheless, having stripped himself of all social or cultural support, he stands there naked and alone, without the means to create any new order or to protect himself from the old, and without as much freedom of mind as he supposes.

Toward the end of his life Li met and talked with the pioneer Jesuit missionary, Matteo Ricci, several times. They admired each other's intelligence, learning, and courage. Li thought it incredible that Ricci could have achieved such a mastery of the Chinese classical tradition. But he was baffled by Ricci's motive in coming all the way to China from his homeland. The thought that Ricci might have something to offer China which she did not already possess in Confucianism was too foolish to be considered seriously.[297] And when Ricci complains that most Chinese were too addicted to the study of traditional philosophy to take any interest in Western science, one wonders if he would have made an exception of Li Chih.[298]

In this connection we may consider all the more remarkable the achievement in the seventeenth century of Huang Tsung-hsi, who in his *Ming-i tai-fang lu* bm saw clearly that Chinese absolutism could never be restrained or individual freedom guaranteed without the establishment of fundamental law and the creation of independent centers for free discussion.[299] We cannot help asking how much the free thought and widespread skepticism of the late Ming contributed to this attempt at reconciling the age-old conflict between Legalist "law" and the Confucian respect for the human person, by challenging Huang to a more radical reexamination of tradition than even Li Chih had attempted.

Yet Huang Tsung-hsi's ideas, too, were suppressed by Manchu absolutism with the able assistance of Confucian scholars. To the extent that this repression arose partly in reaction to the "heresies" of Li Chih, and was justified by the necessity to reestablish traditional law, order, and morality,[300] the shock of Li Chih's challenge to tradition may have had a double effect. While some men were provoked to deeper thought, others reacted to the threat of moral and social anarchy in Li Chih's thought with renewed efforts and more drastic means to preserve Chinese tradition and immunize it against all new ideas. In this, then, lies the tragedy of Chinese individualism and, to a degree, of modern China itself.

From this admittedly limited survey we may perhaps draw a few general, but still tentative, conclusions:

1. A type of individualistic thought with strikingly modern features did arise, in conjunction with larger social and cultural forces, out of a liberal and humanitarian movement within the Wang Yang-ming school in the sixteenth century. Thus Confucianism, though the dominant tradition and, to modern eyes, an authoritarian system, proved capable of fulfilling somewhat the same function as that credited by Professor Butterfield to medieval Christianity in the rise of Western individualism. "If religion produced the authoritarian system, it also produced the rebellion against the system, as though the internal aspect of the faith were at war with the external. The total result over the long medieval period may have been a deepening of personality, a training of conscience, and a heightening of the

sense of individual responsibility, particularly in the matter of religion itself." [301]

2. Within this general movement one form of "positive" individualism was represented by Ho Hsin-yin, who attempted to establish it first in the clan community as an egalitarian concept and then in the context of the larger scholarly community. This attempt failed, in the absence of a strong middle-class base, for want of support from the scholar-official class and because of the inability of the schools, academies, and scholarly associations to maintain their independence of the ruling power. To a degree then, the premonition of Lord Acton that the great danger to individual liberty in the twentieth century would come from the monolithic state was borne out in China even before Acton's time.[302]

3. Another radical form of individualism represented by Li Chih, though distinguishable in the originality of its thought from the traditional forms of dissent, Buddhism and Taoism, tended in the end toward the extreme of what we have called a "private" or "negative" individualism which was incapable of establishing itself in any framework of laws and institutions. Though Li too felt the repressive power of the state, if our analysis is correct, the rejection of Li's ideas by leading scholars and prelates was a more fundamental factor in the failure of his type of individualism. Furthermore, the effect of Li's involvement with Ch'an Buddhism suggests that, while the latter may have contributed to his intellectual independence, it afforded no positive basis for asserting individualism within Chinese society.

These conclusions, however, must be seen in relation to the limited aims of this study. We have been concerned here with that strain of radical thought most nearly resembling individualistic thought in the modern West, and yet in the larger perspective of world history we would have difficulty in holding to the latter as a norm for China. Subsequent history, indeed, has not brought China any closer to such a norm despite even the revolutionary changes of the twentieth century. The possibility must be allowed for that any type of individualism which develops in the future may tend more to keep within the allowable limits of Chinese tradition than to expand to the outer limits of Western forms of individualism. It is not inconceivable, for instance, that a Confucian type of individualism or personalism could eventually prove itself more adaptable to a socialist society than modern Western types of individualism. Undoubtedly we are involved here in rather large speculations concerning a future which defies definition in traditional terms. But insofar as China might derive some value from its own past—and nationalism cannot be discounted as a powerful force in that direction—the Ming experience with a variety of individualistic thought may yet prove to have some relevance. It therefore deserves deeper and more extensive study.

NOTES

1. Cf. de Bary, Chan, and Watson, *Sources of Chinese Tradition* (New York, 1960), pp. 813 ff.
2. *Ibid.*, p. 768. The same view is found in Wing-tsit Chan's "Chinese Theory and Practice," in Charles Moore (ed.), *Philosophy and Culture, East and West* (Honolulu, 1962), pp. 92–93.
3. *Sources*, pp. 858–61.
4. To name only two of the more prominent examples: Hou Wai-lu, *Chung-kuo ssu-hsiang t'ung-shih* [bn] (Peking, 1960), Vol. IVB (hereafter referred to as Hou, *T'ung-shih* IVB), pp. 875–1290; Shimada Kenji, *Chūgoku ni okeru kindai shii no zasetsu* (Tokyo, 1949; hereafter referred to as *Zasetsu*).
5. Such a distinction might well apply to the subject matter discussed by Max Loehr, in his "Individualism in Chinese Art," and J. R. Hightower in "Individualism in Chinese Literature," both appearing in the *Journal of the History of Ideas*, XXII (No. 2, April–June, 1961), 147–68. For the most part they are concerned with "individuality" in arts and letters and touch only negatively on the question of "individualism" in the sense that it is discussed by Herbert Butterfield, for instance, in his paper for the same Conference on "Religion and Modern Individualism" in the West (*Ibid.* [No. 1, January–March], pp. 33–46).
6. This type of individualism as it flourished in the third century B.C. is discussed by Etienne Balazs in an article translated into English under the title "Nihilistic Revolt or Mystical Escapism" and published in his collected papers under the editorship of Arthur Wright. Cf. E. Balazs, *Chinese Civilization and Bureaucracy* (New Haven, 1964), pp. 226–54.
7. That this is an important, if not essential, element in modern Western individualism is implied by Butterfield in his description of it as a "heightening of the notion of individual responsibility and the dissemination of this amongst wider sections of the population" (*Journal of the History of Ideas*, XXII (No. 1) 40) and as "the autonomy of men who are determined to decide the main purpose of their lives and feel a similar responsibility for public affairs . . ." (*Ibid.*, p. 46).
8. Cf. Introduction, pp. 12 ff.
9. In this, of course, he was only fulfilling the implications of a subjectivism already well established in the early Ming and perhaps even in the Yüan period, if Professor Loehr's observations on Yüan painting are an indication. Cf. Max Loehr, "Individualism in Chi-

nese Art," *Journal of the History of Ideas*, XXII (No. 1, January–March, 1961), 157–58.

10. *Ch'uan-hsi lu* (in *Wang Yang-ming ch'üan-chi*, Ta-t'ung ed. [Shanghai, 1935], Vol. I), 2/46 Ch'i wen Tao-t'ung shu.

11. *Ch'uan-hsi lu*, 1/24–25 Te-chang yüeh . . . : cf. Wing-tsit Chan, *Instructions for Practical Living* (New York, 1963; hereafter referred to as *Instructions*), p. 69.

12. *Ch'uan-hsi lu*, 1/25.

13. E.g., *Ch'uan-hsi lu*, 1/2; Chan, *Instructions*, p. 7.

14. *Nien-p'u*, 1/4 Hung-chih 15.

15. *Ch'uan-hsi lu*, 2/118; Chan, *Instructions*, p. 118.

16. *Idem*; Chan, *Instructions*, p. 119. Italics mine.

17. *Idem*. Brackets mine.

18. *Idem*; Chan, *Instructions*, p. 120.

19. There are some who interpret such invocations of the past as mere pious platitudes to conceal or dress up revolutionary ideas. This seems to me a fundamental misunderstanding of the function of traditional values as a measure by which to judge the present. Wang's view of tradition obviously reflects his own concerns and convictions, and his use of it must be understood in relation to the social and cultural tensions of his own time. But that it should be a mere convention or game with him calls into question his integrity as man and thinker, for it is contrary to his own basic teaching on sincerity in thought, word, and deed, and makes of him truly a hypocrite's hypocrite.

20. *Ch'uan-hsi lu*, 2/57 (Ta Ou-yang Ch'ung-i), echoing *Analects* XIV, 25.

21. The whole work reflects this spirit, but we might cite in particular the conversations recorded by Ch'en Chiu-ch'uan, Huang I-fang, and Huang Mien-shu in *chüan* 3.

22. *Ch'uan-hsi lu*, 3/71; Chan, *Instructions*, pp. 194–95.

23. *Ibid.*, 3/74; Chan, *Instructions*, p. 200.

24. *Ch'uan-hsi lu*, 2/58–59 Ta Lo Ch'eng-an; Chan, *Instructions*, p. 159.

25. *Ibid.*, 2/60; Chan, p. 164.

26. Cf. Araki Kengo, "Min matsu ni okeru ju-butsu chōwa ron no seikaku" [bp] (The character of Confucian-Buddhist syncretism in the later Ming period), in *Nihon chūgoku gakkai ho*,[bq] No. 18, pp. 219–20. Araki believes that it was the intellectual revolution springing from Wang's identification of mind as principle which overcame the intellectual isolation and defensive attitude of Zen Buddhists at this time, and gave them an opportunity to reengage in the intellectual life of the late Ming.

27. The classic example is the discussion of the Four Dicta at the T'ien-

ch'üan bridge (cf. *Ch'uan-hsi lu*, 3/90; Chan, *Instructions*, pp. 241 ff.), which left things as ambiguous as at the start.

28. Cf. Huang Tsung-hsi's classification of the late Ming schools in the Table of Contents of *Ming-ju hüeuh-an* (hereafter referred to as *MJHA*), and especially chuan 10–36. The classification of the T'ai-chou school as "left-wing" in contrast to the "right bank" originates, so far as I am aware, with Chi Wen-fu. Cf. p. 223, n. 117 infra. See also, above, Okada, *Wang Chi and the Rise of Existentialism*, pp. 121 ff.

29. For this necessarily brief account of Wang Ken's life and ideas I have consulted the following sources and selected secondary studies:

Wang Ken [Ming-ju] *Wang Hsin-chai hsien-sheng i-chi*,[br] Peking(?), 1911; *Hsin-chai yüeh-yen*,[bs] in Tsao Jung, comp., *Hsüeh-hai lei pien*; *MJHA*, 32 (Wan-yu wen-k'u ed.), 32/62–75.

Wang Yüan-ting, *Wang Hsin-chai nien-p'u*,[bt] in *I-chi*, 3. Biog. in *Ming shih* 283.

Chao Chen-chi, *T'ai-chou Wang Hsin-chai Ken mu-chih-ming*,[bu] in Chiao Hung, *Kuo-ch'ao hsien-cheng lu*,[bv] 114 (*Chung-kuo shih-hsüeh ts'ung-shu* [photographic reprint; Taiwan, 1965], pp. 5032–33; abbr. *Mu-chih-ming*).

Hsü Yüeh, *Wang Hsin-Chai pieh-chuan*,[bw] in *I-chi*, 4/6b–8a (abbr. *Pieh-chuan*).

Keng Ting-hsiang, *Wang Hsin-chai chuan*, in *I-chi*, 4/12a–14a.

Hsu Yü-lüan,[bx] *Wang Ken chuan* from *Yang-chou fu-chih*, reprinted in *I-chi*, 4/16a–17b.

Li Chih, *Hsu Ts'ang-shu* [by] (Wan-li ed. of Wang Wei-yen; Nanking), 22/14a; also Chung-hua shu-chü ed. (Peking, 1959), pp. 432–35.

Chou Ju-teng, *Sheng-hsüeh ts'ung-ch'uan* [bz] (Wan-li ed.), 34, 16/1a.

Chi Wen-fu, *Tso-p'ai Wang-hsüeh* [ca] (Shanghai, 1934), Ch. 2.

Shimada Kenji, *Zasetsu*, pp. 94–112.

Hou Wai-lu, *T'ung shih*, IV B (Peking, 1960), 958–1002.

Kusumoto Masatsugu, *Sō-Min jidai jugaku shisō no kenkyū* [cb] (Chiba ben, Kashiwa-shi, 1962), pp. 489–94.

Jung Chao-tsu, *Ming-tai ssu-hsiang-shih* [cc] (reprint; Taipei, 1966), pp. 150–59.

Wu K'ang, *Sung-Ming li-hsüeh* [cd] (Rev. ed.; Taipei, 1962), pp. 324–28.

Ono Kazuko, "Jukyō no itansha tachi," [ce] in Matsumoto San-nosuke, ed., *Taidō suru Ajia* [cf] (Tokyo, 1966), pp. 8–18.

Forke, Alfred, *Geschichte der neueren Chinesische Philosophie* (Hamburg, 1938), pp. 400–2.

Carson Chang, *Development of Neo-Confucian Thought,* II, 25–27, 113–18. Chang's book is the only extended account of the thought of this period, but the limitations of his approach to Wang Ken's thought are clearly indicated by his introductory remark: "I must restrict myself to dealing with it only insofar as it is a mark of the deterioration of the school of Wang Shou-jen. With this end in view, let me point out a few of the peculiarities of the philosopher from Taichou's teaching. . . ."

30. Chou Ju-teng, *Sheng-hsüeh ts'ung-ch'uan,* 16/3a; Shimada, *Zasetsu* p. 98. *Ken* is hexagram 52 in the *Book of Changes,* where it stands for upright and firm adherence to principle (Cf. Legge, *I Ching* [New York, 1964], pp. 175–77). The commentary on the hexagram, as well as Wang's courtesy name, Ju-chih, and his honorific Hsin-chai (taken from Chuang Tzu's "fast of the mind"), all suggest an undistracted and imperturbable state of self-containment. Professor Frederick Mote suggests to me that Wang Yang-ming may have recommended the change to Ken out of distaste for the bourgeois vulgarity implicit in the original name, Yin ("Silver").

31. Keng, *Wang Hsin-chai chuan,* 2/12ab.

32. Chao, *Mu-chih-ming,* 14/5032a; Hsü Yüeh, *Pieh-chuan,* 4/7b; Keng, *Wang Hsin-chai chuan,* 4/12b; *MJHA,* 32/68; Hou, *T'ung-shih IVB,* p. 261.

33. Chao, *Mu-chih-ming,* 14/5032a; Keng, *Wang Hsin-chai chuan,* 4/12b; Hou, *T'ung-shih IVB,* p. 261.

34. *MJHA,* 32/68, Wang Ken chuan; cf. also Hsü, *Pieh-chuan,* 4/7b.

35. Hsü, *Pieh-chuan,* 4/7b; *Nien-p'u,* 3/2b–3a, 37 *sui;* Hou, *T'ung-shih IVB,* p. 962.

36. *Ch'uan-hsi lu,* 2/62, Ta Nieh Wen-wei; tr. adapted from Chan, *Instructions,* pp. 168–69.

37. *Ch'uan-hsi lu,* 2/63.

38. Chao, *Mu-chih-ming,* 5032b; *MJHA,* 32/68 Wang Ken chuan.

39. Carson Chang's translation of this passage is: "If there is a similarity, then Wang Shou-jen will be a dominating personality for many generations to come. If there is no similarity, then I should follow Wang Shou-jen" (*Development of Neo-Confucianism,* II, 115). Dr. Chang assumes the worshipful tone which would be normal in such a situation, but Chao's epitaph for Wang Ken (cf. n. 38 above) makes it clear that this was taken as an expression of Ken's amazing self-confidence, and the following encounter with Wang Yang-ming bears out that Ken felt he had as much to give as to get from such a meeting.

40. *MJHA,* 32/69 Wang Ken chuan.

41. *Ibid.*

42. Keng, *Wang Hsin-chai chuan*, 4/12b.

43. *Ibid.*; Chou, *Wang Ken chuan*, 16/4b; Huang, *MJHA*, 32/69; Hou, *T'ung-shih IVB*, pp. 967–68.

44. Hou, pp. 968–69.

45. *MJHA*, 32/71 Yü-lu; Kusumoto, *Sō-Min jugaku*, p. 491.

46. Hsi-tzu B 47; cf. Legge, *I-ching* (reprint; New York, 1964), p. 392.

47. *MJHA*, 32/69 Wang Ken chuan. This is Huang Tsung-hsi's paraphrase or summary of Wang Ken's position.

48. *MJHA*, 32/69–70 Wang Ken chuan. Again, Huang's paraphrase.

49. *Ibid.*, 32/70 Yü-lu.

50. Cf. *Ibid.*, 32/71–75 Yü-lu, and *I-chi* 1/12b–13a.

51. The expression *Ming-che pao-shen* is drawn from the *Book of Odes*, No. 260, where it is said of a minister that "he is enlightened and wise and so he protects his person" (Karlgren, *Book of Odes*, p. 229).

52. *Mencius*, 7A, 15.

53. *I-chi*, 1/12b–13a Ming-che pao-shen lun.

54. The *Chuang Tzu* refers to a loyal minister cutting off his flesh to feed his sovereign. In the *Hsin T'ang shu* and *Sung shih* there are examples of filial sons slicing flesh from their thighs to make medicine for their parents. Cf. Ch'an, *Instructions*, p. 107, n. 44. A typical example of this sort of thinking in Ming times was the famous paragon of filial piety, Madam Wang, who, in order to have meat for her parents-in-law, was said to have cut the flesh off her own thighs, cooked it, and served it to them. She was a common figure in moralistic literature and official Confucian indoctrination, and was also represented in painting for moral inspiration down to the nineteenth century. She is included in a set of "Four Illustrations of Filiality" by the Ch'ing painter Ting Kuan-p'eng, modeled after those of an anonymous Yüan artist, at the National Palace Museum, Taipei.

55. Chao, *Mu-chih-ming*, 114/5032a; *MJHA*, 32/68 Wang Ken chuan.

56. Cf. *I-chi*, 2/9ab Hsiao chen.

57. For a much fuller discussion of this problem in relation to Wang Yang-ming, Wang Chi, and Wang Ken, see Shimada, "Subjective Idealism in Sung and Post-Sung China," *Tōhōgakuho*, No. 28, pp. 1–9, 40–46.

58. Huang, *MJHA*, 32/70 Yü-lu.

59. Wang Ken, *Hsin-chai yüeh-yen*, 1b–2b, 4b–5b; Kusumoto, *Sō-Min jugaku*, p. 489.

60. *MJHA*, 32/74 Yü-lu.

61. Cf. Kusumoto, *Sō-Min jugaku*, p. 491.

62. *MJHA*, 32/70 Yü-lu. The way of the concubine (*ch'ieh-fu chih tao*)

is referred to in Mencius, IIIB, 2 as characterized by dutiful compliance.

63. *Ibid.*, 32/74 Yü-lu.

64. *I-chi*, 1/7ab.

65. *MJHA*, 32/70, 72, 74 Yü-lu.

66. *I-chi*, 2/9b–10; *MJHA*, 32/75, Lo hsüeh ko.

67. The common reference in the Confucian tradition is to the disciple Yen Yüan who "loved to learn" (*Analects* VI, 2).

68. *Hsin-chai yüeh-yen*, 1a.

69. The original expression *pai-hsing jih-yung* is from the *I-ching*, Hsi tzu A, p. 40. Hou, *T'ung-shih* IVB, gives considerable biographical evidence on this point.

70. The term derives from *The Mean*, XII.

71. *MJHA*, 32/72, 73, Yü-lu; *Yüeh-yen*, 3–4.

72. "*Chih-chin erh shen*." *Nien-p'u*, 46 *sui*. *I-chi*, 3/4b.

73. Hou, *T'ung-shih* IVB, pp. 974–95; Jung Chao-tsu, in his *Ming-tai ssu-hsiang-shih*, pp. 150–59, emphasizes practical action, but not social reform to the same extent.

74. This is conceded by Hou, p. 983, and by Ono Kazuko, "Itansha," p. 17.

75. Hou, *T'ung-shih* IVB, p. 983.

76. *Chuang Tzu*, Tien-hsia p'ien (Harvard-Yenching Index Series, Supplement No. 20, *A Concordance to Chuang Tzu*, p. 91; tr. in *Sources of Chinese Tradition*, pp. 82–83.

77. *Ch'iu-shan fu.*[cg] I cannot vouch for the ichthyological accuracy of the terms *loach* and *eel*.

78. *I-chi*, 2/10ab, Ch'iu-shan fu.

79. *Mencius*, IIIB, 2; tr. adapted from Legge and from Chan (*Source Book*, p. 72).

80. *Ch'uan-hsi lu*, 2/44 Ta Ku Tung-ch'iao; tr. adapted from Chan, *Instructions*, p. 124.

81. See above, Okada, "Wang Chi and the Rise of Existentialism," p. 129.

82. The term *ta-chang-fu* also means "great soul" (*mahāpurusha*) in Buddhism, and Wang Ken's use of it has the double significance of the Confucian and Buddhist ideals of unselfish service to mankind.

83. Shimada, *Zasetsu*, p. 104. Shimada's discussion of this aspect of Wang Ken shows the depth and skill that make this a classic among studies of modern Chinese intellectual history.

84. Shimada, *Zasetsu*, p. 113; Hou, *T'ung-shih* IVB, pp. 996–98; Okada Takehiko, "Ō-mon genjōha no keitō [ch] (The Filiation of the existen-

tialist branch of the Wang Yang-ming school)," *Teoria*, No. 6, p. 36; Carson Chang, *Development*, pp. 26–27.

85. Ping-ti Ho, *The Ladder of Success in Imperial China: Aspects of Social Mobility, 1368–1911* (New York, 1962), p. 199 (hereafter abbreviated as *Ladder*).

86. Cf. Miyazaki Ichisada, *Ajia shi kenkyu*,[ci] IV (Kyoto, 1964), 306 ff., 722 ff.

87. Cf. Saeki Tomi, *Sō no shin bunka* (Tokyo, 1967), pp. 381 ff.

88. Cf. Yoshikawa Kojiro, *Genmin shi gaisetsu*[cj] (Tokyo, 1963), pp. 220–22; Saeki, *Sō no shin bunka*, p. 387.

89. Cf. André Levy, Vogue et Declin d'un Genre Narratif Chinois—Le Conte Vulgaire du XIIe Siècle (MS.). I am grateful for the opportunity to examine this study in manuscript. It includes an extensive discussion of the cultural background of the rise of the popular tale in the sixteenth and seventeenth centuries.

90. Cf. Ping-ti Ho, "The Salt-Merchants of Yang-chou, a Study of Commercial Capitalism in Eighteenth Century China," *HJAS*, XVII (Nos. 1, 2, June, 1954).

91. J. L. Gallagher, *China in the Sixteenth Century: The Journal of Matthew Ricci 1583–1610* (New York, 1953), pp. 268–69.

92. Miyazaki, *Ajia shi kenkyū*, IV, 322. Professor Ho, in a personal communication, states that the prefectural population was already well over two million by the late fourteenth century and by the late sixteenth century must have been far larger, since by 1776–1850 the population was well over five million.

93. Gallagher, *China in the Sixteenth Century*, p. 317.

94. Ho, *Ladder*, p. 73.

95. According to Levy, *Vogue et Declin*.

96. These are, with the corresponding reference in the *Ming-ju hsüeh-an* for each case: Hsü Yüeh (32/80); Lin Ch'un (32/95); Chao Ch'en-chi (33/99); Lo Ju-fang (43/1); Yang Ch'i-yüan (34/30); Keng Ting-hsiang (35/35); Chiao Hung (35/45); P'an Shih-tsao (35/50); Chu Shih-li (35/61); Chou Ju-teng (36/64); and T'ao Wang-lin (36/74).

97. Yen Chün, Ho Hsin-yin, and Li Chih were particular beneficiaries of such influence in high places, as will be seen below.

98. Ho, *Ladder*, p. 73; citing *Chen-ch'uan hsien-sheng chi*, 13/2ab.

99. Saeki, *Sō no shin bunka*, pp. 388–92.

100. *MJHA*, 32/62.

101. *I-chi*, 1/Fu p'u lun chih t'u 2b.

102. *MJHA*, 32/77.

103. *Idem*.

104. Hou, *T'ung-shih* IVB, pp. 1000–2.

105. *I-chi*, 3/4b.

106. *MJHA*, 32/69.

107. Sakai Tadao, *Chūgoku zensho no kenkyū* ᶜᵏ (Tokyo, 1960), p. 329.

108. *Ibid.*, pp. 373–94.

109. *Ibid.*, pp. 330–31; citing the testimony of Wang Chi, Chou Ju-teng, and Li Chih.

110. *Ibid.*, p. 375; see also below, Sakai, "Confucianism and Popular Educational Works."

111. Takao Giken, *Chūgoku bukkyō shiron* ᶜˡ (Kyoto, 1952), pp. 264 ff.; Kenneth Ch'en, *Buddhism in China* (Princeton, 1964), pp. 443–45.

112. Takao, *Bukkyō shiron*, pp. 235–45; Sakai, *Zensho*, p. 377.

113. Sakai, *Zensho*, pp. 377–78.

114. Ch'en, *Buddhism in China*, p. 439, describes it as "a good example of Buddhist-Taoist mixture." I would suggest, however, that it is more than just another case of popular "syncretism." The real impetus here comes not from within Buddhism and Taoism or from a vague eclectic tendency, but from the dynamic humanist spirit of which the Wang Yang-ming school was the chief expression in the sixteenth century.

115. The range and variety of thought in this school are well represented in Okada Takehiko, *Minmatsu jukyō no dōkō*,ᶜᵐ Kyūshu daigaku bungakubu, Sō-min shisō kenkyushitsu, 1960); and his "Ōmon genjōha no keitō," in *Teoria*, No. 5 (December, 1961), pp. 59–86, and No. 6, pp. 31–50.

116. See Araki Kengo, "Minmatsu ni okeru jubutsu chōwa-ron no seikaku," *Nihon Chūgoku gakkai ho*, XVIII, 210–23.

117. Shimada's discussion of "The Frustration of Modern Chinese Thought" in his *Zasetsu* (1948), centers on the T'ai-chou school as a means of evaluating the potential for modernization in Ming and Ch'ing China. Hou Wai-lou's more recent work ("Shih-liu shih-chi Chung-kuo ti chin-pu ti che-hsueh ssu-ch'ao kai-hsū," ᶜⁿ in *Li-shih yen-chiu* [1959, No. 10] and in *T'ung-shih* IVB) give much attention to the T'ai-chou school as the vanguard of "progressive" thought in the sixteenth century. Earlier, Chi Wen-fu in *Tso-p'ai Wang-hsüeh* (1934) and Jung Chao-tsu with his studies of Ho Hsin-yin (*Fu-jen hsüeh-chih*, VI, Nos. 1, 2) and *Ming-tai ssu-hsiang shih* (History of Ming thought, 1941) had made some of the more unorthodox thinkers better known. Some of this had stimulated Shimada's own thinking on the subject, but he put the problem in a much broader historical and sociological perspective. For a contrasting view among Japanese scholars, see Yamashita Ryūji, "Minmatsu ni okeru han jukyō shisō no genryu," ᶜᵒ *Tetsugaku zasshi* (June, 1951); and Shimada's response in "Ōgaku saharon hihan no

hihan," cp in *Shigaku zasshi*, LXI (1952), 9. Most recently Ono Kazuko has seen the T'ai-chou school as the first stage in the "quickening of Asia" (Cf. Matsumoto Sannosuke, ed., *Taidō suru Ajia* (Tokyo, 1966), pp. 1–45.

118. T. Shan-nung. From Chi-an, Kiangsi Province. Dates unknown.
119. Wang Shih-chen, *Yen-chou shih-liao hou-chi* 35 Chia-lung chiang-hu ta hsia cq (reprinted in *Ho Hsin-yen chi*, p. 143).
120. *Idem.*
121. Original name Liang Ju-yüan.cr From Yung-feng, Chi-chou, Kiangsi Province. Cf. Huang, *MJHA*, 32/63.
122. *MJHA*, 32/62; and in *Ho Hsin-yin chi*, 1, 22.
123. T. Tzu-chih, H. Po-shih. *Chin-shih* 1533. Cf. MS, 283/3186; *MJHA*, 32/50.
124. *Idem.*
125. The good deeds of the *yu-hsia* often flouted law or convention or were undertaken in defiance of the authorities. There is almost as much of the gangster in this conception as of the knight in shining armor. For the tradition of the "knight-errant" in Chinese literature, see James J. Y. Liu, *The Chinese Knight-Errant* (Chicago, 1967).
126. Thinking victory was in his grasp, Hsi allowed himself to be caught off guard by a false surrender trick. Cf. *MJHA*, 32/81.
127. *Ibid.*, 32/63.
128. Jung Chao-tsu, "Ho Hsin-yin chi ch'i ssu-hsiang" (see n. 129 below) 167 citing *Keng T'ien-t'ai chi* 12.
129. The principal sources for the study of Ho Hsin-yin's thought are contained in the edition of Ho's works edited by Jung Chao-tsu, *Ho Hsin-yin chi* cs (Peking, 1960). Prefaced to it is Li Chih's essay on Ho in *Fen-shu* 3 entitled "Ho Hsin-yin lun" (pp. 10–12); an appendix contains several early accounts of Ho's life and thought, of which the following have been most useful here:

> Tsou Yüan-piao, Liang Fu-shan chuan in *Ho Hsin-yin chi*, pp. 120–21 (from *Liang Fu-shan i-chi*).
> Huang Tsung-hsi, T'ai-chou hsüeh-an hsü, from *MJHA* 32 (pp. 122–24).
> Wang Shih-chen, Chia-lung chiang-hu ta hsia, from *Yen-chou shih-liao hou-chi*, 35 (in *Ho Hsin-yin chi*, pp. 143–44.)

The following secondary studies have also been consulted:

> Jung Chao-tsu, "Ho Hsin-yin chi ch'i ssu-hsiang" in *Fu-jen hsüeh-chih* 6 (1937), 1, 2, pp. 129–72.
> Hou Wai-lu, *T'ung-shih IVB*, pp. 1003–30.
> Shimada Kenji, *Zasetsu*, 134–61.
> Okada Takehiko, "Ō-mon genjō-ha no keitō" 2, in *Teoria*, No. 6 (1962), pp. 31–50.

130. Tsou Yüan-piao, *Liang Fu-shan chuan*, in *Ho Hsin-yin chi* 120; *MJHA*, 32/63 (*Ho Hsin-yin chi*, 123).

131. *Ho Hsin-yin chi*, 68–69 Chü-ho shuai-chiao yü-tsu li-yü; *ibid.*, 70–72 Chü-ho shuai-yang yü-tsu li-yü; Tsou, Liang Fu-shan chuan, pp. 120–21; Huang, *MJHA*, *idem*; Jung, "Ho Hsin-yin chi ch'i ssu-hsiang," pp. 130–33.

132. Tsou, *idem*; *MJHA*, *idem*; Jung, "Ho Hsin-yin chi ch'i ssu-hsiang" pp. 135–36; Hou, *T'ung-shih IVB*, p. 1005.

133. *MJHA*, 32/64.

134. *Ibid.*, 32/63.

135. *Ibid.*, 32/64; Tsou, Liang Fu-shan chuan, p. 121. The above brief account of Ho's life is offered only as background for the understanding of his type of individualism. More detailed and consecutive accounts are contained in the writings of Jung and Hou cited above.

136. *Ho Hsin-yin chi*, 54 Ta Chan-kuo . . . pu lo i-ch'i.

137. *Ibid.*, 55.

138. *Ibid.*, 40 Kua-yü.

139. *Ibid.*, 42 Pien wu-yü; Jung, "Ho Hsin-yin . . ." p. 170.

140. *Ho Hsin-yin chi*, 42 Pien wu-yü.

141. *Ibid.*, 72 Chü-ho lao-lao wen.

142. Thus, the legitimate and irreducible desires were seen as those common to all men. *Idem*; Jung, "Ho Hsin-yin . . . ," p. 170; Ono Kazuko, "Jukyō no itansha tachi," in Matsumoto Sannosuke, ed., *Taido suru Ajia* (Tokyo, 1966), p. 21.

143. *Ho Hsin-yin chi*, 72–3 Hsiu Chü-ho-ssu . . . Ling Hai-lou shu.

144. On these attitudes see de Bary, ed., *Sources of Chinese Tradition*, pp. 458–61, 591, 693; and Denis Twitchett, *The Fan Clan's Charitable Estate 1050–1760*, in Arthur Wright, ed., *Confucianism in Action* (Stanford, 1959), pp. 97–133.

145. E.g., Hou, *T'ung-shih IVB*, 1018–19; Ono, "Itansha," pp. 20–22.

146. Cf. *Ho Hsin-yin chi*, 2/33–37 Chü 3/48 Teng Tzu-chai shuo.

147. Cf. Myron L. Cohen, "Variations in Complexity among Chinese Family Groups: the Impact of Modernization," in *Transactions of the New York Academy of Sciences*, Series II, XXIX (No. 5, March, 1967), 638–44.

148. *Ho Hsin-yin chi*, 28–29 Lun yu, Yü-hui.

149. *Ibid.*, 66 Yü Ai Leng-hsi-shu.

150. *Idem*.

151. *Ibid.*, 73–74 Yu shang Hai-lou shu.

152. *Ibid.*, 1–25 Yüan hsüeh, yüan-chiang.

153. *Ibid.*, 11 Ho Hsin-yin lun (from *Li shih fen-shu* 3/87–89).

154. Much of this is summed up in Huang Tsung-hsi's account and evaluation of Ho, *MJHA*, 32/63–64 (*Ho Hsin-yin chi*, 122–24).

155. Cf. Shimada, *Zasetsu*, pp. 133, 142–44; Okada, "Genjōha," pp. 33, 35.

156. *Ho Hsin-yin chi*, 83 Yü Tsou Ho-shan shu.

157. *Ho Hsin-yin chi*, pp. 42, 51–52; Okada, "Genjōha," pp. 32, 34; Ono, *Itansha*, pp. 23–24.

158. *Ho Hsin-yin chi*, 34–35 Chü, 73–74 Yu shang Hai-lou shu; Okada, "Genjōha," pp. 36, 49, n. 5.

159. Original name Lin Tsai-chih.[cv] T. Hung-fu, Ssu-chai, H. Cho-wu, Wen-ling, etc.

Despite the considerable literature on Li Chih, a full-length study of this important figure is badly needed. The brief acount here is confined to aspects relevant to his individualism, and makes no attempt to settle many of the disputed points concerning his life history. It is based on the following sources and secondary works:

Li Chih, *Cho-wu wen-lüeh*, in *Fen-shu* (Peking, 1961), 3/82–87. Brief autobiography.

Yüan Chung-tao, *Li Wen-ling chuan* [cw] from *K'o-hsüeh-chai chin chi*: reprinted in *Fen-shu*, iii–vii. A vivid personal account by a literary friend.

MS 221/2553 Included in biography of Keng Ting-hsiang: 241/ 2746, Biog. of Chang Wen-ta; Wang Hung-hsü, ed., *Ming shih kao* 207/6a; P'an Tseng-hung, *Li Wen-ling wai-chi*.[cx] 1609 ed. of *Hsü Fen-shu*.

Huang Yün-mei, "Li Cho-wu shih-shih pien-cheng," *Chin-ling hsüeh-pao*, II (May, 1932).

Wu I-feng, "Li Cho-wu chu-shu k'ao," [cz] *Wen-shih yen-chiu-so chi-k'an*, I (June, 1932). A bibliographical study.

Chi Wen-fu, Li Cho-wu yü tso-p'ai Wang-hsüeh,[da] *Honan ta-hsüeh hsüeh-pao*, I–II (June, 1934). Li Chih in relation to T'ai-chou school, Wang Chi, etc.

Chi Wen-fu, "Wang Ch'uan-shan yü Li Cho-wu," [db] *Li-shih yen-chiu* (1961–66), pp. 86–89. Wang Fu-chih's criticism of Li Chih.

Jung Chao-tsu, *Li Cho-wu p'ing-chuan* [dc] (Commercial Press, Shanghai, 1937) and *Li Chih nien-p'u* (Peking, 1957). Major studies by a veteran scholar of Ming thought.

Yeh Kuo-ch'ing, "Li Chih hsien-shih k'ao,[dd] *Li-shih yen-chiu*, II (1958). On Li's family background, based on a recently discovered family genealogy.

Chu Ch'ien-chih,[de] *Li Chih* (Wuhan, 1957). Reviewed by Timoteus Pokora in "A Pioneer of New Trends of Thought in the End of the Ming Period," *Archiv Orientalni*, XXIX (1961), 469–75.

Hou Wai-lu, *Tung-shih* IVB, 1031–95. One of the more scholarly and well-documented "Marxist" interpretations, containing much useful information.

Li Hsien-chih, *Li Chih shih-liu shih-chi chung-kuo fan feng-chien ssu-hsiang te hsien-ch'ü* (Wuhan, 1957). Unavailable to me. Cf. R. Crawford's discussion of the relation between Chang Chü-cheng and Li Chih, below, pp. 401–3.

Ch'iu Han-sheng, "T'ai-chou hsüeh-p'ai ti chieh-chü ssu-hsiang-chia Li Chih,[df] *Li-shih yen-chiu* 1964–1, pp. 115–32).

Fung Yu-lan, "Ts'ung Li Chih shuo-ch'i," [dg] *Chung-kuo che-hsüeh-shih lun-wen erh chi* (Shanghai, 1962). Li Chih as an example of Mao Tse-tung's thought on contradictions.

Suzuki Torao, "Ritakugo nempu," [dk] *Shinagaku*, VII, no. 2 (February, 1934), pp. 139–97; VII, no. 3 (July, 1934), pp. 299–347. A pioneering scholarly work done before the reprinting of some of Li's scarcer works.

Hirose Yutaka, *Yoshida shōin no kenkyū* [di] (Tokyo, 1943), pp. 60–149, 182–85. Of interest here mainly for its painstaking research on Li Chih's works preserved or printed in Japan.

Shimada Kenji, *Zasetsu*, pp. 179–251. Li Chih as the central figure in the gestation and abortion of "early modern" thought in China. Unquestionably the most important interpretive study on Li Chih to date in any language known to me.

Shimada Kenji, "Jukyō no hangyakusha,[dj] Ri Shi (Ri Takugo)" in *Shisō*, no. 462 (1962); nos. 1–13 (1597–1609). A brief report on Shimada's more recent thinking on Li Chih since the publication of his *Zasetsu* in 1949.

Yagisawa Hajime, "Ri Shi" in *Chūgoku no shisōka*,[dk] compiled by Tōkyō daigaku chūgoku tetsugaku shitsu (Tokyo, 1963). A brief, general account by a specialist in Ming literature.

Okada Takehiko, "Ōmon genjōha no keitō Pt. II," *Teoria*, No. 6, pp. 36–50. Li Chih in relation to existentialist thought in the Wang Yang-ming school, with special attention to philosophical questions.

Ono Kazuko, "Jukyō no itansha tachi," in Matsumoto Sannosuke, ed., *Taido suru Ajia*, 25–45. A semipopular presentation by a specialist in late Ming thought with a quasi-marxist approach, emphasizing Li's practical and social thought.

O. Franke, "Li Tschi: Ein Beitrage zur Geschichte der Chinesischen Geisteskämpfe im 16. Jahrhundert," *Abhandlungen der Preussischen Akademie der Wissenschaften* (1937, no. 10); "Li Tschi und Matteo Ricci," *Ibid.*, (1938, no. 5). The former is a general introduction to Li's life, works, and thought; the latter a discussion of the brief, cordial, but unproductive contacts between Li and Ricci.

K. C. Hsiao, "Li Chih: An Iconoclast of the Sixteenth Century," *T'ien Hsia Monthly*, VI, no. 4 (April, 1938), pp. 317–41; Biography of Li in *Draft Ming Biographies* (Dittographed) No. VII (Ming Biographical History Project, New York, 1967). The former is a generally sympathetic portrait of Li Chih as seen amidst the intellectual ferment of the '30s in China; the latter reflects the more mature scholarship of the author, an authority on Chinese political thought.

R. Irwin, *The Evolution of a Chinese Novel: Shui-hu-chuan* (Cambridge, Mass., 1953), pp. 75–86. Li Chih in relation to *Shui-hu-chuan* and vernacular literature.

In addition to the bibliographies specifically noted above, the *Nien-p'u* by Jung Chao-tsu has a substantial appendix including a critical bibliography of Li's works (pp. 113–26), as does Hou Wai-lu, *T'ung-shih* IVB, pp. 1048–51. A more succinct bibliography is presented by Hsiao in the draft biography listed above. The reader is referred to them for further information of this type.

Following are the works of Li drawn upon for this study:

Fen-shu,[dl] ed. of Chung-hua shu-chü. Peking, 1961.

Hsü Fen-shu,[dm] ed. of Chung-hua shu-chü. Peking, 1959.

Ts'ang shu,[dn] ed. of Chung-hua shu-chü. Peking, 1959.

Hsü Ts'ang shu,[do] ed. of Chung-hua shu-chü. Peking, 1959.

Ch'u-t'an chi,[dp] 30 *chüan*. Undated Ming edition. National Central Library (hereafter cited as NCL), Taipei.

Li Cho-wu hsien-sheng i-shu,[dq] 3 *chüan* ed. of Wan-li 40. NCL, Taipei.

Li Wen-ling chi,[dr] 20 *chüan* Ming ed., NCL, Taipei.

San I-jen wen-chi,[ds] 18 *chüan* Ming ed., NCL, Taipei.

[Ming-teng] *Tao ku lu*,[dt] 2 *chüan* Ming ed. Collection of Yoshikawa Kojirō (I am grateful to Prof. Yoshikawa for making this rare copy available to me). Preface dated c. 1599.

160. Cf. Yeh Kuo-ch'ing, "Hsien-shih k'ao," p. 80.
161. *Ibid.*, pp. 81–84; Hou, *T'ung-shih* IVB, 1031.
162. Hou, *ibid.*; Ono, "Itansha," pp. 25–27.
163. Hou believes that Li's last testament and burial instructions suggest some connection with Islam, but he does not press the point. Cf. Hou, *ibid.*; Shimada, *Hangyakusha*, 4; Ono, "Itansha," pp. 26–27.
164. Cf. Yeh, "Hsien-shih k'ao," pp. 81–83; Shimada, *Hangyakusha*, 4a, 12b (n. 9).
165. Ono Kazuko, "Itansha," pp. 26–27, acknowledging the decline of foreign trade in Ch'üan-chou, nevertheless emphasizes the venturesome, risk-running life of the smuggler as contributing to the "free"

spirit of the city, which Li reflected and which she associates with a rising capitalist spirit in sixteenth-century China. Li indeed demonstrated a strong defiance of authority, but the covert defiance of Ch'üan-chou smugglers is certainly a far cry from the open independence of European traders and merchant princes in sixteenth-century Europe.

166. *Fen-shu*, 3/83 Cho-wu lun-lüeh.

167. *Idem:* Jung, *Nien-p'u*, 20. Carson Chang's assertion that Li achieved the *chin-shih* degree at this time is incorrect. (Cf. *Development of Neo-Confucianism*, II, 126.) His relatively low rank certainly has a bearing on what follows, though one must allow that Li's behavior might have been much the same even as a *chin-shih*.

168. Shimada discusses this as a problem inherent within the Neo-Confucian revival of the early Ming (*Zasetsu*, pp. 285–89). It is a familiar type to readers of Chinese fiction, especially in *The Scholars* (*Ju-lin wai-shih*) and *Dream of the Red Chamber* (*Hung-lou meng*).

169. *Fen-shu*, 3/83 Chou-wu lun-lüeh; Shimada, *Zasetsu*, p. 181.

170. *Fen-shu*, 3/85.

171. Jung, *Nien-p'u*, 26, citing *Wang Yang-ming hsien-sheng nien-p'u hou-yü*.

172. H. Lu-yüan, 1528–1611. *MJHA*, 14/36. *MJCCTLSY*, p. 458.

173. H. Ta-chou, 1508–1576. *MS*, 193/2256; *MJHA*, 33/99. *MJCCTLSY*, p. 760.

174. *MJHA*, 14/36 Hsü Yung-chien chuan.

175. H. T'ien-t'ai, 1524–1596. *MS*, 221/2552f.; *MJHA*, 35/35; *MJCCTLSY*, p. 418.

176. H. Ch'u-k'ung. *MS*, 221/2553b; *MJHA*, 35/43; *MJCCTLSY*, p. 419.

177. H. T'an-yüan, 1541–1620. *MS*, 288/3237b; *MJHA*, 35/45; *MJCCTLSY*, p. 677.

178. In Yünnan he did, it is true, have some intellectual associations with Buddhist monks, but these were not of a kind likely to sustain his official vocation during a period of great trial. Cf. Jung, *Nien-p'u*, 42–44.

179. *Ibid.*, 45–46.

180. Yüan, *Li Wen-ling chuan*, iii; Jung, *Nien-p'u*, 50–55; Hou, *T'ung-shih IVB*, 1036.

181. Cf. *Fen-shu*, 2/42–43, 3/84. In a draft biography for the Ming Biographical History, Hsiao Kung-chuan shows that, though Li admired his long-suffering wife, he was not much attached to her and forsook her "to seek the Buddha." Jung's evidence to the contrary (*Nien-p'u*, 65) is less persuasive. To imply deliberate neglect on Li's part would be going too far, but it is clear that the sacrifices necessary for him to follow his chosen course fell more heavily on his

family than on him. He seems not to have suffered comparable deprivations.

182. These are discussed by Shimada in *Zasetsu*, p. 184. Cf. also *Hsü Fen-shu*, 1/51 Yü Tseng Chi-ch'üan shu; Yüan, Li Wen-ling chuan, iv; Jung, *Nien-p'u*, 64–65.

183. Cf. *Fen-shu*, 4/184 Yü-yüeh, tsao-wan shou t'a. Extracts from this work, emphasizing the same general point, are also given in Lin Yutang, *The Importance of Understanding* (Cleveland, 1960), pp. 416–17.

184. Yüan, Li Wen-ling chuan, iii–iv, viii.

185. Yüan, *Li Wen-ling chuan*, vi; Shimada, *Zasetsu*, p. 184.

186. The title echoes Ssu-ma Ch'ien's statement that he was storing a copy of his *Shih chi* in a safe place away from the capital in order to preserve it for posterity. Cf. Pokora, "Pioneer," p. 474, n. 18; B. Watson, *Ssu-ma Ch'ien, Grand Historian of China* (New York, 1958), pp. 57, 214, n. 93.

187. *Fen-shu*, 3/130 Tzu tsan.

188. *Ibid.*, 2/78 Wei Huang-an . . . san shou; 3/87 Ho Hsin-yin lun.

189. Hou (*T'ung-shih IVB*, 1051–53) strains greatly to disassociate his hero Li Chih (a "materialist") from the "idealistic" Wang Yang-ming school. He cites the fact that Huang Tsung-hsi classified the T'ai-chou school separately in *MJHA*. But Huang, though he is eager for reasons quite different from Hou to distinguish the T'ai-chou school from the more orthodox Wang Yang-ming school, nevertheless clearly identifies it as a deviant outgrowth of the latter, and so far as Li Chih is concerned the evidence is overwhelming that he thinks of himself as carrying on in the spirit of Wang's teaching. Hou's basic position is questioned by Shimada, in *Tōhō-gaku hō*, 28, pp. 5–8, 37–41, 46–52. Cf. also Ono, "Itansha," p. 44.

190. Fen-shu, 1/1 Ta Chou Hsi-yen.

191. Cf. Hsiao, "Li chih . . . ," 331; and Hou, *T'ung-shih IVB*, 1062.

192. Hou, *ibid.*

193. *Hsü Fen-shu*, 1/3–4 Yü Ma Li-shan.

194. *Fen-shu*, 4/137 Nien-fo ta-wen.

195. *Ibid.*

196. *Fen-shu*, 3/97–98 T'ung-hsin lun.

197. *Ibid.*, 3/98.

198. *Idem.*

199. Cf. Irwin, *Shui-hu-chuan*, pp. 81–86; Pokora, "Pioneer," p. 473.

200. Cf. *Fen-shu*, 3/109 Chung-i *Shui-hu chuan hsü*; Irwin, *Shui-hu-chuan*, p. 86.

201. *Fen-shu*, 3/109.

202. Cf. *Fen-shu*, 5/205 Ch'in fu; 5/215 I-shao ching-chi; 5/217 Fan

min pei hou; 5/218 Shih hua; also Okada, "Ōmon genjōha . . . ,"
p. 47.

203. *Fen-shu*, 3/101 Ssu-wu shuo.

204. This appears as the general introduction to the Ming edition of the
Ch'u t'an chi, but has also been included bỹ Li in the *Fen-shu*,
3/89–90 Fu-fu lun.

205. *Fen-shu*, 2/56–57 Ta i nü-jen hsueh-tao wei chien-tuan shu.

206. *Fen-shu*, 3/90 Fu-fu lun.

207. Li's views on such questions, not marked by much concern for philosophical consistency, are discussed by Okada, "Genjōha," *passim*, but
with specific reference to this passage on p. 44. It would be too great
a digression from the subject of this paper to take up here the in-
triguing question of the relationship between Buddhist-Taoist mysticism and the new "realism" or "empiricism." Chiao Hung, Fang
I-chih, and Ni Yuan-lu are but a few of the other late Ming figures
in whom we find this combination. It is, of course, bound up with
the whole question of how this "realism" or "empiricism" emerged
from the subjectivity of Ming thought, which shows antimetaphysical tendencies as early as Wu Yü-pi and Ch'en Hsien-chang.

208. *Hsü Fen-shu*, 1/17 Yü Wu Te-ch'ang; 2/78–79 Lun chiao-nan.

209. *Fen-shu*, 1/17 Ta Keng Chung-ch'eng.

210. *Ibid.*, 17, 18 Yu ta Keng Chung-ch'eng.

211. Cf. *Mencius*, IIA, 8 and *Shu-ching*, II, 3.

212. *Fen-shu*, 1/40 Ch'i ta Keng Ta-chung-ch'eng.

213. *Wu-hsin.*[du] Cf. de Bary, *et al.*, *Sources of Chinese Tradition*, p. 561;
or Wing-tsit Chan, *A Source Book in Chinese Philosophy*, p. 525.

214. *Ts'ang-shu*, 32/544 Te-yeh ju-chen hou-lun.

215. *Ibid.*

216. *Fen-shu*, 1/36 Ta Teng Ming-fu.

217. *Fen-shu*, 1/4 Ta Teng Shih-yang.

218. *Fen-shu*, 1/37 Ta Keng Chung-ch'eng.

219. *Ts'ang-shu*, vii Tsung-mu ch'ien-lun.

220. *Ibid.*, 1/2 Shih-chi ts'ung-lun.

221. *Hsü Fen-shu*, 1/46 Yü Keng Tzu-chien.

222. *Ts'ang shu*, xx–xxi Tsung-mu hou-lun; 32/544 Te-yeh ju-chen hou
lun.

223. Cf. Carson Chang, *Development*, II, 126.

224. *Hsü Fen-shu*, 1/16 Yü Chiao Jo-hou t'ai-shih.

225. *Ibid.*

226. *Fen-shu*, 3/124–25 Lo Chin-hsi hsien-sheng kao wen.

227. *Ibid.*, 3/88–89 Ho Hsin-yin lun.

228. *Hsü Fen-shu*, 3/94 K'ung Jung yu tzu-jan chih hsing.

229. *Fen-shu*, 4/159 Yin chi wang shih.

230. *Fen-shu*, 2/61 Yü Chiao Jo-hou.
231. *Fen-shu*, 2/46 Yu Yü Chiao Jo-hou.
232. *Ibid.*
233. *Hsü Fen-shu*, 2/78–79 Lun chiao-nan.
234. Hou, *T'ung-shih* IVB, 1054; Ono, "Itansha," pp. 41–42, 44–45.
235. *Fen-shu* 2/47 Yu Yü Chiao Jo-hou.
236. Hou, who cites the foregoing passage (*ibid.*), fails to give the continuation, which puts a very different face on the matter.
237. *Fen-shu, ibid.*
238. Shimada, *Zasetsu*, p. 190; cf. Max Weber, *Gesammelte Aufsätze zur Religionssociologie* (Tubingen, 1922–33), I, 181; II, 360.
239. *Fen-shu*, 2/78–79 Lun chiao-nan; *Tao-ku lu* A/14a.
240. *Fen-shu*, 3/102 Hsü-shih shuo.
241. *Ibid.*, 3/100 *Hsin-ching* t'i-kang.
242. *Hsü Fen-shu* 1/17 Yu Chiao Jo-hou t'ai-shih.
243. *Fen-shu*, 4/191–92 Han-teng yeh-hua 2; Hsiao, "Li chih . . . ," pp. 336–38.
244. *Ts'ang shu* 2, Shih-chi tsung-lun; Hou, *T'ung-shih* IVB, 1092.
245. *Fen-shu*, 3/93–96 Ping shih lun.
246. *Fen-shu*, 1/7–8 Ta Chiao I-yüan shu; *Hsü Fen-shu* 1/46 Yü Keng Tzu-chien.
247. *Hsü Fen-shu*, 2/77–78 San-chiao kuei ju.
248. *Ibid.*, 2/77.
249. *Ibid.*, 2/78.
250. *Ibid.*
251. *Hsü Fen-shu*, 4/102 T'i K'ung tzu hsiang yü Chih-fo yüan.
252. The possibility of some interinfluence is alluded to in Irwin, *Shui-hu-chuan*, p. 106 n. 26 and Pokora, "Pioneer," p. 473. On the importance of the Heart Sutra in the *Journey to the West* (*Hsi-yu chi*), see C. T. Hsia, *The Classic Chinese Novel* (New York, 1968).
253. E.g., *Li Cho-wu hsien-sheng i-shu*, A/8b Yü Chou Yu-shan (*Hsü Fen-shu* 1/14); A/47ab Ta yu-jen shu (*Hsü Fen-shu* 1/10).
254. Shimada, *Zasetsu*, pp. 222–24, citing *Hsü tsang-shu*, 5/85–6 Sun-kuo ming chen, *Wen hsüeh po shih Fang kung*; and 7/1 Yü-shih ch'eng-kung, Li T'u weng yüeh.
255. *Fen-shu*, 4/164 Wu ssu; discussed by Hsiao in his Draft Biography.
256. *Ibid.*, 3/108 Chung-i *Shui-hu chuan* hsü.
257. *Hsü fen-shu*, 1/20 Yü Keng K'o-nien shu.
258. [Ming-teng] *Tao ku lu*, A/14a–19b; *Fen-shu* 3/86–87 Lun cheng p'ien; *ibid.*, 3/93–95 Ping shih lun; Hou, *T'ung-shih* IVB, 1075; Ono, *op. cit.*, 40–42.
259. Carsun Chang, *The Development of Neo-Confucianism*, II, 127. Chang does not put all the blame on society, but see also, p. 142.

260. *Li Cho-wu hsien-sheng i-shu*, A/150ab Yüan Chung-tao pa *Li shih i-shu*.

261. Cf. Franke's article, "Li Tschi . . ." which gives considerable information on this point. Cf. also Busch, "The Tunglin Academy," *Monumenta Serica*, XIV, 82; Shimada, *Zasetsu*, p. 192. Both Li's admirers and his critics testify to this popularity. Ku Yen-wu's note on Li Chih in *Jih chih lu*, 18 (Commercial Press ed. [1934], VI, 121–22) stresses the point; and the editors of the *Ssu-k'u ch'üan tsung-mu t'i-yao* allude to it in condemning his influence (Commercial Press ed., 50/1111; 178/3401; 179/3950).

262. Cf. Hirose, *Yoshida shōin*, pp. 60 ff.; Shimada, *Zasetsu*, pp. 192, 240; Irwin, *Shui-hu-chuan*, pp. 79–80.

263. Some elements in this situation parallel earlier crises leading to the collapse of great dynasties. At the end of the Han in the 2d century A.D. there is an intellectual atmosphere characterized by "cynical authoritarianism, Taoist poetry and revolt against traditions." Cf. Balazs, *Chinese Civilization and Bureaucracy*, p. 225. Thus there appear to be recurring patterns of intellectual frustration and alienation accompanying dynastic decline, which are intermixed in the present case with new trends and more complex social and cultural forces.

264. Shimada, *Zasetsu*, p. 193.

265. The absence of any treatment of Li Chih in the *Ming-ju hsüeh-an* cannot in itself, of course, be considered conclusive evidence on this point. The possibility of censorship must not be excluded. Huang was unhappy over the deletions in the first edition of *MJHA*, and he expresses satisfaction over Cheng Hsing's more complete edition, which is the one generally in use today. But the chapters dealing with Wang Chi and Chao Chen-chi, with both of whom Li was associated, are remarkably short and deletions may have occurred. The effectiveness of the Ch'ing proscription in suppressing even criticism of Li Chih is indicated by the omission of Ku Yen-wu's condemnation of Li from the Kang-hsi 34 edition of the *Jih-chih lu*. On the other hand, it was restored in subsequent editions, and there are brief accounts of Li in both the *Ming shih* and *Ming-shih kao*. The point requires further investigation, but in any case there can be no doubt of Huang's attitude toward Li and the whole "Wild Ch'an" movement. One of his main reasons for writing the *Ming-ju hsüeh-an* was to rescue Ming thought from Ch'an influence and to counteract Chou Ju-teng's *Sheng-hsüeh tsung-ch'uan*, which gave a strong Ch'anist interpretation to Confucian thought. Cf. Hummel, ed., *ECCP.*, p. 353; Chang, *Development*, II, 180.

266. *Jih-chih lu*, 18, Li Chih (Commerial Press ed., VI, 122).

267. Cf. Chi Wen-fu, "Wang Ch'uan-shan yü Li Cho-wu, *Li-shih yen-chiu* 1961–66, pp. 86–89.

268. The views of both Huang and Ku were widely respected among scholars in and out of office. Both declined honors from the state. Shimada appropriately describes Ku's opinion of Li as the "definitive judgment" in the Ch'ing. Cf. *Zasetsu*, p. 253.

269. Cf. Hummel, ed., *ECCP*, p. 818.

270. Chi Wen-fu, "Wang Ch'uan-shan," pp. 86–87.

271. Cf. Busch, "Tunglin Academy," pp. 47–48.

272. Huang Tsun-su (1584–1626) H. Pai-an. *MJHA*, 61/17; Hummel, ed., *ECCP*, p. 351.

273. *MJHA*, 60/5–6 Shih Yü-ch'ih lun-hsüeh; tr. adapted from Busch, "Tunglin Academy," pp .87, 89–90.

274. Tsou Shan, H. Ying-ch'üan, *chin-shih* of 1557. Cf. *MJHA*, 16/55.

275. *MJHA*, 16/64 Ying-ch'üan hsien-sheng.

276. Jung, *Nien-p'u*, 110–11, citing *Ming Shen-tsung wan-li shih-lu*, 369/14; cf. also Ku Yen-wu, *Jih-chih lu*, 18, Li Chih.

277. *Ibid.*, 111; Hsiao, Draft Biography.

278. *Fen-shu*, vi Li Wen-ling chuan.

279. In Li's case the word "sexy" would certainly be misleading if it did not take into account his primary dedication to the "Way" and his scholarship. On the other hand, he believed in the free and uninhibited expression of emotion and gratification of the appetites as Kenkō, being of a more aristocratic and aesthetic type, did not.

280. *Fen-shu*, 3/99–100 *Hsin-ching* t'i-kang.

281. *Taishō daizōkyō*, 25/1509c Ta-chih-t'u lun.

282. Cf. Mochizuki Shinkō, *Bukkyō daijiten*, V, 4704b.

283. See pp. 268–69.

284. Chu-hung, *Chu-ch'uang san-pi* [dv] (1615 ed.), 21a Li Cho-wu 1.

285. *Ibid.*, 21b.

286. *Ibid.*, 22a Li Cho-wu 2.

287. Araki Kengo, "Chōwa ron," p. 220b, citing *Chiai-shu fa-yin*, pp. 342, 358.

288. *Ibid.*, 220b, citing Ch'an-yü wai-chi 1, T'i Cho-wu Fen-shu hou.

289. Cf. W. T. de Bary, "Buddhism and the Chinese Tradition," *Diogenes*, no. 47, 102–24.

290. Cf. Araki Kengo, *Bukkyō to Jukyō* [dw] (Kyoto, 1963), pp. 440–48. Indeed this reaction is also quite apparent even within the T'ai-chou school itself. Several of its leaders, and even some who were themselves deeply involved with Ch'an, strongly criticized Li. Cf. Araki, "Chōwa ron," pp. 216–17.

291. Cf. *Fen-shu*, 1/23 Ta Liu Hsien-chang; Suzuki, *Nempu* B, pp. 27–28; Shimada, *Zasetsu*, p. 206.

292. Chang, *Development of Neo-Confucianism*, II, 127.

293. Cf. *Hsü Fen-shu*, 2/75–76 Chin-kang-ching shuo. The Great Perfect Wisdom, Li says, objectively and impartially reflects all things, showing no preferences. Presumably had such rights existed it would have respected them, as Li says it respects the Confucian relations, but its function is not to *assert* them. Cf. also, Nakamura Hajime, "A Brief Survey of Japanese Studies on the Philosophical Schools of the Mahayana," *Acta Asiatica* (Tokyo, 1960), I, 66, for his discussion of the Madhyamīka in this respect.

294. Cf. de Bary *et al.*, *Sources of Chinese Tradition*, pp. 320–26, where it is translated by Leon Hurvitz.

295. Araki, "Chōwa ron," p. 221; and "Kan Tō-mei" [*Kuan Tung-ming*],ᵈˣ *Nippon chūgoku gakkai ho*, XII, 101–2.

296. Araki, "Kan Tō-mei," pp. 101–2.

297. *Hsü Fen-shu*, 1/36 Yü yu-jen shu: cf. also Franke, "Li Tschi und Matteo Ricci" *Abhändlung der Preussischen Akademie der Wissenschaften*, for a discussion of the limitations of Li's intellectual horizon; and Shimada, *Zasetsu*, pp. 194, 241, n. 39 (a long and thoughtful footnote on the significance of Li's myopia in this respect).

298. Gallagher, Louis J., tr., *China in the Sixteenth Century: The Journals of Matteo Ricci* (New York, 1953), pp. 32–33.

299. Huang Tsung-hsi, *Ming-i tai-fang lu* (Erh-lao ko ed.), Yüan-fa, Hsüeh-hsiao; de Bary *et al.*, *Sources of Chinese Tradition*, pp. 585–86, 590.

300. The main purpose, of course, was to entrench Manchu rule, but one important aspect of this was the re-establishment of Chu Hsi orthodoxy. Cf. L. Carrington Goodrich, *The Inquisition of Chien-lung* (Baltimore, 1935).

301. Herbert Butterfield, "Reflections on Religion and Modern Individualism" in *Journal of the History of Ideas*, XXII (no. 1, January–March, 1961), 39.

302. *Ibid.*, p. 35.

GLOSSARY

a 個人主義

b 銀

c 艮

d 安身

e 淮南格物

f 明哲保身論

g 身

h 心

i 性

j 自然

k 偽

l 百姓日用

m 愚夫愚婦

n 大丈夫

o 豪傑之士

p 泰州

q 韓貞

r 袁黃

s 善書

t 功過格

u 雲谷

v 袾宏

w 王世貞

x 顏鈞, 山農

y 徐樾, 子直, 波石

z 游俠

aa 趙貞吉, 大洲

ab 耿定向, 天臺

ac 聚和堂

ad 意氣

ae 無欲

af 李贄

ag 徐用檢, 魯源

ah 耿定理

ai 焦竑

aj 黃安

ak 芝佛院

al 成一個人

am 袁中道

an 焚書

ao 藏書

ap 羅汝芳

aq 生知

ar 大圓鏡智

as 童心

at 初潭集

au 風水

av 仁者

aw 講學

ax 山人

ay 顧炎武

az 王夫之

ba 日知錄

bb 東林

bc 劉宗周

bd 史孟麟

be 鄒善, 穎泉

bf 色坊子(坊主)

bg 徒徒草

bh 大智度論

bi 淫欲卽是道

bj 煩惱卽菩提

bk 元賢

bl 達觀

bm 明夷待訪錄

bn 侯外廬, 中國思想通史

bo 島田虔次, 中國に於ける近代
　　　思惟の挫折

bp 荒木見悟, 明末に於ける儒佛調
　　和論の性格

bq 日本中國學會報

br 王艮, 王心齋先生遺集

bs 心齋約言

bt 王心齋年譜

bu 趙貞吉, 泰州王心齋艮墓誌銘

bv 焦竑, 國朝獻徵錄, 中國史學叢
　　書

bw 徐樾, 王心齋別傳

bx 徐玉鑾

by 李贄, 續藏書

bz 周汝登, 聖學宗傳

ca 嵇文甫, 左派王學

cb 楠本正繼, 宋明時代儒學思想の
　　研究

cc 容肇祖, 明代思想史

cd 吳康, 宋明理學

ce 小野和子, 儒教の異端者たち

cf 松本三之介, 胎動するアジア

cg 鰍鱔賦

ch 王門現成派の系統

ci 宮崎市定, アジア史の研究

cj 吉川幸次郎, 元明詩概說

ck 酒井忠夫, 中國善書の研究

cl 高雄義堅, 中國佛敎史論

cm 岡田武彥, 明末儒敎の動向

cn 侯外廬, 十六世紀中國的進步的
　　哲學思潮概述

co 山下龍二, 明末に於ける反儒敎
　　思想の源流

cp 島田虔次, 王學左派批判の
　　批判

cq 王世貞, 弇州史料後集卷三五,
　　嘉隆江湖大俠

cr 梁汝元

cs 容肇祖, 何心隱集

ct 鄒元標, 梁山夫傳

cu 容肇祖, 何心隱及其思想

cv 林載貴, 宏甫, 思齋, 卓吾, 溫陵

cw 袁中道, 李溫陵傳

cx 潘曾紘, 李溫陵外紀

cy 黃雲眉, 李卓吾事實辨正

cz 烏以鋒, 李卓吾著述考

da 嵇文甫, 李卓吾與左派王學

db 王船山與李卓吾

dc 李卓吾評傳

dd 葉國慶, 李贄先世考

de 朱謙之

df 丘漢生, 泰州學派的杰出思想家
　　李贄

dg 馮友蘭, 從李贄說起—中國哲學
　　史中唯物主义和唯心主义互
　　相轉化的一个例證, 中國哲
　　學史論文二集

dh 鈴木虎雄, 李卓吾年譜

di 廣瀨豐, 吉田松陰の研究

dj 島田虔次, 儒教の叛逆者李贄

dk 八木次元, 李贄, 中國の思想家

dl 焚書

dm 續焚書

dn 藏書

do 續藏書

dp 初潭集

dq 李卓吾先生遺書

dr 李溫陵集

ds 三異人文集

dt (明燈)道古錄

du 無心

dv 袾宏, 竹窗三筆

dw 荒木見吾, 佛敎と儒敎

dx 管東溟

C. T. HSIA *Time and the Human Condition*

in the Plays of T'ang Hsien-tsu

日月 Before the launching of the "Proletarian Cultural Revolution" T'ang Hsien-tsu [a] (1550–1616) had received attention as a thinker in his own right among Chinese Communist scholars actively concerned with late Ming thought.[1] The greatest playwright of the Ming period, T'ang was of course a leading figure in the literary and intellectual world of his time. Among his older contemporaries Li Chih [b] and Hsü Wei [c] were his friends, and among his younger, the Yüan [d] brothers. He was affiliated with the Tung-lin clique,[e] and his submission of an outspoken memorial to the throne on one occasion speaks for his political bond with that group.[2] Especially as a student of Lo Ju-fang,[f] T'ang claims a place in the history of late Ming thought. Lo Ju-fang was a prominent member of the T'ai-chou school, and his teacher Yen Chün,[g] far more than its founder Wang Ken, stamped that school with its radical character.[3]

T'ang Hsien-tsu studied under Lo at the age of thirteen.[*] While he must have been more a student of classics preparing for the examinations than a philosophic seeker, there is no doubt that T'ang was exposed to Lo's thought through daily contact so that in retrospect he refers to his period of study under Lo as one in which his latent spiritual capacity (*t'ien-chi*)[h] was kept in a state of blaze.[4] In examining the sayings of Lo Ju-fang compiled by Huang Tsung-hsi,[i] we find that his distinctive contribution to Ming thought lies in his application of the term *sheng-sheng*[j] (perpetual renewal of life), taken from the *Book of Changes*,[k] to a system of ethics and metaphysics largely built upon an interpretation of key terms found in *The Great Learning*[l] and *The Doctrine of the Mean*.[m] [5] Lo sees as the animating principle of the universe the phenomenon of life itself, or the endless process of birth and growth. This ceaseless vitality he

---

[*] Throughout this paper I have adopted the customary Chinese system for counting age.

regards as something intrinsically good, and he would equate the term *sheng* [n] (life, vitality) with the term *jen* [o] (humanity, love). To him, the very endowment of life extends to man the supreme ethical attribute *jen*. He reasons thus: "The birth of a person is due to the latent vitality (*sheng-chi*)[p] implicit in the process of creation. Therefore, when a person is born, he partakes in the joy of spontaneous creativity so that we may say the terms *jen* (humanity) and *jen* [q] (man) are identical." [6] He suggests that "those who are expert in discussing *hsin* [r] (mind) would do better to replace that term with the term *sheng*." [7]

As I shall later demonstrate, this vitalistic strain of his teacher's thought is quite evident in T'ang Hsien-tsu's first three plays, *Tzu-hsiao chi* [s] (The purple-jade flute), *Tzu-ch'ai chi* [t] (The purple-jade hairpins), and especially *Mu-tan t'ing* [u] (The peony pavilion). Scattered through his extant letters, numbering about 450, and his voluminous writings in classical prose and verse [8] are numerous instances where T'ang seems to have held the term *sheng* in especial regard. During his period of exile at Hsü-wen, Kwangtung, as a minor official (1591–92), he established an academy called Kuei-sheng shu-yüan [v] and wrote an essay explaining the term *kuei-sheng* [w] (reverence for life). "Therefore the education of a great man starts with 'knowing life,'" he writes. "Knowing what life is, he knows how to respect himself. Then he will also know how to hold in reverence all forms of life in this universe." [9] Since in both traditional and modern estimation T'ang is especially praised for his affirmation of *ch'ing* [x] (love, feelings), we may further say that he attaches supreme importance to *ch'ing* precisely because *ch'ing* appears to him the distinguishing feature of human existence. In the teaching of Yen Chün, *ch'ing* already appears as a term of key importance. Huang Tsung-hsi reports Yen Chün as saying, "Of my many disciples I would discourse on *hsing* [y] (nature) with Lo Ju-fang and on *hsin* (mind) with Ch'en I-ch'üan; [z] as for the rest, I would discourse on *ch'ing*." [10] It is unlikely that Lo Ju-fang could have been uninformed of his teacher's doctrine of *ch'ing* since he expounded it before so many of his disciples.

After the age of fifty T'ang Hsien-tsu seems to have been more inclined to the traditional wisdom of Buddhism and Taoism. To most critics, his last two plays, *Nan-k'o chi* [aa] (The Nan-k'o dream) and *Han-tan chi* [ab] (The Han-tan dream), represent an aberration from his earlier thought because of their otherworldly attitude toward life. The friend whom T'ang held in the greatest esteem during the middle period of his life was the Ch'an priest Ta-kuan,[ac] also styled Tzu-po. T'ang first met him at the age of forty-one (1590) and Ta-kuan died of government persecution in prison in 1603 when T'ang was fifty-four.[11] Ta-kuan was a monk of intellectual stature who commanded almost as much attention among the literati of his time as Li Chih.[12] But his influence on T'ang Hsien-tsu is difficult to estimate. While his active involvement in politics bespeaks his radical temper, in the speculative realm he appears an orthodox Ch'an thinker influenced by the major ideas of Neo-Confucianism. In a letter to T'ang, for example, he defends the greater human relevance of the concept *hsing* (nature) over against his friend's advocacy of *ch'ing*.[13] To many scholars, Ta-kuan would seem to have been an influence which accounts for T'ang's ultimate retreat to Buddhism.[14] Hou Wai-lu,[ad] however, gives greater stress to Ta-kuan's positive influence on T'ang in his role as a political activist. He sees the political satire in *Han-tan chi* as evidence of T'ang Hsien-tsu's active concern with Ming politics despite his ostensible espousal of Taoism. Further, he regards the author as a Utopianist who projects his vision of a happier and more equitable society in the ostensibly Buddhist dream allegory of *Nan-k'o chi*.[15] However, even in Communist China, scholars more competent in Ming drama have questioned Hou's fanciful reappraisal of the playwright as a protosocialist of the Utopian variety.[16]

In the preceding section I have written as if I were complying with the request of a hypothetical scholar who wanted to include a brief section on T'ang Hsien-tsu in his systematic survey of Ming thought. I have therefore supplied the kind of information that would seem germane to his purpose. But T'ang Hsien-tsu, of course, is primarily a playwright: to extract his "thought" from his plays and other writings, to trace its probable derivation, and to relate it solely to the philosophical and political currents of his time is actually to do injustice to the meaning of each individual play and the total pattern of meaning which is revealed when his five plays are studied in organic relation to each other. Whereas the speculative scholars whose sayings are recorded in *Ming-ju hsüeh-an* [ae] are primarily concerned with concepts, and study the problems of ethics and metaphysics at a high level of abstraction, the playwright as thinker, of necessity, dramatizes the philosophic issues either in the tension of actual human conflict or in the fantasy of a dream allegory. In reading the plays of T'ang Hsien-tsu, therefore, we are far less concerned with the fixable meaning of individual ideas than with the dramatic interplay of such ideas. We all feel the profundity of Shakespeare's thought, but we would be hard put to formulate that thought except in terms that would reduce it to a philosophical commonplace. Though T'ang Hsien-tsu is hardly to be ranked with Shakespeare (as many Chinese scholars would like us to believe),[17] his plays, too, give us not so much a paraphrasable statement about life as an impassioned presentation of life with all the illogic of human existence itself. We must attend to every detail of dramatic structure, every nuance of poetic language, to do proper justice to the meaning of the plays.

As stated in the title of my paper, I propose to examine the plays of T'ang Hsien-tsu as a study of the human condition under the curse of time. I am not aware of any major Ming thinker specifically concerned with the problem of time and eternity, but, of course, T'ang is far more importantly a product of the Chinese literary tradition with its characteristic preoccupation with the transience of human life. Indeed, the literary tradition counts so enormously toward an understanding of the playwright that every salient feature of his "thought" mentioned in the preceding section could as well be explained with reference to that tradition alone. Even if T'ang were not philosophically concerned with such concepts as *sheng* and *ch'ing*, he would still have affirmed life and love in conformity with the *ch'uan-ch'i* [af] tradition of Ming drama with its partiality for the welfare of young lovers. Likewise, even if T'ang were personally indifferent to Taoism and Buddhism, Taoist and Buddhist ideas would have crept into his plays as a matter of course, in view of their wide currency in the popular literature of the Yuan-Ming period. Again, even if T'ang were not actively concerned with government affairs, political satire of some inoffensive kind would have been present in his plays because such satire had always been an ingredient in Chinese drama.

I have chosen to stress the theme of time in T'ang Hsien-tsu not only because of its importance in every one of his plays but because it provides a unifying idea to our understanding of his work as a whole. Though scholars are not agreed as to when T'ang started writing each of his first three plays,[18] they generally subscribe to the view that these plays are mainly concerned with love while his last two plays, composed during his early fifties, are "dream" plays which repudiate love and other worldly values in favor of a religious interpretation of life. Because of the modern partiality for worldly values, it has been the fashion to deplore the author's religious stance in the last two plays, however much they may be admired on other grounds. Various explanations have been given for T'ang's change of outlook: his retirement from official life and consequent adoption of a mode of thought more appropriate to a recluse, the influence of Ta-kuan, his grief over the loss of some of his children (especially his eldest son at the age of twenty-three in 1600),[19] and general disillusionment with his times. Whatever the offered explanation, it is commonly believed that there is a definite ideological break between the first three and the last two plays. The oeuvre is therefore disappointing in view of its lack of philosophic continuity.

A careful reading of the plays, however, will show that the case is overdrawn. Not only is the religious note already heard in the first play, *Tzu-hsiao chi*, but in the last two plays, especially in *Nan-k'o chi*, the married lovers are by and large described with as much tender affection as in the earlier plays, even though in the last scenes of each play love is repudiated. What seems to me certain is that T'ang Hsien-tsu had never suffered a drastic change of attitude which induced him in his later age to look upon love or any other human attachment traditionally sanctioned as something disgusting or repulsive. Such attachments remain endearing as long as the tyranny of time over humanity is not raised as an issue. In the last two plays sensuality unaccompanied by love is satirized, but this is nothing exceptional since sensuality has always been scorned in the traditional moral scheme. What seems to me to be the case is that in his last two plays T'ang prefers to see the human condition in the aspect of eternity, and it is only in this perspective that love and all other human values are found wanting. T'ang is not a mystic who can perceive eternity in the dimension of time. To him, eternity appears as an infinity of time which crushes his human consciousness. In his first two plays he is only slightly bothered by this problem so that he can submit himself to the stream of time and celebrate the kind of love which seems to obliterate time in the ecstasy of its enjoyment. Time itself is not yet the villain; the kind of villainy depicted in *Tzu-ch'ai chi* stems from human malice and spite, which is rectifiable in time by recourse to heroic action (*hsia*).[ag] [20] Before the author submits to the defeat of humanity by time in his last two plays, however, he makes a gallant attempt to defy time in *Mu-tan t'ing*. Through the death and resurrection of the heroine, T'ang Hsien-tsu asserts the triumph of love over time, but in the comic framework of the play the heroine is eventually reduced to a creature of time seduced by its rewards.

In *Tzu-hsiao chi* T'ang Hsien-tsu already appears as a master player of the many variations on the time theme to be seen in traditional Chinese poetry: youth versus age, mortal man seen against nature with its cyclical renewal, the intolerableness of time when one's beloved is absent, the temporary obliteration of time when lovers or friends meet after a period of separation. Also present are the various goals sought by the Chinese poet to mitigate or cancel out the evil of time: Confucian fame, Taoist immortality, and Buddhist enlightenment. Most early Chinese poets, of course, simply drown time in a cup of wine: in place of this hedonism, T'ang Hsien-tsu characteristically offers the intenser joy of romantic love.

Tzu-hsiao chi is loosely based on the famous T'ang tale by Chiang Fang,[ah] entitled "Huo Hsiao-yü" (*Huo Hsiao-yü chuan*),[ai] which tells of the betrayal of the title heroine by her lover, the poet Li I,[aj] and her death. In the play T'ang Hsien-tsu turns Li I into an admirable and ardent lover, partly in conformity with the romantic convention of the *ch'uan-ch'i* play which dictates the portrayal of the hero in a favorable light and partly out of his overwhelming sympathy for the heroine. For various reasons, however, T'ang did not complete the play [21] and he eventually chose to readapt the tale under the title of *Tzu-ch'ai chi*. *Tzu-hsiao chi*, which was written in the ornate *p'ien-ch'i* [ak] style then going out of fashion, was excluded from the canon of the "Four Dream Plays of Lin-ch'uan" [al] (T'ang was a native of Lin-ch'uan, Kiangsi), and largely for this reason it has always been dismissed as an immature work.[22] Actually, it is the most undeservedly neglected of T'ang's plays. By the standards of Ming drama, which require an abundance of vicissitudes in the chronicling of the fortunes of young lovers, the play is of course incomplete and short on action. But by modern standards its paucity of action is amply compensated for by its rich imagery, its neat structure, and its passionate orchestration of the theme of love. Far more than the celebrated *Mu-tan t'ing*, it is a sustained paean of youthful passion.

T'ang's dramatic skill is especially in evidence in his exploration of the time theme implicit in the tale: the sharp contrast between the young beauty Hsiao-yü with all the promise of life ahead of her and the aging courtesans and entertainers living as dependents in the households of the great. The latter had enjoyed brief fame before they were bought as concubines by the aristocrats and officials of the capital. But with their beauty fading, any day they may be dismissed from service; they will become lonely and some of them will turn to religion for consolation. Already in T'ang's first play, renunciation is entertained as a serious possibility, and even Hsiao-yü herself is once praised for her potential vocation as a Taoist nun.[23] She is the illegitimate daughter of the Prince of Huo.[am] In the tale her mother, named Cheng Liu-niang [an] in the play, is turned out of the house after the prince's death. She rears her daughter in a state of semi-respectability, though actually training her for the profession of a singer-courtesan. In the play the prince is still alive, but all of a sudden (scene 7), he follows his whim to seek Taoist immortality and dismisses his two concubines, Cheng Liu-niang and Tu Ch'iu-niang.[ao] They have served him for twenty years, and now they have to shift for themselves and to emulate his example if they feel the call for a Taoist career. Ch'iu-niang soon becomes a Taoist nun, living with a younger companion named Shan-ts'ai.[ap] The names of both characters are taken from Po Chü-i's [aq] "The Lute Song" (*P'i-p'a hsing*),[ar] though in the poem *shan-ts'ai* actually signifies a teacher of *p'i-p'a* music.[24] Just as "Huo Hsiao-yü" is the most tragic of T'ang tales depicting the fate of a young courtesan, "The Lute Song" is the most pathetic of T'ang poems about an entertainer who has out-lived her days of glory in Ch'ang-an. T'ang Hsien-tsu recreates the mood of "The Lute Song" to reinforce his sympathy for the aging beauties in his play.

Even earlier in the play (scene 3), General Hua Ch'ing,[as] who has been feeling the stirrings of ambition to achieve great deeds on the frontier, admires a steed owned by the scion of Kuo Tzu-i [at] and he has no compunction in exchanging for that horse his concubine Pao Ssu-niang [au] (Pao Shih-i-niang [av] in the tale), a professional singer who has served him for years. In the tale Pao is a "crafty, smooth-tongued" matchmaker, a type usually treated with contempt in Chinese fiction. But in the play, while she still plays the role of a go-between to bring together Li Yi and Hsiao-yü, she is a great friend of the discarded concubines of the Prince of Huo and shares their fate.

The dramatic bearing of the fate of these aging beauties upon Hsiao-yü is unmistakable. Though she is addressed as a *chün-chu* [aw] (princess), she is being prepared for the vocation of a high-class courtesan. In the tale, upon being introduced to her, Li Yi cohabits with her the same evening; in the play the intervention of a wedding ceremony still leaves no doubt about her dubious status as a long-term mistress rather than as a proper wife. When Li Yi first seeks Pao Ssu-niang's help as a go-between, she recommends Hsiao-yü and cautions him against dissipation: "Shih-lang, why injure your pre-cious-as-gold body among the courtesans? It's better to contract your-self to a famous beauty and let her entertain you as your companion (*hsiang-p'ei tso-k'e* [ax])." [25]

In the tale Hsiao-yü begs Li I to stay with her for eight years— at the end of the term he will be only thirty and still eligible to marry a girl from a respectable and wealthy family. In the play she begs him for ten years of his companionship.[26] Hsiao-yü is an intense romantic who believes that living happily for eight or ten years with the man of her choice is worth a lifetime, but at the same time she is a realist who knows the futility of expecting a famous poet with a promising official career to be hers for life.

Hsiao-yü's fate, therefore, depends entirely upon her lover. If he proves perfidious, she is ruined and will die. But since T'ang has changed his character, he proves in every way worthy of her trust and passion (except in scene 3, where he appears as the friend who advises Hua Ch'ing to exchange his concubine). Soon after their marriage, when Hsiao-yü confides to him her ten-year plan during a stroll in the garden, he protests eternal love for her in some of the loveliest stanzas in the play. For the young couple passionately in love, time creates no problem unless they are apart. Sure enough, soon after Li I has earned the *chuang-yuan* [ay] degree, he is appointed a secretary to the old general Tu Huang-shang [az] at the frontier. Luckily, while he displays ability, he sees no action. But for both the poet and his wife the period of separation is unbearable. In scene 32 he pours forth his longing for her in a lyrical recapitulation of their delirious courtship, their mutual avowal of undying love in the garden, and their touching farewell scene. Peace is soon concluded on the frontier, however, and in the final scene (scene 34) the hero returns home on the seventh day of the seventh month—the one day in the year when the Herd-boy and the Weaver-girl can meet in Heaven.

The young lovers in *Tzu-hsiao chi* overcome the tyranny of time over a three-year period through an act of reunion—and for the moment and possibly for years to come time cannot bother them. But for the older people the situation is quite different. The women have time on their hands because love is denied them and they can only obtain some vicarious satisfaction in the good fortune of their beloved Hsiao-yü. The men, however, seek other ideals because for them a loving relationship can no longer ward off their sense of mortality: they would sooner choose Confucian fame or Taoist longevity. In this connection, the sudden decision of Tu Huang-shang to turn Buddhist upon returning from the frontier is of especial interest. An early follower of Kuo Tzu-i, he has had a long, illustrious career serving as minister and general under three emperors. Now, at sixty, he is being recalled to court. Ssu-k'ung,[ba] a saintly monk over a hundred years old, who has been the general's friend in years past, awaits his arrival at his temple for a visit. Though the general has earlier shown few signs of otherworldliness, he is immediately awakened to the necessity of a spiritual life upon hearing Ssu-k'ung's song about the ten decades of a man's life:

> When a boy of ten, with cheeks as fresh as the hibiscus,
> You play all day and return home only near dusk.
> At twenty, you ride in a shining coach, drawn by spirited horses,
> And heartily talk of poetry and rhetoric.
> At thirty, strong enough to lift a tripod, you feel
> You can fly, sustained by the wind of ambition, determined
> To achieve fame and rank in government service.
> At forty, you straddle over provinces and commanderies,
> And with pendants jangling from your hat, you go in and out of the
>   emperor's courts.
> Full of pomp and circumstance at fifty, you are entertained
> By dancing and singing girls in exquisite silk and gold.
> At sixty you make arrangements to provide for your family.
> At seventy all joy is gone and you hate
> To look at your own visage in the mirror.
> At eighty, your intelligence is gone, and you can no longer
> Recall what you said or did in the past, in your state of retirement.
> Your days are declining at ninety
> And your mind can no longer direct your body—
> Words said out of turn are all inappropriate
> And your deluded mind is easily apprehensive.
> Your tears course down as you remember the past
> And you won't even recognize your sons and grandsons when they come
>   to pay their respects.
> When you reach a hundred, life is totally sans taste;
> Your eyes are now blurred mirrors,
> And your drooling mouth gapes for breath.[27]

The song bears a striking resemblance to Jaques' famous speech in *As You Like It* except that it accords man a much longer span of life. To Jaques, man ends his "strange, eventful history" in his seventh decade as he creeps toward "second childishness and mere oblivion," but nevertheless Jaques does not regret the various roles man has assumed before he reaches that state. For him, it is perhaps a good thing to shun the delusive glory of the court and the battlefield (for he is something of a philosopher), but each stage of a man's life offers Jaques equal wry amusement as his cunning eye selects for emphasis the most comic and absurd detail. In the Chinese monk's song, which is designed for a listener who has achieved unusual success, man's early enjoyments and glories are pointedly contrasted with his dotage when life appears utterly tasteless and meaningless. General Tu reacts to the song in an expected manner, saying, "When a man's life reaches this last stage, what's the use of talking about Heaven and Tao? Even sages and worthies are not spared, and how could I hope to preserve my life? When I think of my past life, it is only the dream of an ephemeron." [28] He therefore seeks repentance and embraces Buddhism to await rebirth in the Western Paradise.

This scene of General Tu's conversion (scene 31) appears as a miniature play upon which *Nan-k'o chi* and *Han-tan chi* are eventually modeled. Though Ssu-k'ung has earlier spoken of the filthiness and decay of the body in conventional Buddhist terms, his song has not deliberately depicted man's life in repulsive colors. It has only realistically called attention to the debilities of age, in contrast to which the earlier pleasures of man appear rather vain and delusive. General Tu, however, is immediately persuaded of the Buddhist logic of forsaking the world. At sixty there is enough vigor left in him to escape the humiliating circumstances of sheer senility; he has had a rich and rewarding life, and by electing Buddhism, he appears a sensible man who chooses wisdom before his intellect and senses have completely withered. But his awakening suggests no genuine spiritual enlightenment.

In General Tu's response to the song we hear a familiar strain in Chinese poetry. In fact, his comment "Even sages and worthies are not spared" (*Sheng-hsien pu-neng tu*)[bb] is adapted from one of the "Nineteen Old Poems." The relevant passage goes:

Man's life is like a sojourning,
His longevity lacks the firmness of stone and metal.
For ever it has been that mourners in their turn were mourned,
Saint and Sage—all alike are trapped.[29]

(The last line is Arthur Waley's rendition of *Sheng-hsien mo-neng tu.*)[bc] Like the early Chinese poets, General Tu appears primarily apprehensive of old age and afraid of death, and he chooses a conventional solution with its promise of a paradise. But among Chinese poets whose hedonism and melancholy betray their fear of death, there are major exceptions who have spoken eloquently of man's existential dignity or who have truly apprehended the mystic light. T'ao Ch'ien's [bd] poem, "Substance, Shadow, and Spirit" (*Hsing ying shen*),[be] seems to have been deliberately written as an answer to the kind of questions raised in "Nineteen Old Poems." Whereas Substance speaks for wine and sensual pleasure to make time pass by agreeably and Shadow speaks for fame and achievement as a Confucian answer to oblivion, the Spirit advises both to accept death calmly:

> You had better go where Fate leads—
> Drift on the Stream of Infinite Flux,
> Without joy, without fear;
> When you must go—then go,
> And make as little fuss as you can.[30]

If hedonism and Confucian endeavor are designed to lull one's fear of death and oblivion, then the stoicism of T'ao implies a release from such fear in that every moment can be enjoyed for its sake without one's worrying whether one is enjoying oneself or whether one is doing something worthwhile in the perspective of human history. One is ready to meet death at any moment because every moment represents a point in a continuum of calm enjoyment unperturbed by a sense of life's transience. I would further suppose that, in electing to live by this existentialism, one does not have to exclude the heights of joy or achievement. If the indwelling spirit prompts a person to fall in love or to engage in an act of creativity, then he should be all the more grateful for its temporary invigoration of his bodily frame.

General Tu's sudden conversion also indicates that for T'ang Hsien-tsu it is the spectacle of mortality alone which impels one to seek a form of permanence which supposedly arrests time. The playwright, being no mystic, cannot see the simultaneous coexistence of timelessness and time. In his "First Fu on the Red Cliff" (*Ch'ien Ch'ih-pi fu*),[bf] another great poet, Su Shih,[bg] transcends the Chinese concern with mutability to indicate his awareness of a higher form of reality coexisting with time: "For if you look at the aspect which changes, heaven and earth cannot last for one blink; but if you look at the aspect which is changeless, the worlds within and outside you are both inexhaustible, and what reasons have you to envy anything?" [31] This is a piece of wisdom with which neither philosophical Taoism nor Ch'an [bh] Buddhism can disagree. And yet, despite his friendship with Ta-kuan which would indicate an intellectual sympathy with Ch'an wisdom and despite his passionate commitment to romantic love as an intense form of existence to be enjoyed in disregard of time, T'ang Hsien-tsu is nevertheless a time-obsessed poet who seeks religion as an *alternative* to life because he is neither sufficiently appreciative of man's existential dignity nor sufficiently aware of the timeless aspect of things in all their apparent mortality.

After affirming love in two other plays (*Tzu-ch'ai chi* and *Mu-tan t'ing*, to which we shall return later), T'ang Hsien-tsu wrote *Nan-k'o chi* and *Han-tan chi* as further elaborations on the theme of the dream of life from which General Tu has earlier awakened. Each play is based on a famous T'ang tale: *Nan-k'o chi* on Li Kung-tso's [bi] "The Governor of Nan-k'o" (*Nan-k'o t'ai-shou chuan*),[bj] and *Han-tan chi* on Shen Chi-tsi's [bk] "Life Inside a Pillow" (*Chen-chung chi*).[bl] T'ang must have been aware of the unpromising dramatic character of these sources, but he chose them nevertheless as vehicles for his new conviction about life.

"The Governor of Nan-k'o" tells of Ch'un-yü Fen,[bm] a onetime military officer now addicted to drinking, and his changed fortune in a dream. Transplanted to an ant kingdom, he marries its princess Yao-fang [bn] and is put in charge of the province of Nan-k'o.[bo] He is a good governor and repels the invasion of a neighboring ant kingdom. After the death of his wife, however, he suffers calumny at court and is advised to return to the human world. Upon awaking, Ch'un-yü identifies the location of the ant kingdoms underneath the acacia tree in his courtyard and finds the predictions and happenings in the dream confirmed. Having realized that "man's life is but a fleeting moment," [32] he turns into a Taoist recluse, forsaking the pleasures of wine and sex. Three years later he dies in his home at the age of forty-seven.

T'ang Hsien-tsu changes the story by enlarging the role of the Ch'an priest, Ch'i-hsüan,[bp] who is only briefly mentioned in the tale, and by translating the awakened hero into a Buddha rather than a mere recluse. Ch'i-hsüan, possibly a glorified portrait of Ta-kuan, is the puppet master in the play who manipulates the lives of the ants as well as that of the hero. In his previous incarnation he was a follower of Bodhidharma ^{bq} who had accidentally spilled hot oil over an ant colony, and his rebirth, in a way, is for the purpose of redeeming these ants.[33] The opening and concluding scenes involving the hero's confrontation with the monk are of decided philosophic interest, though the bulk of the play, which faithfully recounts the hero's dream career as given in the tale, is rather drab. It is the worst of T'ang's five plays.

In *Tzu-hsiao chi* General Tu's awakening from life involves no emotional crisis because he is not called upon to tear himself away from anyone particularly dear to him. At sixty he is already indifferent to love and his election of a life of Buddhist devotion is comparatively easy. In *Nan-k'o chi* Ch'un-yü Fen is primarily depicted as a person committed to love (*ch'ing*): he inquires after the welfare of his deceased father, he loves his wife and children dearly, and as a lonely widower toward the end of his stay in the ant kingdom, he even has a brief fling with three sex-hungry ladies at court. Since in his three earlier plays T'ang Hsien-tsu has affirmed the supreme value of love in the temporal dimension, *Nan-k'o chi* represents his first serious attempt to place the value of love in the scheme of human transience. The three key scenes—scene 8: "Attachment to Love" (*Ch'ing-chu*)^{br}; scene 43: "Transference of Love" (*Ch'uan-ch'ing*)^{bs}; scene 44: "Exhaustion of Love" (*Ch'ing-chin*)^{bt}—are all significantly titled to indicate the schematic design of the play. Though in the very first scenes Ch'un-yü is depicted as a drunkard disillusioned with life (he knows every prostitute in Yang-chou and out of sheer boredom seeks amusement at the Avalambana Festival at a Buddhist temple), the author is so conditioned by the romantic conventions of Ming drama that once he meets two of the ant ladies offering in behalf of their princess a small box made of rhinoceros horn and a pair of gold hairpins before the statue of Kuan-yin ^{bu} at the temple,[34] he appears considerably younger, handsome and well-behaved, a fit mate for a princess. During his stay at the ant kingdom, therefore, he appears no different from any other sentimental hero in a Ming play—a man of feeling firmly attached to Confucian and romantic values without a trace of his earlier disillusionment.

Upon awaking, he examines the site of the ant kingdoms with two of his friends and is overcome with grief when he spots the burial ground of his wife:

Ch'un-yü (*scans the site and cries*): There you see the mound over a foot long and underneath it my wife lies. Alas, my princess! [35]

Overwhelmed by love and nostalgia, Ch'un-yü again goes to see Ch'i-hsüan and avows his wish to have his late father and wife and all the inhabitants of the ant kingdom ascend to Heaven. It is, of course, partly because of his compassion that he is eventually granted Buddhahood. But for Ch'i-hsüan, the ultimate test of his Buddhahood is the eradication of all feelings of love for sentient beings. He stages therefore a mass ascension to Heaven as a harrowing trial for the hero in preparation for his enlightenment.

When Ch'un-yü sees his three ant mistresses ascend to Heaven, he is still amorous:

Ch'un-yü: You three celestials, please descend. I have something to tell you.
Lady A: Our bodies are now celestial. How could we descend?
Lady B: Even if we descend, to us your human body stinks, and it won't do you any good.

Most pitiful the human body,
Most pitiful the human body.
In Heaven we will have a new kind of fulfillment.
How could you, crazy man, still cling to us? [36]

Then it is the princess' turn to ascend. The hero, after apologizing for his infidelity, protests undying love:

Ch'un-yü: Day and night I am drunk with love,
My longing for you never diminishes.
Ah, Princess, is my fear justified
That in Heaven you will seek a new mate?
While in Heaven, could you once again take me as your consort?
Once you are back in Heaven, when will we see each other again?
Please vouchsafe a detailed answer to my three questions.
(*Cries.*) If you cannot answer me,
Then what's so good about Heaven?
Better descend to earth where we loved.[37]

Out of pity the princess descends.

Yao-fang: Ah, how come I have been lowered back to earth?

Ch'un-yü: Ah, my wife.

Yao-fang: The air of Heaven is different from the air of the earth. Please don't stay too close, my brother.

Ch'un-yü: Why did you call me brother?

Yao-fang: Once you were at the temple and you called me sister.

Ch'un-yü: I did call you so.

Yao-fang: Once you said you wanted a token. On the seat of the Kuan-yin statue there lie a pair of gold hairpins with the phoenix design and a small box made of rhinoceros horn. Are these not the tokens which made you fall in love with me?

Ch'un-yü: It is so.

Yao-fang (bows before the Kuan-yin statue, picks up the hairpins and the rhinoceros box, and hands them to Ch'un-yü): Ch'un-lang, Ch'un-lang, cherish this box and these hairpins. I'm going now.

Ch'un-yü (receives the box and hairpins and pulls at the princess. He kneels and cries):

I once searched for you underneath the earth;
Now that you are ascending to Heaven, how can I let you go?
I'll never stop pulling at the sashes of your celestial skirt:
When an ant is going to Heaven, what could I do but be its supplicant?

Yao-fang: It's not yet time for you to ascend to Heaven. Oh, my husband!

Ch'un-yü: I must follow you to Heaven. (*Ch'un-yü and Yao-fang pull at each other and cry. Suddenly Ch'i-hsüan enters with sword in hand. He parts them with his sword and ejaculates the sound "Ya!" to music. Exit Yao-fang hurriedly. Ch'un-yü stumbles and falls.*) [38]

As with lovers in nearly every culture, Ch'un-yü and Yao-fang want a Heaven which will perpetuate their love without change. In Rossetti's "The Blessèd Damozel," while the lover longs for his departed love, the girl herself, now in Heaven, fancies the day when he, too, will arrive there. She will then introduce him to the Virgin Mary and petition Christ to grant her wish:

Only to live as once on earth
    With Love,—only to be,
As then awhile, for ever now
    Together, I and he.

But if the Catholic imagination permits the reunion of lovers in Heaven, the Buddhist imagination allows no such dispensation. Yao-fang, as a mere celestial about to ascend to Heaven, may still speak of romantic love in human accent and wish for some kind of physical and spiritual union with her husband in the lower tiers of Heaven (in a passage omitted from the translation given above),[39] but Ch'un-yü is to become a Buddha and he is not allowed the luxury of attachment. After he has parted the lovers, Ch'i-hsüan forcibly reminds the hero that his wife is but an ant, that his years of happiness with her are but a brief dream, and that her tokens of love are but trifles:

Ch'un-yü (*awakens and examines the tokens*): Ah, the gold hairpins are but twigs of the acacia and the small box is but a pod of the same tree. Pshaw, what's the use of these things? (*He throws away the hairpins and the box.*) Now I, Ch'un-yü Fen, am finally awakened. The ties between king and minister, the ties binding a family, how do they differ from similar ties in the ant kingdom? All pleasure and suffering, all success and failure—they take place as well in Nan-k'o. Everything is in a state of dream, and what's the use of ascending to Heaven? All my life I have been deluded.[40]

One may say that the awakening of the hero is too pat to be convincing. In describing the ant kingdom, the author has elevated the ants to the status of human beings so that naturally the hero gets as much involved with them as he would with his own kind. At the end, however, the author appeals to our prejudice against ants, saying that ants are but ants and their feelings are not worth bothering about. But the farewell scene between Ch'un-yü and Yao-fang is touching precisely because she is in everything but name a human being. When Ch'un-yü realizes that the person he loves is but an ant and throws away her tokens of love, he has not, as the author would have us believe, brought the world of human sentiments to its true scale in the perspective of Buddhist cosmology; rather, he has only cast contempt upon human feelings by a cheap appeal to our customary belittlement of the ant. And in the true scheme of Buddhist compassion (after all, it is to return the ant colony to Heaven that Ch'i-hsüan has resumed incarnation on earth), what is so contemptible about the feelings of ants? Twigs and pods may not compare in worth with gold and rhinoceros horn by the standards of monetary economy. But as sincere offerings of love or thankfulness, how do they differ from the so-called rare objects? In the play, therefore, while T'ang Hsien-tsu realizes that as long as we have emotional attachments we are the slaves of time and cannot obtain true liberation, he brings about the liberation of his hero by the device of an allegorical comparison which doesn't tell us in the end why the feelings are bad. In the bulk of the play, in scenes descriptive of the hero's varied activities as lover, governor, and military commander, he employs the affirmative poetic language appropriate to each of these scenes. He has actually depicted the human or ant world in a favorable light, and then in the end he equates it with a dream. One is not convinced that the state of awakening is preferable to the dream state if the kind of permanence sought for in the former state cannot be arrived at without one's first entertaining an intellectual contempt for all human and animal existence.

Han-tan chi is a much more powerful play than Nan-k'o chi. Though "Life Inside a Pillow" is a shorter and less interesting tale than "The Governor of Nan-k'o," its hero, Lu Sheng,[bv] is an ambitious malcontent exposed to greater extremes of success and humiliation in his dream state. In his dream Ch'un-yü Fen lives by and large a happy and useful life, the kind of life that tends rather to confirm our faith in humanity than otherwise; Lu Sheng, on the other hand, is a man on trial, though he is by no means an archetypal hero on a par with Job or Faust. In the tale, when asked by the Taoist Lü Weng [bw] why he is discontented, Lu Sheng answers, "Born into this world, a scholar ought to achieve great deeds and establish his fame. He should serve as a general when on the frontier and a prime minister when at court. He should preside over sumptuous banquets and order the orchestra to play what he likes. He should cause his clan to prosper and his own family to wax rich, and then he could say that he has fulfilled his heart's desire. I was once ambitious at my studies and applied myself to all the arts, and I thought that rank and title were mine for the taking. But now at the prime of my life I still have to till my own field. What do you call this if not failure?" [41] Lü Weng places a magic pillow under his head and asks him to take a nap. Upon awaking, he has experienced all the rewards and tribulations of a distinguished official and feels no desire to strive further. In the play, Lü Weng is identified with the Taoist immortal Lü Tung-pin.[bx] He receives the awakened hero as a disciple and wafts him to P'eng-lai [by] Island.

T'ang Hsien-tsu adapts the tale quite faithfully, but at the same time he has enriched many episodes of the hero's dream life with political satire so that his play has about it an air of knowing cynicism which agrees well with its central message of Taoist detachment. Whereas both Ch'un-yü and Yao-fang are characters of conventional goodness to be expected in Ming drama, Lu Sheng and his wife, Miss Ts'ui,[bz] are not so innocent. Upon being sent to sleep in scene 4, Lu Sheng right away dreams that he is in the garden of Miss Ts'ui, an heiress of fabulous wealth, and she decides on the spot to marry him despite his shabby condition. The wedding itself is a rather coarse affair: both the groom and the servants talk in *double-entendre* and tease the bride about the anticipated sexual experience. After the wedding, again quite unlike most heroes in his situation, Lu Sheng shows not the least inclination to take the examinations even when his wife asks him to do so. His excuse is as follows: "I don't want to deceive you, my wife. Though I have read the classics and history, for years I have neglected to prepare for the exams. Today, thanks to our heaven-destined marriage, I am in the lap of luxury, and please don't ever mention to me again words like 'rank' and 'fame.' " [42] Miss Ts'ui agrees that it is quite futile to prepare for the examinations, but she assures him that with her kind of connections at court and her kind of money to bribe everyone concerned, "to become a *chuang-yüan* is as easy as turning over the palm of one's hand." [42] After Lu Sheng has bribed his way to the highest academic honors, the trials and challenges of his official career gradually mature him as a responsible statesman. But these early scenes of satire cannot be forgotten, and the ups and downs of Lu's career are mainly the result of political intrigue.

It seems that Lu Sheng, in bribing all around, has neglected the chief examiner Yü-wen Yung,[ca] a man of deep malice who enjoys great power at court. (He belongs to a special type of villain who has earlier appeared in *Tzu-ch'ai chi* and *Nan-k'o chi*, and T'ang Hsien-tsu may have drawn this type after Chang Chü-cheng,[cb] whom he detested for deeply personal reasons.)[43] Upon obtaining the *chuang-yüan* degree, Lu Sheng further slights him deliberately. It is at Yü-wen's recommendation, therefore, that, upon the completion of his three-year term at the Han-lin Academy, he is assigned to two difficult missions which, however, he accomplishes with amazing success. It is again at Yü-wen's instigation that the hero is charged with treason and exiled to Hainan Island. He almost dies there, but with the intercession of his good friends, notably the eunuch Kao Li-shih,[cc] Lu Sheng is eventually recalled to court, and his wife, who has been sold into slavery to endure the indignities of being a seamstress at a government factory, is restored to honor along with their children. Yü-wen himself is exposed for his treachery and sentenced to capital punishment. After twenty years' distinguished service as a prime minister, Lu Sheng is enfeoffed as the Duke of Chao (Chao Kuo-kung)[cd] and is awarded by the emperor thirty thousand ch'ing[ce] of land and a special villa in which are housed twenty-four female entertainers for his amusement. At this moment in his career, Lu tells his wife, "My lady, I have now reached the utmost of my desires." [44]

On the pretext of "robbing the yin[cf] to nourish the yang"[cg]—a Taoist form of sexual regimen much practiced among Ming emperors and aristocrats—Lu indulges himself in the company of the twenty-four girls and falls precipitately into a decline. On his deathbed, attended by Kao Li-shih and the emperor's own physician, he worries over the verdict of history, which may not do adequate justice to his distinguished and meritorious career, and over his youngest son, who has not yet reached seniority and the official eminence of his four elder brothers. He entrusts both his record and his youngest son to the care of Kao Li-shih. But on the whole, he dies content. His last words are: "When a man reaches my age and position, he should be satisfied. Alas, why is my eyesight failing me? I'm going now." [45]

The dreams of Lu Sheng and Ch'un-yü present obvious differences. First, whereas the latter is sent back to earth in mid-career, the former has lived his life to the full and expresses little regret over leaving it. Second, whereas the dream-life of Ch'un-yü is seen in the aspect of a Ming play, with its usual round of romantic and military episodes, the dream-life of Lu Sheng is at once charged with political meaning and conspicuous for a phantasmagoric quality in some of its most powerful scenes.⁴⁶ Third, Lu Sheng's career, far more than Ch'un-yü's, symbolizes the life of political ambition in the full range of its glory and ignominy. Lu's extreme suffering at Hainan Island dramatizes an experience common to many a Chinese official of literary or political eminence—unjust exile to an alien region as the consequence of a power struggle at court.

Lu Sheng's career also suggests that of Faust in a reverse fashion. The Chinese hero first achieves renown as an official in charge of canal-digging over a mountainous region of some 280 li.ᶜʰ Upon the successful completion of this task, he is appointed regional commander of Ho-hsi,ᶜⁱ to guard against the invading tribes. He scores a brilliant victory over the enemy and reaches T'ien-shan, almost 1,000 li from the Yü-men Pass,ᶜʲ where the Chinese forces have been previously stationed. By Act IV, Part II of Goethe's poetic drama, Faust has long enjoyed political eminence as a trusted counselor of his emperor, and in that act he routs the forces of a rival emperor. In Act V he embarks on the project of reclaiming a tract of marshy land from the tyranny of the ocean for the use of a happier humanity. A deed of value to the public, then, crowns the career of a Western seeker of self-fulfillment while it marks the beginning of a distinguished career for a Chinese official. While Faust's work is enmeshed in the individual tragedy of an old couple who refuse to make room for his project, Lu Sheng's task is carried out lightly, in a facetious comic manner (his recipe for turning rocks into water: take a million bundles of dry wood and set them on fire over the rocky mountain area; pour vinegar over the cinders and then drill the mountain until it crumbles into pieces of rock; pour salt over them and they will turn into water).⁴⁷

But the two heroes differ in more fundamental ways. Faust begins as a scholar wearying of life; he presently goes in pursuit of pleasure at the instigation of Mephistopheles, and it is only when he has outgrown his phase of spiritual despair that Mephistopheles begins to lose his hold upon him: for Goethe, therefore, Faust's last act of humanitarian goodness is regarded as a step beyond the kind of individualistic romanticism to which he was committed in his youth. As for T'ang Hsien-tsu's hero, though he is goaded into good deeds by the malice of an evil minister, he is not afflicted with romantic nihilism and he performs them as a matter of course. It is only when he is surfeited with power that he begins to seek sensual pleasure outside of wedlock. But even then his debauchery is regarded primarily as a quest for longevity. Twice, as we have seen, Lu Sheng declares his contentment with his life. With Faust, it is his agreement with Mephistopheles that

If ever I say to the passing moment
"Linger a while! Thou art so fair!"
Then you may cast me into fetters,
I will gladly perish then and there! [48]

For Faust the moment never comes since to him satiety means an end of life and he regards his life as one of endless adventure in a process of unceasing self-realization. Even though at the very end of his life he does bid a hypothetical moment in the indefinite future to "linger a while," he is expressing his contentment with the happy settlement of his reclaimed land by an ideal community which has not yet taken place and probably never will. As D. J. Enright has commented brilliantly, "*Im Vorgefühl*: in anticipation and only in anticipation, can he enjoy this unalloyed contentment." [49] In T'ang Hsien-tsu's plays, the supreme moment comes soon enough: when the lovers consummate their passion and wish to prolong their joy forever, when an official reaches the pinnacle of his success and feels that there is nothing he wants further, or, conversely, when the same official is suddenly awakened from life in a new state of enlightenment.

If on his deathbed Lu Sheng expresses on the whole satisfaction with his life, why does he then, upon awaking, immediately accept life as an illusion and go off with Lü Tung-pin? Why doesn't he want to relive his lucky encounter with an heiress, his moment of triumph as a *chuang-yüan*, his historic deeds of digging a canal and routing an enemy, his last fling with a bevy of beauties, and perhaps even his tribulations during his exile? But after Lü Tung-pin has told him that his dream-wife is but his donkey in disguise and that his children are but the chickens and dogs in the courtyard, Lu Sheng answers promptly enough, in a speech adapted from the tale: "Reverend sir, I, Lu Sheng, am now awakened. Our life and family ties are but like this. How could they pertain to the realm of reality? I have now completely realized the nature of life and death, and the principle lying behind our preordained glory and disgrace, gain and loss." [50]

Lu Sheng's decision to forsake the world, therefore, primarily stems from the fact that nothing in the human condition is permanent. Whereas the true Romantic as exemplified by Faust is characterized by perpetual self-dissatisfaction and ceaseless striving, the would-be Taoist-Buddhist man of enlightenment in T'ang Hsien-tsu is content enough to bask in mundane felicity so long as it proves permanent. It is because neither sexual love nor the progeny it produces, neither Confucian deeds nor the fame they bring guarantees perpetual happiness that he wants to sever his ties with the human world. In *Faust*, the act or deed is assigned primacy: so long as a man is true to himself and engaged in a meaningful quest, it matters little when his end comes. T'ang Hsien-tsu's heroes have an aversion to action (a partial exception is *Mu-tan t'ing*, where everyone is on the move): it is nearly always at the instigation of an evil minister that the hero is sent on a dangerous mission, and while he is Confucian enough to appreciate the kind of honor which the successful completion of his mission will bring him, at the same time he longs for his wife just as the wife, equally lonely at home, will think of him. A long tradition of poetry and drama has prepared T'ang to see the heroic deed as the agent that disrupts the family, that parts a couple happily in love, entailing for them painful emotional deprivation. In a sense, the touching reunion scenes that conclude *Tzu-hsiao chi* and *Tzu-ch'ai chi* are not unlike the scenes of the heroes' final awakening in *Nan-k'o chi* and *Han-tan chi*. For the young lover, with years of happy domestic life ahead of him, the very fact that he has returned home to his wife provides security enough—he has as yet no time to bother his head with the ultimate necessity to release himself from the illusion of the permanence of a loving attachment. Having lived an abundant life in a dream, the heroes of the latter plays immediately seek the higher form of release. For Ch'un-yü Fen, forcibly torn from his dream-life, it is understandable that he still clings to his ties with the ant world, but for Lu Sheng, who has lived to the hilt, his decision to aspire to Taoist immortality is promptly made.

For both of the awakened heroes, their enlightenment suggests little radical alteration of their perception. We do not feel that their normal self-consciousness has yielded to a consciousness of God or a higher reality, which has filled its place. They have merely grown aware of the treachery of time and they adopt one of the traditional religious systems to enable them to escape from time. The dream-device has foreshortened time, and each is brought face to face with the contemptible nature of human bonds because they appear ever so much more transient in the brief time-space of a dream. In *Nan-k'o chi* traditional Buddhist compassion is given lip service, and the hero is transformed into a Buddha partly because he wants to save all sentient beings. But in the process of his awakening, the antness of an ant and the humanity of a human being are slighted.

I have mentioned three types of living in the present without recourse to external religious aid: the Goethean form of romantic striving, the kind of stoical existentialism advocated by T'ao Ch'ien, the cultivation of a mystical awareness recommended by Su Shih and better exemplified in the West by Blake's axiom, "To see a World in a Grain of Sand/ And a Heaven in a Wild Flower." None of these or other possible forms of coming to terms with life without being intimidated by time is suggested by T'ang Hsien-tsu. To cite a contrasting example, Thornton Wilder, an American playwright much influenced by the Chinese and Japanese theater, sees the recurrence of ordinary human events as something worthy of unqualified affirmation. Human life is precious precisely because it is transient, but its transience does not preclude the presence of eternity. In *Our Town* the ghost of the heroine Emily relives her twelfth birthday in a vision and falls all the more in love with the human condition. Her only regret is that, as she sees herself and her parents occupied with routine tasks on the morning of that day, they are too busy to relish their every passing moment in the aspect of eternity:

"I didn't realize. So all that was going on and we never noticed. Take me back—up the hill—to my grave. But first: Wait! One more look.
"Good-by, Good-by, world. Good-by, Grover's Corners . . . Mama and Papa. Good-by to clocks ticking . . . and Mama's sunflowers. And food and coffee. And new-ironed dresses and hot baths . . . and sleeping and waking up. Oh, earth, you're too wonderful for anybody to realize you."
She looks toward the STAGE MANAGER and asks abruptly, through her tears:

"Do any human beings ever realize life while they live it?—every, every minute?" [51]

To Thornton Wilder, the human condition is not desperate because every passing moment is potentially a moment of eternity. For him, therefore, there is no need to crave for bodily permanence. Precisely because T'ang Hsien-tsu lacks that mystical vision, in his plays we see rather the lust for permanence finding expression either in the seemingly time-eclipsing solace of a loving relationship or in the final retreat to some kind of religious anchorage, both solutions, however, decked out in a poetry that makes the author a great inheritor of the varied strands of the Chinese literary tradition.

Mu-tan t'ing, written at the height of his poetical powers, is T'ang Hsien-tsu's sole attempt to defy time. In *Tzu-ch'ai chi*, the author has reworked the story of Huo Hsiao-yü to demonstrate the rectification of evil in the temporal order through the agency of *hsia*. But before the intervention of the Man in the Yellow Jacket (Huang-shan-k'e [ck]), the heroine, despite her generosity and chivalrous temper, is on the point of losing her life because of her languishment over the absence of her lover. She would have died if there had been no intervention. But with her lover finally by her side, she undergoes an instant miraculous recovery. Intrigued by this idea, T'ang Hsien-tsu must have searched for a story to affirm love's triumph over life and death, and he finally found it in a colloquial tale about Tu Li-niang.[cl] This tale receives its first mention in a catalogue compiled about 1560, though its earliest extant version, entitled "Enamoured of Love, Tu Li-niang Returns to Life" (*Tu Li-niang mu-sê hui-hun*)[cm] appears only in an enlarged edition of a late Ming miscellany called *Yen-chü pi-chi*.[cn] [52] But because this drab tale was probably little known even during the late Ming period, scholars have until very recently always assumed that, in a radical departure from the practice of most Ming playwrights, the author of *Mu-tan t'ing* had made up an original story about Tu Li-niang and Liu Meng-mei [co] even though its basic motives are drawn from a few pre-T'ang tales.[53] In his own preface to the play, however, T'ang Hsien-tsu has explicitly acknowledged his indebtedness to the tale:

The transmitters of the story of Prefect Tu have modeled it upon the tales of the daughter of Prefect Li Chung-wen [cp] of Wu-tu [cq] and of the son of Prefect Feng Hsiao-chiang [cr] of Kuang-chou,[cs] both prefects being of the Chin [ct] period. I have further changed the story and expanded it. As for the episode of Prefect Tu incarcerating and inflicting corporeal punishment upon Liu Meng-mei, this rather resembles the story of the King of Sui-yang [cu] meting out identical punishment to Scholar T'an.[54]

In checking the play against the tale "Enamoured of Love, Tu Li-niang Returns to Life," one cannot but agree with T'ang's statement that, whereas the transmitters of the tale have made use of the stories of the two prefects, to be found in *Fa-yüan chu-lin*,[cv] for their basic plot, he has further embellished it with the story of a father punishing his daughter's husband to be found in *Lieh-i-chuan*.[cw]

Mu-tan t'ing is a very long play, but it is never dull.[55] Chinese readers have always delighted in it, though no critics have traced its popularity to its comic exuberance. With a few slight changes, the main plot follows the colloquial tale. Tu Li-niang, the sole child of Tu Pao,[cx] prefect of Nan-an,[cy] Kiangsi, is tutored at home. One spring day, after taking a stroll in the garden of her house, she returns to her chamber and dreams of a youth taking her to the peony pavilion in the garden and making love to her. She becomes lovesick as a result, draws her own portrait for posterity, and before her death requests that she be buried under a plum tree in the garden. Soon afterward Tu Pao leaves Nan-an with his wife to accept a new post at Yang-chou. The youth of Li-niang's dream, Liu Meng-mei, now arrives in Nan-an. He stays in the Tu residence, treasures the portrait he has accidentally found, and is visited at night by the ghost of Li-niang, who calls herself a neighbor. She finally reveals her identity and requests him to exhume her body. Miraculously resurrected, she marries him, and they go north to seek reunion with her parents.

Upon this implausible tale T'ang Hsien-tsu has expended his comic gifts so that nearly all the minor characters become alive. In the tale, the father is a respectable, upright official and nothing more; in the play, in addition to being a good prefect earning the praise of his subjects and a lucky commander pacifying a critical region with minimal effort, he is a stern guardian of Confucian morality and a blind rationalist who refuses to believe in the reality of his daughter after she has been revived and insists on punishing his son-in-law as a grave robber. In the tale, Li-niang's tutor is not even given a name; in the play he is called Ch'en Tsui-liang [cz] (also known as Ch'en Tsüeh-liang [da] or Starveling Ch'en),[56] and is at once a dull-witted tutor utterly insensible of the beauties of nature and the charm of love, a quack doctor and good Samaritan, a guardian of the heroine's grave, a captive of the rebel forces, and a spy accomplishing single-handedly a most important mission. There are other comic characters of earthy coarseness suggestive of the clowns and rustics in Shakespeare. In T'ang's other plays, the military scenes, which seem to be *de rigeur* in the *ch'uan-ch'i* tradition of Ming drama, are usually very dull. In *Mu-tan t'ing*, however, one such scene (scene 47) is uproarious.[57] Readers accustomed to textbook description of the play as one of intense romanticism will be delightfully shocked by its coarse language and its abundance of bawdy jokes.

Tu Li-niang is, therefore, the only serious character in the play. It is she who is obsessed with love and languishes in its deprivation. Though her body is crushed under this unrelieved suffering, her soul rises triumphant over the judges in Hell to claim her rightful happiness in the arms of her lover. Compared with her, even Liu Meng-mei is partly an object of satire. Though he has dreamed of her before he himself enters into her dream, until he finds her portrait he is a brash go-getter intent on official success by whatever means. In comparison, Li I and even Ch'un-yü Fen are more admirable lovers in that their thoughts seldom stray from the objects of their love. Liu Meng-mei is properly tender and passionate in his love scenes with the ghost of Li-niang. But once he marries her and embarks on his journey to Hang-chou to take the examinations, he is again his brash self and obtains the *chuang-yüan* degree with extraordinary luck. Delighting in his new importance, he takes pleasure in harassing his father-in-law for refusing to recognize his worth. By that time Li-niang herself is so overpleased with her husband's changed status (and her father's promotion) that she has almost forgotten the intensity of her passion that made her rise from the grave.

Despite its comedy, *Mu-tan t'ing* has always been read as if the only scenes that matter are those tracing the heroine's essential history—her dream and her quest of the lost dream in the garden, her grief and death, her judgment in Hell, her trysts with her lover, and her resurrection.[58] T'ang's own preface has certainly encouraged this partial reading:

Of all the girls in this world, who is ever so committed to love (yu-ch'ing)[db] as Li-niang? Once she dreams of her lover, she falls ill and her illness worsens until with her own hand she transmits to the world a portrait of her features and then dies. After being dead for three years, she can still in her limbo-like existence seek the object of her love and regain her life. Verily Li-niang can be called a person committed to love (yu-ch'ing jen [dc]). She doesn't know how she has fallen in love, but once in love, she is totally committed to it. While still alive, she wills her death, and while in death, she wills to have her life restored. To stay alive without the courage to die, and to die without the volition to regain life—such is not the condition of one supremely committed to love. Love engendered in a dream—who says it is not real? Aren't there quite a few such dreamers in this world? [59]

In this eloquent statement of T'ang's philosophy of love, we find the reiterative use of the key terms: sheng (life), ch'ing (love), and meng [dd] (dream). (Ssu [de] [death] is also a key word, but its negative connotations only underscore by contrast the powers of sheng and ch'ing.) We have seen that Lo Ju-fang's distinctive contribution to Ming thought lies in his replacement of the term hsin (mind) by the term sheng as the generating and animating force of the universe, and his further equation of sheng with the term jen (humanity, love). Since T'ang Hsien-tsu regarded Mu-tan t'ing as his favorite play, he may have deliberately adapted the story of Tu Li-niang to dramatize the kind of affirmation of life consonant with his teacher's philosophy, and, further, to modify that philosophy by postulating "love" as the primary and essential condition of "life." But at the same time his use of the third key term meng modifies his total commitment to love and life in the world of time. It is only when Li-niang falls into a dream, which is, in a sense, a timeless state because it is not subject to the measurement of waking time, that the intensest form of life and the richest fulfillment of love are intimated to her, and, further, it is only when she is enjoying her dream-like existence as a ghost that she appears most daring and passionate in her quest of love. Once time reclaims her with her resurrection, she is no longer the girl supremely committed to love proclaimed in the preface.

Mu-tan t'ing is T'ang Hsien-tsu's only play in which the Taoist-Buddhist ideals are not once presented for serious consideration: the few Taoist nuns in the play are themselves sex-starved creatures now parading their physical or mental deformity for our comic attention.[60] This is so because the play is solely concerned with this-worldly values, with love and life pitted against the kind of caricature of Confucian values embodied in the father and tutor of the heroine, who are grossly insensible to her state of sexual awakening and regard sexual repression in a girl as natural until the time comes for her to get married. Li-niang triumphs over her father and tutor not by active revolt but, in a fairy-tale fashion, by a total submission to their tyranny. She is a sexually precocious Sleeping Beauty who lies dead for three years until a questing prince arrives at her castle and awakens her with a kiss. But if, in her total innocence, the Sleeping Beauty of the fairy tale lies in a state of deep sleep without a single dream to disturb her, it is only in her dream and in her state of death that Li-niang's libidinous self is freed from all inhibitions and taboos to roam all over the world in quest of her love.

Once revived, Li-niang appears quite a different person, a coy young lady very much aware of the importance of decorum and propriety. It has often been said that she is a far bolder and more impassioned girl than the heroine of *Hsi-hsiang chi* [df] (*Romance of the Western Chamber*) in that she seeks her love through life and death.[61] But her ghostly existence properly takes place in a timeless dimension where her censor-ego remains a non-entity. Without benefit of a dream existence, Ying-ying [dg] nevertheless gives herself to her importunate lover of her own will and experiences "the awful daring of a moment's surrender," something Li-niang could not have brought herself to do in her waking state. After her resurrection, she checks Liu Meng-mei's immediate desire to have sexual union with her.

Li-niang: But, sir, you must surely remember what the ancient classic [*Mencius* [dh]] says about awaiting the parents' command and the match-maker's counsel.

Meng-mei: Though I didn't bore a hole through the wall to peep at you, I have already gone into your grave and got you out. *Hsiao-chieh*, why cite book and chapter to lecture me now?

Li-niang: Sir, this is not like the former times. On the earlier evenings I was only a ghost and today I am a person of flesh and blood. A ghost may respond to passion, but a person must observe the proper rites (*kuei k'o hsü-ch'ing, jen hsü shih-li* di).[62]

Later on, in the same scene (scene 36), after she agrees to an immediate marriage, she surprises her lover with an admission.

Li-niang: Liu-lang, I am still a virgin.

Meng-mei: We have already had several trysts. How is it that your jade body still remains intact?

Li-niang: I was a ghost then; this time I'll serve you with my real body:

It was my wandering ghost that came to you, my lover;
My virgin body is still whole.[63]

The self-conscious young lady who protests her virginity and insists on a basic distinction between ghostly passion and human propriety is not the same person who three years ago died of lovesickness. Even though during her wedding night she tells Meng-mei, "Liu-lang, tonight I have finally realized the joy of living in this human world," [64] the situation has changed. Li-niang has got her man, and Meng-mei has found his dream girl, and from now on their immediate task is to justify their behavior before the eyes of her parents and the world. If he passes the examination with the highest honors (as he does), then the interlude of their ghostly love will be reinterpreted in the light of his success. After all, he is a *ts'ai-tzu* dj (young scholar of literary talent) and she is a *chia-jen* dk (beauty) and a certain romantic impropriety in their past is something to be admired. The last third of the play therefore becomes a more conventional romantic comedy which justifies the earlier imprudence and passion of the lovers because they are now the paragons of the official establishment, living very much in accordance with their newly acquired official dignity. In the last scene of the play (scene 55), Li-niang actually congratulates herself because the lover in her dream is now assured of far greater official success than any young man her parents could have chosen for her. She tells Ch'en Tsui-liang, "Tutor Ch'en, if you didn't give me the idea of strolling in the back garden, how could I have set my heart on one who has plucked the cassia bough off the moon so successfully?" [65] The romantic passion initially seen as a fierce assertion of life in the stifling environment of a deadened Confucian society is changed beyond recognition as the lovers afflicted with that passion pass beyond the phase of love to seek reconcilement with society.

There is no doubt that T'ang Hsien-tsu has intended to embody in Li-niang a passion for love that is beyond time, beyond life and death. But, alas, love appears eternal only so long as it remains unfulfilled. The mood of eternity cannot continue once passion is normalized or abated in the actual sexual embrace. Li-niang and Meng-mei could have become tragic lovers if the fulfillment of their love had meant for them a continuing disregard of conventional success and defiance of conventional morality. But, for one thing, the tragic mode is not available to T'ang Hsien-tsu: with all its fondness for sentiment and pathos, the *ch'uan-ch'i* genre of the Ming theater is a drama in the comic mode. As a poor scholar, Liu Meng-mei has always wanted to succeed in the official world, and Li-niang herself, given her family background and upbringing, would not have been happy with a lover who remained a mere indigent scholar. *Mu-tan t'ing*, therefore, is a comedy of reconcilement: the impulse toward love, in the heroine's case, has brought her greater worldly honor and success than if she had not taken the initiative in self-fulfillment and undergone death and rebirth. Her brief spell of rebellion against time notwithstanding, she is soon happily reconciled to time, and in time she will become a Confucian mother, anxious for the proper education of her children. In comparison with *Nan-k'o chi* and *Han-tan chi*, the distinction of *Mu-tan t'ing* lies in the fact that, whereas the dreams in the later plays contract time and dramatize the transience of life, the dream of Li-niang depicts a timeless condition where love is seen as the sole reality. But outside of her dream state and ghostly existence, the reign of time is absolute.

1. Notably, Hou Wai-lu, *Lun T'ang Hsien-tsu chü-tso ssu-chung* (On four of T'ang Hsien-tsu's plays) (Peking, Chung-kuo hsi-chü ch'u-pan-she, 1962). Like most other eminent scholars on the mainland writing about Ming history or thought, Hou has been harshly attacked since the launching of the "Great Proletarian Cultural Revolution." In his article "Hou Wai-lu chieh-ku feng-chin pei-ch'ing-suan" (Hou Wai-lu was purged for drawing upon the past to satirize the present), *Ming-pao yüeh-k'an*, I, No. 12 (Hong Kong, 1966), Wu Wen-pin reports on two articles appearing respectively in *Kuang-ming jih-pao* (August 10, 1966), and *Hung-ch'i*, No. 10 (August, 1966), which attack Hou especially for his writings on T'ang. According to the first article, it was Chou Yang who took a personal interest in the preparation of the 4-volume *T'ang Hsien-tsu chi* (The works of T'ang Hsien-tsu) and asked Hou to write an introduction to it. The two were therefore conspirators affirming the nobility of T'ang's thought as an indirect critique of the inhumanity of the Communist regime. *T'ang Hsien-tsu chi*, hereafter abbreviated as *THTC*, was published by Chung-hua shu-chü in 1962. Vols. 1–2, "Shih-wen chi" (Poetry and prose), were edited by Hsü Shuo-fang; vols. 3–4, "Hsi-ch'ü chi" (Plays), by Ch'ien Nan-yang.

2. In 1591 T'ang Hsien-tsu submitted a memorial defending the Censorate and criticizing Prime Minister Shen Shih-hsing. Highly displeased, Emperor Shen-tsung exiled T'ang to a minor post in Hsü-wen *hsien*, Kwangtung (cf. *THTC*, II, 1215). The memorial, known as "Lun fu-ch'en k'o-ch'en shu," is reprinted in *THTC*, II, 1211–14. T'ang's submission of this memorial constitutes an important episode (scenes 6–7) in Chiang Shih-ch'üan's (1725–85) biographical play entitled *Lin-ch'uan meng*.

3. The sayings of Lo Ju-fang are preserved in Huang Tsung-hsi, *Ming-ju hsüeh-an* (hereafter abbreviated as *MJHA*), *chüan* 34 (Wan-yu wen-k'u hui-yao ed.; Taipei, Commercial Press, 1965), VII, 1–30. The serious student should also consult *Lo Chin-ch'i hsien-sheng ch'üan-chi* (The complete works of Lo Ju-fang), which is much less accessible. For a concise presentation of Yen Chün's thought, see Huang's introductory essay on the T'ai-chou school in *MJHA*, *chüan* 32 (VI, 62–63). Fung Yu-lan maintains in Derk Bodde, tr., *A History of Chinese Philosophy*, II (Princeton University Press, 1953), 627: "Huang Tsung-hsi is not unjustified in accusing Wang Chi of Ch'anist bias. His similar criticism of Wang Chi's fellow student, Wang

Ken, however, seems less well founded, and would appear to apply more appropriately to Yen Chün. . . ."

4. T'ang Hsien-tsu refers to his spiritual condition under Lo Ju-fang in his preface to *T'ai-p'ing shan-fang chi-hsüan* (*THTC*, II, 1037). The latter work was by Tsou Yüan-piao, an early leader of the Tung-lin group.

5. Cf. T'ang Chün-i, "Lo Chin-ch'i chih li-hsüeh" (The Neo-Confucianism of Lo Ju-fang), *Min-chu p'ing-lun*, V, No. 5 (Hong Kong, 1954), and Mo Chung-kuei, "Lo Chin-ch'i chih ssu-hsiang" (The thought of Lo Ju-fang), a mimeographed report (n.d.) given at the twentieth monthly meeting of the research assistants of the New Asia Institute, Chinese University of Hong Kong.

6. *MJHA*, VII, 34/20.

7. *Ibid.*, p. 26.

8. In addition to the plays and letters, *THTC* contains 2,274 poems (*shih*) and 145 compositions in prose and in verse forms other than the *shih*, including 30 *fu*. These compositions and letters have received scant attention as literature in their own right, though they have been utilized by scholars in their studies of the author's life and thought. Hsü Shuo-fang, especially, has quoted copiously from these writings and other relevant documents in his excellent chronological biography of the playwright, *T'ang Hsien-tsu nien-p'u* (Peking, Chung-hua shu-chü, 1958). Huang Chih-kang, "T'ang Hsien-tsu nien-p'u" *Hsi-ch'ü yen-chiu*, Nos. 2–4 (Shanghai, 1957), is particularly good in relating T'ang's life to the politics of his time. In its serialized form, however, the biography stops at the year 1591 when T'ang was only forty-two years old; the work was completed long ago, but, so far as I know, it has not yet been published as a book. Yagisawa Hajime, *Mindai gekisakuke kenkyu* (Studies in Ming playwrights) (Tokyo, 1959), also includes a chronological biography in its long chapter on T'ang Hsien-tsu. The work has been translated into Chinese by Lo Chin-t'ang as *Ming-tai chü-tso-chia yen-chiu* (Hong Kong, Lung-men shu-tien, 1966).

9. "Kuei-sheng shu-yüan shuo," *THTC*, II, 1163.

10. *MJHA*, VI, 32/63.

11. Cf. the Chronological Biography in *THTC*, II, 1577–78. According to Hsü Shuo-fang ("Ch'ien-yen," *THTC*, I, 4), Ta-kuan had wanted to convert T'ang twenty years before they actually met. Upon Ta-kuan's death, T'ang wrote three four-line poems to express his grief (*THTC*, I, 595).

12. Cf. Hou Wai-lu, "T'ang Hsien-tsu chu-tso chung ti jen-min-hsing ho ssu-hsiang-hsing," *THTC*, I, 6.

13. *Ibid.*, p. 7. On the same page Hou quotes a passage from Ta-kuan

opposing *li* (principle) to *ch'ing*. In Appendix A to *T'ang Hsien-tsu nien-p'u*, Hsü Shuo-fang includes three letters from Ta-kuan to T'ang which are of decided help toward our understanding of this intellectual friendship.

14. See, for instance, "Ch'ien-yen," *THTC*, I, 8, and *Chung-kuo wen-hsüeh shih* (A history of Chinese literature) (Peking, Jen-min wen-hsüeh ch'u-pan-she, 1959), III, 375. The latter work was prepared by the class of 1955 of the Chinese Department of Peking University.

15. Cf. Hou Wai-lu, *Lun T'ang Hsien-tsu chü-tso ssu-chung*, pp. 28–40.

16. See, for instance, Wang Chi-ssu, "Tseng-yang t'an-so T'ang Hsien-tsu ti ch'ü-i," *Wen-hsüeh p'ing-lun*, No. 3 (1963).

17. The fact that Shakespeare and T'ang died in the same year has naturally tempted many Chinese scholars to regard the Ming playwright as if he were the equal of his English contemporary in poetic and dramatic excellence. Aoki Masaru, whose *Shina kinsei gikyoku shi* (A history of the Chinese drama of the more recent dynasties) has been very influential among the Chinese since it was translated by Wang Ku-lu in 1936 (*Chung-kuo chin-shih hsi-ch'ü shih*; Shanghai, Commercial Press), may have been the first to make the comparison. In *Ming Drama* (Taipei, Heritage Press, 1966), p. 163. Josephine Huang Hung has with greater propriety compared *Mu-tan t'ing* to two of Shakespeare's earlier works, *A Midsummer-Night's Dream* and *Romeo and Juliet*. T'ang Hsien-tsu has also been compared to the young Goethe: see the stimulating essay on T'ang and the *Sturm und Drang* movement in China ("T'ang Hsien-tsu yü Chung-kuo chih k'uang-piao yun-tung") in Li Ch'ang-chih, *Meng-yü chi* (Chungking, Commercial Press, 1945).

18. Of T'ang's recent biographers, Hsü Shuo-fang has dated the plays with the greatest precision. According to him, T'ang wrote *Tzu-hsiao chi* between the autumns of 1577 and 1579 when he was twenty-eight to thirty years (*sui*) old, and he began *Tzu-ch'ai chi* in 1586 and most probably completed it by 1587. The play was being readied for the printer in 1595, the year T'ang wrote a preface to it. He wrote the preface to *Mu-tan t'ing* in the fall of 1598 when he was forty-nine years old; Hsü believes that this date marks the completion of the play and argues against the hypothesis held by many scholars that it was completed a few years earlier. Cf. Appendix C in Hsü, *T'ang Hsien-tsu nien-p'u*, pp. 217–26.

According to Yagisawa Hajime (*Ming-tai chü-tso-chia yen-chiu*, p. 426), the first drafts of *Tzu-ch'ai chi* and *Mu-tan t'ing* were completed respectively in 1589–90 and 1588, while their final versions were completed in 1595 and 1598. But *Mu-tan t'ing* could not have been an earlier work than *Tzu-ch'ai chi*: the latter is closely linked to

Tzu-hsiao chi in style and imagery while the former marks in many ways the author's greater maturity as a playwright. As Hsü Shuo-fang has rightly noted, the many references to Kwangtung in *Mu-tan t'ing* would suggest that T'ang had incorporated in the play his experiences in Hsü-wen during his exile there in 1591–92. The first draft could not have been completed in 1588 unless one assumes that it bears very little resemblance to the final version.

To conclude our chronological account, *Nan-k'o chi* and *Han-tan chi* were completed respectively in 1600 and 1601. Yagisawa's supposition (pp. 423–26) that the final versions of these plays were not completed until 1606 and 1613 respectively cannot be taken seriously.

19. Cf. Hsü, *T'ang Hsien-tsu nien-p'u*, pp. 147–48; *Ming-tai chü-tso-chia yen-chiu*, p. 412.

20. As in Chiang Fang's story, the main agent of *hsia* in *Tzu-ch'ai chi* is Huang-shan-k'e or the Man in the Yellow Jacket.

21. In his preface to *Tzu-ch'ai chi* (THTC, II, 1097), T'ang Hsien-tsu states that, while engaged in the writing of *Tzu-hsiao chi*, he had become the target of malicious rumor and had to publish the play in its incomplete form to show that it had nothing to do with contemporary politics. The preface further quotes a comment by a friend to the effect that *Tzu-hsiao chi* is "a book for perusal and not a play for the stage." It seems to me that *Tzu-ch'ai chi* was certainly written to make the story of Huo Hsiao-yü more conformable to the structure of a *ch'uan-ch'i* play and hence more actable by contemporary standards. According to some early commentators, the play that caused the spread of malicious rumor against T'ang could not have been *Tzu-hsiao chi*, which in its present form is politically innocuous, and must have been an overtly satiric work about the four temptations of man —*chiu sê ts'ai ch'i* (drinking, sex, covetousness, anger)—which the author had withheld from publication. Huang Chih-kang, who believes this, accordingly slights *Tzu-hsiao chi* as a work dashed off in a hurry to quiet dangerous gossip (see "T'ang Hsien-tsu nien-p'u," *Hsi-ch'ü Yen-chiu*, No. 4 [1957], pp. 106–7). Hsü Shuo-fang argues against this theory along with other myths surrounding the composition of the play in Appendix D to *T'ang Hsien-tsu nien-p'u*. According to early Ch'ing biographers, T'ang eventually completed *Tzu-hsiao chi*, but the manuscripts were burned after his death by his third son K'ai-yüan. Hsü (p. 231) believes on the contrary that, if such manuscripts did exist, they must have been consumed in the fire that destroyed T'ang's collection of calligraphy and painting in 1613.

22. But it must be remembered that *Tzu-ch'ai chi*, with its ornate poetic imagery and its antithetical and often stilted prose passages, was also composed in the *p'ien-ch'i* style. In "T'ang Hsien-tsu ho t'a-ti ch'uan-

ch'i" (*Yüan Ming Ch'ing hsi-ch'ü yen-chiu lun-wen chi*) (Peking, Tso-chia ch'u-pan-she, 1957), p. 349, Hsü Shuo-fang singles out for attack a highly hyperbolic passage on tears (*Tzu-hsiao chi*, scene 24 [*THTC*, IV, 2543]), not realizing that the same passage occurs intact in *Tzu-ch'ai chi*, scene 25 (*THTC*, III, 1674), except for the revision of the last two lines to even greater stiltedness. If *Tzu-hsiao chi* deserves criticism for this passage, then so should *Tzu-ch'ai chi*. Actually, this passage is not unpleasing as poetry, and it is not typical of either play in its deliberate cultivation of a conceit.

23. She is so praised by Tu Ch'iu-niang in scene 29 (*THTC*, IV, 2561). In scene 10, after Li I has declared his marital interest through a matchmaker, Hsiao-yü tells her mother that she does not want to marry but would rather keep her company and live a life of Taoist cultivation. This avowal, of course, cannot be taken seriously. With all her religious sympathy, she is primarily a romantic heroine. If T'ang Hsien-tsu had completed the play in adherence to the plot outline given in scene 1, Hsiao-yü would soon after the reunion scene that completes the extant version have suffered many trials before she and her husband were finally reunited and restored to honor. But the résumé gives no indication that she would have turned religious.

24. In "The Lute Song" the merchant's wife recalls her glory in Ch'ang-an in the following lines:

> When my recital was over, even *shan-ts'ai* would frequently acknowledge my excellence;
> When my toilet was done, even Ch'iu-niang would very often show her envy.

In the preface to the poem Po Chü-i states that she "had learned to play the *p'i-p'a* from two *shan-ts'ai* named Mu and Ts'ao"; the *shan-ts'ai* of the first line would seem naturally to refer to either or both of her instructors. In *Yüan Po shih chien-cheng kao* (Canton, Lingnan University, Chung-kuo wen-hua yen-chiu-shih, 1950), Ch'en Yin-k'o gives further references to Ch'iu-niang in the poems of Yüan Chen and Po Chü-i and believes that she must have been a celebrated courtesan of her time. In *Tzu-hsiao chi* T'ang Hsien-tsu has given Ch'iu-niang the surname Tu; in "Tu Ch'iu-niang shih" Tu Mu celebrates a beauty of the same name much loved by the T'ang emperor Hsien-tsung. In *Tzu-hsiao chi*, scene 29, Ch'iu-niang admits that she was of an envious temper in her youth, and both she and Shan-ts'ai, depicted as a woman ten years her junior, recall their earlier days in terms suggested by Po Chü-i's poem.

25. Scene 9 (*THTC*, IV, 2473).

26. Scene 20 (*Ibid.*, p. 2531).

27. Scene 31 (*Ibid.*, p. 2570).
28. *Ibid.*, p. 2571. Tu Huang-shang is a historical figure whose biography appears in *Chiu T'ang-shu, chüan* 147, and *Hsin T'ang shu, chüan* 169. He died at the age of seventy-one *sui* (according to *Chiu T'ang shu*) or seventy (*Hsin T'ang-shu*) without undergoing a religious conversion.
29. Arthur Waley, tr., *Chinese Poems* (London, Allen & Unwin, 1946), p. 62.
30. *Ibid.*, p. 103.
31. A. C. Graham, tr., "The Red Cliff, I," in Cyril Birch, ed., *Anthology of Chinese Literature* (New York, Grove Press, 1965), p. 382.
32. "Nan-k'o t'ai-shou chuan," in Wang P'i-chiang, ed., *T'ang-jen hsiao-shuo* (Hong Kong, Chung-hua shu-chü, 1958), p. 40.
33. Cf. scene 4.
34. In scene 8.
35. Scene 42 (*THTC*, IV, 2260).
36. Scene 44 (*THTC*, IV, 2271).
37. *Ibid.*, p. 2273.
38. *Ibid.*, pp. 2273–74.
39. In scene 44 (*Ibid.*, p. 2273) Yao-fang tells Ch'un-yü of a tier of heaven known as Tao-li-t'ien where husband and wife could still have sexual intercourse, though without the accompanying "clouds and rain." She says further that, higher up, husband and wife are no longer sexual partners though, when prompted by love, they still embrace, smell, or smile at each other. Beyond these tiers of heaven, however, is Li-hen-t'ien where no human love is possible.
40. *Ibid.*, p. 2274.
41. "Chen-chung chi," in *T'ang-jen hsiao-shuo*, p. 37.
42. *Han-tan chi*, scene 6 (*THTC*, IV, 2307–8).
43. Biographies of Yü-wen Yung appear in *Chiu T'ang-shu, chuan* 105, and *Hsin T'ang-shu, chüan* 134. T'ang Hsien-tsu's refusal to accept Chang Chü-cheng's patronage and his consequent failure to achieve the *chin-shih* degree as long as Chang was in power were dwelt upon by Tsou Ti-kuang in his biography of his good friend (*THTC*, II, 1511–14) and have been made much of by all subsequent biographers, including the Ch'ing playwright Chiang Shih-ch'üan. (Chang died in 1582, and the following year T'ang became a *chin-shih* at the age of thirty-four.) Other villains implacably opposed to the young heroes in T'ang's plays and possibly modeled after Chang Chü-cheng include the Minister of the Right in *Nan-k'o chi* and Grand Commander of the Armies (*t'ai-wei*) Lu in *Tzu-ch'ai chi*. The latter eventually keeps Li I as a captive guest in his house in his attempt to force him to marry his daughter; in this respect, he is not unlike Prime Minister

Niu in Kao Ming's *P'i-p'a chi*, who incarcerates the hero Ts'ai Po-chai in his house and forces him to marry his daughter. The villains in T'ang's plays may have autobiographical significance, but at the same time they must be seen against the villains in *P'i-p'a chi* and other earlier plays in the *ch'uan-ch'i* tradition.

44. Scene 27 (*THTC*, IV, 2412).

45. Scene 29 (*Ibid.*, p. 2420).

46. The phantasmagoric note is especially pronounced in scene 22, which despicts Lu Sheng's banishment to Kwangtung and his subsequent voyage to Hainan Island.

47. Scene 11 (*THTC*, IV, 2329).

48. Translation by Louis MacNeice (*Faust*, Oxford University Press, 1951), quoted in Maynard Mack, general editor, *World Masterpieces*, II (New York, Norton, 1956), 1448.

49. D. J. Enright, *A Commentary on Goethe's Faust* (New York, New Directions, 1949), p. 150.

50. Scene 29 (*THTC*, IV, 2423).

51. Thornton Wilder, *Three Plays* (New York, Harper, 1957; Bantam Books, 1958), p. 62. Page reference is to Bantam ed.

52. "Tu Li-niang chi" (The story of Tu Li-niang) is listed among over a hundred titles of fiction in the catalogue of Ch'ao Li's private library entitled *Pao-wen-t'ang fen-lei shu-mu*. During his trip to Tokyo in 1931 Sun K'ai-ti discovered this catalogue and duly lists its titles of fiction in *Chung-kuo t'ung-su hsiao-shuo shu-mu* (Peiping, 1933). On the same trip Sun found in the Naikaku Bunko a late Ming edition of *Yen-chü pi-chi* bearing the full title of *Ch'ung-k'e tseng-pu yen-chü pi-chi* and in the Archives and Mausolea Division of the Imperial Household (Kunaichō Toshoryō) an early Ch'ing edition known as *Tseng-pu p'i-tien t'u-hsiang yen-chü pi-chi*. In *Jih-pen Tung-ching so-chien Chung-kuo hsiao-shuo shu-mu t'i-yao* (Peiping, 1932), Sun notes that *chüan* 9 of the earlier set contains the story "Tu Li-niang mu-sê hui-hun" while *chüan* 8 of the later contains one entitled "Tu Li-niang mu-tan-t'ing hui-hun chi." I have examined photostatic copies of both tales and found the second to be of little direct concern to the student of T'ang's play about the same heroine, *Mu-tan t'ing*, since it bears all the earmarks of being a condensation of the first. The shorter tale, however, is simply titled "Tu Li-niang chi" (Sun K'ai-ti must have transcribed the longer title from the table of contents), and for the present I would not rule out the possibility of its being an earlier tale of which "Tu Li-niang mu-sê hui-hun" was an expansion. I am preparing an article on this question.

Though Sun K'ai-ti had early noted these titles about Tu Li-niang, their possible connections with T'ang's play were not explored until

T'an Cheng-pi wrote for W*en-hsüeh i-ch'an*, No. 206 (*Kuang-ming jih-pao*, April 27, 1958), a short article entitled "Ch'uan-ch'i *Mu-tan t'ing* ho hua-pen 'Tu Li-niang chi.' " T'an believes "Tu Li-niang chi" to be the primary source of *Mu-tan t'ing*, though he has seen neither version of the story noted by Sun K'ai-ti. In his aforementioned article "Tseng-yang t'an-so T'ang Hsien-tsu ti ch'ü-i" (1963), Wang Chi-ssu reports his discovery of a set of *Ch'ung-k'e tseng-pu yen-chü pi-chi* in the Peking University Library and states his conviction that *Mu-tan t'ing* was indeed based on the tale of Tu Li-niang to be found in that miscellany. My own examination of a photostatic copy of presumably the identical tale in the Naikaku Bunko set has led me to the same conclusion. T'ang, however, must have read the tale in a miscellany or story collection printed earlier than *Ch'ung-k'e tseng-pu yen-chü pi-chi*, and at present we have no way of knowing whether the two versions are identical.

53. Whenever they had occasion to discuss the sources for *Mu-tan t'ing*, all literary historians writing at length on Ming drama tended to over-stress the importance of the three pre-T'ang tales alluded to in T'ang's preface to the play. Aoki Masaru seems to have set the precedent in his survey of Chinese drama (Cf. *Chung-kuo chin-shih hsi-ch'ü shih*, pp. 240–41). Ch'en Wan-nai is among the latest scholars to have re-peated this error; see his *Yüan Ming Ch'ing hsi-ch'ü shih* (History of the drama of the Yüan, Ming, and Ch'ing periods) (Taipei, Chung-kuo hsüeh-shu-chu-tso chiang-chu wei-yüan-hui, 1966), pp. 475–76.

54. "*Mu-tan t'ing chi* t'i-tz'u," THTC, II, 1093.

55. It has 55 scenes and runs to 247 pages in THTC. *Tzu-ch'ai chi*, T'ang's second longest play, is shorter by two scenes and twelve pages.

56. The character *tsüeh* (Mathews, No. 1703) is usually romanized *chüeh*. I have adopted the *tsüeh* form to indicate that the tutor's nickname is a pun on his given name. In the *Analects*, XV, 1, we are told that Confucius once starved in Ch'en (*tsai Ch'en tsüeh-liang*). The name Ch'en Tsüeh-liang has therefore a further dimen-sion of humor as a quotation from the Confucian classic.

57. In that scene an envoy from the Chin headquarters lusts after the rebel Li Ch'üan's wife and makes progressively more impudent de-mands upon her through the help of an interpreter. Both the envoy's gibberish and the interpreter's translations are exceedingly funny.

58. As given in scenes 10, 12, 14, 20, 23–28, 30, 32, 35.

59. THTC, II, 1093.

60. For instance, in a long self-deprecating monologue in scene 17, the Taoist nun Shih mocks her own misery as a *shih-nü*, that is, a woman with a hymen as impenetrable as a stone (*shih*).

61. See, for instance, "Ch'ien-yen," THTC, I, 8–10, and Liu Ta-chieh,

Chung-kuo wen-hsüeh fa-chan-shih (The development of Chinese literature) (Peking, Chung-hua shu-chü, 1963), III, 1002–3.

62. *THTC*, III, 1973. In this conversation both Li-niang and Meng-mei are alluding to a passage in *Mencius*, III B: "If the young people, without waiting for the orders of their parents, and the arrangements of the go-betweens, shall bore holes to steal a sight of each other, or get over the wall to be with each other, then their parents and all other people will despise them." James Legge, tr., *The Chinese Classics* (London, Trübner & Co., 1861), II, 144.

63. *THTC*, III, 1976.

64. *Ibid.*, p. 1977.

65. *Ibid.*, p. 2075.

GLOSSARY

a	湯顯祖	ai	霍小玉傳
b	李贄	aj	李益
c	徐渭	ak	駢綺
d	袁氏兄弟	al	臨川
e	東林黨	am	霍王
f	羅汝芳	an	鄭六娘
g	顏鈞	ao	杜秋娘
h	天機	ap	善才
i	黃宗羲	aq	白居易
j	生生	ar	琵琶行
k	易經	as	花卿
l	大學	at	郭子儀
m	中庸	au	鮑四娘
n	生	av	鮑十一娘
o	仁	aw	郡主
p	生機	ax	相陪作客
q	人	ay	狀元
r	心	az	杜黃裳
s	紫簫記	ba	四空
t	紫釵記	bb	聖賢不能度
u	牡丹亭	bc	聖賢莫能度
v	貴生書院	bd	陶潛
w	貴生	be	形影神
x	情	bf	前赤壁賦
y	性	bg	蘇軾
z	陳一泉	bh	禪
aa	南柯記	bi	李公佐
ab	邯鄲記	bj	南柯太守傳
ac	達觀，紫柏	bk	沈既濟
ad	侯外廬	bl	枕中記
e	明儒學案	bm	淳于芬
af	傳奇	bn	瑤芳
ag	俠	bo	南柯
ah	蔣防	bp	契玄

bq	達摩
br	情著
bs	轉情
bt	情盡
bu	觀音
bv	盧生
bw	呂翁
bx	呂洞賓
by	蓬萊
bz	崔小姐
ca	宇文融
cb	張居正
cc	高力士
cd	趙國公
ce	頃
cf	陰
cg	陽
ch	里
ci	河西
cj	玉門關
ck	黃衫客
cl	杜麗娘
cm	杜麗娘慕色還魂
cn	燕居筆記

co	柳夢梅
cp	李仲文
cq	武都
cr	馮孝將
cs	廣州
ct	晉
cu	睢陽王
cv	法苑珠林
cw	列異傳
cx	杜寶
cy	南安
cz	陳最良
da	陳絕糧
db	有情
dc	有情人
dd	夢
de	死
df	西廂記
dg	鶯鶯
dh	孟子
di	鬼可虛情, 人須實禮
dj	才子
dk	佳人

LIU TS'UN-YAN *Taoist Self-Cultivation*

in Ming Thought

I. GENERAL INTRODUCTION

明　An important aspect of Ming thought, as yet insufficiently studied and appreciated, is the profound influence of Taoism throughout this period. True, the Ming period produced no outstanding Taoist philosopher, yet in all of Chinese history Taoism was never more powerful or more pervasive among all social strata than during this time. It is well known among historians how infatuated with Taoist superstition the Emperors Hsien-tsung (1465–87) and Shih-tsung (1522–66) were, and that they thus greatly influenced their ministers and subjects. In fact, however, this state of affairs had existed to a greater or lesser extent through all Ming reigns since that of Emperor Ch'eng-tsu (1403–24).[1] The only difference was that some emperors believed not only in Taoists but in Tibetan lamas as well, while others believed in Taoist priests only. These Taoist priests were in league with other dubious elements and had wide social connections. They engaged with eunuchs in official corruption and in enriching themselves through building grandiose Taoist monasteries and through their lucrative monopoly on the conducting of expensive Taoist services and sacrifices offered on behalf of souls in purgatory. Some Taoist priests, such as Li Tzu-hsing,[a] Shao Yüan-chieh,[b] and T'ao Chung-wen,[c] were even appointed to ministerial posts. These Taoists invariably cultivated intimate friendships with powerful politicians, often through affiliations based on the simple fact that both came from the same province or county. Thus the political influence of these Taoist priests ramified from the metropolis to every corner of the Ming empire.[2] The Taoist priest T'ao Chung-wen was so influential that Yen Sung[d] had to turn to him for help in undermining the position of Hsia Yen,[e] Yen Sung's superior at the imperial court.[3] It is said that afterwards, when Yen Sung became the all-powerful prime minister and long enjoyed the favor of Emperor Shih-tsung, Lan Tao-hsing,[f] a Taoist sorcerer, had only to play a trick on the emperor with the planchette in order to sabotage Yen Sung's career.[4]

In spite of the influence Taoists wielded in Ming politics we could still ignore them were it not for the fact that Taoist activities and attitudes also, directly and indirectly, affected the thought of Ming scholar-officials. As a result, in Ming Confucianism there was an indelible Taoist tinge, even deeper than in the Sung. These scholar-officials had become so accustomed to Taoist ideas that it would hardly occur to them that such ideas were foreign to Confucianism and should be purged.[5] Further, on the lower levels of Chinese society Taoist ideas spread widely and penetrated deeply by means of Taoist exhortative pamphlets such as the *Kung-kuo ko* [g] (Ledgers of merit and demerit) and *Pao-chüan* [h] (Precious scrolls) and through popular fiction.[6]

Before proceeding to discuss further the influence of Taoism in Ming thought, let us consider the basic concepts of Taoism which gained wide currency at this time. We shall then see how even the leading Confucian scholars of the period accepted and used these concepts or were given to other traditional Taoist practices.

II. MAIN CONCEPTS OF TAOISM IN THE MING

These concepts are mainly on the practical side of self-cultivation, for on one hand the Taoist thinkers in this period could not excel their predecessors in philosophical discourse, and on the other hand religious Taoism had since Sung-Yüan times displaced philosophical Taoism in many respects. The concepts may be explained under the following twelve terms:

1. Golden Pill (*Chin-tan*).[i] This is the internal pill (*nei-tan*),[j] which was highly esteemed by the Taoists in their cultivation of the *ch'i* [k] (vital breath), and is to be differentiated from the external pill (*wai-tan*),[l] which is also called *chin-tan* but indicates exclusively the products of the alchemists. The external pill was still used as a means of cultivation by some in the Ming dynasty. Among the Neo-Con-

fucians concerned, Fang Yü-shih [m] of the T'ai-chou branch of the Wang Yang-ming school was perhaps the most famous one, for it was said that his knowledge in this field was able to arouse voracious desires in the multimillionaire Yen Shih-fan,[n] son of the notorious Grand Secretary Yen Sung.[7] While the practice of the internal pill is not that of the external pill, in the process of its cultivation a large number of technical terms were borrowed from the texts for the study of the external pill. For instance, the terms *ting* [o] (tripod) and *lu* [p] (furnace) when used in the cultivation of the internal pill, ceased to convey their original meanings. The former came to mean the "nature" (*hsing*),[q] the male (trigram *ch'ien*),[r] and the "guest" (*k'o*),[s] and the latter, the "life" (*ming*),[t] the female (trigram *k'un*),[u] and the "master" or "self" (*chu*).[v] The term "crescent-shaped furnace" (*yen-yüeh lu*)[w] came to mean the kidneys.[x] When the study of the internal pill became identical with dual cultivation (*shuang-hsiu*)[y]—i.e., cultivation through the process of sexual intercourse, a degenerate practice which had been in vogue since Sung-Yüan times—these apparently innocent terms were generally invested with the esoteric meaning. For instance, the "crescent-shaped furnace" (kidneys) came to represent the vulva in this connection.

The cultivation of the internal pill, though easily confused with the idea of dual cultivation in its sexual aspects, should not be interpreted as being identical with the study of the "bedchamber art" (*fang-chung*).[z] The *fang-chung* scholars of the Former Han, during the Northern and Southern dynasties, and of the T'ang mainly concerned themselves with hygienic arrangements in Chinese family life, and to some extent they also made contributions to the Chinese pharmacopoeia. But they did not often recommend the cultivation of the *ch'i*. The cultivation of the *ch'i* is, therefore, the most important characteristic in the study of the internal pill.

2. Vital Breath (*Ch'i*). Before we come to the Taoist cultivation of the *ch'i*, we must first understand the Chinese belief that the *ch'i* naturally tends toward diffusion, and consequently must be regulated and conserved. Thus in individual cultivation the problem is to prevent its indiscriminate emission, and especially through breath control to hold it in. To inhale *ch'i* is mainly an external, physical exercise. But, during the process of inhalation, if the adept contem-

plates his surroundings, and believes that in so doing he is brought into contact with something other than himself, this may lead to a belief that communion between himself and the universe is possible. If the universe is perpetual and firm, so will his fleshly body be, since he has identified himself with the universe through this means. For instance, in the Taoist scripture *T'ai-shang ling-pao wu-fu-hsü* [aa] we have:

The taking in of the essence of the moon is done to nourish one's kidney-root,[ab] that grey hair can be turned black. It is good for one to meditate at midnight, thinking that around his kidneys there is white *ch'i* flowing through the body, upward to the door of the brain,[ac] and downward to the two soles of his feet. This is the natural course, easy to grasp but difficult to follow persistently.

Therefore, it might be easier for him if he constantly chants this to the moon on the fifteenth day of the month, saying,

Thou Ruler of the Moon, Mistress of the
Primordial *yin*,
Be harmonious with me,
That together we may give birth to a little child
in my cinnabar field.[ad] 8

The scripture *Ling-pao wu-liang tu-jen shang-ching ta-fa* [ae] describes the internal circulation of the *ch'i* within one's body. In the passage quoted below we find that imagination also plays an important role during meditation, in which the image of an immortal may appear to the meditator, and may eventually become identical with him:

In the three fields [af] of the human body there is the "real earth." When it is the hour of *tzu* [ag] [11 P.M.–1 A.M.], [a meditator] should concentrate his "real *ch'i*" [ah] which he gathers from his kidneys on his lower field [i.e., the cinnabar field]. He should imagine that this *ch'i* is a round, tangled, and colorful ball which goes up to combine with the real *ch'i* on the top of his head (*ni-wan* [ai]). The *ch'i* then descends from the Jade Tower (*yü-lou*,[aj] throat) and stops a while at the Yellow Court (*huang-t'ing*,[ak] a part of the abdomen) to be mixed up with the *ch'i* round the heart. Again, [going down to the perineum] it passes through the coccyx, whence it rises upward, taking the two courses parallel to the spine (*chia-chi* [al]) to return to the Yellow Court, passing through the *ni-wan*. Imagine that at the Yellow Court there is a Heavenly Honored Immortal, resembling one's own features. Inhale the real *ch'i* at the hour of *tzu* and the hour of *wu* [am]

[11 A.M.–1 P.M.], each time three rounds. After the hour of *wu*, lower this *ch'i* down a little so that it may stay at the Yellow Court, using the flame of the heart. Imagine again that the Heavenly Honored Immortal is sitting quietly in the midst of a conflagration, undisturbed, as if forgetting his own existence.[9]

Why is the *ch'i* so important? In a chapter entitled *Fu-ch'i chih-lun* [an] (The subjugation of the ch'i) in his *T'ien-hsien cheng-li* [ao] (The true principle upheld by a heavenly immortal), Wu Shou-yang [ap] (*c.* 1563–*c.* 1632) says:

The great pass which divides life and death is the *ch'i*. The difference between a sage and an ordinary man is [that the sage is able] to subdue the *ch'i* [while the ordinary man is unable to do so]. The meaning of the character *fu* [aq] (to subdue) is twofold: it is to conceal, and it is also to subdue. Only by subduing his *ch'i* is one able to redirect the course of the sperm and convert it into the vital *ch'i*, and to condense the spirit and diversify it into the vital spirit. It is because one wishes to calm down and subdue the *ch'i* that it is necessary to refine one's spirit.[10]

Why is the *ch'i* to be subdued, and to be subdued from beginning to end? He says:

Because, when one is born, the two *ch'i* [i.e., the vital *ch'i* and the breath] are combined in their base within the cinnabar field, and this base is called the "root of *ch'i*." [ar] The *ch'i* has long been subdued in quietude and it begins to move, which is the breathing. Therefore, the *ch'i*, which comes out from long subjugation in quietude [before birth] to become the respiration of a man, is the breath which takes its natural course and it is to be understood as a natural consequence. When one wishes to become an immortal, it is necessary for him to reverse the natural channel and return to the state of subjugation in quietude through the same breath. [as] These are the natural and the reverse courses of subjugation of the *ch'i*.

When the mouth and the nose become the exclusive organs for breathing [after birth], the real *ch'i* in one's body is compelled to be evaporated and disseminated outside; when it is injured, one is taken ill; when it is exhausted and ceases to exist, one dies. For [a layman] does not understand that subduing the *ch'i* is a means for its animation, nor does he know the practice of subduing it.[11]

3. Breath Regulation (*T'iao-hsi*) [at]. How does one subdue the *ch'i?* The term *t'iao-hsi* (regulating the breath) has been used in many Taoist texts, and also since the Sung dynasty in the writings of some Confucian scholars who had been influenced by Taoist thought. But

some Taoist scholars, particularly in Ming times, did not think it was a suitable term to describe the process of subduing the *ch'i*, for they were able to distinguish the slightest and most subtle difference between the breath which exists after one's birth and the vital *ch'i* which, according to their theory, is gradually diminishing and disappearing in the course of life. Wu Shou-yang explains:

The importance of subjugation of the *ch'i* lies in the fact that it is a practicable way for the initiated to attest his ability in the course of cultivation. But this heavenly mechanism (*t'ien-chi*) [au] is so marvellous that it is entirely different from what is commonly meant. The reason the ancients called it regulating the breath was that they wished people to grasp the idea of inhaling and exhaling but to ignore the actual form, and the breathing they meant was nothing other than the very soft movement of respiration which is so fine and so slow that it seems to be nonexistent. In name it may reluctantly be called regulating the breath, but in fact it should be as empty as the Great Void, so that it can be consistent with quietude and concealment in the pre-primordiality (*wu-chi* [av]).[12]

4. Embryo Breath (*T'ai-hsi*)[aw]. To inquire further into the breathing of the *ch'i* within one's body, we must understand the Taoist term *t'ai-hsi* (the breath of a baby in embryo). This is the state that a true Taoist should be most desirous of and should try to attain. Wu Shou-yang's *T'ai-hsi chih-lun* [ax] is probably the best work depicting this, though it is not the only one.[13] He says:

Before the embryonic state [literally, the beginning of one's person] is formed, the two *ch'i* are but one, the primordial essence in the Great Void. At first there is neither embryo nor breathing; but when the rudimentary form inhales and exhales with its mother, it grows gradually and becomes an embryo, and when an embryo is formed, it is able to take breath. When the embryo is fully developed, it does not breathe with mouth and nose, but simply follows the tempo of the respiration of its mother, through the connection of its umbilicus with her body. During a whole day of breathing, it is neither depressed nor suffocated; for it does not feel that it has [its own] breathing. This is what may be called the condition of the true breath of an embryo. When the body of the baby is severed from that of the mother, the connection by the umbilical cord is cut off, and for this reason the baby has to breathe through its mouth and nose. This function is the same as it was within the mother's womb, though the apertures are different. [This being the case,] how could one who wishes to follow the practice of redirecting [the sperm] and converting it [into the vital *ch'i*] not turn his ordinary breath into that of the baby in embryo? [14]

5. Consolidation of the base (*Chu-chi*)[ay]. The original term for the consolidation of the base, i.e., the combination of the sperm, the spirit, and the *ch'i*, is *chu-chi*. The Taoists believed that it is only with the combination of the three that the base for one's cultivation can be consolidated. When the base is safely built, the sperm will then be stable, and the *ch'i* will then be ready to be reversed. To be free from emission is a prerequisite for the reversion or, in more general terms, the cultivation of the *ch'i*.[15]

6. Refining of the drug (*Lien-yao*)[az]. In Taoist cultivation, the term "drug" or *yao* indicates the formless, vital sperm (*yüan-ching*).[ba] It is to be "refined" in the "true hour of quietude," [bb] the time when one's mind and body are both at their highest state of tranquillity. This is again an allegory for the hours between the end of *hai* and the beginning of *tzu* [bc] (approximately 11 P.M. to midnight). The Taoists believed that just at that time, when it is yin and the quietest moment, there is the inception of movement and a change to yang. The movement of the vital *ch'i* is then said to be reversible. When the "true pivot of the nature" (*chen-chi tzu-jan*)[bd] revolves again, it is called "the drug." The Taoists alleged that "since there is the drug and a natural mechanism of life, there should be an enlightenment for one to perceive the coming of the drug. The enlightenment should be the substance for the refining of the drug, while emptiness and humility are the function of the refinement." [16] To be able to perceive the exact moment of the coming of "the drug" and to "refine" it was of vital importance for the Taoist cultivators who aimed at longevity and identifying themselves with an immortal.

7. The Hour of *Hai-mo Tzu-ch'u* [bc]. *Hai-mo Tzu-ch'u* is the hour between the end of *hai* and the beginning of *tzu*. Why is it so momentous for cultivation? The theory originated from a part of the Han theory for interpreting the *Book of Changes*—which had been incorporated into the *Chou-i ts'an-t'ung-ch'i* [bf] (Ideas of Taoist cultivation tallying with the *Book of Changes*)—in terms of the influence of each of the sixty-four hexagrams upon a certain period of the year. The plan is to assign the hexagrams *k'an, li, chen,* and *tui* [bg] to the four cardinal points north, south, east, and west to represent

the four seasons, in terms of the increasing and diminishing of the two forces, yin and yang. Each of these four hexagrams has six lines, therefore, each line is taken to represent one of the twenty-four Solar Terms.[bh] Besides, twelve among the remaining sixty hexagrams are chosen to illustrate the waxing and waning of the yang and the yin through the year. These twelve hexagrams are known as the twelve sovereign hexagrams,[bi] and each of them has four accessory hexagrams. These forty-eight accessory hexagrams, together with the twelve sovereign hexagrams whence they are derived and the four hexagrams representing the four cardinal points and four seasons, form the complete cycle of sixty-four hexagrams.

Let us now see why these twelve hexagrams had been regarded as so important by the Han scholars, particularly Meng Hsi[bj] and Ching Fang,[bk] [17] and the Taoist scholars of later times who believed in the apocryphal treatises of the Classics. The twelve sovereign hexagrams chosen, according to the Han dynasty work *I-wei chi-lan-t'u*[bl] (Apocryphal treatise of the *Book of Changes*)[18] are:

fu [bm]	*chüeh*	*p'i*
lin	*ch'ien*	*kuan*
t'ai	*kou*	*po*
ta-chuang	*tun*	*k'un*

The lines of a hexagram are read from the bottom up. *Fu* has one unbroken yang or line as its first line, while the other five lines are all broken or yin. This shows that the yang then begins to reappear, while the yin has reached its zenith. In terms of weather, no matter how severe the cold winter is, it is preparing to yield to the opposite dominating force, and there is nothing that can be done about it. Traditionally, the time is given as midnight of the winter solstice, which falls in the eleventh month of the lunar calendar. The rotation continues through hexagram *lin*, which begins with two yang lines while the other four lines remain yin, to the hexagram *ch'ien* which has no yin lines and is apparently the zenith of the yang when in the fourth month. One line of yin appears in the first line of the next sovereign hexagram *kou;* following the natural sequence it develops gradually to the last sovereign hexagram *k'un,* which is composed of six yin, and is at the highest point of its influence in the tenth lunar month. Then the yang appears again at the bottom of the following sovereign hexagram, *fu.* This describes the mutation of the yang and yin in the twelve sovereign hexagrams. Hence we have in the *Ts'an-t'ung-ch'i:*

The early hours of the day correspond to *fu,* when the *ch'i* of the yang principle begins to grow. With no one to distress it in its exits and entrances, it shows slight strength as it is growing. The time is the hour *tzu* and in musical pitchpipes it is *huang-chung.*[bn] An omen can be seen clearly. Warmth is to be distributed and all the people receive this attention. . . .[19]

The author of the *Ts'an-t'ung-ch'i* believes that, since this is a natural course of phenomena, the same rule should be observed by those who practice the physiomental cultivation of breath control as a means at least of prolonging life, if not of becoming immortal. Furthermore, although this theory illustrates the waxing and waning of the yin and yang throughout the year, it can be crammed into the course of one day;[20] hence the hour *hai-mo tzu-ch'u* is the moment corresponding to the hexagram *fu,* the time when the *ch'i* of yang begins to reappear.

8. Taking a bath (*Mu-yü*).[bo] In Taoist cultivation the term *mu-yü* (to bathe) means to rest the *ch'i* in the body for a long while. In the *Hsing-ming shuang-hsiu wan-shên kuei-chih* [bp] (preface 1615), we read:

The line "cleansing their minds, retired and laid them up in secrecy" [bq] as found in the *Book of Changes* [21] was the origin of the term "taking a bath" used by the immortals of the T'ang-Sung period. . . . The heart [or mind], being fire in its nature, is then to be enshrouded by water sent down from the back; that is the meaning of "cleansing." The heart is placed in the front of one's body, and it is covered by water from the back, which is opposite to the front; that is the meaning of "retiring." It is the natural course for beginners to follow in subduing their minds. When

CHART I. *The Combination of the Five Directions and the Five Elements*
(according to the *na-chia* 納甲 theory initiated by Ching Fang 京房
and elaborated by Yü Fan 虞翻 of the Three Kingdoms period)

北 = Water 水 = *yin-kuei* 壬 - 癸
|
西 = Metal 金 = 庚 - 辛 *keng-hsin* ——— 中 = Earth 土 = 戊 - 己 *wu-c*
|
南 = Fire 火 = 丙 - 丁 *ping-*

the mind has been brought under control too rigidly, one begins to be
flighty and unstable. There is flame in his mind. Therefore, as a temporary
measure, it is advisable for him to remove his mind of fire from the south,
and place it at the back, which is water in the north. When water and fire
come to supplement each other, the confusion of thoughts will automatically cease. This is exactly what Po Yü-ch'an [br 22] has said: "Cleansing
the mind and removing one's worries from it is what is meant by 'taking
a bath.' " [bs 23]

9. Temperature (*Huo-hou*)[bt]. This is applied to the movement of
breath, or the state of "neither breathing nor yet of arresting breath."
In discussing "refining the drug" Wu Shou-yang says:

If one earnestly employs his mind to increase its temperature, then he will
have paid too much attention to the temperature itself, and will have forgotten that the drug is easily exhausted. If one becomes too negligent of
the temperature and is unaware of its existence, then he will easily fall
asleep or be distracted. When the temperature is cooled down and the fire
extinguished, the drug tends to be dissipated and is no more. Then the
great drug can never be produced. If the temperature is not attended to
continuously, then the drug may become spoiled even if it would have
been produced otherwise. If the temperature is constantly increased and
yet one is still not satisfied, even if the drug has been produced, it will still
be spoiled. The spoiled drug should not be taken. Sages and talented men
of later generations should notice that during the cultivation one should
make the spirit agreeable and balanced with the *ch'i*, and the temperature
applied should suit the state of the drug. The movement is the product of
the ordinary breath multiplied by the true *ch'i*, and the movement of the
true *ch'i* will consolidate the base of the true breath. Then the temperature one employs will not be extreme; there will be neither forcible action

良 = Wood 木 = 甲 - 乙 *chia-yi*

nor remissness. By refining the drug in this way, one is able to grasp the remarkable principle of revolving the *ch'i* round the body, and producing the drug of longevity, namely, the Golden Pill.[24]

10. The Secret (*Chi*).[bu] The character *chi* in Taoist texts means generally "a clue to the unseen," and the practice of Taoist cultivation in order to prolong one's life has been compared since Sung-Yüan times to the strategy of "stealing a march on heaven" (*tao-chi*).[bv] For the Taoist philosophers believed that the practice of their principle was to live by entirely reversing the natural course which carries us on from cradle to grave, so that death, as the natural consequence of life, could be averted. The idea of "stealing" is derived from these few lines from the *Yin-fu Canon:* [bw]

Heaven and Earth are the despoilers of All Things;
All Things are the despoilers of Man;
Man is the despoiler of All Things. . . .
The motive power of the three despoilers is invisible and unrecognized by the generality of men. When the superior man receives it he is enabled to invigorate his body; and when the inferior man receives it he makes light of his life.[25]

11. "Capturing the yin to replenish the yang" (*Ts'ai-yin pu-yang*).[bx] In the *Shuo-kua* (Treatise of remarks on the trigrams), V, of the *Book of Changes* the trigram *k'an* represents the second son of a family, while the trigram *li* is a symbol for the second daughter.[26] The Taoist philosophers of the Internal Pill School, in their texts, preferred to explain the trigram *li* as the flame of one's heart,

CHART II. *The Combination of the Eight Trigrams and the Movement of the Moon* (according to Ching Fang and Yü Fan)

(For the link between and *yi*, etc., see Cha

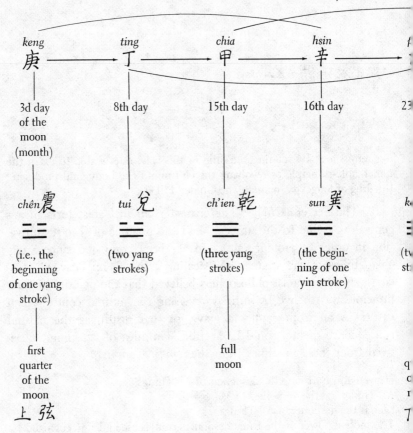

keng 庚	*ting* 丁	*chia* 甲	*hsin* 辛	
3d day of the moon (month)	8th day	15th day	16th day	2
chên 震	*tui* 兌	*ch'ien* 乾	*sun* 巽	*k*
(i.e., the beginning of one yang stroke)	(two yang strokes)	(three yang strokes)	(the beginning of one yin stroke)	(t st
first quarter of the moon 上弦		full moon		q c r 丁

i.e., the mind, and the trigram *k'an* as the water contained in one's kidneys (secretions). When they came to the point of *t'iao k'an-li* [by] (regulating the *k'an* and the *li* in one's own body as a part of Taoist cultivation), they simply regulated and controlled the breath to a

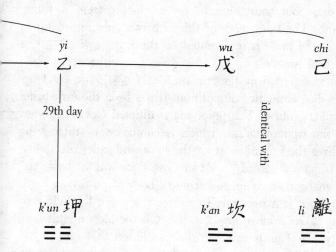

last day of the moon
(month) when the sun
and the moon meet at
yin 壬 (i.e., on the
30th day) and disappear
at *kuei* 癸 , both yin
and *kuei* denote the
North (see Chart 1);
thenceforth they go
further to the Center,
i.e., *wu-chi*[1] 戊己
where the identifying
trigrams would be
k'an-li 坎 離 ☵ ☲

坎 = 戊
離 = 己

[1]*Wu-chi* 戊己 as a compound was equivalent to
chung 中 in Han times. For instance, the *wu-chi
chiao-yü* 戊己校尉 a commander who was
placed at the center of a garrison region.

state of partial suspension of vital functions of the body, as a means
of bringing about calmness and exaltation of the mind.

As previously noted, the Taoist priests of ancient times had invented a theory of inhaling air or *ch'i* (facing either the sun in the

morning or the full moon at night) so that they could benefit from the essences emitted from the heavenly bodies. This, I think, served as a basis for the belief that in the same way a man may, during intercourse, draw out something to his advantage from a young woman's womb. The framework of this idea can be summed up in the belief that the male is represented by the trigram *li* (☲), a sign composed of two yang lines and one yin line in between, while the female is represented by the trigram *k'an* (☵), the exact opposite of *li* in diagrammatic composition. It has been the firm belief of Taoist thinkers, and on this point the traditional Confucian view agrees, that the trigram *ch'ien*, which is composed of three yang lines, symbolizes the utmost in strength, vigor, and indestructability. Now if the trigram *li* already has two yang lines within itself, and if it is to be changed to *ch'ien* to become a body of pure yang made of three yang lines, it is necessary to replace the yin in its middle by a line of yang taken from somewhere else. On the basis of this kind of plausibility, the Taoists came to the conclusion that one should borrow the yang line from the body of the trigram *k'an* to fulfill the requirement. This is perhaps the fundamental structure of the "Golden Pill" theory among those who believed that sexual intercourse might have something to do with the perpetuation of one's life. In the W*ang-wu chen-jen k'ou-shou yin-t'an pi-chüeh ling-p'ien* ᵇᶻ (Occult formulae on the female pill according to the verbal instructions given by Immortal Wang-wu) we have the following passage which gives the reasons why such a practice could be useful for bringing a man longevity:

The art of longevity can be likened to grafting, to continuing one's own life by adding to it elements from another life. In grafting, although a shoot of another stock is inserted in the slit, it is the vital *ch'i* and the sunshine which play the important part in bringing out the wonderful results. An analogy to this may be seen in the method for preserving and extending human life. When the vulva is open and menses have just been cleared, then it is a suitable time for the veins to act harmoniously and prepare the ground for the forces of yin and yang to meet. It is also the time for the female to become pregnant. It is only logical to believe that at this time, when a woman may be going to bear the fruit of a new life, one may divert its course to oneself, and obtain a new infusion of life to continue the old one. But the most important thing to bear in mind is that no sperm be discharged. As the ancient saying goes, "To discharge it in the natural way is to give birth to a new life, to preserve it in one's body is to keep oneself vigorous and active." It is most effective in springtime, when all lives are flourishing and vying in growth. If during the contact a man is able to bring about "one conception" (*i-kan*)[ca] to his merit, his life will be prolonged twelve years, which is the time needed to circle heaven and earth once. Should he obtain ten "conceptions," his life would last one hundred and twenty more years, and he would have no difficulty in following the Yellow Emperor and ascending to the sky.[27]

The following table taken from the *Ch'i-pi-t'u*, or *Ta-huan-tan ch'i-pi-t'u*[cb] (The secret of the reviving pill), quoted in Ch'en Chih-hsü's[cc] (*c.* 1335) *Shang-yang tzu chin-tan ta-yao*[cd] [28] may give us some vague idea of the cryptic terms used by the advocates of such practice:

LI	K'AN
To be received by *chi*[ce]	To be received by *wu*[cf]
Sun	Moon
Fire	Water
Heart	Kidneys
Cinnabar	Lead
Dragon	Tiger
Mercury	*ch'i*

12. The Dual Cultivation of Nature and Life (*Hsing-ming shuang-hsiu*).[cg] The term *hsing-ming shuang-hsiu* is a difficult one to explain. It has two different meanings, but sometimes these two meanings can be unified in the person who practices such cultivation. First, its general meaning is always the union of the spirit (*shen*)[ch] and the *ch'i* within one's own body. Second, it denotes exclusively the dual cultivation of male and female through sexual intimacy, in which *ming* (life) is male and *hsing* (nature) is female.

Ma Chüeh[ci] (*c.* 1183), alias Ma Tan-yang, one of the seven earliest disciples of the founder of the Ch'üan-chen[cj] sect of Taoism in the north, once said:

The spirit and the *ch'i* may be called the *hsing* and the *ming*. The *hsing* and the *ming* are the dragon and the tiger, the lead and the mercury, the water and the fire, the Baby[ck] and the Amazed Maid,[cl] [29] the yin and yang. Therefore, the true *yin* and genuine yang are but the spirit and *ch'i*;

all the other variant terms can be abandoned. In order to keep the spirit and nourish the *ch'i*, it is important for one to cut off all entanglements in life. He should be pure both inwardly and outwardly, should practice breathing, that is, his breathing should be slow and long drawn-out, and not be alarmed by anything. If he is able to keep his sperm for three years, he will produce a pill in the lower cinnabar field [cm]; six years, in the middle cinnabar field [cn]; and nine years, in the upper [literally great] cinnabar field.[co] [30]

Wang Tao-yüan [cp] (*alias* Wang Chieh, Master of Hun-jan), a well-known Ch'üan-chen priest of early Ming times, wrote an essay entitled "On the Interconnection of the nature (*hsing*) and life (*ming*)" [cq] in which he asserts:

Hsing is the master of one's person. In daily life, to respond to myriad things is the function of the *hsing*. *Ming* is the root of one's person, and is the body which does various works. . . . In the response of *hsing* to matters, *ming* is the body and *hsing* is its function. In the transformation and changes of the *ming*, *hsing* is the body and *ming* is its function.[31]

In 1406, when Chang Yü-ch'u [cr] (the 43d Celestial Master) wrote his *Tao-men shih-kuei* [cs] (Ten principles in Taoist cultivation), he said:

In recent years people take Zen Buddhism as seeking for cultivation of the nature (*hsing*); Taoism, for cultivation of the life (*ming*); the Ch'üan-chen sect of Taoism, for dual cultivation of both the nature and the life, and the Cheng-i [ct] sect of Taoism, for cultivation of rituals and ceremonies. But is not the learning of the *tao* simply the cultivation of nature and life and nothing else? Even the teaching of rituals and ceremonies is only for the learning of these two things.[32]

Chang's opinions agree with the view found in the *Hsing-ming shuo* [cu] (On the nature and the life) included in the *Hsing-ming shuang-hsiu wan-shen kuei-chih.*[cv] The anonymous author of this treatise says:

What is *hsing*? It is primordiality, the true suchness, and the illustrious spirit. In man, it is to be called nature.

What is *ming*? It is the primordial vital sperm, enshrouded by the mists of the generative force. It comes from Heaven, and is to be called life.

But these two things cannot be separated. *Hsing* cannot be established without the participation of *ming*. *Ming* cannot be sustained alone without the coordination of *hsing*. The Taoist cultivators tend to take the *ch'i* for *ming* and aim at the cultivation of *ming*, . . . hence they put much emphasis on the study of *ming* at the expense of *hsing*. The Ch'an Buddhists tend to take the spirit for *hsing*, . . . hence they put much emphasis on the cultivation of *hsing* at the expense of *ming*. However, although the spirit has its root in the nature (*hsing*), the nature cannot be the spirit exclusively, though the spirit becomes efficacious through it. Although the *ch'i* has its root in life(*ming*), life cannot be the *ch'i* only, though the *ch'i* is produced by it.[33]

This may be considered the basis for the outgrowth of the theory of dual cultivation.

III. TAOIST INFLUENCES ON LEADING MING THINKERS

Among Confucian thinkers of the Ming, Wang Yang-ming clearly had the widest influence, and we may consider him typical of the age in that, although he disavowed any allegiance to Taoism, his thinking was strongly affected by it. He himself admitted that out of his fifty odd years thirty had been spent in the study of Taoist literature. It was not until 1505, when he became acquainted with Chan Jo-shui,[cw] a disciple of Ch'en Hsien-chang's, that he began to change his views, and it was as late as 1521 that he formally put forward his philosophical theory of "innate knowledge" (*liang-chih*).[34] Yet, in his *Ch'uan-hsi lu* (*Instructions for Practical Living*) there are *passim* not only Taoist terms but also some passages quite incomprehensible except to readers familiar with Taoist thought and terminology. Read, for instance, the following dialogue between Wang Yang-ming and his disciple:

Disciple: In the Way of the Immortals what are the vital *ch'i*, the vital spirit, and the vital sperm? [cx]
Master: They are but one thing. The *ch'i* represents it in a state of pervasion. When it is condensed, it becomes the sperm. The spirit is the active functioning of both the *ch'i* and the sperm.[35]

Elsewhere in the *Instructions* Lu Ch'eng [cy] (the disciple who put the above question) asked Wang Yang-ming about "the place where the vital spirit, the vital *ch'i*, and the vital sperm are stored" and about "the sperm of the true yin and the *ch'i* of the true yang." [cz] Now we are almost certain that none of the great Neo-Confucians, the Ch'eng brothers, Chu Hsi, or even Lu Hsiang-shan, would have ever condescended to talk about anything so un-Confucian. One would therefore expect a stern rebuke from the great master Wang Yang-ming to a question like this. But he replied:

Innate knowledge (*liang-chih*) is one. Its active function is called the spirit, its pervasion the *ch'i*, and its condensation the sperm. How could these things be taught in concrete form? The sperm of the true yin is the mother of the *ch'i* of the true yang; the *ch'i* of the true yang is the father of the sperm of the true yin.[da] The yin is rooted in the yang, and *vice versa*; they are not two different things. If you are clear about my theory of innate knowledge, then questions of this kind will be solved without further explanation. Otherwise, there will still be a lot of things such as the "Three Passes" (*san-kuan* [db]), the "Seven Rounds" (*ch'i-fan* [dc]), and the "Nine Turns" (*chiu-huan* [dd]) mentioned in your letter which remain undefined and uncertain.[36]

I have quoted Wang Yang-ming's own words to show the manner in which Taoist elements appear in his thought and that of other Confucians of the Ming dynasty. Only with a better understanding of these elements can we arrive at a real understanding of both Yang-ming himself and the various branches of his philosophical school in Chekiang, T'ai-chou, and Kiangsi. Then, too, we may understand why Wang Chi's *hui-yu* [de] (seminar lecture notes) are full of Taoist terms;[37] why Lo Hung-hsien (Nien-an)[df] and Lo Ju-fang (Chin-hsi)[dg] would at one time dally with Buddhism and at another with Taoism; and why their behavior was so eccentric.[38] For instance, Lo Ju-fang often mentioned the Buddhist "heaven of Trāyastriṃśat" [dh] in his conversation with scholar-officials. Under Hu Ch'ing-hsü,[di] he had studied alchemy and dual cultivation in terms of sexual life. Nevertheless he was honored as the great Neo-Confucian master of the T'ai-chou branch of Wang Yang-ming's school. That such an anomaly could have been overlooked by all except a few of his contemporaries indicates both the wide influence and the general tolerance of ideas and practices drawn from Taoism and Buddhism.

In pointing to such influences on the Wang Yang-ming school I do not ignore the efforts of a group of traditional Confucians in the

Ming to guard the "orthodox" learning of the Ch'eng brothers and Chu Hsi from heterodox contamination. These efforts, however, only confirm the extent to which Taoism and Buddhism had made inroads on Confucianism.

Such is the case, for example, with Hu Chü-jen,[dk] who denounced the Taoist practice of breath control and "gazing at the end of one's own nose." [dl] [39] There was also Ts'ao Tuan,[dm] who hated any worship inconsistent with Confucian tradition. When there was a funeral in the home of a disciple, Ts'ao Tuan forbade a Buddhist mass. To "release a soul from suffering" in the netherworld, he argued, presupposes sins committed by the departed during his lifetime, and a filial son should not impute such things to his parent. In those days all candidates in state examinations worshiped the god Wen-ch'ang,[dn] but Ts'ao Tuan refused to do so. Originally Wen-ch'ang had been a Tsin dynasty general named Chang Ya-tzu [do] from Szechuan, who was killed in action. Later, Taoists turned him into a star in the South Dipper and made him patron of examinations. Begun in the T'ang dynasty, the worship of Wen-ch'ang had by Ming times become a well-established convention among scholars.[40] Therefore when Ts'ao Tuan refused to do obeisance to him, a colleague said to him: "Since Wen-ch'ang is the deity ruling over scholars, I am afraid you cannot but pay homage to him." Ts'ao Tuan retorted in anger: "If *he* rules over scholars, whom shall Confucius rule over?" [41]

Another scholar of this type was Huang Tso,[dp] who in his letters to Ts'ui Yüan-yeh [dq] and Cheng I-chai [dr] strongly denounced contemporary scholars as "Buddhists in Confucian disguise" [ds] and severely criticized Chou Tun-i and Chu Hsi for having accepted the teachings contained in the *Yin-fu ching* and the *Chou-i ts'an-t'ung-ch'i*.[42] On the other hand, Ho T'ang [dt] could be strongly anti-Buddhist while taking a much less rigid position toward religious Taoism.[43]

The existence of such frequent protests from the orthodox, however, betrays the prevailing heterodox trend of Ming thought as a whole. The intellectual scene, especially in the fifteenth and sixteenth centuries, was dominated by scholars who had been influenced to a greater or lesser extent by Taoist and Buddhist ideas and in the latter half of the period also by the philosophy of Wang Yang-ming. In his own time, for example, Hu Chü-jen stood in opposition to Ch'en Hsien-chang and Lou Liang.[du] Lou Liang died early, and his writings were lost in the aftermath of the rebellion of Prince Ch'en-hao,[dv] to whom his daughter was married. Ch'en Hsien-chang, however, was much more influential than his "orthodox" opponent Hu Chü-jen. And despite Ts'ao Tuan's vigorous denunciation of Buddhism and Taoism, the impact he made was insignificant in comparison with the role played by contemporaries of his who were influenced by these heterodoxies.

Yang-ming himself admitted that he had been fascinated by Taoism and that for three decades he had been occupied in studying Taoist texts. There is an astonishing story about him as a young man. On his wedding night he slipped away from his bride and the bridal chamber his father-in-law had prepared for him in Nan-ch'ang, and went to the Taoist monastery T'ieh-chu Kung,[dw] where he listened to a Taoist priest's teaching on longevity until dawn.[44] Singularly eccentric as this episode of his early life is, I am inclined to doubt that he was ever actually converted to Taoism. In the first place, he did not believe that a human being could "bodily ascend to heaven"[dx] and thus become an immortal. Yet this idea had been the essence of religious Taoism. Many persons found the appeal of Taoism irresistible simply because it offered them the promise of physical immortality or at least longevity. Throughout Chinese history many emperors had succumbed to this temptation. Among Yang-ming's intimate friends Hsü Chen-ch'ing (alias Hsü Ch'ang-kuo[dy]), a man of literary talent, also got caught up in it. In 1510 Hsü Chen-ch'ing raised the subject in a conversation with Wang Yang-ming and Chan Jo-shui, for Hsü knew that Yang-ming had been well acquainted with Taoism. At that time, Yang-ming chose not to refute the superstitious belief in immortality but tactfully said: "If a person is able to cultivate his mind, to nourish his nature, and to follow what is natural in life, he may be said to have done his best."[45] Yet two years before this, when Yang-ming was living in Kweichou Province in exile, he had, in fact, strongly criticized the absurdity of such things in "answering someone's letter about the immortals."[dz 46]

In the second place, we have reason to suppose that Wang Yang-ming never believed in the Taoist theory of "capturing the yin to replenish the yang." Versed in Taoist literature as he was, Wang Yang-ming must have read the *Wu-chen p'ien* [ea] (To understand the truth) written by Chang Po-tuan [eb] (d. 1082), an early Taoist master of the Southern Branch. [ec] Although this work was said to deal with the secret of the internal pill, most commentators and annotators since the Southern Sung had classified it under the category of "capturing the yin to replenish the yang." Ostensibly these commentators and annotators opposed the "bedchamber art," but in their hearts they obviously knew more about it than they were willing to admit. Probably irritated by their hypocrisy, Yang-ming chose to be frank over this matter. In a poem written at Nanking in 1514 reciprocating another by a friend, he vehemently denounced the *Wu-chen p'ien*, and more particularly the commentaries and annotations. [47]

On the other hand we do find occasional references to this work in his own writings, not necessarily unsympathetic in tone. In a letter to Nieh Pao [ed] written in 1526 Yang-ming used the following words which were precisely those found in the *Yü-lu* (Classified conversations) of Chan Jo-shui, a quotation from the *Wu-chen p'ien*: "If there is no rice [literally 'genuine seed'] in the pan, it is boiling water in the vessel with fire underneath." [ee] [48] There would be nothing surprising if these words had been used simply as metaphors, but in this case they are undoubtedly cryptic references to mental cultivation.

The method of cultivation used by Ch'an Buddhists is called meditation (*dhyāna* or *ch'an*) and that used by Taoists is breath control. The latter method, as we have seen, is to direct and concentrate breathing through one's whole constitution in such a way that one's spirit remains collected and does not scatter. When breath control reaches the perfect stage, a physical and mental equilibrium will result. This is the mental stage every Taoist cultivator of the internal pill seeks to bring about.

Confucians, who aspire to become sages rather than immortals, have had their own method of mental cultivation. If we read the Confucian *Analects*, the *Book of Rites*, and other early texts, our impression is that Confucians emphasize primarily the moral and social aspects of personal cultivation. The further idea that Confucians also needed methods of mental cultivation as distinct from moral cultivation originated with Sung scholars. Ever after Chou Tun-i mooted the idea of "calmness" (*ching*)[ef] and Ch'eng Hao the idea of "stabilizing" (*ting*),[eg] the Sung Confucians had taught scholars to "nurture the roots" through sitting still and meditating.[40] Later Ch'eng Hao and his younger brother, Ch'eng I, changed the principle of "calmness" into that of "reverence." [eh] [50] In so doing these Neo-Confucians merely invented a system of mental cultivation which the Confucians had never before possessed. They probably thought that Confucianism could not compare favorably with Taoism and Ch'an unless it possessed its own version of mental cultivation. So they were obliged to adopt such a system of mystical practice from other religions and present it in respectable language taken from the Confucian Classics.

Needless to say, both Chu Hsi and Lu Hsiang-shan recognized the importance of meditation. The former not only wrote the *T'iao-hsi chen*[ei] (Instructions for breath control)[51] but also made commentaries and annotations on the *Yin-fu ching* and the *Chou-i ts'an-t'ung-ch'i*; he was thus more inclined towards Taoism, at least in regard to mental cultivation.[52] This was probably the reason why Wang Yang-ming, in answering Hsü Ch'eng-chih's letter, said: "Hence some people suspect him [Chu Hsi] of toying with trifles." [53] For his own part, however, Yang-ming readily admitted that he had studied Taoism for longevity (*yang-sheng*[ej])[54] as distinct from immortality, and the art of longevity consists mainly of mental cultivation and meditation. Despite Yang-ming's admonishing his students against trying to become immortals or Buddhas, he did not forbid such men as Lu Ch'eng[ek] and Wang Chia-hsiu[el] to study Taoist methods of cultivation for the sake of achieving long life.

In the life chronology (*nien-p'u*) of Wang Yang-ming, compiled jointly by Ch'ien Te-hung[em] and Lo Hung-hsien,[en] are recorded many occasions when Yang-ming on his own initiative visited Taoist priests.[55] Mention is also made of his prescience as a result of prolonged meditation in a grotto at Shao-hsing.[eo] Wang Yang-ming, however, never conceded that he had adopted or engaged in heterodox practices. Nor did Ch'en Hsien-chang or Chan Jo-shui, whose methods of mental cultivation approximated those of Ch'an Buddhism. To explain and justify their methods of mental cultivation, as distinct from those of the Buddhists and Taoists, they were simply obliged—as were their eminent predecessors—to find among Confucians in the past someone whose words they could interpret as providing authority for their own ideas.

Four centuries before the time of Ch'en Hsien-chang and Wang Yang-ming, Ch'eng I had expounded the meaning of the character *ching* (reverence) in the following vein:

"Reverence" merely means pondering in a state of unperturbed mind.[ep] "There must be [constant] practice [of righteousness]," and one ought to "accumulate righteousness." [eq] If one is merely "reverential" but does not "accumulate righteousness," that will amount to no practice at all.[56]

The Chinese phrases *pi yu-shih yen* and *chi-i*, which are rendered respectively as "there must be [constant] practice [of righteousness]" and "to accumulate righteousness," originated in *Mencius*. The original passage which contains these phrases, although philosophically important, is so worded as to be open to more than one interpretation. Many a Confucian master of later ages took advantage of this textual ambiguity. The following is adapted from James Legge's translation of this classical text:

This is the Great Morale [er]: It is exceedingly great, and exceedingly strong. Being nourished properly, and sustaining no injury, it pervades all between heaven and earth. This is the Great Morale: It is something suitable to match with righteousness and the Path. Without it, man is in a state of cowardice. It is produced by the accumulation of righteousness; it is not to be matched by impulsive acts of righteousness. If the mind does not feel complacency in conduct, [the Great Morale] becomes enfeebled. I therefore said, "Kao tzu [es] has never understood righteousness, because he takes it to be something external."

There must be [constant] practice [of this righteousness], but without the object of thereby strengthening [the Great Morale]. Let not the mind forget [its work], but let there be no conscious assisting of the growth [of that Morale].[57]

In instructing people to practice meditation, Ch'en Hsien-chang often used the expression "neither to forget nor to assist." [et] For this, people branded him a follower of Ch'an, but he passed off such

criticism by pointing out that the resemblance between his philosophy and Ch'an Buddhism was only superficial. Nevertheless, in 1511,
when Chan Jo-shui was about to set out on an official mission to
An-nan, Yang-ming composed a valedictory essay, in which he referred to the fact that some people detected a similarity between
Chan Jo-shui's philosophy and Ch'an Buddhism.[58]

Previous to this, Yang-ming had been unable to link up his own
methods of mental cultivation, which were Taoist in origin, with
Confucian theory. But after Ch'en Hsien-chang and Chan Jo-shui
had set a precedent, he could follow suit. Thus his originally Taoist
practice of mental cultivation came to include some Ch'an ingredients. In 1506, when Yang-ming was banished to Kweichou Province,
Chan Jo-shui wrote a farewell poem in which the phrase "neither to
forget nor to assist" was used in reference to Wang's method of
spiritual cultivation.[59] Circumstances such as these show that before
Yang-ming formulated his theory of innate knowledge his philosophical views were much in line with those of Chan Jo-shui and Chan's
teacher, Ch'en Hsien-chang.

Before Wang's exile he had already attained the stage of "spiritual
enlightenment" (te-tao) as known in Taoist-type cultivation. His life
chronology gives 1502 as the year in which this happened. "Spiritual
enlightenment" is, however, merely a preliminary stage before advancing to that known as "forming a sacred embryo in one's cinnabar
field." [eu] These are Taoist technical terms with which Yang-ming
had become well acquainted in his boyhood, and these are also the
objectives which he had pursued for many years.

By the time he was living in the hills of Kweichou, however, since
his faith in these things had already been shaken, his spiritual experiences were no longer described in Taoist terms. From what he
records of the first flash of intuitive insight into "innate knowledge"
it may well have resulted from a Taoist kind of cultivation, but he
put it in terms memorized, as he said, from the Confucian Classics.
Thus the sense of exaltation he felt at the moment when enlightenment suddenly dawned on him is described by him in Confucian
terms as follows:

Before I came to the Southern Capital (Nanking), I still had something
in me of the over-cautious and the "Pharisee." [ev] Now that I have a real

grasp of innate knowledge and am able to distinguish between right and wrong, I can act with a free hand and there is no need for me to conceal anything whatsoever. I now have the mind and ambition of a frank and forward man [ew] and I would not care even if all the people in the world should criticize me and say that my actions do not tally with my words.[60]

The profound significance of Wang's enlightenment is indicated in what his outstanding disciples Wang Chi and Nieh Pao and his admirer Lo Hung-hsien said about meditation.[61] This they understood to be a regular practice of sitting still, pondering for hours at a time. It was not, as Yang-ming had once said, merely "in order to patch up the imperfections which one has had since childhood and to regain our abandoned mind," [62] for as soon as "childhood training" is mentioned, one immediately thinks of "sweeping the floors, answering the door, and replying to questions." Thus Wang Chi practiced meditation in seclusion. Lo Hung-hsien reached a vague stage of awakening after meditating for ten days. The imprisoned Nieh Pao, "living long in idleness and absolute tranquillity, suddenly saw the truth." [63] So these scholars all regarded meditation as a serious practice, not to be compared to mere childhood training. The mental state actually experienced in their meditation no doubt had its origin in Ch'an Buddhism, though Yang-ming frequently denied that his meditative methods were those of the Ch'an cult. He could not easily deny, however, that they had some root in Taoism, with which he was generally known to be well acquainted.[64]

Earlier I have referred to the occasion on which Yang-ming strongly condemned the *Wu-chen p'ien*. In his letter to Lu Ching, written in 1521, Yang-ming, however, conceded that there was some point to what was said in the Epilogue [ex] to this work.[65] Since Lu Ching had been a Taoist devotee before becoming Yang-ming's disciple, Yang-ming was perhaps merely being tactful in making this comment. But later Huang Wan,[ey] one of Yang-ming's most outstanding students, in his *Ming-tao p'ien* (To expound the way), expressed grave doubt about his master's attitude in admitting that "the Epilogue to the *Wu-chen p'ien* accords with the ideas of the sages." [66] This shows that in the eyes of one of his own students Yang-ming had not entirely shaken off Taoist influence.

When Yang-ming was living in exile in Kweichou, he admitted, in "answering someone's letter about the immortals," that his own study of Taoism for many years had left him with his teeth loose and his hair gray. So he was disillusioned with the Taoist promise of immortality,[67] though the influence of Taoist mental cultivation remained with him. In a still later phase of his development he wished further to free himself from the influence of Ch'en Hsien-chang and Chan Jo-shui, for he was well along towards establishing his own philosophical school. At Shao-hsing, in 1526, he wrote a letter of reply to Nieh Pao in which he still quoted *Mencius*. He said that so long as scholars understood the idea that "there must be [constant] practice [of righteousness]," it would be sufficient. His argument ran like this: If their practice were sustained, they need not be told "not to forget"; if they were not overeager for results, they need not be cautioned "not to assist." [68] Here, though Wang still couches his argument in the terms of Mencius, it seems clear that he is moving away from Ch'en Hsien-chang and Chan Jo-shui, and preparing to blaze a new trail.

It had been a different matter, however, when both Yang-ming and Chan Jo-shui, in describing respectively how they arrived at a mental state of cultivation, quoted the same passage from the *Wu-chen p'ien:* "If there is no rice in the pan, it is boiling water in the vessel with fire underneath." Within the sphere of the Three Teachings—Confucianism, Buddhism, and Taoism—for an adherent of one religion to be "eating off one plate with his eye on the other two" [fa] was a common occurrence. Upon hearing the stock phrase "neither to forget nor to assist," a student seized the opportunity and asked Chan Jo-shui whether the phrase alluded to "medium firing," [fb] that is, to being neither too strong nor too weak.[69] And it occasioned no wonderment, for this cryptic term, which had since Sung times been used by Taoist priests for "temperature" [fc] (meaning the regulated speed of breathing in mental cultivation), was by the mid-Ming period no longer a guarded secret.

Under such circumstances Yang-ming was obliged to admit that in a certain sense the Three Teachings were really one:

The Way is so great that it is boundless. If one maintains the view that there are divergent ways, then no way can be great. At the time when the study of the mind was pure and illuminating, all scholars in the world enjoyed the same teaching and all did their best to make a contribution of their own. This may be likened to the construction of this hall. Originally it was one great hall [which had no partitions]. Later on, sons and grandsons began to live apart, and the hall was partitioned into the central chamber and the lateral compartments. In still later years hedges divided up the courtyard, although members of the various branches of the family would still help one another. Then, many years afterwards, they began to quarrel and even developed a hostile attitude towards one another. Who could tell that at one time they all belonged to one large family and that they could still live as one family once the fences were removed from the courtyard? There is a similarity between this family and the division of the Three Religions. In the beginning those who shared the same interest, or whose temperaments were more or less the same, concentrated themselves on one particular section of learning. After four or five generations, the development of this branch of study had become so specialized that it seemed to be entirely different from the other branches. Those young scholars whose inclinations lay in this direction came to study under this particular school. Their bias then blocked the way and made communication between the various schools difficult. And when there was a clash of interests either for fame or for profit, they became opponents and fought against one another. Such has always been the tendency. Therefore it is said: "When a good man sees it, he thinks that it is good; when a wise man sees it, he thinks that it is wise." If a man emphasizes one point, it is impossible for him not to be biased.

The above is my translation of what Wang Yang-ming said to his student Chu Te-chih,[fd] in the *Yü-lu* of Chu Te-chih as quoted in the *Ming-ju hsüeh-an*. But this particular passage as given in the *Ming-ju hsüeh-an* actually comes from the *Hsiao-lien hsia*[fe] (A sheathed sword for nocturnal practice) written by Chu Te-chih. Although only the title of this book is recorded in the *Ssu-k'u ch'üan-shu* (The great compendium of Chinese literature), classified under the heading *tsa-chia* (miscellaneous works) in the *tzu* (philosophy) section, its text is partially quoted in the *Ku-chin t'u-shu chi-ch'eng* (A comprehensive encyclopedia of works past and present) under the heading *ching-kung*[ff] (Taoist cultivation in terms of the internal pill) which forms the 299th *chüan* of the section *Shen-i tien*[fg] (On the supernatural). The *Hsiao-lien hsia* is therefore classified as a book on Taoist cultivation.[70] This shows that even during Yang-ming's lifetime, some of his disciples were permitted to dabble in heterodox studies.

Yang-ming's intention had been to demonstrate that there was basically no difference between Confucianism on one hand and Buddhism and Taoism on the other, except that the Buddhists' and Taoists' outlook on life was escapist, and they were therefore selfish. Although the Buddhist outlook on life is, in fact, not entirely that of a recluse and some Taoist activities are even altruistic and social in nature, Yang-ming's observation was nevertheless penetrating. If, like his friend Hsü Chen-ch'ing, Yang-ming had persisted in the Taoist search for immortality—an obsession from which his many students and juniors were not entirely free—he would not have been able during his later life to make so brilliant a political and military contribution to his society, nor to found a philosophical school which inspired so much creative thought.

There was, however, a positive side to the contact between the Taoists and the Confucians during the Ming, as seen in two related developments. One was the dialogue stimulated by the interaction between Confucian and Taoist ideas, and another was the conscious attempt to reconcile and unify these two systems of thought. Here these two types of contact may be only briefly illustrated.

As an example of the first type there is the discussion concerning the differing conceptions of human nature in Confucianism and Taoism. Often this dialogue is conducted in an atmosphere relatively free of sectarianism and with a genuine readiness to discuss issues on their own merits. The possibility that Taoist cultivation may have something to offer the Confucians is at least seriously entertained, if not always accepted. Thus, for instance, in a preface by Hsüeh Hui [fh] (d. 1541) to Chuang tzu chu, which in turn is cited in the Ming-ju hsüeh-an, we read:

The Taoist priests are fond of speaking about the nourishment of life, but in discussing it they have often stepped beyond its field of the nature and life (hsing-ming chih wai). They do not know that the nature and life are the only things one should be concerned about in the nourishment of life. However, although the Confucian scholars in the world talk in general terms of knowing the nature and heaven (chih-hsing chih-t'ien), the study of the nourishment of life is usually despised by them. They do not appreciate the point that if one's life is well preserved then the tao of the nature and life is also preserved and will last long.[71]

Another example may be found in the recorded conversations of Wang Yang-ming's follower, Wang Chi, which includes a conversation between himself and Liu Shih-ch'uan (Pang-ts'ai)ᶠⁱ in which Liu said:

A man is born with the nature and life. By the nature, I mean the mastery of one's mind. [My] nature is inaction (*wu-wei*). Therefore, it needs to be brought out. The fluidity of my mind is life, and life is substantial. Therefore, there is the necessity of transformation and change (*yün-hua*). Constant knowledge is a substance, hence it does not tend to produce thought; constant change is the realization of the action [of life], hence a thought cannot be formed of it. Since these two things cannot be severed, it is necessary to study dual cultivation so that the learning can be complete.

Wang Chi answered:

Innate knowledge itself is a doctrine combining the nature and life into one. It is the master, it is again the fluidity. Therefore, in the method of extending knowledge (*chih-chih kung-fu*), there is but one action. If one insists upon the need of "bringing it out" and of "transformation and change," and sets store by differentiating "not producing a thought" from "a thought cannot be formed of it," this would separate one thing into two. To do so is to bisect the wholeness; how could the two then return to one? [72]

It is clear then that Taoist dual cultivation could be seriously considered within Wang Yang-ming's school, though Wang Chi opposed the dualism it implied because this would destroy the unity of innate knowledge, which had been a cardinal point of Wang Yang-ming's teaching.

In connection with the second development, the attempt to unify Taoism with Confucianism, two men deserve mention: Lin Ch'ao-en and Yüan Huang.

Lin Ch'ao-en ᶠʲ (1517–98) was a native of Fukien Province. His paternal grandfather served as an official under Wang Yang-ming.[73] Lin Chao-en was said, while a child, to have met the great man. At one time Lin Chao-en also sought enlightenment from Lo Hung-hsien. Eventually Chao-en set up his own syncretist religious organization which, with Confucianism as its principal doctrine and Buddhism and Taoism as its subsidiary teachings, aimed at gradually eliminating all denominations and sectarianism. He styled himself "Master of The Three Religions" ᶠᵏ and collected many disciples around him. "The Three-Religion Church," founded under his leadership throughout Southeast China, had a wide influence during his lifetime and for about a century and a half after his death.[74]

Later Yüan Huang [fl] appeared on the scene. His father was an admirer of Wang Yang-ming, and he himself was a student of Wang Chi. Yüan Huang's main contribution consisted in turning the blend of Confucian-Taoist thought to the advantage of moral reform. For this purpose his principal instruments were the Ledgers of Merits and Demerits, a kind of Taoist literature which had been in circulation since the end of the twelfth century, and some exhortative pamphlets written by himself, representing a confluence of Confucian and Taoist ideas.

By further exploiting superstitious beliefs in the Buddhist theory of retribution and in the Taoist idea of canceling past wrongs by accumulative good deeds, Yüan Huang extended his influence widely and deeply into the middle and lower social classes. If we check his Ssu-hsün [fm] (Four admonitions) against Wang Yang-ming's works we find some passages which coincide not only in spirit but in letter.[75] At the instance of some publishers, Yüan Huang also compiled several books to meet the need of candidates for state examinations. Their underlying intent was to advance Wang Yang-ming's philosophy and to displace the Ch'eng-Chu commentaries which had been used since the early Ming as guides for candidates interpreting Confucian Classics. In the official Ming History it is recorded that someone petitioned the throne to destroy the Ssu-shu shan-cheng [fn] (An abridged reader of the Four Books) compiled by Yüan Huang.[76] It may seem that the petitioner was making too great an issue out of a minor work, and yet this book clearly challenged the established orthodoxy. The only extant copy of this work, which is kept in the Japanese Cabinet Library,[fo] has revealing notations in the margin above the text on many pages: "Following the teaching which my late master heard personally from Yang-ming." Elsewhere Yüan asserted that Chu Hsi was not a well-read man, an example of his firm and unequivocal way of pronouncing his opinions.[77]

Lin Ch'ao-en and Yüan Huang had no place in Huang Tsung-hsi's Ming-ju hsüeh-an. He probably excluded them from the company of Confucian scholars because of their strong Taoist coloration. Yet they were not unconnected with several scholars whose names do appear in the Ming-ju hsüeh-an. Of course Huang Tsung-hsi would never have condescended to include the names of Lu Hsi-hsing [fp] and

Wu Shou-yang in his book on Ming thought. The former, a Confucian of the Chia-ching period, became a Taoist priest for several decades, and the latter had been one throughout his life.[78] While Huang Tsung-hsi's attitude in these cases is understandable, one cannot help noting his inconsistency. Many of the Confucian scholars to whom he did assign a place in his *Ming-ju hsüeh-an* were not untinged by Taoist thought and practice. Nor indeed was he. As our final piece of evidence of the pervading influence of Taoist concepts, we may consider in what terms Huang himself set forth the place of the leading Neo-Confucian philosophers:

It has been said by those who are learned that, when the Five Planets met in the Region of *K'uei*, the great Sung scholars of Lien [Chou Tun-i], of Lo [the Ch'eng brothers], of Kuan [Chang Tsai], and of Min [Chu Hsi] were born. When the Five Planets met in the Region of *Shih*, the doctrine of Master Wang Yang-ming flourished. When the Five Planets met in the Region of *Chang*, the Way of Master Liu Tsung-chou became known. Could I say that it was not from Heaven? Could I say that it was not from Heaven? [79]

What language is it that Huang Tsung-hsi uses here, if not the language of Taoism?

NOTES

1. Yang Ch'i-ch'iao,[fq] "Ming-tai chu-ti chih ch'ung-shang fang-shu Chi-ch'i ying-hsiang," *New Asia College Academic Annual*, IV (1962), 73–147; particularly pp. 83–60.
2. For Li Tzu-hsing,[fr] see Li's biography in the *Ming shih* (Dynastic history of the Ming) (hereafter abbreviated MS), 307/769–70; also the biographies of Lo Ching, *ibid.*, 152/357; of Wan An, *ibid.*, 168/393; of Li Chün, *ibid.*, 180/421; of Ma Wen-sheng, *ibid.*, 182/428; of Min Kuei and Keng Yu,[fs] *ibid.*, 183/431. For Shao Yüan-chieh and T'ao Chung-wen, see MS, 307/771; see also biographies of Kao Chin, 209/502; of Liu T'ien-ho, 200/479; of Ou-yang Te. 283/700; and of the sons of Emperor Shih-tsung,[ft] 120/298. *Erh-shih-wu shih*, K'ai-ming ed., and other photostat editions based on it.
3. Biography of Hsia Yen, MS, 196/467.
4. Biography of Tsou Ying-lung,[fu] MS, 210/508; see also biography of Liang Ju-yüan [fv] (alias Ho Hsin-yin) in *Ming-ju hsüeh-an* (hereafter abbreviated MJHA), VI, 32/64, *Wan-yu wen-k'u* ed. Cf. Yü Shen-hsing,[fw] *Ku-shan pi-chu*, 4/8b–9a (Library of Congress Microfilm FR 1002).
5. There have been some individual cases of scholars who were opposed to Buddhism or Taoism. See below, pp. 309–10, for Hu Chü-jen and Ts'ao Tuan.
6. For the early development of the *Kung-kuo ko* (Ledgers of merit and demerit), see Yoshitoyo Yoshioka,[fx] "Shoki no "Kōka kaku" ni tsuite," *The Memoirs of the Institute for Oriental Culture*, Twentieth Anniversary Issue (1962), Pt. 3, pp. 107–86.
7. See MJHA, VI, 32/66.
8. This is a comparatively early Taoist text, which may have been compiled at approximately the same time as the scripture *T'ai-p'ing ching*.[fy] *Tao-tsang* [fz] (hereafter abbreviated TT), 183, *chüan shang*, 19a–b.
9. TT, 93, 46/7a–8.
10. Wu Shou-yang's works may be a little later than those of other Taoist scholars in the Ming. But I think his writings are more systematic, and therefore more suitable for the purpose of illustrating the basic Taoist concepts which prevailed throughout the period. See *Fu-ch'i chih-lun*, 8, in *T'ien-hsien cheng-li, Tao-tsang chi-yao*,[ga] Pi 4/68b–71a.
11. *Ibid.*
12. *Ibid.*, 71a–72b.
13. See also *Hsiu-chen pi-lu*,[gb] quoted in the *Ch'ang-sheng ch'üan ching*,[gc] *Hsü tao-tsang* [gd] (hereafter abbreviated HTT), 1082, 29a; cf. Frederic

Henry Balfour, trans., "The Respiration of the Embryo," *China Review*, IX (1880), No. 4.

14. *T'ai-hsi chih-lun*, 9/73b–76b.

15. See Wu Shou-yang, *Chu-chi chih-lun*,[ge] 6/61a–b.

16. *Ibid.*, 63a. *Lien-yao chih-lun*,[gf] 7.

17. Biography of Meng Hsi,[gg] *Han shu*, 88; biography of Ching Fang,[gh] *Han shu*, 75.

18. With the commentary of Cheng Hsüan; [gi] *Yi-hai chu-ch'en* [gk] (*ko*), Series *keng*.

19. Cf. Lu Hsi-hsing,[gl] *Ts'an-t'ung-ch'i ts'e-su*, in *Fang-hu wai-shih*, (Taipei reprint ed.), *hsia*, pp. 472–73.

20. See Yü Yen,[gm] Commentary on the *Ch'in-yüan-ch'un* (a *tz'u* poem on Taoist cultivation), *TT*, 60/2b.

21. The original line can be found in the *Hsi-tz'u* (Great appendix), Pt. 1. See *Chou-i chu-su* [gn] SPPY ed., 7/16a; Legge, trans., *The I Ching* (Dover reprint, 1963), p. 372.

22. One of the Five Patriarchs of the Southern Branch of Taoism who lived in the early part of the thirteenth century.

23. *Hsing-ming . . . Kuei-chih*, Bk. *heng*,[go] p. 15a (Taipei reprint ed.).

24. *Lien-yao chih-lun*, 7/65a–67a.

25. *Po-tzu Ch'üan-shu*.[gp] See James Legge, trans., *The Texts of Taoism* (Julian Press, 1959), Appendix II, "Classic of the Harmony of the Seen and the Unseen," pp. 702–3.

26. *Chou-yi chu-su*, 9/4b; Legge, trans., *The I Ching*, pp. 429–30.

27. Quoted in *Yün-chi ch'i-ch'ien*,[gq] *TT*, 690, 64/14a.

28. *TT*, 736, ch. 4.

29. Baby (*ying-erh*) is another name for *ch'ien* [gr] (lead), and Amazed Maid (*ch'a-nü*) is another name for *kung* [gs] (cinnabar of mercury). See Ch'en Chih-hsü, *Shang-yang-tzu chin-tan ta-yao t'u*,[gt] *TT*, 738/9b–10a. Originally such terms were used in the preparation of the external pills, which was the work of the alchemist. See Yüan Hsiao-cheng's [gu] commentary to *Liu Tsu* [gv] (The works of Liu Chou [mid-6th century]), *TT*, 673, 3/14b.

30. *Tan-yang Chen-jen chih-yen*,[gw] *TT*, 989, 3a.

31. *Huan-chen chi*,[gx] *TT*, 739, *chüan chung*, 4a–5b.

32. *TT*, 988, 7a.

33. *Hsing-ming . . . kuei-chih*, Bk. *yüan*, 8a–10b.

34. See epitaph of Wang Yang-ming written by Chan Jo-shui, in *Wang Yang-ming ch'üan-chi* [gy] (hereafter abbreviated YMCC), 37/16b; *Pieh Chan Kan-ch'üan hsü* [gz] (written in 1511), 7/4b; *Ta Jen-wen shen hsien*,[ha] 21/4a–b; and Wang Yang-ming's *Nien-p'u*, compiled by Ch'ien Te-hung and Lo Hung-hsien, ed. Sao-yeh Shan-fang,[hb] in YMCC, 33, under this year.

35. *Ch'uan-hsi lu, shang,* YMCC, 1/15b; cf. Wing-tsit Chan, trans., *Instructions for Practical Living and Other Neo-Confucian Writings* (New York, 1963), Part I, "Conversations Recorded by Lu Ch'eng," sec. 57, p. 44. Cf. also *Nan-yu hui-chi,*[hc] in *Wang Lung-hsi yü-lu* (hereafter abbreviated WLCYL), ed. Kuang-wen, 1960, 7/4a–b.

36. *Ibid., chung* 2/18a–b; cf. Chan, *Instructions,* Part II, "Letter in Reply to Lu Yüan-ching,"[hd] sec. 154, p. 133.

37. For instance, *Tung-yu hui-yü,*[he] in WLCYL, 4/6a; *Liu-tu hui-chi,*[hf] *ibid.,* 4/17b–19a; *Chih-chih i-pien,*[hh] *ibid.,* 6/10a; *Nan-yu hui-chi, ibid.,* 7/2a, 5b–6a; *Hsin-an Tou-shan shu-yüan hui-yü,*[hi] *ibid.,* 7/12a; *T'ien-ken yüeh-k'u shuo,*[hj] *ibid.,* 8/9a.

38. See MJHA, biographies of Lo Hung-hsien and of Lo Ju-fang,[hk] IV, 18/3, and VII, 34/3, respectively.

39. See *Chu-yeh Lu*[hl] (Ts'ung-shu chi-ch'eng ed.), 7/81–82; also quoted by Huang Tsung-hsi in MJHA, I, 2/16.

40. See Chou Hung-mu's[hm] memorial to the throne in 1488, MS, 50/116 (*Li* 4); also *Yü-ch'ing wu-chi tsung-chen wen-ch'ang ta-tung hsien-ching,*[hn] TT, 51, 2/7b–9b; *Ch'ing-ho nei-chuan,*[ho] TT, 73, 13b–18a; and *Tzu-t'ung Ti-chün hua-shu,*[hp] TT, 74, 4/35a. Tzu-t'ung is another name for Wen-ch'ang, which was originally a star in the South Dipper. See *Yüan-shih T'ien-tsun shuo Tzu-t'ung Ti-chün pen-yüan-ching,*[hq] TT, 27, and *Nan-tou yen-shou teng-i,*[hr] TT, 81. In the *Tung-chen t'ai-chi pei-ti tzu-wei shen-chou miao-ching,*[hs] TT, 29, however, Wen-ch'ang is not the God of Examinations, but an extremely violent deity who in his wrath is capable of crushing one's head into pieces. I am inclined to think that the description found in the last work may be that of the earliest form of the god.

41. Ts'ao's biography in the MJHA, IX, 44/2.

42. *Huang T'ai-ch'üan chi,*[ht] quoted in MJHA, X, 51/12.

43. See *Yin-yang kuan-chien pien*[hu] in the MJHA, IX, 49/92. The article *Yin-yang kuan-chien*[hv] is included in the *Hsüeh-hai lei-p'ien*[hw] (Han-fen lou ed., 1920), Bk. 31; *Pai-ling hsüeh-shan*[hx] (Han-fen lou ed.), Bk. 3.

44. See *Nien-p'u,* under the year 1488. See also Lo Hung-hsien's 4th letter to Ch'ien Te-hung, YMCC, 36/8a.

45. Epitaph of Hsü Ch'ang-kuo,[hy] YMCC, 25/3b–4a.

46. *Ta jen wen shen-hsien* (written in 1508 at Lung-ch'ang), YMCC, 21/4a.

47. *Shu Wu-chen p'ien ta Chang T'ai-ch'ang*[hz] (1), YMCC, 20/14a.

48. *Ta Nieh Wen-wei*[ia] (2), YMCC, 2/34a–b; a reply to Fu-hsien,[ib] in Chan's *Yü-lu,* quoted in MJHA, *Kan-ch'üan* 1, Bk. 7, p. 92. Cf. *Meng tzu Kao tzu chih-hsüeh,*[ic] WLCYL, 8/11b–12a. The original line of Chang Po-tuan can be found in TT, 61, 4/9b.

49. See Chou, *T'ai-chi-t'u shuo,*[id] in *Sung-Yüan hsüeh-an,* 12/1a–b;

Ch'eng, *Ta Heng-ch'ü Hsien-sheng ting-hsing shu*,[ie] *Ming-tao wen-chi*[if] (SPPY ed.), 3/1a–b. See also Wm. Theodore de Bary, *et al.*, *Sources of Chinese Tradition* (New York, Columbia University Press, 1960), p. 514; Wing-tsit Chan, *A Source Book in Chinese Philosophy* (Princeton University Press, 1963), pp. 525–26; and *I-ch'uan yü-lu*, in *Erh-Ch'eng hsien-sheng ch'üan-shu*[ig] (1687 ed.), 18/25b–28a.

50. *I-ch'uan yü-lu* in *Erh-Ch'eng hsien-sheng ch'üan-shu*, 15/19a, 18/10b–11a, 27b; cf. Chang Po-hsing,[ih] *Chin-ssu lu chi-chieh* (Commercial Press, 1937), 4/156.

51. *Hui-an hsien-sheng Chu Wen-kung wen-chi*[ii] (SPTK ed.), 85/6b.

52. See *TT*, 58 and 624; see also *Chu tzu yü-lei*[ij] (photostat ed.; Taipei, 1962, based upon 1270 ed.), 125/12a–b; *Ssu-k'u ch'üan-shu tsung-mu* (I-wen ed.), 146/2884; Pao Chung-chi's' preface (dated 1208) to the *Chou-i ts'an-t'ung-ch'i ting-ch'i-ko ming-ching-t'u*,[ik] *TT*, 624, 7a; Yü Yen's colophon (dated 1284) to his *I-wai pich-ch'uan*,[il] *TT*, 629; *Pa Lü-ch'iu Sheng Yin-fu ching shuo*,[im] in *Hui-an hsien-sheng Chu Wen-kung wen-chi*, 82/19b.

53. *Ta Hsü Ch'eng-chih*[in] (2), YMCC, 21/6a.

54. *Yü Lu Yüan-ching*,[io] YMCC, 5/7a.

55. Noticeably in 1488, 1501, 1502, and 1507.

56. *Erh-Ch'eng hsien-sheng ch'üan-shu*, 18/33b.

57. Cf. Legge, trans., *The Works of Mencius*, *The Chinese Classics*, Bk. II, Part I, Ch. 2, pp. 189–90.

58. YMCC, 7/4b.

59. YMCC, 37/17a.

60. *Ch'uan-hsi lu, hsia*, YMCC, 3/22b; cf. Chan, trans., *Instructions*, Part III, sec. 312, p. 239.

61. See Wang, *San-shan li-tse lu*,[ip] WLCYL, 1/8a–b; *Chiu-lung chi-hui*,[iq] 3/2a–b; *T'ien-chu shan-fang hui-yü*,[ir] 5/12a–b; Lo, *Yü Yin Tao-yü, Lo Nien-an wen-lu*[is] (1886 ed.), 2/7; Nieh Pao, *Ta K'ang Tzü-yi Wen-hsüeh, Shuang-chiang Nieh hsien-sheng wen-chi*[it] (Yün-ch'iu Shu-yüan ed., 1564; Library of Congress Microfilm FR 921), 8/31b–32a.

62. *Yü Ch'en-chung chu-sheng*,[iu] YMCC, 4/1a.

63. See n. 61; see also *MJHA*, III, 16/85.

64. That the earlier Taoist patriarchs might have been influenced by Ch'an may be shown by Tao Kuang's[iv] commentary on the *Wu-chen p'ien*. See Weng Pao-kung's Annotated Commentaries to the *Wu-chen p'ien*,[iw] *TT*, 62, 8/21a. Tao Kuang himself was one of the patriarchs. Cf. his biography included in *TT*, 64/17a–b.

65. *Yü Lu Yüan-ching*,[ix] YMCC, 5/7a.

66. *Ming-tao p'ien*[iy] (1550 ed.) (Library of Congress Microfilm FR 296), 1/11a–12a.

67. YMCC, 21/4a–b; cf. note 46.

68. *Ta Nieh Wen-wei* [iz] (2), YMCC, 2/34a–b; cf. n. 48.
69. Cf. n. 48.
70. MJHA, V, 25/64; cf. YMCC, *Nien-p'u*, under the year 1523; *San-shan li-tse lu*,[ja] WLCYL, 1/12a. The complete version (in one *chüan*) of the *Hsiao-lien hsia* [jb] is, however, included in the *Pai-lin hsüeh-shan*,[jc] Bk. 8. For this particular passage see 3a–b.
71. MJHA, X, 53/75.
72. MJHA, III, 12/6–7.
73. Lin Fu [jd] (1474–1539) had been an administration commissioner in Kwangsi under the direct command of Wang Yang-ming. Cf. *Ti-fang chin-chi yung-jen su*,[je] YMCC, 14/11b.
74. See Lieh-che Tu Fang,[jf] "Lin Chao-en," Draft Ming Biographies, #6 (dittograph; Columbia University, 1966); Mano Senryū,[jg] "Rin Chō-on to sono chosaku ni tsuite," in *Studies on the Ming Period Presented to the Late Taiji Shimizu* (Tokyo, 1962), pp. 421–56.
75. See my monograph "Yüan Huang and His 'Four Admonitions,'" *The Journal of the Oriental Society of Australia*, V (Nos. 1 and 2 [Sidney, 1967]), 108–32.
76. Biography of Ch'en Yu-hsüeh,[jh] MS, 281/694.
77. Comments on the *Analects*, Pt. 2, 6a; Pt. 1, 20a; Pt. 2, 37b; on the *Great Learning*, 1b.
78. See Wu Shou-yang, *T'ien-hsien Cheng-li*,[ji] and also his *Yü-lu* in the *Tao-tsang ch'i-yao*, *pi* 1–5.
79. MJHA, XII, 62/36.

GLOSSARY

a	李孜省	ai	泥丸
b	邵元節	aj	玉樓
c	陶仲文	ak	黃庭
d	嚴嵩	al	夾脊
e	夏言	am	子午
f	藍道行	an	伏氣直論
g	功過格	ao	天仙正理
h	寶卷	ap	伍守陽
i	金丹	aq	伏
j	內丹	ar	氣根
k	氣	as	逆修 . . . 當必由呼吸之氣而返
l	外丹		還藏伏爲靜
m	方與時	at	調息
n	嚴世蕃	au	天機
o	鼎	av	無極
p	鑪(爐)	aw	胎息
q	性	ax	胎息直論
r	乾	ay	築基
s	客	az	煉藥, 藥
t	命	ba	元精
u	坤	bb	至靜之眞時
v	主	bc	亥之末, 子之初
w	偃月鑪	bd	眞機自然
x	腎		既有藥物生機, 必有先天得藥
y	雙修		之覺. 而以覺靈爲煉藥之主,
z	房中		以沖和爲煉藥之用
aa	太上靈寶五符序	be	亥末子初
ab	腎根	bf	周易參同契
ac	腦戶	bg	坎離震兌
ad	丹	bh	二十四節氣
ae	靈寶無量度人上經大法	bi	十二辟卦
af	三田	bj	孟喜
ag	子	bk	京房
ah	眞炁	bl	易緯稽覽圖

bm 復 臨 泰 大壯 夬 乾 姤 遯 否 觀 剝 坤

bn 黃鍾

bo 沐浴

bp 性命雙修萬神圭旨

bq 洗心退藏於密

br 白玉蟾

bs 洗心滌慮爲沐浴

bt 火候

bu 機

bv 盜機

bw 陰符經

bx 采(探)陰補陽

by 調坎離

bz 王屋眞人口授陰丹秘訣靈篇

ca 一感

cb 契秘圖(大還丹契秘圖)

cc 陳致虛

cd 上陽子金丹大要

ce 納己 爲日 爲火 爲心 爲丹砂 爲龍 爲汞

cf 納戊 爲月 爲水 爲腎 爲鉛 爲虎 爲氣

cg 性命雙修

ch 神

ci 馬珏, 馬丹陽

cj 全眞

ck 嬰[兒]

cl 姹[女]

cm 下丹結

cn 中丹結

co 大丹結

cp 王道淵, 王玠, 混然子

cq 性命混融論

cr 張宇初(第四十三代天師)

cs 道門十規

ct 正一

cu 性命說

cv 性命雙修萬神圭旨

cw 湛若水, 甘泉

cx 元氣元神元精

cy 陸澄

cz 眞陰之精, 眞陽之氣

da 眞陰之精卽眞陽之母, 眞陽之氣卽眞陰之父

db 三關

dc 七返

dd 九還

de 會語

df 羅念菴(洪先)

dg 羅近溪(汝芳)

dh 三十三天

di 胡淸虛

dk 胡居仁

dl '視鼻端白'

dm 曹端, 月川

dn 文昌

do 張亞子

dp 黃佐, 泰泉

dq 崔垣野

dr 鄭抑齋

ds '陽儒陰釋'

dt 何瑭

du 婁諒

dv 宸濠

dw 鐵柱宮

dx 飛昇

dy 徐禎卿, 昌國

dz '答人問神仙'

ea 悟眞篇

eb 張伯端

ec 南宗

ed 聶豹, 文蔚, 雙江先生

ee '鼎中若無眞種子, 如將水火煮空鐺'

ef 靜

eg 定

eh 主敬

ei 調息箴

ej 養生

ek 陸澄

el 王嘉秀

em 錢德洪

en 羅洪先

eo 紹興

ep 敬只是涵養一事

eq 必有事焉, 集義

er 浩然之氣

es 告子

et 勿助 勿忘

eu 結聖胎

ev 鄉愿

ew 狂者的胸次

ex 悟眞篇後序

ey 黃綰(宗賢)明道編

ez 顧憲成, 小心齋劄記

fa '吃一望二'

fb 文武火

fc 火候

fd 朱得之

fe 宵練匣

ff 靜功部

fg 神異典

fh 薛蕙

fi 劉獅泉, 邦采

fj 林兆恩

fk 三教先生

fl 袁黃, 了凡

fm [了凡]四訓

fn 四書删正

fo 日本內閣文庫

fp 陸西星, 長庚

fq 楊啓樵, 明代諸帝之崇尙方術及其影響, 新亞學術年刊

fr 李孜省

fs 羅璟傳(附柯潛傳), 萬安傳, 李俊傳, 馬文升傳, 閔珪傳, 耿裕傳

ft 明史佞幸傳

　　高金傳 (附楊最傳)

　　劉天和傳

　　歐陽德傳

　　世宗諸子

fu 鄒應龍傳

fv 梁汝元(何心隱)

fw 于愼行, 穀山筆塵

fx 吉岡義豐, 初期の功過格について, 東京大學創立二十周年記念論集

fy 太平經

fz 道藏

ga 道藏輯要, 畢集

gb 修眞秘錄

gc 長生詮經

gd 續道藏

ge 築基直論

gf 煉藥直論

gg 孟喜傳

gh 京房傳

gi 鄭玄注

gk 藝海珠塵 庚集

gl 陸西星, 參同契測疏, 方壺外史, 下

gm 兪琰, 沁園春丹詞註解

gn 周易注疏, 四部備要

go 亨集

gp 百子全書

gq 雲笈七籤

gr 鉛

gs 汞

gt　陳致虛, 上陽子金丹大要圖

gu　袁孝政

gv　劉子(畫)

gw　丹陽眞人直言

gx　還眞集

gy　土陽明全集

gz　別湛甘泉序

ha　答人問神仙

hb　掃葉山房

hc　南遊會紀, 王龍溪語錄, 廣文影
　　印本

hd　陸元靜(澄)

he　東遊會語

hf　留都會紀

hg　答楚侗耿子問

hh　致知議辨

hi　新安斗山書院會語

hj　天根月窟說

hk　羅汝芳

hl　居業錄, 叢書集成

hm　周洪謨

hn　玉清旡極總眞文昌大洞仙經

ho　清河內傳

hp　梓潼帝君化書

hq　元始天尊說梓潼帝君本願經

hr　南斗延壽燈儀

hs　洞眞太極北帝紫微神呪妙經

ht　黃泰泉集

hu　陰陽管見辨

hv　陰陽管見

hw　學海類編, 涵芬樓

hx　百陵學山

hy　徐昌國墓誌

hz　書悟眞篇答張太常

ia　答聶文蔚(二)

ib　答孚先問

ic　孟子告子之學

id　太極圖說, 宋元學案

ie　答橫渠先生定性書

if　明道文集, 四部備要

ig　伊川語錄, 二程先生全書

ih　張伯行, 近思錄集解, 商務印書
　　館

ii　晦菴先生朱文公文集

ij　朱子語類

ik　周易參同契鼎器歌明鏡圖鮑仲
　　祺序

il　兪琰跋易外別傳

im　跋閻丘生陰符經說

in　答徐成之(二)

io　與陸元靜 傳習錄下

ip　王(龍溪)三山麗澤錄

iq　九龍紀誨

ir　天柱山房會語

is　羅(洪先), 與尹道輿, 羅念菴文錄

it　聶(豹), 答亢子益問學, 雙江聶先
　　生文集, 雲丘書院刻本

iu　與辰中諸生

iv　道光

iw　翁葆光, 紫陽眞人悟眞篇註疏

ix　與陸元靜

iy　明道編

iz　答聶文蔚(二)

ja　三山麗澤錄

jb　宵練匣

jc　百陵學山

jd　林富

je　地方緊急用人疏

jf　房杜聯誌

jg　間野潛龍, 林兆恩と其の著作に
　　ついて, 明代史論叢 (清水[泰
　　次]博士追悼記念), 大安版

jh　陳幼學

ji　天仙正理

TADAO SAKAI *Confucianism and Popular*

Educational Works

明月 Confucianism existed on several levels in Ming China. This paper will discuss its development through the interaction of traditional Confucian teachings and popular thought as affected by social changes in the Ming period. The conventional view of this process would be in terms of the downward penetration of Confucian teachings made into an official ideology and systematically propagated by the state among its subjects. Actually the process was much more complex. The maintenance of the official ideology itself was affected by new currents of thought among the educated classes, and the content of Confucianism was also influenced by popular trends. Thus it was not just a question of traditional Confucianism being disseminated downward but of popular thought penetrating upward. In this process of interaction new forms of thought made their appearance. I shall discuss these in connection with two main types of literature which circulated widely in the Ming, the popular encyclopedias and the popular morality books.

POPULAR ENCYCLOPEDIAS

The official "orthodoxy" was most prominently established in connection with the civil service examination system (*k'o-chü*).[a] This included also the system of state schools by which students were prepared on the prefectural, subprefectural, and county levels to take the official examinations. The subjects of study in these schools consisted chiefly of those meeting the requirements for the civil service, and were called the "examination course" or "examination studies" (*chü-yeh*).[b] The principal texts were the Confucian Classics, and most particularly the Four Books, with the commentaries of the Ch'eng-Chu school. These had been compiled in *Ssu-shu ta-ch'üan*[c]

(The great compendium of the Four Books) and *Wu-ching ta-ch'üan* ᵈ (The great compendium of the Five Classics), published during the reign of the Yung-lo emperor (1403–27). Even in the independent academies (*shu-yüan*) and other private schools these texts were an important subject of study, because most persons who sought an education did so with a view to passing the official examinations, whatever else they might think or read.

There was an increasing tendency, however, for this type of study to become very routine and mechanical. Candidates merely memorized the texts and their commentaries so that they could produce the right words or phrases in the examinations. They did not necessarily think deeply about them or form any real convictions about them. Therefore, this type of study, instead of conducing to the further development of Confucianism or the application of its ideas and values to political life, became highly formalized. And, as larger numbers of persons sought to acquire this kind of formal training, the demand arose for the type of book that would most easily provide the necessary instruction. The concomitant development of printing resulted in the production and wide distribution of popular encyclopedias especially intended for civil service candidates.

These encyclopedias consisted mainly of model essays of the type required for the examinations—the famous eight-legged essays. Insofar as the content of the essays represented a kind of routine Confucianism the encyclopedias became a means of popularizing Confucianism in this form. There were also other types of encyclopedia which covered a variety of subjects and were called *Jih-yung lei-shu* ᵉ (Encyclopedias for daily use).[1] Following is a list of the different classifications represented by or included in such encyclopedias, with examples of each:

1. General.
   San-t'ai wan-yung cheng-tsung ᶠ (Orthodox teaching for a myriad uses), 1599.
   Wan-pao ch'üan-shu ᵍ (A complete book of a myriad treasures), 1614.
2. Examination studies.
   Ku-chin wen-yüan chü-yeh ching-hua ʰ (Essential learning for ex-

amination studies, past and present), by Yüan Huang (late Ming edition).

3. Letters and formal documents, public and private:
   Han-mo ta-ch'üan [i] (Great compendium of model letters), 1307.
   Ch'i-ch'a ch'ing-ch'ien [j] (The essence of letters), 1324.

4. Poetry:
   Shih-hsüeh hui-hsüan [k] (Anthology for the study of poetry), compiled by Hu Wen-huan in late Ming.

5. History and customs:
   Ku-shih ch'i-pao ta-ch'eng [l] (Complete collection of the seven treasures of ancient things), late Ming edition.

6. Children's education:
   Yu-hsüeh i-chih tsa-tzu ta-ch'üan [m] (Great compendium and dictionary for the elementary instruction of children), late Ming.

7. Household affairs:
   Chü-chia pi-yung shih-lei ch'üan-chi [n] (Complete collection of matters necessary for household use), 1560.[2]

These encyclopedias had first made their appearance in the Sung period, had been further developed in the Yüan or Mongol period, and became highly popular in the Ming, especially in the late sixteenth and early seventeenth centuries. Originally intended for a relatively restricted group of educated people, largely members of the ruling classes, they served diverse needs, both public and private, of such people. In the Ming, however, as the reading public expanded it came to include larger numbers of persons outside the official class, and the contents of the encyclopedias consequently reflected a greater range of needs and concerns among the common people. That is, the encyclopedias being intended to answer all uses, they naturally reflected social change by the nature of their contents. This was particularly shown in the encyclopedias for daily use. In addition to those listed under Nos. 3 and 7 above, the following may be considered typical examples of this type:

8. *Shih-lin kuang-chi* [o] (Broad record of many matters). Yuan and Ming editions.

9. *Wu-ch'e pa-chin* [p] (Collection of excerpts from all kinds of books), 1597.

10. *Wen-lin kuang-chi* ꟙ (Broad record of many writings), 1607.
11. *Chi-yü ch'üan-shu* ꟛ (Complete book of many treasures). Late Ming edition of Li Kuang-yü.
12. *Lei-shu tsuan-yao* ꟝ (Compilation of the essentials of the encyclopedias). T'ien-ch'i period (1621–27).

The preface to the Complete Collection . . . for Household Use (No. 7), which was written in the Wan-li period (1573–1620), says: "This book deals with matters concerning the four classes of people and the many branches of learning. It provides all kinds of knowledge and the essence of what is contained in a host of other books—all things which the householder cannot well do without. . . . It being thus of the most real and practical use, its title is most appropriate." [3] The preface to the Broad Record of Many Writings (No. 8) also contains the statement: "Everything that concerns the immediate needs of the common people is brought together here." Elsewhere it states: "It is not only those of well-known and well-to-do families who may gain knowledge from this book, but also common people living in the towns and villages. . . ." The Introduction (*fan-lei*) of the Collection of Excerpts from All Kinds of Books (No. 9) says: "This is meant to serve the practical needs and convenience of the four classes of people." The Introduction to the Orthodox Teaching for a Myriad Uses (No. 1) also has the statement: "Everything which is needful for everyday use in this world has been hunted up and included in this book." Further, the Introduction to the *Wen-lin chü-pao wan-chüan hsing-lo* Ƛ (Myriad stars of collected literary treasures) (Wan-li period) asserts: "This compilation is for the reference of people in ordinary life. Its effectiveness is not limited to study of the Six Classics and Four Books, but applies to life in the ordinary world." The postface of the *Shih-hui yüan ch'iao tuei ku-shih* ꟟ (Material used in essay antitheses by the foremost *chin-shih* (1520) states: "This is valuable not only for the young and ignorant but also for classical studies and for the various needs of everyday life." Likewise the postface of the Complete Collection of the Seven Treasures of Ancient Matters (No. 5 above), emphasizes the utility of its contents not only for the young and ignorant, but also for teachers and scholars who may supplement their learning thereby.

The broad appeal of these works to people of all classes and their emphasis on practical utility in daily affairs is suggested by many of the titles of these encyclopedias. Often we find in them such expressions as "for the rapid use of the four classes," [v] "for the convenience of the four classes," [w] and "for ready reference in daily needs of the four classes." [x] Although the term "four classes" was more a conventional term than an exact description of social strata, it nevertheless indicated the aim of these encyclopedias to serve all who could read on any level of society. There are constant references also to young and old, rich and poor, learned and ignorant, high and low, etc., which make abundantly clear that the aim of these books was to reach the widest possible audience.

Moreover, the contents of the encyclopedias for daily use suggest the different ways in which Confucian teaching was incorporated in them. Subheadings include such classifications as "Confucian teachers" (*shih-ju*), "Literature and history" (*wen-shih*), "School" (*hsüeh-hsiao*), "Instruction for small children" (*hsün-t'ung*), "Study for the young" (*yu-hsüeh*), and "Confucian teaching" (*ju-chiao*),[y] the contents of which are mostly a kind of elementary Confucianism.

In the second type of encyclopedia mentioned above, that for examination studies, we find as typical examples *Wen-hai p'o-lan* [z] (Waves from the sea of writings) (1574), *Ku-chin chü-yeh wen-t'ao ch'u-hsi p'ing-lin* [aa] (Notes and comments on examination writings, past and present) (1597), and Essential Learning for Examination Studies, Past and Present listed under No. 2 above. In the introduction to the latter, the author, Yüan Huang (1533–1606), explains that he has selected from a number of existing compilations those excerpts which would be most useful to candidates for the examinations, in order to make them readily available for study.

Through these works candidates could familiarize themselves with the form and style of the essay (*shih-wen*)[ab] used in the examinations. During and after the Chia-ching period (1522–67) booksellers did a considerable business selling engraved editions of these formal essays and also model exercises based on hypothetical examination problems known as *ni-t'i*.[ac] [4] These exercises contained model questions and answers with which students could practice. However, several prominent scholar-officials protested against this kind of superficial and mechanical preparation for the examinations, which might give the candidate the technical skills needed to qualify without his undertaking any genuine study of the Classics in depth.[5]

In addition to this type of encyclopedia, popular editions of the Four Books with explanatory notes and classified summaries of the Classics (in various combinations) were also published in great numbers. About forty examples of the first type have been preserved in Japan and studied by the present author.[6] Among them we may cite as typical examples *Ssu-shu hsün-erh su-shuo* [ad] (The Four Books with popular commentaries for the instruction of children) and *Ssu-shu shan-cheng* [ae] (The Four Books with a summary of the orthodox commentaries), both of them compiled by the above-mentioned Yüan Huang. Of the latter type we may cite *Liu-ching tsuan-yao* [af] (A compilation of the essentials of the Six Classics) by Yen Mao-yu. These summary books were characterized by simplicity, brevity, orderly arrangement of topics, and ease of comprehension by those without much classical education.

Publications of this type, which had begun in the Sung period, reached a new height of popularity in the fifteenth and sixteenth centuries. It is true that, despite the increasing numbers of such books printed and sold, many of the common people still could neither use nor buy them. Most of them remained illiterate or too poor to afford books even at the relatively low prices which prevailed in this period. Nevertheless, a rise in general prosperity at this time enabled more persons than ever before to achieve some degree of reading ability and to buy not only this type of exercise book but other popular publications including fiction and the so-called morality books (*shan-shu*).[ag] This cultural growth followed great progress in agriculture and handicrafts, and the spread of silver currency and commercial prosperity. This affected the social status not only of merchants and landowning peasants, but also of persons who had no definite occupation but did odd jobs, the so-called [persons] lacking [fixed means of] support (*wu-lai*.[ah]) They had previously been considered vagabonds or loafers, but during this period under the influence of commercial capital they became organized into mutual-aid societies (*pang*),[ai] their labor power was systematized, and they achieved a more definite status in society. Consequently we find that these "vagabonds" in some cases were able to improve themselves, in the same way as merchants and peasants, by studying the kind of simplified Confucianism available in these popular works, and to acquire certain of the skills required in the civil service examinations.[7]

Another development which affected the training of prospective officials was the sale of studentships at the Imperial Academy, a practice begun in 1451 through the *li-chien* [aj] system. This system was most widespread during and after the Lung-ch'ing period (1567–72). The title so purchased, *chien-sheng*,[ak] entitled a man to minor official appointment and also put him in a better position to take further examinations if he so chose. It meant that persons from the lower classes who had managed to improve themselves and had the funds to purchase such appointments rose rapidly to a higher status, without first having to engage in long scholarly preparation. Later on, in the T'ien-ch'i period (1621–27), it became possible also to purchase the lowest civil service degree of *sheng-yüan*.[al] At the beginning of this period one education officer in Fukien sold such degrees in large numbers and was accused of regarding their sale as if it were "money growing on a tree." It was also charged that at his lectures a sort of broker in official positions was in attendance.[8]

In general the status of persons who had purchased such ranks was lower than those who had qualified through the examinations, although considerably higher than that of ordinary commoners. They were, in other words, a kind of intermediate group. Sometimes in their native places or home localities, where it was known how they had acquired their status, they were not held in very high esteem, but elsewhere, and especially in urban areas their status was greatly enhanced over that of other commoners, and they enjoyed certain tax exemptions as well. These titleholders contributed to the demand for popular works of Confucian culture and simplified means of preparing for the higher examinations. Often lacking the cultural and educational background of those who qualified in the regular way, they tried hard to improve themselves in order to live up to their new status or to achieve higher rank.[9]

Another sign of the times was the fact that even household slaves of wealthy families found it possible to acquire some education and compete in the civil service examinations.[10] Thus the social base from which candidates were drawn was definitely widened, and this was made possible not only because of increasing affluence but also because the means whereby the lower classes might educate themselves were available through the various types of new publications printed and sold in much larger numbers.

POPULAR INFLUENCES IN MING THOUGHT AND THE EXAMINATION SYSTEM

As these social changes made their effects felt, certain popular attitudes came to be reflected in the conduct and content of the examinations. Taoism and Ch'an Buddhism, and the tendency toward syncretism of these two with Confucianism, manifested themselves in the examination halls during the Lung-ch'ing and Wan-li periods (i.e., from 1567 to 1620). Partly this resulted from the influence of the Wang Yang-ming school. Although the examinations were officially based on the Ch'eng-Chu commentaries on the Classics, the minds of both administering officials and competing candidates were strongly influenced by currents of heterodox thought. For instance, Yang Ch'i-yüan [am] (1547–99), a "radical" in the Wang Yang-ming school and much drawn to Taoism and Ch'an Buddhism, who was an advocate of the "combined practice of the Three Teachings" (*San chiao chien-hsiu*),[an] nevertheless in 1578 managed to place first in the metropolitan examinations at Peking. This, it has been said, set a precedent for the acceptance of Ch'an Buddhist ideas in the examinations.[11] In the metropolitan examinations for 1568, the chief examiner Li Ch'un-fang [ao] (1510–84), in presenting a passage from the *Analects* as a subject in the examinations, had already used an expression from the *Chuang Tzu*—namely, *chen-chih*,[ap] (true knowledge), in setting the theme for the candidates to write on. From this it was clear that he used this Taoist concept in interpreting the passage from the *Analects*.[12]

As this tendency grew, it drew protests from defenders of the official orthodoxy. In 1588 a memorial from the Board of Rites complained that the Six Classics were being displaced in the examinations by Buddhism and Taoism. "Recent examinees have forgotten the orthodox teaching and busy themselves with hunting up words and phrases in the Classics and [Four] Books only in order to memorize them. The worst of them have even come to respect Buddhism and Taoism." [13] Despite the issuance of prohibitions against these practices, they continued to prevail because of the widespread influence of heterodox thought among those involved in the conduct of the examinations. This reflected not only the continuing influence of the syncretism of the Three Teachings among the great mass of the people, but more particularly the strong popular character of the thought of the Wang Yang-ming school.

This popular character, which affected both the examination system and new publications such as the encyclopedias for daily use, was expressed in Wang Yang-ming's doctrine that every man can become a sage irrespective of rank, wealth, and scholarly learning. This was a development of the idea found in *The Book of Mencius* and in the teaching of the Sung school: that any man can become a Yao or a Shun. However, prior to the Ming period and especially in the thought of Chu Hsi, there remained a clear distinction between those who actually achieved a high degree of wisdom and virtue and the great mass of ordinary men.[14] In the Wang Yang-ming school, on the other hand, there was a definite emphasis on the popularization of learning so that all men, high and low, could achieve self-fulfillment, and the Way or True Learning could answer to the needs of ordinary people in their everyday lives. Wang Yang-ming said: "That which corresponds to the mind of the ignorant man and woman may be called 'common virtue.' That which differs from the ignorant man and woman may be called 'heterodox.' " [15] This attitude, expressed in the saying "The streets are full of sages,"[16] was spread abroad by Yang-ming's followers, especially those in the school of Wang Ken.

Such ideas fitted in well with the popular consciousness that developed with social changes in the Ming. One reason for this was the fact that the so-called School of the Mind, from Ch'eng Hao and Lu Hsiang-shan in the Sung down to Wang Yang-ming himself, reflected the actual experience of these thinkers themselves in contact with the common people.[17] In other words it arose in part from their own dealings with ordinary people on the lower levels of society, not just bureaucrats and gentry. The family trade of Lu Hsiang-shan was pharmacy. His older brother was a military man with practical abilities who had been in charge of the local militia. When Hsiang-shan himself was a magistrate, among other accomplishments he was particularly effective in maintaining the *pao-wu* [aq] system of collective security and curbing the activities of robbers. This could not have been achieved had not Lu shown an ability to handle people and gain control over the so-called vagabond element, which could be a source of trouble and instability.

Wang Yang-ming, too, as a young man had engaged in the military arts and participated in the brotherhood of the *jen-hsia*,[ar] who pledged themselves in blood to help one another and others in distress. This kind of brotherhood was especially active among the "vagabonds" and other lower-class elements who had no fixed status or property in the local community. As a youth Wang Yang-ming was called "indomitable" and "dauntless," and he went through a somewhat wild stage before settling down to a career as a member of the official class. But these youthful experiences undoubtedly stood him in good stead later. He proved to be the most effective military leader among the Ming civil officials. During his service in remote Kueichow he had to live and work among so-called barbarian peoples, "vagabonds," and exiles. As an official in charge of the post and relay system at Lung-ch'ang, he had to organize and direct men of these types. No doubt his success was due in considerable measure to his ability to gain their confidence and active cooperation. And it was in just such circumstances that he came to formulate his own basic philosophy in terms of the identity of mind and principle, that is, that every human mind is identical with the ultimate principle of life based on a common moral consciousness.

It is important to recognize that this idea, and Wang's doctrine of the unity of knowledge and action, arose not from academic philosophical discussion but from his own direct experience of life. It is important to recognize also that much of that experience was in working with common people. During his period as provincial governor in the border region between Kiangsi and Fukien, Wang also had great success in pacifying an area that had been wracked by recurrent rebellions. This, again, he was able to do because of his effectiveness in organizing the peasants in a system of mutual aid and collective defense. It was accomplished through the so-called *pao-chia* system and the adoption of a local compact (*hsiang-yüeh*)[as] by which the people took responsibility for self-government and the enforcement of common moral standards. One of Wang's basic policies was to bring under his control the poorer peasants and vagabonds who had often been active in peasant rebellions.

Wang Yang-ming's thinking, then, was intimately related to his experience as an official and a military man dealing with all classes of people. He was able to gain their support and cooperation only because he understood them, and this understanding of the ordinary man was also expressed in his philosophy. It was no accident, therefore, that his philosophy should have become the basis for new movements in popular thought and new developments in popular culture.[18]

THE MORALITY BOOKS

The spread of Wang Yang-ming's thought gave a further stimulus to education among the lower classes and contributed to the increased demand for the popular morality books (*shan-shu*). This type of book, which had made its appearance in the Sung period, became much more popular in the Yüan and Ming. Together with the encyclopedias for daily use, the morality books served a wide public, especially in the late Ming. By calling them "popular" I mean that these books served not only the lower levels of society, but all types and classes of people irrespective of social status, economic position, and religious affiliation. In fact, so basic was their appeal to the common denominator in ethical thought that they were read and used even by scholars identified with the Ch'eng-Chu school.

The underlying idea of the morality books is that virtue is rewarded and vice punished. Besides identifying good deeds and their rewards, and bad deeds and their retributions, the morality books give homely tales drawn from the popular consciousness and imagination to illustrate them. Probably the best known representative of this type is the *T'ai-shang kan-ying p'ien*[at] (Treatise of the most exalted one on moral retribution),[19] which was published for the first time in the Southern Sung period and republished often in the Ming. From the beginning it had a connection with a popular deity, Tzu-t'ung Shen, to whom candidates for the civil service examinations prayed for good fortune. Li Chih-chi, the author of the Treatise, was said to have achieved success in the examinations after doing some religious service to this god.[20] Thus, though the examinations and officialdom were primarily associated with Confucianism, the author and subsequent candidates who used his book readily resorted to a Taoist kind of religious worship, and in order to achieve their ambitions performed various good deeds defined on the basis of popular religious and moral consciousness. Much of its content was in fact Confucian—that is, it represented Confucianism as practiced among the common people, supplemented and supported by religious notions drawn from Taoism and Buddhism.

From the title Treatise of the Most Exalted One on Moral Retribution it may be seen that the rewards and punishments discussed in this book were thought to be dispensed by a supreme being. This idea had its ground in the ancient belief that Heaven presides over the moral order, rewarding the good and punishing the wicked.[21] But in the Ming a new attitude comes to prevail. Instead of relying on the belief that everything is dependent on the favor of a god, the morality books are based on the idea that one can control one's own destiny by achieving virtue and eschewing vice. One can judge the value of his own actions and be assured of an appropriate reward.

Such is the idea underlying the morality books known as Kung-kuo ko [au] (Ledgers of merit and demerit). According to this system the value of human deeds could be calculated with so many credits or merits attached to each good deed and so many debits or demerits for the evil deeds. Using the point system provided him in the Ledgers, each individual could evaluate his deeds one by one, add the merits and demerits, and then strike the balance for himself. The greater the balance of merits, the greater the reward he might expect, and vice versa. A conscientious person would go through this process each day, and also calculate how he stood at the end of each month and each year. In general, one sought to build up as large a balance of merits as possible, and certain extraordinarily virtuous actions could count heavily in erasing an accumulation of demerits. Mechanical though the system was, however, it was based fundamentally on the idea that the individual did the evaluating for himself and took charge of his own fate.[22]

The Ledgers of Merit and Demerit had been in existence since the Sung, but their most flourishing days came in the late Ming through the activity of Yüan Huang,[av] mentioned above as a compiler and publisher of popular encyclopedias and manuals for civil service candidates. He was a man of extraordinary energy and ability, and his own personal experience had much to do with his belief in the individual's capacity to determine his own fortune. His immediate forbears, though persons of some means and culture, had been debarred from official service because an ancestor had supported the cause of the Chien-wen Emperor against the Yung-lo Emperor. When the latter won out and Yüan's ancestor was condemned, it meant, according to Ming law, that his descendents for three generations would be ineligible to enter the civil service. Consequently they turned to medicine. It was only in Yüan Huang's generation that the ban was lifted. Nevertheless Yüan too was forced to take up medicine when, on his father's death, his mother insisted that he carry on the family trade. A fortuneteller, however, predicted that Yüan would become an official after all, but would fail to achieve the highest degree, would have no children, and would die at the age of fifty-three. On the strength of the favorable indication in the first part of this prophecy, Yüan took and passed the prefectural and provincial examinations. He remained, however, quite fatalistic about his future in regard to the other matters involved. Then in 1569 he was persuaded by a Ch'an priest that it was wrong to accept this gloomy forecast passively. The priest recommended instead that he practice the system of merits and demerits. The accumulation of virtuous acts would overcome the dire prophecy. As a result, so Yüan thought, of taking this advice and acting on it, he was eventually blessed with a son, passed the *chin-shih* examination in 1585, and became an official of some importance, first as a magistrate and then in the Board of War. Even his later dismissal from the official rolls on false charges did not shake Yüan's conviction that success could be achieved through the system of merits and demerits.[23]

It may be seen from this account that Yüan practiced the system in the same eclectic atmosphere which had surrounded the morality books from the beginning, namely, the popular acceptance of Confucian, Taoist, and Buddhist ideas as blending harmoniously together. Yüan remained in close contact with leading Buddhist priests of the late Ming, such as Yün-ku [aw] and Ta-kuan.[ax] In the company of Buddhists he prayed for the success of his efforts and the fruition of his good deeds. As regards Taoism, which was intimately connected with his family trade of medicine, Yüan utilized different Taoist methods and arts, such as the Golden Pill,[ay] the Fu-erh [az] system of medical prescription, the Bedroom method (fang-chung),[ba] and the Breath control system (T'ai-hsi).[bb] Even after he had overcome his earlier fatalism, which was based on a Taoist type of prognostication, Yüan continued to study and employ these other Taoist arts.

In these respects Yüan Huang reflected a well-established tradition of popular syncretism. The sixteenth century was a period in which the Combined Practice of the Three Teachings and the Unity of the Three Teachings were especially popular notions, and Yüan's many writings were influential in popularizing these ideas still further. But the main point of Yüan's teaching was his positive belief in the individual's ability to "establish his own destiny" (li-ming),[bc] or carve out his own fortune in life. This was an idea which had come to Yüan from the teaching of Wang Ken: "Though they say that our destiny lies with Heaven, what creates that destiny [i.e., the means by which it is brought about] lies within ourselves." [24] Yüan's father had been associated with Wang Yang-ming, Wang Chi, and Wang Ken, and Yüan Huang himself had studied under Wang Chi. Responding to this influence, Yüan Huang took the Ledgers of Merit and Demerit, originally a system of Taoist-Buddhist popular morality, and made them serve as a concrete method whereby practical application could be given to the idea of "establishing one's own destiny." [25]

Drawing thus upon the religious syncretism of the common people and the popular character of the Wang Yang-ming school, Yüan Huang was able to formulate a philosophy and way of life which combined strong moral effort and self-discipline with a simple religious faith. Through his own example as well as his numerous publications, Yüan also related his system closely to the worldly aspirations of the people and particularly to the prevalent ambition to rise to the official rank through the examination system. But Yüan's method was applicable to all walks of life, and one of the great values of his and other morality books to the student of Chinese history and thought is the way in which these books reflect social change in the sixteenth and seventeenth centuries, precisely because they were concerned with the daily lives of the common people.

THE MORALITY BOOKS AND SOCIAL CHANGE

In the late Ming one can see in the morality books the effects of two significant developments in Chinese society. If the morality books were to be applicable to the daily life of the people, they necessarily had to adapt to the increasing specialization of functions among the common people and they also had to take into account the effects of a spreading money economy in the Ming. As a result we find that virtuous conduct comes to be defined both in general terms, in regard to those actions appropriate for all men in all circumstances, and in more specific terms for those actions appropriate to particular occupations. Further, the attempt is made to distinguish between virtuous acts which do not involve any monetary expenditure and those which do.

In the Sung, as I have already noted, Confucian thought affirmed the basic principle that any man might become a sage, but tended at the same time to be highly conscious of distinctions between good men and bad, high and low, rich and poor, etc.[26] In other words, any man might prove himself by rising to the top, but there was a clear hierarchical order which he had to ascend. And though the conditions for achieving Confucian fulfillment were the same for all, insofar as education and learning were involved it was accepted that the lower orders of society would have more difficulty obtaining the necessary books or schooling. In other words there was as yet no conscious inclination to question traditional notions of social structure or to ask whether or not traditional concepts were appropriate to the existing reality. An evidence of this is the persistence of the ancient habit of describing society in terms of the traditio:al four classes: scholar-officials, peasants, artisans, and merchants. These classifications were conceived primarily from the administrative point of view. They were the categories under which the government dealt with, regulated, and taxed the people.

On the other hand, we can already see in the morality books of the late Sung period an embryonic recognition that morality appropriate for the common people has to take into account their actual statuses and functions. This arose out of the close relationship between the early morality books and popular religions, especially the popular forms of Buddhism like the Pure Land faith which were concerned with the salvation of souls, without distinction as to wealth or rank. Thus the morality books contained popular lectures on religious salvation directed at "ordinary people" (fan-min)[bd] and at "ignorant men and women" (yü-fu yü-fu).[be] [27] But democratization in religion also involved recognition of the greater specialization of function among the common people than among the ruling elite. In popular Buddhist texts, such as Lung-shu ching-t'u wen [bf] (The preachings of Lung-shu concerning the Pure Land), we find people classified according to such categories as subordinate office helpers, physicians, monks, women, rich men, household slaves, farmers and peasants, dealers and merchants, craftsmen, fishermen, and wine sellers.[28]

Such being the genesis of the morality books, as the emphasis shifted in the Ming from religious salvation in another world to a man's conduct in this world, there was bound to be more attention given to the actual circumstances in which meritorious deeds would be performed. To some extent the traditional nomenclature is still used in a rather general and imprecise way, but in the classification of good and bad deeds there is a definite trend toward more realistic and specific social differentiation. A particularly good example of such differentiation is found in the Kuang-shan p'ien kung-kuo ko [bg] (Ledger of merit and demerit for the diffusing of good deeds) published in the mid-Ch'ing period, but the pattern is already established in the seventeenth-century book *Pu-fei-ch'ien kung-te li* [bh] (Meritorious deeds at no cost).

To appreciate the full significance of this latter work, we must consider the factor of wealth in relation to the performance of good works, both Confucian and Buddhist. It was in the very nature of traditional Confucian morality that general ethical principles should be given specific interpretation and application through the prescribed ritual or decorum, which also allowed for a certain degree of social differentiation. Nevertheless, because of the Confucian preoccupation with the duties and privileges of the ruling class, there was a tendency to establish as the norm the ritual requirements of that class. And in any case Confucian morality stressed the performance of a proper ritual on the important occasions of family life and in the development of the individual to assume family responsibilities. Thus coming of age, marriage, funeral, and ancestral rites were particularly observed. While it had been a basic principle of the prescribed ritual that it should not exceed what was appropriate to the social and economic circumstances of the persons involved, this principle became more difficult to apply when it came to concern proper conduct among the common people as distinct from the ruling elite, because of the former's greater heterogeneity.

A further problem arose from the prevalence of Buddhism and Taoism among the common people, since the rituals associated with these religions were completely unregulated by Confucian norms, and expense became a much greater factor. In religious rituals and funeral ceremonies the lower classes felt a strong compulsion to demonstrate their virtue or faith by sparing no expense in honoring the gods, the buddhas, or their departed parents. In the Ming period, moreover, rising economic prosperity, commercialization, and the spread of a money economy only intensified the strain on the common man trying to find some standard for what constituted proper conduct in these regards.

In the morality books we see an attempt to ease this strain by making a distinction between good deeds which do or do not involve any expense to the performer. That is, while many of the meritorious works recommended are those which offer the ordinary man some standard in regard to the performance of traditional Confucian cere-monials that involve some material outlay, many others are specifi-cally identified as works which do not require the performer to spend money. The Meritorious Deeds at No Cost is particularly designed to meet the latter need.

The rationale for this, however, is already expressed in Yüan Huang's Li-ming p'ien [bi] (Establishing one's own destiny), as we see in the following:

The virtue of modesty (ch'ien-hsü)[bj] is essential for poor scholars and those seeking to enter the civil service without much means. Poor scholars cannot hope to achieve merit [and thus succeed in the examinations] through works that involve the expenditure of money, but the essential thing in the achieving of merit is the attitude of mind. Modesty, which is an attitude of mind, does not require any expense.[29]

This emphasis on the attitude or quality of mind shows the influ-ence on Yüan Huang of Wang Yang-ming's thought. As he attempts to practice "the establishing of one's own destiny" through the prac-tical method of the Ledger of Merit and Demerit, he tries to estab-lish a more interiorized morality in place of a purely materialistic standard.

Following this effort of Yüan Huang, other morality books ap-peared which emphasized a nonmonetary standard for the perform-ance of meritorious deeds. At the end of the Ming Ti-chi lu [bk] (A record of the practice of good deeds), by Yen Mao-yu, recommended that people practice good deeds which involve no expense, stating that they are especially appropriate for the "ignorant," and for "common people of the lowest class, such as woodcutters and shep-herds." In a postface to this work there is mention of "saving many lives without going out of doors, practicing many good deeds at no monetary expense, bestowing the favor of gods and buddhas without preaching."[30] This work also describes the position of the local gentry (hsiang-shen),[bl] that is, members of the official class residing in their home towns, and explains the difference in the moral practice of the local gentry and the common people. It was as a result of such a de-velopment that there appeared in the early Ch'ing period the afore-mentioned work Meritorious Deeds at No Cost. The preface to this book says:

People seek after the joys of the other world and neglect life in this world. They think it meritorious to heap praises on the Buddha, to spend money for Buddhist rituals, or to go to great expense for Taoist services. They never think it a waste of money to spend it on such religious observances.[31]

In general, the view was neither to disallow such expenditures altogether, nor to insist that the only truly good deeds were those which involved no expense. In the Ledgers of Merit and Demerit there are good deeds listed in which the value of the deed is proportionate to the expense involved. For instance, *Hui-tsuan kung-kuo ko*[bm] (A synthetic compilation of ledgers of merit and demerit) lists good deeds involving such expense which were recognized among the common people in the late Ming—early Ch'ing periods:

Aid your relatives, teachers, or friends, if they are in need of clothing, food, or money for ceremonies such as marriages and funerals.

Save good people from enmities or calamities [arising from financial troubles?].

Save people from falling into servile status [through debt or crime] and becoming separated from their families.

Help the poor, widowers, widows, and orphans of your own locality.

Help travelers who have fallen into trouble to return to their home locality.

Help the poor with the expense of marriage and funeral ceremonies.

Help those seriously sick to get medical treatment.

Pay taxes in full for the indigent.

Give money and goods to beggars, the disabled, the crippled, and the aged.

Have compassion on poor people who are forced to turn to begging and give them some employment.

Establish endowed schools and educate the people.

Establish a foundling hospital to care for foundlings.

Establish a charitable estate [for one's clan?].

Donate a public cemetery for the poor who have no burial place.

Establish old people's homes and institutions to provide for their security at your own expense.

Take in dependent, disabled, and crippled persons, and give them money and goods.

In case of famine provide free kitchens and rice gruel for the poor.

When there is a plague establish free medical facilities and give medicine to the poor.

In summer provide mosquito nets and tea to the poor.

In winter give bedding to the poor.

Provide burial for those who die without relatives.

Repair roads, set up benches and resthouses in the shade, and build ferry-boats.

Print and publish morality books; distribute them to others so as to lead them toward the good.

Print good medical prescriptions and give them to others to rescue them from disease.

Aid in the repair of temples and shrines which have long been dilapidated.

Buy, save, and release living creatures.[32]

In the Ledgers of Merit and Demerit such good deeds as the above were valued in terms of the expense involved for the performer. For instance, expense amounting to one hundred copper cash counted as one merit point. This was in accordance with the system earlier developed in connection with these Ledgers when they were first used in the Taoist religion and employed in the type of Ledger Yüan Huang received from the monk Yün-ku. The Synthetic Compilation explains this aspect of the system as follows:

Generally speaking, the expense of one hundred copper cash counts as one meritorious deed. If the same good deed is performed by a poor person, the number of merits increases in proportion to the degree of poverty. In the case of a really poor man, even if he incurs an expense of no more than five or ten coppers, it is counted as equal to one hundred coppers spent by the rich.[33]

This statement bespeaks the view of morality as primarily a thing of the mind. It recognizes the value of money, but subordinates monetary value to spiritual value, the outward object to the inner intention. Thus, even in the case of material gifts and virtuous acts reckoned in monetary terms, a spiritual element was present in this system of merits and demerits.

SOCIALLY DIFFERENTIATED "NO-COST" MORALITY

Against this background we can now take up the contents of the seventeenth-century work Meritorious Deeds at No Cost, which combines both of the new developments mentioned earlier: that is, the idea that it should be possible to achieve merit through the performance of works which do not involve any material expense, and the principle that such good works should be adapted to the social and economic status of the performer on a realistic basis.

The classifications used in the Meritorious Deeds at No Cost generally are based on occupational status. It is divided into the following sections: [bn]

1. Local gentry (*hsiang-shen,* i.e., officials residing in their home locality)
2. Candidates for officialdom (*shih-jen*), including educated persons who have not attained office and may be serving as teachers, tutors, etc.
3. Peasants (*nung-chia*)
4. Craftsmen (*pai-kung*)
5. Merchants and dealers (*shang-ku*)
6. Physicians and pharmacists (*i-chia*)
7. Subordinate office workers [of humble status] (*kung-men*)
8. Women (*fu-nü*)
9. Soldiers (*shih-tsu*)
10. Buddhist and Taoist monks (*seng-tao*)
11. Household slaves and servants (*p'u-pi kung-i*)
12. People in general (*ta-chung*)

Concerning these classifications it should be noted that the term Local Gentry (*hsiang-shen*) represents members of the official class (i.e., persons having official rank and status) who are residing at home and have social responsibilities in their own locality even though they are not charged with administrative duties there. In other words, the present work does not presume to prescribe for them in the political sphere or to discuss their official functions, but deals only with their social responsibilities in their home community. This aspect of Chinese social life appeared first in the Sung but developed distinct features in the Ming. It was in the late Ming that the term *hsiang-shen* came into use.

The term Scholars (*shih-jen*) represents those engaged in the different stages of preparation for the civil service examinations. As persons with some education and as candidates for the bureaucracy, they stand higher than the common people although they do not qualify as officials. Many of them served in educational capacities, and the meritorious works recommended for them emphasize that role.

Peasants (*nung-chia*) include those directly engaged in farming, whether landowners or peasants, but not absentee landlords. Similarly, the term Craftsmen (*pai-kung*) means those actually engaged in the production of handicrafts, whether independent or employed, but would not apply to nonworking owners of factories. Absentee landlords or factory owners would be thought of as coming under either the first two classifications or the general group at the end.

Under each of these classifications the work lists good deeds involving no cost with a comparatively high degree of specificity, though it must be acknowledged that in certain cases the context of the original recommendations is no longer so clear that we can always be sure of the exact meaning. Therefore, in order to provide the reader with some idea as to the type of meritorious deeds included, I present here the listings under the first five classifications and the last. Because the last is a catch-all for persons who do not fit the preceding classifications, it is to be expected that a certain amount of duplication will be encountered. The same is also true to some extent within the specialized classifications because their ways of life were different in many respects, although not necessarily in all.[34]

1. Local gentry

Take the lead in charitable donations.

Rectify your own conduct and transform the common people.

Make a sincere effort to inform the authorities of what would be beneficial to the people of your locality.

Make every effort to dissuade the local authorities from doing what would be detrimental to the people of your locality.

If people have suffered a grave injustice, expose and correct it.

Settle disputes among your neighbors fairly.

When villagers commit misdeeds, admonish them boldly and persuade them to desist.

Do not let yourself be blinded by emotion and personal prejudices.

Be tolerant of the mistakes of others.

Be willing to listen to that which is displeasing to your ears.

Do not make remarks about women's sexiness.

Do not harbor resentment when you are censured.

Protect virtuous people.

Hold up for public admiration women who are faithful to their husbands and children who are obedient to their parents.

Restrain those who are stubborn and unfilial.

Prevent plotting and intrigue.

Endeavor to improve manners and customs.

Encourage fair and open discussion.

Prevent the younger members of your family from oppressing others by taking advantage of your position.

Prevent your household slaves and servants from causing trouble by relying on your influence.

Try not to arouse the resentment of others by showing partiality to the younger members of your own family.

Do not provoke incidents which result in harm or loss to others.

Do not be arrogant, because of your own power and wealth, toward relatives who are poor or of low status.

Persuade others not to seek gain through oppression or honors through intrigue.

Do not encroach on others' lands and dispossess them.

Do not scheme to buy up others' property.

Do not mix debased silver with good.

Do not ignore your own relatives and treat others as if they were your kin.

Influence other families to cherish good deeds.

Do not officiously take charge of the affairs of those outside your own household.

Do not disport yourself with lewd friends.

Do not look for pretexts to injure others.

Do not allow yourself to be overcome by personal feelings and therefore treat others unjustly.

Do not let your feelings of pleasure and displeasure influence others or suggest to them how they can benefit themselves.

Restrain others from arranging lewd theater performances.

Do not scheme to seize geomantic advantages (*feng-shui*)[bo] for yourself or deceitfully deprive others of them.

Instruct your children, grandchildren, and nephews to be humane and compassionate towards all and to avoid anger and self-indulgence.

Do not deceive or oppress younger brothers or cousins.

Do not force others off the road by dropping stones in dangerous places.

Do not scheme to deprive others of some advantage in order to suit your own convenience.

Encourage others to read and study without minding the difficulties.

Urge others to esteem charity and disdain personal gain.
Do not underestimate the value of others [or underpay them].
Do not let what you hear from servants and slaves cause you to turn against relatives and friends.
Persuade others to settle lawsuits through conciliation.
Try to settle complaints and grievances among others.
Do not force others to lend you their property.
Do not force others to enter into deals on credit.
Curb the strong and protect the weak.
Show respect to the aged and compassion for the poor.
Do not keep too many concubines.
Do not keep catamites.
Do not marry off household slaves to wicked men or cripples for your own selfish gain.
Choose a favorable time for marrying off household slaves.
Do not force "good" people to become base [i.e., lose their freedom].

2. Scholars

Be loyal to the emperor and filial to your parents.
Honor your elder brothers and be faithful to your friends.
Establish yourself in life by cleaving to honor and fidelity.
Instruct the common people in the virtues of loyalty and filial piety.
Respect the writings of sages and worthies.
Be wholehearted in inspiring your students to study.
Show respect to paper on which characters are written.
Try to improve your speech and behavior.
Teach your students also to be mindful of their speech and behavior.
Do not neglect your studies without reason.
Do not despise others or regard them as unworthy of your instruction.
Be patient in educating the younger members of poor families.
If you find yourself with smart boys, teach them sincerity; and with children of the rich and noble, teach them decorum and duty.
Exhort and admonish the ignorant by lecturing to them on the provisions of the local compact and the public laws.
Do not speak or write thoughtlessly of what concerns the women's quarters.
Do not expose the private affairs of others or harbor evil suspicions about them.
Do not write or post notices which defame other people.
Do not write petitions or accusations to higher authorities.
Do not write bills of divorce or separation.
Do not let your feelings blind you in defending your friends and relatives.
Do not incite gangs (*pang*) to raid others' homes and knock them down.

Do not encourage the spread of immoral and lewd novels [by writing, reprinting, expanding, etc.].

Do not call other people names or compose songs making fun of them.

Publish morality books in which are compiled things that are useful and beneficial to all.

Do not attack or vilify commoners; do not oppress ignorant villagers.

Do not deceive the ignorant by marking texts in such a way as to overawe and mislead them.

Do not show contempt for fellow students by boasting of your own abilities.

Do not ridicule other people's handwriting.

Do not destroy or lose the books of others. . . .

To those of some understanding explain the teachings of the Ch'eng-Chu school; to the uneducated give books on moral retribution.

Make others desist from unfiliality toward their parents or unkindness toward relatives and friends.

Educate the ignorant to show respect to their ancestors and live in harmony with their families. . . .

3. Peasants

Do not miss the proper times for farm work.

Have regard for [the lives of] insects.

When fertilizing the fields, do not harm living creatures.

Do not obstruct or cut off paths. Fill up holes that might give trouble to passersby.

Do not instigate landlords to buy up lands.

Do not steal and sell your master's grain in connivance with his servants.

Do not damage crops in your neighbors' fields by leaving animals to roam at large, relying on your landlord's power and influence to protect you.

Do not encroach [on others' property] beyond the boundaries of your own fields and watercourses, thinking to ingratiate yourself with your landlord.

Do not disturb others' graves or interfere with the geomantic advantages of others.

In plowing, do not infringe on graves or make them hard to find.

Do not suggest to your master that he willfully cut off watercourses and extort payments from neighbors.

Do not take your landlord's seed crops for your own benefit.

Do not damage the crops in neighboring fields out of envy because they are so flourishing.

Do not instigate your landlord to take revenge on a neighbor on the pretext that the neighbor's animals have damaged your crops.

Do not through negligence in your work do damage to the fields of others.

Do not become lazy and cease being conscientious because you think your landlord does not provide enough food and wine or fails to pay you enough.

Fill up holes in graves.

Take good care of others' carts and tools.

Do not kill mules and cattle, pigs and sheep, even if they eat your crops.

Keep carts and cattle from trampling down others' crops.

Do not desecrate the gods of the soil by plowing or hoeing the land or irrigating or spreading manure on days of abstention [*wu*, i.e., the fifth day of each ten-day cycle, which is the first of two days identified with Wood in the Five-Agent cycle].[bp]

4. Craftsmen

Do not profane sacred images when carving or drawing.

Whenever you make something, try to make it strong and durable.

Do not be resentful toward your master if he fails to provide enough food and drink.

Do not utter inauspicious words.

When making things, do not leave them unfinished or rough.

Do not use superstitious charms.

Do not compel others to work.

Do not reveal and spread abroad the secrets of your master's house.

Do not make crude imitations.

Finish your work without delay.

In your trade with others, do not practice deceit through forgery.

Do not mix damaged articles with good.

Do not break or damage finished goods.

Do not recklessly indulge in licentiousness.

Do not spoil the clothes of others.

Do not steal the materials of others.

Do not use the materials of others carelessly.

Take good care of the shop roofs, awnings, and tents. . . .

5. Dealers and merchants

Do not deceive ignorant villagers when fixing the price of goods.

Do not raise the price of fuel and rice too high.

When the poor buy rice, do not give them short measure.

Sell only genuine articles.

Do not use short measure when selling and long measure when buying.

When sick people have urgent need of something, do not raise the price unreasonably.

Do not deceitfully serve unclean dishes or leftover food to customers who are unaware of the fact.

Do not dispossess or deprive others of their business by devious means.

Do not envy the prosperity of others' business and speak ill of them wherever you go.

Be fair in your dealings.

Treat the young and the aged on the same terms as the able-bodied.

When people come in the middle of the night with an urgent need to buy something, do not refuse them on the ground that it is too cold [for you to get up and serve them].

Pawnshops should lend money at low interest.

Give fair value when you exchange silver for copper coins. Especially when changing money for the poor, be generous to them.

When a debtor owes you a small sum but is short of money, have mercy and forget about the difference. Do not bring him to bankruptcy and hatred by refusing to come to terms.

When the poor want to buy such things as mosquito nets, wadded clothing, and quilts, have pity on them and reduce the price. Do not refuse to come to terms.

12. People in general

Do not show anger or worry in your parents' sight.

Accept meekly the reproaches and anger of your parents.

Persuade your parents to correct their mistakes and return to the right path.

Do not divulge your parents' faults to others.

Do not let your parents do heavy work.

Do not be disgusted with your parents' behavior when they are old and sick.

Do not yell at your parents or give them angry looks.

Love your brothers.

Keep close to your relatives.

Be attentive and obedient to the principles of Heaven and the laws of the ruler.

In everything you do fear Heaven, Earth, the gods, and the spirits.

Do not harbor ulterior motives when you undertake something in cooperation with others.

If you are poor, do not entertain thoughts of harming the rich.

If you are rich, do not deceive and cheat the poor.

Do not scheme to induce rifts among relatives.

Do not lightly suspect others of evil intentions.

Do not recklessly destroy natural resources.

Buy and sell with the same measures.

When weighing, do not press down the scales [with your hands].

Do not speak of others' humble ancestry.

Do not talk about the private [women's] quarters of others. [Commentary:

When others bring up such things, if they are of the younger generation, reprimand them with straight talk, and if they are older or of the same generation as you, change the subject.]

Do not use debased silver.

Do not damage the livelihood of others by trying to buy things through coercive or devious means.

Do not be proud of your own skill and look down on others' clumsiness.

Do not try to undo others' success.

Respect women's chastity.

Help others to preserve their family succession.

Do not envy the rich or deceive the poor.

Do not presume upon your own strength to oppress the weak.

Do not instigate quarrels.

Do not climb down or drop stones into others' wells.

Do not divulge others' secrets.

Do not put curses on those from whom you have become estranged.

Do not poison someone because you are covetous of his wealth.

Do not stir up your mind with lewd and wanton thoughts.

Do not besmirch others' honor or chastity.

Do not intimidate others to satisfy your own ambition.

Do not assert your own superiority by bringing humiliation upon others.

Do not harbor evil thoughts while speaking of doing good.

Do not dwell on others' faults while dilating on your own virtues.

Try to promote friendly relations among neighbors and relatives.

When you meet fishermen, hunters, or butchers, try to have them change their occupations.

Do not get angry with household slaves when they give you cause for anger, but instead instruct them with kind words.

Propagate among others the law of moral retribution.

Disseminate morality books which teach retribution and reward.

Make others desist from lawsuits.

Do not waste grain.

Do not gossip about others' wrongdoing.

Warn others lest their children should get drowned.

If you find someone else's valuables, return them to him.

Do not be avaricious.

Take good care of paper on which characters are written.

When you hear someone speaking about the failings of others, make him stop.

When you hear a man praising the goodness of others, help him to do so.

When you see others in worry and grief, be sympathetic and comfort them.

When you see a man about to go whoring or gambling, try to dissuade him.

Do not speak deceitful words.

Do not say sharp or cruel things.

When others entrust their property to you, do not violate the trust.

Do not deceive cripples, fools, old men, the young, or the sick.

When you see a man who has suddenly fallen ill without any one to look after him, hire a doctor to take care of him.

Do not make unreasonable demands for yourself, but be content to live modestly and within your means.

For bad deeds, find fault with yourself; for good deeds, give credit to others.

Do not speak ill of a man you have broken off with.

Help those who have been unable to marry to get married.

Make peace between husbands and wives who are about to separate.

Do not forget the kindness of others; do not remember the wrongdoing of others.

Do not help others in wrongdoing.

Do not speak ill of Buddhist and Taoist monks.

If you find a dead body in a stream, report it to an officer and have it buried.

If someone has died on the road, take up a collection so he can be buried in a coffin.

If you find human bones lying on the ground, gather them up and bury them.

If you see a family in mourning, be kind and help them.

Show the way to those who have become lost.

Help the blind and disabled to pass over dangerous bridges and roads.

Advise others where a river is shallow or deep to cross.

Cut down thorns by the roadside to keep them from tearing people's clothes.

Remove tiles and stones from the road so that others will not stumble over them.

Put stones in muddy places [to make them passable].

Lay wooden boards where the road is broken off.

At night, light a lamp for others.

Lend rainwear to others in case of rain.

Look after the household slaves lest they suffer from heat or cold, hunger or illness.

Establish uniform weights and measures all over your locality.

Do not let your young children mistreat household slaves.

Do not listen to your wife or concubines if they should encourage you to neglect or abandon your parents.

Do not intercept others' letters.

When undertaking construction work, take into consideration your neighbors' geomantic advantages.

When you are given gifts, acknowledge by your manner that you do not deserve such favors.

Praise the good deeds of others.

Clear others of false charges.

Do not kill animals without good reason.

Do not humiliate or ridicule the aged, the young, or the crippled.

Do not trample down others' crops along the pathways.

Do not change the family names of children left in your charge.

If coffins in graves become exposed, cover them with earth.

Do not destroy public cemeteries.

Do not curse the wind and the rain.

Do not be tardy in giving others of your goods [in time of need].

Do not irreverently move your forebears' remains, vainly hoping to [obtain geomantic advantages and] enhance your own fortunes.

Do not say words which are harmful to morals and customs.

Do not stealthily peep at others' womenfolk when they are exposed by a fire in their home.

When helping to put out a fire, do not take advantage of it to steal others' belongings.

Do not be impudent toward your superiors.

Do not instigate quarrels among relatives.

Do not attempt to force reconciliations among those inferior to you.

Show reverence to sacred images.

Do not obstruct others in doing good.

Do not encourage others to do evil.

Do not destroy the nests of birds or the dens of animals.

Do not steal the eggs of fowl.

Refrain from shooting birds during the three months of spring.

Do not sell faithful dogs to dog butchers.

Do not eat the meat of plow oxen and dogs.

Do not squeeze too much from tenant farmers.

Make every effort to save those in extremity and be generous to those who are in need.

Do not hide and keep what you have borrowed.

Even if you see that the good sometimes suffer bad fortune and you yourself experience poverty, do not let it discourage you from doing good.

Even if you see bad men prosper, do not lose faith in ultimate recompense.

Never fail to give rice cakes or drugs first of all to your parents and only after that to your children and grandchildren.

When you save a poor family, always save the main family line first and after that the branch families.

In all undertakings, think of others.

Consider others in your use of all things.
Give others what you yourself would like, not what you would dislike.
A good deed is worth doing, no matter how slight.
An evil deed should never be done, no matter how slight.

The above may suffice to give a general impression of the type of moral practice recommended by Meritorious Deeds at No Cost. Each of the remaining classifications has its own peculiar interest from the sociological standpoint, but the examples given suggest both the common elements among the different occupational groups and the differences in emphasis among them. It will be noted that the most typically Confucian virtues are stressed in connection with the Scholars (*shih-jen*), whose function it is to perpetuate traditional values and perform educational functions in the community. Among the other groups, aside from repeated injunctions in favor of filial respect to parents, the moral precepts are based on common human concepts of equity, reciprocity, and harmony as applied to the different circumstances of life in each group.

In conclusion it may be said that the morality books reflect the following attitudes in late Ming–early Ch'ing society. First, there is the belief that it should be possible for all men to lead a good life and achieve fulfillment regardless of social status. In other words, one need not be a member of the Confucian elite to be a good man, nor need one be well to do. Second, there is a definite method which men may follow in order to achieve true success in this life. Rewards may be expected from the practice of this method, some of them material, and others spiritual, but in any case they represent an improvement in one's general well-being. Third, the system involves both universal principles and their particular applications among people who are increasingly conscious of their different social roles and functions. On the other hand, there is virtually no class consciousness or awareness of class interests to be asserted or defended. Fourth, specifically bourgeois values or virtues are not much in evidence. The section dealing with Merchants and Dealers occupies only a small part of the whole, roughly proportionate to their limited strength in society as a whole. The moderate stress on thrift suggests peasant frugality, not the accumulation of great wealth or capital; the well to do are urged to be generous, and there is a traditional disapproval of usury. Fifth, although there is a strong emphasis on this-worldly morality, religion and retribution in the afterlife are seen as reinforcing the moral order. Religious piety is enjoined, and the prevalent belief in the essential harmony of the Three Teachings is clearly reflected.

NOTES

1. Concerning *Jih-yung lei-shu*, see Tadao Sakai, *Mindai no nichiyō ruisho to shomin kyōiku* [bq] (included in Hayashi Tomoharu, ed., *Kinsei chūgoku kyōikushi kenkyū* [Tokyo, 1958]; hereafter abbreviated as Sakai, *Nichiyō ruisho*).

2. For further examples of the above, see Sakai, *Nichiyō ruisho*.

3. The sources of quotations from prefaces and introductions in this paragraph may be found by consulting the titles as given in the list of Chinese characters. Cf. Sakai, *Nichiyō ruisho*, pp. 134, 76, 79, 82, 83, 122.

4. Ku Yen-wu, *Jih-chih-lu* (Tsao-yeh shan-fang ed.), 16/9a–10b Ni-t'i.

5. Cf. Tadao Sakai, *Chūgoku zensho no kenkyū* [br] (Tokyo, 1960) pp. 137–48, 199–206. (Hereafter abbreviated as Sakai, *Zensho*.)

6. Cf. *Naikaku bunko kanseki bunrui mokuroku* (Tokyo, 1956) pp. 36–40.

7. Cf. Sakai, *Zensho*, pp. 157–87.

8. *Jih-chih-lu*, 18/10b–11b, Chu yeh.

9. Sakai, *Zensho*, pp. 137–48, 199–206.

10. Cf. *Ibid.*, p. 177.

11. *Jih-chih-lu*, 18/10b–11b, Chu yeh.

12. *Ibid.*, 18/10b–11a.

13. *Wan-li shih-lu*, Wan li 15, 2d month Ting mao (Minkuo 29 photographic ed., 183/6b); cf. Sakai, *Zensho*, p. 269.

14. *Hui-an hsien-sheng Chu Wen-kung wen chi* [bs] (SPTK ed.), 76/23a.

15. *Ch'uan-hsi lu* [bt] (Meiji rangai ed. of Satō Issai), 3/16b.

16. *Ibid.*, 3/26a.

17. Cf. Tadao Sakai, "Ōgaku no shominsei ni kansuru shakai teki rekishi-teki igi," [bu] in *Ryūkoku shidan*, No. 55–56 (December, 1966), pp. 193–203.

18. For further details and documentation on this aspect of Lu Hsiang-shan and Wang Yang-ming, see *ibid.*

19. Cf. Sakai, *Zensho*, p. 363.

20. *Ibid.*, p. 431.

21. *Ibid.*, chap. 5.

22. *Ibid.*, pp. 356–57.

23. *Ibid.*, chap. 4.

24. Cf. Shimada Kenji, *Chūgoku ni okeru kindai shii no zasetsu* (Tokyo, 1949), p. 111.

25. Cf. Sakai, *Zensho*, pp. 347–49.

26. Cf. Sakai, *Ōgaku no shominsei*, p. 193.

27. *Hsi-shan hsien-sheng Chen Wen-chung wen-chi* (SPTK ed.), 27/11b.

28. "Lung-shu ching-t'u wen" (*Taishō daizōkyō*, 47), 6/269–274.
29. Cf. *Li-ming p'ien* (Wan-li ed.), 23a; *Yin-chih lu* (Edo ed.), 9b Ch'ien-hsü li-chung.
30. *Ti-chi lu*, P'ing chuan (chuan 8), finis to *Kung-kuo ko*.
31. *Pu-fei-ch'ien k'ung-te li* (Edo ed.), p. 49a.
32. *Hui-tsuan kung-kuo ko* (Tao kuang ed.), 8/25a–26b.
33. *Ibid.*, 8/25a (original commentary).
34. *Pu-fei-ch'ien k'ung-te li* (Edo ed.), pp. 49a–52a, 55a–57a.

GLOSSARY

a 科舉

b 舉業

c 四書大全 36 卷, 明永樂中胡廣等奉勅撰

d 五經大全 113 卷, 同上撰

e 日用類書

f 三臺萬用正宗 43 卷, 萬曆 27 年 (1599), 余文台刊本, 日本蓬左文庫藏

g 萬寶全書 34 卷, 萬曆 42 年 (1614), 存仁堂刊本, 日本宮內廳書陵部藏, 他種刊本, 37 卷本, 35 卷本等

h 古今文苑舉業精華, 明袁黃編, 明刊本, 日本尊經閣文庫藏

i 翰墨大全, 元劉應李編, 元大德 11 年 (1307) 序刊

j 啓劄青錢 51 卷, 劉氏日新堂, 元泰定甲子 (1324) 重刊本, 日本德山市毛利文庫藏 10 卷, 元版, 一部明補修刊本, 日本內閣文庫藏

k 詩學彙選 2 卷, 明胡文煥編

l 故事七寶大成 20 卷, 明吳道明編, 集義堂明刊本, 日本故仁井田陞博士藏

m 幼學易知雜字大全, 明末編刊, 日本故仁井田陞博士藏

n 居家必用事類全集 10 卷, 明內府刊本, 萬曆刊本, 日本內閣文庫藏 明嘉靖 39 年 (1560) 田汝成叙刊, 日本寬文 13 年 (1673) 刊本

o 事林廣記, 日本元祿 12 年 (1699) 刊本 (原本元刊本) 元刊本, 日本內閣文庫, 宮內廳書陵部等藏 明刊本數種

p 五車拔錦 33 卷, 萬曆 25 年 (1597) 鄭氏刊本, 日本故仁井田陞博士藏

q 文林廣記 31 卷, 萬曆 35 年 (1607) 序刊, 陳氏積善堂刊本, 日本宮內廳書陵部藏

r 積玉全書 32 卷, 李光裕增補版, 明刊本, 日本宮內廳書陵部藏

s 類書纂要 3 卷, 明璩崑玉編, 葉文懋增補, 錢國煥刊, 明天啓版 12 卷本, 明崇禎 7 年 (1634) 序刊本

t 文林聚寶萬卷星羅 40 卷, 萬曆 28 年 (1600) 序刊本, 日本蓬左文庫藏

u 施會元巧對故事 12 卷, 萬曆丁未 (35) 年 (1607) 刊本

v 四民捷用

w 四民便用

x 四民日用備覽

y 師儒, 文史, 學校, 訓童, 幼學, 儒教

z 文海波瀾 2 卷, 明李廷機撰, 萬曆 2 年 (1574) 黃鳳翔序, 日本內閣文庫等藏

aa 古今舉業文弢註釋評林, 明劉日寧選, 董其昌, 朱之蕃評註, 萬曆 24 年 (1596) 叙, 萬曆 25 年 (1597) 刊, 日本尊經閣文庫藏

ab 時文

ac 擬題

ad 四書訓兒俗說,袁黄編,萬曆35年
(1607)序刊, 日本內閣文庫藏

ae 四書刪正6卷,袁黄編, 明刊, 日
本內閣文庫藏

af 六經纂要, 顔茂猷編, 日本尊經
閣文庫藏

ag 善書

ah 無賴

ai 幇

aj 例監

ak 監生

al 生員

am 楊起元, 復所

an 三敎兼修

ao 李春芳

ap 眞知

aq 保伍法

ar 任俠

as 鄕約

at 太上感應篇30卷,宋李昌齡傳,鄭
清之賛(道藏, 太清部834-839
册)

au 功過格

av 袁黄, 了凡

aw 雲谷禪師

ax 達觀禪師

ay 金丹

az 服餌

ba 房中

bb 胎息

bc 立命

bd 凡民

be 愚夫愚婦

bf 龍舒淨土文12卷,南宋王日休著
(大正藏卷47収)

bg 廣善篇功過格, 清康熙辛丑
(1721)序

bh 不費錢功德例, 陳弘謀編, 訓俗
遺規—乾隆七年(1742)序—卷
4収

bi 立命篇(収謙虛利中),萬曆丁未
(1607)刊, 日本內閣文庫藏
陰隲錄(収謙虛利中),日本元祿
14年(1701)刊本

bj 謙虛

bk 迪吉錄(平卷収)功過格, 顔光衷
(茂猷)著,明末刊

bl 鄕紳

bm 彙纂功過格, 清陳錫嘏序, 康熙
10年代刊本, 日本內閣文庫藏
流布本, 道光刊本, 卷八費錢行
功格

bn 士人, 農家, 百工, 商賈, 醫家, 公
門, 婦女, 士卒, 僧道, 僕婢工
役, 大衆

bo 風水

bp 戊日(十干)

bq 酒井忠夫,明代の日用類書と庶
民敎育(林友春編「近世中國
敎育史研究」収, 1958)

br 酒井忠夫, 中國善書の研究,
1960

bs 晦庵先生朱文公文集100卷,續
集11卷,別集10卷,目錄2卷
(四部叢刊集部収), 卷70中庸
章句序

bt 傳習錄三卷附佐藤一齋欄外書,
明治版

bu 酒井忠夫,王學の庶民性に關す
る社會的歷史的意義(小笠原,
宮崎兩博士華甲記念史學論
集, 龍谷史壇56, 57號収)

ROBERT CRAWFORD *Chang Chü-cheng's*

Confucian Legalism

日月 Chang Chü-cheng [a] was born on May 24, 1525, in Chiang-ling [b] County in Hupei Province, the only son in a family of poor, unsuccessful scholars. The founder of the family, Chang Kuan-pao, [c] had been a soldier with Chu Yüan-chang when he first rebelled and, in return for his military merit, was given the hereditary position of battalion commander in Kueichou. [d] His great-grandfather, being a second son, could not inherit the title and moved to Chiang-ling. He was apparently a scholar but there is no record of his having received any degree. Chang's father, Wen-ming, [e] was unsuccessful seven times in the examinations.

Change received his *chin-shih* in 1547 and was appointed to a position in the Hanlin Academy.[1] The beginning of his political career corresponds in time to a low point in dynastic fortunes and to an intellectual revolt that, in its most radical form, threatened the foundations of the imperial order. Each of these forces had their effect upon his views and his policies.

Chang did not formulate a systematic body of thought. He was an activist, and rather contemptuous of formal philosophy. His purpose was to revive what he considered the spirit of the period of the dynasty's founding emperor and to revitalize the dynasty's vital essence. Nevertheless, he was a politician with ideas, and, although his philosophical position is only loosely and vaguely stated in his public and private papers,[2] it is important to an understanding of this great statesman, who by his vigor and ruthlessness gave a tottering dynasty a new, if temporary, lease on life. Moreover, his views, representative of those of a large number of leading contemporaneous officials, reveal the extent to which the rejection of Neo-Confucianism had also penetrated the world of action. This trend reflected a belief that the essence of true Confucianism lay in the pursuit of reality, and rejected abstract thought divorced from factual knowledge or practical action. Its subjectivism and relativism emphasized individual judgment and rejected the notion of eternally valid institutions. In short, these views represent many elements of what has been called the school of practical statesmanship [3] and of those forces Professor de Bary characterizes as leading toward a kind of pragmatism in seventeenth-century China.[4]

One of the great difficulties in analyzing Chang's thought is the paucity of data which might serve to trace his intellectual development. What we have is largely a final statement in which the dominant element is an absolute commitment to the dynasty and an idealization of autocracy. "If it is to the benefit of the state," he was fond of saying, "I would do it regardless of life or death." [5] Chang's keen concern over the fate of the dynasty as the guiding factor in his thought is clear.

The Ming political climate had been precisely expressed by the Korean Confucianist Ch'oe Pu as "among those who serve, the state is all, the family forgotten." [6] Chang's grandfather had admonished him to devote himself totally to the well-being of the people and to "take pride in your country." [7] Chang may also have felt a deep sense of gratitude to a state whose institutions he viewed as perfect and which had enabled him, a scholar of humble beginnings, to rise to the pinnacle of power.[8]

An important feature of Chang's intellectual milieu was the development and spread of the Wang Yang-ming school of Confucianism. Wang propounded a doctrine of the individual mind as the ultimate source of morality, finding within itself and not in the outside world the norms of action. His doctrine of intuitive knowledge thus pointed away from external authority—political and intellectual. His moral subjectivism formed the basis for a new appreciation of the individual; and his doctrine of the unity of knowledge and action brought a revived interest in practicality and activism.[9]

Whether Chang Chü-cheng was influenced by Wang's philosophy is not clear. He is never mentioned by his contemporaries as having been a disciple of Wang's school and specific doctrinal influences do not appear in his writings. Indeed, there is evidence that Chang rejected some of Wang's key doctrines.[10] On the other hand, throughout his life he had close associations with members of Wang's school such as Hsü Chieh,[f][11] his tutor while in the Hanlin and later his political benefactor, Nieh Pao,[g][12] and Keng Ting-hsiang.[h][13] It is also clear that he had in common with members of Wang's school a rejection of contemporary Neo-Confucianism; an inclination to activism, subjectivism, and relativism; and an emphasis upon the autonomy and independence of one's own mind. While these ideas need not have been derived directly from Wang's philosophy, but could have been drawn from earlier philosophers, the circumstances would seem to indicate some influence or at the very least a sympathetic response. Certainly the famous Wang Yang-ming radical Li Chih[i] had some very kind words for Chang. In discussing Chang and Ho Hsin-yin,[j] a member of the T'ai-chou group of the left wing of the Wang school, Li wrote

If we do not discuss their ruin but discuss their accomplishments; do not investigate their lives but investigate their minds; do not upbraid their faults but reward their merits; then these two old ones are both my teachers. They do not compare with the world's petty and opportunistic, those who bury their heads in books, have a high opinion of themselves, and steal the name of sage in order to conceal their own covetousness for position and their subservience.[14]

To the extent that Chang may have been influenced by Wang's philosophy, the juxtaposition of these influences with legalist elements in his thought might point, in contradistinction to the major anti-authoritarian thrust of Wang's ideas in the philosophical realm, toward an authoritarianism for which the way had been opened by Wang's moral subjectivism. It might also indicate that there had been an evolution in Chang's thought in which the more liberal trends in Wang's school came to be viewed by him as incompatible with political realities and his own ambitions. It is worthy of note that similar relationships exist in the thought of Chang's onetime friend and colleague, Kao Kung, who had preceded Chang as chief grand secretary.[15] As regards an evolution in Chang's thought, even to his contemporaries it appeared that some change had occurred. In a letter to Keng Ting-hsiang, Chang himself noted the disappointment of the scholar-officials with his policies. "We considered," he wrote of their feelings, "that Mr. Chang in wielding authority would constantly carry out the way of the Sage Emperors (Ti) and Kings (Wang). Now [we] see that his discussions are merely of a kind to enrich the state and strengthen the army." [16]

All things considered, it is doubtful that any single school molded Chang's outlook. He was consciously eclectic and his views developed primarily out of his great concern over dynastic problems. He was also pragmatic, indeed cynical, in his approach to the political function of ideology or beliefs. In an essay on the fundamental norms of government, Chang noted the political manipulation of the people's beliefs in demons, gods, and calamities by some of the early sages and then declared

Generally, [taking] the way of spirits to establish instruction was used in order to guide the stupid. Respect for demons and fairies was not abolished by the sages. Those who are wise know their intention [for not doing so] and do not [themselves] cling to the theory. Hence they may be called enlightened. [17]

As for himself, Chang disclaims any belief in omens or divination and yet his actions "obtain auspicious results." [18] In spite of such disclaimers, however, he did use the appearance of a comet in 1577 to carry out an intercalary capital evaluation to expel critics. On another occasion he sought to submit an auspicious omen to flatter the emperor. [19] Such statements lead to the suspicion that for Chang ideas were tools for meeting the world. The demands of the world— specifically the political world—and the necessity of dealing practically with those demands were the keystones in Chang's philosophy. He read widely and freely incorporated in his writings ideas from philosophers of all schools, especially from the pre-Han and Han periods. He frequently asserts that strict adherence to schools of thought, debates over their validity, and abstract philosophizing all obscure true learning. His position and an accompanying relativism toward right and wrong are stated in one of his attempts to defend himself against charges of anti-intellectualism:

Now, to learn is a matter that lies within the sphere of our prime duty; we cannot leave it aside for a single moment. Those who say that they love *Tao-hsüeh* [Neo-Confucianism] are in error; those who say that they dislike it are also mistaken; and those who, making an arbitrary choice among alternatives, say that there should not be the designation of one who dislikes *Tao-hsueh* commit the worst of errors. . . . To say that it is improper not to like the *Tao-hsüeh* approach to learning is not so good a plan as to free oneself of prejudices and predilections and to recognize directly that which is primary and genuine as learning.[20]

HISTORY AND THE MING DYNASTY

From the time he became chief grand secretary on July 26, 1572, until his death on July 9, 1582, as Chang Chü-cheng's *Ming shih* biographer notes, "the emperor abandoned all his own opinions and delegated [authority] to Chü-cheng. Chü-cheng then frankly took over the empire as his personal responsibility." [21] The same biographer also points out that he was "courageous and determined in assuming responsibilities, regarding himself as a man of heroic stature." [22] Something of the same flavor is found in Chang's own description of his career:

Since I have taken control of affairs, I devote everything to the public interest. I empty my mind and examine things, rectify myself, and am stern with subordinates. The laws are properly applied, and I am not lenient [even] with those in high position and close [to the court]. If there is a talented man who can be used, [even if he] is low in status and distant [from the court] I do not ignore him. I devote attention to strengthening the dynasty and restricting private interests, reducing discussion and criticism, and checking names and realities, in order to venerate the sovereign and shelter the people. I take the lead in initiating affairs. At the same time, I realize that the inked marking string is not suited to a crooked tree and a bright mirror is detested by an ugly woman. So I investigate the times and calculate the tendency, and the administration is definitely proper.[23]

By the time he assumed his duties, Chang was convinced that the Ming dynasty was in a state of rapid decline. As early as 1547 he saw signs of a decline that had begun after the first hundred years of the dynasty;[24] and in 1568 he wrote "since the Chia-[ching] and Lung-[ch'ing] periods, imperial control has degenerated and the laws have deteriorated. We are rapidly falling into the degeneracy of Sung and Yüan."[25] He saw it as his responsibility to arrest the decay and to restore the dynastic vigor and brilliance of the Hung-wu and Yung-lo periods.

Chang's study of history had convinced him that each dynasty had its own particular nature which differed from preceding periods. It was the task of the "superior man" to strengthen the basis of his state, preserve its laws and institutions, and take "care of its primal spirit." [k][26]

The nature of the Ming dynasty, according to Chang, was determined by its founding emperor. It rested on strictness and compulsion (wei-ch'iang),[l][27] was institutionally eclectic, and was the product of the best that previous history had to offer. "Ever since the Three Dynasties (san-tai)," says Chang, "for the perfection of laws and institutions none have surpassed [our] brilliant dynasty." The six ministries imitated the Hsia dynasty; the Three Dukes and the Three Solitaries continued the Chou system; the "common pattern of government" took its framework from Han Kao-tsu; the basic laws were taken from the laws and ordinances of T'ang Tai-tsu; the court ceremonies came from the royal family law of Sung; and the calendar came from the Yüan. In utilizing these institutions, however, Ming T'ai-tsu "followed the times to regulate their suitability and established the administration to fit the people." [28] He took nine tenths from recent dynasties and one tenth from the first dynasties. Within the realm of specific policies, levying a merchant tax and establishing the salt office came from Sung Hung-yang [m] and K'ung Chin; [n] the systems of seniority and achievement by which to regulate the periodic evaluations were from Ts'ui Liang [o] of Later Wei; the three due periods of the two taxes came from the land tax system of Yang Yen; [p] and the *pao-chia* system, the policy that each household should raise one horse, and the use of essays on the principles of the Classics came from the New Regulations of Wang An-shih.[29] Thus, concludes Chang, as to

what in former times were called vile practices and bad administration, we at present use them all and contrary [to the past] they bring results, wealth, and strength and accomplish the task of tranquillity. Therefore, if they are properly used, even the laws of commoners can bring about the same results as sages and wise men.[30]

The Ming dynasty was thus institutionally eclectic and, like the period of Emperor Hsüan of the Han dynasty, had its own pattern.[31]

The reigns of the Hung-wu and Yung-lo emperors were praised by Chang as establishing the essential nature of the Ming dynasty. The middle periods preserved the former achievements. Using the hexagram Peace (*t'ai*)[q] to convey his meaning, Chang wrote "for developing Peace no rulers were as good as T'ai-tsu and Ch'eng-tsu. For protecting Peace, none were as good as the two reigns of Hsüan [tsung] and Hsiao [-tsung]." [32] Later reigns, however, revealed a steadily accelerating process of decay. Chang's analysis of the causes of the decline amounted to nothing less than a total condemnation of the administration, particularly of the Chia-ching period.

In Chang's view, the dynasty had passed through three stages of decline. The first stage was a deterioration of "excellent customs" and a loosening of authority. This was followed by a growth in the power of the princes, who "perverted authority and injured the upright," and by a disregard for the laws. The third stage saw taxation become unequal, the people losing their employment and becoming victims of "monopolies." [33] In 1549, while still in the Han-lin Academy, he submitted a "Memorial on Current Government." At that time he detected five evils in the government, all five of which originated in one basic evil: lack of communication between ruler and minister. He chided Emperor Shih-tsung for not attending court for nine years and for surrounding himself with eunuchs and favorites, with the result that ministers could not take up urgent matters. He accused the imperial family, powerful persons, and officials of arrogance, greed, treachery, and exploitation of the people.[34] In a letter to Keng Ting-hsiang, probably written in 1578, six years after he had become chief grand secretary, Chang repeated an earlier condemnation of the Chia-ching and Lung-ch'ing periods, asserting that during the middle years of the Chia-ching period "merchants held power" and only the continuing influences of the early years of the dynasty had staved off collapse. The Lung-ch'ing period, he conceded, had seen some improvement, but discipline had not yet been restored, corrupt practices were still esteemed, and writings without substance still multiplied daily.[35]

Throughout his writings, but especially in his "Memorial on Six Affairs" submitted September 20, 1568, Chang points to a number of specific factors weakening the dynasty and concludes that these were the consequences of a lack of communication between minister and sovereign, the indecisiveness of the emperor, a weakening of imperial authority, and disrespect for the dynastic laws and institutions.[36] In Chang's mind, the latter two problems were the most serious. But the accumulated weaknesses were not yet irremediable. The course of history could yet be altered and the dynastic brilliance of the Hung-wu period recaptured. To do so, it was necessary to reestablish imperial authority,[r] to strengthen and enforce the laws, to check names against realities, and to apply rewards and punishments consistently.

But if specific dynastic problems called forth these legalistic solutions, Chang found the source of the problems themselves and justification for his solutions in a philosophy of history based on the principle of constant change in time and circumstances. History, for Chang, demonstrated a kind of law of reversal which followed a logical but not inevitable pattern.

Chang was a very close student of the Book of Changes and it is likely that this classic is the source of his position that the operation of yin and yang when applied to the world of men demonstrates that "When affairs of the world reach their extreme [point of development] then they must reverse. If they reverse, they must return to the beginning. This is the natural principle of the creative and transforming [forces]." [37] This was not, however, a mechanistic movement over which man had absolutely no control. Before a situation has developed too far, says Chang, "[a person] of middling talents can put a plan into effect. But if a trend becomes established, [even] a wise man will not be able to do anything about it." [38]

The relationship between the individual and the external forces of his environment is given fuller treatment by Chang in an essay criticizing those who believe that destiny and righteousness coincide. Why, he asks, if destiny and righteousness correspond, is it possible that those who are benevolent do not necessarily live long and those who live long are not necessarily benevolent; that sages do not necessarily possess the empire and those who do possess it are not necessarily sages? It is not, he replies, because some are predestined by Heaven to occupy high position and others lowly status; nor is it because of sheer individual determination. "Heaven," he declares, "shuffles things in an absolutely unfathomable way." [39] Reason cannot divine it. But, while even a sage cannot alter the decrees of destiny, righteousness can be practiced and destiny cannot take that away from a person. It is like agriculture, he concludes:

Plowing, weeding, and sowing are human actions. Rain, sunshine, abundance, or deficiency are heavenly actions. Even a Shen Nung [s] or a Hou-chi [t] could not guarantee an abundant harvest. Yet the success of agriculture is not possible without [human] effort.[40]

There is, then, a necessary interdependence between Heaven and man, and within limits imposed by his environment man plays an essential role. Indeed, within these limits he is not only master of his own fate but is also in a position to influence the course of events about him.

As applied to institutional and political history, Chang's "law of reversal" provides for belief in an orderly and predictable fluctuation between two fixed poles of simplicity (*chih*) [u] and ornateness (*wen*).[v] He rejects Tung Chung-shu's three-way alternation among faithfulness, simplicity, and ornateness. Citing the *Shih-chi* as evidence, he concludes that the Hsia dynasty esteemed simplicity in addition to faithfulness and the Shang dynasty esteemed ornateness in addition to simplicity. With Confucius as evidence, Chang also points out that the Chou dynasty esteemed simplicity as well as ornateness. Therefore, there are only the two poles of simplicity and ornateness, and both are operative in the same dynasty.[41] Chang thus concludes that

Generally [speaking], affairs of the world are always simple in the beginning and towards the end they inevitably become complex (*chü*).[w] When the sun first rises, its light is very brilliant and its atmosphere elegant (*ch'i*).[x] As it reaches the middle of the sky, its light is dazzling. But when it reaches the center, that is the beginning of [its] decline. . . . In the beginning of a state all affairs are simple (*ts'ao-ch'uang*) [y] and people's feelings are simple. Generally there is much simplicity (*chih*) and little ornateness (*wen*). The establishment of rites and music and the elaboration and multiplication of affairs are all in the middle period of a state. At that time people feel there is great peace and prosperity and do not know that the germinating point of decay and confusion commences in these. Hsia and Shang were both like this, not only Chou. The sages knew this and did not wait until decay developed but constantly opposed it. They cut [wood] to make it rough, and broke down the round to make it square. In the control of things it is better to be clumsy than clever. In employing people it is better that they be practical than flowery. It is like the branches of a tree. If one repeatedly prunes it, there is the opportunity of returning to [its] basic [form] and to the beginning.[42]

In applying this concept to Chinese history, Chang began with the Hsia dynasty on the ground that the cycle prior to Yao and Shun could not be known. Through Hsia and Shang to Chou, the first knowable cycle, decline was already extreme and the world became overelaborate (*to-shih*).[z] The exhaustion of the "Kingly Way" of Chou resulted. This development then of necessity reverted and resulted in the Ch'in dynasty. Ch'in abolished all the ornate institutions of the previous dynasties and ruled only by law. This, says Chang, was an "occasion of returning to the beginning." But Ch'in could not hold the empire and it passed to the Han dynasty. The government of Western Han was simple and austere and close to the ancient form, "thanks actually to Ch'in which cleared the ground for it." [43] But Kung Yü [44] and the like took "the dregs of Chou elegance and used them in the corrupt and declining periods of Yüan

and Ch'eng. They did not understand the change in the times."
During the remainder of the Han, the T'ang and the Sung periods,
"elaborateness was excessive and the world daily became more divorced from reality." Sung marked the extreme of decadence and
then the cycle of necessity reversed and resulted in the Yüan dynasty. Yüan abolished the rites and institutions of the former kings
and ruled solely by means of simplicity. "This was an occasion of
returning to the ancient." But Yüan could not retain the empire
and the Ming dynasty succeeded it. The government of Ming was
able to be "simple, strict and realistic" (*chih-p'o*),[aa] thanks to Yüan
which had cleared the ground for it.[45]

In this process, then, when ornateness reached its extreme, there
was a reversion to simplicity, first through an interim dynasty which
prepared the way, and then through a dynasty truly ruling by the
principle of simplicity; but then the development of ornateness began
all over again. It is clear from this interpretation that ornateness involves music, rites, and the like, and refers to Confucianism. If left
to themselves, these institutions bring collapse. The opposite principle, simplicity, is equivalent to austerity, basic principle, sternness,
and law, and refers to Legalism. It is this latter principle of ruling
that, for Chang, constitutes the true ancient way of government.

The operation of this cycle is not a purely mechanistic repetition
of identical institutions. The principles of simplicity and ornateness
are inherent in every period. The dominance of one over the other
sets the basic pattern of government, but in adapting institutions to
the principle, which in the beginning is always simple, there is a
wide range of latitude. As the cycle progresses in time, each period
encounters different circumstances. Each period has its own unique
qualities, and the good institutions of the preceding age may be bad
for the period following, or what was bad in the preceding period
may be good for the next even though the same determining principle predominates in both periods. In practice there should be a
high degree of institutional relativism. "Laws and institutions,"
Chang writes, "are not constant." [46] The same suggestion is expressed
in his dictum that "the times which the worthy sages of ancient
times encountered were not the same and the manner in which they

handled them also differed." [47] No age, at least from Chou to Ming, is superior. Each age has contributed institutions which may or may not be useful for later periods. "Past and present," Chang wrote, "differ in circumstances so that what was once vulgar becomes proper." Changes in times necessitate appropriate changes in response, and the criterion for determining the nature of the response is not age, source, or any absolute inherent rightness, but suitability to the times and to the people or customs,[48] or, more specifically, to whatever creates wealth and strength. Chang cites Hsün Tzu to the effect that one cannot pattern the government after the ancient kings [49] and concludes that

Law is neither ancient nor modern. It is merely what is suitable to the times and what is acceptable to the people. If it is suitable to the times and the people accept it, even if it is established by commoners it should not be abolished. If it does violence to the times and is rejected by the people, then even if it was created by sagely wisdom it should not be followed.[50]

Chang is not prepared, however, to grant too much to the people since he also argues that they must at times be told what is good for them.

The possibilities for freedom inherent in this relativism are already limited by the tyranny of the moment. But Chang further qualifies the concept. According to him, principle (li)[ab] and circumstances (shih)[ac] operate continuously in history and are interdependent and inseparable. Principle and circumstance must change pari passu. The principle of any matter must fit the circumstances before it can be undertaken. The concepts of the highest good of The Great Learning and of the mean in the Doctrine of the Mean, says Chang, both indicate the natural and exactly right place in events and principles. He rejects Chu Hsi's interpretation of the passage "to rest in the highest good" as implying stagnation and suggests that what is meant is not to exceed the mean.

[In] heavenly principle and human feelings, [when one has] attained to what they properly permit, without excess or deficiency, then one has reached the highest good. However, events and principles are not constant at all times and in all situations. One should move with them in order to abide with the mean. For what was formerly considered good may not be considered good in the present; what is considered good in one [situation] may not be considered good in another.[51]

As with Wang Yang-ming, the mean for Chang changes according to the time.[52] But each period has its own complex of principle and circumstance which differs quantitatively and qualitatively from previous periods, and the mean rests within that complex. What this means to Chang is clear from his praise of Emperor Hsüan of the Han dynasty. He praises this emperor for his excellent administrative policies of firmness and of carefully checking names against realities; but, more specifically, he admires Hsüan because he, unlike Emperor Yüan, understood the specific nature of Han. Indeed, Emperor Hsüan's administrative techniques were praiseworthy because they were in accord with the nature of the Han dynasty and, according to Chang, always remained within the Han pattern. This is the rationale for Chang's praise of such Han statesmen as Chia I,[ad] Ch'ao Tso,[ae] and Wei Hsiang,[af] all of whom are portrayed in the histories as Legalist-Confucianists.[53]

It is a logical conclusion from Chang's argument that, since principle and circumstances constantly change and are a unity, one can neither go back in time nor undertake anything new until circumstances justify it. It is probably this belief that lies behind Chang's assertion that

The laws cannot be lightly changed and at the same time cannot be unthinkingly followed. If they are unthinkingly followed, then one will inherit worn-out [laws and institutions] and errors, and there will be a danger of decline which cannot be revitalized. This is the mistake of not wanting things to be done perfectly. If [the laws and institutions] are lightly changed [on the other hand], then [people will] hate the old and like the fashionable and there will be the calamity of change without order.[54]

What Chang thus seems to be saying is that, as principle and circumstances develop in history, only the given moment is real, and that the context of the given period determines what is fitting to it. Since the mean moves only within boundaries set by the nature of the period, it thus defines appropriate action; and therefore only the laws and institutions of the reigning dynasty, which fit and define the specific nature of the dynasty, are true. Consequently, they must be carefully studied and accepted.

As we have seen, Chang considered the Ming as having its own particular pattern and as being institutionally eclectic. Its institutions were the sum of the best history had to offer, and the function of the "gentleman" was to follow and preserve the particular nature of his dynasty. Chang complains, however, that "Decadent Confucians do not understand the changes in the times. They praise the Three Dynasties and want to introduce the same practices that corrupted the way of Han." They do not realize, says Chang, that the framework of Ming "in the founding of the state" differed from former periods. "It originated in a policy of the application of both authority and kindness." [55] As Chang uses the terms "authority" and "kindness" in his writings, it is clear that for him the Ming system is Legalist in application and Confucian in principle. Still, "impractical and abstract scholars," not understanding the changes in the times,

excitedly praise the Three Dynasties. But to criticize the affair of Chien-wen [losing his throne by his brother's usurpation] and condemn the laws and commands of our two *tsu* [Hung-wu and Yung-lo] are remnant practices of the evil ministers and traitors of Sung times. These decadently unrealistic and impractical arguments definitely cannot be used.[56]

The scholars, in Chang's view, want to develop ornateness—that side of the historical cycle leading to collapse—and they suggest changing the laws and institutions, and engage in empty, theoretical, and impractical discussions. To correct this corrupting tendency, Chang calls for combining study of the two concepts, nature and destiny,[ag] with practical considerations.[57] But what standard is to be applied to determine what is practical at any given stage? According to the principles outlined above, for Chang the guidelines must be furnished by the laws and institutions of Ming, and only the edicts of the reigning sovereign and the demands of one's office can be legitimate objects of study.[58] According to the *Li-chi*, he wrote,

"In learning, the official puts duties first and the scholar puts his purpose (*chih*)[ah] first." When scholars have not yet met their time, they discuss matters with each other and make clear the means by which to cultivate themselves and govern men, because another day they will be required to apply it. When a scholar is appointed to office and has official duties, he takes his duties as his study. He carefully and attentively seeks thereby to fulfill his duties and avoid blame and to fulfill the orders of his superiors. He should never abandon his duties and open a new school of thought and consider it as learning.[59]

Moreover, declares Chang, this was the doctrine expounded by Confucius. He traveled about and discoursed with his disciples only because he had not obtained office. Yet, even in these circumstances, what he taught was concerned entirely with practical matters. His "general theme," said Chang, "was to model himself after Wen and Wu and restore Eastern Chou. He took living in the present but looking back to the ancients as a rebuke and considered loyalty as the standard." [60] When he was old he compiled the *Spring and Autumn Annals* in order to preserve the statutes of Chou.[61] His purpose, Chang says, was

to follow Chou and that is all! What is recorded in the *Spring and Autumn Annals* are entirely the institutions of the Chou. Now Confucius was a man of Yin. Why didn't he desire to implement the rites of the Yin? Did the laws of the Chou so far surpass those of the previous dynasty that they could not be changed? [It is because] living in the Chou and being an official of Chou, he did not dare turn his back on Chou.[62]

If Confucius occupied office under the Ming dynasty, he would do the same for Ming. He would not leave his "original work to open another door, thereby himself committing the fault of returning to the past." [63] As Professor Hsiao Kung-ch'üan points out, Chang assumed the positive value of governmental decrees; it was not necessary to question whether or not their content was in harmony with the very best standards. Consequently, learning itself "no longer had a definite value." [64] Scholars should take only "walking on actual ground as merit (*kung*),[ai] esteeming basic stuff (*pen-chih*)[aj] as conduct, obeying and maintaining the established laws (*ch'eng-hsien*)[ak] as the standard, and obeying the sovereign with a sincere heart as loyalty." [65]

THE STATE AND THE STATESMAN'S CRAFT

Chang spent little time theorizing about the origin of the state. The state is and must be accepted. But he is not without some theory of its origin. In Chang's view, the state, by which he means the emperor, originated from man's struggle to satisfy his own personal needs. In the world, he declared,

there were the strong who oppressed the weak, the many who suppressed the few, those who cherished knowledge but did not teach others, those who monopolized profit and did not share it, and inaccessible countries with different customs so remote they could not benefit from virtue and receive enrichment.[66]

Under these circumstances, Heaven gave the empire "to one man, calling him the Son of Heaven"; and caused him to bring order out of chaos, to bring about unity and uniformity, "to equalize and see to it that [the people's] desires were satisfied in proper measure." Only when the material wants of the people were satisfied and their distress relieved did "Heaven's purpose have a place in which to lodge." [67] The continuance of political authority is also justified by the assumption that man's selfishness does not cease and that only by strong authority can each member of the community be guaranteed life and security. The origin and continuance of the state is thus a material and not a moral question, and its origin defines the purpose of the state, the function of the ruler, and the type of government necessary to fulfill the original purpose. Like Mencius, Chang emphasizes the economic role of society. With Hsün Tzu and the Legalists he agrees that man is basically selfish and that strong government is necessary. With both Mencius and Hsün Tzu he agrees that the people are the end of government and that rulership is a bestowed trust. He departs from these two streams of Confucianism, however, in recommending techniques to implement the purpose of the state. Here Mencius' love is metamorphized into Hsün Tzu's strictness. Hsün Tzu's *li* is exchanged for law, and specific Legalist techniques replace the moral and ethical approach as the best means to achieve the desired end.

Chang develops the theme that the people are the foundation of the state and the emperor is responsible to them in an essay entitled "A Ruler Protects Himself in Order To Protect the People." [68] In essence, Chang's approach is a combination of love and enlightened self-interest. The people and the world love the emperor not only because they love the sovereign but also because having him is to their advantage. The sovereign, he wrote, takes care of his person not only because he desires longevity, peace, stability, and a long reign, but also because it is advantageous to the empire. The body of the ruler, says Chang

is not the body of one man but the body of myriads of men. Heaven for the sake of the people loves the sovereign. If the ruler does not think about conserving his body in order to protect the people, does he not thereby prove himself unworthy of the purpose Heaven has entrusted to him? [69]

The relationship of sovereign and people, says Chang, is like the relationship between father and son. The father considers the son of importance for carrying on the ancestral sacrifices and as a means for later prosperity. Therefore he loves him and worries about him. The son dare not forget this and only fears "lest one day through disgrace or injury to his own person he may cause his parents worry." Similarly, Heaven loves the sovereign. It invests him with the natural talents of astuteness, understanding, sageness, and wisdom; bestows upon him the throne, wealth, and honor; and causes the people to obey his commands all because of its love for the people.

For Chang, the sovereign's authority is absolute and unlimited, at least in this world, and he must place restraints upon himself in order to fulfill his function. Unlimited use of imperial authority by an emperor for personal gratification will lead to oppression of the people and to final calamity. Chang's restraints are, as he frankly admitted, self-imposed or symbolic.[70] Beyond the customary warnings of rebellion, Chang offers no new solution to the age-old problem of abusive emperors, of which, he admits, history has seen many. The emperor is still the one who controls the commands, the ministers carry them out, and the people obey.[71]

Concerning restraints upon the people and the ministers, Chang is less reticent. In this case, abnegation of desires is not the means to keep them in check.[72] He minimizes the role of moral education and, through a utilitarian view of human nature, emphasizes imperial manipulation of the "handles" of reward and punishment. Chang was a realist concerning imperial authority. It was an established fact. There is, however, no reason to assume that he was merely rationalizing a fact. His view of the emperor was part of the value system of the society. There is also no reason to believe that his expressed concern for the well-being of the people was a mere pious platitude. It is a recurrent theme in his essays and poems and perhaps recalls the difficult days of his own youth. In recalling his temporary retirement in 1554, Chang once wrote

When I was a youth I was bitterly poor and my family's income was only several *shih*. At twenty I entered office and there were only several tens of *mou* of land. In the Chia-ching [period] I returned home because of illness. . . . At that time all about me old farmers tested the soil for dryness or moisture to see whether the planting and harvesting would be early or late, and looked up to the sky to see if there was a halo around the sun in order to know whether the year would be auspicious or bad. Each showed that he was subjected to wind, rain, and the broiling sun, and at the end of a year of toil barely escaped starvation. If the year's harvest was bad men could not take care of their wives and sons, but officials pressed them for taxes more urgently than putting out a fire. Widows wept at night and thieves roamed at night. This always gave me a pitiful feeling, it was so sad, and a feeling of alarm, it was so fearful. Other times it was a good year and the grain flourished and the weather was good. The farmers cried out happily and I celebrated with them for a whole day. I also rejoiced because it was good and clamored with them because I was pleased.[73]

Chang devoutly believed that autocracy was the only possible form of government capable of ensuring the peace and prosperity Heaven intended for the people. This did not mean that he was satisfied with the *status quo*. He manifested a great deal of dissatisfaction with the government of his day. His solution, however, was to make autocracy work as it was meant to do.

Throughout his life, Chang's credo was subordination to the emperor. "The way of the minister is to honor and obey [the emperor]," he was wont to say. He defined obedience as

To [devote one's] complete ambition and exhaust one's strength in order to assist in public affairs and not dare to have the intention of esteeming one's own virtue in the slightest—this is obedience. When danger and barbarians suddenly increase, to accept the orders of superiors and not have the slightest intention of selecting when to advance or retreat according to the possibilities of advantage [for oneself]—this is obedience. Within, to have the skill of changing and adapting to [the emperor]; and without, not to have the reputation of correcting and saving [the emperor]—this is obedience. To bear all hatred and slander oneself and attribute all good and fame to the emperor—this is obedience. [Although a person's] merit covers the universe, to subordinate his own fame and be all the more respectful—this is obedience.[74]

Yet the actual sovereign–minister relationship should be a cooperative venture. His frequent use of the hexagrams *Ch'ien* and *K'un* to express this relationship implies mutual dependence. But his most explicit definition of the relationship is found in his discussion of the hexagram *T'ai* (Peace). "The meaning of [the hexagram] *T'ai*," he wrote, "is definitely the sovereign–minister relationship." In the hexagram *T'ai*, Chang wrote,

nine in the second place takes hard as central and responds to [six] in the fifth place, which takes soft as central. It empties itself in order to follow [nine in the second place]. This is what is meant by the union of sovereign and minister. . . . [Nine] in the second place is the way of the minister and takes fulfilling one's duties as loyalty. [Six] in the fifth place is the way of the soverign and takes entrusting affairs to the minister as the greatest [concern]. If [nine] in the second place is equal to its duties, then [six] in the fifth place can refrain from action. Therefore, it is said, "this brings blessings and supreme good fortune" and that is all. This is what is called the union of ruler and minister, and produces *T'ai*.[75]

The meaning of the hexagram is indeed that the wills of emperor and minister should be united in striving toward a common goal; that within this union good men dominate at court; and that one must constantly strive to hold in check the forces of decay, even though knowing they will return. But there is the clear implication that within the union the influence of the minister is very strong if not dominant. Whether Chang intended this meaning, except perhaps for the ten-year-old emperor he served, is doubtful. His most frequent discussions of the meaning of this relationship call only for the necessity of mutual cooperation. Palace and court are separate, says Chang, and the wise sovereign, realizing that "their sentiments are easily divergent and their tendencies scattered," condescends to maintain contact by holding court and heeding advice. To achieve the union of the *T'ai* hexagram, says Chang, the best way is to "properly institutionalize the practice of court sessions." However, Chang qualifies any intimate relationship achieved through such sessions by providing six very Legalist procedures for the emperor to follow in his conduct toward his ministers.

In his association with his ministers, says Chang, the emperor should 1) examine world affairs; 2) examine talents and character; 3) make known his kind intentions; 4) keep state affairs secret; 5) fix state policies; and 6) stimulate loyalty and sincerity. The first rule, Chang explained, means that the emperor should summon experts on any matter regarding which he wishes information and then use his investigation to measure achievements. "Then you cannot be deceived." The second rule means that he should unexpectedly question officials during the court sessions. If officials were permitted to leave court and memorialize, they could "adorn their phrases," and if they were given time to think, "then the essentials could be concealed." Direct questioning would determine their ability. The third rule means that, as the emperor's intentions are like a target which all vie to hit, he should order memorialists to examine the regulations, thereby revealing his intention of maintaining the laws and achieving good government. The fourth rule means that, by direct discussion, there would be no opportunity for information to leak out beforehand and modifications or changes in policy "could not be spied out." The fifth rule means that, as there can be very divergent opinions among even capable and devoted officials, only if the emperor personally decides all issues can anything be achieved. The last rule means that, if one is friendly and intimate with officials and trusts them with great responsibilities, they will be loyal. In addition to these six rules, which have as their basis imperial suspicion of officials, Chang recommends constantly applying the laws and institutions and the use of the imperial "awe-inspiring and unfathomable authority."

Enough has already been said to indicate the nature of Chang's state. He makes his position clearer, however, in his discussion regarding government by firmness (*kang*)[al] or leniency (*ku-hsi*)[am] and in his definitions of "dictatorship" (*ts'ao-ch'ieh*)[an] and "revitalization" (*chen-tso*).[ao]

Professor Hsiao Kung-ch'üan has written that Chang's political views can probably be summed up in the one word "firm." [77] This means taking as the fundamental tasks "venerating the sovereign's authority, fixing state policies, revitalizing discipline, and eliminating defects." [78] Professor Hsiao adds that the reason for this approach by Chang derived from the circumstances of a young emperor being on the throne and of a decline in the effectiveness of government.[79] Unquestionably these factors did play an important part in Chang's thinking. In several of his writings, Chang draws a distinction between the style of government required for times of peace and times of disorder. Since, in his view, the Ming dynasty was approaching the point where decline could not be reversed, the situation called for vigorous governmental action. But "firm government" was for Chang a principle, rather than a temporary expedient.

To Chang the *Book of History*'s dictum that the teaching of the five constant relationships rested in gentleness [ap] meant only that because human intelligence differed one must be patient and kind. It did not mean spoiling people or being lenient as apparently some scholars were arguing.[80] Leniency, as used by these scholars, said Chang, was really laxity or improper leniency. In terms of human nature, this was pampering human nature (*hsün-ch'ing*),[aq] and differed from being in accord with human nature (*shun-ch'ing*).[ar] When one pampers human nature, one disregards the rightness or wrongness of principle and the permissibility of an affair and merely accommodates human whims.[81] In terms of Chang's historical cycle, laxness or leniency is equated with ornateness. All governments, he declared, begin in strictness and end in laxness and the spirit of the people begins in energy and ends in indolence.[82] A government based on leniency becomes a haven for the powerful and unscrupulous who "take advantage of the laws to realize selfish profits" [83] and to exploit the people. On this basis, Chang attacks many of the historical figures the Confucians usually admire. Ch'in Shih-huang-ti's misfortune, he says, was that he did not have a son capable of maintaining and developing his laws. Hu Hai was young and stupid and Fu Su was benevolent and weak. Had the latter lived, he would have changed the laws to restore the system of the Three Dynasties. Later scholars, says Chang, see only Fu Su's remonstrance against burning the books and burying the scholars. They "do not know that the one who confused Ch'in was Fu Su." [84] In the Ming dynasty, Ai-wen, Hung-wu's first heir apparent, was benevolent and soft. Chien-wen followed "the vile customs of decadent Sung and daily took the regulations of Kao Huang-ti and changed them [like] Fu Su of Ch'in." If he had not "brought an early ruin upon himself, it would also have resulted in the end of the state." [85]

A government of firmness, on the other hand, in terms of the historical cycle is equated with simplicity. In terms of human nature it is equated with being in accord with human nature. By this Chang means "to grant [things] according to what is commonly desired by human desires. [This is] what *The Great Learning* calls 'what the people love, [the ruler] loves; and what the people hate, [the ruler] hates.' " [86]

In using the term "revitalization," Chang means a government of firmness. By "revitalization," he says,

I mean in an orderly and all-inspiring manner to publish the laws in order to reveal them to the people and cause them not to dare transgress them. [This is what] Confucius called "leading the people by means of virtue and regulating them by means of rites." [87]

This differs from "dictatorship," which imposes severe punishments and harsh laws and cruelly uses the people.[88] Presumably, by harsh laws and severe punishments Chang means arbitrarily cruel laws and punishments, or punishments according to laws not made known to the people; for he himself frequently uses the term harsh punishments as something desirable. In a letter to Chou Yu-shen, for example, Chang declared:

When people who lust for bodily pleasures cannot attain their desire they often find that thievery is the only means to do so. Plowing, hoeing, and hard work in the fields and being completely restrained by traditional moral codes are bitter pills in life. . . . If we do not believe that harsh punishments and clear laws can suppress the villainous and instead preach abstention from desire [expecting the people thereby] to cast aside what is pleasurable and follow what is bitter, this can be done only after everyone in the empire is [like] Yu, I, Tseng, and Shih.[89]

Chang's distinctions here are very fine, and were apparently not even clear to his contemporaries, since charges of dictatorship were frequently leveled against him.

While a government of leniency, which resembles benevolence, becomes a haven for exploiters and evil men, firm or strict government is, for Chang, truly benevolent. Such a government would ensure a just distribution of tax burdens, prevent exploitation of legal privileges which increased the burden on the people, and ensure a sufficient income for all, including the state. For Chang, stern government is a loving government,[90] not unlike the compassionate parent who lances the child's abscess to prevent further infection or shaves the baby's head to prevent a recurrence of sores.[91] The assumption is, as it was for Han Fei Tzu (from whom the analogy is borrowed), that the people do not always know what is best for themselves. In a letter to an official in Wu-chung discussing inequality in taxes and labor services in that area, Chang argues that by using repressive measures "the stubborn and the strong of past years will bow their heads and respectfully accept restraint." The people of Wu will then begin to know that there are laws and that regulations will be enforced. "This will be to the good fortune of the people of Wu, but they will not realize it." Moreover, says Chang, strict enforcement of the law is also a matter of self-interest even for the wealthy and powerful who will be restrained by them:

Now, wealth is the storehouse of resentment; profit is the womb of calamity. The ability of the wealthy to keep their wealth, without anyone daring to seize it, depends upon there being the laws of the dynasty. If the wealthy do not apply law to restrain themselves, but [instead] rely upon their wealth and power to fleece [the people] thereby accumulating resentment [toward themselves], the people will also not fear the public law and, cherishing their resentment, will give vent to their anger. If such wealthy men lived in a well-ordered world, the kingly laws would not be lenient [toward them]. In a confused world, they would be the first upon whom great robbers would cast a covetous eye. How could they keep their wealth for long [then]? Now [since the laws are enforced, such persons] uphold the commonweal and obey the laws, release one one-hundredth of their accumulated [wealth] in order to pay their tax arrears of many years past, so that the officials who were sent to press them [for payment] have ceased their operations. The appellation of "mild and docile" is applied to them by the government treasury. Henceforth, they will maintain propriety in order to hold on to their power and obey the law in order to keep their wealth. Even if they have [a pile of] gold and grain [as high as a] mountain, no one will dare cast a covetous eye upon it. To the end of their lives they can enjoy the amenities of their wealth, and their wealth can be passed on to their heirs. This is to their advantage. Is it not also generosity? [92]

People, like a child, concludes Chang, must be compelled to discover what is really in their interest. Left to themselves, they would only follow their ephemeral, capricious, human desires.[93] A government of leniency, which pampers human nature, leads ultimately to conflict among the people. A government of firmness, on the other hand, which may temporarily seem to oppress the people by driving them along the path of their true interest and by restraining their capricious desires, accords with human nature by guaranteeing to all the security of life and prosperity which human nature desires. Such a government is, therefore, truly benevolent. Chang believed that to spare the rod is to spoil the child. Logically, this leads to the position that the state, or he who controls the state, determines the true interest of the people. As Chang's position and power increased he came to conclude that he embodied the interest of the state—and thus of the people—and that criticism of him was therefore an attack upon the state.

Since the best government is a firm government, in Chang's view, the state must always be strong. Only in this way will its authority be recognized *de facto* as well as *de jure*. "If the authority of the state is strong," he said, "all undertakings will be auspicious. If the authority of the state is weak, then all undertakings will turn out badly." [94] He compared state authority with the primal spirit (*yüan-ch'i*) of the human body. If this spirit is vigorous, in times of sickness medicines will be effective; if not vigorous, nothing can prevent death. As applied to the state, the term refers to the laws, institutions, and effective imperial authority. It is the function of the statesman to preserve and nurture the state's "primal spirit" in order to strengthen the state and make its benevolent paternalism effective.

Having determined the desirable nature of the state, in formulating procedural principles for its proper functioning Chang fuses Confucian texts with Legalist techniques.

Turning to "The Great Plan" in the *Book of History*, Chang borrows the sections dealing with the establishment of the royal standard, the reverent practice of the five functions together with the orderly practice of the three virtues, and intensive cultivation of the eight regulations. These Chang cites as "the grand norm for governing the world for ten thousand generations."

As explained in the text and commentaries of the *Book of History*, these principles can justify: 1) the dominance of imperial authority; 2) the people as the basis of the state; 3) an active and vigorous government as the *sine qua non* for providing the people with the institutions and protection necessary for their peace and security and for the preservation of social order; and 4) such techniques as minute investigation of affairs and people to distinguish good from evil; acceptance of advice by the emperor; and the necessity of laws for punishment and execution, as well as the teaching of rules of propriety and righteousness, to prevent the strong and weak from contending.[95] In Chang's thinking, the practice of the three virtues of correctness and straightforwardness, strong rule, and mild rule probably played a dominant role. As the *Book of History* explains these virtues, they mean

In peace and tranquility, correctness and straight-forwardness [must sway]; in violence and disorder, strong rule; in harmony and order, mild rule. For the reserved and retiring there is the strong rule; for the lofty and intelligent there is the mild rule. It belongs only to the sovereign to confer dignities and rewards, to display the terrors of majesty, and to receive the revenues of the kingdom. There should be no such thing as a minister conferring dignities and rewards, displaying the terrors of majesty, or receiving revenues. Such a thing is injurious to the families and fatal to the states;—small officers become one-sided and perverse, and the people commit assumptions and excesses.[96]

Basic to this position is the effective implementation of imperial authority through laws and institutions which are the means of ensuring that the sovereign's authority permeates every aspect of the state. While Chang's emphasis is upon effective authority and not upon the Confucian view that what is required of the emperor is moral excellence, he does not ignore the question of moral principles. His *Ssu-shu chih-chieh* [as] (Correct explanations of the Four Books), written for the education of the young Wan-li Emperor, does not differ in this regard from other Confucian commentaries. Indeed, the book is, for the most part, a stylistically simplified version of Chu

Hsi's commentaries. But Chang distinguishes moral education from administrative expertise. The same distinction is manifest in his advice to Emperor Mu-tsung. Here Chang stresses the emperor's ability to manipulate the administration:

I have heard that in the emperors' and kings' governing of the empire there were great fundamentals and there were urgent tasks. To rectify the heart and cultivate the person, to establish absolutes to serve as models and guides for the ministers and people, [these are] the great fundamentals of realizing good government. To detect the minute [before it becomes big] and to weigh the situation, to adapt governmental policies to suit the people, [these are] the urgent tasks for correcting the times. [But] even if the great fundamentals are established, if one is unable to adapt governmental policies in order to make the administration efficient, [the situation can be] compared to a lute being out of tune.[97]

Since the emperor is head of the state and responsible for its operation, he must be master of the governmental functions. He must give direction to the whole by personally making all decisions after consultation with his ministers and after careful investigation of details. In formulating policies and appointing officials to implement them, both emperor and ministers must remember that nothing is completely good or bad and that all persons have strong points as well as shortcomings. What is important is the proportion of advantage or disadvantage in a particular situation.[98]

To be effective, the emperor must tighten imperial authority. He should not relax the provisions of the laws and must see that they are applied to all regardless of position, for only he is able to make the empire obey and achieve good order, which he does through "the laws and regulations and that is all." It follows logically that it is necessary for the emperor to ensure the implementation of imperial commands among the people and that the emperor alone should have the power to command. Without these two powers, the emperor would be without authority and there would be no law, only chaos.[99]

Laws and commands, while decided upon by the emperor, must be conveyed to the people by officials. To establish laws and to listen to advice is easy, Chang declared. The difficulty lies in being certain that the desired results are actually achieved.[100] The only way to ensure that officials act according to orders, and act effectively, is for the emperor to hold and use the handles of rewards and punishments. "The means by which the ruler of men controls his ministers is by rewards and punishments, promotion or dismissal and that is all." [101] The means by which to ensure a reliable and consistent application of reward and punishment is by checking names against realities. If the emperor does this, he will be assured that the talented men of his day, who do not differ in kind or in number from ancient times, will clamor to serve him and will do so effectively and efficiently.

The sum of Chang's views on government by firmness is given in his advice to Emperor Mu-tsung:

Exercise the decisiveness of imperial firmness [at] and shed brilliance on the empire to illuminate it, tighten the laws and regulations in order to [make] reverential the mass of functionaries, and grasp the reigns of power to make everything correct. In conferring or taking away punishments or rewards, in all cases make [the officials] comply with impartiality and then it will not be necessary to cater crookedly to private [interests] and predilections.[102]

THE CONFUCIAN LEGALIST

Some of Chang Chü-cheng's contemporaries saw him as a Legalist, as Chang himself implies. Specific assertions to this effect are absent from the earliest biographical accounts,[103] but Wang Shih-chen,[au] who knew Chang personally, states that Chang "was fond of the laws of Shen Pu-hai and Han Fei." [104] The *Ming-shu*, which, with trivial exceptions, is identical with Wang's biography of Chang repeats the statement,[105] but the *Ming-shih kao* and *Ming shih* do not. Several modern scholars have revived this characterization. Ch'en I-lin, for example, writes that "although Chang came to power as a Confucian, he deeply understood that only Legalism could save the situation." [106]

Chang does express ideas that have been generally associated with the classical Legalists. Yet these ideas were not peculiar to the Legalists. Many can be traced to Taoists, Confucius, Hsün Tzu, and Mencius. Many were ideas widely held among followers of the Pragmatists (*kung-li*)[av] of Sung, the school of Neo-Confucianism which stood apart from the Ch'eng-Chu school. Li Hsien-chih, in a recent study of Li Chih,[108] even characterizes Chang as a pragmatist (*shih-hsing chia*).[aw]

The most obvious Legalist ideas in Chang are his emphasis upon rewards and punishments, and checking the correspondence between names and reality.[109] The criterion for checking names against realities is dynastic law, strict adherence to which was the basis for consistent application of rewards and punishments. The basis for the conduct of government is thus for Chang the objective standard of dynastic laws rather than an ethical standard. Not that he denies the relevance of ethical considerations; he simply makes law the basis without which morality would be ineffective. "Without checking names against realities," he declared, "even if a Yao or Shun were on the throne with Yü and Kao as assistants, it would be difficult to bring things to a conclusion and achieve results." [110]

A number of scholars, both ancient and modern,[111] have pointed to the Confucian-Legalist amalgam that developed in Han and post-Han times and to the tensions this fusion created. Hsiao Kung-ch'uan, in a recent study, concludes that, as a result of this marriage, autocracy was imbued with moral values and placed on a secure footing. Confucianism became autocracy's conscience and as such played an important role in humanizing the state and society.

Other Chinese statesmen reflect views identical to those of Chang and like him have been characterized as Legalists. They found it necessary to commit themselves totally to dynastic institutions in order to be effective, but saw no necessary contradiction in trying to make these serve Confucian ends. Chang himself saw this polarity as the essence of at least the Han and Ming dynasties and found no contradiction therein. In a statement reminiscent of Wang An-shih and Ch'en Liang of the Sung dynasty, Chang's answer to his critics was that the distinction between the way of the king and that of the hegemon lay in their motivation:

When Confucius opened his mouth to discuss government, he said "sufficiency of food" and "sufficiency of weapons." Shun ordered the twelve shepherds, saying: "Food! Take care for its timeliness." Chou Kung, in establishing the government, said "You should be able to manage your armor and weapons." How could I not desire the enrichment [of the state] and the strengthening [of the army]? The scholarship of later generations does not enlighten and [the scholar's] high-flown arguments are without reality. They make a show of *jen* and *i* and call it "the way of the king." If one is concerned with enriching [the state] and strengthening [the army], then they call it "the technique of the hegemon." They do not know that the distinction between king and hegemon, between righteousness and utility lies in the intentions and not in the effects. Why must *jen* and *i* be kingly, while enriching [the state] and strengthening [the army] are hegemonic? [112]

An even more precise statement of Chang's view of the Confucian–Legalist interrelationship, and a demonstration of his most basic difference with Legalism as such, is found in his conception of law and punishments.

In Han and post-Han Confucianism, law and punishments and the Confucian emphasis upon moral influence had been interrelated and made interdependent. Law and punishments emerged as the handmaidens of the moral order which was primary.[113] No less a Confucian than Chu Hsi asserts this relationship in his commentary on the chapter Conducting Government in the *Analects*.[114] Chang's commentary on the same chapter repeats Chu Hsi with some amplification:

Cheng [ax] means laws and ordinances. It is the means by which to rectify those who are unrectified. . . . What Confucius said [was that] the sovereign occupies a place above the ten thousand people. If he desires all to return to rectitude, he must have laws and regulations, prohibitions and ordinances in order to govern them. This is called "conducting government." However, if [the sovereign] does not devote attention to cultivating virtue as the basis of conducting government, then he is himself unrectified. How can he rectify [other] people? Even if there were ordinances, they would not be followed. Therefore, the sovereign in conducting government [should] desire only in his personal conduct actually to carry it out in order to lead them by his personal example.[115]

In another essay, Chang also wrote that laws, ordinances, regulations, and punishments are essential for governing; rules of propriety are to prohibit violations from occurring; and law is applied after misconduct. To enforce rules of propriety and righteousness, he wrote, is to enlighten the people. If education in ethical conduct does not prevail and virtue is not established, the rules of propriety and music cannot flourish and punishments will not be pertinent.[116] Moral education and observable example must be coupled with force in order to achieve uniformity. Legalist techniques may be used, but the motivation is still Confucian.

Chang also departs from pure Legalism by adhering to the Confucian conception of the purpose of the state, which is to promote the well-being of the people and enable them to pursue the perfection of virtue. The state should be a benevolent despotism, for the way to help the people—to be truly benevolent—is to enforce the laws rigidly, thus ensuring a fair distribution of burdens. Moreover, he would argue, the despotic state is acceptable to the people because in a properly functioning state the interests of the people and the state are identical and mutually dependent. Only when the state is wealthy and strong, he says, can both the people and the state derive the income necessary for security and for encouraging the teaching of righteousness and the rules of propriety.

If the door to private interests is closed, then the public house will be strengthened. Therefore, to punish avaricious officials is the means by which to [ensure] a sufficiency for the people. To clear away tax arrears is the means by which to [ensure] a sufficiency for the state. [To guarantee that] officials and people both have a sufficiency and that both above and below are benefited is the means by which to plan for the strengthening of the foundation of the state, to maintain peace [within] and expel aggression [from without], to encourage the custom of frugality, and to encourage the teaching of the rules of propriety and righteousness.[117]

Like the reformers and pragmatists of Sung, Chang believed that one must take human nature as it is with its desire to seek pleasure and avoid pain. This is no doubt the reason for his emphasis on rewards and punishments. Like Mencius and the Sung pragmatists, he gives much greater emphasis to wealth and strength than do conventional Confucianists:

When wealth is insufficient, contention arises; when faith is short, falsehood appears. Contention and falsehood are the assistants of great villains. What do we use to guard the narrow passes on our frontier? We use men. What do we use to gather men? We use money. Hence, propriety and morality begin when money is sufficient. Then, even if there are great villains and bandits, they will not dare take a chance and attack.[118]

Or again:

> Confucius in discussing government first mentioned [the necessity of] sufficient food [for the people]. Kuan tzu was assistant to a hegemon. He also said that propriety and righteousness are born of wealth and sufficiency.[119]

But Chang goes further, for he equates economic policies with specific moral qualities. He writes:

> not to spare labor and expense to establish profit for a hundred generations approaches righteousness. To accumulate [wealth] and be able to disperse it approaches wisdom. Not to brag about one's merit approaches sincerity.[120]

THE REJECTION OF MING SCHOLARSHIP

Chang Chü-cheng saw himself as a Confucian but drew a distinction between himself and other contemporary Confucians. His utilitarianism, relativism, and statecraft already set him apart from the more conventional Confucians; but the basic distinction he drew was between "empty discussion" and "the pursuit of reality." For Chang, true Confucianism lay in the latter and contemporary scholarship was a distortion of the original eminently practical Confucianism.

Chang's approach to learning is best reflected in a letter to his son recalling his unsuccessful attempt in the 1544 *chin-shih* examination.[121] "If one wants to seek out the precepts of the ancients and join them to present developments," he wrote, "only a person of exceptional talent can do so, and ever since the beginning of the Ming [dynasty] not many [such persons] have been seen." As a youth, he continued, he felt that many famous scholars had been ordinary men, "so I abandoned studies of the Sung commentaries and the eight-legged essay (*pen-yeh*)[ay] and hastened to the [study of] ancient institutions and regulations." After 1544, however, Chang returned to the "former path." He does not record here that he had also become interested in Buddhism, taking instruction from Li Chung-ch'i.[az] In a letter to Li he once noted that "when I was young, I studied Tao (*hsüeh-tao*)[ba] and harbored thoughts of escaping from the world. I was, however, restrained by the times and have since been managing affairs among people." [122]

After having passed his *chin-shih* examination, Chang did not abandon his earlier interests. His biographers all note that after receiving in 1547 this degree and an appointment in the Hanlin Academy, then headed by Hsü Chieh, who acted as his "tutor" and later as his political mentor, Chang rejected the common practice of discussing poetry and writing essays modeled after those of Han and T'ang and devoted himself to "seeking out past affairs of the state and the essentials of governmental matters (*ku-tien*)." [bb] [123] From this study emerged his dictum: "Learning which does not examine nature (*hsing*)[bc] and destiny (*ming*)[bd] cannot be called learning. If principles are not combined with practical matters (*ching-chi*)[be] they cannot be profitably applied." [124]

Chang regularly characterized the scholars of his day as decadent, unrealistic, impractical, intellectually partisan, reactionary, and guilty of perpetuating irrelevant dregs. He was especially critical of the spread of the academies. While economic and political motives may also have been involved in Chang's attempted suppression of this movement, his intellectual outlook certainly reinforced his decision. As we have seen, for Chang the *raison d'etre* of study and knowledge was their application to state affairs. To charges that he was anti-intellectual, Chang replied:

Truly this is a great slander. I am now one who assists a brilliant sovereign. How [could I] in a single word or in a single matter turn my back on the Way of Yao, Shun, Chou [kung], and Confucius? But in what I do, I wholeheartedly want personally and vigorously to carry it out. Therefore, those who [engage in] empty discussions cannot be tolerated.[125]

Chang's goal in his total integration of knowledge and practical action was to "reform the intellectual world by reintegrating it into the existing institutional and political order." [126]

Knowledge for Chang was the product of the investigation of phenomena. It was not gained intuitively. His emphasis is upon the principle inherent in affairs as well as in things. He expresses this position in a letter to a provincial official regarding the necessity of studying practical matters:

In studying, once one knows the method, one must investigate practical matters. . . . Now, as to human nature and the principle of things, although [some people] say that intuition can illuminate them, yet, after all, this is [like] looking at the flowers through a gauze window. . . . The sages were able to make all under heaven to be one family and the Middle [Kingdom] to be one person. They did not merely think about it. [In considering something] one must thoroughly understand its parts and its difficulties and only then can it be undertaken. If human nature and the principle of things are not understood, it is exactly because the study was not thorough. Confucius said, "The way is not far from man." Now, I cannot stand those who take empty opinions as implicit proof.[127]

Chang probably had in mind those of the Wang Yang-ming school who had come to believe that study in any form was unnecessary. While this might be argued in ethical matters, the theory would be dangerous if applied to the practical world. Chang's position also supports the usual Neo-Confucian insistence on study. Indeed, in his Correct Commentary on the Four Books, Chang specifically endorses Chu Hsi's interpretation of the passage "extension of knowledge through the investigation of things." [128] Yet, in spite of his support of Chu Hsi in this matter, Chang condemns discussions of the doctrines of Chou Tun-i, the Ch'eng brothers, Chang Tsai, and Chu Hsi as "all the remnant practices of the evil ministers and traitors of the Sung period and the remnant arguments of old Confucians and the decadent." [129] He recommends that scholars "attain to the principle (li)[bf] in phenomena (shih)[bg] and then they will understand the doctrines of Confucius." [130]

Chang also attempted to shift attention away from ethical and metaphysical speculation and turn it to practical matters. Unlike Chu Hsi, who was concerned in his investigation of things with ethical principles and ethical insight, Chang was concerned with a knowledge of external relationships and causes. Some of Chang's statements, however, indicate a much more complex situation than might appear at first glance. Concepts derived from Buddhism provided him with a metaphysical foundation for his approach to both politics and knowledge.

Chang had studied Buddhism; but he rejected the life of pure contemplation and fused the concepts found in Hua-yen Buddhism with his activist instincts. In a letter probably written in 1567, he said, "By chance I read the *Hua-yen pei-chih ch'i* [bh] and I had an inspiration and made a vow. I vowed to serve the world and not seek profit and advantage for myself." [131] The original inspiration for this Boddhisattva ideal of service to mankind may not have been his discovery of this book. In later life, faced with criticism of himself and his policies, Chang recalled that as a very young man he had "vowed to use my body as a mat and let people sleep on me. Even if they were to urinate on me and dirty me, I would not stop." [132] The vow is reminiscent of the charge given to him by his great-grandfather.[133] One might also suspect that Chang's frequent assertions of a selfless devotion to mankind were but egotistical equations of the well-being of mankind with his own political dominance and an excuse to suppress criticism. While this may in part be true, the evidence still suggests that he was a devout Buddhist,[134] and his reference to the Hua-yen teaching is a rare personal acknowledgment of specific intellectual influences.

Hua-yen Buddhism accepted the phenomenal world as absolute.[135] This position derived from the theory that all dharmas are empty. Emptiness has two aspects—static as principle and dynamic as phenomenon. Therefore, principle and phenomenon are interfused unimpededly and all phenomena are mutually identified with each other, representing the absolute mind or principle in its totality. Since all phenomena are manifestations of the one ultimate principle, they are in perfect harmony with each other. "All things in the universe, animate and inanimate, are representations of the same supreme mind, and can perform the work of the Blessed One." [136] This is a totalistic system with everything leading to one point— Buddha—in the center. It thus provides a religious sanction for totalitarianism.

Chang has not given us any systematic discussion of Hua-yen doctrines, but their influence on his thought seems clear. In a letter to Hu Lu-shan, Chang wrote,

Now [being] empty [in the proper sense, one is] therefore able to respond; [being] quiescent [in the true manner, one is] therefore able to be stimulated. The [*Book of*] *Changes* says, "The superior man receives people by virtue of emptiness; he is quiescent and does not move; but when he is stimulated, he comprehends all situations under heaven." If one is truly empty and truly quiescent, one will be adequate to meet all situations. Simply because [contemporary scholars] do not make efforts to gain [knowledge as something with which] one truly identifies oneself—because they do not understand that phenomena and principles are identical, being different names for the same manifestation [of reality]—and seek only what they call "emptiness" and "quietude" in sheer abstraction, it is to be expected that [what they have is] "vast but unrelated to reality" and that they [find themselves] obstructed and uncomprehending.[137]

The realm of true emptiness is where principle and phenomena are one. In practice, this gave Chang a basis for complete detachment without regard for commonly accepted standards of right and wrong. The moral subjectivism in Chang's thought is nowhere better illustrated than in his statement:

In recent days in quietude I realized that the basic substance of the mind (*hsin-t'i*)[bi] is originally clean and bright and without the slightest corruption. The dirt and suffering are self-inflicted. If one understands this principle, then everything can be made understandable and becomes wisdom and everything can be done in good conscience. Consequently, by not giving rise to a pure heart, not giving rise to a defiled heart, not giving rise to an attached heart, and not giving rise to a detached heart, one can encompass the world and there are no obstacles.[138]

Chang's subjectivism, like that of the followers of Wang Yang-ming, provided him with a strong sense of independence and of the validity of individual judgments and efforts. "Throughout my life," he wrote, "I have learned to take my own mind as a guide and not seek for what others know. The censure or praise of one time does not worry me; the approval or condemnation of all times is also something I do not consider." [139] He thus criticized the practices of commenting on texts, appealing to authority, and relying on others for one's beliefs. One should rely upon personal judgments in deciding truth. He also disavowed any intention to impose "praise or blame" upon facts. Facts are valuable in themselves and any value judgment should emerge from the material itself.[140] His call to scholars is thus for independence in one's study.

The subjectivism and self-reliance in Chang's thought gives him a common ground with members of Wang Yang-ming's school. Indeed, some scholars have pointed to specific intellectual influences. Li Hsien-chih has argued that Chang had a great influence on Li Chih.

Chang once wrote to Nieh Pao that "in studying, one should rely upon the mind for penetrating explanations. If one follows another person blindly, this is just what the Buddhists mean when they say 'to examine exhaustively another's excellences will not in the end make them part of oneself.' " [141] Chu Tung-jun concludes that the first part of Chang's statement was in the philosophical tradition of Wang Yang-ming's idealism.[142] On another occasion, while discussing philosophy, Chang wrote:

Since Confucius died, trifling discussions have reached the extreme. Students are immersed in observing and hearing irrelevant dregs, people support strange views, and each displays his theory of the world. Therefore, the study of cultivating oneself, rectifying the heart, of the true and valid, has disappeared and the study of epigraphy and stylish writing flourishes. There were various Sung scholars who strongly condemned these evil practices but argumentation daily became extreme. Although they are called great scholars of vast learning, they labor to old age without exhausting matters, while independent scholars are frequently, on the contrary, considered by the world as something laughable. Alas! if learning is not based on the mind but is borrowed from without in order to benefit oneself, then [I can] only observe that the more one labors the more one is ruined.[143]

T'ao Hsi-sheng observes that the concluding remark in this passage "comes close to the essentials of Yang-ming's philosophy." [144]

In a poem on the Seven Worthies, Chang wrote:

They followed their own inclinations,
    and in the path they followed
    They did not take the same road. . . .
But one who walks alone does not harbor regrets
    [Even though] he will sink into oblivion
    for a thousand years.
Those who are alone do not feel depressed
    because their hearts are satisfied.
They roam beyond ordinary beings.

He continues by arguing that the *yü-lan* does not lose its fragrance because no one picks it, nor does jade lose its brilliance because it lies undiscovered in dark caves.[145]

Chang's position is, then, that one should be inner-directed and not concerned with the opinion of others in determining one's course of conduct toward what is, after all, a common goal; and that the goodness of something exists independent of a perceiver. This tends to indicate that Chang's subjectivism is not based on Wang's subjective idealism but on the objective idealism of Hua-yen doctrines, which holds that an objective world exists independent of a subject and all things in the objective world are manifestations of one all-embracing absolute mind.[146] It is in this light, then, that we can understand Chang's statement that "having confidence in my own mind and relying upon what is genuine [in me], I seek the one idea that is original and primary." [147]

The differences between Chang and the Wang school should not obscure the common elements in their outlook and what this reveals about the Ming state and society at the time. After all, even Li Chih had a great deal of praise for Chang.[148] But one difference is critical. Confined as it was to the intellectual realm, Li Chih's relativism and subjectivism led toward personal freedom. Chang's relativism and subjectivism, carried out in the practical world of politics, led, contrarily, to a statism best expressed in his own words:

Every time I think about my motives in acting for the state and being a scholar-official, I personally know I am sincere and single-minded. In making decisions, I may not agree with prevalent customs but the essential thing is my desire to fulfill my motive of acting for the state and being a scholar-official.[149]

CONCLUSION

There is something of the tragic in Chang's thought and career. His overwhelming concern was for the preservation of the dynasty. He did not, however, attempt to explain, even to himself, why the Ming dynasty with all its problems was still appropriate to the time and should not also pass into history, leaving to its successor the best products of its experience as earlier dynasties had done. His relativism and subjectivism, his philosophy of history and of change were all aimed at a revitalization of the dynasty, but this entailed the preservation of institutions and practices of which even he had been critical. His philosophy of history led him to the belief that a "law of reversal" operated in the historical process, and one of his great concerns was the place of the individual in that process. He objected alike to strict determinism and to any suggestion that external forces played no part in restricting man's ability to guide his own destiny. He had a considerable faith in the ability of the independent and self-reliant individual to control his own fate by his will. But he was also careful to temper his optimism by recognizing the necessity for a stoic acceptance of the consequences, good or bad, of one's actions, and he defined this acceptance as righteousness.[150] In adhering to these positions during the course of his life Chang emerges as a tragic figure. All the biographical sources and Chang's own writings agree in picturing him as a hero selflessly battling to stem the tide of dynastic decay. Yet he was more constrained by historical developments than he realized. In his own terms, he was struggling against the point of no return in his law of reversal. Eunuchs, cliques, corruption in the army and the government, and powerful interests inside and outside the court were so entrenched that little could be done to solve the problems. Paradoxically, his convictions and his efforts led him to attempt a revitalization of the centralism and authoritarianism which were, to a large extent, root causes of the very decline he fought to avert. More specifically, his policies and conduct did much to create the character of the Wan-li Emperor, the clique struggles that followed immediately upon Chang's death, and the consequent growth of eunuch power. Toward the end of his tenure as chief grand secretary—and of his life— even he began to realize that he might quite well become a victim of the very system he idealized. Yet he persisted in his policies. In the end, although dying a natural death, he was indeed victimized by the forces he had held in check for ten years.

NOTES

1. Chang T'ing-yü, *et al.*, *Ming-shih* (SPPY ed.), 213/8a–14a. (Hereafter cited as MS.) See also *Index to Eighty-nine Ming Dynasty Biographical Collections* (Peking: Chung-hua Publishing Co., 1959), V, 78 (hereafter cited as *Index*) and Robert B. Crawford, *The Life and Thought of Chang Chü-cheng, 1525–1582*, (University of Washington, unpublished PhD dissertation).

2. Chang Chü-cheng, *Chang-wen-chung kung ch'üan-chi* (Kuo-hsüeh chi-pen ts'ung-shu ed.; Shanghai: Commercial Press, 1937). This is a punctuated edition. All items used have been checked against other editions. Hereafter cited as CW.

3. Liang Ch'i-ch'ao, *Intellectual Trends in the Ch'ing Period*, trans. by Immanuel C. Y. Hsü (Cambridge: Harvard University Press, 1959), pp. 19–48. See also David S. Nivison, *The Life and Thought of Chang Hsüeh-ch'eng (1738–1801)* (Stanford University Press, 1966), for some interesting parallels in thought.

4. Cf. above, p. 22.

5. CW, "Letters," 11/417–18.

6. John T. Meskill, *A Record of Drifting Across the Sea. P'yohae rok* (University of Arizona Press, 1965), p. 112.

7. CW, "Letters," 3/262–63.

8. See for example, *ibid.*, "Essays," 8/636.

9. Wang Yang-ming, *Instructions for Practical Living and Other Neo-Confucian Writings*, trans. by Wing-tsit Chan (New York, 1963; Frederick G. Henke, *The Philosophy of Wang Yang-ming* (London: The Open Court Publishing Co., 1916); Hsiao Kung-ch'üan, "Li Chih: An Iconoclast of the Sixteenth Century," *Tien-hsia Monthly*, Vol. 6, No. 4 (1938). See also Hsiao's biography of Li Chih in Draft Ming Biographies, No. 7, 1967. See also Heinrich Busch, "The Tung-lin Academy and Its Political and Philosophical Significance," *Monumenta Serica*, Vol. XIV (1949–55); and Professor de Bary's introduction, above, infra, p. 32.

10. Some of these differences are noted below.

11. MS, 213/1b–5a; *Index*, III, 28.

12. MS, 202/7b–8a; *Index*, II, 290.

13. In Chang's letters he is referred to by his *hao*, Keng Ch'u-tung. MS, 221/3b–4a; *Index*, III, 184.

14. T'ao Hsi-sheng, *Chung-kuo cheng-chih ssu-hsiang shih* (Peking: New Life Publishing Co., 1935), IV, 347, quoting Chi Wen-fu, *Tso-p'ai Wang-hsüeh*. On Ho Hsin-yin, see *Ming-shih kao*, 285/20b (here-

after cited as *MSK*); see also *Ho Hsin-yin chi* (Peking: Chung-hua Publishing Co., 1960), pp. 1–115.

15. Kao Kung, 1511–1578; *chin-shih* 1541. See *MS*, 213/5a–8a; *Index*, II, 167; Chi Wen-fu, *Wan-ming ssu-hsiang shih-lun* (Shanghai: Commercial Press, 1944).

16. *CW*, "Letters," 11/417–18.

17. *Ibid.*, "Essays," 11/672.

18. *Ibid.*, "Letters," 9/386–87.

19. *MSK*, 197/15a; Fu Wei-lin, *Ming-shu* (Chi-fu ts'ung-shu ed.), 150/10a, 15a.

20. *CW*, "Letters," 11/422.

21. *MS*, 213/8b.

22. *Ibid.*, 213/8a.

23. *CW*, "Letters," 9/306–7; Yang To, comp., *Chang Chiang-ling nien-p'u* (Shanghai: Commercial Press, 1938), p. 118.

24. *CW*, "Essays," 9/651.

25. *Ibid.*, "Letters," 10/403; 12/438.

26. *Ibid.*, "Essays," 11/674.

27. *Ibid.*, "Essays," 11/675.

28. *Ibid.*, "Essays," 3/551–52.

29. Sang Hung-yang, 152–80 B.C. He came from a wealthy merchant family of Lo-yang and at thirteen became a palace attendant. He then became an official in charge of grain in the Ministry of Agriculture, when K'ung Chin was minister. In 110 B.C. he was made acting minister of agriculture, in charge of the monopolies, to replace K'ung Chin. He became minister of agriculture in 100 B.C. Subsequently, he was made grandee secretary and was holding this position when he was called upon to defend the government's monopolies in 81 B.C. Cf. Esson M. Gale, trans., *Discourses on Salt and Iron, passim*; Swann, *Food and Money in Ancient China*, pp. 40, 63, 64–68, 271–72, 285, 314, 317–21; S. C. Chen, "Sang Hung-yang, Economist of Early Han," *JRASNCB*, LXVII (1936), 16–70.

K'ung Chin was an iron merchant from Nan-yang. Along with Tung-kuo Hsien-yang, he was appointed an assistant in the Ministry of Agriculture in 120 B.C. In 117 B.C., they proposed the salt and iron monopolies and were placed in charge of them. He became minister of agriculture in 115 B.C. and held that office until replaced by Sang Hung-yang. Cf. Swann, *Food and Money . . .* , 63, 271–72, 275, 277, 285, 311, 314, 337, 347n, 412; Gale, *Discourses . . .* , 55, 65, 86.

Ts'ui Liang. For his biography see *Wei-shu*, 66. He was for ten years in charge of the selection and promotion of officials in the Board of Civil Offices.

Yang Yen, 727–81. The tax system referred to here was introduced in 780 and ended the "equalized land distribution" system initiated at the beginning of the T'ang dynasty. Yen's tax system continued down to mid-Ming, when the single-whip tax was introduced. For his biography, see *Hsin T'ang-shu*, 145; Giles, *Biographical Dictionary*, No. 2417, pp. 917–18.

30. *CW*, "Essays," 3/552.
31. *Ibid.*, 3/553.
32. *Ibid.*, 3/547.
33. *Ibid.*, 9/651.
34. *Ibid.*, "Memorials," 12/175–78; *Nien-p'u*, 7–11.
35. *Ibid.*, "Letters," 12/438.
36. *Ibid.*, "Memorials," 1/1–8. See also "Essays," 11/687–88; 11/678.
37. *Ibid.*, 11/675.
38. *Ibid.*, 11/673–74.
39. *Ibid.*, 6/601. Chang is here quoting Chia I's "Fu-niao" *fu* as given in his *Han shu* biography. Cf. *Ch'ien Han shu*, 48/3a. This *fu* is translated by Richard Wilhelm in *Die Chinesische Literatur* (Potsdam, 1926), pp. 111–112, and by Giles in *Adversaria Sinica*, II, No. 1, pp. 1–10.
40. *CW*, "Essays," 6/602.
41. *Ibid.*, 11/673.
42. *Ibid.*, 6/602.
43. Chang may here be referring to the *Shih-chi*, where Ch'in is spoken of as having prepared the way for Han. Cf. *Shih-chi hui-chu k'ao-teng*, 16/3a.
44. Kung Yü, 123–43 B.C. He rose to the position of grandee secretary under Emperor Yüan of Han and was one of the most influential Confucians at this time of the triumph of Confucianism. For his biography, see *Ch'ien Han shu*, 72/6a–9b; Giles, *Biographical Dictionary*, No. 1037, p. 397; Homer Dubs, tr., *History of the Former Han*, II, 285–91. Chang's criticism of Kung Yü makes it clear that "elegance" or "ornateness" does not refer to lavishness at court, since Kung Yü was instrumental in securing a number of reforms to reduce court expenditures.
45. *CW*, "Essays," 11/675.
46. *Ibid.*, 3/551.
47. *Ibid.*, "Letters," 8/346. For similar statements see James Legge, tr., *The Texts of Taoism* (New York: The Julian Press, 1959), pp. 406–7; J. J. L. Duyvendak, *The Book of Lord Shang* (London, 1928), pp. 172–73.
48. *CW*, "Essays," 3/551–53.
49. Cf. Homer Dubs, tr., *The Works of Hsüntze* (London, 1927), pp.

110, 73–75. But Hsün Tzu's position differs from Chang's. For Hsün Tzu, it is a question only of lack of material for thoroughly understanding the periods of antiquity; and he takes the position that history is static. In Chang's view, history is dynamic. One cannot follow the past because ancient and modern times differ in nature.

50. *CW,* "Essays," 3/551.

51. *Ibid.,* 11/671.

52. Chan, tr., *Instructions for Practical Living,* pp. 42–43.

53. Chia I, 200–168 B.C. Bodde, *China's First Unifier* (Leiden, 1938), p. 6, gives his dates as 198–165. Swann, *Food and Money . . . ,* p. 28, gives them as 201–169. See Wm. Theodore de Bary, *et al., Sources of Chinese Tradition,* pp. 166–68; see also *Ch'ien Han shu,* 48/1a–15b. For several of his memorials, see Swann, pp. 152–57, 233–39. See also Burton Watson, tr., *Records of the Grand Historian of China* (Columbia University Press, 1961), I, 508–16.

Ch'ao Tso, d. 154 B.C. His biography in *Ch'ien Han shu* records that he studied the laws of Shen Pu-hai and Shang Yang. While in the Ministry of Ceremonies, Ch'ao Ts'o was sent to study the *Book of History* under Fu Sheng and is thus often cited as an example of a statesman who covered Legalism with Confucianism. See *Ch'ien Han shu,* 49/4a–13b; Watson, tr., *Records . . . ,* I, 527–32; Giles, *Biographical Dictionary,* No. 204, pp. 85–86.

Wei Hsiang, lieutenant chancellor under Emperor Hsüan of Han. His biography says he was stern and implies that his philosophy, like that of Chia I and Ch'ao Ts'o, was a fusion of Legalist and Confucianist principles. See *Ch'ien Han-shu,* 74/1a–9a.

54. *CW,* "Essays," 3/551.

55. *Ibid.,* 5/307.

56. *Ibid.,* 11/676.

57. *Ibid.,* 6/598.

58. *Ibid.,* "Letters," 9/379.

59. *Ibid.,* 9/384. For the quotation from the "Hsüeh-chi" in the *Li-chi,* or *Books of Rites,* see Legge, tr., *Li Ki (The Sacred Books of the East,* Vols. XXVII–XXVIII), p. 85. Legge translates the passage as "In all learning, for him who would be an officer the first thing is (the knowledge of) business; for scholars the first thing is the directing of the mind."

60. *CW,* "Letters," 9/384. For the statement by Confucius, see Legge, tr., *The Chinese Classics,* I, 410.

61. *CW,* "Letters," 9/379.

62. *Ibid.,* 9/384–85.

63. *Ibid.*

64. Hsiao Kung-ch'uan, *Chung-kuo cheng-chih ssu-hsiang shih* (Taipei: Chung-kuo hsin-wen Publishing Co., 1954), IV, 539.

65. *CW*, "Letters," 9/385.

66. *Ibid.*, "Essays," 6/591.

67. *Ibid.*, 6/591–92.

68. *Ibid.*, "Essays," 6/591–94.

69. *Ibid.*, 6/591–92.

70. *Ibid.*, 6/592–93.

71. *Ibid.*, "Memorials," 1/3. Chang is paraphrasing Han Yü's "Yuan-tao."

72. *Ibid.*, "Letters," 9/375–76. Chang is specifically criticizing Confucius' statement to Chi-k'ang: "If you, sir, were not covetous, although you should reward them to do it, they would not steal." See Legge, tr., *Chinese Classics*, I, 258.

73. *CW*, "Essays," 9/650. See also *CW*, "Letters," 15/512–14.

74. *Ibid.*, "Essays," 11/674–75.

75. *Ibid.*, 3/548. The three quotations from the *Book of Changes* are found, respectively, in the *I ching* (German trans. by Richard Wilhelm, rendered into English by Cary F. Baynes; 2 vols., New York: Pantheon Books, 1950), I, 51, II, 80; I, 52, II, 81; I, 53, II, 82.

76. *CW*, "Essays," 3/549–50.

77. Hsiao, *Chung-kuo cheng-chih ssu-hsiang shih*, IV, 539–40.

78. *CW*, "Letters," 14/491.

79. Hsiao, *Chung-kuo cheng-chih ssu-hsiang shih*, IV, 539–40.

80. *CW*, "Letters," 3/262.

81. *Ibid.*, "Memorials," 1/3.

82. *Ibid.*, "Essays," 3/552.

83. *Ibid.*, 6/592.

84. *Ibid.*, 11/675.

85. *Ibid.*, 11/676.

86. *Ibid.*, "Memorials," 1/3. For Chang's quotation see Legge, tr., *Chinese Classics*, I, 374.

87. *CW*, "Memorials," 1/3. For the quotation, see Legge, tr., *Chinese Classics*, I, 146.

88. *CW*, "Memorials," 1/3.

89. *Ibid.*, "Letters," 9/375. See also "Essays," 11/679.

90. Chang's position in this regard is reminiscent of Kuo Yen's declaration that "The law is an expression of love for the people," Duyvendak, tr., *The Book of Lord Shang*, p. 169, and note 5. See also Legge, tr., *Chinese Classics*, III, 39, for a similar statement by Shun.

91. *CW*, "Letters," 9/378. Chang quotes here Han Fei's "Hsien-hsüeh" (W. K. Liao, tr., *The Complete Works of Han Fei Tzu*, II, 309).

92. *CW*, "Letters," 9/378.
93. *Ibid.*, "Essays," 3/551.
94. *Ibid.*, 11/674.
95. *Ibid.*, 11/672. See Legge, tr., *The Chinese Classics*, III, 324–44.
96. Legge, tr., *Chinese Classics*, III, 333–34.
97. *CW*, "Memorials," 1/1.
98. *Nien-p'u*, p. 114.
99. *CW*, "Memorials," 1/2–4.
100. *Nien-p'u*, p. 115.
101. *Ibid.*, p. 114.
102. *CW*, "Memorials," 1/3.
103. Cf. Kuo T'ing-hsün, *Pen-ch'ao fen-sheng jen-wu k'ao* (author's preface undated; preface by Ch'en Chi-ju dated 1622), *chuan* 7–8.
104. Wang Shih-chen, *Chia-ching i-lai shou fu chuan* (Lo-shu shan-fang ts'ung-shu ed.), 79/20b–27b, in *Chih-hai* (Shanghai: Ta-t'ung Book Co., 1935).
105. *Ming-shu*, 150/13b–14a.
106. Ch'en I-lin, *Chang Chü-cheng p'ing-chuan* (Shanghai: Chung-hua Book Co., 1944), p. 111. See also Chi Wen-fu, *Tso-p'ai Wang-hsüeh*.
107. Hsiao, *Chung-kuo cheng-chih ssu-hsiang*, IV, 449–81.
108. Li Hsien-chih, *Li Chih shih-liu shih-chi chung-kuo fan feng-chien ssu-hsiang te hsien-ch'ü che* (Wuhan: Hupei People's Publishing Society, 2d ed., 1957), pp. 32–33.
109. *Nien-p'u*, p. 114.
110. *CW*, "Memorials," 3/40.
111. For the views of Ssu-ma Ch'ien and Pan Ku, see Robert B. Crawford, "The Social and Political Philosophy of the *Shih-chi*," *JAS*, XXII (No. 4, 1963), 401–16; Dubs, *A History of the Former Han Dynasty*, II, 301. For Chu Hsi, see Carsun Chang, *The Development of Neo-Confucianism* (New York, 1957), I, 318. Yeh Tzu-ch'i of Ming recognized this amalgam. Cf. Vincent Shih, "Some Chinese Rebel Ideologies," *T'oung Pao*, XLIV (Nos. 1–3, 1956), 196. For Huang Tsung-hsi's view, see Wm. Theodore de Bary, *A Plan for the Prince: The Ming-i tai-fang lu* of Huang Tsung-hsi (Columbia University PhD dissertation, 1953), pp. 154–56. See also Ku Yen-wu, *Jih chih-lu* (Shanghai: Wan-yu wen-k'u ed., 1934), 13/2b. For modern scholars, see, for example, Hsiao Kung-ch'üan, "Legalism and Autocracy in Traditional China," *Tsing Hua Journal of Chinese Studies*, New Series, IV (No. 2, February, 1964), 108–22; Charles O. Hucker, "Confucianism and the Chinese Censorial System," in David S. Nivison and Arthur F. Wright, eds., *Confucianism in Action*, p. 15; Benjamin Schwartz, "Some Polarities in Confucian Thought," *ibid.*, pp. 50–62.

112. *CW*, "Letters," 11/417–18. For Chang's quotations, see, respectively, Legge, tr., *Chinese Classics*, I, 254; *Ibid.*, III, 42, where it is translated as "The food!—it depends on observing the seasons"; Karlgren, tr., *The Book of Documents*, p. 68. Chang's references to "the way of the king" and "the technique of the hegemon" are probably not a quotation from any work in particular but rather a statement of the general argument over the difference between a government of *wang* or *pa*. See Chang, *Development*, I, 316–17, for Ch'en Liang's views.

113. See Hsiao, "Legalism and Autocracy"; Ch'ü T'ung-tsu, *Law and Society in Traditional China* (Paris: Mouton and Co., 1961), pp. 226–79.

114. Chu Hsi, *Ssu-shu chi-chu* (Shanghai: Commercial Press, 1933–35), "Lun-yü," 1/4b.

115. Chang Chü-cheng, *et al.*, *Ssu-shu chih-chieh* (microfilm copy of the edition in the Library of Congress), 4/23b–24a. See also *Ibid.*, 4/25a–26b.

116. *CW*, "Essays," 9/651–52.

117. *Ibid.*, "Letters," 6/320.

118. *Ibid.*, "Essays," 9/652. See also *Ibid.*, "Memorials," 1/6; *Nien-p'u*, pp. 115–16.

119. *Ibid.*, "Letters," 6/319–59. For the first of Chang's allusions, see n. 112 above; for the indirect quotation of Kuan Chung, cf. Lewis Maverick, ed., *Economic Dialogues in Ancient China: Selections from the Kuan-tzu* (Carbondale, Ill., 1954), pp. 31, 93–94, for example. This particular assertion is not made in any of these essays, although it is, in effect, stated throughout the extant essays. It does appear in *Shih-chi*, 129. Here it reads: "Thus [Kuan tzu] said, 'When the granaries for the people and the granaries for stipends are full, [the people] know the [meaning of] moral discipline and moderation; when their clothing and their food are sufficient, [the people] know [the meaning of] honor and disgrace. Moral discipline is produced by sufficiency, while it is destroyed by want.' " Cf. Rhea Blue, "The Argumentation of the Shih-huo chih: Chapters of the Han, Wei, and Sui Dynastic Histories," *Harvard Journal of Asiatic Studies*, XI (Nos. 1–2, June, 1948), 24. Blue takes the last sentence as part of the quotation from Kuan tzu.

120. *CW*, "Essays," 10/659.

121. *Ibid.*, "Letters," 15/511–12.

122. *Ibid.*, 6/313; *Nien-p'u*, p. 5.

123. *Ming-shu*, 150/1b.

124. *CW*, "Essays," 6/598.

125. *Ibid.*, "Letters," 10/402.

126. David S. Nivison, *The Life and Thought of Chang Hsüeh-ch'eng* (*1738–1801*) (Stanford, 1966), p. 169.

127. CW, "Letters," 15/518–19. For Chang's quotation see Legge, tr., *Li Ki* (Sacred Books of the East, Vol. XXVII), p. 379.

128. *Ssu-shu chih-chieh*, 1/4a–5b.

129. CW, "Letters," 11/417–18.

130. *Ibid.*, 9/379–80.

131. *Ibid.*, 5/289.

132. *Ibid.*, 5/295.

133. *Ibid.*, 3/262–63.

134. Busch, *Tunglin Academy*, p. 22, refers to the Buddhist services held for Chang when he was ill.

135. See Feng Yu-lan, *History of Chinese Philosophy*, II, 335–59; Kenneth K. S. Ch'en, *Buddhism in China, a Historical Survey* (Princeton University Press, 1964), pp. 313–20.

136. Ch'en, *Buddhism in China*, pp. 319–20.

137. CW, "Letters," 2/238.

138. *Ibid.*, 15/520.

139. *Ibid.*, 12/446.

140. *Ibid.*, 12/437.

141. *Ibid.*, 15/514.

142. Chu Tung-jun, *Chang Chü-cheng ta-chuan* (K'ai-ming Book Co., 1945), p. 48.

143. CW, "Essays," 9/652–53.

144. T'ao Hsi-sheng, *Chung-kuo cheng-chih ssu-hsiang shih*, IV, 349.

145. CW, "Poems," 1/696.

146. Feng Yu-lan, *History of Chinese Philosophy*, II, 359.

147. CW, "Letters," 11/427.

148. See quotation by Li Chih in T'ao, *Chung-kuo ching-chih ssu-hsiang shih*, IV, 347.

149. CW, "Letters," 8/347.

150. *Ibid.*, "Essays," 6/601–2.

GLOSSARY

a	張居正	v	文	aq	徇情
b	江陵	w	巨	ar	順情
c	張關保	x	氣	as	四書直解
d	歸州	y	草創	at	乾剛
e	文明	z	多事	au	王世貞
f	徐階	aa	質朴	av	功利
g	聶豹	ab	理	aw	實行家
h	耿定向	ac	勢	ax	正
i	李贄	ad	賈誼	ay	本業
j	何心隱	ae	鼂錯	az	李中溪
k	元氣	af	魏相	ba	學道
l	威強	ag	性命	bb	古典
m	桑弘羊	ah	志	bc	性
n	孔僅	ai	功	bd	命
o	崔亮	aj	本質	be	經濟
p	楊炎	ak	成憲	bf	理
q	泰	al	剛	bg	事
r	紀綱	am	姑息	bh	華嚴悲智偈
s	神農	an	操切	bi	心體
t	后稷	ao	振作		
u	質	ap	寬		

RAY HUANG *Ni Yüan-lu: "Realism" in a*

Neo-Confucian Scholar-Statesman

明 Ni Yüan-lu,[a] a Confucian scholar-official of the late Ming, has never been rated a great statesman. Much of his service in the Ming court consisted of routine assignments of an academic nature. Not until 1643 was he appointed Minister of Revenue, and by then state affairs had already deteriorated beyond redemption. As the empire's chief fiscal administrator Ni recommended to the Ch'ung-chen Emperor a series of reforms, but these came too late to avert the dynasty's downfall. Less than a year after Ni's elevation to ministerial office, Peking fell into the hands of the rebel leader Li Tzu-ch'eng.[b] True to the Confucian doctrine that loyal subjects survive or perish with the dynasty they serve, Ni hanged himself.

Despite this record of frustration and failure, however, Ni Yüan-lu's writing is worth the attention of present-day historians. His memorials to the throne contain much valuable information about Ming fiscal administration during the dynasty's waning years. Thirty-nine of those memorials still extant in his *Complete Works* were submitted when Ni was Minister of Revenue.[1] They reveal the mind of a top bureaucrat struggling with the desperate problems of his time. The classical bibliographical guide, *Szu-k'u ch'üan-shu tsung-mu t'i-yao*, speaks of him as "especially interested in administrative matters. His ideas and managerial planning, his methods of auditing military supplies, could all be practically applied, unlike the empty talk of bookish scholars."[2] Other essays in the *Complete Works* set forth the writer's philosophical position. In addition, Ni published in 1640 two volumes of commentaries on the *Book of Changes*. The combination of metaphysical speculation and down-to-earth discussion on fiscal management offers a rare example of the interplay of late Ming philosophy with socioeconomic thought.

Ni Yüan-lu was born in 1594 in Shang-yü[c] County, Chekiang

Province. His family traced its origin to north China during the Sung period. In the twelfth century the family followed the Sung court to Chekiang. Ni's ancestors served in various official capacities under the Sung, Yüan, and Ming. From Yüan-lu's own description we can see that his family was quite affluent for a great many years.[3]

The life and official career of Yüan-lu's father, Ni Tung,[d] influenced the son's future in many ways. Ni Tung passed the civil service examination and became a *chin-shih* in 1574. As a new *chin-shih*, the elder Ni had great admiration for Tsou Yüan-piao,[e] later a leader of the Tung-lin party. In 1577 Tsou was flogged and banished from court because he offended the then omnipotent grand secretary, Chang Chü-cheng.[f] While Tsou was on his way to exile, Ni Tung paid him courtesy calls and entertained him, thus inevitably making himself also *persona non grata* with the fearsome Chang Chü-cheng. Thereafter Ni Tung and Tsou Yüan-piao regarded each other as "friends in time of distress." Their friendship was further strengthened when, after Chang Chü-cheng's death, they both held official positions in Nanking.

In his adolescent years Yüan-lu, too, learned to admire and respect his father's hero. When Ni Tung died in 1615, Yüan-lu traveled all the way to Honan to secure a tombstone commendation composed by Tsou. The younger Ni related later that his father's thought had been influenced by Tsou Yüan-piao.[4] But indications are that Tsou's influence on Yüan-lu himself may have been even greater. Chiang Shih-ch'üan,[g] who edited Yüan-lu's papers in the eighteenth century, commented: "Throughout his life he [Yüan-lu] regarded himself as a disciple of Tsou Yüan-piao, and at the same time as a close associate of Liu Tsung-chou [h] and Huang Tao-chou." [i][5] Among them the influence of Liu Tsung-chou seems to have been the greatest, though a search of their writings fails to produce any correspondence between Liu and Ni. An explanation of this may be that both were banished from the court in the same year and later recalled to Peking in the same year. During the period of banishment both lived in their native Chekiang. Thus personal contacts may have taken the place of correspondence.

There is little doubt that Ni Yüan-lu learned a great deal about civil administration from his father. Whether he learned it through oral instruction or through examining the personal papers left by

Ni Tung, we have no way of knowing. In an elaborate essay, also inscribed on stone tablets on his father's grave, Yüan-lu cited his deceased parent's benevolent administration as county magistrate and prefect, giving detailed accounts of how the elder Ni handled criminal cases as well as civil suits. The lack of practical administrative experience in the early years of his own career was presumably compensated for somewhat by his study of his father's example. At all events, the reforms initiated by Ni Tung at the Ministry of War's Nanking office left a strong impression in Yüan-lu's memory.

The elder Ni had been placed in charge of the Bureau of Equipment at Nanking in 1586, with a fleet of 864 service vessels under his control. Originally designated to transport horses and heavy equipment for the army, the craft were subsequently used merely to haul supplies to the palace in Peking. Crews to man these vessels were drafted from some 60,000 hereditary military families in and outside of Nanking. Conditions in the Ming military colony system were such that in the later sixteenth century most of the hereditary families were on the brink of starvation, yet they had to fulfill their service obligations. Above all, the earlier administrative procedure which held military personnel financially responsible for the maintenance of their equipment remained in force. As a result, each time a ship came due for overhaul or refitting some crew members were forced to abandon their families and desert, while others sold their wives. Suicides were frequent. Faced with such a distressing situation, Ni Tung initiated and carried through a sweeping reform. Within three years he reduced the number of service ships to 500. Additional funds were secured to supplement dockyard maintenance. Crew members were recruited instead of drafted, and their pay was increased. The over-all efficiency of the fleet was improved.[6] Yüan-lu was so impressed with his father's innovation that, as we shall see later, upon becoming Minister of Revenue he attempted an extension of the reform on a nation-wide scale.

Passing the civil service examinations had not been an easy task for young Yüan-lu. Even though he succeeded on the provincial level at the age of sixteen, three subsequent trips to take the metropolitan examination in Peking ended in failure. When he finally cleared this hurdle in 1622, he was already a mature young man of twenty-nine. Appointed a Bachelor in the Hanlin Academy, Yüan-lu could expect to be groomed for important positions. He became successively a compiler, a librarian-assistant (among whose duties was that of assisting on occasions when the classics and histories were read and explained to the emperor by the senior Academy members), custodian of examination papers at palace examinations, and in 1627 commissioner for the provincial examination in Kiangsi. In those years he saw the eunuch Wei Chung-hsien [j] rise to power and visit on Tung-lin members and their associates a bloody persecution. Throughout these years, however, Ni kept silent.[7]

A turning point came when the Ch'ung-chen Emperor succeeded his half-witted brother in 1628. Wei Chung-hsien committed suicide, and his "brain-truster" Tsui Ch'eng-hsiu [k] followed suit. The new monarch would have preferred not to investigate further lest pursuit of the matter reopen the partisan controversy which had already plagued the whole court. An early supporter of Wei Chung-hsien, however, opportunistically proposed that things be resolved by purging both the Tung-lin and anti-Tung-lin groups. Ni Yüan-lu rose to defend the Tung-lin partisans, and his memorials apparently caused Ch'ung-chen to have second thoughts about the issue. The anti-Tung-lin pro-Wei group was prosecuted. Banished Tung-lin members were recalled, and those who had died were posthumously restored to full honor. The "history" of recent events written under Wei Chung-hsien's patronage, the San-ch'ao yao-tien,[l] was proscribed and its plates destroyed. At the same time Ni Yüan-lu was promoted to the position of expositor in waiting. Many of the Ch'ung-chen Emperor's proclamations honoring the deceased Tung-lin officials were composed by him. The compilers of the Wan-li shih-lu [m] (Veritable records of the Wan-li period) also employed his services in chronicling these affairs. Indeed, many historians consider Ni's defense of the Tung-lin the most commendable service he rendered to the Ming court.[8]

In 1629 Ni was transferred to the National University at Nanking to become director of studies. The following year he returned to Peking. Once again serving as compiler in the Han-lin Academy but concurrently holding several honorary titles, he was able to remain close to the throne. The Ch'ung-chen Emperor included him in state banquets. In 1633 he was called to lecture on the classics and histories in the presence of the monarch. Now and then he submitted memorials advising the throne on current issues of state, including the selection of court personnel, fiscal policy, and military affairs. Some of these recommendations were accepted by the emperor, others rejected. But at least one of Ni's petitions which had originally been denied by the Grand Secretariat was favorably received by the emperor. Ch'ung-chen personally reversed the reply and directed ministerial officials to follow Ni's advice.[9] The normal procedure, according to Ming court practice, would have been to appoint Ni Yüan-lu himself as a Grand Secretary—a position in which he was not uninterested. However, such an appointment never came.

Many years later, Yüan-lu's son, Ni Hui-ting,[n] compiled a chronological biography of his father, in which he indicated that Yüan-lu's failure to be elevated to the high position was due entirely to the jealousy of Wen T'i-jen,[o] the Grand Secretary who dominated the Ch'ung-chen court from 1630 to 1638.[10] Nevertheless we must remember that the Ch'ung-chen Emperor was extremely suspicious by nature. All his life he feared two things in his entourage: the receiving of bribes and the revival of partisan feuds. Ni Yüan-lu's incorruptibility was established; yet his close association with Tsou Yüan-piao, Wen Cheng-meng,[p] Yao Hsi-meng,[q] Liu Tsung-chou, and Huang Tao-chou, not to mention his pro-Tung-lin memorials, marked him as a strong partisan.[11] Even though Ch'ung-chen ordered the reinstatement of Tung-lin adherents after his enthronement, his misgivings about factionalism at court persisted. It is understandable, then, that he should have personally honored Ni Yüan-lu as a scholar-official of high calibre and yet hesitated to entrust him with a position of great power. As a matter of fact, Ni's political enemy Wen T'i-jen succeeded in rising to power primarily by posing as a nonpartisan.

By today's standards Ni Yüan-lu could be called critical and quarrelsome, yet he was no more so than most of his fellow courtiers. When the conflict with Wen T'i-jen became unbearable, Ni requested retirement. In 1633 and 1634 he submitted his resignation seven times; but leave was not granted him. In 1635 his lectures before the throne were discontinued and he was "kicked upstairs" to become Chancellor of the National University. Then, a year later, he was impeached on a freakish charge.

According to the "authentic biography" written by Chiang Shih-ch'üan in the eighteenth century, Yüan-lu had previously been married to a daughter of a certain Ch'en house. Having charged her with being disrespectful toward his mother, Yüan-lu dismissed her, an act which, in the seventeenth century, was quite legal and had the effect of a legitimate divorce. Afterwards he married a daughter of a Wang house. One of Wen T'i-jen's henchmen deliberately misconstrued these actions in an attempt to show that the Ch'en woman was the legal wife and the Wang girl no more than a concubine, and that consequently Yüan-lu had committed a misdemeanor by entering the Wang daughter in the official records as his wife. Whatever the truth of this charge, it brought about not only Ni's disgrace but also his involuntary retirement from the court for more than five years.[13]

Finally, in 1642, the tide turned. Another former enemy of Wen T'i-jen's, Chou Yen-yü,[r] came to power in Peking and persuaded the emperor to recall the banished officials. Most of those recalled belonged to the pro-Tung-lin group, among them Ni Yüan-lu.[14] By this time the route from Huaian to Peking was no longer safe for travel, with Manchu cavalry columns already raiding far into Chinese territory. Ni recruited "several hundred death-defying young men" from his home locality and with three hundred mounts dashed into the isolated capital, arriving there early in 1643.[15] He was appointed Vice-Minister of War—the first administrative position that he ever held. In addition to this, he was also ordered to resume his lectures on the classics before the throne. That summer saw him promoted to become Minister of Revenue over his own protests; the lectures, also, continued. He was so overloaded with duties that often he had to work until midnight.[16]

With all his diligence and devotion, Ni Yüan-lu was unable to hold his ministerial assignment through the last days of the dynasty. In early 1644 another Grand Secretary suggested to the emperor that Ni was too bookish a scholar, unfamiliar with "matters of grain and money." The vacillating Ch'ung-chen ordered that Ni be relieved as Minister of Revenue and remain only as the monarch's lecturer. Yet until a replacement could be nominated he retained responsibility for the affairs of the Ministry. Almost two more months elapsed before a vice-minister was ordered to take over.[17] In another three weeks both emperor and minister were dead, by their own hands.

From a modern point of view the fiscal and other policies recommended by Ni Yüan-lu could by no means be regarded as radical innovations. They represented only piecemeal remedies for an outmoded system. However, some of Ni's policies, if fully implemented and promoted, could have had far-reaching consequences. The significance of these policies must be appraised in the light of Ming governmental customs and usages. Ever since the Hung-wu Emperor had established the dynasty, little allowance had been made for alterations and adjustments in governmental institutions. Practically every edict issued by the founding emperor was considered permanently binding. To these a body of precedents and operating procedures had been added in the reigns of his successors. All these were faithfully followed in later eras as if they were, in Charles O. Hucker's words, "a kind of dynastic constitution."[18] Sometimes merely to suggest revisions of the established order could be considered heretical and lead to severe punishment. Further, under the dynasty's autocratic system the emperor kept all power in his own hands. The minister functioned as no more than an adviser and secretary. He had little authority in decision-making.

Yet upon being appointed Minister of Revenue, Ni had gained the Ch'ung-chen Emperor's agreement on three principles: first, fiscal management must be realistic, rather than merely look splendid on paper; second, justice must be observed; and third, attention must be focused on important and vital issues. When Ch'ung-chen gave his consent, Ni put these principles down in writing and hung them in his office. He even renamed the minister's office the "Hall of the Three Principles."[19] Apparently he regarded these principles as a compact between himself and the monarch, an attitude quite unprecedented in the history of the dynasty.

Within his office Ni installed an executive officer. Previously the minister had attended to all office details. For instance, Pi Tzu-yen,[s] minister in the early years of Ch'ung-chen's reign, according to his biographer, personally composed his own official reports, producing several thousand words each day.[20] Li Jü-hua,[t] the last minister under the Wan-li Emperor, constantly busied himself with matters that should have been handled by his subordinates.[21] Yüan-lu felt that the chief fiscal administrator should never let office routine occupy his attention. After some deliberation, he conferred the position of executive officer on a brilliant but entirely unknown student named Chiang Ch'en.[11] Under this executive five aides selected from the ministry staff formed an inner control group.[22]

For the empire's fiscal administration Yüan-lu was anxious to establish a geographical base. He recognized that the economic center of the empire lay to the south, far removed from its political center. While Vice-Minister of War, he had envisioned such an area on the lower Yangtze. His memorial to the throne reads:

Today the northwest is declining while the southeast section remains a stronghold of our financial resources. It is suggested that Kiukiang be established as a pivot point, Wuchang be utilized as a forward post, and Huai-an and Yangchow be the rear echelon. [It is further suggested] that a commissioner who commands wide public respect be appointed to administer the area. In ordinary times he shall promote trade and commerce; in times of emergency he can [be called on to] cope with the situation in the north as well as in the south.

By the time Ni became Minister of Revenue, however, the situation had changed considerably. He therefore suggested a base of operations farther south in Fukien Province:

Kwangtung, Fukien, Chekiang, and South Chihli should be organized as a territorial unit. . . . Among the four provinces, Fukien occupies a central strategic position. In addition, its regional naval forces are superior to those of the other provinces. I would suggest that the Governor of Fukien be elevated to Governor-General to command the four provinces.[23]

In making these suggestions Ni Yüan-lu almost anticipated the operations of the resistance movement later carried on in the south by the Ming loyalists, who actually did use such bases against the invading Manchus. It is also noteworthy that he included trade, commerce, financial resources, and the population center in his strategic considerations.

The major task confronting Yüan-lu after he took over the Ministry of Revenue was to keep the army adequately supplied. He began with a thorough audit. Up to then the fiscal system had been in such chaos that the army commands used one set of figures in reporting their strengths to the Ministry of War and another in their reports to the Ministry of Revenue. The revenue derived from several sur-taxes, added to the land tax, was classified as "Manchurian Military Supplies," "Bandit-suppressing Supplies," and "Training Supplies." Each agency followed its own schedule of collection and the proceeds were not consolidated. Yüan-lu, with the approval of Ch'ung-chen, introduced an integrated collection schedule. In the eighth lunar month of 1643 he succeeded in producing a military budget for the next year. Anticipating an income of less than sixteen million taels of silver and an expenditure of more than twenty-one million taels, he proposed to make up the deficit by increasing the sale of salt, com-muting punishments to fines, and selling official ranks. He further urged Ch'ung-chen to promote the commissioners in charge of mili-tary supplies in the field and make them simultaneously responsible to the Ministry of War and the Ministry of Revenue. By maintaining a close contact with the Ministry of War he hoped that pay and rations would eventually be delivered according to the army's actual strength rather than its paper strength. This goal would have taken two years to achieve. But even during Ni's nine months in office, two of the army commands reduced their inflated strength by a total of 1,300,000 men.[24]

On the other hand, Yüan-lu advocated delegation of power. Pro-vincial governors should be given enough authority to act, and not be constantly handicapped by the touring supervising secretaries and inspecting eunuchs. "Today's governors," he argued, "are comparable to the dukes in ancient times. . . . Who else can handle what the provincial governors cannot handle? Who else can be trusted, if the provincial governors cannot be trusted?" [25] At one point he tried to persuade Ch'ung-chen to give army commanders a free hand in raising funds in their own territories, including the power of coining money, collecting inland duties, initiating land-reclamation projects, controlling the gabelle, and engaging in other revenue-generating projects as they saw fit.[26]

Like his friend Liu Tsung-chou, in earlier years Yüan-lu had ap-pealed for a lightening of the burden of the tax-paying population. In 1635 he had petitioned Ch'ung-chen to remit all the overdue payments from the two previous fiscal years,[27] but after he became Minister of Revenue no such petition was submitted by him. Nor did he attempt to overhaul the existing land tax structure. On only one issue was he consistent. He strongly argued that the palace supplies collected in kind from the southern provinces, including silk wadding, lacquer, wax, tea, metals, etc., should be commuted to money payments. The annual quota of these articles has been mentioned by a contemporary source as having a total value of some five million taels of silver.[28] In 1635 Ni had argued for their commutation to no avail. In 1643, as Minister of Revenue, he brought up the topic again: this time he included in the suggested commutation list even military items such as bows and arrows. Ni's recommendations were opposed by the eunuchs in charge of the warehouses, and in the end the commutation was applied only to eight items out of his suggested list of fifty-eight.[29]

Until this time about two and a half million piculs of husked rice had been transported on the Grand Canal to Peking. Customarily referred to by Western scholars as the "grain tribute," this consignment was handled by special army transportation corps whose boats often took a whole year to make the round trip on the waterway. Consequently each picul of grain delivered cost the taxpayer more than two piculs. Dissatisfied with the slow and costly delivery system, at one point Ni toyed with the idea of abandoning the operation altogether. He figured that, if the tax payment were commuted to twice the value of the nominal quota in the south, the taxpayers would actually be better off and the revenue would still be more than enough for the government to purchase the grain in Peking. One consideration restrained him from making such a move: the canal operation, ineffective though it was, had been contributing to the price stability of foodstuffs in north China, and its sudden discontinuance could disturb the food market. In the summer of 1643 he conceived an alternative. He would barter salt produced at the government salterns near Huaian for grain, thus shortening the canal transportation for government agencies by at least one third.[30] Further studies were made with a view to substituting transportation along the coast for the canal traffic. Transportation of grain to north China by the sea route had been done in the early Ming reigns of

Hung-wu and Yung-lo, but such operations had been terminated after the Grand Canal was opened for traffic in 1415. In the fifteenth and sixteenth centuries several Ming officials, including Ch'iu Ch'ün,[v] Liang Meng-lung,[w] and Wang Tsung-mo,[x] championed their revival without success. To resume the use of the sea route now was not easy; neither the time nor the dynasty's financial resources was favorable for such an undertaking. Nevertheless Minister Ni personally contacted the outstanding mariner Shen T'ing-yang.[y] Shen made a test run with six ships along the coast, arriving in north China in a little over a month. With this success Yüan-lu persuaded the emperor to proceed with the coastwise operation on a large scale. It was planned that the next year half of the tributary grain should be carried to Peking by sea.[31] But before this time came the dynasty collapsed.

Efforts to broaden state revenue proved to be most difficult. Yüan-lu once complained: "Methods of increasing state income, since they involve long-range planning, may require several decades to materialize; even short-range projects may take years. *Sometimes investment is essential.*" [32] As time was pressing and capital nowhere available, he had to resort to such improvised actions as the commutation of punishments to fines and the sale of official ranks. But he also strongly recommended that maritime trade with foreign states should be legalized for revenue purposes. He estimated that in Fukien alone the custom duty could produce an annual income of over 10,000 taels.[33] The proposal seems to have met no favorable reaction from Ch'ung-chen. Ni further suggested that the institution of hereditary military families be abolished. The Ming military colony system had already degenerated beyond recognition in the late period: yet the hereditary military families were still subject to a series of stringent restrictions. The problems of the personnel operating army supply ships in Nanking (described above, p. 417) exemplify their hardships. We have not the slightest doubt that Yüan-lu's contemplated abolition of the whole system was at least in part conceived of as an extension of his father's reform some fifty-eight years before, although now, as Minister of Revenue, he based his argument entirely on state interest. As Ni described it, when a member of a hereditary military household was called to service, he and his immediate family had to be relocated in the assigned colony. According to custom, from ten to twenty years later this member was allowed to return to his home locale to serve his family temple, but not before several hundred taels of silver had been extorted from him for the alleged purpose of replacing his original military equipment. Ni estimated that by 1644 there were some 1,700,000 households across the empire classified as hereditary military families. His formula was based on emancipation for a fee. Each household's service obligation would be permanently removed upon the payment of one hundred taels of silver. This way, he declared, "Ten million taels can be raised immediately." [34] As a rough, preliminary proposal, this memorial did not mention how the military colonies would be disposed of. In any case, the suggestion drew only a rebuke from the emperor. Ch'ung-chen's rescript indicated that the hereditary military families were part of the "ancestral system" and that to consider their elimination was completely inadmissible.

The issue of government notes was also a part of Ni Yüan-lu's fund-raising program. Originally, when he brought the device to Ch'ung-chen's attention, Ni added that, in order to keep the notes in circulation, more copper cash would have to be coined, and coining money required capital. However, when Schall von Bell, the Jesuit astronomer serving the Ming court, urged Ch'ung-chen to revive government mining, Yüan-lu rose against this proposal. His argument was that such an undertaking would raze houses and disturb graves, and would inevitably "hurt geomantic features everywhere." [35] The monarch paid no attention to Ni's protest, in this case showing greater realism than his adviser, whose motives in opposing Schall von Bell were probably questionable. The latter was deeply resented by many Confucian officials. His removal was also suggested by Liu Tsung-chou.[36]

As the court was still unable to collect enough copper, Ch'ung-chen thought of nationalizing the metal. He personally directed that within three months all copper objects throughout the country, except military weapons, mirrors, antiques, locks, musical instruments, and bells and cymbals used in religious institutions, be surrendered to the imperial mint. Obviously, such an edict would have been practically impossible to enforce. Yüan-lu made the counterproposal that the possession of copper objects not be outlawed altogether, but only that the casting of new bronze articles be prohibited. He further suggested to Ch'ung-chen that when penalties were commuted to fines, half of the fine should be payable in copper. His reasoning was that such a policy, by suddenly increasing the demand for the metal, would artificially boost its market price. When copper became expensive, people would automatically abstain from using it. Hopefully, he predicted: "Within a year, all available copper will have flowed into the imperial mint." [37] To this suggestion the emperor gave his consent.

However, discussions of monetary policy brought forth further disagreement between the emperor and the minister. Ch'ung-chen intended immediately to make the new paper money legal tender. Yüan-lu believed that the circulation of the notes could not be pushed through by edicts alone; the public's confidence in it would have to be built up first. Previously notes issued by the Ming government had failed because they had no backing and were not convertible. Despite stringent government orders their value decreased sharply. Since the new currency had no more backing than the old, Ni advised Ch'ung-chen that the prudent course was to make it acceptable in tax payments and fines, while leaving private transactions for the time being unaffected. The conversion of copper cash and silver into paper money should be on a voluntary, rather than a compulsory, basis. The impatient Ch'ung-chen, however, rejected this advice and ordered merchants in Peking to bid for the notes yet to be manufactured, apparently at a small discount. We know very little about what actually took place later. Ni Hui-ting gave the following description of the public reaction: "When pressed hard, some of them [the merchants] carted away their goods and left [the capital]. The currency thus failed." [38]

The government's notes were printed on a special kind of paper made of mulberry tree fiber. It was estimated that to meet the need about two and a half million pounds of mulberry branches would be required. Ch'ung-chen had dispatched several trusted eunuchs to Shantung, South Chihli, and Chekiang to purchase the material. Demands were made on three thousand papermakers and printers in Peking for production of the notes. When the news broke out, rumors ran wild. Some peasants understood that their mulberry trees would be stripped of their bark, the leaves destroyed before the feeding season of the silkworms. Fearful that such rumors would agitate people and provoke rebellion, Yüan-lu petitioned the emperor to recall the eunuchs who had been sent on the procurement mission. Reluctantly, Ch'ung-chen consented. The whole paper money adventure was called off.[39] The episode has since become a controversial historical point. Huang Tao-chou, who composed Ni Yüan-lu's tombstone inscription, suggested that Yüan-lu's failure to give Ch'ung-chen's monetary policy wholehearted support caused his dismissal as Minister of Revenue.[40] But Ku Yen-wu, one of the outstanding scholars of the seventeenth century, complained in one of his essays that it was Ni who "insisted on" issuing the worthless paper money.[41]

Other reforms championed by Ni were intended to curb existing abuses. The tax agents affiliated with the various government offices, in Yüan-lu's opinion, should themselves be taxed if not eliminated. The appearance of those agents, actually tax farmers of a sort, is a strange phenomenon in the late Ming period. They were either civilians having no official status or holders of some nominal appointment with or without pay. In either case they purchased their positions with fees, and thereafter were empowered to check in tax payments from local collectors. The Minister of Revenue disclosed that in the larger provinces these agents numbered one or two thousand, and even in an independent commissary there could be as many as one thousand. Their fees ranged from thirty or fifty to a hundred or two hundred taels of silver. He asked: "If we can neither eliminate them nor tax them, how can we do justice to farmers and merchants?" [42]

Ni's crusade against bureaucratic abuses benefited inland traders, but his over-all attitude toward merchants was still somewhat ambiguous. At one point he wrote: "Kings in ancient times did not like their people to pursue petty profits, and therefore they taxed the merchants." [43] This seems to reaffirm the Confucian prejudice against mercantile interests. But the statement was written in connection with his observation that tax agents were worse than merchants. In other instances not only did he present merchants in a much more favorable light, but he also manifested a personal interest in their welfare. Busy though he was, he took the time to interview about ten merchants engaged in inland trade. After the inquiry he reported to the emperor on the extent to which governmental abuses hurt inland trade: "When a single piece of silk goods or a skirt is omitted [from the custom declaration], the penalty is applied to the whole list. . . . The list could contain as many as two or three thousand articles owned by scores of merchants." Then he petitioned the emperor to issue an edict to liberalize the treatment of merchants. In conclusion, he stated: "When merchants and travelers can move about freely, complaints are not heard on the road, and our goal of enriching and strengthening the nation can be brought within reach." [44] Also, as we have seen in connection with his idea of establishing a territorial base as the empire's fiscal foundation, Ni emphasized that "to promote trade and commerce" should be one of the major functions of the territorial commander. His opinion that merchants provide a useful service to society finds further expression by a letter he wrote to the Ministry of Revenue in 1635, while he was the emperor's lecturer. Arguing the wisdom of purchasing palace supplies rather than having them collected in kind from the taxpayers, he named one of the advantages of the former course of action as: "Merchants from all corners will gather around the capital, awaiting government procurement orders. Goods will be amply stored. . . . The government office will turn into a market and official funds will begin to circulate among the population. The imperial city itself will also benefit by the prosperity [thus created]." [45]

Governmental finance, to Yüan-lu's mind, sometimes followed the same principle as private enterprise, wherein "capital," "investment," and "profit" were involved. We have already noted several of his remarks to this effect. On the whole, however, he seems to favor private enterprise over government-managed business. One of his memorials to Ch'ung-chen pleaded that the community granaries operated by the government should be replaced by privately owned ones. Government-operated institutions of this kind never worked, he pointed out, because they "rely on the government for capital, yet each group makes its own rules; they charge interest on loans, yet cannot stop fraud, even though those administering [the granaries] are not [supposed to] share in the profit." [46] Before his recall to

Peking in 1642 Ni actually started organizing a "grain-lending" company in his home locality. It was to be a joint-stock company, controlled by five subscribing families. Twenty percent annual interest would be charged on all loans. Because of his sudden return to the capital, however, the plan was shelved.[47]

Although Yüan-lu never fully approved the idea that man is basically self-seeking, many of his suggestions seem to assume such a premise. While persuading Ch'ung-chen to allow military commanders a free hand in fund-raising in their respective domains, he maintained that each general must keep a group of "death-defying braves" who were willing to share his fortune through thick and thin, and that this cost money. "An officer commanding one thousand troops should have one hundred men who are willing to die for his cause," he advocated. "But these hundred are not to be treated lightly. Their food and allowances must be ten times more generous [than what is allowed to ordinary soldiers]." Understandably, Ni based such conclusions on his own recent experience, for he himself had just arrived in Peking with three hundred such recruits. He also cited history to justify his proposal. "In the Sung dynasty all generals had bullion at their disposal," he continued. "That is why throughout the Sung there were as many famous generals as clouds [in the sky]." [48] This is tantamount to saying that the best way to promote *esprit de corps* in the army is to satisfy the fighting man's mercenary nature.

The strain of realism in Yüan-lu's political thought sometimes reveals itself in his personal papers. His comments on Chang Chü-cheng may be cited as an example. Although Chang was his father's enemy, Yüan-lu could not help but regard him with some admiration. He said:

Both accomplishments and failings may be attributed to the person of Chiangling [Chang Chü-cheng's home town]. . . . Hypocrisy, intrigue, an overbearing manner which enabled him to awe the emperor—these were his failings. A reinforced frontier, a disciplined officialdom, quick rewards and decisive punishments, and a willingness to start afresh and remake the world—these were his accomplishments. His failings caused the downfall of his own household; yet his accomplishments manifested themselves in the nation. This cannot be effaced with the sharpest knife or the strongest fingernails.[49]

In a letter to Yang Sze-ch'ang,[z] he mentioned Chang Chü-cheng again. This time he wrote:

Since the Chiangling Grand Secretary failed in the Wan-li reign because he was too severe, later administrators [have all tried to] exercise power slyly and without attracting attention. In such circumstances infirmity is taken for mellowness, slowness to react is taken for prudence, feebleness is taken for a peaceable disposition, and occupying the position but doing nothing is taken as stability.[50]

The writer's passion for positive action is clearly expressed in these passages. In a letter to Mei Chih-huan [aa] dated 1630 he says: "Generally speaking, dealing with the affairs of the world is handicapped not so much by lack of ideas as by lack of effective action, and not so much by lack of moral standards as by lack of [sound] management." [51]

The insatiable urge to act, when seen against the background of his life history, makes his role as a diligent and alert student of current affairs understandable. His personal knowledge on a wide range of practical issues was hardly rivaled by any of his contemporaries, as the *Szu-k'u t'i-yao* has pointed out. His fiscal proposals are always supported by factual evidence. When recommending that palace supplies be commuted to money payments, he cites the articles collected from his home locality in order to back his argument. For legalization of maritime trade, he emphasizes that the prohibition has never been effective, since ivory and the horns of rhinoceros, "originating from nowhere but the Western Oceans," are now found in abundant supply in the Chinese market.[52] On land tax abuses, he not only discloses the kind of abuses, but also estimates the actual amount extorted from the taxpayers.[53]

All such practical knowledge Yüan-lu included in his broad concept of "learning." In a 1632 letter to Huang Tao-chou he emphasized: "The essence and function of the Way of the great sages derive from the same origin. While theorizing about man's nature and destiny involves learning, discussing practical worldly affairs also involves learning." Then he enumerated the topics of study that he had in mind, which included agriculture, water control, frontier defense, money, and taxation. "Do you think," he questioned, "we can declare that we have exhausted our fields of study by [simply] examining trigrams and drawing *T'ai-chi* [ab] circles [i.e., studying the *Book of Changes*], by picking up [minute] details from the Books of *Music* and *Rites*, and by making [minor and inconsequential] revisions in the Books of *Odes* and *History?*" [54] In 1635, as chancellor of the Imperial College, he also included in the university curriculum what he called subjects of "management," including military affairs, agriculture, water control, law, and astronomy.[55]

Although not revolutionary or strikingly original, these attitudes and activities of Ni Yüan-lu do distinguish him from most other seventeenth-century Chinese scholar-officials. His sense of organization, his advocacy of decentralization and delegation of power, his recognition of the law of supply and demand, his awareness of self-interest and the profit motive, and his reservations on the use of legislative power in economic matters enable us to see him as closer to ourselves in much of his thinking than to his contemporaries. Can we, then, go further and identify him as a political realist, a pragmatic thinker, an empirical social scientist, or a spokesman for the "budding" bourgeois capitalism in the late Ming period? In the latter connection his affiliation with the Tung-lin partisans could easily be construed to make Ni a political spokesman of the "new bourgeoisie" if one were inclined to accept the view that has been put forward by several economic and social historians in mainland China: that the Tung-lin members were allied with the rising bourgeoisie on the lower Yangtze in the early seventeenth century.[56]

Before one can deal with such questions one must consider Ni's political and economic thought in the context of his Neo-Confucian background. There are, to be sure, difficulties that lie in the way of this. First of all, nowhere in Ni's writings do we find a systematic exposition of even his economic views. Second, while his ideas on practical issues are most often to be found in memorials submitted to the throne while he was Minister of Revenue (i.e., toward the end of his career), the essence of his metaphysical views has to be extracted from earlier writings. The collection of his belles-lettres (*wen-chi*), first published in 1642 and now incorporated in his Complete Works, contains many papers which are undated. They were meant to serve the diverse interests and needs of a Confucian scholar, among which the least important was to construct a consistent philosophical system. Furthermore, Yüan-lu's thought drew upon a variety of sources and he cannot be identified easily with a single school or tradition. For one thing, he made no secret of his devotion to Buddhism. In 1629 he spent a whole day copying the Diamond Sūtra from cover to cover and let the manuscript be deposited in a Buddhist temple.[57] In 1642, to cope with famine in his native Chekiang, he organized a community chest; his appeal for charity was couched in Buddhist terms and reflected Buddhist doctrines.[58] His poetry and painting often reveal Taoist sentiments. His recommendations on military strategy clearly indicate that he was influenced by Sun Tzu and by such classical works as the *Intrigues of the Warring States* and the *Spring and Autumn Annals*. Thus his "Neo-Confucianism" was of a liberal rather than narrow sort.

But it is safe to say that as a thinker Yüan-lu is in the mainstream of late Ming thought. Like many of his contemporaries, he adopted Wang Yang-ming's monistic view with certain modifications. The attempt to reconcile Sung rational idealism and Wang Yang-ming's teaching of innate knowledge was a general trend in this period.[59] If the remarks of his biographer that Yüan-lu was a disciple of Tsou Yüan-piao and a close associate of Huang Tao-chou and Liu Tsung-chou have any significance at all, they show that Ni was closely identified with this same trend. Tsou belonged to the Chiang-yu school of Wang's teaching, a moderate group which is usually considered to have held faithfully to Yang-ming's teaching and avoided the excesses of the so-called left wing.[60] Both Huang and Liu are likewise considered to have interpreted Wang Yang-ming's teaching in the light of Chu Hsi's philosophy, i.e., to have sought a common ground for the two as a basis for the reaffirmation of traditional ethics.[61]

The development of Ni's own thought, however, increasingly reacted against Sung scholasticism. In his later years he vigorously attacked the Sung school, as is clear in his study of the *Book of Changes*. He started writing his two-volume commentary on the *Changes* in 1636, when he was banished from the court, giving it the title: A Child's Book of Changes (*Erh I*).[ac] His preface reads in part:

When Han scholars worked on the *Book of Changes*, they excelled in the discussion of minor points; but omitted the essentials. They were like children striving to learn affairs. The Sung scholars combed and raked through [the whole work], attempting to grasp it comprehensively. As a result they only made pedants of themselves. Pedants are worse than children. Those who go to excess in straining to acquire knowledge are no better than children who have never tried.[62]

Here Ni reflects the Wang Yang-ming school's rejection of the rationalistic theories and ponderous scholarship of the Chu Hsi school. He presents the essential message of the *Changes* which had eluded both the philological commentators of the Han and the metaphysical commentators of the Sung. And what is essential here, what is recognizable to anyone's innate knowledge, is simple and obvious enough for the child to understand. The "child" then is a symbol of unspoiled, unaffected human intelligence, responding directly and without preconception to reality. For Wang Yang-ming that response to reality had been understood as an experience of truth and primarily moral truth. For Ni Yüan-lu's understanding of it, we may examine his preface further in the full translation which follows:

The Book of Changes that derived from the Three Sages was made decisive by Confucius. The Three Sages dealt with essence: Confucius dealt with function. Those who deal with essence employ the [round] compass. Those who deal with function, the [square] ruler. Prior to King Wen and the Duke of Chou, all people knew their [own] qualifications and capacities. All those making use of the *Changes* were gentlemen. Therefore, the best method was to handle the *Changes* in the spirit of the round, enabling people to become cultured. [But] in the period when the Chou was declining, the shrewd and the cunning rose every day. If the *Changes* had been permitted to remain elastic and compliant, then the most righteous would have had to share the *Changes* with the most vicious. Had that been the case, inevitably there would have been bogus versions to adulterate the *Changes*. Fearful that the spirit of the round might fail, Confucius, therefore, followed the eternal principle and squared the *Changes* with a ruler. [He] devised the sixty-four hexagrams, each representing one virtue. Every hexagram's usefulness was clarified. [His] division was similar to the official dividing pathway set in the rice field. The Greater Symbol (*ta-hsiang*)[ad] uses the character *i* [ae] (in order to) because it is referring to function. The way Confucius made use of the *Changes*— he derived practical function from its usefulness—was like controlling mercury with oxides. *Yü* [af] was applicable to music; therefore, the hexagram of *yü* was devoted to use in music. *Ko* [ag] was applicable to astronomy;

therefore, the hexagram of *ko* was devoted to use in astronomy. *Shih* [ah] and *tsui* [ai] were devoted to use in military affairs. *Shih-ho*,[aj] *pi*,[ak] *feng*,[al] and *lü* [am] were devoted to use in the penal code. The way Confucius handled the *Changes* was to create utility out of them. The *Changes* responded [to him] as an echo to sound. He made a comprehensive study of each hexagram's virtue, applied the Sets of Lines (*hsiao*) [an] and Explanations (*t'uan*) [ao] thoroughly to it, with such divine dexterity that one would think it had been perceived in a dream. This was because Confucius could think deliberately and precisely. Furthermore, his words were incisive, yet capable of grasping technique and preventing stumbles. A few words of his could completely cover the whole hexagram, like an inch on the sundial representing a thousand li. His literary skill was a result of his magnificent talent and copious energy. Do I dare ask: "If all this had definitely been the original intent and purpose of King Wen and the Duke of Chou, why did they not work this out themselves? Why did one have to wait for Confucius to do it?"

Therefore, those who work on the *Changes* must understand the Greater Symbol. If you separate yourself from the Symbol to work on the *Changes*, you will only exhaust your wits without ever getting anywhere. The *Changes* has been a controversial subject among scholars for more than a thousand generations. When all this talent in a thousand generations has been employed to establish a single [*Book of*] *Changes* and yet there is still dispute, how can there be a standard [interpretation of the] *Changes*? And yet it is regarded as a crime to contradict even the casual remarks of the Ch'eng brothers and Chu Hsi! Now I am only following Confucius' interpretation, without daring to inject my own ideas into it. But suppose King Wen and the Duke of Chou should take to chastizing rebels; Confucius would have to apologize. However, if we took Confucius [on our side] to question the Ch'engs and Chu, the Ch'engs and Chu would have to bow their heads. Thus it is that the Way may be clarified and made easy to practice.[63]

In this passage Ni ostensibly pays tribute to Confucius and the *Book of Changes*, while actually raising a fundamental question as to what constitutes ultimate authority in the Confucian tradition. Can there be any fixed and final interpretation of the *Changes*? If received authority be accepted as the sole standard, Confucius would have to be considered out of order for daring to add anything to what King Wen and the Duke of Chou had said. But the general acceptance of Confucius' explanation demonstrated that superior intelligence, responding to the change in historical circumstances, is the real basis of interpretation, and not rigid adherence to the past.

If this is so, moreover, one may also dispense with the volumes of commentary that have intervened between Confucius and the later reader. Confucius alone may be taken as a reliable guide to the *Changes*, and reason and practicality alone may be taken as reliable guides to Confucius. There is, then, nothing really presumptuous in Ni's offering his interpretation of Confucius, any more than in Confucius' offering his of the *Changes*.

In his Child's Book of Changes, Ni by and large kept his promise to introduce nothing but what he thought Confucius would have meant. The numerous historical examples supporting his argument in the first volume (designated as *Nei-i* [ac] or Interior Commentary with Practical Applications) are with only two exceptions [64] dated prior to Confucius' time, and drawn exclusively from the *Book of History*, *Book of Odes*, and *Spring and Autumn Annals*. In the second volume, the *Wai-i* [ap] or Exterior Commentaries, later historical examples are given, but the distinction which Ni draws between these two types of evidence establishes clearly the order of his priorities. Plausibility in terms of later experience is not inconsequential as a factor in interpretation, but it must yield precedence to historical evidence as a basis for judging what Confucius must have meant. In these respects, then, Ni anticipates the main tendencies which developed in seventeenth- and eighteenth-century thought: namely, the return to Confucius and to the Classics rather than later philosophers as the authentic sources of truth, and the emphasis on historical scholarship, rather than rationalistic speculation or metaphysical theory, as a means of determining the authentic teaching of Confucius.

When this preface was reproduced in Ni's Complete Works, first appearing in 1772, the remarks insinuating that Confucius might have to apologize to King Wen and the Duke of Chou were deleted, no doubt because the editors feared that they would provoke condemnation as being impious or heretical. In the late Ming, however, such rationalism and skepticism were not unprecedented. Li Chih [aq] in the late sixteenth century had questioned even more boldly the sacrosanct status of the early sages, including Confucius.

A Child's Book of Changes contains much of the mystic symbolism and pseudoscience surrounding the traditional study of that text (for instance, the heavenly firmament, including its longitude and latitude, totals 357,000 li, or about 136,000 miles).[66] Nevertheless at the end of every paragraph, Ni turns back to the theme of righteous living and sound government. It is also noteworthy that in the author's preface, where he enumerates the possible applications of the several hexagrams, he points to music, astronomy, military affairs, and the penal code—all instruments of government useful to the traditional Chinese state. And throughout his work Ni invokes "utility," "function," and "applicability" as basic criteria of truth. True, he employs a well-established Neo-Confucian formula by which "substance" and "function" are taken as simply different aspects of the same truth, but one cannot fail to observe that in identifying King Wen and the Duke of Chou with "substance" and Confucius with "function," Ni is far more eloquent and enthusiastic in his discussion of the latter.

The universe, as Yüan-lu saw it, is produced from the void. The void generates the myriad things. The myriad things are constituted of a single primal substance—the *ch'i* [ar] (hereafter referred to as "ether")—a concept developed by Chang Tsai in the eleventh century and widely accepted in the late Ming. Ether not only sustains man's physical being, but also determines his capacity and personal traits. This primal substance, therefore, can be classified by kinds. Appearing in Yüan-lu's writing are the terms "righteous ether," "ether of magnanimity," "ether of unyielding loyalty," and "ether of chastity and uncompromisingness." [67] But ether itself is neither good nor evil; its moral quality seems to depend upon its inner arrangement or balance. Harmony purifies ether. In an edict composed for the Ch'ung-chen Emperor to reinstall deceased Tung-lin members to full honor Yüan-lu wrote: "Our purpose is to reach the ultimate harmony . . . until the ether of various phantoms is transformed into brightening clouds." [68]

When Ni worked on the Child's Book of Changes in 1636, he no longer frequently used the term "ether." It was now replaced by the concept of *ts'ai* [as] (hereafter referred to as "powers," but meaning also "talent," "ability," or "capacity to perform"). Powers are a manifestation of the ether or life force in man, as can be seen from the following passage quoted from Ni's writing:

Powers are to virtue what water is to fire. Ether, which constitutes things, [has a tendency to] break out of vessels in order to gain its [own] contours. The self-suppressing mind, [on the other hand,] would cut back [one's own] corners to maintain [one's] quality.[69]

Here by virtue (te)[at] Ni actually meant "function," "utility," or "the capacity of rendering a service to others without seeking compensation." In an earlier passage, as we have observed, he used the word to denote the usefulness of a hexagram. At one point he defined virtue as the ability to carry an external load. Earth's virtue, for instance, is strictly construed in this sense. Since a horse can carry a heavy load, that is also the horse's virtue.[70]

Powers, in the main, epitomize man's self-seeking urge, or drive. The universe lives on its own powers or resources; it also endows all things with powers which enable them to live. Man receives a generous share of this gift. In Yüan-lu's own words,

by nature all men know how to perpetuate themselves; without being taught, they all know sexual reproduction. They all know how to acquire subsistence for survival; without being taught, they all know how to seek food and drink. They all know how to administer themselves; without being taught they all know how to honor their parents and respect their elders.[71]

That men by their natural instinct will honor their elders may appear a doubtful assumption to the modern Western mind. Apparently Yüan-lu, like many other Chinese writers, accepted this powerful element in Chinese cultural conditioning as being a natural instinct.

Powers, like ether, are not evil per se. They are not to be suppressed. On the contrary they should be promoted, but at the same time carefully rectified by learning. Though powers are to virtue "what water is to fire," the two components, in consequence of Ni's monism, are not constituted of radically different substances. Powers, in fact, generate virtue. No one can produce virtue unless he already possesses the powers. To carry an external load requires inner strength. One cannot help others unless he has the capacities required. The most gifted is most likely to provide a greater public service. Another statement of Ni's reads: "Powers are what introduce [or initiate] virtue." [72] Speaking of government officials, he went on to say: "If an official does not have the powers, who is to benefit by his virtue? . . . Powers, therefore, are to virtue what the crossbar is to a carriage." [73] This runs parallel to his early reasoning that ether is neither good nor evil, that its quality depends on its inner arrangement or balance. Now the emphasis is on man's self-seeking urge as either harmful or useful, depending upon its orientation.

Virtue is both inborn and acquired. When ice grows thicker, it increases its virtue until it will support wagons. "Gentlemen follow their natural instinct to attain virtue, from a small start [until] they reach the height. Because it is a [matter of] gradual accumulation and no resistance is involved, it is therefore natural." [74] The height of human virtue is benevolence (*jen*) and righteousness (*i*).

The Confucian values were closely related to and integrated with a broader cosmic order presented by Yüan-lu. That man's virtue is comparable to the virtue of a horse, a sheet of ice, and the earth expresses his organic view.

But the operation of the universe is not determined by ether or virtue. It is the work of the yang and the yin. The ceaseless cycle of exaltation-decline-depression-return always applies. For individuals, predestination is involved. "When the universe commands [a person] to be a hero, a hero he becomes. It is not due to his ambitious maneuvers and exertions." [75]

Should man, then, resign himself to his fate and do nothing? Far from it, says Ni. Fate is by no means absolute. Good fortune can be exploited, and the effects of bad fortune can be minimized if not totally evaded.[76] The opening paragraph of his Exterior Commentary reads:

The *Changes* is a book to save the world. It does not want man to remain ignorant, accepting his losses and gains passively. When the pivot is under control, how to make the turn is at your command. When an opportunity is seized, the development can be directed. When the *Book of Changes* is mastered, all changes are within one's grasp.[77]

Nevertheless there is a limit to what man can do. It is essential to time one's actions, Ni advised, with the movement of the cosmic ether. In times when everything is flourishing, even the mediocre should strive to achieve merit. In difficult times, even the most talented can only hope to avoid blundering.[78] Similarly, "sages, know-

ing that misfortunes are everywhere, do not dare to press for unattainable luck. [But] if a gentleman retreats too easily, his talent
cannot be fully used." [79]

Thus, though Ni places great stress on man's natural endowment,
and sees his physical powers as delimiting his moral potentialities,
he does not see them as determining them. In other words, within
the general framework of predestination, man still exercises some
measure of free will. Another conclusion which we can draw from
the above quotations is that, to Ni's way of thinking, the operation
of the universe is independent of the human mind, its processes having nothing to do with man's virtue or the absence of it. This in
turn means that there are really two sets of human values. One is
virtue, or Confucian value, which Yüan-lu considered as "instinctive
and spontaneous." Another set of values involves success or failure;
it is by and large determined by destiny (sou [au]), but man should at
least exploit every possibility of attaining the maximum success and
avoiding fatal errors.

Man, therefore, is simultaneously engaged in two kinds of pursuit.
On the one side he has to follow his natural instinct to increase his
spiritual worth, which is its own reward; on the other he cannot
ignore worldly gain or achievement. For him, worldly success has a
value and a purpose in itself. This can be seen in the following passage taken from the Child's Book of Changes: "What the *Book of
Changes* wishes to see is accomplishment. With distinguished accomplishment the *Changes* becomes king of the world. The *Changes*
does not wish to see virtue stand by itself. When virtue stands by
itself, the *Changes* can only relieve virtue of sorrow and worry." [80]

The writing of the Child's Book of Changes engaged Yüan-lu in
four years (1636–40) of active work. According to his disciples, its
planning and contemplation occupied his attention for a decade.[81]
This confirms our observation that Ni's fiscal policies, in general
pragmatic and success-oriented, cannot be dismissed simply as emergency measures hastily conceived to meet an immediate situation.
They arise directly from the author's personal convictions as expressed in relation to the *Changes*.

But a natural consequence of the duality of purposes in life is that
they may work against each other. In a letter to a friend written in
1628 Ni spoke of the Ch'ung-chen Emperor: "His Majesty . . . seems

to place priority on strengthening the nation and enriching the country over benevolence and righteousness. Yet no one can tactfully dissuade him from doing this." [82] On the other hand, in a letter to Mei Chih-huan in 1630, quoted earlier, Ni expresses the opinion that there is too much talk of morality and too little attention to solid achievement.

The precarious balance which Ni sought to maintain between virtue and the powers is more difficult to achieve in practice than to assert in writing, more suitable as a personal moral guide than as the basis of a nation's fiscal policy. Unwilling to make a distinction between private morality and public morality, Yüan-lu unavoidably fell into his own trap. Often he would abandon altogether his realistic approach to political problems and fall back on the traditional belief that moral rearmament was the cardinal issue in national affairs. In early 1664, while he was still Minister of Revenue and concurrently serving as the emperor's lecturer, he continued to dwell on virtue to the very end (when he himself and the Ch'ung-chen Emperor had only thirty-five days more to live!). During one of Ni's lectures on the classics, the emperor could not refrain from asking: "If virtue is really of such preponderant importance, how could it be usefully employed to solve the nation's pressing problems, while pay and supplies to the soldiers on the frontier are in arrears?" To this question Ni had no satisfactory answer; the end was frustration on the part of both the emperor-student and the minister-instructor.[83]

Though some of his economic policies would no doubt have been conducive to the growth of trade and investment, and thus perhaps of capitalism, Ni's overriding belief in the primacy of moral virtue shows how fundamentally his Neo-Confucian outlook differed from that of the typical exponent of "capitalism" in the West. "The spirit of capitalism," as Max Weber puts it, holds pecuniary acquisition as an end in itself, not as a means to something else, not as an evil; the acquisition is not to be stopped at the level of a satisfying standard of living or at the level of the traditional sense of contentment.[84] Yüan-lu's concept of virtue, on the other hand, requires each individual to maintain a built-in brake upon his self-seeking urge. While planning for the grain-lending association in his home locality, he did not expect profits to be reinvested so as to increase the capital of the enterprise. That profits would be distributed annually to the members is indicated by his assertion that each subscriber's share of the annual profit would be comparable to the return on 240 *mou* of top-quality land, a sound investment that the subscriber could pass on to his posterity as a trust fund.[85]

Many of Ni's ideas, instead of being conducive to the growth of capitalism, were actually detrimental to it. For instance, to cope with the flood disaster in Chekiang, he drafted the so-called Clan Compact of the Ni clan, which called for contributions amounting to 4.17 percent of the annual income of its members. The proceeds were to be distributed as relief to the poor of the clan. The dual purpose of the Compact was that "no poor member of our clan need receive charity from outside, nor well-to-do members of our clan be bothered by government officials." [86] His underlying thought is that the clan as a social organism must be complete and self-sufficient, so as to provide within itself for the needs of its members. His approach was thoroughly traditional in seeking to provide for these needs though the "patriarchal bureaucracy"—and could have served only as a negative force in the development of a free economy.[87]

Thus, despite the comparative "realism" in Ni's approach to fiscal problems, he was far from achieving practical success as a statesman or establishing a scientific basis for his social thought. Joseph Levenson, in his analysis of the failure of early Ch'ing empiricism, suggests that social scientists usually follow the steps of natural scientists, and that there is little hope that social science can mature before natural science.[88] Joseph Needham considers that the differentiation between natural law and the laws of nature, accomplished in the days of Suarez, Kepler, and Descartes (all of whom lived and worked approximately in Yüan-lu's time), marked a major breakthrough in European intellectual history which eventually enabled Westerners to overtake the Chinese in scientific inquiry.[89] Yüan-lu not only lacked the necessary exposure to natural science which might have equipped him to be a competent social scientist; he also failed to make a distinction between substance and concept, let alone between laws of nature and natural law. Like most Chinese scholars, he was devoid of any training in logic, and therefore often took some random analogy as a major premise and drew conclusions from it. Wing-tsit Chan criticizes Wang Yang-ming for confusing reality with value;[90] this criticism, I believe, can also be applied to Ni Yüan-lu.

While recognizing these weaknesses in Ni, however, we cannot dismiss him as simply one more Neo-Confucian or deny him credit for perceiving more clearly than most of his contemporaries the need for basic fiscal reforms. Most Confucians of his time failed to see that the major difficulty faced by the Ming court derived not so much from rising military costs as from the dynasty's institutional inadequacy.[91] The whole fiscal organization of the empire was too antiquated to cope with the problems arising from a national emergency. Many state institutions, such as the gabelle, the military colonies, and the grain transport on the Grand Canal, were too outmoded to be of any help in mobilization of resources. While the centralization of fiscal authority was tight and thorough, funds were scattered. A great gap existed between the organization on paper and actual practices. Tax laws could not be enforced. Domestic and international trade were not promoted and explored as new sources of revenue. Ni's reforms, though narrow in scope and not integrated, represented at least some remedy of the existing system. His programs, as well as his intentions, reflected a tendency to break away from the traditional concept of fiscal management, based on a preconceived scheme dictated from above and designed for an unchanging agrarian economy.

Thus the examination of Ni's thought reveals how it was possible for his "realism" to discern some of the underlying economic factors at work in the late Ming, and to suggest constructive remedies for the problems they created. On the other hand, his proposals were far from radical or revolutionary. He could recognize self-interest as a basic motivation in economic life, and yet he could not have tolerated the idea that man's selfish drives should be allowed free play or that the whole social and moral fabric of Chinese society should be revamped to allow greater freedom for the individual. His utilitarianism, therefore, operated only within the traditional limits of Confucian concern for effective governmental administration. It is unlikely that, even had he survived the fall of his dynasty, his type of "realistic" or "utilitarian" thought would have engendered a significant new trend toward liberal or scientific thought in the Ch'ing period. Its more typical outcome and logical fulfillment was perhaps best exemplified by his own end—his readiness to sacrifice himself for the achievement of Confucian virtue.

NOTES

1. Ni Yüan-lu, *Ni Wen-cheng kung, ch'üan-chi* [av] (1772 ed.) (hereafter cited as Complete Works), Memorials, chs. 1–12.
2. *Ssu-k'u ch'üan-shu tsung-mu t'i-yao* (1930 ed.), 172/16.
3. Complete Works, Belles-lettres, 13/1; Ni Hui-ting, *Ni Wen-cheng kung nien-p'u* [aw] (hereafter cited as Chronological Biography) (Yüeh-ya-t'ang Collectanea ed.), 1/1.
4. Complete Works, Belles-lettres, 13/3–4, 19. For Tsou Yüan-piao's confrontation with Chang Chü-cheng, see Charles O. Hucker, "The Tung-lin Movement of the Late Ming Period," in John K. Fairbank, ed., *Chinese Thought and Institutions* (Chicago, 1957), p. 140.
5. Chiang Shih-ch'üan, "Ni Wen-cheng kung pen-chuan," in Complete Works, 7.
6. Complete Works, Belles-lettres, 13.6–8; Chronological Biography, 1/1.
7. George A. Kennedy's article on Ni in Arthur W. Hummel, ed., *Eminent Chinese of the Ch'ing Period, 1664–1912* (Washington, D.C., 1943–44), p. 587, states: "While supervising examinations in Kiangsi in 1627 he [Ni] offended the party of the eunuch, Wei Chung-hsien, but was saved from punishment by the latter's downfall at the close of that year."

   This involved one of Ni's examination questions which could be interpreted as a hidden attack on Wei. Referring to the incident, Ni's son said only: "People were shocked." We have found no evidence that Ni was persecuted. As an apologist for his father, Ni Hui-ting also mentioned: "Since he was assigned to study [in the Hanlin Academy], he was restrained from speaking up." See Chronological Biography, 1/8–9.
8. Complete Works, Memorials, 1/1–14; Chronological Biography, 1/9–18; *Ming shih-lu* (photolithographic ed., 1940), Ch'ung-chen, 1/1–2, 7; *Ming shih* (Po-na ed.), 265/3–8; and Hsieh Kuo-chen,[ax] *Ming-Ch'ing chih-chi tang-she yün-tung k'ao* [ay] 2d ed.; Shanghai, 1935), pp. 72–73. In *Ming shih*, ch. 265, for instance, Ni's biography is composed of 2,763 words, of which 1,682 words are quotations from Ni's three memorials arguing in favor of the Tung-lin. *Cf.* Kennedy, in Hummel, *ECCP*.
9. Chronological Biography, 2/5–6.
10. *Ibid.*, 2/3, 6, 3/1; Hsieh Kuo-chen, *Tang-she yün-tung*, pp. 78–83.
11. Complete Works, Poetry, 6/5, Chiang Shih-ch'üan, 7.
12. *Ming shih*, 308/29; Hsieh Kuo-chen, 79.

13. *Ming shih*, 265/8, Chronological Biography, 3/1; Chiang Shih-ch'üan, 3, Hsieh Kuo-chen, p. 83. However, *Ming shih-lu*, Ch'ung-chen, 9/8, indicates that Ni resigned.

14. *Ming shih*, 308.25; Hsieh Kuo-chen, 87.

15. Chronological Biography, 4/1–3. For the disposition of the Manchu army inside the Great Wall, see *Ming shih-lu*, Ch'ung-chen, 15/17.

16. Chronological Biography, 4/3, 9. *Cf.* Kennedy, p. 587.

17. Chronological Biography, 4/19, 21; *Ming shih*, 265/9.

18. Hucker, *The Traditional Chinese State in Ming Times, 1368–1644* (Tucson, Ariz., 1961), p. 78.

19. Chronological Biography, 4/4; Complete Works, Memorials, 7/2.

20. Chiang P'ing-chieh,[az] *Pi-shao-pao-kung chuan*[ba] (ed. of *ca.* 1672), p. 26.

21. Lu Shan-chi,[bb] *Jen-chen-ts'ao*[bc] (*Ts'ung-shu chi-ch'eng* ed.), ch. 6.

22. Chronological Biography, 4/8–9.

23. Complete Works, Memorials, 6/2; Chronological Biography, 4/17, 27.

24. Chronological Biography, 4/5.

25. Complete Works, Memorials, 7/12.

26. Complete Works, Memorials, 6/2.

27. Chronological Biography, 2/9.

28. Sun Ch'eng-tse,[bd] *Ch'un-Ming meng-yü lu*[be] (Ku-hsiang-chai ed.), 35/21. Feng Ch'i,[bf] writing around 1600, indicated that the total value was about four million taels. *Feng Tsung-po chi*[bg] (ed. of *ca.* 1607), 51/34.

29. Chronological Biography, 4/8.

30. *Ibid.*, 4/20.

31. Sun, *Meng-yü lu*, 37/29.

32. Complete Works, Memorials, 9/1.

33. *Ibid.*, 9/6.

34. *Ibid.*, 11/6–7; Chronological Biography, 4/22.

35. Chronological Biography, 4/17.

36. *Ming shih*, 255/11.

37. Complete Works, Memorials, 9/11; Chronological Biography, 4/15.

38. Chronological Biography, 4/23.

39. *Ibid.*, 4/24.

40. Huang Tao-chou, "Tomb-stone Inscription," preceding Complete Works, p. 4.

41. Ku, *Jih-chih lu* (Wan-yu wen-k'u ed.), 4/103.

42. Complete Works, Memorials, 9/5.

43. *Ibid.*

44. *Hsü Wen-hsien t'ung-k'ao*[bh] (1936 ed.), p. 2938.

45. Chronological Biography, 2/10.

46. Complete Works, Memorials, 6/7.
47. Chronological Biography, 3/13.
48. Complete Works, Memorials 6/2–3.
49. Ibid., Belles-lettres, 14/8.
50. Ibid., Correspondence, 19/1.
51. Ibid., 18/18.
52. Ibid., Memorials, 9/5; Chronological Biography, 4/13.
53. Complete Works, Memorials, 8/6–7.
54. Ibid., Correspondence, 18/3–4.
55. Chronological Biography, 2/16.
56. See Albert Feuerwerker, "From 'Feudalism' to 'Capitalism' in Recent Historical Writing from Mainland China" (a review article), The Journal of Asian Studies, XVIII, No. 1 (November, 1958), 107–16.
57. Chronological Biography, 1/20.
58. Ibid., 3/8–9.
59. David S. Nivison, " 'Knowledge' and 'Action' in Chinese Thought Since Wang Yang-ming," in Arthur F. Wright, ed., Studies in Chinese Thought (Chicago, 1953), p. 122. Ku Hsien-ch'eng, another leading scholar of the seventeenth century, took the same position by reconciling the teachings of Chu Hsi and Wang Yang-ming. See Heinrich Busch, The Tung-lin Shu-yüan and Its Political and Philosophical Significance (Monumenta Serica XIV), pp. 97–120.
60. Ming-jü hsüeh-an (Wan-yu wen-k'u ed.), 3/52.
61. Carson Chang, The Development of Neo-Confucian Thought (New York, 1962), II, 173–78; 251–54.
62. Ni Yüan-lu, Erh-I nei-i-i (Ts'ung-shu chi-ch'eng ed., hereafter cited as Interior Commentaries), p. 1.
63. This text appears in Interior Commentaries. With the revision mentioned in this paper, the same text is reproduced in Complete Works, Belles-lettres, 6/12–13. English translation and romanization of the special terms in this passage follow Joseph Needham, Science and Civilization in China (Cambridge, 1956), II, 312–21.
64. In Interior Commentaries, out of the hundreds of examples, only Empress Lü, Empress Wu, and Wang An-shih are mentioned on page 18. On page 58 the Han, T'ang, Chin, and Sung are mentioned. There are more later historical examples in Erh-I wai-i (Ts'ung-shu chi-ch'eng ed., hereafter cited as Exterior Commentaries). Those examples, however, are cited by the author to exemplify the original thought of Confucius, or what he believes to be Confucius' original thought.
65. See Jung Chao-tsu, Li Chih nien-p'u (Peking, 1957), pp. 8, 35, 61.
66. Exterior Commentaries, p. 94.
67. Complete Works, Belles-lettres, often mentions the different kinds

of ether. For instance, "righteous ether" appears on 1/1. "Ether of magnanimity" appears on 9/1. "Ether of chastity and uncompromisingness" appears on 8/13. "Ether of unyielding loyalty" was quoted by Chiang Shih-ch'üan from Ni and appears on Chiang, *Pen-chuan*, 2. Note that the concept of different kinds of ether would place Ni closer to the teaching of Ch'eng I than to that of Ch'eng Hao. Of the two brothers, Ch'eng I stressed the difference in individual endowment, while Ch'eng Hao did not assert this difference. The former foreshadowed Chu Hsi, and the latter, Lu Hsiang-shan and Wang Yang-ming. See Wm. Theodore de Bary, *et al., Sources of Chinese Tradition* (3d ptg., paperback, New York, 1964), I, 470–71, 473, 481, 492, 495, 504, 507–8, 515. For the different concepts of ether held by the Ch'eng brothers, see also Fung Yu-lan, *A History of Chinese Philosophy*, tr. by Derk Bodde (Princeton, 1953), II, 518.

68. Complete Works, Belles-lettres, 1/15.
69. *Ibid.*, 11/11.
70. Interior Commentaries, p. 2; Exterior Commentaries, p. 28. Note that A. C. Graham equates *te* with "inner power" or "mana." See Graham, *Two Chinese Philosophers* (London, 1958), p. 112.
71. Exterior Commentaries, p. 84.
72. *Ibid.*
73. Complete Works, Belles-lettres, 4/15.
74. Interior Commentaries, pp. 2, 52.
75. Exterior Commentaries, p. 184.
76. *Ibid.*, p. 171.
77. *Ibid.*, p. 1.
78. *Ibid.*, pp. 171–72.
79. *Ibid.*, p. 1.
80. *Ibid.*, p. 171.
81. Note by Wang K'un,[bi] Interior Commentaries, p. 1.
82. Complete Works, Correspondence, 18/13.
83. Chronological Biography, 4/25–26.
84. Weber, *Protestant Ethic*, as summarized by C. K. Yang in his introduction to Weber's *The Religion of China* (New York, 1964), p. xvi.
85. Chronological Biography, 3/13; Complete Works, Belles-lettres, 6/19.
86. Chronological Biography, 3/10.
87. *The Religion of China*, pp. 90, 95 f.
88. Levenson, *Confucian China and Its Modern Fate* (Berkeley, 1958), pp. 7–14.
89. Needham, *Science and Civilisation*, II, 540–42.
90. Chan, in his introduction to Wang's *Instructions for Practical Living and Other Neo-Confucian Writings* (New York and London, 1963), p. xxxiii.

91. These features are discussed in my paper "Fiscal Administration during the Ming Dynasty," presented to the research conference on Ming government in August, 1965, and included in *Chinese Government in Ming Times: Seven Studies*, ed. by Charles Hucker (New York, 1969).

GLOSSARY

a	倪元璐	af	豫
b	李自成	ag	革
c	上虞	ah	師
d	倪凍	ai	萃
e	鄒元標	aj	噬嗑
f	張居正	ak	賁
g	蔣士銓	al	豐
h	劉宗周	am	旅
i	黃道周	an	爻
j	魏忠賢	ao	象
k	崔呈秀	ap	兒易外儀
l	三朝要典	aq	李贄
m	萬歷實錄	ar	氣
n	倪會鼎	as	才
o	溫體仁	at	德
p	文震孟	au	數
q	姚希孟	av	倪文貞公全集
r	周延儒	aw	倪文正公年譜
s	畢自嚴	ax	謝國楨
t	李汝華	ay	明清之際黨社運動考
u	蔣臣	az	蔣平階
v	邱瀋	ba	畢少保公傳
w	梁夢龍	bb	鹿善繼
x	王宗沐	bc	認眞草
y	沈廷揚	bd	孫承澤
z	楊嗣昌	be	春明夢餘錄
aa	梅之煥	bf	馮琦
ab	太極	bg	馮宗伯集
ac	兒易內儀以	bh	續文獻通考
ad	大象	bi	王鯤
ae	以		

LEON HURVITZ *Chu-hung's One Mind*

of Pure Land and Ch'an Buddhism

明 Yün-ch'i Chu-hung (1532–1612) was by common agreement the most important Buddhist cleric of Ming times.
The present paper, however, makes no pretense to be an exhaustive
study of either the man or his thought. It is confined to his synthesis
of Pure Land and Ch'an Buddhism, and is based primarily on two
major works, Yün-ch'i Chu-hung's Phrase-by-Phrase Commentary on
the Buddha's Scripture Concerning the One of Immeasurable Life
(*Fo shuo A-mi-t'o ching su ch'ao*)[a] and his Random Jottings by a
Bamboo Window (*Chu chuang sui pi*[b]); with its two sequels, the
Second Series (*Erh pi*) and Third Series (*San pi*).[1]

Born into the Shen[c] clan, Chu-hung is referred to by the courtesy
name Fo-hui[d] and the style (*tzu*) Lien-ch'ih,[e] but he is most commonly known under the honorific title Yün-ch'i Ho-shang,[f] after the
monastery in which he settled.[2] His birthplace was Jen-ho[g] County
in Hang-chou, northeast Chekiang. At seventeen he began his course
of scholarship, becoming a *chu sheng*, presumably with the goal of
an official career, on which, however, he never was launched. Instead,
he succumbed to what must have been a stronger desire to leave
the world, when, at the age of thirty-one, he formally entered the
Buddhist clergy. Among his teachers were Chen-yüan,[h] a Hua-yen
scholar, and Te-pao,[i] a Ch'an specialist. Next Chu-hung went to
Chin-ling (Nanking) to the Wa-kuan-szu,[j] a monastery famous for
approximately a thousand years, then even further south, settling
eventually on Mount Yün-ch'i[k] at the age of thirty-six. Because of
his beneficent influence on the local population, we are told, a monastic community quickly sprang up about him. Chu-hung, himself
a strict practitioner, insisted on the same high standard on the part
of the monks with whom he shared his dwelling. Han-shan Te-
ch'ing,[l] the other great name in the Ming Buddhist community, says
that the Buddha himself did not contrive to maintain so well-disci-

plined a group of followers as did Chu-hung. Chu-hung devoted much of his energy to the lay apostolate, and one of the things which he attempted to teach his countrymen was the sinfulness of taking animal life. Already he was attempting to influence the local people to stop killing even for food. In religious terms, his followers in later times said that his philosophy was Hua-yen, his discipline Ch'an, and his ideal the Pure Land. He was, in fact, a principled and convinced opponent of sectarian splintering, and his own personal faith might be called eclectic.[3]

By the Ming period the well-known schools of Chinese Buddhism (T'ien-t'ai, Hua-yen, etc.) were becoming mere names, and the only meaningful divisions were those of contemplation (ch'an [m]), textual study (chiang [n]), and strict adherence to the monastic code (lü [o]). At that, Chu-hung himself tells us that, while in his boyhood the distinction still meant something, by the time of the production of the Chu ch'uang erh pi it was virtually a dead issue.[4] According to the late Ming monk Tao-p'ei,[p] all that was left was Ch'an, and of that only the Lin-chi school, although the Ts'ao-tung school was also contriving to stay alive somehow.[5] Still, the situation even within Ch'an was one of decay. In addition, granted the syncretistic tendencies within the Chinese church, beginning in Ming times there was a pronounced tendency to amalgamate Ch'an with the Pure Land. Special note should be taken of Fan-ch'i,[q] Shao-ch'i,[r] Ching-lung,[s] and Hsiu-shan,[t] [6] the second and fourth of whom used the Pure Land as a subject in their kung-an (Japanese, kōan).

Contemporaneous with Chu-hung, and more or less his equals in moral and religious stature, were Chen-hsia of Tzu-po [u] (1543–1603) and Te-ch'ing of Han-shan (1546–1623), of whom the latter is ranked along with Chu-hung as one of the greatest Buddhist monks in Ming times. Te-ch'ing was, in fact, very like Chu-hung in many ways: he wished to save the failing fortunes of the Faith, he was an earnest practitioner of contemplation, an earnest student of Hua-yen, and a keen scholar of Confucian and Taoist, as well as Buddhist, writings. He also was a simultaneous practitioner of Ch'an and Pure Land meditation, organizing lay fellowships in the case of the latter and also, under the influence of one of his teachers, using the Pure Land as a subject for his kung-an. In fact, he went so far as to say that the Pure Land is the best such subject, holding, likewise, that the best form of Buddha-recollection (*Buddhā nusmṛti*) is that associated with Ch'an contemplation (*ts'an ch'an nien fo* ᵛ), the conventional act of calling upon the Buddha (*ch'eng ming nien fo* ʷ) being good enough for persons of middle and inferior faculties (*chung hsia chi* ˣ). The two men certainly knew of each other, and Te-ch'ing wrote an encomium of Hung (*Yün chi' t'a ming* ʸ), but there is no certain knowledge as to whether they ever met.

As has already been suggested, Hung deplored sectarian rivalry. He was a syncretist or, if you will, a peacemaker. For him, the basis of the monastic life was the code (*chieh-lü*,ᶻ Sanskrit, *vinaya*); his practice was an amalgam of Ch'an contemplation (*dhyāna*) and Buddha-recollection, the latter in the Pure Land tradition; his doctrine was that of the Hua-yen school. In a letter to Yüan Kuang-yen ᵃᵃ (whom I cannot otherwise identify), he says:

The *dhyāna* principle and the Pure Land lead to the same goal by different avenues. What is known as Ch'an contemplation (*ts'an ch'an*) serves merely to clarify birth and death (i.e., *saṃsāra*), while Buddha-recollection simply aims at putting an end to birth and death. The essence [of both] lies in entry into one [and the same] gateway. Nowadays those clever by nature take pleasure in talking *dhyāna*, delighting themselves merely with the motion of their lips. On the other hand, those who cling to dull Buddha-recollection contemplate, for their part, only superficially, and never observe the mind. Frequently [as a result] both miss [the essence].[7]

In another letter, addressed to Wang Kuang-yao ᵃᵇ (also unknown to me), he says:

In antiquity, those who did not strive for the Pure Land did, however, as a matter of fact concern their thoughts with *dhyāna*. When *dhyāna* was perfected, the Pure Land was [*eo ipso*] complete. Now, however, those who do not strive for the Pure Land do not, in fact, concern their thoughts with *dhyāna* [either]. With their mouths they talk *dhyāna* to their great conceit but of *dhyāna* and the Pure Land they achieve neither.[8]

In order to make clear Chu-hung's notions about the Pure Land, it would be well to give a bare summary of Kumārajīva's translation of the *Lesser Sukhāvatīvyūha*, since Chu-hung's views on the Pure Land are intimately associated with this particular scripture.

The Buddha Śākyamuni is at Śrāvastī, surrounded by the usual retinue, of whom śrāvakas, bodhisattvas, and devas are specified. He then tells them, Śāriputra in particular, the following: "West of here, many millions of worlds away, is a land called Chi lo [ac] (Extremely Pleasant), presided over by a Buddha named A-mi-t'o (Amita, i.e., Immeasurable). The land itself is wondrous, consisting of . . . (there follows a physical description). It has no inferior creatures, its birds being transformations effected by Amita for purposes of salvation. All of its human inhabitants are *avaivartika* (not subject to backsliding), most of them *ekajātipratibaddha* (one who will attain Buddahood in the next rebirth), i.e., all bodhisattvas. Any living being who hears of that land should vow to be reborn there. How? If, upon hearing the name of Amita pronounced, he (or she) contemplates that name steadily for as much as seven days, he will be reborn there immediately upon terminating his present life. I know, for I have seen it happen. For that matter, Amita is only one of many Buddhas in the West, not to mention all the others in the North, South, East, Up, and Down. Anyone who believes this sermon of mine will attain *anuttarasamyaksaṃbodhi* (unexcelled right and perfect enlightenment); one who believes it should vow to be reborn in that land. My supreme wisdom and my worthiness of credence, in spite of the apparent incredibility of what I have just said, are attested by all the other Buddhas." The assembly, overjoyed at having heard this, takes respectful leave. A mantra follows.

Because of his Hua-yen orientation, Chu-hung wishes to assign the *Sukhāvatīvyūha* its place in the scheme of gradations (*p'an chiao* [ad]) devised by Fa-tsang (643–712), the systematizer of the Hua-yen doctrine. This scheme consists of: 1) the Lesser Vehicle and four facets of the Greater Vehicle, viz: 2) the preliminary (*shih chiao* [ae]); 3) the final (*chung chiao* [af]); 4) the sudden (*tun chiao* [ag]); and 5) the rounded doctrine (*yüan chiao* [ah]). The *Sukhāvatīvyūha*, says Chu-hung, belongs properly to (4), but certain aspects of it "spill over" into (3) and (5). The reason for (4) is that, difficult as it is for the "ordinary fellow on thin ground" (*po ti fan fu* [ai]; Sanskrit, *tanubhūmiḥ pṛthagjanaḥ?*) to get to "holy ground" (*sheng ti* [aj]; Sanskrit, *āryabhūmi*[?]), he does so *all at once* by the mere recitation of a Name and, having done so, does not backslide (*pu t'ui* [ak]; Sanskrit, *na vivartate*). The reason for (3) is that, by these means, even the worst sinner (*icchantika*) is not beyond the reach of salvation. As for (5), Chu-hung gives ten reasons, of which the two most important are these:

1. While the *Avatamsaka* tells us that everything in the inanimate world (*bhajanaloka*), whether shaped or shapeless, conveys the Buddha's Message, the *Sukhāvatīvyūha* now tells us that the waterfowl and the trees in the forests preach the basic constituents of sensation, knowledge, and enlightenment (*indriyas, balas,* and *bodhipakṣas*).

2. While the *Avataṃsaka* says that every grain of sand contains the adornments of the dharma spheres of all ten directions, the *Sukhāvatīvyūha* says that it is possible to see on any jeweled tree in the Pure Land (*Sukhāvatī*) the Buddha-lands of all ten directions as if in a mirror.

Chu-hung goes on to say that all are within reach of salvation except those "without faith, without the wish, and without the [proper] conduct" (*wu hsin wu yüan wu hsing*[al]). "Faith" is, of course, unqualified belief in the efficacy of the vow to be reborn in the Pure Land. "Wish" means just that. The "action" in question is constant mindfulness of the wish to be reborn there. It goes without saying that faith, wish, and action, all three, are indispensable for rebirth in the Pure Land.

The *Sukhāvatīvyūha* says that one's rebirth in Sukhāvatī is assured "if one takes hold of the Name for a time from one day to seven days, with mind undisturbed." In other words, says Chu-hung, the essential act is, having heard the Name, to "take hold" of it (*chih ch'ih*[am]). *Chih,* according to him, means the acceptance of it upon hearing it and, once having accepted it, the steadfast refusal to be deprived of it. *Ch'ih,* on the other hand, refers to the constant retention of it in the memory. There are three kinds of *ch'ih*: *ming ch'ih, mo ch'ih,* and *pan ming pan mo ch'ih.*[an] The first is intonation in a clear voice. The second is contemplation. The third is recitation with movement of the lips but without uttering a sound, or alternation of *ming ch'ih* with *mo ch'ih,* whether at fixed intervals or at random.

Buddhānusmṛti, says Chu-hung, is of four kinds: *ch'eng ming,*[ao] *kuan hsiâng,*[ap] *kuan hsiâng,*[aq] and *shih hsiang.*[ar] The first is the well-known resort to calling upon the Name, prescribed in the *Sukhāvatīvyūha.* The second is contemplation of an image of Amita. The third is the evocation of the vision of Amita before one's mind's eye and the contemplation of him there. The fourth and last is the contemplation of Amita as transcending all notions of birth and extinction, existence and emptiness, subject and object, indeed all names and even all thoughts. While he holds that the progression of these four is from the shallowest to the deepest, Hung is as far as anyone else from maintaining that the *Sukhāvatīvyūha* is shallow in content. For, says he, the "calling upon the Name" prescribed in that scripture embraces the other three practices as well. The reason, says he, is that it must be carried out "with mind undisturbed" (*i hsin pu-luan* ᵃˢ). The "one mind" (*i hsin*) may be of two kinds: particular (*shih i hsin* ᵃᵗ) or universal (*li i hsin* ᵃᵘ). While the former is not really profound, the latter is to be identified with Truth itself (*i hsin chi shih shih hsiang* ᵃᵛ), i.e., with superiority to all marks and signs (*wu hsiang* ᵃʷ). The particular/universal distinction applies to the "taking hold" as well as to the "one mind." The former has to do with "uninterrupted mindfulness" (*i nien wu chien* ᵃˣ), i.e., with constant mental dwelling on the four syllables A-mi-t'o-fo ᵃʸ in continuous and uninterrupted succession; whether walking, standing, sitting, or lying; without allowing the *kleśas*, or indeed anything else, to disturb the unity of these thoughts; thus arriving at the one mind of particularity mentioned above. The latter has to do with "uninterrupted total embodiment" (*t'i chiu wu chien* ᵃᶻ), i.e., with reaching a state wherein the object of contemplation coalesces with one's own mind, eventuating in the one mind of universality also mentioned above. This also has two facets, one referring to the recognition of the absence of contradiction between the cognizing intellect and the cognized object, the other to the absence of all contradictions. Thus, says Chu-hung, shallow though it may appear, calling on the name of the Buddha (*ch'eng ming nien fo*) is very profound indeed. In point of fact, this "one mind" and the Ch'an school's "direct pointing" (*chih-chih* ᵇᵃ) at the mind were one and the same thing, as far as Chu-hung was concerned.[9]

Chu-hung goes even further, holding that the *Sukhāvatīvyūha* belongs to the consciousness-only (*vijñānamātra*) strain of Buddhism, since, in his view, the scripture in question says that everything is a figment of the consciousness (*vijñāna, shih* ᵇᵇ), a proposition that can be considered with reference to four points of view. 1. Everything

is real, there being no deceptive appearances (*wei pen wu ying*^{bc}).
This is typical of the Hīnayāna scriptures, which give us to understand that the Buddha was really there, that he really preached, etc.
2. There are both reality and deceptive appearances (*i pen i ying*^{bd}).
This is typical of the "early" Mahāyāna. The Buddha's predications
were absolutely true, but the beings placed upon them constructions
ranging from the partially true to the totally false. 3. Everything is
deceptive appearance (*wei ying wu pen*^{be}). This is typical of the
"late" Mahāyāna. Apart from the mind, there is nothing—no Buddha, no predications, absolutely nothing. 4. There is nothing whatsoever. Deceptive appearances are as nonexistent as substantial reality. This is the position of the "sudden teaching" (*tun chiao*), a
teaching quite beyond words, a doctrineless doctrine, so to speak.
The Venerable One says nothing, and I hear nothing. There is
consciousness (*vijñāna*) and nothing else.

The *Sukhāvatīvyūha* belongs to (3) and (4) simultaneously. The
beings, yearning in their hearts for escape from the world, in their
mind's eye see the Buddha preaching to them about the Supremely
Pleasant Land and him whose base it is. In their belief, they vow to
be reborn there. In reality, however, there is neither preaching nor
listening. Therefore consciousness is the substance of this doctrine.[10]

The above was part of a larger effort to counter the attempts of
the learned Buddhists to pooh-pooh Pure Land salvationism as cater-
ing to the unlettered, the idea of the learned being that the lettered
would gravitate toward T'ien-t'ai, Hua-yen, or even Ch'an. Chu-
hung's objection to this was on several levels. The Buddha's single
goal in coming into the world was universal salvation. A device that
proves salutary in one case may not prove salutary in another. Any
device that works is justified. Besides, the efficacy of contemplating
Amita and invoking him is attested throughout the Canon; anyone
calling himself a Buddhist is obliged to believe in Amita. Next, Pure
Land euphoria is definitely not the goal of contemplation-invocation.
Rebirth in the Pure Land is but the first step toward the attainment
of Buddhahood and all that it means, viz., the role of universal
Saviour. So much the less reason, then, for the shoddy spectacle of
sectarian dogfights staged by the self-styled pious Buddhists of our
land.

Chu-hung gives the "true meaning of this Scripture" in terms of five pairs of opposites. 1. The first is the teaching versus its content. "What does this mean? It means just this: The Buddha wishes to convey clearly and unambiguously the primary recompense, Buddha-hood, and the secondary recompense, the Pure Land, . . . which have fallen to the lot of Amita Buddha. . . . If the practitioner be-lieves and desires them, then he will be reborn in that land. . . . This scripture is no mere collection of empty words and phrases, of written characters strung together." 2. The inner meaning (i ^{bf}) of this scripture contains both particulars ($shih$) and universals (li). "What does this mean? The Buddha wishes to clarify the general truths contained in these concrete facts. This is his goal. It is no mere statement of concrete specifics." 3. This general truth is an object ($ching$ ^{bg}) of intuitive observation, as opposed to the wisdom ($chih$) which intuits it. The practitioner venerates this object. "What does this mean? Knowing Amita's own being, i.e., that the Pure Land is mind alone, he desires, having made the same into a true object of intuition, to initiate the action which consists of observing the Pure Land and of holding to his Name, both single-mindedly and unwaveringly. This is his goal. It is no mere statement of an abstract understanding of this general truth." 4. The action just mentioned is now counterposed to the goal of total calm ($chih$ chi ^{bh}). The prac-titioner honors the aforementioned action, which consists of observ-ing the Pure Land. "What does this mean? Indeed, though the mind is fundamentally calm, it gives rise to many taints, and attachment to objects arises within the mind. Unless one cultivates the above-mentioned action based on observation, then, however much one may forcibly suppress unwarranted thoughts, the final outcome will not be one of undifferentiating concentration and wisdom ($ting$ hui $p'ing$-$teng$ ^{bi}; Sanskrit, $dhyānaprajñāsamatā[?]$). Now, however, if, by relying on right observation and holding to his name, one arrives at the One Mind, then one will revert to the substance of empty calm (i.e., of a Calm devoid of all attributes, $k'ung$ chi ^{bj}); this is his goal. It is no mere placing of false and arbitrary constructions." 5. The Calm, finally, is counterposed to the manifest functions ($yung$ ^{bk}) of the one who has attained it. The practitioner reveres this Calm. "What does this mean? Indeed, by relying on false constructions and attachments, one makes nothing of salvation. If the false is done away with and the mind unified, then the pure Ultimate shines through, just as, for example, when the dust is cleared away, the mirror is bright, and there is no image that cannot be seen therein. What is meant is as follows: Having been reborn in the said Land, and having attained the unconditioned state (*anutpattikadharmak-ṣānti*),[11] one returns to the realm of birth and death and, by resort to numberless devices, performs in a great way the functions of a Buddha, saving many beings. One's wondrous functions are as numerous as the sands of Ganges: this is one's goal. It is no mere self-immersion in emptiness and calm." [12]

One of the headings of the Commentary says that the Buddha, in the *Sukhāvatīvyūha*, "makes it clear that precisely those whose minds are full of thoughts of Amita are capable of no-thought." This can be properly understood only in the light of the use of the Chinese *nien* [bl] to express two ideas, that of "mindfulness" or "recollection," corresponding to the Sanskrit *smṛti*, and that of "thought" in the most general sense, not corresponding, so far as I am aware, to any Sanskrit original. While in the former sense it is the supreme desideratum in Pure Land salvationism, in the latter sense it is an obstacle to salvation in all Buddhist schools, most particularly in Ch'an. It is precisely because Chu-hung is so committed to both approaches that he makes—and clearly by intention—the apparently paradoxical statement that "the mind which possesses *nien* can enter into absence of *nien*," i.e., that precisely the mind that is intent on the recollection of Amita can achieve the freedom from thought that is an indispensable precondition to Buddhist intuition. Nonetheless, for Chu-hung, Chinese that he was, *nien* was a single word, representing at bottom one idea. Clearly, for him freedom from *nien* in the very midst of *nien* was no more of a paradox than the presence of *nirvāṇa* in the very midst of *saṃsāra*. Whether well or ill, the body is the body, is it not? Whether rebellious or obedient, the people are the same people, are they not? "To remove thought (*nien*) and seek for the mind (*hsin*) is, in the case of the physician, to feel obliged to destroy the body in order then to cure the disease; it is the same as to slaughter the nation in order to pacify the people. Is this rational?" [13] Closely allied to this is the idea that contemplation of the Buddha banishes the random thoughts that, stuffed indiscriminately in his mind, distract the ordinary man from the proper goal of salvation. When now, thanks to the power of keeping his Name, proper mindfulness (*cheng nien;* [bm] Sanskrit, *samyak-smṛti*) has but arisen, the random thoughts automatically vanish. It is just as, when the lion comes out of his den, the hundreds of beasts hide their tracks; as, when the sun shines from high on the frost, the thousands of trees lose their whiteness.[14]

The particular category to which a given Chinese master assigned a given scripture depended, as we have said, on his general schema of *p'an chiao*. For all of them, however, the status of the Lotus Sutra (*Saddharmapuṇḍarīka; Miao fa lien hua ching* [bn]) was a high one. The reasoning was as follows: There is only one form of salvation, viz., Buddhahood itself. The ordinary mentality, however, cannot grasp this. The Buddha, accordingly, as a temporizing device (*upāya; fang pien* [bo]), preached three courses or vehicles (*yāna*), in order to appeal to persons of sharp, middle, and dull faculties, respectively, but for the ultimate purpose of converting them. When this groundwork had been laid, he told his listeners that there is only One Vehicle (*ekayāna*) i.e., Buddhahood itself. This alleged resolution, known in Chinese as "uniting the Three and reducing them to One" (*hui san kuei i* [bp]), is traditionally regarded in China as the Buddha's sole reason for coming into the world, the "Great Message of the Thus-Come One's entire teaching career." [15] The soul-gladdening message of the Buddha-destiny of all the living is, in the view of Chu-hung, common to the Lotus and the *Sukhāvatīvyūha*. In the latter, "if one will but single-mindedly keep his name, immediately one will attain to freedom from backsliding." This is nothing other than a flat indication that the mind of the ordinary fellow is the stuff of ultimate Buddhahood. If one can believe this thoroughly, what need to pass through three vehicles, to traverse at length through many kalpas? In no more than a single thought one can have a sudden and direct intuition of *bodhi*.[16]

The inevitable corollary is that the Pure Land is in the mind, that the place in which one is situated is pure or impure depending on the state of one's mind. We have already seen the prescription of single-mindedness. "Once one has achieved single-minded imperturbability, one understands for the first time that the lotus-blossoms and the rows of trees, as well as all the sundry ornaments, are no-where out of the mind. What need to hear the Golden Sayings with one's ear in order to be able only then to speak of the perfection of the adornments of the Pure Land? . . . It is for this reason that one says that the Pure Land is before one's very eyes." [17]

If the Pure Land is in the mind, a bridge is furnished from Pure Land salvationism to Ch'an. "The Ch'an doctrine and the Pure Land reach the same destination by different routes. Since the latter does not separate itself from the One Mind, it is identical with Buddha, identical with *Dhyāna*. Therefore he who clings to Ch'an and den-igrates the Pure Land is denigrating his own Original Mind (*pen hsin* [bq]); he is denigrating the Buddha. He is denigrating his own Ch'an doctrine. He simply is not thinking." [18]

In India, the Buddhists had inherited from their non-Buddhist ancestors the notion of cosmic cycles, the idea being that the pas-sage of time brought with it steady degeneration, until the world should be consumed by a cosmic holocaust and the next cycle should begin. Within this scheme, the emergence of a Buddha was supposed to take place relatively late, when the degeneration was already rather well advanced. At that, the interval between the Buddha's *nirvāṇa* and the cosmic holocaust could be divided into three parts. 1. In the first, the era of the True Dharma (*saddharma; cheng fa* [br]), the Buddha's message would take full effect. 2. In the second, that of Counterfeit Dharma (*pratirūpakadharma; hsiang fa* [bs]), the outward forms would be observed, but would be devoid of any real inner content. 3. In the third and last era, that of Decay of the Dharma (*saddharmavipralopa; mo fa* [bt]), there would be a total loss. In *mo fa* a man's merit is so paltry that salvation on the basis of it alone is out of the question. The Buddhas and bodhisattvas, on the other hand—and this applies to Amita in particular—have superabundant merit. Faith in them is all that is necessary for rebirth in a Pure Land, where the achievement of Buddhahood is much easier than here on this earth (*Jambudvīpa*). Moreover, in this degenerate age no other form of salvation is really possible. Amita Buddha, says Chu-hung, in his infinite compassion holds out this form of salva-tion to suffering mankind, and Śākyamuni Buddha, in his own infi-nite compassion, informs suffering mankind of the availability of it. [19]

The Buddha has not only made this salvation possible, but has also provided the means for the achievement of it. "Among an infinity of gateways to salvation, the one gateway of Buddha-contemplation is the easiest. Simply put, these easy means are four in number. The first is the possibility of constantly seeing a Buddha in an age in which one cannot meet one. The second is the possibility of extricating oneself from the spinning of the wheel in transmigration (*lun hui* [bu]; *saṃsāra*) while still engaged in actions similar to those of the unenlightened. The third is the possibility of achieving the perfection of Wisdom (*prajñāpāramitā*) through the cultivation of no other act than this one of Buddha-contemplation. The fourth is the possibility of securing quick release without going through many kalpas." [20]

Chu-hung tells us that only three persons are beyond the reach of Amita's saving grace: 1) the one who does not believe him; 2) the one who, though believing, does not earnestly wish for rebirth in his Land; 3) the one who, though wishing for it, does not exert himself by thinking constantly and single-mindedly of the Pure Land.[21] Further comment on this is the following: "If one but keeps the Buddha's Name, one will without fail be reborn in his Land. Be one's station high or low, be one saintly or common, be one even a believer or a doubter, a praiser or a vilifier, if one but knows that the Buddha is there, one thereby achieves roots of goodness. In the course of many kalpas and many rebirths, all such persons shall benefit from salvation." [22]

A straw man now asks how doubters and vilifiers can also be saved. The answer says, in part, "Doubt arises from knowledge, and knowledge arises from hearing. If one hears and knows that there is a Buddha, only then can one have doubts. If one has never heard or known, whence can doubts arise? Thanks to hearing and knowing, the one word 'Buddha' is lodged in the soil of one's consciousness. When thereafter seed is strewn on that earth, and when straightway thereafter rain and dew infuse it, there is, finally, a day on which the plant sprouts. The vilifier of the Buddha is, in principle, exactly like this. For this reason I have said, 'If one but knows that that Buddha is there, one thereby achieves roots of goodness,' eventuating in salvation. If one neither hears nor knows, there can be no sowing." [23]

This, surely, is almost the ultimate in salvation: To be saved, all one needs is to hear his Name.

As has already been stated, a common charge against the salvation-ists was that the rebirth they desired was, though subjectively Ma-hayanistic, nonetheless, in effect, no different from *arhattva*, being a sort of euphoric paradise. Disgust with pain and the quest for joy seem nothing other than being intent on self-benefit. Under the circumstances, what talk can there be of "bodhisattvas"? The answer is as follows: The quest for rebirth in the Pure Land is precisely for the purpose of seeing Buddha and hearing the Dharma, thus attaining to the abovementioned unconditioned state (*anutpattikadharma-kṣānti*). Having attained this, the practitioner comes back to this world and saves the suffering beings. This is bodhisattva conduct, not the way of the auditor (*śrāvaka*).[24]

There is considerable treatment of "single-mindedness (*i hsin*), mentioned earlier, of which it would not be out of place to reproduce a certain portion here. Single-mindedness as a matter of universal truth (*li i hsin*) consists of direct intuition in the following two senses. 1. One must understand thoroughly that the recollector and the recollected are in no sense two separate things, since they are only One Mind. 2. This One Mind neither exists nor does not exist, nor both nor neither, since none of these four terms (*ssu chü* [bv]; *catuṣkoṭi*) is applicable to the One Mind. This is a matter of universal truth (*li*), not of particular experience (*shih*) alone. The perfection of this power of observation is what is called *li i hsin*. The "direct intuition" just mentioned signifies direct introspection, the limit of which is one's own mind. The two senses just mentioned are further commented on as follows. 1. Thusness and Knowledge are not two. Outside the mind of the recollector there is no Buddha whom I can recollect. This is to say that outside of Knowledge there is no Thusness. Outside of the Buddha who is recollected there is no mind that can recollect a Buddha. This is to say that outside of Thus-ness there is no Knowledge. It is neither Thusness nor Knowledge; that is why it is only One Mind. 2. Calm and Intuition are difficult to conceive. If one says that they exist, then the objection is that the mind that recollects is in substance empty, while the Buddha who is recollected is absolutely unattainable (*pu k'o te* [bw]; *aprāpya*). If one says that they do not exist, then the objection is that the mind that recollects them is bright and unobscured, while the Buddha who is recollected is plain and obvious. If one says that they both exist and do not, then the objection is that he who has recollections and he who has none both disappear. If one says that they neither exist nor do not, then the objection is that he who has recollections and he who has none both exist. All avenues of speech and thought are cut off; there is no form to which one can give a name. Therefore, there is only One Mind. This being the case, the identity of both the actor and his object fades; views of existence and nonexistence vanish. What dharma can there possibly be that might adulterate and render confused a substance that is both pure and original? Because one sees this truth (*ti* [bx]; *satya*), one names it *li i hsin*.[25]

The One Mind, devoid of content, will make some think of Ch'an. Chu-hung is no exception, for he says in so many words that this One Mind is the very thing at which Bodhidharma was "directly pointing" (*chih chih*; cf. p. 456). Chu-hung further comments that the Ch'an people usually denigrate the Pure Land, but that the only difference between what they are "pointing at" and the One Mind just mentioned is one of terminology. Well has it been said that *dhyāna* is the *dhyāna* of the Pure Land, and vice versa. Still other protagonists of Ch'an say that the latter does not resort to the written word (*pu li wen tzu*), while the Pure Land salvationists call upon all mankind to utter the four-syllable name A-*mi-t'o-fo*. Yet, says Chu-hung in rebuttal, in comparison to the four rolls of the Laṅkāvatāra Sūtra,[26] the four syllables of the salvationists are modest indeed. However, he says, all this is rather beside the point. "Non-reliance on the written word" does not mean "annihilation of the written word" (*tuan mieh wen tzu* [by]). The essential is to refuse to commit oneself to the written word, yet, at the same time, not to adhere to this refusal.[27] A bit later on, Chu-hung says that this contemplation of Amita is to be identified with the One Mind (a point he has made before), and that this total commitment is *eo ipso* Buddhahood. He concludes with a scriptural quotation which says that the mere hearing of the Name is enough for salvation.[28]

After saying that faith is crucial,[29] Chu-hung goes on to say that, if hearing the Name had no beneficial consequences, it would be no different from music. The hearing, however, induces the practitioner to contemplate the Three Jewels, with all that that implies.[30]

The One Mind is, of course, nondual, and is a denial of contradictions. Thus greed (*t'an* [bz]; *rāga*), anger (*ch'en* [ca]),[31] and folly (*ch'ih* [cb]; *moha*) are in and of themselves disciplined conduct (*chieh*; *śīla*), contemplation (*ting* [cc]; *dhyāna*), and wisdom (*hui* [cd]; *prajñā*); thus the good way and the evil way are both in the nature of hallucination. Hallucination having no own-being, all is One Mind alone. If the One Mind does not come into being, then all dharmas come to rest.[32] Thus even the One Mind is no more than a device, which, once it has served its purpose, must be done away with.

Says Chu-hung, "Now men who hear of the Buddha but cannot bring themselves to keep his Name are, roughly speaking, subject to four obstacles. And, if these four obstacles can be smashed, they are then able to keep the Name and thus to reach the One Mind." He further comments:

1. "Since the Mind is the Buddha, what need to throw oneself away in order to contemplate him?"

They who think thus do not understand that the identity of the Buddha with the Mind is no obstacle to Buddha-contemplation. That is why they think thus. But, since the Mind is equal to the Buddha, why is the Buddha not equal to the Mind? If one merely clings to contemplation of the Mind, and does not allow contemplation of the Buddha, then the Mind and the Buddha are two, and the doctrine becomes untenable. For this reason, Buddha-contemplation and Mind-contemplation should not be an obstacle to each other.

2. "Why not contemplate all the Buddhas universally? Why one Buddha alone?"

They who speak thus do not understand that it is only when concentrated on one subject exclusively that the mind achieves *samādhi*; that is why they speak so. Indeed, because the beings are of shallow intelligence, when the object is complex, they are not equal to it. Therefore they who direct their attention undividedly can concentrate their spirit, while they who exert their minds in different directions waste their efforts. It is because the Buddhas are of the same body of Dharmahood that, if one contemplates one of them, one is *eo ipso* contemplating them all.

3. "All Buddhas can be contemplated. Why not contemplate the one of one's choice? Why must it be Amita?"

They who speak thus do not understand that that Buddha has a particular nexus with the beings; this is why they speak so. Indeed, it is because that Buddha's Name is a thing men desire to call upon that even an evil man will, at times quite unintentionally, find the invocation slipping out of him. On the other extreme, a man will encounter a happy incident, and quite unintentionally find himself contemplating the Buddha and joyfully praising him. Or a man might encounter unpleasantness and unhappiness and unintentionally find himself contemplating the Buddha in his suffering. For the impulses to this sort of devotion may be spontaneous, having no specific causation.

4. "Why not contemplate the Buddha's excellences and wisdom, his primary and secondary marks, his luster? Why only his Name?"

What they who speak thus do not understand is that keeping his Name is most appropriate in this latter age, for it is quite past comprehension. As to the meaning of "appropriate," the Mahāprajñā-pāramitā scripture preached by Mañjuśrī [33] says, "The beings are stupid and dull. What they see they do not understand. If they but cause thought and voice to succeed each other without interruption, they will automatically achieve rebirth." Not only is this practice in accord with the faculties of the dull, but its superhuman functions are also not to be calculated. Now one trains the mind to call upon the Name of the Buddha, thereby arriving at the One Mind. How can reason comprehend this? [34]

Chu-hung's imaginary interlocutor asks a question which must have plagued the salvationists:

The ordinary man, if he fears transmigration enough, will bend every effort toward salvation, never letting a single moment go idly by. However, once he hears of a way of getting out of the Triple Sphere (*Tridhātu*) "horizontally," of a "short cut" to self-cultivation, of the expunction of sin by recollection of the Buddha, of rebirth in that Land thanks to ten repetitions of a formula, than he thinks, "After all, there is a Buddha to whom I can have recourse. What need to fear the consequences of my deeds?" With this in mind, he stops exerting himself, and falls into the hands of one of Yama's henchmen. This is the fault of the salvationists, who have led him astray. Both the Ch'an and the philosophical schools make no pretense of a royal road to salvation. When the salvationists say that "life and death are in the mind," what nonsense they talk!

Chu-hung's answer is as follows:

Most men, in cultivating a way of life, stop short of reputed difficulties and direct themselves to practices alleged to be easy. Some, on the contrary, gird their loins when they hear of difficulties, and slacken when they are told how easy it all is. The saints of yore tailored their preaching to the times. The ability or inability to take the predications to heart was a purely individual matter. The Way of Buddha-recollection directly outpasses the Triple Sphere. The Buddha, in his extreme compassion, opened this door to the beings. If the practitioner proves lazy and commits wrong, it is he who is deceiving himself, not the Buddha who is deceiving him.[35]

We are told that other Buddhas heaped praise on Śākyamuni for his ability, in the face of great difficulties, to preach the Dharma, "difficulty" referring to the reluctance of mankind to accept the doctrine preached. Chu-hung says that men's reluctance to believe is due to their inherent evil, which impels them to reject their own salvation. He comments further: [36]

By "difficult of belief" are meant roughly ten things: [37]
1. Now they dwell in a filthy land, where, through long custom, their minds are at ease. Suddenly hearing of that Land of pure adornment, they suspect there is no such thing. This is the first point of difficulty.
2. Even if they believe in that Land, they suspect that it is possible to be reborn in the Buddha-fields (*buddhakṣetras*) of all ten directions, and question why they must necessarily be reborn in the Extremely Pleasant Land. This is the second point of difficulty.
3. Even if they believe that they may be reborn there, yet they suspect that the distance between this world and the Extremely Pleasant Land is ten thousand million *kṣetras*, and question how, in the face of such extreme distance, they can go thither. This is the third point of difficulty.
4. Even if they believe distance to be no obstacle, yet they suspect that ordinary fellows (*fan fu* [ce]; *pṛthagjanāḥ*) on the face of the broad earth are so terribly burdened by the impediments of their own sin (*tsui-chang* [cf]; *pāpāvaraṇa*[?]) that they question how they can be reborn in that Land as if nothing had happened. This is the fourth point of difficulty.
5. Even if they believe that rebirth there is possible, they suspect that it may be possible through refined methods and meritorious acts of all kinds, and question how by merely keeping to his Name one can possibly be reborn there. This is the fifth point of difficulty.

6. Even if they believe in keeping his Name, yet they suspect that it is necessary to keep his Name for many years, many kalpas, in order to achieve the desired result, and question how it is possible in a mere day, or even in seven, to be reborn without further ado. This is the sixth point of difficulty.

7. Even if they believe in the possibility of rebirth in seven days, yet they suspect that those who are born into the seven destinies [38] cannot escape rebirth from a womb (*t'ai* [cg]; *jarāyu*), egg (*luan* [ch]; *aṇḍa*), moisture (*shih* [ci]; *saṃsveda*), or self-production (*hua* [cj]; *upapāduka*), and question how in that Land all can be reborn from self-production on a lotus blossom. This is the seventh point of difficulty.

8. Even if they believe in rebirth on the lotus, yet they suspect that the person whose conversion to the Way is of recent date is subject to backsliding at many points, and question how, upon rebirth in that Land, he is immediately free from backsliding. This is the eight point of difficulty.

9. Even if they believe that he will not backslide, yet they suspect that this is a device for attracting beings of inferior faculties, and that persons of superior knowledge and sharp faculties (*li ken* [ck]; *tīkṣṇendriya*) have no need to be reborn there. This is the ninth point of difficulty.

10. Even if they believe that those of sharp faculties are also reborn there, yet they have their doubts, since of the other scriptures some say that there is a Buddha, some that there is none; others say that there is a Pure Land, still others that there is not. Thus their doubts are not resolved. This is the tenth point of difficulty.

Hence "difficult of belief." As for the infinity of time and space [separating this world from the Pure Land], it is not merely those in the three lowest destinies who find it difficult to believe, for some men and gods also doubt it; not merely fools and those gone astray, for some of the wise and knowing also doubt it; not merely those of callow faculties, for some of long practice also doubt it; not merely ordinary fellows, for in some cases those in the Two Vehicles also doubt it. For these reasons it is called a "dharma difficult of belief for all the worlds."

One of the supplements to the Commentary is a series of forty-eight questions (equal in number to the vows of Dharmākara) from an imaginary interlocutor and the answers thereto. The last of the answers concludes with a passage which in a sense summarizes Chu-hung's whole attitude toward the Pure Land:

In the invocation in six syllables (*nan-wu a-mi-t'o-fo* [cl] for *namo 'mitā-bhāya buddhāya*), each syllable reveals the inner meaning of Bodhi-dharma's arrival from the West. What need to turn from the Lesser to the Greater, to change the cramped space into a free passage, in order then and only then to have access to those superior faculties and propagate this mysterious conversion? Hence we know that the single road of Buddha-recollection is in and of itself the subtle gateway of entry into the absolute and universal truth, fully according with the Five Schools,[39] broadly co-inciding with the various doctrines, so that one's exactitude and subtlety shall be unfathomable, one's breadth and greatness unlimited. The person of sharp intelligence encounters it and directly passes over to Yonder Shore. It seems coarse, yet is fine; though apparently easy, still it is difficult. You whose vow is universal, whose thoughts are profound, take care not to make light of it! [40]

The *Chu ch'uang sui pi* (Random jottings by a bamboo window) and its two sequels, the *Erh pi* and the *San pi*, are, as indicated in the word *sui pi* itself, random jottings on a great number of subjects. What appear below are paraphrases of those entries that concern Ch'an contemplation and Buddha-recollection, as well as two other aspects of Chu-hung's thought for which he is famous: his insistence on strict monastic discipline and his condemnation of sectarian polemics. The first personal pronoun, unless otherwise indicated, refers to Chu-hung himself.

There are some who say, if the mind is the Pure Land, then the much-touted Pure Lands are all imaginary. True, but susceptible of misinterpretation. For, if the mind is the object, then there is no object apart from the mind, but there is also no mind apart from the object. The object and the mind being perfectly identical, why cling to the mind and deny the object? For one who does that does not really understand the mind. Others will say the Pure Land that one sees at the moment of death is only one's own mind. Therefore there is no Pure Land. Those who speak thus do not think of the ancient and modern devotees of the Pure Land, escorted into the Pure Land with much pomp and fanfare in a spectacle borne witness to by others besides themselves. Not only that, but the scent of the perfume borne by the escorting multitude would be detected at the place of death for days afterward. Do you still say that there is no Pure Land? Besides, if you maintain the real existence of Hell, how can you consistently deny that of the Pure Land? [41]

There was a monk practicing nothing but Buddha-recollection. There was another monk very proud of his Ch'an contemplation,

who said to him, "You Buddha-recollectors must wait for rebirth in
the West in order to see Amita Buddha and only then gain enlightenment. We meditators gain enlightenment in this very life. The
difference in speed is obvious. Stop your recollecting and begin
meditating!" The other monk, unable to decide, asked me. I told
him: "Among faculties there are sharp and dull. Among energies
there are diligent and slack. It depends upon the individual. Hence
it is not right to say, on the mere basis of relative speed, that one is
right and the other wrong. It is like two men going to a place where
there is a jewel to be found. One man goes on horseback, the other
by ship. Both set out the same day, but arrive at different times. This
is what is meant by 'sharp and dull, diligent and slack.' Ch'an contemplation and Buddha-recollection are of a piece with this. If one
speaks of slowness, some men contemplate the Buddha for *kalpas*
on end before the lotus blossoms out. There are some meditators
also who, in spite of bitter efforts throughout many lives, cannot see
their own true nature. If the talk is of speed, there are some meditators who have their intuition on the spot, who, without passing
through incalculable *kalpas*, acquire the dharma body (*dharmakāya*).
There are some Buddha-recollectors also who, as soon as they die,
are reborn in the highest status." [42]

. . .

One of my worthy predecessors has said that egress from household
life (*ch'u chia*,[em] *pravrajyā*) is a matter for a great man (*ta chang
fu*, [en] *mahāpuruṣa*), not a matter within the reach of a general or a
minister of state. Now a general through his prowess stills disorder;
a minister of state through his learned accomplishments fosters
peace. All great matters under Heaven are the doing of generals and
ministers of state. Yet to say that egress from household life is not
within their power is to indicate that that egress is no small matter!
Now the shaving of one's head and the dyeing of one's garments are
all that is usually meant by "leaving the household." Yet this is no
more than leaving a gate with two large gateposts. It is not so good as
leaving the burning house of the three worlds. A man can be called
a "great man" only when he has left the house of the three worlds.
Yet not even then. For he cannot really be called by that name until
he has left the three worlds in the company of other living beings.
A song by one of the ancients says:

The most excellent one's
House-leaving is good.
The two words "house-leaving" are understood by few.

The "most excellent one" is the great man. The great man's status is not easily obtained. What wonder that so few know the meaning of "house-leaving"? [43]

. . .

There is also a common saying: "When one son leaves the household life, nine clans are reborn as gods!" Both of these sayings praise the monastic life, but do not say wherein its advantages lie. Can they possibly mean that the monk neither tills the soil nor weaves, yet has the advantage of guaranteed food and clothing? Or that he neither buys a house nor rents a room, yet has the advantage of a guaranteed dwelling? Or, again, that kings and ministers who keep the dharma make him offerings in faith and do him honor? Or, again, that from above he is not belabored by officials, nor from below bothered by commoners, but has the advantage of a guaranteed life of cleanliness, leisure, seclusion, and joy? In ancient times there was a *gāthā* [44] which said:

One grain of rice from a donor
Resembles Mount Sumeru in size.
If you do not requite it with the Way,
Resume your hair and horns and go home.

It also is said: "One day old Yama will reckon up with you the amount of rice and money you got and see what you gave in return." This is what doubles the monk over with fear. What talk can there be of "advantage"? Now, what is meant by the monk's "advantages" is the following: By virtue of his smashing of the *kleśas*, his severance of ignorance (*wu ming,*[co] *avidyā*), his acquisition of the unconditioned state (*anutpattikadharmakṣānti*), his self-extrication from the pains of life and death, his is the supreme status among men and gods, and his parents and kinsmen bask in the benefit thereof. Otherwise, had he a thousand boxes full of wealth, the honor of being a teacher to seven emperors, what "advantage" would he have? I am truly in great anxiety and fear as I tell all these things to those who share my vocation.[45]

When men first leave household life, the differences in their states of mind are quantitative, not qualitative, for they are all full of idealistic dreams. Then, after a while, some get tainted by connections, some by fame, some by profit, so that some build palaces, others dress in parti-colored robes, yet others acquire land and sundry property, still others amass followers. They heap up much gold and fine fabrics, they exert themselves to establish profitable alliances; they are, in short, no different from laymen. The scriptures say that, when one man becomes a monk, Māra trembles with fear. But, if *this* is what it means to become a monk, then Māra should receive them joyfully, with wine on the table. Those who feel inclined to leave the household life should be on their guard. I once saw an ascetic monk emerge from the mountains to be buried under the weight of the lavish offerings of a few score of pious lay folk; and this was a relatively mild case! For this reason I say that one must leave the house of the *kleśas* a second time, sever the net of pollution a second time. This is the house-leaving that follows house-leaving. The house in which one lives before one has left it is an easy one. The house in which one lives after one has left it is the difficult one. It is for this reason that I am in trepidation both morning and night.[46]

There are persons who have left the household life, yet still dwell at home. There are householders who have nevertheless left the household life. There are householders who live at home. There are, finally, persons who have left the household life and have no home. Persons who live in family dwellings and have father and mother, wife and children, yet whose hearts are constantly fixed on the Way, and who are not tainted with the filth of the world, are persons who have left the household life, yet who still live at home. Persons who dwell in monasteries, who have the burden of neither father nor mother, wife nor children, yet who are intent on fame and profit, and are thus no different from laymen, are householders who have left the household life. Those who dwell in secular habitations, who are fettered all their lives, and who have no thought for salvation are householders who dwell at home. Those who dwell in monasteries, who exert themselves all their lives, and who do not backslide for a single moment are those who have left the household life and have no home. . . . These are of course supreme. Better than the householder who has left the household life is the householder who lives at home. . . .[47]

The Buddhist monastic code requires the monk to be an ascetic, to beg for his food, to use rump-wiping rags for his clothing, to lodge among graves or at the foot of trees. Now we live among the multitudes, lay donors send us offerings, we have enough to wear and enough to eat, and we dwell securely in our monasteries. Yet we seek after yet more luxury. Is this proper? One bowl could be mended four times, one pair of sandals could last thirty years, and still the high standards of our virtuous predecessors would not deteriorate. In my shame I reproach myself, and convey these reproaches to my brethren.[48]

Doctrinal study necessitates fine distinctions, and the choice of the religious life compels one to specialize. Yet the insistence that I am right and the other fellow wrong will never do. In fact, there is less excuse for it now than there ever was. (There follow examples of how this or that school of Chinese Buddhism will malign all the rest.) Cases of such polemics are too numerous to count. I regret all this profoundly. I can only urge all you brethren to abandon your insistent postures, to empty your hearts of their prejudices, to study the Truth to its very limits, and to make Enlightenment your rule. After the achievement of Great Enlightenment there will still be time for leisurely discussion.[49]

All men know that the Buddhist religion is dependent on the protection of kings and their ministers, yet few know that the monks who are so dependent must be very careful. This means three things:

1. Monasteries which originally were the property of the Church later were seized by men of power. It is only right for the Church to want to have the lands back. Yet the land titles can be ambiguous, and this grows only worse with the passage of time. May the Church regain them by force? In other words, may the Church persuade an even more powerful man to intimidate the present occupants into giving them up? No, for the Buddha, who regards all living beings with equal compassion, will never countenance that sort of thing, even if the end is the restitution of monastery lands.

2. The writings of learned Buddhists are in accord with the Mind of the Buddha and the meaning of the scriptures. It is only right for

Buddhists to propagate and publicize them. However, is it right for non-Buddhists to twist the meaning, then to praise the alleged, but in fact nonexistent, message of these writings? If all a monk cares about is to have a prologue or epilogue written by a famous gentleman, and gives no thought to how this writing may mislea.! future generations, then he stores up sin, not merit.

3. Monks occupy themselves with and gain an insightful understanding of the Message; they equip themselves with great knowledge and gain a hold on the Truth that is both earnest and accurate. One trusts and cultivates them. This is only as it should be. Would it also be right to esteem and trust an empty-headed visitor to the land of *dhyāna*, a mean, inferior, ordinary fellow? If a monk merely cultivates the high and mighty, hoping for their patronage, and uses their lavish gifts of fine clothes to cover his gaping spiritual wounds, he is simply aggravating his malady, and is accumulating sin, not merit.

These are the three ways in which kings and ministers protect the dharma and monks ruin it. Oh, how sad! [50]

There are practitioners of quietude who sit alone in a single room and get irked when they hear human voices. Now human voices can be stopped, but what would these people do if crows and magpies were chirping in the courtyard? Crows and magpies can be chased off, but what would they do if tigers and leopards were howling in the forest? Even tigers and leopards can be left to a hunter, but what would they do if the wind were to whistle, the rivers to flow, the thunder to rumble, and the rain to come down in torrents? For this reason it is said that, while the fool clears away the object of sensation (*ching*,[cp] *viṣaya*) and not the thought, the wise man clears away the thought and not the object. If in spite of one's wishes the object can ultimately not be got rid of, then the Way to the very end cannot be learned. To place the blame on the nonquiescence of the object, rather than to find fault with the weak will of the practitioner, is a serious mistake indeed! [51]

For a long time now Buddhists and Confucianists have been engaged in mutual backbiting. At first, in my view, this was not such a wicked thing. For, when Buddhism first entered the Middle Land, its worshipers were many. The Confucianists, concerned as they were with the practical governance of the world, quite naturally spoke ill of it. Once they had begun to do so, persons suspicious of Buddhism became numerous. The Buddhists, for their own part, concerned as *they* were with the cultivation of the supramundane way, no less naturally counterattacked. Then came the vicious anti-Buddhist diatribes of Fu I and Han Yü, since which time the attacks have been but imitations of theirs. Now this *is* excessive. Why so? Because, when clouds already cover the sun, there is no further need for smoke or mist. On the other side were the anti-Confucian polemics of Ming-chiao [eq] and K'ung-ku, [cr 52] since which time the attacks have likewise been mere imitations, which is no less an excess [than the anti-Buddhist attacks]. Why? Because, when the sun has dispelled the darkness, there is no further need for candlelight. Now, if one will consider this question from the point of view of reality rather than that of prejudice, one will see that Buddhism and Confucianism, far from embarrassing each other, complement each other. Put very simply, my meaning is as follows: In general, when a man does evil and somehow contrives to escape the law-enforcement authorities in this life, yet fears rebirth in Hell in the next, he reforms and does good. This means that it is the Buddha who, without anyone's knowing it, aids the secular power to reach where it otherwise would not. Those monks who cannot be held in restraint by the monastic code in their fear of the penal code will not dare act as whim dictates. This means that Confucianism quite openly aids the Law of Buddha to reach where otherwise *it* would not. Now those monks whose sole concern is for the allegedly unflourishing state of Buddhism do not understand that, when Buddhism is too flourishing, it is to the misfortune of the monks themselves. It is by a bit of checking and restraining that Buddhism is enabled to endure long in the world. If they understood this, rather than damn each other they would praise each other. [53]

The purviews of Buddhism and Confucianism being distinct, one can neither divorce them nor identify them. Why? Because Confucianism is concerned with the mundane, Buddhism with the supramundane. Where the former is concerned, the Classics suffice, but they break down when that scope is exceeded. Where the latter is concerned, Buddhism points the way to leaving the world, but it has all too little to say about the former. What cause for wonder in that?

If you say that Confucianism is the same as Buddhism, then the Classics are complete in themselves, and there is no need either for the Buddha or for Bodhidharma. If you say that Buddhism is the same as Confucianism, then why not use the scriptures as guides to the governance of the world? What need for the sage-kings and sage-philosophers of yore? Hence divorcing them and identifying them are equally wrong. Yet, those of superior accomplishments will allow both, divorcement and identification. This must also be understood.[54]

NOTES

1. Although Chu-hung is renowned, among other things, for a debate conducted by him in writing with P. Matteo Ricci on the relative merits of Buddhism and Christianity, I have not been able to procure a copy of this debate.

2. The primary source for Chu-hung's biography is an account of him in the *Shih-shih chi-ku lüeh hsü-chi*,[cs] which is contained in the *Dai-Nippon zoku-zōkyō*.[ct] Since this was not available, I derived my information from the standard reference works and from Takao Giken,[cu] *Unsei daishi Shukō ni tsuite* [cv] (in *Naitō Hakushi shōju kinen shigaku ronsō*,[cw] [Kyoto, 1930]).

3. Takao, pp. 224–27.

4. *Ibid.*, p. 217.

5. *Ibid.*

6. Biographies of these men are all contained in the *Zoku-zōkyō*, unfortunately not available to me.

7. Quoted in Takao, p. 238.

8. Quoted *ibid.*, p. 239.

9. *Ibid.*, 243–48.

10. *Fo-shuo A-mi-to ching su-ch'ao* (*Zoku zōkyō* ed.) (hereafter abbreviated *FACSC*), 1/47b–48b.

11. *Anutpattikadharmakṣānti* (*wu sheng fa jen*) [cx] is a peculiarly Mahayanist notion. The earlier schools held that the dharmas emerge (*utpadyante, sheng* [cy]) and submerge (*nirudhyante, mieh* [cz]) at every moment or *kṣaṇa* (*nien nien sheng mieh* [da]). The Mahāyāna says that no predications are possible, including that of the emergence of the dharmas. Before understanding this truth intuitively, however, the practitioner must accept it on faith or "acquiesce" (*kṣamate, jen* [db]) in it. *Anutpattikadharmakṣānti* is characteristic of bodhisattvas on high levels of development, and is a precondition of Buddhahood. Cf. also *FACSC*, 1/34a.

12. *FACSC*, 1/51b–52b.

13. *Ibid.*, 1/29a.

14. *Ibid.*, 1/8b.

15. *Ibid.*, 1/6b.

16. *Ibid.*, 1/18b–19a.

17. *Ibid.*, 1/9.

18. *Ibid.*, 1/10a.

19. *Ibid.*, 1/19b–20b.

20. *Ibid.*, 1/20b–21a.

21. *Ibid.*, 1/44a–45a.

22. *Ibid.*, 1/45b.
23. *Ibid.*, 1/45b–46a.
24. *Ibid.*, 1/34a.
25. *Ibid.*, 3/66.
26. Referring to the Chinese version.
27. *FACSC*, 3/70b–71a.
28. *Ibid.*, 3/71b–72b.
29. *Ibid.*, 3/17b–18a.
30. *Ibid.*, 3/18b–19b.
31. The second of the three *kleśas* is *dveṣa* (hatred), but all Chinese translators render it with some word meaning "anger," indicating, possibly, a divergent tradition.
32. *FACSC*, 3/23a.
33. *Wen-shu-shih-li so shuo Mo-ho-po-jo-po-lo-mi ching* [dc] (Chinese version of the *Saptaśatikā nāma prajñāpāramitāsūtram*).
34. *FACSC*, 3/61a–62b.
35. *Ta ching t'u ssu shih pa wen*, in *Yün-ch'i fa-hui* X (Kuang-hsü ed.), 28b–29a.
36. *Ibid.*, 1/58b–59b.
37. "Difficult of belief" (*nan hsin* [dd]) signifies incredulity or incredibility, as the case may be. The word itself is lifted out of the sūtra text: "For the sake of the beings he preaches this dharma, difficult of belief (i.e., defying belief) in all the worlds."
38. *Ch'i-ch'ü*,[de] going back to a presumable *sapta gatayaḥ*. This is a bit puzzling, since the usual number is five or six. The five are *deva* (*t'ien*), *manuṣya* (*jen*), *tiryañc* (*hsü-sheng*), *preta* (*o-kuei*), and *naraka* (*ti-yü*). In systems that count six, *asura* (transcribed *a-hsiu-lo*, but usually with the first syllable omitted) is inserted between *deva* and *manuṣya*. My guess is that the "seventh destiny" is *antarābhava* (*chung-yu* [df]), this interval between incarnations.
39. 1) San-lun; 2) T'ien-t'ai; 3) Hua-yen; 4) Fa-hsiang; 5) Lü.
40. *Ta ching t'u ssu shih pa wen*, in *Yün-ch'i fa-hui* X, 29b.
41. *Chu ch'uang erh pi*, 58a–59a.
42. *Chu ch'uang san pi*, 20a–21a.
43. *Chu ch'uang erh pi*, 53a.
44. Here used loosely, in the sense of a verse of Chinese origin but of Buddhist content.
45. *Chu ch'uang san pi*, 55a–56a.
46. *Chu ch'uang erh pi*, 53b.
47. *Chu ch'uang san pi*, 23ab.
48. *Ibid.*, 8b–9a.
49. *Chu ch'uang erh pi*, 70b–71a.
50. *Chu ch'uang san pi*, 41b–42b.

51. *Chu ch'uang erh pi*, 46b.
52. Ming-chiao Ta-shih is the honorific title of the Sung monk Ch'i-sung [dg] (1011–72). According to his biography in *Fo-tsu li-tai t'ung-tsai*,[dh] 19 (T49/688c–89a), however, his response to the anti-Buddhist attacks of the Confucianists was an attempt to demonstrate the absence of contradiction between the two systems rather than a counter-attack.

K'ung-ku was the *hao* of the Ming monk Ching-lung.[di] His biography is to be found in *Hsü chi ku lüeh*,[dj] 3, *Hsü teng ts'un kao*,[dk] 9, and *Wu teng yen t'ung*,[dl] 23, none of them, unfortunately, available at the time of writing.

53. *Chu ch'uang erh pi*, pp. 46–56.
54. *Ibid.*, p. 57.

GLOSSARY

a   佛說阿彌陀經疏鈔

b   竹窗隨筆, 二筆, 三筆

c   沈

d   佛慧

e   蓮池

f   雲棲和尚

g   杭州仁和縣

h   眞圓

i   德寶

j   瓦官寺

k   雲棲山

l   憨山, 德清

m   禪

n   講

o   律

p   道霈

q   梵琦

r   紹琦

s   景隆

t   秀善

u   紫柏眞下

v   參禪念佛

w   稱名念佛

x   中, 下機

y   塔銘

z   戒律

aa   袁廣漢

ab   王廣堯

ac   極樂

ad   判教

ae   始教

af   終教

ag   頓教

ah   圓教

ai   薄地凡夫

aj   聖地

ak   不退

al   無信無願無行

am   執持

an   明持, 默持, 拌明拌默持

ao   稱名

ap   觀像

aq   觀想

ar   實相

as   一心不亂

at   事一心

au   理一心

av   一心卽是實相

aw   無相

ax   憶念無間

ay   阿彌陀佛

az   體究無間

ba   直指

bb   識

bc   唯本無影

bd   亦本亦影

be   唯影無本

bf   義

bg   境

bh   至寂

bi   定慧平等

bj   空寂

bk   用

bl   念

bm   正念

bn   妙法蓮華經

bo   方便

bp   會三歸一

bq 本心

br 正法

bs 像法

bt 末法

bu 輪廻

bv 四句

bw 不可得

bx 諦

by 斷滅文字

bz 貪

ca 瞋

cb 癡

cc 定

cd 慧

ce 凡夫

cf 罪障

cg 胎

ch 卵

ci 濕

cj 化

ck 利根

cl 南無阿彌陀佛

cm 出家

cn 大丈夫

co 無名

cp 境

cq 明教

cr 空谷

cs 釋氏稽古略續集

ct 大日本續藏經

cu 高雄義堅

cv 雲棲大師袾宏に就いて

cw 内藤博士頌壽記念史學論叢

cx 無生法忍

cy 生

cz 滅

da 念念生滅

db 忍

dc 文殊師利所說摩訶般若波羅密
經

dd 難信

de 七趣

df 中有

dg 契嵩

dh 佛祖歷代通載

di 景隆

dj 續稽古略

dk 續燈存稿

dl 五燈嚴統

ANNA SEIDEL *A Taoist Immortal of the*

Ming Dynasty: Chang San-feng

明 Ming thought was strongly, though unconsciously, influenced by the pervasive attitudes and powerful undercurrents represented by popular Taoist beliefs. To expose this religious background of Ming thinkers, which is often unstated but implicit in their work, I choose to deal here, not with Taoist philosophy or any eminent Taoist thinker, but rather with a time-honored Taoist concept in its Ming incarnations: belief in the immortals. These represented a numerous though heterogeneous group of eccentrics whose ideal of perfection was more than a simple psychological defense against the pressure of rigid orthodoxy. In the eyes of their disciples they were masters of esoteric techniques of religious experience and self-cultivation; to the non-initiated (among whom we must count ourselves) they have appeared as inspired fools or weird magicians. They are distinct not only from orthodox Confucianists, who almost succeeded in effacing them from the historical records, but also from the two main Taoist currents, the Cheng-i [a] and Ch'üanchen [b] sects, the institutionalized structures of which they rejected. They would have been forgotten had not the emperors' penchant for magicians secured a historical role for some of them, and had not Taoist sects and popular religion transformed them into legendary figures, enduring and everpresent teachers, or helpful deities.

The local gazetteers and the notebook literature of the Ming abound in legends, contradictory reports, and even miraculous tales by surprised eyewitnesses, who were in other respects quite Confucian and scholarly. A study of the immortal Chang San-feng [c] may serve as a guideline in these profuse and heterogeneous sources, for he is an especially rich and famous example of the cult of the immortal and well suited to reveal the multiple facets of the hagiography of a Taoist saint.

The memory and even the cult of Chang San-feng are still alive today in three different forms. In the 1940s Professor Yoshioka visited and described the shrine of the Immortal San-feng in the White Cloud Monastery of the Ch'üan-chen sect in Peking, where he met three monks from the sect of this patriarch.[1] Chang is thus considered one of the patron saints of the Ch'üan-chen sect. Furthermore his name is associated with the Taoist boxing school T'ai-chi ch'üan,[d] of which he is supposed to have been the founder. The recent prolific literature on these boxing techniques claims to transmit the authentic teachings of the first patriarch Chang San-feng. Three boxing societies celebrated the patriarch's birthday in Hong Kong on May 29, 1966.[2] Moreover, there is The Collected Works of Chang San-feng, reedited in Shanghai in 1919. This compilation goes back to a seventeenth-century Taoist master of a spirit medium cult in Szechwan and consists mostly of revelations allegedly made by the patriarch Chang San-feng to the adepts of this sect through "spirit writing."[3]

Going back to the Ming period we find that Chang San-feng figures in none of the genealogies of Ch'üan-chen masters. His biographies and legends lack even the faintest allusion to his being a boxing master and lack equally any hint of his being venerated by adepts of mediumism.

To make it clear right from the start: we know next to nothing about Chang San-feng's historical existence and his thought—and for purposes of this study these questions are beside the point. Whatever the core of historic fact was, the relevant question here is what beliefs crystallized around this figure, why, and how. We will study the process of the making of a saint. This approach, it is hoped, may throw some light on the belief in immortals and the religious atmosphere of Ming times.

In Ming sources Chang San-feng is a Taoist master who died in the first years of the dynasty, came back to life, and continued to live and to manifest himself for centuries. His fame attracted the attention of three emperors: T'ai-tsu invited him to court; Ch'eng-tsu tried to find him and built a temple on Mount Wu-tang in his honor; Ying-tsung, finally, canonized him. Chang San-feng was one of the immortals involved in the miraculous events which accompanied the founding of the dynasty and his fame contributed to the important religious role of the holy mountain Wu-tang in Ming times.

First I shall examine this period of history and its legends as a background for Chang San-feng's role in it; next I shall analyze the different aspects of the saint.

TAOIST LEGENDS CONCERNING THE EARLY MING DYNASTY

Chang San-feng's Biographies

The *Kuo-ch'ao hsien-ch'eng lu* [e] contains in four biographies what was known or believed about Chang San-feng in the sixteenth century. The records in the *Ming shih* and the more detailed *Ming shu* add nothing to this earlier source.[4] Leaving aside what is obvious legend, what then is the picture of him given here?

He was born in I-chou,[f] the present district of Liao-yang in Liao-ning Province.[5] His childhood names were Ch'üan-i [g] and Chün pao.[h] He styled himself "Master of Triple Abundance Capable of Endurance and Preserving Harmony," [i] whence comes his most common name, San-feng.[6] Each of his biographies describes him as exceedingly tall (seven feet); looking as if he had the longevity of a turtle and the immortality of a crane. He had enormous eyes and ears, a beard bristling like the blades of halberds, and hair tied into a knot at the back of his head. Summer and winter he wore only one garment and a bamboo hat; he could sleep in the snow without catching cold, could eat huge quantities of food at one sitting or fast for months, and could climb mountains as if flying. The foot rule he is always said to have carried in his hands is perhaps an early iconographic detail.[7]

Little is reported about the early part of his life. He was an itinerant eccentric under the Mongol dynasty. He is supposed to have studied Buddhism together with Liu Ping-chung [j] (1216–74) and the Taoist Leng Ch'ien [k] under the Ch'an master Hai-yün [l] (1201–56).

The prominent events which interest his biographers must have taken place towards the end of his life, when he was an accomplished master in the art of interior alchemy and had gained a reputation as an uncanny eccentric capable of magic feats. In the first years of the Ming he established himself in the Wu-tang [m] Mountains in northern Hupeh. He lived in a retreat north of Chan-ch'i [n] Peak in the vicinity of the Yü-chen [o] Temple. For this shrine he predicted a brilliant future. Not far from there, on a rampart called Hui-hsien kuan,[p] he built another retreat and left it in charge of his disciple Chou Chen-te.[q] Three other disciples [8] he ordered to live at Tzu-hsiao [r] Peak and at the Southern Precipice (Nan-yen [s]). Together with Chou Chen-te they reappear in Ch'ing legends as the four immortals of Mount Wu-tang—having attained immortality through Master San-feng. A fifth disciple, Ch'iu Hsüan-ch'ing,[t] who lived on Wu-lung [u] Peak, is worth noting for his later prominence in connection with San-feng. He was from Fu-p'ing [v] District in Shensi, had become a Taoist in his youth, and studied the teachings of the Ch'üan-chen sect under San-feng on Mount Wu-tang. At the age of fifty, after a period of wandering in Shensi and Hupeh, he was called to the capital, where he refused high positions in the censorate. He was in Emperor T'ai-tsu's good graces and stayed at court until his death in 1393.[9]

In the wars at the end of the Mongol dynasty, the sanctuaries on Mount Wu-tang had been demolished and up until 1390 soldiers still ravaged the region. This is given as the reason why in that year San-feng "angrily flapped his sleeves and left." In 1391 T'ai-tsu sent the Taoist San-shan [w] to search for him and invite him to court—without success. One might well suppose that Ch'iu Hsüan-ch'ing, like San-shan a disciple of the Master,[10] was similarly bidden (in 1391 or 1392) to attempt to reach San-feng. Legends tell of a conversation between the emperor and the disciple Ch'iu, who tried to show the futility of the search by hinting that San-feng was enjoying himself beyond the seas and that "flowing water and drifting clouds do not gather." [11]

From Wu-tang, San-feng went to Szechwan and had a conversation with Prince Ch'un of Shu.[x] This encounter is not mentioned in the biography of Prince Ch'un, who was the eleventh son of T'ai-tsu, and who resided from 1390 until 1423 in Ch'eng-tu where San-feng is supposed to have met him in 1392. Its omission in his short and laconic biography in the Annals is not sufficient to prove that the meeting did not take place.[12]

The third event is dated by the Ming Annals, the *Hsien-ch'eng lu*, and the *Ming-shih kao*, later than his stay at Wu-tang; two sources give what appears to be the very suitable date of 1393.[13] Around that

time San-feng died in the Chin-t'ai ʸ Monastery of Pao-chi ᶻ in western Shensi, after having announced his departure and taken leave of
his followers, with whom he left some hymns. When the people of
Pao-chi were just about to bury him, they heard him knock on the
inside of his coffin and discovered that he had come to life again.
This pseudo-death in Pao-chi is dated by a number of other versions
at the end of Yüan and before his activities on Mount Wu-tang.[14]
Still others date his meeting with the Prince of Shu after his resurrection in Pao-chi.

Historical data become more precise when the records switch from
the life of San-feng to the imperial honors bestowed on him. As we
have seen, T'ai-tsu sent the Taoist San-shan on a mission to him and
invited his disciple Ch'iu Hsüan-ch'ing to court. Ch'eng-tsu ordered
the censor Hu Yung,[aa] among others, to bring San-feng to court.
When this mission proved unsuccessful, the emperor tried to win
the favor of the reluctant hermit by a sumptuous reconstruction
of the demolished sanctuaries on Wu-tang, thus fulfilling the prophecy made by San-feng concerning the brilliant future of this site.
Chang San-feng never appeared at court but continued to manifest
himself as an immortal teacher of Taoist hermits. In 1459 Emperor
Ying-tsung canonized him as "The Immortal Penetrating Mystery
and Revealing Transformation." [ab][15]

The facts to be retained from this survey of San-feng's earliest
biographies can be summarized very briefly. He was a Taoist master
loosely connected with the local center of the Ch'üan-chen sect on
Mount Wu-tang and he was very famous in the Hung-wu and
Yung-lo eras (1368–1424), since he attracted the attention of these
two emperors. He continued to work upon the imagination of ama-
teurs of the miraculous in the following centuries, to the point of
being canonized and wrapped in a wreath of legends. In order to
understand the emperors' interest in him, we have to take a look at
the role of several Taoist immortals in these first decades of the
dynasty.

The Four Taoists of the Early Ming Dynasty

Chang San-feng was not the only Taoist favored by the first Ming
emperors. Chapter 299 of the *Ming shih*, "Experts on Occult Meth-

ods," [ac] lists together with him some eighteen physiognomists, astrologers, diviners, and physicians who played a more or less obscure role in the first decades of the dynasty.

The introduction presents, with some reservations as to the authenticity of the traditions, an appraisal of Chou Tien,[ad] Chang San-feng, and Chang Chung [ae] as men who had impressed the emperors and delivered unfailing prophecies. A closer look at the biographies of Chou Tien and Chang Chung shows that their prophecies concerned the heavenly mandate of the founder of the dynasty and that they impressed the emperor by their magic help during his struggle for power. It is in fact their role in the establishment of the dynasty that has prompted the historian to mention these mysterious figures in the Official Annals. And it is with these two immortals that Chang San-feng is associated in Ming literature,[16] as well as with a fourth, Leng Ch'ien, who has no biography in the Annals. How then did Chang San-feng—who never saw an emperor—come to have a place among these court magicians? This question merits attention all the more since the impulse behind San-feng's later career as a legendary immortal derived precisely from his renown at court. The court's attitude towards men of this kind can be examined by taking a brief look at the three immortals who did have dealings with the emperors.

Chang Chung (T. Ching-hua [af]) was from Lin-ch'uan,[ag] south of Po-yang Lake in the province of Kiangsi.[17] He failed the *chin-shih* examinations towards the end of the Yüan, and on his subsequent travels met a mysterious stranger who taught him the science of numbers, initiating him in the art of divination. In this capacity and under the sobriquet "Master Ironcap," [ah] he endeared himself to Chu Yüan-chang, the future emperor, in the years of Chu's struggle against Ch'en Yü-liang. Chu Yüan-chang had established himself since 1356 in the region around Nanking. In 1360 Ch'en Yü-liang, who controlled the Upper Yangtze region, declared himself emperor of a new Han dynasty. Around this time the diviner Chang Chung and Chu Yüan-chang met for the first time. The future emperor honored the guest by sharing a cake with him, and was rewarded with a prophecy confirming that he was predestined to found the new dynasty: "You have a dragon's pupil, the eyes of a phoenix, and an extraordinary appearance. Like a god you spread brilliant light, like the wind you sweep the dark shadows. Today you will receive the mandate." [18]

In 1362, when Ch'en Yü-liang besieged Nan-ch'ang, Chu Yüan-chang had a dream which seemed a good omen. He found himself in a narrow pathway bordered by burning lamps. The Taoist Ironcap stood at the side of the road and trimmed the lamps. Following this dream Chang Chung was again invited to come to Chu, and predicted a decisive victory in fifty days.[19] When Chu Yüan-chang moved his troops up the Yangtze from Nanking to the Po-yang Lake, where the decisive battle against the army of Ch'en Yü-liang was fought, Chang Chung accompanied the ships and his magic revived the winds to secure the advance of the fleet. In a second battle, foreseeing the death of Ch'en Yü-liang, he prompted Chu Yüan-chang to carry out a mourning ceremony for Ch'en, in order to undermine the courage of the enemy troops.[20]

According to several anecdotes in the *Ming shu*, Chang Chung lived after the establishment of the dynasty as a hermit on Mount Chung [ai] near Nanking. He predicted the early death of General Hsü Ta [aj] to the general, and snubbed General Lan Yü [ak] because he foresaw that he would conspire against the emperor and be executed. Having revealed to the monks of the Buddhist Monastery Chi-ming [al] the emperor's plan to demolish their stupa, Ironcap fell out of favor. Once the plan was known and the monks had begged for their stupa to be spared, the emperor desisted, but Chang Chung threw himself off the great middle bridge at Nanking and drowned. On the same day, as was reported later to the capital, he was seen walking through the T'ung [am] Pass in Shensi. Sung Lien,[an] who knew him, wrote his biography on imperial order in 1364 and revised and augmented it in 1370.[21]

Thus we have a picture of one of the magicians with whom T'ai-tsu surrounded himself before his rise to power in order to strengthen by supernatural signs the belief of his followers in his divine predestination.

Chou Tien, who came from the same region in northern Kiangsi, also enjoyed the hospitality of Chu Yüan-chang between 1360 and 1364. There are two strikingly common features in their stories: first, in 1360 Chou Tien also recognized in the face of Chu Yüan-chang the new emperor; second, when the fleet came to a standstill on its voyage up the Yangtze, Chou Tien blamed the soldiers' lack of courage and made the winds revive. Apart from that, his biography is more fabulous, and at the same time better attested, since T'ai-tsu himself wrote an account of his dealings with Chou Tien.[22] He was not an expert in divination, but an inspired simpleton and buffoon; his initiation took the form of a fit suffered at the age of fourteen which turned him into Chou "the Madman" (Tien). Living as a beggar in Nan-ch'ang, he had the habit of greeting people—everyone except Ch'en Yü-liang—with the slogan: "I announce the Great Peace" (T'ai-p'ing). When Chu Yüan-chang pacified Nan-ch'ang, Crazy Chou followed him back to Nanking, pestering him with his T'ai-p'ing prophecy. Chu Yüan-chang's attitude toward him is ambivalent. He shared meals with him, gave him new clothes, accepted from him a medicinal plant for his health, and lodged him in a monastery on Chiang shan [ao] near Nanking. On the other hand, he tried to sober the pestering fool by a kind of sauna treatment, which as reported in the Annals and the *Ming shu* version seems much like an attempt to kill him. They "cooked" him in a large jar but he emerged from the pot after three treatments with only drops of perspiration on top of his head.[23] T'ai-tsu showed the fool not admiration, but an amused and cruel curiosity. He made the monks lock Chou up for a month without food just to see if he really could get along without it, and when an ill-omened prophecy threatened to discourage the soldiers preparing for the battle on Po-yang Lake, he ordered him to be killed. Chou Tien came back with the men who had not been able to drown him, invited the emperor to a formal dinner, and humiliated him with his readiness to suffer death at his hands.

After this farewell we lose track of Chou. He became a recluse on Mount Lu [ap] (Kiangsi). In 1383 he sent a "barefoot monk" to the emperor with a message concerning "the prosperity of the state," and four years later he sent a magic drug which cured the ailing emperor. All attempts to bring him back to court failed.

Chou Tien had the additional capacity of healing and, unlike the expert Chang Chung, he represented or feigned the inspired fool who almost unconsciously manifests the will of Heaven. Once he drew circles in the sand, when walking with Chu Yüan-chang, and declared: "You will destroy a bucket and make a bucket." *Ming shu* interprets *t'ung* [aq] (bucket) as a pun for *t'ung* [ar] (dynastic rule). Both men indicate a faint trace of Taoist activity in the years of Chu Yüan-chang's rise to power, a trace that later orthodoxy almost succeeded in effacing.

Leng Ch'ien (Ch'i-ching [as]) was their contemporary.[24] His birthplace is given variously as Chia-hsing [at] (Chekiang) or Wu-ling [au] (Hupeh). Painter and musician, he lived at the end of the Mongol dynasty as a Taoist hermit on a mountain called Mount Wu [av] or Mount Hsü [aw] near Hangchow. Perhaps it was on the recommendation of his friend Liu Chi,[ax] the chief adviser of T'ai-tsu, that the emperor in 1367 appointed him *hsieh-lü-lang,*[ay] or court musician in charge of music, dance, and the fashioning of musical instruments. As he was a Taoist, all his pupils and successors in service in the early years of the dynasty were enrolled among the Taoists.

His reputation as a painter is the basis of two legends which interest us here. One of them explains why he fell out of favor and disappeared;[25] the other concerns the picture scroll of "the Immortals' Beauty on P'eng-lai" (*P'eng-lai hsien-i t'u* [az]). The picture bears a colophon written by Chang San-feng to the effect that Leng had painted it for him in 1340. Chang San-feng says that Leng had studied Buddhism together with him and Liu Ping-chung, the Buddhist adviser of Kubilai,[26] had later devoted himself to Confucianism under the guidance of Chao Meng-fu [ba] (1254–1322), and was initiated into Taoism by a mysterious stranger who taught him the Taoist treatise *Wu-chen p'ien.*[bb] [27] Thus the instruction in the three doctrines is complete and the whole is probably legend, interesting because it antedates the life of the Immortal Leng and shows him as a partisan of the San-chiao [bc] movement. Chang San-feng writes further that he will soon meet Sir Leng on "The ten continents and the three islands" (the Taoist paradises) and that therefore he confers this scroll on Lord Ch'iu of Ch'i-kuo [bd] [28] in order to make the extraordinary genius of Sir Leng known to posterity. The colophon is dated 1412 in *Hsien-ch'eng lu* and 1402 in *Yeh chi.*[be] Lang Ying [bf] (1487–1566) in his *Ch'i-hsiu lei-kao* [bg] quite convincingly demonstrates the spuriousness of the picture—which he regrets not having seen—and the colophon, but in the same short essay this rational critic tells us that Chang San-feng had come back to life after his death at the end of the Yüan dynasty, and in 1459 (the year of his canonization) had visited Emperor Ying-tsung. He himself has seen a picture of Chang San-feng painted on that occasion.[20]

Thus, the so-called four Taoists of the early Ming period represent the best-known thaumaturges grouped together retrospectively as witnesses to the dynasty's rise, as beneficiaries of imperial favor and as proof of the Taoists' loyalty to the emperor. Among them Chang San-feng is the only one who had no personal contact with the court. Nevertheless his fame, as we shall see, is based on his prestige at the Ming court.

Ch'eng-tsu's Search for San-feng and the Imperial Honors Bestowed on Mount Wu-tang

In the Yung-lo era the high commissioner Hu Yung spent thirteen years (1407–16; 1419–23) in extensive travels to find the whereabouts of Chang San-feng. The biography of Hu Yung [30] makes it clear that the hidden aim of this search was to determine if Emperor Chien-wen was still alive. Indeed, Ch'eng-tsu did have more urgent problems to deal with than the finding of Taoist immortals. He was a son of T'ai-tsu and had been invested Prince of Yen. When his young nephew, the son of the deceased heir apparent, had succeeded T'ai-tsu, the Prince of Yen staged a coup d'état and enthroned himself as emperor. Rumors spread that the young ex-emperor had not died in the burning palace, but was in hiding disguised as a Buddhist monk. The official mission to seek "Chang La-t'a,[31] the Immortal" was thus intended to find possible traces of the ex-emperor. At the same time there suddenly began and ended a series of southeast maritime expeditions motivated, according to the Official Annals, by the same search for Chien-wen.[32]

Ch'en Wan-nai,[bh] who has recently collected evidence on the life of Chien-wen after his escape, thinks that the name of Chang San-feng was only a cover for the real motive, which was a state secret.[33] If this is correct, it is still significant that Chang was famous enough to serve such a purpose. That Ch'eng-tsu had no interest in Chang, however, seems unlikely in view of another incident in connection with San-feng. Having failed to find him, Ch'eng-tsu paid homage to the mountain where San-feng had lived and taught and was still thought to be hiding.

Wu-tang is the collective name for a number of peaks south of Chün [bi] District in northern Hupeh. It had been since the thirteenth century if not earlier a Taoist sanctuary dedicated to Hsüan-wu,[bj] the God of the North. Hsüan-wu was, as early as Han times, the emblem of the seven zodiacal constellations of the Northern Sky, and the essence of the element water and of the supreme Yin, symbolized by the tortoise and the snake. Under the Sung, Hsüan-wu became the God of War. Emperor Chen-tsung (998–1023) changed his name to Chen-wu [bk] on account of the taboo on the personal name, Hsüan-lang,[bl] of Sung T'ai-tsu. Emperor Hui-tsung (1101–26) saw the god in visions and dedicated a cult to him. From this period dates the oldest representation of the god as a black-armored warrior standing on the tamed tortoise and snake.[34] Taoist hagiography, no earlier than the T'ang period, identifies this stellar deity with a legendary immortal of Han times, the heir of the Prince of Ching-lo,[bm] an exorcist and alchemist who obtained immortality on Mount Wu-tang and upon whom the Heavenly Emperor conferred rule over the North.[35] An important hall of the Po-yün kuan in Peking is still dedicated to Chen-wu, whose statue is enthroned there, flanked by the god of literature and Chang Tao-ling, the ancestor of the Celestial Masters.

The cult of Chen-wu was of paramount importance in Ming times. T'ai-tsu built a temple on Mount Chi-ming [bn] near Nanking in order to thank the deity for help in the battles preceding the establishment of the dynasty. In 1416 Ch'eng-tsu, prompted by similar motives, built a temple in the capital for the "Perfect Lord and Assistant Saint of the Polestar" [bo] and instituted monthly sacrifices.[36] Four years earlier he had issued an imperial decree ordering the reconstruction of the demolished sanctuaries on Mount Wu-tang where Chen-wu had achieved immortality and manifested himself.

In his article on Mount T'ai-ho in the Ming period, Mano Senryū gives a useful presentation and discussion of the sources on these religious activities.[37] In 1413 the then Celestial Master Chang Yü-ch'ing [bp] was sent to bestow honorific titles upon the four new temples on the four main peaks, the same sites where Chang San-feng had installed his disciples.[38] On the highest peak, T'ien-chu,[bq] the so-called Copper Hall, which had been there in Yüan times, was replaced by a "Golden Hall" with gilded decorations and a golden statue of Chen-wu.[39]

In 1413 Sun Pi-yün,[br] a Taoist of the Wu-tang sect, who had already been invited to court in 1394, was made superior of the Nan-yen Temple; the three other temples received two abbots each. The shrine of Wu-tang with its 200 monks was endowed with 27,700 mou of land, to be administered by nine officials (t'i-tien [bs]) of the sixth rank. Chen-wu was honored with the title "Dark Emperor" and his mountain ranked among the sacred peaks of the empire with the title "Supreme Harmony." [bt] [40] T'ai-ho shan became the official name of the mountain.

The official reason given for this extraordinary and costly project was to honor the memory of the deceased Emperor T'ai-tsu and his empress, the parents of Ch'eng-tsu, and to assure divine protection for the officials and the people. This pious declaration served a political end. Ch'eng-tsu had to appease the general agitation caused by his overthrow of the legitimate Emperor Chien-wen. He did it by underlining ceremoniously his filial piety and by demonstrating his concern for the welfare of his subjects.[40]

A more personal motive, which may also explain the choice of Wu-tang, was his desire to establish contact with the mysterious Master Chang San-feng. One of his officials, Chang Hsin,[bu] marquis of Lung-p'ing,[bv] had known Chang San-feng in Kuei-chou, where he had had his first appointment. Chang Hsin inspired the whole project, with whose execution he was eventually charged, through a painting of the divine manifestations on Wu-tang presented at an imperial audience. It so pleased the emperor that he ordered the restoration.[41]

In addition, from 1405 until 1417 four imperial messengers in addition to Hu Yung were dispatched to find Chang San-feng.[42] In the spring of 1412, having ordered the restorations on Wu-tang, Cheng-tsu wrote two letters. The first was given to Hu Yung to be taken on his travels and later presented to a monk from Lung-hu shan.[43] In this letter the emperor expresses his ardent desire to meet "the perfect Immortal, Master Chang San-feng" and to receive from him personally the rule of right conduct. He alludes to other messengers sent in the past who had searched all the famous mountains in order to extend a respectful invitation, with letters and incense offerings, for the Immortal to come to court. Then follows a conventional passage contrasting the Immortal's high excellence and unfathomable mystery with the coarse and ordinary disposition of the imperial writer whose only merit is his sincere desire to learn from the Master. The letter concludes by reiterating the invitation to Chang to descend in his cloud chariot in order to assist the emperor who looks up to him in admiration.

The second missive has the same conventional tenor; it was written to announce to the Master the construction of a sanctuary on Wu-tang in his honor. "I have heard that the Yü-chen Temple on Mount Wu-tang is the holy place where the Perfect Immortal, Master Chang San-feng, has cultivated himself. Not having met the immortal old Master, I cannot but venerate the site where he roams on his crane. I desire to construct a sacrificial altar to propagate his brilliance." This document was given to Sun Pi-yün on March 18, 1412.[44]

The desire to meet a Taoist hermit was probably merely the ostensible aim of an enterprise intended to legitimize the reign of Ch'eng-tsu. It was by now a time-honored custom of Chinese emperors to call worthy sages to their court, and of the latter to show their reluctance to go. Seen in this light, the tenor of the two letters in question is in no way extraordinary. It is, however, of interest that San-feng was the one who attracted this attention.

Moreover, it may not be farfetched to link this dual motive for the establishment of a state cult with the imperial sacrifices *feng* and *shan*,[bw] which had been abolished since Sung times. The official purpose of these sacrifices had been to announce to Heaven the establishment of a new dynasty. Usually they were executed not by the founder of the dynasty but under a subsequent, stabilized reign. As far back as Han times, the underlying motivation was the concern of the emperor for his personal immortality, conferred by deities accessible through the *feng* and *shan* sacrifices. Wu-ti of the Han was promised the immortality of the Yellow Emperor if he succeeded in performing the *feng* and *shan* ceremonies. He celebrated two *feng* sacrifices, one at the foot of T'ai-shan, and another secretly and alone on the summit.[45] Ch'eng-tsu's dual motive of stabilizing his rule and meeting a saint is, notwithstanding the changed religious mentality of the Ming, an echo of this tradition.

San-feng's Friend Li Ching-lung

While Ch'eng-tsu's efforts to reach the Immortal never succeeded, Li Ching-lung,[bx] an ill-fated subject of his, enjoyed the blessings of San-feng's friendship. His father Li Wen-chung,[by] a cousin of Emperor T'ai-tsu and one of his best generals, had been made duke-of-domain in Ts'ao [bz] and fourth meritorious servant of state when T'ai-tsu was enthroned and, after his death, was ennobled as Prince of Ch'i-yang.[ca] [46] His son, Li Ching-lung, was a favorite of Emperor Hui-ti and the chief general entrusted with the unsuccessful military campaign against the rebelling Prince of Yen. Consequently, with the installation of the Prince of Yen as Emperor Ch'eng-tsu, the Li family faced a period of disgrace and hardship. In 1404 Ching-lung was stripped of all his honors except, out of regard for his imperial blood, his noble rank; his income was discontinued and he was forced to return to his private residence.[47]

In former days both Li Wen-chung and Ching-lung had kept a hospitable house and among the numerous personalities who had enjoyed their friendship was said to be the itinerant Chang San-feng. According to the Li Family Genealogy, Chang San-feng foresaw Ching-lung's misfortune and invited him to follow the example of the famous Immortal Ch'ih-sung Tzu [cb]: to leave society with him and to strive for immortality. Upon Ching-lung's refusal, San-feng gave him three farewell presents, a self-portrait, a gourd, and a wooden box, prophesying that these objects would help him in later days of hardship.

When in custody and faced with starvation, Ching-lung sowed the grains he found in the gourd and cereals grew miraculously fast and nourished his whole family. The wooden box contained the Immortal's cloak made of leaves which proved to have the power to cure any kind of disease. The emperor reinforced surveillance, suspecting that people secretly supplied the Li family with food. When, two years later, an imperial inspection found them all well nourished and unchanged, the emperor yielded before this evident supernatural interference; he ordered a regular grain supply given to them and requested the miraculous gourd for the treasury.[48]

The Li family had a numerous posterity and continued to fill important posts. Li Hsüan [cc] became commander of the imperial body-guard in 1492; his grandson Li Hsing,[cd] in 1532, became marquis of Lin-huai [ce]; five members of the family figure in the list of meritorious servants of state in the Ming Annals. All these blessings they attributed to the help of Chang San-feng, whose self-portrait became the object of a cult and is reproduced in the Genealogy.

In the sixteenth century Yao Fu [cf] visited in Nanking a great grandson of Li Ching-lung, Li O,[cg] who showed him a bamboo hat and a shabby leaf cloak of Chang San-feng's and told the story a little differently: Li Ching-lung had put on hat and cloak and called out the name of the Immortal in the backyard of his residence, whereupon grain grew around him and ripened fast enough to nourish the family.[49]

With this story we are already in the early stage of legendary adornment. A Ch'ing-time colophon on San-feng's self-portrait by Chu Ch'i-ch'ien [ch] presumes that Li Ching-lung successfully exploited his connection with Chang San-feng in order to soften the hostile attitude of the emperor, who yearned for a meeting with this Immortal who had once honored the home of the Li family.[50] Whatever the historical core of Li Ching-lung's miraculous story, one of the Taoist visitors on the Li estate was considered to be Chang San-feng, and his cult in the family dates from the Yung-lo era. The story, moreover, fits well into the Immortal's hagiography, which we shall now study.

THE MAKING OF A SAINT

The evolution of the legend can roughly be divided into three chronological phases. The Taoist master, known only to his disciples, probably died before the imperial inquiries in the Yung-lo era spread his fame throughout the empire. He then became invested with the traditional features of a Taoist immortal, features which characterized a whole group of eccentrics in the sixteenth and seventeenth centuries.

At this stage the legend branched off in different directions. Esoteric school traditions claimed him as a patron of special techniques: boxing and sexual practices. Popular religion associated him with the gods of wealth, while a mediumistic sect conjured up the picture of a saint. What we shall trace here is the slow adaptation of the life of an eccentric to the patterns of Taoist hagiography.

The Immortal Chang San-feng

The biography of San-feng given at the beginning is only a selection of the most basic data repeated wherever he is mentioned. Except for those corroborated by other sources, these data are not necessarily those most likely to reflect his real existence but can just as well be taken as the standard "biography" ascribed to a saint.

Ming authors of local gazetteers and literary note books give a more highly colored version of him as an immortal who manifested himself throughout centuries and in many different parts of the empire. Some made him into a contemporary of the Chin Tartars (1115–1234), others, a Taoist of Sung times. As a rule there is a tendency in the hagiography of famous Taoists to push the date of their births always further into the past. Thus San-feng as well as Leng Ch'ien is considered to have been a friend of Liu Ping-chung (1216–74), a century before the Ming; and San-feng is said to have studied Taoism at the T'ai-ch'ing Temple at Lu-i,[ci] the birthplace of Lao Tzu, together with a certain Chang I [cj] whose great-great-grandson Chang Ch'ao-yung [ck] he met in the Hung-wu era in Pao-chi. This legend already existed in the sixteenth century and seems to go back to Chang Ch'ao-yung who, as a thirteen-year-old boy, met an old Taoist Chang Yüan-yüan [cl] (Hsüan-hsüan,[cm] one of San-feng's names) who told him that he had been friends with his great-great-grandfather when he was young.[51]

In Sung times, a Chang La-ta [cn] (variant of the nickname La-t'a [co]) is said to have met the reputed Taoists Ch'en T'uan [cp] (?–989) and Lü Tung-pin [cq] and to have obtained immortality by eating a magic date given him by the latter. In the Yung-lo era, this Master Chang accepted the invitation of Ch'eng-tsu, came to court, and displayed some of his magic powers. All bystanders had to leave before he approached the emperor with a jug and said: "What I want is to enter this jug and contemplate the process of creation." He shrank up and disappeared, to emerge again after having continued the conversation from inside the vase. The emperor was stunned. Chang spat water which, all of a sudden, became a river. He slipped into an anchored boat, rowed away, and vanished together with the whole vision.[52]

These two feats belong to the traditional stock of Taoist magic. The jug symbolizes the alchemical container where, mythologically speaking, the yin and yang ingredients of the drug harmonize in a microcosmic repetition of primordial creation. The Taoist wants to reintegrate in order to achieve the state of unity before creation, the state where heaven and earth were united in the primordial chaos. The symbol of this state is the gourd whose two bellies are heaven and earth united. In Taoist mythology the gourd is literally a microcosmic "heaven and earth" where the Taoist can enter and find the way to paradise.[53] Equally the disappearance of a magician who walks into a visionary landscape or landscape picture or enters a jug is the stock in trade of Taoist legends.[54]

Moreover, these two themes appear in the biographies of two other Taoists who most probably have been confused with Chang San-feng. It was Leng Ch'ien who slipped into a jug and was gone when the angry Emperor T'ai-tsu had the jug broken. Another contemporary of Chang San-feng and friend of the Taoist Ironcap Chang Chung was an eccentric and comedian by the name of Chang Chin-po.[cr] He amused Emperor T'ai-tsu by producing clouds in five colors out of a little copper flask. In the middle of winter he threw dry lotus seeds on the ice of a river, folded paper into a boat and ferried across the water singing and plucking the blooming lotus flowers until suddenly he vanished.[55]

It seems likely that the story of this Master Chang has been incorporated into the hagiography of Chang San-feng—who never went to court. However, all these themes are related. Chang San-feng was said to have given to Li Ching-lung a jug full of seed-grain which grew with magical speed and in great abundance. Another gourd he left with a Chang family in Kan-chou, in return for their hospitality.

When in the Ch'eng-hua era (1465–87) this gourd broke, a little drum was found inside—the drum given to San-feng by Yang Kuei-shan [cs] who had buried him and witnessed his revival in Pao-chi. The drum is mentioned in this account to allude to his roamings inside the gourd.[56] In 1535 Lu Ch'üan [ct] saw in the Yü-chen Temple in the Wu-tang Mountains a statue of the Immortal "Filthy [La-t'a] Chang" and noticed his bamboo hat and wooden staff.[57] One of the letters of invitation from Emperor Ch'eng-tsu and the patent of canonization by Emperor Ying-tsung were preserved in this sanctuary.[58]

San-feng's apparitions are not confined to Mount Wu-tang. In the Hung-wu era (1368–98) he roamed through Szechwan and stayed with a Chiang [cu] family in Ch'eng-tu; there he used to sit in meditation on a rock, plant plum tree branches in front of him, and make flowers grow immediately.[59] In the same period a "Dirty Immortal" (La-t'a hsien) lived in the Kao-chen [cv] monastery on Mount Fu-ch'üan [cw] near P'ing-yüeh [cx] (Kweichow); there still exists a Li-tou Pavilion [cy] where he meditated in seclusion during the day and at night venerated the deity of the Dipper. At this place he met Chang Hsin and predicted that one day he would be a marquis.[60]

During the Yung-lo period he was seen on Mount Yün-men [cz] in Shantung; the grotto he lived in received the name "Grotto of the Immortal Chang." In Jih-chao [da] (Shantung) he helped the peasants weed their fields; when sent on an errand, he came back incredibly fast and was recognized as an Immortal by an old woman who saw him take off through the air riding a crane.[61]

In Anhui he instructed the Taoist Chang Ku-shan [db] who later became one of the administrators of the Wu-tang monasteries.[62] On Mount T'ai-p'ing [dc] in Hupeh he took a little boy on an excursion through the air and invited an old man to share a meal which he brought in an instant from a shop 140 miles away.[63] A stone bed and a grindstone with which he used to grind drugs are noted in another gazetteer as relics of his presence there.[64] In Fu-feng [dd] (Shensi) San-feng drew his picture on a wall of the Ching-fu [de] Temple. The brick bed he sat and slept on there never became cold in winter. When people later on examined it, they found that on the back of every brick was written the character "fire." [65] Back in Szechwan, he cultivated himself in the K'un-lun Grotto high on a cliff on Mount Pa-yüeh.[df] People saw him enter the grotto on a donkey. In the grotto a bamboo staff, a stone chair, a stone bed, jade tablets, and a well are remnants of his stay.[66]

In the early years of the Yung-lo era he came to Nei-chiang [dg] (Szechwan) and stayed in the home of the Taoist Priest Ming-yü.[dh] When the visitor was asked for his name, he said his name was P'ang,[di] and therefore people simply called him Lao P'ang. Priest Ming-yü was good at charms both verbal and written, while the visitor excelled in other achievements, such as traveling on mountain peaks without falling, or walking on water without sinking. He said to his host: "What I can offer you is the Way (*Tao*), and what you can offer me is method (*fa*)." Thereupon he wrote the treatise *Tao-fa hui-t'ung shu* [dj] expounding the theory that the Way and method really complement each other. After about a year's time, Emperor Ch'eng-tsu's high commissioner Hu Yung came to Nei-chiang and met him in the house of Priest Ming-yü. Thereafter, nobody knew what became of the famed Taoist.[67]

A stranger remarkable for his bristling beard, his utter filthiness, and his strange manners appeared in the Yung-lo era in the western suburb of Ch'ang-an. He said his name was Chang, whereupon people called him "Filthy Chang" (Chang La-t'a). He used to scrape the dirt off his body and roll it into pills which cured people's diseases. Liu Kua-tang [dk] roamed around with him. Later, when Chang had disappeared, Liu described him to the high commissioner Hu Yung, who told him that this man must have been Chang San-feng.[68] Again, in Ch'ang-an, a certain Chang K'o [dl] saw San-feng in winter time in the temple of the Duke of Chou. He did not greet this filthy old fellow, but when San-feng prepared his meal with fresh vegetables which he said he had just fetched from Ch'eng-tu (Szechwan), K'o went outside, found no traces in the snow, and recognized him as an Immortal. Asked for a wish, the licentiate K'o complained about his bad memory. San-feng blew into his ears, pronounced a formula, and K'o never again forgot whatever his eyes saw or his ears heard. In the examinations of 1414 he came out first on the list.[69]

Chang San-feng's canonization by Emperor Ying-tsung in 1459

was said to be due to the fact that he roamed the mountains, sometimes hidden, sometimes manifest, and "the whole empire was full
of his traces." Lang Ying (1487–1566), who describes a picture
painted of the Immortal on this occasion, reports that hope for a
visit by San-feng to Emperor Ying-tsung had been the motive for his
canonization.[70]

If we are to venture a guess about these extensive roamings of
Chang San-feng, it seems that there must have been several people
who either assumed this identity intentionally or were so identified
mistakenly by others, or whose deeds were attributed to San-feng by
later authors—as in the case of Chang Chin-po's visit to Emperor
T'ai-tsu.

A visitor to the priest Ming-yü in Nei-chiang told people that his
name was P'ang, but without explanation he was identified as Chang
San-feng. The untidy eccentric in Ch'ang-an whom Liu Kua-tang
described to the high commissioner "must have been" Chang San-
feng. Hu Yung traveled during ten years and covered many provinces.
His inquiries in the Yung-lo period might have led to the identification of many a mysterious stranger who went "we know not where"
with the Chang San-feng whom Hu Yung had described to people
in the course of his search. Whenever an eccentric named Chang, or
someone who evaded giving his name, appeared, or a ragged, dirty,
old mendicant passed by, uttered prophecies, cured diseases, or simply
took up his abode in a temple for a while, it would not be unusual
for him to get the nickname La-t'a and be identified with Chang
San-feng.

At this point we can place San-feng in the context of a distinct
social and religious type. In the *Ku-chin t'u-shu chi-ch'eng* there are
some 230 biographies of *shen-hsien* [dm] of the Ming dynasty. Among
them is a "Filthy Immortal" (La-t'a hsien) who lived in Hsiu-ning [dn]
(Anhui) during the Chia-ching period (1522–67). He never washed
and his entire body was covered with dirt. In snow and ice he ran
around barefoot. When people asked for his name, he just laughed,
so they called him the Filthy Immortal. He built himself a retreat
on Ch'i-yün [do] Mountain, shut his gates, and passed his time in meditation; sometimes he did not eat for days. Asked to tell the future,
he waved his hands and told people to mind their own business; only

when someone insisted did he speak up and admonish him to practice the virtues of loyalty and filial piety.[dp] [71] This man, so far as we
know, has never been identified with San-feng, but the resemblance
between their legends is striking.

An Immortal Liu La-t'a [dq] led an equally strange life in Han-yang [dr]
(Hupeh) and also limited himself to sermons on loyalty and filial
piety when talking to people.[72] Most of these Immortals have entered
the records under some eccentric nickname: they have abandoned
their social status with its code of behavior and they have become
Crazy Chou,[ds] Filthy Chang, Ironcap Chang, mountain recluse
Ma,[dt] Ironbelt Li,[du] Bare-Belly Li,[dv] the barefoot Immortal,[dw] Master
Big-Belly,[dx] Crazy Immortal Chang,[dy] and so forth.

Let us take a look at their common features. They lead vagrant,
mendicant lives. Old but not at all decrepit, they are immune to heat
or cold, can live without food, travel with magical speed, foretell the
future, and cure diseases. Except in rare cases involving persevering
and congenial disciples, they never speak about their own beliefs and
techniques but rather encourage young people to study for the examinations, take office, and respect the traditional Confucian virtues of
loyalty and filial piety. They also discourse on the syncretism of the
Three Religions (San chiao), very popular in the Ming period.

A last remark about the deaths of these Immortals. Very rarely are
there indications of their age at the time of "departure" (seventy-six,
over eighty, ninety, ninety-three, ninety-nine, over a hundred years);
more frequent is the statement, made by themselves or others, that
they have already lived through several centuries, that they were born
in Sung or even T'ang times. The majority of the biographies contain no such information; the age of an Immortal is beyond telling.

There are two traditional ways for a Taoist to leave the world and
attain immortality: "flying up to heaven in broad daylight" (pai-jih
sheng-t'ien [dz]) and the shih-chieh [ea] process. The first method,
though mentioned in the biographies, seems to have become in Ming
times a euphemism for the death of a saintly Taoist, similar to such
expressions as yü-hua [eb] (transformed into a feathered being, i.e., an
immortal), hsien-hua,[ec] tso-hua [ed] (transformed while sitting [in correct posture]), ch'eng-yün shang-sheng [ee] (to ascend on the clouds)
and so forth. The clearest example of a shih-chieh process is the

reputed death and resurrection of Chang San-feng in Pao-chi. He is, of course, far from being the only one: Ironbelt Li "died" in 1556; a year later he was seen peddling drugs on a bridge in Yang-hsien.[ef] [73] The "Taoist with the lifted-up foot," [eg] who used to hop around on one foot, was, in the Wan-li period (1573–1619), duly buried at the Dragon King's Temple in T'ien [eh] (Yünnan); later on, people from T'ien met him on Mount Wu-tang, unchanged in manner or dress.[74] The Taoist who has, through physical and mental self-cultivation, created within himself the "embryo of immortality," at his apparent death leaves his body "like the cicada its husk" and enters with his new *physical* body into a new life. It is in this reborn state that Chang San-feng and his equals are immune to hunger and cold, and capable of traveling through the air, walking on water, and so forth.

However, the most frequent ending to an immortal's biography comes from the famous expression of Ssu-ma Ch'ien in describing the end of Lao Tzu: "Nobody knows what became of him." [ei] This seems the wisest conclusion for us to draw, too. All these different ways of death, departure, transformation, and immortality are different means of expressing the same belief: the Immortals are still alive, they can still be found as hermits in holy mountains or disguised as eccentric old fools among the people. The belief that certain Taoists can, by using the appropriate techniques, live in the world through several centuries, is still found today. In an assembly of a Tantric sect in Taiwan in 1965, a Chinese professor of law, with a Western educational background, pointed out a bearded old man whom he "knew" to be three hundred years old.[75]

The Patron Saint of the T'ai-chi ch'üan Boxers

Some readers may be surprised that this hagiography contains not even the faintest allusion to the Taoist techniques of boxing, whereas Chang San-feng is known today, if at all, as the founder of the boxing school *T'ai-chi ch'üan*.[ej] [76]

The earliest data on a boxing master Chang San-feng [ek] is found in the biography of a famous boxing master Chang Sung-ch'i [el] who lived in the sixteenth century in Ning-po. He called himself a disciple of an alchemist [em] Chang San-feng, a recluse in the Wu-tang Mountains who refused the invitation to court of Hui-tsung of the

Sung (1101–26). In a dream the Dark Emperor en (Hsüan-ti) taught him the boxing technique which enabled him alone to overcome a hundred robbers. The name of Chang Sung-ch'i's technique is not T'ai-chi ch'üan but "esoteric school" *nei-chia* eo in opposition to the older Buddhist boxing tradition of the Shao-lin ep Monastery which he called "exoteric school" *wai-chia*.eq The *nei-chia* technique was inspired by Taoist conceptions of yielding and defeating the enemy less by force than by knowledge of his weak spots. Rivaled by Buddhist boxers of the Shao-lin branch who traced their tradition back to Bodhidharma, Sung-ch'i chose a famous Taoist as the patron saint of his "esoteric school." [77]

The second historical source, the Epitaph for Wang Cheng-nan er composed by Huang Tsung-hsi es (1610–95), gives us the line of transmission from Chang San-feng to Huang Po-chia,et the son of Huang Tsung-hsi. In the twelfth century San-feng's boxing technique had spread in Shensi and a certain Wang Tsung eu excelled in it. He transmitted it to Chen Chou-t'ung ev from Wen-chow,ew who propagated it in Chekiang. Chang Sung-ch'i, in the sixteenth century, taught Yeh Chin-ch'üan ex from Ssu-ming ey (Chekiang), who in turn transmitted it to Tan Ssu-nan,ez the teacher of Wang Cheng-nan, for whom the epitaph was composed. Cheng-nan was a military man. After the fall of the Ming dynasty he retired from his post of area vice commander (*fu tsung-ping kuan* fa) and was introduced by his disciple Huang Po-chia to the circles of retired scholars in the region of Ning-po and Yü-yao.fb [78] This boxing tradition of north Chekiang still represents the "esoteric school" or Wu-tang tradition, more a method of military training than of physical self-cultivation. The T'ai-chi ch'üan school has nothing to do with it.

The history of T'ai-chi ch'üan has recently been studied by Tseng Chao-jan.fc He traces its tradition back to a Yang Fu-k'uei fd (*tzu:* Lu-chan fe), who lived toward the end of the nineteenth century (died 1872). Yang Fu-k'uei combined the teachings of the Shao-lin school with the boxing technique of a Ch'en ff family of Huai-ch'ing fg (Honan) who had cultivated during fourteen generations the tradition of one Wang Tsung-yüeh fh from Shansi. Yang Fu-k'uei's disciple Wu Ho-ch'ing fi wrote treatises on T'ai-chi ch'üan which he ascribed, in order to give them more weight, to the patriarch Wang

Tsung-yüeh.[79] Thus we can read in a Western publication on T'ai-chi ch'üan that in the fifteenth century Wang Tsung-yüeh documented and augmented the boxing theories of the Sung philosopher Chang San-feng in a *T'ai-chi ch'üan ching*.[80]

Why did Chang Sung-ch'i choose San-feng as the patron of boxing and how did this patron of the "esoteric school" become the founder of T'ai-chi ch'üan? As to the second question we agree with Tseng Chao-jan in his opinion that there must have been a conscious or unconscious confusion of Wang Tsung from Shensi (supposedly disciple of San-feng and teacher of Ch'en Chou-t'ung) with Wang Tsung-yüeh from Shansi (supposedly founder of the boxing tradition of the Ch'en family)—a confusion which established a link between the "esoteric school" located in northern Chekiang and the later T'ai-chi ch'üan school developed in Honan. The first question is of more interest here. Chang Sung-ch'i's master is a Chang San-feng of the Sung dynasty. This antedating, as we have seen before, is designed to enhance the prestige of the Immortal, a prestige apparently considerable enough to compete with the fame of Bodhidharma, the patriarch of the Shao-lin boxers. Moreover, Chang San-feng was a saint of the Wu-tang Mountains, the sanctuary of the War God Chen-wu, and it was Chen-wu who revealed the military skill of boxing to San-feng in a dream. The connection with the god of war might also have accounted for the choice of Chang San-feng as a patriarch of boxers.

The Master of Sexual Practices

The esoteric teachings of military and sexual arts are closely related in Taoism; for instance, the emblems of the war god Chen-wu, tortoise and snake, are sexual symbols. Chang San-feng is considered also a master of the art of sexual self-cultivation. The study of these techniques is one of the most difficult and mysterious chapters of Taoism. The Taoist Canon contains many treatises on this subject and still more polemics and warnings against them. These texts are written in a very esoteric language intended to conceal their real meaning from the uninitiated outsider. The only thing we can ascertain is that the constant polemics against these practices prove their uninterrupted existence from before Han times until today. I shall limit myself to a brief presentation of the data collected in connection with Chang San-feng.

A thirteenth-century treatise on self-cultivation, the *San-chi chih-ming ch'üan-t'i,*[fj] contains a warning against the "method of the Three Peaks and the Yellow Valley" (*San-feng huang-ku chih shu* [fk]). From the context it becomes clear that this term designates a method of sexual intercourse: the adept should cultivate the original essence (*yüan-ching* [fl]), not the essence stimulated by debauchery as in the above method; equally he should cultivate the original breath (*yüan-ch'i* [fm]), not the breath of the respiration through mouth and nose, etc.[81] San-feng,[fn] in this context, is not a personal name but an esoteric term for a method ascribed to a Wang Ku-tzu [fo]; the "Three Peaks" designates three different sexual practices.[82]

The nineteenth-century compiler of the *Collected Works of Chang San-feng*, Li Hsi-yüeh,[fp] disavows all connection between the Immortal Chang San-feng and the tradition of sexual cultivation. He explains the confusion by the fact that a Chang Shan-feng [fq] of the Liu Sung dynasty (420–77) instructed disciples in the *fang-chung yü-nü fang* [fr] before entering orthodox Taoism, and was punished for it by the Heavenly Emperor. Also, according to Liu Hsi-yüeh, the prime patriarch of all sexual practices (*yin-tao* [fs]), P'eng tsu,[ft] has in the heavenly hierarchy the title *T'ai-ch'ing ching-ming san-feng chen-chün.*[fu] [83] Thus Li reduced the problem to the phonetic resemblance of *san-feng,*[fr] *san-feng,*[fw] and *shan-feng.*[fx] However, the fact remains that in the sixteenth or seventeenth century the famous Immortal Chang San-feng was credited with an esoteric knowledge of these techniques and several texts having a more or less hidden sexual meaning were ascribed to him.[84]

Etymologically speaking, the characters *feng* [fy] and *feng* [fz] (mountain peak) have strictly no relation to each other. The original meaning of *feng* [fy] is "luxurious vegetation," "beautiful appearance," and if there is a character interchangeable with *feng,*[fy] it is *feng* [ga] (abundance), the original religious meaning of which is a sacrificial vessel filled with offerings for the gods. Thus we are not astonished to find also a Chang San-feng.[gb]

The God of Riches

Chang San-feng became a god of wealth, in the seventeenth century or later, through the belief that he was the master of a certain Shen Wan-san,[gf] a popular deity of wealth. In this legend San-feng is a real alchemist manipulating pots and pills. His maxim was: "Both method and material have to be employed" (*fa-ts'ai liang-yung* [gc]). This can well be interpreted in terms of mental hygiene, the material being the human person who needs to assimilate doctrine in order to reach perfection. This is in fact the meaning of the phrase in a series of twenty-four poems of San-feng, "The rootless tree" (*Wu-ken shu* [gd] = the human body), where he describes the successive mental achievements of adepts in terms of flowers which grow on this "rootless tree." [85] In terms of alchemy *fa-ts'ai* [ge] denotes the necessary combination of technical knowledge and costly ingredients used in the transmutation of cinnabar. The alchemist Ko Hung (284–363) had already complained that, though he knew the methods, poverty hindered him from employing them and accomplishing the fusion.

Chang San-feng found Shen Wan-san,[gf] a fisherman from Ch'in-huai [gg] River (Kiangsu), who sold his property—and even his daughter—to furnish the master with the necessary mercury and lead. They worked together and, when the fusion was perfect, they both gained immortality. A more visible result of their connection was the immense wealth the fisherman procured for himself with San-feng's alchemical recipes. Shen Wan-san figures in history as the richest man of Wu [gh] in the Hung-wu era. He financed the construction of fortifications around Nanking when the state treasury of T'ai-tsu was empty. Later he fell out of favor and was banished to Yünnan on account of his presumptuous offer to distribute bounty money to the victorious soldiers of T'ai-tsu. On T'ien-ch'ih [gi] Lake south of K'un-ming he again joined Master San-feng and, his whole family partaking in the alchemical labors, they all became immortal.

The historical core of this story is Shen Wan-san (whose real name was Shen Hsiu [gj]), the richest man in Wu, banished by T'ai-tsu because his financial power was considered to rival that of the state. He is mentioned in the Annals of the Empress because he owed his escape from a heavier penalty to her intercession.[86] The legends of San-feng's miraculous activities in the same Hung-wu era came in handy to explain the origin of Shen Wan-san's impressive wealth.[87] Moreover, the banishment of Shen Wan-san to Yünnan became linked with T'ai-tsu's search for the master in 1391. The Taoist San-shan,[gk] charged with this mission, was in legend Shen Wan-san who was qualified for the task by his earlier contacts with Chang San-feng.

Shen Wan-san became one of the gods of riches and was canonized as Guardian of the Territory of Nanking. He also has a legend independent of Chang San-feng: he became rich through a bowl which, as a poor fisherman, he once caught in his net, and which magically collected treasures (*chü-pao p'en*).[gl][88] Chang San-feng,[gm] nicknamed Chang La-t'a, a Taoist in possession of the cornucopia *chü-pao p'en*, has become the protecting spirit of riches.[89]

That an immortal pictured as an utterly destitute, filthy mendicant should become a protecting spirit of riches is a paradox not infrequent in mythology. The introduction of San-feng into the hagiography of Shen Wan-san is probably not much older than the early eighteenth century when we find it in the *Li-tai shen-hsien t'ung-chien* [gn][90] and in the legends collected by the adepts of Chang San-feng's spirit medium cult in Szechwan. These adepts considered Shen Wan-san not only to be the most prominent disciple of the master but even to be present among them in the guise of Wang Hsi-ling [go] (1674–1724), the compiler of the Collected Works of Chang San-feng. When Wang "met" Master San-feng for the first time on Mount O-mei, a sudden enlightenment made Wang realize that he had formerly sojourned in the world as Shen Wan-san.[91]

A closer look at this compilation will complete the survey of Chang San-feng's hagiography.

The Deity of a Spirit Medium Cult

The Collected Works of San-feng contains most of the material discussed in the preceding pages, such as the biographies from the Ming Annals and the *Ming shu*. Some additional biographies seem suspiciously more detailed and consistent. The account written by Wang Hsi-ling contains astonishing "historical details" found in none of the earlier sources. He claims to know about San-feng's birth in 1247, his official career under the Mongols, the persons with whom he associated (Liu Ping-chung and Duke Lien Hsi-hsien [gp] who recommended him to the post of magistrate in the district of Po-ling [gq] south of Peking), his subsequent withdrawal and study of Taoism, and his meeting with an immortal master in 1314. On one point Wang Hsi-ling seems more credible than the Ming Annals: San-feng did not die and come back to life but the people of Pao-chi mistook for death a state of trance during which the yang spirit of the master had left the body for an ecstatic excursion. In 1359 (a hundred and twelve years old) the master met Shen Wan-san in Chin-ling (Nanking) and taught him the Tao of alchemy. In the Hung-wu era he visited the Prince of Shu and so forth.

Where did Wang Hsi-ling get all his information? He certainly had at his disposal more material than can be found today in the libraries of Paris and the United States. He himself says that he found, in a Yang-chou bookstore in 1720, an old book of poems by San-feng handed down from the Taoist of the Flower Valley,[gr] the great-great-grandson of San-feng.[92] But in his own biography we learn that he met Chang San-feng himself, earlier than 1720 and neither in Yang-chou nor in the Wu-tang Mountains, but on Mount O-mei in Szechwan. He served as intendant (*kuan-ch'a* [gs]) in Chien-nan,[gt] south of Ch'eng-tu, and was the medium of a Taoist center in the nearby Lo-shan [gu] District where he received "Master Chang San-feng's secret method of cultivating and nourishing the self," and revelations concerning the above-mentioned "facts" of Chang's life.

Did he bring along the teachings of San-feng from Yang-chou or did he join an existing spirit medium cult? The local gazetteer of Lo-shan District does not mention Chang San-feng earlier than in a note concerning the grave of Wang Hsi-ling on the nearby Ling-yün [gv] Mountain.[93] On the other hand, his disciple Li Hsi-yüeh writes that Wang Hsi-ling was received into a sect (*men* [gw]) of San-feng.[94] In any case he was the chief propagator and compiler of San-feng's historical records and teachings; in reference to the latter he insists on having received them "by oral transmission" (*k'ou-ch'uan* [gx]). The present edition is based on his work and was published by his disciples in Lo-shan at the beginning of the nineteenth century, the preface of Li Hsi-yüeh bearing the date 1844.

Apart from the biographies and three doctrinal treatises ascribed to the master, the collection contains innumerable poems dictated by the planchette, conversations between the master and his disciples in the eighteenth century, and three sutras of prayers and litanies representing the liturgy of the "Sect of the Hidden Immortals" (*Yin-hsien p'ai*)[gy] in Lo-shan.

On closer examination three strata appear in this confusing mass: the historical records compiled by Wang Hsi-ling; the revelations of Master San-feng to Wang; the additional revelations to the disciples in the Chia-ch'ing and Tao-kuang eras (1796–1850).

The third layer is of no interest here. The first I have tried to identify with the aid of Ming sources. What became of it in the vision of Wang Hsi-ling and the Hidden Immortal's Sect?

There was a striking silence in earlier tradition as to the teacher of San-feng and the doctrinal transmission of which he was heir. This gap is now filled. San-feng met his master Huo-lung [gz] in 1314 in the Chung-nan Mountains [ha] (Shensi, south of Sian). This Huo-lung is an obscure figure, often identified with Chia Te-sheng,[hb] the first disciple of Ch'en T'uan, the well-known Taoist recluse of the Sung period. Ch'en T'uan, under the name of Hsi-i,[hc] is in fact the master of Huo-lung. Further back in tradition comes Ma-i [hd] ("the Hemp-clad Taoist," 4th century)[95] who received the doctrine in the Chung-nan Mountains from the Guardian of the Pass, Yin Hsi,[he] the disciple of Lao Tzu. This genealogy from Lao Tzu to San-feng reflects the local legends of the three Taoist mountains Chung-nan, Wu-tang, and Hua-shan [hf] in southern Shensi and northern Hupeh. Ch'en T'uan lived on Mount Wu-tang and was transported to Hua-shan by the five dragon gods of the Wu-lung Peak. On Hua-shan he learned alchemy from the Immortal Ma-i.[96] In the Chung-nan Mountains Lao Tzu transmitted the *Tao-te-ching* to Yin Hsi and tradition located there the Lookout Tower of the Guardian from which he saw Lao Tzu approach in a purple cloud.[97] More recently, Wang Che,[hg] the founder of the Ch'üan-chen sect, had received his revelations on Mount Chung-nan. These six, from Lao Tzu to San-feng, are the six patriarchs of the sect, the "Hidden Immortals" or the "likes of dragons" (*yu-lung* [hh]) as Confucius had characterized Lao Tzu after their presumed meeting.

San-feng is the last patriarch and immediate teacher of the sect. What he reveals about himself is never in blatant contradiction to historical fact but is rather an elaboration on it. Wang Hsi-ling, who was well read, poses as historiographer presenting the esoteric side of San-feng's life. The search of the high commissioner may serve as an example of his procedure:

When Hu Yung had searched for nine years he came again to Hunan and put up in the mountains. One evening around midnight when everything was quiet, the tea had become cold, and the lamp shone brightly, he suddenly heard a knock on the door. The door opened by itself and he saw a Taoist resembling Old Feng.[hi] Hu wanted to call out to him but the master quickly covered his mouth with his hands, dusted a bench to sit on, and they conversed intimately; then he left. In Ming times nobody knew about this event. Yesterday the master descended into my studio (shu-chung[hj]) and told me all about it. I, Ling,[hk] moistened my brush and noted it.[98]

This is one of the very few passages in Wang Hsi-ling's commentaries which indicate clearly the origin of his surplus information. To judge from the almost indistinguishable mixture of history and legend in this part of the book, the three treatises of San-feng may well contain some authentic material but it can only be identified with the help of other sources.[99]

Why did this cult develop around San-feng and why in Szechwan rather than, for instance, in the Wu-tang Mountains? The prefaces indicate that the works of San-feng were compiled after the model of the Lü-tsu ch'üan-shu [hl] (Collected works of the Patriarch Lü). They proudly state that San-feng can well bear comparison with Lü Tung-pin. One of the sutras from Lo-shan defends the occult power of San-feng as equivalent to the might of the Patriarch Lü: "Nobody should pretend that the immortals perch only in Han-san [hm]; San-feng has often descended on our cloud altar in the mountain." [100] Han-san is the name of a temple in Wu-ch'ang (Hupeh) where an apparently more important mediumistic sect received during the same K'ang-hsi period (1662–1722) the revelations of the Patriarch Lü and edited the Lü-tsu ch'üan-shu. The two centers were in communication. San-feng has written a preface to the T'ai-i chin-hua tsung-chih [hn] [101] and has commented on the Pai-tzu pei [ho] of Lü

Tung-pin.[102] A poem written by the planchette in Han-san tells of a meeting of the two patriarchs on Lake T'ung-t'ing in Honan: taking leave of Lü Tung-pin, San-feng says that he will go to Hsi-ch'uan,[hp] the part of Szechwan comprising Lo-shan.[103] The Patriarch Lü also revealed himself together with San-feng to an adept in Lo-shan in 1839.[104] It is in this context of Ch'ing cults that San-feng got a place in the school tradition of Lü Tung-pin. Since Ch'en T'uan, they say, was not only a disciple of Ma-i but also studied under Liu Hai-ch'an,[hq] Chang San-feng received through them the teachings of Lü Tung-pin. In view of all this, it is very likely that he was the local variant of this more famous patron saint of spirit medium cults in the K'ang-hsi era.

The Collected Works of Chang San-feng was well known in Taoist circles in the nineteenth century. Its editor Li Hsi-yüeh became the patriarch of a Western school which corresponded to an Eastern school venerating Lu Ch'ien-hsü.[hr] [105] Both, of course, were additions to the historic Northern and Southern schools of Wang Che and Liu Hai-ch'an.[106] San-feng himself is quoted as an authority in several treatises on inner cultivation.[107] His cult seems to have been widespread. The list of Taoist sects of the Ch'üan-chen school, which Fu Ch'in-chia [hs] found in the White Cloud Monastery, shows the existence of eight sects of the Patriarch.[108] The Yin-hsien p'ai of Lo-shan, not mentioned there, is the predecessor if not the common origin of these more recent groups.

CONCLUSION

In the late Yüan and early Ming dynasties lived an eccentric Taoist master rendered famous by the interest several emperors took in him. Once invested with the traditional features of a Taoist Immortal, his relation to the War God Chen-wu resulted in his being credited with the invention of Taoist boxing techniques; the confusion of his name with an expression in the esoteric terminology of sexual cultivation made him into a master of such practices; the real meaning of his name and some coincidences of date and place established a connection with the legend of a minor popular deity of riches; finally, a spirit medium cult of early Ch'ing times brought together all these heterogeneous elements into the coherent and completely hagiologic picture of a patron saint.

Needless to say, this breakdown of the making of a saint into three phases—Taoist Master, Immortal, and popular Saint—is somewhat arbitrary and superficial. There are no clear lines of demarcation among the three. The popular religion incorporated innumerable orthodox Taoist deities and in Taoism the Master and the Immortal coincide: even the gods are gods because and insofar as they possess primordial revelation or, even better, embody this revelation. The Immortals carry out their task of salvation by making humanity participate in this revelation.

On the other hand, the transmission of a famous master's doctrine gradually transforms him into a saint: the study of a sacred text is joined with veneration of its author, who attained immortality through this doctrine. The process seems less involved in the case of the Ming Immortals. They wrote, if at all, highly technical treatises on mental hygiene and magic practices or left some hymns and poems, which, as in the case of Chang San-feng, are difficult to disentangle from mediumistic revelations and seem to count for little in the making of the saint.

How are we to understand the Taoist conception of communication with "Immortals" who have long since disappeared? Is the account of such a meeting with an Immortal who lived centuries earlier a metaphor for inspiration through his writings? This answer would be too simple since study of a text alone never leads to perfection and initiation by the master in person is always indispensable. Methods become effective only through the student's total commitment to the master who is already on the level of perfection. A proof of this is the over-all importance of the "oral formula" (k'ou-chüeh [ht]) in Taoist scriptures. Wang Hsi-ling received the teachings of San-feng by "oral transmission." Therefore, it was, I believe, precisely the absolute necessity of communicating with the master himself which led to the apparitions of Immortals seen by lone mountain recluses (hallucinations?), to the identification of mysterious strangers with Immortals of previous ages, and to the use of mediumism as a means to obtain this personal guidance.

Taoist mediumism is attested to at least as far back as T'ao Hung-ching [hu] (456–536), who compiled the revelations of Taoist deities "dictated" to a circle of adepts around 365. In this sect of Mao shan,[hv] the distinction was already apparent between, on one hand, popular spiritistic cults and, on the other, the revelations made by orthodox deities of the Taoist pantheon through the writing brushes of their mediums, mostly calligraphers.

Nevertheless, San-feng was not primarily a saint of the popular religion. His disciples in Szechwan were members of the gentry, officials of minor rank, or monks. The texts revealed to them show their knowledge of history, their skill in poetry, and their familiarity with the techniques of mental hygiene. They criticize the use of spirit-writing for the purpose of fortunetelling. Charms and spells should not be employed to force the Immortals to descend. A purely external skill in spirit-writing, without sincere devotion to the deities and an irreproachable life, is evil; in the houses of virtuous adepts the Immortals will descend without special inducement. Their intention, moreover, is not to reveal the future but to give advice on how to please the gods by good deeds and how to cultivate the self. Such an attitude distinguishes them from the popular religious figures.

Only a thorough comparison of these religious eccentrics of Ming times with the "Immortals" of previous dynasties could determine if we are right in supposing that the "Immortals" studied here represent a movement of religious revival. Revivals always start on the margin of established religion. We must know more about the decisive changes in the Taoist religion under the Sung dynasty which led to systematization of the Cheng-i [hw] sect and its priesthood and created, simultaneously with the flourishing of Ch'an Buddhism, the monasticism of the northern Ch'üan-chen [hx] sect.

From this time on an important group of inspired individuals seems to have rejected these two established structures in favor of the solitary pursuit of true religion through a life of poverty and wandering. The impulse of this constant search for an ultimate religious experience was, as I have tried to show through the example of Chang San-feng, slowly integrated into the Taoist hagiography, into monastic life—as is the case with the twentieth-century monks of the sects of San-feng in the White Cloud Monastery—and incorporated also into the vast Taoist pantheon where the adepts of mediumism recruited their deities.

Thus, if I have not answered any questions about Chang San-feng's historical existence and thought, nevertheless, at this point we have learned something about what became of his life in later times and in this sense are better off than those writers who "do not know what became of him."

NOTES

1. Yoshioka Yoshitoyo,[hy] Dōkyō no kenkyū [hz] (Tokyo, 1952), pp. 298, 332, 335.

2. Wah Kiu Yat Po [ia] (Hong Kong), May 30, 1966, sports news column. I thank Dr. Hoklam Chan for this reference.

3. Chang San-feng ch'üan-shu (hereafter abbreviated CSFCS), 8 ch. (Chiang-tso shu-lin [ib] Shanghai, 1919), based on the edition of Li Hsi-yüeh [ic] (Szechwan, 1844); same edition in Tao-tsang chi-yao,[id] section pi,[ie] 7–12, 162–67.

4. Kuo-ch'ao hsien-ch'eng lu [if] (Taiwan, 1965), 118/109a–115b; contains San-feng's biography from Yü-t'ang man-pi,[ig] by Lu Shen [ih] (1477–1544); Ming-shih, 299/8a–9a; Ming-shu (Ts'ung-shu chi-ch'eng ed.), 160/3162–63; Ming-shih kao, ch. 281. Chang San-feng is the last to have a biography (short and spurious) in Hsiao-yao hsü ching [ii] (Tao-tsang, 1081), 2/39b.

5. If we are to believe the compiler of CSFCS, his family was from the Southeast and only his grandfather Yü-hsien,[ij] an expert on divination and astrology, had moved from under the Southern Sung rule up to the North, then held by the Chin Tartars. This is legend, inspired by the wish to connect his genealogy with the family of the Celestial Master Chang (CSFCS, 1/2b).

6. The correct graph of his name is san-feng.[ik] The variant san-feng [il] (Three Peaks) appears almost exclusively in legends alien to his original hagiography; see p. 507. Apart from the names given in the Harvard-Index of Ming Biographies we found further the names (ming) T'ung [im] and Shen-yu,[in] and the religious name K'un-yang Tzu.[io]

7. Fang-ch'ih,[ip] often erroneously given as tao-ch'ih,[iq] may have a significance similar to the rod of the officiating Taoist priest who "measures the dimensions of the universe" which is a way of dominating it. In CSFCS, 2/6a, a text dictated by the planchette explains that San-feng uses the Tao-ch'ih "to cut open the primordial chaos."

8. Yang Shan-teng,[ir] Liu Ku-ch'üan,[is] Lu Ch'iu-yün.[it]

9. These data on Ch'iu Hsüan-ch'ing come not from Ming-shih but from Ming shih-lu [iu] (photographic edition: Taiwan, 1962), 225/3298. I owe this reference to Mano Senryū,[iv] Min Cho to Tai wa san ni tsuite,[iw] Ōtani gakuho,[ix] XXXVIII No. 3 (Dec. 1958), p. 72. Mano also mentions a biography of Ch'iu Hsüan-ch'ing in T'ai-yüeh T'ai-ho shan chih.[iy]

10. San-shan was later identified with the disciple Shen Wan-san; see p. 509.

11. CSFCS, 1/8b.

12. *Yü-t'ang man-pi* gives the date 1392 for the meeting.

13. *Kuo-ch'ao hsien-ch'eng-lu*, 118/110a, biography by Lan Tien ᶦᶻ (16th century); *Che-chiang t'ung-chih* (тscc, 256, 33/8b).

14. *Ming-shu*, 160/3162; *Hsiao-yao hsü-ching*, 2/40a; *Kuo-ch'ao hsien-ch'eng lu*, 118/113b; *Wu-tang shan chih* ʲᵃ (тscc, 256, 33/8b).

15. Tentative translation; *T'ung-wei* can also mean "to understand mystery," and *hsien-hua* is a conventional expression for the manifestations of a supernatural being.

16. Chu Yün-ming ʲᵇ (1460–1526) considers Chou Tien and San-feng the most outstanding immortals of the dynasty (*Yeh-chi*,ʲᶜ in *Li-tai hsiao-shih*,ʲᵈ 79/57a); so does Yao Fu ʲᵉ (*Ch'ing-ch'i hsia-pi* ʲᶠ [*Shuo-k'u* ed.]). Hu Ying-lin ʲᵍ sets the four of them apart from the two main currents of the Ch'üan-chen sect (*Shao-shih shan-fang pi-ts'ung* ʲʰ [Peking, 1958], 42/579). They are also treated together in *Chiang-ning-fu chih* ʲᶦ (1913 ed.), 51/10b–11a. Several collections of legends of Ming "immortals" group these four in one chapter; see, for instance, *Huang-Ming yung-hua lei-pien* ʲʲ Bk. 8, ch. 131 (reproduction of Ming ed.; Taipei, 1965). Hsü Tao,ʲᵏ *Li-tai shen-hsien t'ung-chien*,ʲˡ chüan 21, is a legendary narrative of the activities of leading Taoists in the early Ming period and contains detailed accounts of the four.

17. *Ming-shih*, 299/7b–8a; *Ming-shih kao*, 281/7a; *Kuo-ch'ao hsien-ch'eng lu*, 79/14a; *Ming-shu*, 160/3160 ff.

18. *Ming-shu*, 160/3161.

19. *Chiang-ning-fu chih* (тscc, 256, 33/11b–12a); also alluded to in *Ming-shu*, 160/3162, according to which General Teng Yü invited Chang Chung to visit him. The gesture of trimming the lamp has in the Taoist ritual the meaning of reinforcing the vital energy of the donor of the lamp, whose life it represents. By trimming the wicks the Taoist Ironcap reveals himself as the protector of the emperor's vital spirit.

20. This last story is also found in *Ch'i-hsiu lei-kao* ʲᵐ (Shanghai, 1961), 9/137, by Lang Ying ʲⁿ (1487–1566), who presents Chang Chung and Chou Tien as the two immortals who helped Chu Yüan-chang to defeat Ch'en Yü-liang.

21. *Kuo-ch'ao hsien-ch'eng lu*, 79/15b; Sung Lien says in a final note that this biography was kept in a golden box from which he took it in 1370 to copy and complete it. Yang I ʲᵒ reports that in 1366 Ironcap presented a blueprint to Chu Yüan-chang when the latter ordered the construction of the new capital in Nanking; see *Kao-po i-tsuan* ʲᵖ (Shuo-k'u ed.), B.1a; preface 1531.

22. *Chou Tien hsien chuan* ʲᵠ (*Kuo-ch'ao hsien-ch'eng lu*, 118/99a–103b). Listed in *Ssu-k'u t'i-yao*, 147/38b. The biographies in *Ming-*

shih, 299/6b–7b: *Ming-shu*, 160/3159 ff., and *Yeh-chi* (in *Li-tai hsiao-shih*, 79/2a) are based on this text.

23. Under the Ming, the execution of criminals by boiling in big caldrons was still practiced.

24. *Kuo-ch'ao hsien-ch'eng lu*, 118/119a; *Ming-shu*, 151/3000; *Ming hua lu*, 2/2a; *Kao-po i-tsuan*, ch. A, 3a–3b; several legends in тscc, 256, 33/10b–11a; and the biography of Leng Ch'ien prepared by Professor Weng T'ung-wen for the Ming Biographical Project.

25. "The magic of the crane painting." In order to help a needy friend he painted a door on a wall with a crane as guardian. They went through this door and the friend was to help himself to the treasures found there. Despite the warning of Leng he took too much and, when the following day a theft from the imperial treasury was discovered, the two were arrested. Leng Ch'ien disappeared (*Ming shu*, 151; *Kuo-ch'ao hsien-ch'eng lu*, 118/119a). In *Hsien-ch'eng lu* the story continues thus: the arrested Leng Ch'ien asked for a drink, emptied a jug, disappeared into it, and even the emperor's promise to spare him punishment for the theft could not make him leave his hiding place. When the jug was broken, he had disappeared. According to *Chiang-ning fu-chih* (51/11a), he was seen later on in the Wu-tang Mountains.

26. *Yüan shih*, ch. 157; Liu Ping-chung was a close disciple of Hai-yün, a Ch'an monk of the Lin-chi branch. In 1247 he was appointed chief of monks by Kuyuk Khan; later he became a close friend of Kubilai. His association with Leng and San-feng pertains to legend, Liu Ping-chung having become a prominent legendary figure.

27. *Yeh-chi* (in *Li-tai hsiao-shih*, 79/56a) has the most accurate version: he received the "Great Alchemy of the Central Yellow" [jr] and the "Essentials of the Enlightenment of Truth of Master Chang." [js] The *Wu-chen p'ien* by Chang Po-tuan [jt] (983–1082) is one of the most important treatises on inner cultivation of the northern School of Taoism from the Sung on.

28. Ch'iu Fu [ju] (1343–1409), *Ming-shih*, ch. 145; a general who fought for the rebellious Prince of Yen. Once enthroned, Ch'eng-tsu put him at the top of the list of meritorious servants of state and even intended to make him heir apparent. One of Lang Ying's reasons for rejecting the legend is that a visit of San-feng to a personage so near to the emperor would not have passed unnoticed.

29. *Ch'i-hsiu lei-kao*, *hsü-kao* (1775 ed.), 4/17b–19a. Other picture scrolls representing San-feng existed: *Shan-hu wang* [jv] (Wan-yu wen-k'u ed.), 23/1358, mentions such a picture in the inventory of a Ming library; see also n. 50.

30. *Ming-shih*, 169/2b; *Ming-shu*, 119/2380.

31. La-t'a ʲʷ (Sloven Chang) was a popular name for him on account of his negligence in appearance and manner.

32. The voyage to the West of the eunuch Cheng Ho ʲˣ in 1405 was motivated by the rumor that Chien-wen had escaped abroad.

33. Ch'en Wan-nai, *Ming Hui-ti ch'u-wang k'ao-cheng* ʲʸ (Kao-hsiung; Taiwan, 1960). In 1949 Ch'en Wan-nai had found the genealogy of a Hsiang ʲᶻ family from Wu-ch'ang ᵏᵃ which claimed to descend from Chien-wen, who is supposed to have adopted the name Hsiang. The book is an attempt to justify this genealogy by comparison with the historical records.

34. Reproduced in Bulletin de l'Ecole Française d'Extrême-Orient (hereafter abbreviated *BEFEO*), VIII (1914), fig. 16; Maspero (*ibid.*, p. 28) thinks that this deity Chen-wu might be one of the four generals of the Emperor of the North Tz'u-wei pei-chi ta-ti,ᵏᵇ painted by an empress in 1127.

35. W. A. Grootaers, "The Hagiography of the Chinese God Chen-wu," *Folklore Studies*, XI, No. 2 (1952); he treats literary accounts as well as the popular hagiography of this god in the Chahar region. Also some legends in H. Doré, *Recherches sur les superstitions en Chine*, IX, 479. For the peaks and sites of Wu-tang with their legends, see *Wu-tang fu-ti tsung-chen chi*,ᵏᶜ compiled by Liu Tao-ming ᵏᵈ in 1286; *Tao tsang* 609.

36. *Ming-shu*, 50/961; *Ming-shih*, 50/15b–16a; 18b–19a.

37. See n. 9. Mano Senryū has subsequently published a study bearing on the administrative aspects of the imperial cult at Wu-tang and its connection with the increasing influence of the eunuchs; in *Tōhō Shūkyō*,ᵏᵉ XXII (Nov., 1963), 29–44.

38. North of Chan-ch'i Peak the Hsüan-t'ien yü-hsü kung ᵏᶠ; the other three are named after their peaks: T'ai-hsüan tz'u-hsiao kung,ᵏᵍ Hsing-sheng Wu-lung kung,ᵏʰ Ta-sheng Nan-yen kung.ᵏⁱ

39. *T'ai-yüeh T'ai-ho shan chih*, ch. 3, quoted from Mano Senryū. The descriptions of the temples are contradictory; *Ming T'ai-tsung shih-lu*,ᵏʲ 207/2113, mentions only the construction of a small "Copper Hall" on T'ien-chu Peak which, according to *T'ai-ho shan chih* had already been there in Yüan times. Lang Ying says that this sanctuary has only gilded decorations and is not, as people say, of pure gold (*Ch'i-hsiu lei-kao*, p. 586).

40. *Ming T'ai-tsung shih lu*, 207/2113; dated 1417.

41. Chang Hsin (*Ming-shih*, 146/6b) may have received a Taoist family tradition; his uncle was Chang Yü ᵏᵏ (*Ming-shih*, ch. 145), a general in the army of Ch'eng-tsu who was capable of using Taoist techniques to predict the outcome of a battle. The divine manifestations on Wu-tang (*Ming T'ai-tsung shih-lu*, 140/1686) are the appari-

tions of the "Heavenly Emperor of the North" recorded, together with other auspicious miracles which accompanied the arrival of Chang Hsin on Wu-tang, in the illustrated *Ta Ming Hsüan-t'ien shang-ti jui-ying t'u-lu*,[kl] *Tao tsang* 608. Chang Hsin, moreover, used this project to avert attention from an impending lawsuit in which he was involved. In 1418 he presented magic plants from Wu-tang to the throne. This gesture also shows that in the whole enterprise his personal relation with the court was at stake (*Ming T'ai-tsung shih-lu*, 200/2086).

42. *Yü-t'ang man-pi* (in *Hsien-ch'eng lu*, 118/114b). In 1405 Tsung-tao, Prince of Huai-an,[km] a former disciple of San-feng; in 1412 the abbot Sun Pi-yün with the letter mentioned below; in 1417 the medical officer Su Ch'in [kn] from Pao-chi; in the same year a Taoist from Mount Lung-hu. The genealogy of the Celestial Masters notes two imperial orders, addressed to the forty-third Celestial Master Chang Yü-ch'u,[ko] to search out and invite the immortal Chang San-feng to court in 1408 and 1409 (*Han T'ien-shih shih-chia*,[kp] 3/29a, *Tao-Tsang*, 1066).

43. The text of this letter quoted in: 1) *Ming shu*, 160/3162, said to have been written in the spring of 1412 and given to Sun Pi-yün; 2) *Kuo-ch'ao hsien-ch'eng lu*, 118/110a, and *Huang-Ming yung-hua lei-pien*, Bk. 8, 131/9b–10a, as said to have been given on the same occasion to Hu Yung; and 3) *Yü-t'ang man-pi* (*Hsien-ch'eng lu*, 118/115a), said to have been given to the Taoist from Mount Lung-hu in 1417.

44. The text of this second letter is quoted in: 1) *Hsien-ch'eng lu*, 118/110b, and 2) with indication of date in тscc, ch. 115 (*Wu-tang shan, I-wen*, 1/5b). At the same time Sun Pi-yün was appointed deputy director (*yu-cheng-i* [kq]) in the official Taoist hierarchy—one of the titles given to priests attached to state temples (*Ming T'ai-tsung shih-lu*, 125/1568).

45. His sole companion at the second sacrifice died soon afterwards in mysterious circumstances—either in Wu-ti's place or simply as an undesirable witness of the emperor's dealings with the gods. See E. Chavannes, *Les Mémoires Historiques* (Paris, 1898), III, 500.

46. *Ming shih*, 126/1a, 105/5a–5b, *kung-ch'en piao*.

47. *Ming shih*, 126/6b; 105/5a–b; *Hsien-ch'eng lu*, 5/92a; *Ming shu*, 157/3092.

48. *Ch'i-yang shih-chia wen-wu t'u-hsiang ts'e* [kr] (Peiping, 1937). I wish to thank Professor F. Mote and Dr. Hoklam Chan who kindly procured photocopies of this book from the Princeton University library. The colophon to San-feng's self-portrait by Teh-yao [ks] and the colophon copied from him by Chu Ch'i-ch'ien state that San-feng

invited Ching-lung's father to become an immortal and that the father received the presents and handed them on to his son. The genealogy and all other sources give the version which I have followed (*Chiang-ning fu-chih*, in TSCC, 256, 33/8a; *Ch'ing-ch'i hsia-pi*, 3a; *Ch'i-yang Wu-ching wang pieh-chuan*,[kt] quoted in the genealogy, p. 14). In the last mentioned source, Ching-lung sows the grains while shouting the name of the Immortal.

49. *Ch'ing-ch'i hsia-pi*, 3a–3b.

50. *Ch'i-yang shih-chia wen-wu t'u-hsiang ts'e*, p. 39; Chu Ch'i-ch'ien describes the picture of San-feng in the Li family shrine.

51. *Yü-t'ang man-pi* (*Hsien-ch'eng lu*, 118/114b), Lu Shen quotes this from Traces of San-feng, written by Chang Ch'ao-yung. Ch'ao-yung became archivist in the Imperial Supervisorate of Instruction (*Chan shih fu* [ku]) and later accompanied the censor Hu Yung on his travels. The same legend figures in *Ju-chou chih* [kv] (TSCC, 256, 33/9a–b), where the encounter of San-feng and Ch'ao-yung is said to have taken place in Honan.

52. *I-lin* [kw] (TSCC, 256, 33/6b–7a). In *Chiang-ning fu chih* (*ibid.*, 8a) this audience is alluded to: "In the beginning of the Yung-lo era he received a letter of cordial invitation and went to see [the emperor]. On account of his obstinate behavior the emperor wanted to kill him and he disappeared suddenly." It is Leng Ch'ien who, after his theft, disappeared into a jug to escape punishment.

53. In Taoist mythology there are several immortals called Hu-kung [kx] (the old man with the gourd). Each of them had a gourd, suspended on his staff, which he used as a container for herbs. He could also pass the night in it or invite an adept to take an excursion inside the gourd; see R. A. Stein, "Jardins en miniature d'Extrême-Orient," *BEFEO*, XLII, 53–60.

54. Leng Ch'ien disappeared by entering a jug; see note 25. A T'ang emperor admired a miniature landscape together with the Taoist Hsüan Chiai who suddenly shrank up, entered the sculpture which represented the P'eng-lai paradise, and disappeared. The emperor was told later that on the same day the Taoist had been seen crossing the sea on a yellow mare off the East coast (going to P'eng-lai); see R. A. Stein, "Jardins," p. 40. Chang Chung threw himself from a bridge in Nanking and, the same day, was seen walking through a mountain pass in Shensi; see pp. 488–89.

55. *Keng-chi pien* [ky] (Shuo-k'u ed.), 3/15a–b; *Li-tai shen-hsien t'ung-chien* (1712 ed.), 21, 9/1a, 3a; Wang Chien-chang,[kz] *Li-tai shen-hsien shih* [la] (1936 ed.), p. 126, embellished version. He is mentioned also in *Yeh chi* (in *Li-tai hsiao shih*, 79/57a).

56. *Kuo-ch'ao hsien-ch'eng lu*, 118/119a; *Wu-tang shan chih* (in TSCC, 256, 33/8b).
57. *Wu-tang yu-chi* (in TSCC, ch. 155, I-wen, 2/12b).
58. *Ch'u-pao wai-p'ien*,[lb] 1/22a.
59. *Szu-ch'uan tsung-chih*[lc] (in TSCC, ch. 256, 33/9b–10a).
60. *Kuei-chou t'ung-chih*[ld] (1741 ed.), 32/11b.
61. *Ch'ing-chou fu chih*[le] (in TSCC, ch. 256, 33/9a).
62. *An-huei t'ung-chih*[lf] (1878 ed.), 348/16a; *Ying-chou fu-chih*[lg] (1752 ed.), 8/118a–b.
63. *Teh-an-fu chih*[lh] (in TSCC, ch. 256, 33/8b).
64. *Hsiang-yang fu chih*[li] (in TSCC, ch. 256, 33/8b).
65. *Fu-feng-hsien chih*[lj] (1818 ed.), 14/3a–b.
66. *Ch'ung-ch'ing-fu chih*[lk] (in TSCC, ch. 256, 33/10a).
67. *Szu-ch'uan tsung-chih* (*ibid.*, ch. 9b–10a). The story figures also in *CSFCS*, 1/5a, with the variation that, at the approach of Hu Yung, San-feng left, taking Ming-yü with him. The *Tao-fa hui-t'ung shu* figures in *CSFCS*, 2/4b–5a, followed by a spurious colophon elaborating on the idea of the treatise that *Tao* is the root of *fa* and *fa* only the manifestation of *Tao*, that is, that you have to grasp the fundamental doctrine before you can excel in external magical practices. This was probably, as Mrs. Fang Lien-che has kindly suggested, how the Ch'üan-chen sect of that time (mentioned in the treatise) regarded the difference between themselves and the older Cheng-i[ll] sect. Mrs. Fang found this story and also the treatise in a *Nei-chiang-hsien chih*.[lm]
68. *Ch'ang-an-hsien chih*[ln] (Chia-ch'ing 1796–1820 ed.), 35/4b; *Feng-hsiang fu-chih*[lo] (1766 ed.), 7/89b.
69. *Feng-hsiang-fu chih*, 7/90a.
70. *Ch'i-hsiu lei-kao, hsü kao*, 4/19a.
71. *Hsiu-ning-hsien chih* (in TSCC, ch. 258, 35/4b–5a). Another hint that La-t'a is not necessarily identical with San-feng is found in a note added by Yang I to his biography of San-feng copied from an old I-chou[lp] gazetteer (same version as in *Hsien-ch'eng lu*): he is reluctant to identify La-t'a Chang with Chang San-feng. His arguments are not convincing but it is interesting that in 1531 an author raised this question; see *Kao-po i-tsuan*, A, 2a.
72. *Han-yang-fu chih* (in TSCC, ch. 258, 35/5a–b).
73. *Wu-chin-hsien chih*[lq] (in TSCC, ch. 258, 35/1a).
74. *Yün-nan t'ung-chih* (in TSCC, ch. 258, 35/8b).
75. K. M. Schipper, who was present at this meeting, kindly furnished this information.
76. Out of six recent pamphlets on boxing picked up at random in a

New York Chinatown bookstore, five claim to retain the boxing tradition of the patriarch San-feng, and the *T'ai-chi ch'üan ch'üan-shu* [lr] by Tseng Chao-jan [ls] (Hong Kong, 1964) contains a critical study on the question whether or not San-feng can be considered the founder of T'ai-chi ch'üan (discussed below). Among the others I mention only *Chang San-feng tao-shu hui-tsung* [lt] (Taipei, 1961) and *Chang San-feng Wu-shu hui-tsung* [lu] (Taipei, 1964).

77. *Ning-po-fu chih* [lv] (in TSCC, ch. 810, *Ch'üan-po pu*, 3b–4a; lacking in the Chung-hua ts'ung-shu ed., 1957).

78. *Wang Cheng-nan mu-chih ming*, in *Nan-lei wen-an*, [lw] 6/29a, also reproduced by Tseng Chao-jan, *T'ai-chi ch'üan ch'üan shu*, pp. 215–16; composed between 1669 (death of Wang Cheng-nan) and 1695.

79. *Ibid.*, pp. 37–38.

80. Sophia Delza, *Body and Mind in Harmony: T'ai Chi Ch'üan*, (New York, 1961), pp. 179, 183.

81. *San-chi chih-ming ch'üan-t'i* (*Tao tsang* 133), 23b–24a. The text was written after 1244 (which is the latest date mentioned [p. 12a]).

82. *Ibid.*, p. 18b; I thank Professor Liu Ts'un-yan for drawing my attention to this text.

83. CSFCS, 1/6a; I have looked in vain through P'eng-tsu's numerous biographies in the Taoist Canon for a title containing the expression *san-feng*.

84. According to Professor Liu such a double meaning is contained in *Wu-ken shu*, [lx] a series of 24 poems edited in CSFCS with a commentary by Liu Wu-yüan [ly] dated 1802. The *Wu-ken shu* poems are mentioned in *Kuei-chou t'ung-chih* as having been composed by San-feng during his stay at P'ing-yüeh. Another text with such a hidden sexual meaning is *San-feng tan-chüeh*, [lz] in *Cheng Tao pi-shu*, [ma] compiled by Fu Chin-ch'üan, [mb] preface dated 1813; reedited in *Hui-t'u Tao shu shih-ch'i chung* [mc] (Shanghai, 1921). An initial collection of legends traces the contents of *San-feng tan-chüch* back to the disciple Shen Wan-san.

85. In poem 9 (p. 7a–b), *ts'ai* [md] is explained as "the good treasure (*ts'ai*) of unified and undistracted meditation, a kind heart, and utmost determination."

86. *Ming-shih*, 113/4b.

87. In late Yüan times a Shen family in Chia-ting [me] (Kiangsu) became immensely rich through maritime trade with aborigines on the islands; see *Cho-keng lu* [mf] (Chin-tai pi-shu ed.), 27/16b–17a. Should this be the family of Wan-san, we would have a more rational explanation of this wealth. According to another version, a wealthy Lu Tao-yüan [mg] distributed his property among his trustees, one of them being Wan-san; see Yang Hsün-chi [mh] (1456–1544),

Su-t'an [mi] (Shuo-k'u ed.), p. 7a. Lang Ying says that his wealth was due to "the art of refining"; see *Ch'i-hsiu lei-kao*, 8/126. In *T'ung-su pien* [mj] (1751 ed.), 37/32b, his wealth is attributed to the alchemical instructions of San-feng. The full legend figures in *San-feng tan-chüeh* and in *CSFCS*, 1/3a, 4b, 7a–8b; 2/3a–b.

88. H. Doré, *Recherches*, XI, 961 ff. takes this version from a *Shen Wan-san chuan*.

89. E. T. Werner, *A Dictionary of Chinese Mythology*, pp. 36 ff. Unfortunately I have not found Werner's source of information.

90 *Li tai shen-hsien t'ung-chien*, ch. 21, 6/3b–5b; ch. 21, 9/3a; ch. 21, 9/6a–7a.

91. *CSFCS*, 1/13b.

92. Preface to *CSFCS*, ch. 5.

93. *Lo-shan-hsien chih* [mk] (1934 ed.), 5/58b–59a.

94. *CSFCS*, 1/13b.

95. *CSFCS*, 1/4a–b. Ma-i is the style (*tzu*) of Li Ho,[ml] an immortal of the Chin [mm] dynasty; see *Hsiao-yao hsü-ching* (*Tao tsang* 1081), 1/28b. *Nan-yang-fu chih*,[mn] in TSCC, ch. 237, 14/1b.

96. *T'ai-Hua Hsi-i chih* [mo] (*Tao-tsang* 160).

97. Hagiography of Yin Hsi in *Chung-nan shan shuo-ching t'ai li-tai chen-hsien pei-chi*,[mp] pp. 1a–3a, *Tao-tsang*, 605. The Tsung-sheng [mq] Temple on Mount Chung-nan was regarded as the ancient lookout tower (*lou-kuan* [mr]) of Yin Hsi; see *Hsüan-yüan shih tzu t'u* [ms] (*Tao tsang* 72), p. 1a.

98. *CSFCS*, 2/7a.

99. Such an authentic work may exist. Two treatises by San-feng are listed in the catalogue of the Ming Annals: *Chin-tan chih-chih* [mt] and *Chin-tan pi-chih*.[mu] *CSFCS* does not contain these titles. They might figure in an old manuscript *Chang San-feng tsu-shih chi*,[mv] listed in the catalogue of Teng Pang-shu,[mw] *Chün-pi lou shu-mu* [mx] (1910 ed.), 5/27a, and preserved in the library of the Academia Sinica in Taipei. I thank Professor Jao Tsung-i for this valuable reference.

100. *Ling-chen ching*,[my] revealed by San-feng (*CSFCS*, 7/8b).

101. *Lü-tsu ch'üan-shu tsung-cheng* [mz] (1852 ed.), 10/3b–4a.

102. *CSFCS*, 3/8b–9b.

103. *Hai-shan ch'i-yü* [na] (*CSFCS* ed.), 5/7b; this text is an account of the appearances of Lü-tsu from T'ang until Ch'ing times. The last chapter, on the manifestations in the Ch'ing era, (latest date 1812) is a good source for the activities of the sect in Wu-ch'ang; see Yoshioka Yoshitoyo, "Roso no shinkō to Chūgoku no minshu shin" [nb] *Nippon bukkyō gakkai nempō*, XXI (1955), 107–8.

104. *Lo-shan-hsien chih*, 9/63b–64a.

105. Under this name the Ming scholar and Taoist priest Lu Hsi-hsing [ne] is one of the immortals converted by the patriarch Lü (*Hai-shan ch'i-yü*, 6/2a–b). He is supposed to have been a friend of San-feng's great-great-grandson Hua-ku Tao-jen (*CSFCS*, 1/2b). Lu Hsi-hsing (1520–1601?) was the author of the *Feng-shen yen-i* [nd]; see Liu Ts'un-yan, *Buddhist and Taoist Influences on Chinese Novels*, Vol. I (Wiesbaden, 1962).

106. *Nan-pei ho-ts'an*,[ne] 2/5a, in *T'ung-i chai ssu-chung* [nf] (1903 ed.).

107. Among others, *San-chiao tsung-chih*,[ng] 1/35b, 43a ff., in *T'ung-i chai ssu-chung*; *Yang-hsing pien*,[nh] pp. 2a–9a, in *Yang-hsing yao-chih ho-pien*.[ni]

108. Fu Ch'in-chia, *Chung-kuo tao-chiao shih* [nj] (Shanghai, 1937), pp. 224–25.

GLOSSARY

a	正一	aj	徐達
b	全眞	ak	藍玉
c	張三丰	al	鷄鳴
d	太極拳	am	潼
e	國朝獻徵錄	an	宋濂
f	懿州	ao	蔣山
g	全一	ap	廬
h	君寶	aq	桶
i	保和容忍三丰子	ar	統
j	劉秉忠	as	啓敬
k	冷謙	at	嘉興
l	海雲	au	武陵
m	武當	av	吳山
n	展旗	aw	胥山
o	遇眞	ax	劉基
p	會仙館	ay	協律郎
q	周眞得	az	蓬萊仙奕圖
r	紫霄	ba	趙孟頫
s	南巖	bb	悟眞篇
t	邱玄靖	bc	三教
u	五龍	bd	淇國丘公
v	富平	be	野記
w	三山	bf	郎瑛
x	蜀王椿	bg	七修類稿
y	金臺	bh	陳萬鼐
z	寶雞	bi	均
aa	胡濙	bj	玄武
ab	通微顯化眞人	bk	眞武
ac	方支	bl	玄朗
ad	周顛	bm	淨樂
ae	張中	bn	鷄鳴
af	景華	bo	北極佐聖眞君
ag	臨川	bp	張宇清
ah	鐵冠子	bq	天主
ai	鍾	br	孫碧雲

bs	提點	de	景福
bt	太嶽太和山	df	巴岳
bu	張信	dg	內江
bv	隆平侯	dh	明玉
bw	封禪	di	龐
bx	李景隆	dj	道法會同疏
by	文忠	dk	劉寡蕩
bz	曹國公	dl	張恪
ca	岐陽王	dm	神仙
cb	赤松子	dn	休寧
cc	**璿**	do	齊雲
cd	性	dp	忠孝
ce	臨淮侯	dq	劉邋邊
cf	姚福	dr	漢陽
cg	蕚	ds	周顛
ch	朱啓鈐	dt	馬山人
ci	鹿邑	du	李鐵箍
cj	張毅	dv	李赤肚
ck	朝用	dw	赤脚仙
cl	元元	dx	大腹子
cm	玄玄	dy	張顛儸
cn	剌達	dz	白日昇天
co	邋邊	ea	尸解
cp	陳摶	eb	羽化
cq	呂洞賓	ec	仙化
cr	張金箔	ed	坐化
cs	楊軌山	ee	乘雲上昇
ct	陸銓	ef	陽羨
cu	姜	eg	提脚道人
cv	高眞	eh	滇
cw	福泉	ei	莫知所終
cx	平越	ej	太極拳
cy	禮斗亭	ek	三峯
cz	雲門	el	張松溪
da	日照	em	丹士
db	張古山	en	玄帝
dc	太平山	eo	內家
dd	扶風	ep	少林

eq	外家	gc	法財兩用
er	王征南墓誌銘	gd	無根樹
es	黃宗羲	ge	法財
et	白家	gf	沈萬三
eu	王宗	gg	秦淮
ev	陳州同	gh	吳
ew	溫州	gi	滇池
ex	葉近泉	gj	秀
ey	四明	gk	三山
ez	單思南	gl	聚寶盆
fa	副總兵官	gm	三豐
fb	餘姚	gn	歷代神仙通鑑
fc	曾昭然	go	汪錫齡
fd	楊福魁	gp	廉希憲
fe	露禪	gq	博陵
ff	陳	gr	花谷道人
fg	懷慶	gs	觀察
fh	王宗岳	gt	劍南
fi	吳河清	gu	樂山
fj	三極至命筌蹄	gv	凌雲
fk	三峯黃谷之術	gw	門
fl	元精	gx	口傳
fm	元氣	gy	隱仙派
fn	三峯	gz	火龍
fo	王谷子	ha	終南山
fp	李西月	hb	賈得升
fq	山峯	hc	希夷
fr	房中御女方	hd	麻衣
fs	陰道	he	尹喜
ft	彭祖	hf	華山
fu	太清景明三峯眞君	hg	王嚞
fv	三丰	hh	猶龍
fw	三峯	hi	丰
fx	山峯	hj	署中
fy	丰	hk	齡
fz	峯	hl	呂祖全書
ga	豐	hm	涵三
gb	三豐	hn	太乙金華宗旨

ho 百字碑

hp 西川

hq 劉海蟾

hr 陸潛虛

hs 傅勤家

ht 口訣

hu 陶宏景

hv 茅山

hw 正一

hx 全眞

hy 吉岡義豐

hz 道教の研究

ia 華僑日報

ib 江左書林

ic 李西月

id 道藏輯要

ie 畢

if 國朝獻徵錄

ig 玉堂漫筆

ih 陸深

ii 消搖墟經

ij 裕賢

ik 三丰

il 三峯

im 通·

in 伸猷

io 崑陽子

ip 方尺

iq 刀尺

ir 楊善登

is 劉古泉

it 盧秋雲

iu 明實錄

iv 間野潛龍

iw 明朝と太和山について

ix 大谷學報

iy 太嶽太和山志

iz 藍田

ja 武當山志

jb 祝允明

jc 野記

jd 歷代小史

je 姚福

jf 青溪暇筆

jg 胡應麟

jh 少室山房筆叢

ji 江寧府志

jj 皇明泳化類編

jk 徐道

jl 歷代神仙通鑑

jm 七修類稿

jn 郎瑛

jo 楊儀

jp 高坡異纂

jq 周顚仙傳

jr 中黃大丹

js 張氏悟眞之旨

jt 伯端

ju 邱福

jv 珊瑚網

jw 邇邊

jx 鄭和

jy 明惠帝出亡考證

jz 襄

ka 武昌

kb 紫微北極大帝

kc 武當福地總眞集

kd 劉道明

ke 東方宗教

kf 玄天玉虛宮

kg 太玄紫霄宮

kh 興聖五龍宮

ki 大聖南嚴宮

kj 明太宗實錄

kk 張玉

kl 大明玄天上帝瑞應圖錄

km	淮安王宗道	ly	劉悟元
kn	蘇欽	lz	丹訣
ko	張宇初	ma	證道秘書
kp	漢天師世家	mb	傅金銓
kq	右正一	mc	繪圖道書十七種
kr	岐陽世家文物圖像冊	md	財
ks	德燿	me	嘉定
kt	岐陽武靖王列傳	mf	輟耕錄
ku	詹事府	mg	陸道原
kv	汝州志	mh	楊循吉
kw	異林	mi	蘇談
kx	壺公	mj	通俗編
ky	庚己編	mk	樂山縣志
kz	王建章	ml	李和
la	歷代神仙史	mm	晉
lb	楚寶外篇	mn	南陽府志
lc	四川總志	mo	太華希夷志
ld	貴州通志	mp	終南山說經臺歷代眞仙碑記
le	青州府志	mq	宗聖
lf	安徽通志	mr	樓觀
lg	穎州府志	ms	玄元十子圖
lh	德安府志	mt	金丹直旨
li	襄陽府志	mu	秘旨
lj	扶風縣志	mv	祖師集
lk	重慶府志	mw	鄧邦述
ll	正一	mx	群碧樓書目
lm	內江縣志	my	靈眞經
ln	長安縣志	mz	呂祖全書宗正
lo	鳳翔府志	na	海山奇遇
lp	懿州	nb	呂祖の信仰と中國の民衆神
lq	武進縣志	nc	陸西星
lr	太極拳全書	nd	封神演義
ls	曾昭然	ne	南北合參
lt	張三丰道術滙宗	nf	通一齋四種
lu	武術滙宗	ng	三教宗旨
lv	寧波府志	nh	養性編
lw	南雷文案	ni	養性要旨合編
lx	無根樹	nj	中國道教史

INDEX

Absolutism, 223

Action (*hsing*), 455; (*tung*), 77–78

Advancing, 18–19

Ai-wen, 388

Alchemy, 508

Amazed Maid (*ch'a-nu*), 305, 323 *n* 29

Amita Buddha, 454–56, 461–62, 464, 466, 470

A-mi-t'o-fo, 456, 464

Anger (*ch'en*), 465, 478 *n* 31

Analects, 67, 178–79, 181, 338

Anatpattikadharmaksānti (wu-sheng fa-jen), 477 *n* 11

Archery, 58

Army, 422–23

Arts and Letters, 146, 226 *n* 5

As You Like It (Shakespeare), 258

Avatamsaka, 455

Bare-Belly Li, 503

Barefoot Immortal, 503

Bedchamber art (*fang-chung*), 293, 311, 344

Bell, Schall von, 426

"Blessèd Damozel, The" (Rossetti), 264

Bodhidharma, 505–6

Book learning, *see* Learning

Book of History, 390–91

Book of Rites, 159

Book To Be Hidden Away, A (*Ts'ang-shu*) (Li Chih), 193, 201–3, 210

Book To Burn, A (*Fen-shu*) (Li Chih), 192, 194

Boxing schools, 484, 504–6

Breath, embryo (*t'ai-hsi*), 296–97

————, original (*yüan-ch'i*), 507

Breath regulation (*t'iao-hsi*), 295–96, 311, 344

Buddha, Name of the, 466

Buddha-contemplation, 459–60, 462, 465–66

Buddhahood, 460, 464

Buddha-recollection (*Buddhanusmrti*), 453, 455–56, 469–70

Buddhism: assimilation of, 1; and Confucianism, 5, 16; and Ch'en Hsien-chang, 69; and emptiness, 76; and quiet-sitting, 90 *n* 44: and Li Chih, 190–92; and law, 221–22; and T'ang Hsien-tsu, 250–51; popular forms of, 346; and Chang Chü-cheng, 497–501; *see also* Ch'an (Zen) Buddhism; Pure Land movement; Yün-ch'i Chu-hung

Calligraphy, rushdragon (*mao-lung*), 63

Calmness (*ching*), 312

Capitalism, 441–42

Censorship, 214–15, 243 *n* 265

Chan Jo-shui, 60, 62–64, 74, 84, 311: on Wang Yang-ming, 71, 307; Ch'an Buddhist influence on, 314

Ch'an (Zen) Buddhism, 1–3; influence of, 139; individualism in, 147; ideas of learning in, 155–57; Wang Yang-ming's invigoration of, 156, 227 *n* 26; synthesis with Pure Land, 176–77; anti-intellectualism of, 196; and Li Chih, 224; and meditation, 311; and influence on Confucian cultivation, 314; schools of in Ming period, 452; *see also* Buddhism; Wild Ch'an movement

Ch'an Fu-min, 122

Chang, Celestial Master, 517 *n* 5

Chang Ch'ao-yung, 498

Chang Chin-po, 499

Chang Chü-cheng: and Yen Sung, 180–81; and T'ang Hsien-tsu, 267, 285–86 *n* 43; background of, 367; and autocracy, 368; philosophic eclecticism of, 368–71; philosophy of history of, 372–74, 408 *n* 49; on destiny, 375; and law of reversal, 375–79; on the origin of the state,